the
# Bedford Book of Genres

# the Bedford Book of Genres

## a guide & reader

**THIRD EDITION**

**Amy Braziller**
Red Rocks Community College

**Elizabeth Kleinfeld**
Metropolitan State University

bedford/st.martin's
Macmillan Learning
Boston | New York

*Vice President:* Leasa Burton
*Program Director, English:* Stacey Purviance
*Senior Program Manager:* Laura Arcari
*Director of Content Development:* Jane Knetzger
*Executive Development Manager:* Maura Shea
*Senior Development Editor:* Sherry Mooney
*Editorial Assistant:* Annie Campbell
*Director of Media Editorial:* Adam Whitehurst
*Media Editor:* Julia Domenicucci
*Marketing Manager:* Vivian Garcia
*Director, Content Management Enhancement:* Tracey Kuehn
*Senior Managing Editor:* Michael Granger
*Senior Content Project Manager:* Kendra LeFleur
*Senior Workflow Project Manager:* Jennifer Wetzel
*Production Supervisor:* Brianna Lester
*Director of Design, Content Management:* Diana Blume
*Interior Design:* Carie Keller
*Cover Design:* William Boardman
*Cover Images:* Office building, mf-guddyx/E+/Getty Images; Llama poster, Microstocker.
    Pro/Shutterstock; Pop art of stressed out man, jameslee1/DigitalVision Vectors/
    Getty Images; School lunch infographic, USDA
*Director, Rights and Permissions:* Hilary Newman
*Text Permissions Researcher:* Udayakumar Kannadasan, Lumina Datamatics, Inc.
*Photo Permissions Editor:* Angie Boehler
*Photo Researcher:* Krystyna Borgen
*Director of Digital Production:* Keri deManigold
*Media Project Manager:* Emily Brower
*Composition:* Lumina Datamatics, Inc.
*Printing and Binding:* LSC Communications

Library of Congress Control Number: 2020933308

ISBN 978-1-319-24508-5

Printed in the United States of America.
1  2  3  4  5  6      25  24  23  22  21  20

**Acknowledgments**
Acknowledgments and copyrights appear on the same page as the text and art selections they cover; these acknowledgments and copyrights constitute an extension of the copyright page.


At the time of publication all internet URLs published in this text were found to accurately link to their intended website. If you do find a broken link, please forward the information to sherry.mooney@macmillan.com so that it can be corrected for the next printing.


*For information, write:* Bedford/St. Martin's, 75 Arlington Street, Boston, MA 02116

# ABOUT THE AUTHORS

**Amy Braziller** is an English faculty member and former department chair at Red Rocks Community College. She received her BA from Empire State College and her MA from New York University. She has presented on teaching writing and new media at numerous national and regional conferences. Her research focuses on the intersections between classroom and personal writing. Amy, who is at work on a series of personal essays related to her punk rock days in New York City, blogs about food, film, music, GLBT issues, and social media distractions at amybraziller.com.

**Elizabeth Kleinfeld** is the Writing Center Director and Professor of English at Metropolitan State College of Denver. She received her BS from Bradley University and her MS in English and PhD in Composition and Rhetoric from Illinois State University. She is an associate editor for *WLN: A Journal of Writing Center Scholarship* and has published articles on new media, writing centers, and student source use in various journals and collections, including *Computers & Composition Online* and *Praxis*. Her research interests include disability studies, feminist pedagogies, and teaching for social justice. Her current research focuses on restorative justice models of plagiarism mitigation.

# PREFACE FOR INSTRUCTORS

The multimodal world the third edition of *The Bedford Book of Genres* reflects is a beautiful, sometimes chaotic, always changing stream of color, sound, image, animation, and more. When we began envisioning the first edition, way back in the mid-aughts, multimodality was largely uncharted territory for textbooks. Today, multimodality is a given, with the ubiquity of Instagram-style stories, photos, captions, and stickers; news delivered via tweet; and we would have envied even tweed-jacket wearing instructors carrying smartphones equipped with cameras just a few years ago.

We continue to believe that our students can and should be writing essays, as well as podcasts, infographics, videos, digital stories, blogs, ads, graphic novels, TED-style talks, editorials, profiles, presentations, and more . . . in short, all the new genres that have come into existence in the time since we first wrote a preface for this book. Having taught following the principles of the first two editions, we believe more strongly than ever that our students benefit from learning how to read and respond to any rhetorical situation in a variety of genres. When they can choose the mode and genre for their compositions, our students are excited, curious, and really into their projects. They bring fun, imagination, and personality into their academic work. And they see what they do in terms of skills that can travel with them and work they can showcase in their portfolios.

In response to feedback from users of the second edition, the third edition of *The Bedford Book of Genres* reorganizes material so that Part 2 now focuses on writing processes. This new focus helps students to understand and plan for the entire scope of their work and develop effective writing strategies from the very beginning. Reviewers also have helped us understand the need to include more extensive composition projects to prompt students to put all the pieces together and challenge themselves to implement the skills they developed throughout each chapter. As a result, the Part 3 genre chapters now end with longer assignments that build on the writing practice activities sprinkled throughout the chapters. Just as in the first and second editions, this edition includes student work along with detailed analyses of student processes.

We hope you and your students will be inspired by this book to experiment and have fun.

# A Rhetorical Road Map for Reading & Composing—in Any Genre

This book supports students in two key ways. First, it provides the basics that students need to read any text, to follow any author's rhetorical moves, and to recognize the elements at work in any genre. Second, it offers a framework for analysis and composition to help students understand their own rhetorical situations, to make smart choices as composers themselves, and to select and work in genres that are best for their purposes.

No one is an expert on every genre. We can all start from different places, and with any level, or lack, of technical skills. With these factors in mind, we do not cover every genre there is—that would be impossible. Instead, we've put together a compendium of common genres. And we present them for students to read and analyze, and for them to use as models or jumping-off points for their own creations.

# How This Book Is Organized

**GUIDE**

This is the heart of the book, where we introduce students to the rhetorical situation and genres, then move them from analyzing the work of others to composing their own texts. The Guide is divided into four parts; the first part provides more focused instruction for first-year writing students to fully grasp the concepts of the rhetorical situation and how it drives composing choices. The second part emphasizes the writing process, beginning with brainstorming and freewriting, and then moving to revising, remixing, and reflecting, helping to prepare students for composition situations they will encounter in college and beyond. The third part digs into the characteristics of specific genres and includes new guided readings and extensive coverage of podcasts. The fourth and final part is our thematic reader, giving students an engaging array of readings that span the genres in the book. These thematic readings showcase how a single topic or concept may be treated across genres and encourage students to practice their critical reading skills in a variety of rhetorical contexts.

## Part 1 | Rhetoric & Reading

1. Rhetorical Situations & Choices
2. Genres
3. Reading as a Writer: Rhetorical Situations & Genres Together

In Part 1, students learn about rhetorical situations and explore the rhetorical choices that go into composing in genres. Students learn how to read rhetorical situations and to apply a rhetorical lens for analyzing a variety of genre texts so that they can understand authors' choices (with a focus on purpose, audience, rhetorical appeals, modes, and media). At the same time, they learn to identify what makes a genre a genre. Students learn to analyze conventions, to examine the common elements of a given genre and the typical use of style, design, and sources. The guided readings, dozens of texts that we've annotated to point out composers' rhetorical situations and how they work with their chosen genre (explained in detail on p. xi), are a big part of how this all happens. Chapter 3 in particular has been revised to emphasize the connections between reading and writing, preparing students to move into Part 2, The Writing Process. Part 1 concludes with a case study examining one event, two rhetorical situations, and two genres.

## Part 2 | The Writing Process

4 Composing: Drawing on Experience & Evidence

5 Revising & Remixing

6 Reflection: The Author's/Artist's Statement

In a newly created Part 2, which draws together the key composing coverage in *The Bedford Book of Genres*, students take the critical reading and rhetorical skills they established in Part 1 and put them into practice in their own writing. They learn to develop their own writing process by exploring the steps taken by other student and professional writers, considering the important role of revision, and embracing reflection as a valuable tool for composing in any genre.

## Part 3 | Genres

7 Academic Genres

8 Workplace Genres

9 Public Genres

10 Assembling a Multigenre Project

Through a variety of guided readings, students get a glimpse of the rhetorical situations and choices real writers deal with. Students deepen their understanding of academic genres by examining genres such as researched arguments and critical analyses. Students learn about workplace genres by studying business memos and infographics. Moving beyond college and the workplace, students then explore public genres such as podcasts and editorials. Along with updated readings and a new guided reading on podcasts in Chapter 9, the first three chapters in Part 3 now close with full-length writing assignments that encourage students to practice composing in new genres using a variety of technologies. In the final chapter, students learn how to assemble a multigenre project by putting a variety of genres together.

## Part 4 | Composing with Sources

**11** Exploring Topics & Creating a Research Proposal

**12** Evaluating & Choosing Sources

**13** Integrating & Documenting Sources

**14** Composing: Drawing on In-Depth Research: A Student Case Study

Part 4 takes students through the research process, from choosing a topic to doing preliminary research, formulating research questions and writing a proposal. Students are then guided to evaluate and choose sources, and finally how to integrate into their writing, and document them. Chapter 12 features a new student project evaluating sources on the topic of teenage anxiety.

### READER

## Part 5 | Reader

**15** Identities: The Culture of Identity

**16** Mind & Body: Connections

**17** Activism: Making Your Voice Heard

**18** Creativity: It's Complicated

In the Reader, we offer a thematic approach to a variety of topics and genres. The chapter on identity has been fully updated to focus on personal and cultural identity and the role that technology plays in understanding those identities. The chapter on Mind & Body now includes a reading that explores the role of advertising in challenging stereotypes. In the activism chapter, we've also updated many of the readings to reflect the changing times and issues students face, such as the student loan debt crisis. Updated for the new edition, the readings in all of our thematic chapters offer models for composing, sources to draw upon, and hopefully some moments that are thought-provoking, entertaining, and inspiring too. (For more on this, see pp. 453–540.)

# Features

## Flexible and Easy to Navigate—with an Emphasis on the Rhetorical Situation

*The Bedford Book of Genres* is designed to be an accessible guide that supports students as they analyze and compose their own texts in any mode or media. It also serves as a reference that they can easily refer back to as they work on their own or with peers.

We wanted to make this book flexible enough to support a variety of approaches to first-year composition. Whether you ask your students to compose in different genres or not, we hope you will take advantage of the guidelines provided for applying rhetorical analysis, as well as the variety of texts and genres that students can use for practicing rhetorical analysis.

Those of you who like to emphasize visual rhetoric in your class might focus on the many visual examples in the book, including photos, posters, and infographics.

If your primary focus is on interesting topics and themes, you might want to teach the book through a thematic lens. In addition to the thematic chapters and clusters in the Reader, we have provided an Index of Themes (pp. T-1–T-6) that sorts the rich contents of the book into plenty of relevant and exciting categories that will spark student attention and imagination.

## Guided Readings That Help Students Analyze Various Genres

Annotated guided readings throughout the Guide highlight the rhetorical moves that writers and composers make in different genres and modes, and point out common genre conventions. We've designed the annotations—presented in the margins of over two dozen texts—to help students see what choices authors make and what the consequences of those choices are. As students notice what professional writers and composers do, they become more aware of what they can and should do in their own work.

These guided readings demystify genres and help students recognize familiar strategies composers make across genres, such as appealing to readers' sense of pathos or logos. They also help students understand aspects of composing in genres and modes they might not be familiar with and to look at features such as design.

**How to find and use a guided reading**   The guided readings are clearly listed in the book's table of contents and in chapter opening brief contents; they are designed with large headings and framed with annotations, and the genre of the reading is named in a tab at the top of the page.

The annotations in the margins of the guided readings are structured around two main ideas: (1) the composer's specific rhetorical situation and choices (purpose, audience, rhetorical appeals, modes/media); and (2) the typical conventions of the genre (common elements, style, design, and sources). We see this as a kind of grid that students might apply whenever they read or compose any kind of text in their composition course and beyond.

As your students begin to learn about reading genres critically, you may ask them to annotate texts that you or they bring to class (texts not included in the book); they might want to model their analyses on the structure of the annotations that appear in the margins of our guided readings. You'll find guided readings throughout Parts 1, 2, and 3.

**Guided processes that offer advice about multimodal composing built around interesting student projects**   As mentioned on p. vii of this Preface, we follow several of our former students throughout the book, showing work they did in our classes in various stages, from brainstorming to finished project. Allowing students to see how other real students approach composing in genres lets students see that there is no one-size-fits-all way to compose. Seeing, for example, how Gwen Ganow, featured in Chapters 4 and 5, moves from a very early rough draft through a variety of later drafts shows how important revision is, and more important, what revision looks like for a real student writer. Chapter 6 stars Michael Kipp, using his Artist Statement as an example for students' own reflective practice.

Presenting real students' work also gives us a chance to show that we envision the students who will use this book as interesting and complex and as desiring a challenge to compose using various techniques for a variety of outcomes.

**How to find and use a guided process**   Like the guided readings, the guided processes (found in Chapter 4 and Chapters 11–13) are easy to locate in the table of contents, in the chapter opening brief contents, and on the page. Guided processes walk your students through the steps other students have taken to research, compose, and revise, working in genres that were in some cases new and unfamiliar to them. They show that students don't have to begin as experts to research a topic and make a point about it in a new and interesting way.

The guided processes also work as reference materials that students can refer back to as they work through their own projects.

## Clear Guidance on Reflection

We believe that the Author's/Artist's Statements that students compose—in which they explain how and why they created their specific genre composition(s) and reflect on those choices—are crucial. And through our review programs, we've found conference panels, hands-on workshops, and conversations with many of you, that you think the same. These Statements give students a venue in which to discuss their work in terms of choices and intentions and even to make a case for the sources they drew on (we ask our students to include Works Cited pages with their Statements).

Most significantly, these reflective pieces give students a place to think critically about their composing processes, about how they worked with (or outside of) a genre's typical conventions, and how they positioned themselves rhetorically in terms of their audience and purpose. Even if, say, a student is not pleased with her genre composition (maybe her collage is less than perfect, or her brief documentary or her video ad is not exactly what she'd hoped, or she didn't plan her time well, or she didn't have ample resources), she can still do the thoughtful work in her Statement that we want to see in a first-year writing course. Being able to reflect on and constructively critique one's own work is a lifelong skill that will serve our students well beyond our classrooms. Due to its importance in helping students develop meta-cognitive awareness, the third edition, like the second edition, devotes an entire chapter (Chapter 6) to this genre for reflection.

## Thematic Readings—with a Unique Mix of Genres & Modes—for Students to Draw On

While some themes in our Reader are found in other textbooks, the readings themselves take an unusual approach to the topic. For example, in Chapter 15, "Identities: The Culture of Identity," we include very current issues, such as personal pronoun choice, and in Chapter 16, "Mind & Body: Connections," we include a piece on disability. In Chapter 17, "Activism: Making Your Voice Heard," we include protest signs and activist speeches. Chapter 18, "Creativity: It's Complicated," includes several pieces on the growing acceptance of failure as part of a creative process. When we chose the readings, we made sure to offer a variety of voices and genres, including research-based essays, blog entries, infographics, advertisements, and photographs.

Students can use these chapters to help them hone their critical reading skills, study the rhetorical choices composers make in various genres, and integrate different pieces for research-based writing on these topics. Each chapter begins with an introduction to the theme. Each reading includes both analytical questions and a composing project prompt. Each chapter closes with two long-term projects.

## New to This Edition

**A new organization emphasizing the writing process.** A new Part 2, "The Writing Process" gathers the writing coverage from the previous edition into a cohesive guide for students on every stage of writing, from early brainstorming, through drafting and revision, to the final reflection. This new part makes more explicit connections between reading processes. At the same time, the cohesive organization makes it simple for students to find the guidance they need and encourages them to experiment to discover the strategies that work best for their rhetorical situation and chosen genre.

**New project-length writing Part 3 assignments.** Each of the key genre chapters in Part 3— "Academic Genres," "Workplace Genres," and "Public Genres"—now closes with new, project-length writing assignments that prompt students to explore one or two of the genres they discovered in the chapter in greater depth, putting their rhetorical understanding into practice and exploring both print and multimodal applications.

**In-depth research coverage in Part 3** includes an up-to-date guide to MLA and APA, incorporating the latest version of the American Psychological Association style guide so that students are working with the most current guidelines. In addition, Chapter 12, "Evaluating & Choosing Sources" features a new student writer, Donovan Rodriguez, evaluating three sources as he tackles the issue of teenage anxiety. His careful and contextual analysis models effective source-based critical thinking and use a variety of genres, including a video source.

**A thoroughly revised Reader.** We've updated readings in all four Reader chapters, adding pieces on current topics—for example, how we curate our identities online and addiction—and featuring composers and figures of interest to today's college students, such as soccer player Abby Wambach and climate activist Greta Thunberg. The chapter on identity has been fully updated to focus on personal and cultural identity and the role that technology plays in understanding those identities. The chapter on Mind & Body now includes a reading that explores the role of advertising in challenging stereotypes. In the activism chapter, we've also updated many of the readings to reflect the changing times and issues students face, such as the student loan debt crisis. We've also updated readings in other parts of the book to appeal to college students. For example, Chapter 7 features a journal article on how a recent manifestation of Spiderman brings social justice into the superhero canon, and Chapter 9 includes both a brand new Guided Reading featuring a podcast on China's decision to stop accepting recycling from the United States and an article that explains why aliens might actually look more like a plate of spaghetti than little green men.

**Achieve for Readers and Writers.** Achieve is an exciting, new, and comprehensive set of interconnected teaching and assessment tools. It integrates the most effective elements from Bedford/St. Martin's market leading digital solutions you may be familiar with—including LaunchPad, LearningCurve, and iClicker—in a single powerful, easy-to-use platform. We are proud to present Achieve for Readers and Writers, which rests on three core values: *Engaging students for better outcomes, supporting students of all levels, and partnering with teachers and learners.*

Achieve for Readers and Writers comes with a curated course option that you can adapt to fit your needs; add, hide, and rearrange resources and assignments—conveniently available in a searchable library—until the course works for you. Resources in Achieve for Readers and Writers include:

- *LearningCurve adaptive quizzing* offers personalized question sets and feedback for each student based on correct and incorrect responses. Questions are conveniently tied back to the e-book to encourage students to access help when they need it.

- *Pre-built writing assignments and other activities* have been designed to deliver a coherent learning experience, and will make prep, practice, and review easy and engaging.

- *Source Check plagiarism detection* allows students to scan their papers for potential plagiarism *before* they submit them for review, allowing students to learn academic writing habits and citation practices in the context of their own writing.

- *Diagnostics and study plans* help establish a baseline for student performance—a mark from which students can make progress throughout the course. Promoting personalized learning, Achieve helps students create actionable study plans to strengthen their skills and build their confidence.

- *Reporting and insights* that do the heavy lifting for you with powerful analytics that highlight student engagement, provide opportunities for intervention, and allow you to visualize trends in student progress across assignments.

Based on leading scholars' work on writer development, the pre-built writing assignments in Achieve for Readers and Writers give teachers deeper visibility into students' writing processes so they can target instruction and feedback to help writers grow and develop across drafts, across assignments, and across courses. Students do the work of the course in a contained and active writing space that includes a suite of powerful writing tools. Actionable insights make students' progress toward outcomes clear and measurable.

- *Revision* The Revision Plan helps writers turn feedback into concrete strategies and take ownership of their revision planning. For students, the Revision Plan creates accountability; for teachers, it provides insights about how well students understand the feedback they receive.

- *Reflection* The writing tools increase students' rhetorical awareness and promote the transfer of skills and habits from draft to draft. How? By prompting students to articulate the choices they make as writers and to communicate their confidence in the drafts they write. You can choose and customize reflection prompts to fit your course and assignment goals.

- *Instructor feedback tools* Powerful and customizable commenting tools allow you to focus your feedback on success criteria—draft goals that you set—and efficiently mark patterns of error. Feedback links to e-book content to give students point-of-need support in the context of their own writing.

- *Peer review tools* When you empower students to seek feedback from and offer feedback to one another, you invite them to become *writers*, not just students of writing. Achieve's tools scaffold and support students' development as peer reviewers—and allow you to easily facilitate and monitor the process.

- *Pre-built assignments and units that make your life easier.* A flexible assignment building tool allows you to assign ready-made writing prompts or create your own.

Get ready for insights and *aha!* moments. Get ready to **achieve more**.

# Acknowledgments

As with the first two editions, we could not have written this book without the support and good cheer of many people. Obviously, if our own students hadn't gamely agreed to work on projects in multiple genres and modes, our teaching, and thus the book, would have stalled immediately, and so our first and heartiest thanks go to all the students who have taken our first-year writing classes. We are grateful to all the students whose work appears in these pages, especially to Gwen Ganow and Michael Kipp, whose work is featured in Chapters 4, 5, 6, and 10.

Our insightful and super-organized editor, Sherry Mooney, helped us reenvision this book and kept us focused. Leasa Burton, Laura Arcari, and Vivian Garcia asked challenging questions that helped shape the direction of this edition. Kendra LeFleur expertly managed the production of this edition. Hilary Newman and Angela Boehler ably oversaw the permissions.

We could not have done this without the support of our loved ones. Amy is so thankful for her partner Nan Walker's constant encouragement and support. Elizabeth is grateful to her partner, Tom DeBlaker, and daughter, Lily, for their patience and good humor.

We'd like to thank our reviewers, many of whom generously offered comments through the entire development of the book—and who have become part of the community surrounding this project: Sylvia Basile, Midlands Technical College; Erin Breaux, South Louisiana Community College; Alexandra DeRosa, University of Toledo; Andy Frazee, Georgia Institute of Technology; Holly Hassel, North Dakota State University; Savanti Ganguly Puckett, Johnson County Community College; Jen Richrath, Illinois Central College; Theodore Rollins, Johnson County Community College; Matthew Schmeer, Johnson County Community College; and Jessica Ulmer, Midlands Technical College. We want to thank our enthusiastic colleagues, particularly the ones who used the book and gave us classroom-inspired feedback. Their belief in our vision and excitement at the prospect of the second edition helped spur us on.

And most important, we'd like to thank each other for sharing a brain, food, cocktails, and the good fortune to collaborate on this journey.

Amy Braziller & Elizabeth Kleinfeld

# Bedford/St. Martin's Puts You First

From day one, our goal has been simple: to provide inspiring resources that are grounded in best practices for teaching reading and writing. For more than 35 years, Bedford/St. Martin's has partnered with the field, listening to teachers, scholars, and students about the support writers need. We are committed to helping every writing instructor make the most of our resources.

## How can we help *you*?

- Our editors can align our resources to your outcomes through correlation and transition guides for your syllabus. Just ask us.
- Our sales representatives specialize in helping you find the right materials to support your course goals.
- Our Bits blog on the Bedford/St. Martin's English Community (**community .macmillan.com**) publishes fresh teaching ideas weekly. You'll also find easily downloadable professional resources and links to author webinars on our community site.

Contact your Bedford/St. Martin's sales representative or visit **macmillanlearning.com** to learn more.

## Print and Digital Options for *The Bedford Book of Genres*

Choose the format that works best for your course, and ask about our packaging options that offer savings for students.

### Print

- *Paperback.* To order the paperback edition, use ISBN 978-1-319-245085.

### Digital

- *Achieve for Readers and Writers.* Achieve puts student writing at the center of your course and keeps revision at the core, with a dedicated composition space that guides students through drafting, peer review, source check, reflection, and revision. Developed to support best practices in commenting on student drafts, Achieve is a flexible, integrated suite of tools for designing and facilitating writing assignments, paired with actionable insights that make students' progress toward outcomes clear and measurable. Fully editable pre-built assignments support the book's approach and an e-book is included. For details, visit **macmillanlearning .com/college/us/englishdigital**.

- *Popular e-book formats.* For details about our e-book partners, visit **macmillanlearning .com/ebooks**.

- *Inclusive Access.* Enable every student to receive their course materials through your LMS on the first day of class. Macmillan Learning's Inclusive Access program is the easiest, most affordable way to ensure all students have access to quality educational resources. Find out more at **macmillanlearning.com/inclusiveaccess**.

## Your Course, Your Way

No two writing programs or classrooms are exactly alike. Our Curriculum Solutions team works with you to design custom options that provide the resources your students need. (Options below require enrollment minimums.)

- *ForeWords for English.* Customize any print resource to fit the focus of your course or program by choosing from a range of prepared topics, such as Sentence Guides for Academic Writers.

- *Macmillan Author Program (MAP).* Add excerpts or package acclaimed works from Macmillan's trade imprints to connect students with prominent authors and public conversations. A list of popular examples or academic themes is available upon request.

- *Mix and Match.* With our simplest solution, you can add up to 50 pages of curated content to your Bedford/St. Martin's text. Contact your sales representative for additional details.

- *Bedford Select.* Build your own print handbook or anthology from a database of more than 800 selections, and add your own materials to create your ideal text. Package with any Bedford/St. Martin's text for additional savings. Visit **macmillanlearning .com/bedfordselect**.

## Instructor Resources

You have a lot to do in your course. We want to make it easy for you to find the support you need—and to get it quickly.

*Instructor's Manual for The Bedford Book of Genres* is available as a PDF that can be downloaded from **macmillanlearning.com**. In addition to chapter overviews and teaching tips, the instructor's manual includes sample syllabi, correlations to the Council of Writing Program Administrators' Outcomes Statement, sample lesson plans, teaching strategies, and advice for assessing student work.

| 2014 WPA Desired Outcomes | Relevant Features of *The Bedford Book of Genres* |
|---|---|
| **RHETORICAL KNOWLEDGE** | |
| **Learn and use key rhetorical concepts through analyzing and composing a variety of texts.** | *The Bedford Book of Genres* is designed to help students read and compose—in any genre.<br><br>In **Part 1, "Rhetoric & Reading,"** authors Amy Braziller and Elizabeth Kleinfeld help students recognize rhetorical situations. Students learn how to apply a rhetorical lens for analyzing a variety of genre texts so that they can understand authors' choices—with focuses on purpose, audience, rhetorical appeals, modes, and media.<br><br>The framework of the book—the consistent analysis of rhetorical situations and genre conventions—supports students as they read a variety of texts and create their own work. A wide offering of **guided readings** with annotations point out composers' rhetorical situations and how they work with their chosen genre. Two new chapters open the text to provide sharp focus to purposes as responses to rhetorical situations. Part 1 also emphasizes how students can work with the guided reading feature and gets students started with composing by drawing on their own experiences.<br><br>In **Part 3, "Genres,"** the authors offer readings and instructions in three categories—academic, public, and workplace genres—to highlight how context shapes writers' choices about genres.<br><br>Highly visual, annotated models called **guided readings** and **guided processes** help students analyze and compose in various genres, in print and online, and in multiple modes. The authors' annotations focus on two main things: (1) a given composer's rhetorical situation (with a focus on purpose, audience, rhetorical appeals, and choice of modes/media); and (2) the conventions of the genre he or she is working in (with a focus on its elements, and use of style, design, and sources). The guided processes show student readers how other students approached research and composing. Some examples of guided processes include models for **how to choose a topic and create a bibliography** (Chapter 5), **how to preview and evaluate a source** (Chapter 6), **how to quote from, paraphrase, and summarize a source** (Chapter 7), and **how to work with sources and compose in multiple genres** (Chapters 11–15). Essential to the student work is the reflective analytical piece—the **Author's or Artist's Statements** that they compose to accompany their genre compositions. |
| **Gain experience reading and composing in several genres to understand how genre conventions shape and are shaped by readers' and writers' practices and purposes.** | A consistent focus on the rhetorical situations of readers and composers—and on how genres function in different scenarios—is central to this book's pedagogy. This focus is built solidly into the framework of the **guided readings, guided processes, checklists, and assignments.**<br><br>Additionally, the idea that genres are fluid, and not fixed, is introduced in **Chapter 1, "Rhetorical Situations & Choices,"** and continues throughout the text. Students get a sense that they can adapt a genre, depending on their own rhetorical situations as composers. |

*(Continues on next page)*

| | Chapters 2 through 4 on **composing in genres** give students an overview of how purpose, audience, context, and other rhetorical concepts are interconnected, with guidance on choosing and composing in specific genres. Annotated guided readings highlight the rhetorical moves that writers and composers make in different genres and modes, and point out common genre conventions, demystifying genres and helping students recognize familiar strategies composers make across genres, such as appealing to readers' sense of pathos or logos. |
|---|---|
| | **Part 2, "The Writing Process,"** offers students targeted guidance for composing, including how to respond to an assignment or a particular rhetorical situation, how to revise, and how to reflect on a writing process to grow as a writer. These chapters follow student writers and artists as they respond to unique rhetorical situations. Specifically, **Chapter 4, "Composing: Drawing on Experience & Evidence,"** helps students decide which genres will work best for their contexts. |
| | Additionally, the guided readings and the thematic approach feature examples of many genres, including multimodal genres. For more avenues into the book, see the Contents, the Index of Genres, and Index of Themes. |
| **Develop facility in responding to a variety of situations and contexts, calling for purposeful shifts in voice, tone, level of formality, design, medium, and/or structure.** | In the Guide section of the book, **guided readings** and **guided processes** highlight the rhetorical situations and genre conventions of a large variety of texts. |
| | The annotations surrounding the guided readings and processes focus on rhetorical situations with a specific emphasis on *purpose, audience, rhetorical appeals,* and *modes/media.* They also focus on the conventions of the genre at hand with specific emphasis on *elements of the genre, style, design,* and *use of sources.* This provides a type of grid that students might apply whenever they read or compose any kind of text, in their composition course and beyond. |
| | For example, **Chapter 4, "Composing: Drawing on Experience & Evidence,"** follows student Gwen Ganow of Red Rocks Community College as she drafts, annotates sources, chooses a genre, and composes in that genre. Gwen's project-in-progress shows readers how she thought through options for composing and using voice, tone, and other techniques in her work, through multiple revisions. |
| | **Chapter 5, "Revising & Remixing,"** follows Gwen as she remixes her composition from one genre to another, demonstrating how voice, tone, formality, design, and other elements, may change from one genre to the next. |
| **Understand and use a variety of technologies to address a range of audiences.** | In **Part 3, "Genres,"** the authors encourage students to use a variety of technologies for composing—from creating "low tech" compositions such as print texts or collages made of found objects—to creating more complex digital texts, such as videos and multigenre projects. These chapters give clear guidance on how to use various strategies, tools, and genres to research, compose, review, revise, and share work aimed at specific audiences. |

| | |
|---|---|
| | Chapter 5, "**Revising & Remixing**," guides readers through integrating peer feedback and remixing work into new genres. Students learn to share documents in electronic environments and to use track changes to draft, collect feedback, and revise. In the **guided process** beginning on page 92, student Gwen Ganow remixes her project from an essay into a PowerPoint presentation, giving readers a practical example for how they might use digital media to compose and remix their own work to suit different contexts. |
| | Chapter 10, "**Assembling a Multigenre Project**," features guided readings of three student projects that address different audiences and use different technologies. |
| **Match the capacities of different environments (e.g., print and electronic) to varying rhetorical situations.** | Attention to rhetorical situations and how composers choose genres, modes, and media to best reach their audiences and achieve their purposes is foundational to *The Bedford Book of Genres*. See the guided readings, guided processes, assignments, and checklists throughout the text. |
| | See **Chapter 1, "Rhetorical Situations & Choices,"** especially the introduction to rhetorical situations (pp. 8–11) and academic text conventions (pp. 13–17). |
| | See **Chapter 4, "Composing: Drawing on Experience & Evidence"** (pp. 46–71), which follows Red Rocks Community College student writer Gwen Ganow. She has a specific context for composing, and readers can see her process as she chooses the genres and media that will best suit her purposes, audiences, and use of rhetorical appeals. |

## CRITICAL THINKING, READING, AND COMPOSING

| | |
|---|---|
| **Use composing and reading for inquiry, learning, thinking, and communicating in various rhetorical contexts.** | The purpose of this book is to help students read, analyze, and compose in any genre and in any context. The authors provide a framework that students can use when reading and analyzing the work of others and in composing their own. By focusing on (1) the rhetorical situation and (2) the conventions of a given genre, students learn to think critically and compose thoughtfully. |
| | While **Part 1, "Rhetoric and Reading"** focuses on how to use reading for inquiry, learning, thinking, and communicating, **Part 2, "The Writing Process"** does the same for composing. |
| **Read a diverse range of texts, attending especially to relationships between assertion and evidence, to patterns of organization, to interplay between verbal and nonverbal elements, and how these features function for different audiences and situations.** | Part 1, "Rhetoric & Reading," offers a range of texts that represent various genres, including verbal and nonverbal. The annotations surrounding the **guided readings** in these chapters make clear how composers use rhetorical appeals and draw on evidence and sources, for example. |
| | The Reader portion is divided into four sections —identities, mind & body, activism, and creativity—and provides a thematic approach to a variety of topics and genres, as well as offering models for composing and sources to draw upon. Each reading includes both analytical questions and a composing project prompt. Each chapter closes with two long-term projects. |

*(Continues on next page)*

| | |
|---|---|
| **Locate and evaluate primary and secondary research materials, including journal articles, essays, books, databases, and informal internet sources.** | Students learn to conduct research, evaluate sources, and draw on them as they compose. See **Part 4, "Composing with Sources"** especially:<br><br>**Chapter 11, "Exploring Topics & Creating a Research Proposal,"** covers how to use sources to develop and refine a topic idea, a research question, a bibliography, and a proposal for further research. Readers follow student Jasmine Huerta through her project on diabetes.<br><br>**Chapter 12, "Evaluating & Choosing Sources,"** covers how to locate, preview, and evaluate primary and secondary sources. Readers follow student Emily Kahn as she previews a source for her project on women in comics, and student Donovan Rodriguez as he evaluates in-depth three different sources for his student anxiety project.<br><br>**Chapter 13, "Integrating & Documenting Sources,"** shows students how to use parenthetical citations and signal phrases, and how to quote, paraphrase, and summarize a source. Readers follow student Paul Pierre through part of his project on nonviolent protest. The second part of Chapter 13 provides a thorough guide to **documenting sources in MLA and APA styles**, with models for documenting even the trickiest electronic sources, such as blogs and video games, as well as objects found in the physical world. APA style coverage has been updated to align with the 2019 APA style manual. |
| **Use strategies—such as interpretation, synthesis, response, critique, and design/redesign—to compose texts that integrate the writer's ideas with those from appropriate sources.** | The role of sources is highlighted in the book, consistently identified in the annotations surrounding the guided readings and guided processes. Students are introduced to the rhetorical situations and genres, then moved from analyzing the work of others to composing their own texts.<br><br>See **Part 4, "Composing with Sources,"** where **guided processes** show strategies used by student writers as they research, compose, and revise. For example, in **Chapter 13, "Integrating & Documenting Sources,"** we follow student Paul Pierre as he quotes from a source, paraphrases a source, and summarizes a source during his research for his project on nonviolent protest.<br><br>In **Chapter 4, "Composing: Drawing on Experience & Evidence,"** see also the guided process that begins on page 54 and follows Red Rocks Community College student Gwen Ganow as she analyzes and integrates sources into her work. Her annotations critically examine each source in terms of the author's purpose, audience, use of rhetorical appeals, and more. |
| **PROCESSES** | |
| **Develop a writing project through multiple drafts.** | **Part 2, "The Writing Process"** guides students in how to craft a writing project and carry it successfully through multiple drafts. In particular, **Chapter 5, "Revising & Remixing,"** emphasizes and demonstrates the importance of drafting and revising multiple times on the way to a final composition. |

| | Part 2 follows student writer Gwen Ganow's work-in-progress, beginning with her early drafts and brainstorms and on to her revisions, work with sources, peer review, Author Statement (in multiple drafts), final composition, and even a remix of that composition into another genre. |
|---|---|
| **Develop flexible strategies for reading, drafting, reviewing, collaboration, revising, rewriting, rereading, and editing.** | These strategies are built into the framework of the book, most visibly in the **guided readings and processes** in Chapters 1 through 10. See especially Chapters 7 through 9, which encompass composing in various genres, and **Chapter 5, "Revising & Remixing,"** which provides guidelines for drafting, revising, and remixing a project into a new genre.<br><br>Chapter 5 also features sections on **Revising Based on Your Own Observations** and **Revising Based on Peer Review** that offer strategies for revision and collaboration. |
| **Use composing processes and tools as a means to discover and reconsider ideas.** | **Chapter 11, "Exploring Topics & Creating a Research Proposal,"** makes clear how to use basic research to discover and test ideas.<br><br>The **guided processes** in this chapter follow student Jasmine Huerta as she moves from a research question to a proposal and working bibliography. Huerta is seen moving from an early idea to a revised, more workable idea.<br><br>**Chapter 12, "Evaluating & Choosing Sources,"** follows student Emily Kahn as she previews a source for her women in comics project, and student Donovan Rodriguez as he evaluates in depth three sources related to his teenage anxiety project.<br><br>See also **Chapter 4, "Composing: Drawing on Experience & Evidence,"** which follows student Gwen Ganow as she drafts and revises her project on superheroes, refining her ideas along the way. |
| **Experience the collaborative and social aspects of the writing processes.** | **Chapter 5, "Revising & Remixing,"** encourages students to collaborate with peers at different points in their composing processes.<br><br>**"Choosing a Topic Through Basic Research"** in **Chapter 11** prompts students to begin a research project by reading for ideas and discussing them with peers. The authors encourage students to use discussion as a way to discover what they want to say about a given topic.<br><br>Guidelines for **revising a draft based on peer review** appear in Chapter 5, with a checklist of questions and follow-up questions to ask peers responding to a draft. See also the chapter's **guided process** for **integrating peer feedback**, beginning with a draft and ending with a finished composition. |
| **Learn to give and act on productive feedback to works in progress.** | In addition to the coverage outlined in the previous entry, the first guided process in Chapter 10, **Integrating Peer Feedback: Draft to Finished Composition** follows student Gwen Ganow as she edits multiple drafts and integrates peer review. |

*(Continues on next page)*

| | |
|---|---|
| **Adapt composing processes for a variety of technologies and modalities.** | This book is designed to help students think of themselves as composers—as authors, artists, and academic writers within specific rhetorical situations—with a variety of genres to choose from when they write and create. |
| | Built into the pedagogy of the entire text (see the guided readings, guided processes, and checklists in particular) is support for making sound choices about genres, technology, and modality. |
| | Students learn to compose any kind of text in whichever modality or technology they choose by applying a basic framework: (1) look at the rhetorical situation first (What do you want to say? Who is your audience?); and (2) think critically and creatively about which genre(s) and modalities would work best in that situation. |
| **Reflect on the development of composing practices and how those practices influence their work.** | Students reflect on their own composing processes and final works in their **Author's/Artist's Statement** (see Chapter 6). Students compose these Statements to accompany their genre compositions. In these documents, student composers discuss their processes—how and why they did what they did, how successful they think they were, and even what they might do differently in a future iteration of the project. |

## KNOWLEDGE OF CONVENTIONS

| | |
|---|---|
| **Develop knowledge of linguistic structures, including grammar, punctuation, and spelling, through practice in composing and revising.** | In the **guided readings and processes**, annotations consistently help students read (and compose) with an eye and ear for style, tone, word choice, and other considerations. This helps them keep multiple audiences in mind. |
| | To complement the book's coverage of composing and revising, and to provide help with grammar, punctuation, and spelling, consider packaging *The Bedford Book of Genres* at a discount with a Bedford handbook. |
| **Understand why genre conventions for structure, paragraphing, tone, and mechanics vary.** | See the guided readings in the following chapters: |
| | Chapter 2, "Genres," Chapter 3, "Reading as a Writer," Chapter 4, "Composing," Chapter 7, "Academic Genres," Chapter 8, "Workplace Genres," and Chapter 9, "Public Genres." |
| | The annotations that surround the guided readings point out specific aspects of genre conventions, including the adaptability and flexibility of genres. |
| **Gain experience negotiating variations in genre conventions.** | Please see above. |
| **Learn common formats and/or design features for different kinds of texts.** | The annotations surrounding the guided readings highlight (1) the composer's rhetorical situations and (2) the conventions of the composer's chosen genre. The conventions of genres that are identified include common elements and use of style, design, and sources. |

| Explore the concepts of intellectual property (such as fair use and copyright) that motivate documentation conventions. | Research coverage appears in **Part 4, "Composing with Sources"** (Chapters 11–15) in which the authors and several of their students take readers through steps for exploring a topic, evaluating and choosing sources, and integrating and documenting them. For example, see the guided processes for how to preview a source, how to evaluate a source, how to quote from a source, how to paraphrase a source, and how to summarize a source. Students will find advice for how to avoid plagiarism, especially the kind that can happen inadvertently when working with digital sources. Of particular interest in our research material is the section on MLA and APA documentation in Chapter 13, in which the models show students how to cite today's sources, such as videos, games, wiki articles, and artifacts. |
|---|---|
| **Practice applying citation conventions systematically in their own work.** | See above. **Chapter 13, "Integrating & Documenting Sources"** gives students readable guidance on how to use parenthetical citations and signal phrases, how to cite sources at the end of their papers, and also how to safeguard against plagiarism. Guided processes show how to quote from a source, paraphrase, and summarize, and the guide to MLA and APA styles uses a visual, handbook-style approach that takes the mystery out of how to use these styles correctly. |

# BRIEF CONTENTS

# CONTENTS

## 8   Workplace Genres   174

## 9  Public Genres  212

## 10   Assembling a Multigenre Project   298

**PART 4  COMPOSING WITH SOURCES**   315

## 11   Exploring Topics & Creating a Research Proposal   316

# 12 Evaluating & Choosing Sources 338

# 13 Integrating & Documenting Sources 372

**READER**

## 18   Creativity: It's Complicated   521

# the Bedford Book of Genres

# Guide

# PART 1
# RHETORIC & READING

# 1

# RHETORICAL SITUATIONS & CHOICES

What is *rhetoric*? It refers to the ability to communicate effectively and with a purpose. So what is a *rhetorical situation*? It's the context in which you create a composition. To put it simply, as a writer, you have a specific purpose and an audience. You need to know what you want to say; you also need to know your readers' expectations and accommodate them in some way. For example, when you write a review of a restaurant on yelp.com, you know that Yelp readers want to know your opinion of the meal; they also expect specific details about the individual dishes, service, and ambience you experienced.

Thinking about the rhetorical situation before you begin composing can help you make all sorts of important decisions about your composition, including what level of vocabulary to use (simpler words for an audience of middle schoolers than for a college-educated audience), what kinds of examples to use (more technical examples for an audience of experts than for an audience of laypeople), and what kind of color scheme to use (high-contrast color scheme for people who have color blindness if you anticipate they might be part of your audience).

In 1968, Lloyd Bitzer, a communications scholar, first articulated the modern concept of a rhetorical situation.* He identified three aspects of rhetorical situations:

- **The exigence:** The motivation for the writer or composer. For example, our exigence for writing this chapter is that we want college students to understand the importance of rhetorical situations in their own reading and writing. In this book, we use the term "purpose" to convey the idea of exigence.
- **The audience:** Whoever will receive the message conveyed by the writer or composer. Our audience right now is you, students in a college writing course.
- **The constraints:** The situational factors that a writer or composer must take into account. One of our constraints is that a textbook relies on the written word, so although we might want to explain rhetorical situations to you through an interpretive dance, we are instead using written words.

You consider rhetorical situations all the time, even if you are not consciously aware of doing so. When you make choices about the way you tell a story about a snowboarding adventure you had—perhaps including more colorful language and slang when you tell the story to your friends and then choosing more formal language when you tell the story to your insurance agent—you are responding to a particular rhetorical situation. There is no one "right" way to tell the story of your adventure. The way you tell the story depends on your audience. Likewise, your purpose in telling the story makes a difference: If you are telling the story to illustrate that you are an adrenaline junky, you may highlight the level of risk or danger involved in snowboarding, but if you are telling the

---

*Bitzer, Lloyd F. "The Rhetorical Situation." *Philosophy & Rhetoric*, vol. 1, no. 1, 1968, pp. 1–14.

story to convince a nervous friend to try snowboarding, you might emphasize that you avoided injury on your adventure by taking a few precautions and using high-quality equipment.

Already today, you've probably been involved in several rhetorical situations. If you think of rhetorical situations broadly to include any communication event, then any interaction you had this morning with roommates, family, fellow public transportation riders, or the barista at your favorite coffee shop counts. Think about how you communicated differently with these different people. You might have been more polite with some, more direct with some, or more verbose with some. You may not have even realized you were making choices in your level of politeness, directness, or verbosity because you probably understand the concept of rhetorical situations instinctively.

In this book, we will constantly ask you to think explicitly about the rhetorical situations you find yourself in so that you can be more deliberate about the choices you make in your day-to-day interactions and in your writing. As you think about rhetorical situations, we will ask you to consider your purpose, your audience, your use of rhetorical appeals, and your choice of modes and media. In other words, we will ask you to think carefully about rhetorical choices.

# Understanding Rhetorical Situations & Choices

## Purpose | Why Are You Composing?

Every time you write—or compose anything, in any genre—you do so for a reason. You might be trying to convince someone to change their mind about something or take action. You might be telling a story to build rapport with someone or entertain them. You might be giving someone information to help them make a decision. Or you might have another purpose.

There are many reasons to write, and sometimes these reasons overlap. As writers, we often have several purposes for creating a single text. Let's look at a possible example. Let's assume that you love farmers' markets and want to establish one in your town. Your purpose is to start up a weekly local farmers' market. To make this happen, you need to (1) present your idea to others and (2) persuade them that it's worth acting upon. You expect that some people will object. In this context or rhetorical situation, you have more than one purpose. To persuade others, you need to explain your idea, say what's great about it, provide supporting statistics, and tell a persuasive story about how a similar plan succeeded in a neighboring town. You also have more than one audience. Some people will agree with you 100 percent; others won't be so sure; still others—maybe grocery store owners or city planners—will reject your idea altogether.

# Audience | Whom Are You Composing For?

Every time you compose, you do so for multiple audiences: a primary audience, who are your intended readers, and a secondary audience, who are other people who might end up reading what you wrote. For example, we are writing this book for you, students, so you are our primary audience; however, writing instructors and writing program administrators are likely also going to read this book. Audiences are made up of people—and people can be easily bored, pressed for time, or generally disinterested. You need to grab their attention and keep it. Let's look at an example: Imagine you are traveling across the country and want to tell stories of your adventures (your purpose) to your friends, family, and even strangers interested in travel (your audience). You decide that the best way to reach your audience is to create a blog where you can write about your experiences, show maps and photos, and connect to other social media sites. That is what the world-traveling blogger Gilad Hizkiyahu (who also calls himself Giladhiz) decided to do (see p. 10).

Gilad clearly understands his audiences (his primary audience of travelers and a secondary audience of folks like us who happened upon his blog while looking for examples) and wants them to stick with him. To this end, he does the following:

- Provides a photo of himself and an "About the Author" section so that readers can make a personal connection with him
- Addresses his readers directly: "So, dear friends and accidental surfers, allow me to begin with the reasons that brought me to plan and go on that trip"
- Writes in a casual, readable, and humorous style, meant to hook his readers and keep them interested in his ongoing adventures
- Structures his posts with subheadings to guide readers, and provides options for navigating content and for e-mailing or connecting by social media

## CHECKLIST | Composing with a Purpose

As you begin to compose, ask yourself:

- ☐ Why am I writing? What do I want to communicate? To whom?
- ☐ What do I want my audience to believe or do after reading my composition?
- ☐ Is what I'm communicating objectionable or controversial to anyone? If so, how will I address this?

- ☐ If I'm trying to convince someone of something, what are the best ways to do so for my particular readers?
- ☐ If I'm trying to build rapport with someone, how can I share something about myself or my experiences to help my readers relate to me?
- ☐ If I'm helping someone make a decision, what information does my reader need, and how can I communicate it clearly?

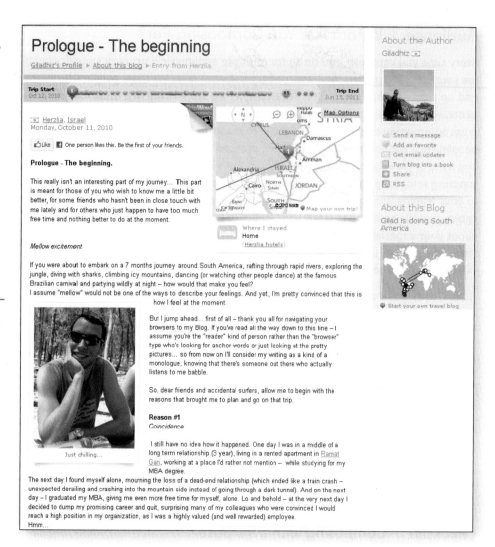

► TRAVEL BLOG

**Gilad Hizkiyahu** (also known as Giladhiz), from *Gilad Is Doing South America*.

*Credit: Gilad Hizkiyahu*

**WRITE**

When you write, do you think of who will read your writing? When you compose a status update on social media, do you think of who will experience what you've created? Write about a time you considered your audience when writing a tweet, a photo caption on Instagram, or a post on another social media platform.

## Rhetorical Appeals │ Ethos, Pathos, and Logos

Regardless of what your purpose is, you need to get your audience on board. This means that all writing has a persuasive element because you are trying to convince the reader to see things the way you do. We persuade our audiences by using what are called *rhetorical appeals*. They are often used in combination:

- **Ethos** is the credibility, authority, and trustworthiness the writer or composer conveys to the audience.

- **Pathos** is an appeal to an audience's emotions or values.

- **Logos** is the logic and connection of facts and evidence to the point being made.

# Modes & Media

**What do we mean by mode?**  When you want to communicate an idea to an audience, you have to decide whether to express it in writing, visually, through sound, or in some other way. Do you want to write down your idea? Express it visually with paint on canvas? Tell the story orally? Whichever method of expression you choose is the composition's mode.

There are many modes, but for the purpose of this book, we work with three modes: **written** or **text-based**, **visual**, and **audio**. The term *multimodal* refers to more than one mode used in a composition. For example, a photo essay usually uses two modes (text and visuals), while a TED talk might use three modes (visuals, and text on slides, and the audio delivery of the speech).

**What do we mean by media?**  Media is how the composition is delivered to its audience. Will your audience read your piece in a book (print), or will they read it in an e-book (digital)? Will your audience watch your TED talk by going to the TED Talk website (digital), watch you deliver it on stage (face-to-face), or read a transcript of it (print)?

For the purpose of this book, we work primarily with three types of media: **print, digital**, and **face-to-face**. Media also includes film, television, software, MP3s, and more.

A particular mode can be delivered in multiple media. For example, a musical performance can be delivered live on stage or recorded for viewing on your laptop or phone. An obituary might be printed in a newspaper or published online.

The modes of Gilad's blog, *Gilad Is Doing South America*, are both written and visual, and the medium is digital. A simple way to distinguish mode from medium is to think of mode as the "how" and medium as the "delivery system." A separate concept is genre, which we will cover in Chapter 2. For now, keep in mind that the genre—in Gilad's case, a blog—is what the composer presents as a final product.

WRITE

Go back to the paragraph you wrote from page 8 about a rhetorical situation you were involved in earlier today. Write another paragraph in which you discuss the mode and media choices you made and why you made them. How might the situation have unfolded differently if you had made different choices?

## CHECKLIST | Composing for an Audience

As you begin to compose, ask yourself:

- Who is my audience in terms of demographics? How do they identify in terms of gender? What is their age range? Where do they live? What do they like? Do they have particular religious beliefs? Are they from a particular social class? Are they of a particular race or ethnic background?
- What is my audience's stake in the issue I'm presenting? Do they care? Why or why not?
- What does my audience value? Will my message be in line with—or contradictory to—their values?

How can I present my message so that my audience will consider it, and perhaps even be persuaded by it?
- What level of education does my audience have? What kind of language will best reach them?
- Who is my primary audience, and what do they need to know?
- What possible secondary audiences might read this, and how do I need to take them into account?

# Reading Rhetorical Situations

In your classes, you might have heard your professors say that the course emphasizes critical reading. This might even be noted on the course syllabus. Reading the rhetorical situation of a text is an important aspect of critical reading. Doing so allows you to dig beneath what is being said to understand the choices the writer made while composing.

Reading rhetorically is an active way to read. You are interacting with the text, noticing and asking questions about the assumptions the composer made. For example, if you are reading a letter to the editor arguing that a homeless shelter should be closed because it is expensive to operate, you might notice that the writer's argument hinges on the assumption that a homeless shelter should not cost the public so much to operate. That means the writer must believe that there is an appropriate amount of money that should be spent on housing the homeless. You might ask where the writer got his or her information about how much the shelter costs to operate. Are the figures current? You might also ask about other perspectives, such as those of the homeless people who rely on the shelter, or the people employed by the shelter.

Initially, when you pick up something to read, you probably read it to understand the message the writer is trying to convey. For example, if you read a Yelp review of a nearby restaurant, you might read it to see whether the writer says you should eat there. However, if you were to read this review rhetorically, you would examine how the writer got her point across. You wouldn't only be concerned with whether you want to eat at the restaurant, but you would dig into *how* the author convinced or failed to convince you to eat at that restaurant. To read something rhetorically, you read to understand not just what the writer is telling you, but also how the writer conveys information and makes her point. When reading rhetorically, you might ask who the composer is, why the piece was written (purpose), whom the composer is addressing (audience), and how language is used to convey the message or appeal to the audience.

## Reading to Understand Purpose

Knowing why a piece was written helps you understand how you might experience it and what you can reasonably expect to get from it. Is the purpose to persuade you about an issue? Help you make a decision? Provide a constant stream of belly laughs? Share a story? Knowing that a Yelp review about a restaurant is intended to help you make a decision about whether to eat at that establishment keeps you focused on looking at the reasons the writer gives for eating there rather than lingering on a clever turn of phrase.

## Reading to Understand Audience

Understanding whom a piece is written for helps you determine what extra information you might need to digest the text. Are you the intended primary audience? If not, how does the piece pertain to you? If the audience of a piece about a landslide is a geologist, you might need to look up some terms to understand the information. What additional resources will you need to understand or relate to the piece?

## Reading to Understand Rhetorical Appeals

Consider who the writer is. Is this person qualified to write about the subject? Is the Yelp reviewer someone who eats out a lot? Once you've determined whether the writer is credible (*ethos*), read to see how the writer establishes that credibility. Is credibility established through the level of information or details provided? Through the language used? Is it established because the writer has written numerous pieces about the subject? Another thing to consider is how the writer connects with you (*pathos*). Are you hooked? Is it because of the emotion used to help you feel the situation? Consider your reactions to the text and why you continue to read or view it. Finally, ask yourself how the author makes his case (*logos*). Is it supported with evidence? Are ideas organized in a particular way to help you consider the question at hand?

## Reading to Understand Modes & Media

Why has the writer chosen to use text? Is it because that's the most efficient way to convey the information to their intended audience? Did the writer include pictures? If so, ask yourself why the visuals were included. Perhaps the Yelp review you're examining incorporates a photo of the delicious onion soup dumplings to illustrate the unique qualities of the chef. This might help convince you to try the restaurant more than if just words were used. If you are listening to a podcast about the homeless, you might ask how listening to the story affects you. Did the writer choose to record words so you could hear the voices of the homeless?

In addition to examining the modes used, read to understand the choices made in media. Is the piece available digitally so that it can be accessed anywhere there is an internet connection? You might want to access a Yelp review from your computer at home when planning a trip, or from your phone when you land in an unfamiliar city and are starving, seeking some comfort food for dinner.

While reading rhetorically might seem like a lot of work, it ultimately helps you gain a better understanding of the decisions the composer has made. This not only helps you discern the messages in a seemingly difficult text, but it also helps you consider the ways you might deliver your own messages. Throughout the text, you will see numerous guided readings that illustrate ways to read rhetorically.

# Reading Academic Texts

You've probably been reading for most of your life and probably read countless texts every day—road signs, text messages, food labels, and more. But reading complex academic texts such as textbooks, peer-reviewed journal articles, and scholarly books requires a special set of skills. When you read road signs, you are simply reading for information. Academic texts, however, usually make an argument of some sort; if you simply read them for information, you might miss the point the authors are making. For example, if you read the previous material about reading rhetorical situations and just took away that it includes noticing purpose, audience, appeals, modes, and media, you would be missing the point that understanding the rhetorical situation helps you see why a writer made certain decisions.

This is a textbook, which means that our rhetorical situation is an academic one. Academic genres may have elements that might not be commonly experienced, so we are providing some strategies you can use to make these complex texts more digestible. You will be able to use some of these strategies with workplace and public genres as well.

## Previewing

Rather than diving in to read from the beginning, it can be helpful to skim through a complex text from beginning to end to get a sense of its organization and purpose. Skimming will help you understand what the topic is and what argument is being made. For example, simply skimming through to read the headings can help you see whether a text will cover both a problem and a solution or only discuss the problem.

## Looking for Key Terms

As you preview, you may notice that some technical terms are used in the headings or are in bold or italics in the text. Since these terms are being emphasized, you should make sure you comprehend them or you will have trouble making sense of the text once you begin reading it more closely. Identify key terms and be sure to look up definitions if you are unsure of what they mean. For example, if you see the word *hegemony* several times in your skimming and aren't absolutely certain what it means, you should look it up, because it is clearly essential to an understanding of the text.

## Identifying Knowledge Claims & Evidence

After you skim the text, you will need to read it at least once, slowly and carefully. As you read, notice the difference between facts and knowledge claims. A fact is something that is uncontested; a knowledge claim is open to debate. For example, it is a fact that millennials spend more time reading on the internet than reading books; it is a knowledge claim that this is problematic. Once you identify something as a knowledge claim, you want to search for the evidence that supports that claim. For example, in the 1968 article mentioned earlier, Lloyd Bitzer makes a knowledge claim that some rhetorical situations are so dramatic that we "can predict with near certainty" what the response will be. He then supports that claim with a discussion of the rhetorical response to President Kennedy's assassination.

## Considering the Composer's Perspective

Many people have written about farmers' markets, but consider how different an article on farmers' markets written by an economist might be from an article written by a city planner. The economist will likely be considering the economic impact on communities, consumers, large- or small-scale farmers, while the city planner will more likely be thinking about how weekend farmers' markets impact traffic patterns and put pressure on a community's parking options. Understanding the perspective of the composer will help you understand why particular knowledge claims are made and not others.

## Annotating the Text

One way to force yourself to read slowly and deliberately is to annotate the text you are reading. Annotating is different from highlighting, which is simply noting important words or sentences in the text. Annotating means making notes directly on the text. You can do this by writing on a hard copy or using software to add notes to a digital copy. With highlighting, you are limited to noting what the author has said; annotating allows you to summarize the writer's ideas in your own words, which is a good way to understand and remember them. Additionally, you might want to ask questions, write down definitions of words you looked up right next to the words themselves, and write down connections or contradictions you notice between the text you are reading and other texts.

## Annotated Example | Reading an Academic Text

Following is an example of an academic text: an assignment to create a bibliography that you might get from your instructor. This assignment sheet is from Elizabeth's second-semester composition course. The annotations in the margins (in black) show you how you might read the assignment using the strategies we've described.

**Composition 201**

Metropolitan State University of Denver

▼ The following annotations are ones that you might make as a student while critically reading this assignment so that you can complete it successfully.

This is an assignment sheet that gives step-by-step instructions for completing the assignment.

After you have conducted general research on your topic and have a sense of the issues, subtopics, agreements, and disagreements discussed by people committed to your topic, you are ready to delve more deeply into your topic. Peer-reviewed journal articles are a good place to do research when you are ready to move beyond what the general public knows about your topic and find out what experts are discussing. Showing that you're knowledgeable about experts in the field helps you establish your ethos as a researcher.

I will need to check the syllabus to confirm when the due date is for this assignment.

1. Find 14 peer-reviewed journal articles on your topic. If you are not sure if your articles have been peer-reviewed, ask me or a librarian for help.
2. For each article, do the following:
   a. Read the entire article. Journal articles are not "quick reads," so be sure you have plenty of time and are in a space where you can concentrate. I highly recommend that you annotate as you read.
   b. Write a bibliographic entry in MLA or APA format.
   c. Write a one-paragraph summary of the main argument or point the article makes and the support offered. This should be a well-developed paragraph of at least five sentences. Journal articles make complex arguments, so you will not be able to do an article's main argument justice in fewer than five sentences. All quotations and paraphrases should include in-text citations.
   d. Write a one-paragraph discussion of how the article aligns with, departs from, extends, or complicates what other sources on the bibliography say. Again, this should be a well-developed paragraph, with some examples to support your assessment. All quotations and para-phrases should include in-text citations. Note that you may not end up using all of these articles as sources in your research paper. That's normal—most researchers consult many more sources than they end up using. You may also end up using or consulting non-peer-reviewed journal articles; that's fine, but ONLY peer-reviewed journal articles should appear on your annotated bibliographies.

A knowledge claim made by this text is: "Peer-reviewed journal articles are a good place to do research when you are ready to move beyond what the general public knows about your topic and find out what experts are discussing." This is then supported with the evidence that this type of research "helps you establish your ethos as a researcher."

The term "peer-reviewed" comes up 5 times in this short document. It must be a key concept that I will need to understand to complete the assignment.

Credit: Elizabeth Kleinfeld.

Are you reading an academic text, such as an assignment or a scholarly essay? Keep the following questions in mind:

☐ **Purpose.** Is the writer trying to convince you of something? Is the writer sharing a story? Is the writer giving me information? You might even notice other purposes that we haven't mentioned here, such as entertaining you. Is the writer reporting, telling a story, entertaining, and persuading all at the same time? Don't worry. Sometimes the purposes for writing or composing overlap.

☐ **Audience.** Who seems to be the author's primary audience? Secondary audience? How do you know? Why do you think someone would read (view, listen to, etc.) the text? How does the author capture and sustain audience attention?

☐ **Rhetorical appeals.** How does the author use the rhetorical appeals—ethos, pathos, and logos—to reach his or her audience? How does the author convey credibility? What kinds of evidence does the author offer to support the point of the piece?

☐ **Modes & media.** What choices has the writer made about mode (how to convey an idea)? If multiple modes are used, how do they interact with each other? What choices has the writer made about media? For example, has the writer made the piece available in print form or digitally? How do the writer's choices about modes and media reflect his or her purposes and audiences?

---

**PRACTICE**

# Reading Any Text Rhetorically

Locate three texts you have read today—maybe a text message, an advertisement, an assignment sheet, or another text for one of your courses. For each one, identify the purpose, audience, rhetorical appeals, and mode and media. Is reading these texts through a rhetorical lens different from how you read them in the first place? Write one paragraph for each piece to explain.

# 2 GENRES

In Chapter 1, "Rhetorical Situations & Choices," we explained that composition scholar Lloyd Bitzer was concerned with describing the rhetorical situation, but he doesn't address how to respond to the rhetorical situation. That's where "genre," the key word in this chapter's title, comes in. Genre is how the speaker chooses to respond to the rhetorical situation.

The concept of genre has existed since the ancient Greeks used it to classify literature, and following the Greeks, today the word is sometimes oversimplified to mean "category" or "type." Scholar Carolyn Miller, however, gives a modern-day definition of genre as a social response to a rhetorical situation.* The word "social" highlights that genre is a form of communication between a speaker and an audience; it involves social interaction.

For example, let's say you are working on an assignment for your biology class the night before it is due, and you realize you don't understand the assignment. The rhetorical situation you find yourself in involves a purpose (you need to figure out what the instructor wants you to do) and an audience (your instructor). You also need to take into account that it's too late to call your instructor because office hours have been over for many hours, and you know you probably should have read the assignment more closely when you first got it and asked questions then, instead of waiting until the last minute. As you consider your options for communicating with your instructor (genre responses) about this pickle you're in, you are considering *social responses to your rhetorical situation*:

1. You could write an e-mail in which you apologize for waiting until the last minute and ask for clarification.

2. You could text a classmate and hope that she can explain the assignment.

3. You could wait until tomorrow and go to the instructor's office first thing in the morning to ask for clarification.

4. You could make some educated guesses about what the instructor wants, do the assignment as best you can, and keep your fingers crossed.

5. You could just take a 0 on the assignment.

Notice that each of the first four options includes a particular form of communication: an e-mail, a text, an in-person conversation, and an assignment that may or may not be completed correctly. But even the fifth option, not submitting anything, is a genre of communication: doing nothing in this case is a deliberate choice, and so it counts as a social response to the rhetorical situation.

WRITE

Think of a rhetorical situation you found yourself in recently in which you considered two or more possible responses. Write a brief paragraph in which you describe the two (or more) options you considered, and explain why you went with the one you did.

---

*Miller, Carolyn R. "Genre as Social Action." *Quarterly Journal of Speech*, vol. 70, no. 2, 1984, pp. 151–167.

# Reading Genres

Why bother thinking about genres? Because they represent possibilities. We wrote this book to acknowledge that in college and beyond, there are many more genres available to us besides the five-paragraph essay or the traditional term paper. As respectable and time-honored as those genres are, there are a whole lot of other options out there. We wrote this book to help you understand and create in a variety of genres—and we invite you to produce works that matter to you and enjoy doing so. As an added bonus, paying attention to genre will make you a better writer and artist because you'll be focused on the needs of your audiences and your own purposes as a composer. Below, we highlight two examples of genres as social responses. As you read other genres in this book, keep in mind that they are all social responses.

## The Blog as a Social Response

Because genres are responses to social situations, they are dynamic, changing over time as people and their needs change over time. Before digital composing, writers who wanted to record their thoughts wrote with a pen in a journal or diary, in a physical notebook. Then blogs were created, and since then, blogs have changed. The original blogs were more stream of consciousness and had smaller audiences than many blogs today. Blogs changed because the people using them, both composers and audiences, realized that blogs could be interactive, could be shared, could be multimodal, and more. Thus, the genre of blog continues to change.

Christine Goforth, who hosts the blog *The Dragonfly Woman*, identifies herself as an "aquatic entomologist with a blogging habit." In her first blog entry, dated May 28, 2009, she explains why she adopted the name "Dragonfly Woman" and how she went from being a kid terrified of insects to a woman obsessed with dragonflies.

The "About DW" page on Christine's blog states that she is now a "bona fide entomologist/scientist" who manages citizen science for the North Carolina Museum of Natural Sciences. She explains her rhetorical situation, speaking directly to her readers. In several paragraphs, she acknowledges her audience and purpose:

> If you arrived here, you probably wanted to learn a little more about the crazy woman who tells strange stories and goes on and on about aquatic insect respiration on this blog. I'd hate to disappoint, so here is everything you ever wanted to know about me or my blog condensed down into a few bullet points.
>
> I am a bona fide entomologist/scientist—I have an undergraduate degree in biology and a grad degree in entomology. I don't know whether that makes me seem any more reliable or trustworthy to my readers or not, but there it is. I study aquatic insects, especially behavior and respiration in giant water bugs and dragonflies. If you've spent any time here in the summer, you'll know I also run a citizen science project called the Dragonfly Swarm Project.

I am NOT a taxonomist, so I *will* get the occasional identification wrong. If you happen to notice a mistake, *please* let me know (use that Contact Me button above). It's frustrating enough to read all the misinformation about insects online without being part of the problem.

I cover a variety of topics, but everything is at least tangentially related to insects. I had originally intended for this blog to be purely educational, but it's evolved into more of a celebration of insects, scientifically, culturally, and personally. I like it better this way.

**Christine Goforth**, from her blog *The Dragonfly Woman* (thedragonflywoman.com)

By acknowledging that she is not a taxonomist, Goforth makes it clear that her purpose is not to be meticulous with identifying insect species, but rather to use her blog to host a "celebration of insects, scientifically, culturally, and personally." In keeping with the celebratory theme, the tone of the blog is enthusiastic and even a bit folksy, as she tries to entice people who might be more like the scared kid she was into becoming more appreciative and less fearful of insects. By sharing her personal excitement about bugs, she helps her audience see them as beautiful and fascinating. All of this also helps her develop ethos and come across as a credible source.

Goforth uses the genre of the blog because she wants to reach out to many more people than she could through her job at the museum in North Carolina. She can tell museum-goers that her blog is a place for them to pursue their curiosity about insects, and she can also count on getting traffic to her blog from people who search online for topics she covers, including "giant water bugs" and "terrestrial insects." Since the blog also includes many links to other blogs and websites on insects, it is a rich resource for anyone interested in entomology.

While blogs are no doubt a familiar genre, think for a moment about the different genres you read and compose in each day. As a student, you write research papers and presentations; these are two examples of academic genres. In each case, you know what is expected of you as a writer because you understand certain features of the genre. You know that in order to write a research paper, you must gather a variety of reliable sources and cite them in a specific way.

▼ **BLOG**

**Christine Goforth**, *The Dragonfly Woman*. In her post titled "Well-Nigh Wordless Wednesday: Itty Bitty Wasp," she writes: "I was walking past my back door about a month ago and caught sight of something out of the corner of my eye. I went to inspect and discovered this: [see image] A very tiny wasp! I'm betting it's one of the parasitic wasps, based on the diminutive size and enormous hind legs. I grabbed my iPhone and my "macro" lens and snapped a few photos because it was simply too adorable to pass up. Apparently my glass could do with a bit of cleaning, though." See thedragonflywoman.com.
*Credit: Christine L. Goforth.*

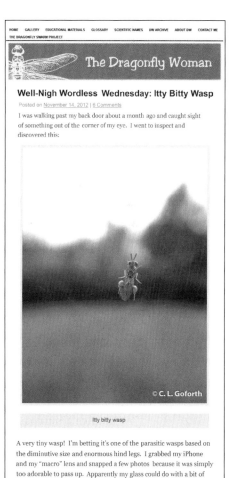

In other situations, you choose the genre to compose in, depending on what you want to say, who you want to say it to, and how you want to say it. Your choice of genre also depends on your own skills and interests as well as the materials available to you. For example, your band is playing next week, and you need to advertise the event. Your purpose is to persuade your potential audience to come to your show. You might choose to present your ad as a poster. Depending on your supplies and desired effect, you could create a handmade poster to tape up at school or design one to post on Facebook. Alternatively, you might choose to advertise by creating and posting a short music video.

## The Memoir as a Social Response

One of the best ways to become a better writer or composer is to read like one—to pay attention to what other writers and composers do, how and why they work in a particular genre, and how they make that genre work for them. Let's look at an example from history. Annie L. Burton (ca. 1858–unknown) was born a slave and as an adult decided to write about her experiences; her 1909 memoir is titled *Memories of Childhood's Slavery Days*. She writes:

> Our clothes were little homespun cotton slips, with short sleeves. I never knew what shoes were until I got big enough to earn them myself. If a slave man and woman wished to marry, a party would be arranged some Saturday night among the slaves. The marriage ceremony consisted of the pair jumping over a stick. If no children were born within a year or so, the wife was sold. At New Year's, if there was any debt or mortgage on the plantation, the extra slaves were taken to Clayton and sold at the court house. In this way families were separated.

While we can't fully know Burton's purpose in writing her memoir, we can assume she wrote to help her readers understand how a formerly enslaved African American woman experienced and resisted expected social and economic roles. What we do know, however, is that she was motivated by her faith. In her memoir, she states:

> For God has commanded me to write this book, that someone may read and receive comfort and courage to do what God commands them to do. God bless every soul who shall read this true life story of one born in slavery.

Thus one purpose of the memoir was to give readers "comfort and courage to do what God commands them to do." Another purpose might have been to help women readers understand what it was like to be a woman and a slave.

Since a purpose of slave narratives is to build empathy in readers, Burton probably intended to reach white people who had not suffered the indignities of slavery. Her audience might have also included literate former slaves, most likely in the North because her book was published in Boston. Her current audience might include students like you, scholars, and historians who want to read a firsthand account of slave life.

Memories of Childhood's
Slavery Days

By

Annie L. Burton

BOSTON
ROSS PUBLISHING COMPANY
1909

Burton likely took into account various constraints and situational factors, including the attitudes of white readers toward African Americans. While she had the education and writing skills to sustain an ambitious writing and research project, she chose to tell her own story simply. As Burton considered her rhetorical situation—she wanted to communicate a message of resistance and faith—and pondered an effective social response, she must have noticed that a very popular genre of the day was memoir. Because memoirs were widely read, Burton could expect a good-sized audience for her piece, and she stood to make some profit from it. The memoir allowed Burton to tell her personal story the way she wanted to tell it, to make her point about resistance, and to set it in a historical context.

So Burton chose her genre—the memoir—as a social response to her rhetorical situation. If she had been trained in music, she could have written a ballad or an opera, or if she had been born a little later, she might have told her story as a documentary film.

In her memoir, Burton wrote in the first person, portrayed real people, described settings, conveyed conflict, and told stories from her own life. These elements are features of the memoir genre and of any autobiography.

## Some Genre Conventions

Do you want to be a great writer or composer? If so, you need to know something about the genre you're composing in; you need to know its basic qualities and agreed-upon conventions, and you need to be familiar with some examples. As Scott McCloud shows in his book *Understanding Comics*, writers and artists who work on comics use visual images and text to convey ideas, balloons to indicate dialogue, and simple but dynamic drawings and design to hold the reader's attention. Let's say you want to tell a story and convey it graphically. You don't need to be McCloud, Picasso, or Art Spiegelman, but you do need to understand how artists, graphic novelists, and memoirists work with visuals and text to tell stories. It helps to have some familiarity with the genre (read a few examples!) and perhaps have one example in mind as a model.

Or let's say you want to draw an annotated map of your neighborhood. It would help to know some of the established conventions of mapmakers, such as using color to represent specific geography, or symbols to identify features or places. If you're using a blog or social media to share your thoughts on specific news items, you will have more authority when you link directly to the material you're responding to. Hyperlinking is a convention of the blog genre.

Keep an open mind as you choose genres to compose in. Consider collaborating with classmates who have more detailed knowledge of the genres you're less familiar with. Often students in our writing classes will discuss and figure out together the

▶ COMIC

**Scott McCloud**, from his book *Understanding Comics: The Invisible Art.*

Credit: Excerpt from p. 66 "See that space BETWEEN . . ." from UNDERSTANDING COMICS by SCOTT MCCLOUD, copyright © 1993, 1994 by Scott McCloud. Reprinted by permission of HarperCollins Publishers.

conventions of specific genres and media (e.g., video or PowerPoint) and go from there. Other times, they keep it simple but thoughtful, creating scrapbooks, print-based texts, or audio essays.

## Common Elements

In this book, we ask you to pay attention to the main features of a given genre: the specific elements that are common to most examples of the genre. For instance, most press release writers try to be as brief and objective as possible and to aim at answering the questions who? what? why? where? and when? For those reasons, we consider brevity, objectivity, and thoroughness to be elements of the press release genre. (For an example, see Paul Henderson's press release "Wall Arch Collapses" on p. 41.)

## Style

*Style* refers to the particular ways we communicate. In this book, we pay attention to the techniques that individual writers use—and to what extent these techniques reflect the style of others composing in the same genre. We look at how much detail writers include and how precise that detail is. We listen for tone (seriousness, humor, etc.) and voice (the presence of the author) and analyze how these qualities affect the overall composition. How a writer uses sources is part of style as well. A writer who has cultivated a serious, academic style will probably use serious, academic sources as evidence. A writer with a more casual, chatty style might depend more on conversations with friends for evidence.

As a writer, you use style when you compose. The trick is to make sure that the style you're using is appropriate to your purpose and accessible and persuasive to your audience. For example, the writer and traveler we mentioned in Chapter 1, Gilad Hizkiyahu, uses a particular style on his blog. Because he is interested in attracting "accidental surfers" to his blog—that is, people who stumble upon his blog accidentally—he takes a casual and funny approach to his travels rather than a serious, scholarly tone. Such a tone would probably appeal to an audience interested in the economics or politics of his travels, but because Gilad's purpose is to share his quirky, funny adventures, his casual, humorous style makes more sense.

## Design

*Design* describes the visual features of a composition, including the use of headings, format, color, and illustration. Design is aesthetic but also functional. As we discuss throughout the book, the design features you and other writers choose can be important in achieving purposes and reaching audiences. Take a look at how Gilad uses images in his blog. Maps show readers exactly where this traveler is, the timeline indicates the duration of his trip, and the photos of Gilad help readers connect with him

▶ TRAVEL BLOG

**Gilad Hizkiyahu,**
Excerpt from *Gilad Is Doing South America*. Notice Gilad's photo caption: "Just chilling . . ." He writes, "So, dear friends and accidental surfers, allow me to begin with the reasons that brought me to plan and go on [this] trip. Reason #1: *Coincidence*. I still have no idea how it happened. . . ." The blogger chooses informal language and humor to draw in his readers.

*Credit: Gilad Hizkiyahu.*

Just chilling...

But I jump ahead… first of all – thank you all for navigating your browsers to my Blog. If you've read all the way down to this line – I assume you're the "reader" kind of person rather than the "browser" type who's looking for anchor words or just looking at the pretty pictures… so from now on I'll consider my writing as a kind of a monologue, knowing that there's someone out there who actually listens to me babble.

So, dear friends and accidental surfers, allow me to begin with the reasons that brought me to plan and go on that trip.

**Reason #1**
*Coincidence*

I still have no idea how it happened. One day I was in a middle of a long term relationship (3 year), living in a rented apartment in Ramat Gan, working at a place I'd rather not mention – while studying for my MBA degree.

personally. His photos documenting his travels let readers see what he saw. Because one of his purposes is to allow others to share in his travels vicariously, the photos are particularly important.

## Sources

*Sources* are the people, conversations, documents, books, journal articles, movies, and other works that we refer to for facts, perspectives, and models as we compose. For example, sources Gilad drew on for his travel blog in Chapter 1 include Google Maps, the people he meets, and tourist information, such as brochures from historical sites. In this book, we consider sources because sources shape what writers create.

WRITE

How might the use of sources help boost—or undermine—your ethos as a composer? Brainstorm a quick list of five ways the sources you choose could boost your ethos and five ways the sources you choose could undermine your ethos.

When you compose in certain genres, such as academic and research essays, you need to document the sources you refer to. In other cases, such as novels, comics, and music lyrics, while you've read and used sources, you're not required to document them formally. Whether or not sources need to be documented depends on the rhetorical situation. Sources referred to in a research essay aimed at academic readers should be documented because readers will want to know where ideas and information came from; the purposes of song lyrics are different, though. Listeners of a song aren't listening for information, so the sources of information are less important. Throughout the book, we look at the conventions of specific genres in this regard, and in Chapter 13, we provide specific guidelines for using documentation styles.

To compose in different genres, you first should be able to identify them, see how other writers use them to achieve purposes and reach audiences, and learn some of the basic features so you can experiment with them.

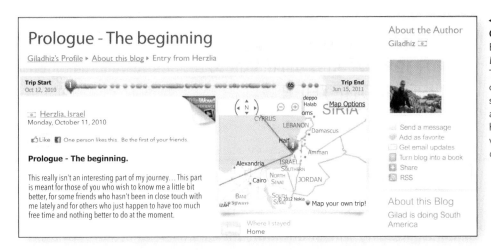

## Prologue - The beginning

Giladhiz's Profile ▸ About this blog ▸ Entry from Herzlia

**Trip Start**
Oct 12, 2010

**Trip End**
Jun 15, 2011

🖭 Herzlia, Israel
Monday, October 11, 2010

👍Like  One person likes this. Be the first of your friends.

**Prologue - The beginning.**

This really isn't an interesting part of my journey… This part is meant for those of you who wish to know me a little bit better, for some friends who hasn't been in close touch with me lately and for others who just happen to have too much free time and nothing better to do at the moment.

**About the Author**
Giladhiz 🖭

Send a message
Add as favorite
Get email updates
Turn blog into a book
Share
RSS

**About this Blog**
Gilad is doing South America

◀ **TRAVEL BLOG**
**Gilad Hizkiyahu,** Excerpt from *Gilad Is Doing South America.* The design that Gilad chose for his blog showcases his text and visuals and allows him to link out to various sources.
*Credit: Gilad Hizkiyahu.*

## CHECKLIST | Reading Genres

Are you looking at a text and wondering what genre it is? Ask yourself the following questions:

☐ **Common elements.** What do I already know about this genre? What are some of the typical features of this genre? How is the content organized? How does the author use words, images, or other media to convey a purpose and reach an audience?

☐ **Style.** What is the author's tone? How would I describe the language of the piece? How much detail does the author use?

☐ **Design.** What does the composition look (sound, feel, smell) like? How do words, visuals, and other media work together in the genre physically? How would you describe the format of the composition? Would the format change if the mode were changed? For example, if a newspaper editorial moves from a print medium to an online medium, what changes occur in the genre?

☐ **Sources.** What sources does the author draw on? How do I know? How does the author incorporate and give credit to sources? Is there documentation? Hyperlinking?

PRACTICE

# Choosing a Social Response

Think back to the opening discussion about identifying different social responses to the situation of being confused about your biology homework. Now write down a challenging situation you've encountered recently. List five different actions you could have taken in response. Which actions would have generated a form of communication? Which would have been most effective? Why?

# 3

# READING AS A WRITER:
## RHETORICAL SITUATIONS & GENRES TOGETHER

**BRIEF CONTENTS**

# What Do Rhetorical Situations Have to Do with Genres?

Now that you have an understanding of what constitutes a rhetorical situation and a beginning concept of genres, it's time to examine how they work together. When composing, a writer is always working within a rhetorical situation. That means the writer considers the purpose of their piece, whom they want to reach, how best to appeal to their reader, and what sources and evidence to use, along with other considerations mentioned in Chapter 1. The next step for the writer is to choose how to best respond to their rhetorical situation. Which genre or genres are the best social response to their situation?

## Genres Respond to Rhetorical Situations

If we examine a particular event, we can see that there are numerous ways someone might choose to respond. After the April 15, 2019 fire at the historic Notre-Dame Cathedral in Paris, France, people chose to respond in a variety of ways. In a televised address, French President Emmanuel Macron said, "Notre-Dame is our history, our literature, part of our psyche, the place of all our great events, our epidemics, our wars, our liberations, the epicentre of our lives . . . So I solemnly say tonight: we will rebuild it together." British Prime Minister Theresa May tweeted, "My thoughts are with the people of France tonight and with the emergency services who are fighting the terrible blaze at Notre-Dame cathedral." In Paris, locals and tourists gathered along the Seine River to sing hymns in response to the gravity of the situation. Many people posted pictures on social media of themselves visiting Notre-Dame prior to the fire, such as former first lady Michelle Obama. Her caption begins: "I will never forget the first time I walked into the Notre-Dame Cathedral." Others, such as Linda Sarsour, a civil rights activist, responded to the event by highlighting another fire that was occurring at the same time. She tweeted, "Jerusalem's Al-Aqsa mosque fire burns at the same time as flames engulf Notre-Dame Cathedral in Paris."

Consider different ways people might protest against something. They might make signs and march, give a speech, create a public service announcement, circulate a petition, or write a letter to the editor. The genre is chosen based on the rhetorical situation.

There are times, however, when genre is stipulated for you. In academic settings, you are often given an assignment and told to compose a research essay, write a poem, or create a lab report based on an experiment. In business settings, you might need to create a proposal, write a recommendation report, or prepare a presentation. We will discuss academic genres in more detail in Chapter 7.

In the rest of this chapter, we highlight different ways writers respond to rhetorical situations. Examining the key rhetorical and genre choices of others will help you make more deliberate and effective choices in your own writing.

# A Meme Responds to a Rhetorical Situation

A meme is a concept that spreads quickly from person to person via the internet through blogging, e-mail, or social media. Memes are easily replicated and altered; for example, when Elizabeth sees that a blogger has posted a photo of his ferret wearing a party hat and looking irritated, she can take that concept and post a photo of her dog wearing a cowboy hat and looking irritated on her Instagram account. Amy might then see Elizabeth's meme and post to her Facebook status a photo of her cat wearing a baseball cap and looking irritated.

The rhetorical situation that the original blogger and Elizabeth and Amy are responding to is simple: They all have pets they think are just adorable and find their pets' reactions to being anthropomorphized hilarious. They are participating in a long tradition of pet owners sharing the silliness of their own pets (purpose) with other pet owners (audience).

A related example is the *Hipster Llama* meme (see p. 31). *Hipster Llama* appears in many variations online. Like most memes, its authorship is not identified. Rather, the meme can be revised, remixed, and shared repeatedly and anonymously online. To unpack this particular meme, let's first consider that a person or persons composed it (or revised an existing version of it). Like all composers, the meme creators worked within a **rhetorical situation**. Let's start by asking: What are the meme creators doing, and why? What are some decisions they have made as composers? Following is a preliminary reading:

- The composers are providing a commentary (**purpose**).
- They are communicating to like-minded readers on the internet (**audience**).
- They are using humor and satire to connect with their audience (drawing on the **rhetorical appeal**, pathos).
- They are working with both text and imagery (**mode**) and delivering the composition digitally online (**medium**).

Now, let's think about the composers' **choice of genre**. What are memes? How do they function? What are their typical qualities and conventions?

- Memes often parody or poke fun at something or someone. They take many forms, but often feature an image and a brief caption written in informal language (**elements and style**).
- Often an image is prominent, and the words—typically what the subject of the meme is saying or thinking—are presented in a large display font (**design**).
- Memes draw on current topics and popular culture (**sources**).

Here we provide a partial reading of the *Hipster Llama* meme. Notice the structure of the annotations in the margins. This is a "guided reading," a feature we discuss in detail in the next section.

# Guided Reading | Meme

## Author Unknown, *Hipster Llama*

| RHETORICAL SITUATION & CHOICES | GENRE CONVENTIONS |
|---|---|

### PURPOSE

The composer of *Hipster Llama* memes poke fun at hipsters, making fun of things hipsters say, their values, and specifically, their haircuts. This particular meme focuses on the stereotype that hipsters are more concerned with exploring their aesthetic sides than on focusing on paid work, and are perhaps more concerned with their personal style than what they produce.

### AUDIENCE

Because hipsters are often self-referentially ironic, it's likely that hipsters themselves are an audience. People who make fun of hipsters are also clearly part of the audience.

### RHETORICAL APPEALS

The humor in the meme is an appeal to pathos because laughter is considered an emotional response. The composer's knowledge of hipster hairstyles and attitudes is an appeal to ethos.

### MODES & MEDIA

**Modes = text and visual.**
The meaning of the meme depends upon both the text and the visual working together.

**Medium = digital.**
Memes circulate on the internet and so are digital.

◀ What is the composer of *Hipster Llama* doing?

The composer of *Hipster Llama* chose to create a meme. What are the conventions of a meme? To what extent is the composer adhering to them? ▶

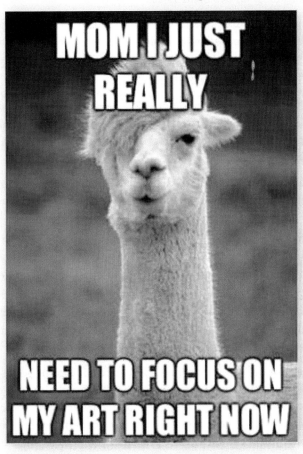

### ELEMENTS OF THE GENRE

**Humor:** Memes are designed to be humorous. The composer of the *Hipster Llama* memes use humor to poke fun at a particular group.

**Repetition:** This meme is part of a series. Viewers can instantly recognize the use of the llama and the fact that this is a part of a larger series.

**Social media:** Memes are distributed online. They can be sent by e-mail, posted on a blog, or shared on social media sites such as Facebook, Twitter, and Instagram.

### STYLE

The text in this meme uses a *conversational tone*. Additionally, the text in a meme is fairly brief, as is the case here.

### DESIGN

**Visual with text.** The llama is the center of focus, with the text complementing it. A meme usually begins with a funny photo and then attaches a caption that amplifies the humor. Here the visual shows the *Hipster Llama* accompanied by words he might say.

**Font:** The font is usually bold, san serif, and not too flashy.

### SOURCES

Memes usually draw on ideas in popular culture, respond to news events, or highlight a celebrity. Memes are often remixes of a visual and a quote that already exist. Here, the meme focuses on the concept of the hipster, a popular culture concept.

# Visualizing Rhetorical Situations & Genres

## What Is a Guided Reading?

Guided readings throughout this book (such as the one provided on the previous page for *Hipster Llama*) highlight the moves that writers and composers make in different genres and modes, and they also point out common genre conventions. These readings are presented with critical annotations in the margins of the page or screen. The annotations focus on two main ideas:

1. The composer's **rhetorical situation and choices** (purpose, audience, rhetorical appeals, modes/media) and

2. The typical **conventions of the genre** the author chose to compose in (common elements, style, design, and sources).

We've designed the annotations to help you see how authors respond to their rhetorical situations. Seeing the choices and decisions that experienced authors made can help you learn how to think through and respond to the rhetorical situations you will find yourself in.

Guided readings appear in the table of contents at the beginning of the book, in the brief contents that open chapters, and are also listed in the adjacent directory.

## Ways to Apply Guided Readings

As you read in different genres on your own, you might use the headings we've used for the guided readings to remind you of things to observe. We are big fans of annotating, as you might have noticed, and we hope you might try annotating the pieces you read the same way we've annotated the guided readings. We find that annotating a reading helps us articulate our thoughts and move them from being fuzzy, half-formed ideas to concrete observations and analysis.

When you are composing, find a guided reading in the genre you're using (or one close to it), and refresh your mind about the different choices you should consider. Consider your purpose, and as you compose, ask yourself if that purpose will be evident to your reader. Pay close attention to the genre conventions. These will help guide you and remind you of certain stylistic principles you need to consider.

# Sample Grid | A Framework for Reading Any Text Rhetorically

When you are reading or composing, consider applying the framework of the guided reading to what you're analyzing or creating. The image below is the grid we use for the guided readings in this text. It's a grid that you can use for approaching any text and for evaluating your own compositions.

## RHETORICAL SITUATION & CHOICES | GENRE CONVENTIONS

**PURPOSE**
What is the composer trying to do? Inform? Persuade? Tell a story? Something else? Does he or she have multiple purposes? And how can you tell?

◀ **What is the composer doing?**

**What genre has the composer** ▶ **chosen to work in? To what extent is he or she adhering to that genre's conventions?**

**ELEMENTS OF THE GENRE**
What are some of the patterns you notice across several examples of this genre? Is there a typical organization pattern or approach? Do sentences or paragraphs seem to be notably short or long? Does one element always seem to appear, such as an anecdote, or an abstract, or notes in the margin?

**AUDIENCE**
Who is the composer communicating to? Are there secondary audiences?

Place the text that you're reading or evaluating right here in the middle.

Next, read through the annotations in the margins to look more closely at the composer's rhetorical choices and how the composer works within his or her chosen genre.

**RHETORICAL APPEALS**
How does the composer entice his or her audience(s)? To what extent does the composer establish his or her ethos? Is logos evident in the text? Does the author appeal to readers' emotions (pathos)?

**STYLE**
Is it in the first or third person? Is the tone formal or informal? What is the level of vocabulary used?

**DESIGN**
How is formatting used? Are images included? Is color used?

**MODES & MEDIA**
What is the mode (visual, text, audio)? Why do you think the composer chose that mode? Or perhaps more than one mode is used; if so, why do you think the author made that choice? What is the medium (print or digital)? Why do you think the composer chose that medium?

**SOURCES**
What kind of source material is used (personal experience, internet research, interviews, etc.)? How are sources referenced within the piece?

# Using Genres to Inform, Narrate, or Persuade

Whether you're writing an academic genre, a workplace genre, or a genre for public audiences, you often need to decide how to make your points. Authors often make their points by giving information, telling stories, and/or persuading.

**INFORMING**

Purpose: Why share information?

Audience: How do we inform others?

Rhetorical appeals: How do we use them to inform?

**TELLING STORIES**

Purpose: Why tell stories?

Audience: How do we connect through stories?

Rhetorical appeals: How do we use them to tell stories?

**PERSUADING**

Purpose: Why write to persuade?

Audience: How do we persuade others?

Rhetorical appeals: How do we use them to persuade?

## Giving Information

Information is everywhere, all the time: online, on your phone, in e-mail, on social networking sites, on TV, and on radio. It's on billboards, road signs, and menus. But not all information is equal: some is reliable; some is not. How do we make sense of it all? The trick is to (1) figure out which sources of information are the best, and (2) analyze, use, and share that information according to your needs as a reader or writer.

In daily life, you draw on a variety of sources for information.

- You want to plant tomatoes on your back porch, so you consult a reference book or online guide by the American Horticultural Society on varieties that grow best in your region.

- You want to avoid the flu, so you read the U.S. Department of Health and Human Services' latest recommendations online or stop in at your pharmacy for information about the flu vaccine.

- You need to create a presentation using software you don't know how to use, so you refer to a Microsoft PowerPoint tutorial or ask an experienced colleague for a quick lesson.

- There's something wrong with your car and you don't know what the flashing light on your dashboard means, so you flip through your owner's manual, search YouTube for tutorials, or call a knowledgeable mechanic.

In each of these cases, you've found convenient but also authoritative sources.

- *Authoritative sources of information.* Here's another scenario. Let's say you want to prepare for a disaster. You do a quick search on YouTube and turn up a video by a guy in a gas mask who lives in a desert bunker. His instructions seem to have some merit but overall are rambling and confusing. Though the video may be riveting, it is a poor source of information because the author lacks credibility (or ethos) and logic (logos). A better, if less colorful, source would be a government organization such as Homeland Security, FEMA (Federal Emergency Management Agency), or the American Red Cross. These are considered excellent sources because the organizations are long established and made up of experts. The material they publish is researched, written, and reviewed by authorities in the field of emergency preparation; approved by the government; and tested out in actual emergencies.

- *Author bias.* No author is purely objective. Personal viewpoints, inclinations, and prejudices can creep into any communication, whether it's a recipe or a government document. Bias can show up in the language that writers use. Bias can also be apparent in the writer's tone. For example, imagine that an article appears in your local newspaper about a family lost during a snowmobiling trip. You might expect the reporter to simply present the facts. However, after reading closely, you see the reporter's opinion has subtly found its way onto the page: The family's lack of preparation influenced the writer and affected his or her tone and the use or omission of details. On the other hand, imagine that the reporter thinks the family did the best they could have—they were as prepared as possible, but no one could have survived that avalanche. In that case, the writer would use a more sympathetic tone.

Presenting information is not a neutral activity. All writing has a persuasive quality, and informative writing is no exception. Keep this in mind as you read and compose.

**Purpose: Why share information?**  When we write with a primary purpose to inform, we share facts and details with our readers. One type of informative writing is instructions. If you've ever purchased a piece of furniture that required assembly, you've probably worked with a set of instructions. The instructions were likely designed by an engineer or technical writer with two goals: (1) to help you put together parts of an object, and (2) to persuade and assure you, through simple images and language, that the task will be easy.

Another example of informative writing is a brochure. You've probably seen these at your doctor's or dentist's office—brochures about how to control asthma or whiten your teeth. Consider the teeth-whitening brochure: It may provide facts about various methods; however, it might also offer reasons for whitening, pricing information, and a photo of an attractive model with sparkling-white teeth. Is the material in the brochure presented only to inform, or is there another motive at work? Could the brochure creators also be trying to convince you to whiten your teeth?

When you read informative pieces, notice what else is going on. An author of a scientific report, for example, may present facts, but as a way to influence you to share an opinion or take an action.

**Audience: How do we inform others?**   As writers, we need to know our audiences — who they are and what they want. For example, in Mooney's memo in Chapter 8, she included specific information that her colleagues would need to accomplish the tasks. Additionally, she uses a bulleted list to make the information easier to scan. Mooney uses very precise language and only includes pertinent information for her audience.

**Rhetorical appeals: How do we use them to inform?**   When we write to inform, how do we get our audiences invested? Whether you're composing a research paper, fact sheet, or flowchart, you will use rhetorical appeals: ethos, logos, and pathos.

- *Ethos*—how you, as an author, are perceived by your audience—is extremely important when informing. That's why it's essential to draw on reliable sources of information in your research and to convey that knowledge with authority and as neutrally as possible. If your audience thinks you are unreliable, or that you have some unstated motive, you will not have established your ethos.

- *Logos*—or your use of logic as an author—is also significant. "How to" or instructional genres, such as recipes, make heavy use of logos. When cooks create recipes, they direct the reader in what to do, in a specific order. Chopping ingredients, mixing them, and cooking them must be presented to readers as logical steps.

- *Pathos*—your appeal to your readers' emotions—is generally not a priority when you're writing to inform. On the other hand, if you want to inform but also persuade your readers, you can appeal to their emotions by using humor, for example. Generally humor is appropriate for less formal informational genres, but you also have to consider your specific purposes and audiences.

## Telling Stories

Constructing narratives is a universal impulse; stories help us make sense of our lives and connect with others. Regardless of the specific genres our stories take—and whether they're fact or fiction, comedies or tragedies, or something in between—they generally include real people or made-up characters, a setting, a conflict, and action.

In your composition course, you may be asked to write a literacy narrative: a story about how you learned to read and write. But there are other, less formal ways to share stories. For example, even a single page from a photo album or scrapbook suggests part of the story of someone's life.

An obituary is another narrative genre that tells a story. Writers of obituaries—sometimes the deceased himself or herself (some people write them well in advance), sometimes a friend or family member—tell the story of the deceased through key biographical details. A related genre, the eulogy, is a speech delivered at the funeral or memorial, usually written by friends or family members. Through eulogies, writers share stories about the deceased's life, character, and accomplishments. Even an epitaph, the inscription on a gravestone, can tell a story about a life.

**Purpose: Why tell stories?**   As we worked on this book, we always began our sessions with an exchange of stories about what happened during the course of the day. Our students do this before class, talking about what happened in other classes or at their jobs. Stories help us reconnect with others.

Stories also help us chronicle events. A story can be true, such as a factual news report or an autobiography, or it can be made up, such as a short story, novel, or other work of fiction. Some stories change history, such as the *Narrative of the Life of Frederick Douglass, an American Slave, Written by Himself*. Douglass's autobiography, which he published in 1845 while living in the North as an escaped slave, helped spark the abolitionist movement in the United States.

Stories also entertain and instruct us. For example, while most well-known fairy tales make for interesting reading, they were actually created to teach children some kind of lesson. Stories can also serve to persuade others. For example, in a job interview, you might tell relevant stories about your previous experience that show you're qualified for the position you're discussing.

**Audience: How do we connect through stories?**   We write stories in order to explore our experiences and share them with others. For a story to resonate, readers must be able to connect with it personally. As writers, we strive for ways to make that happen. For example, in his memoir, *Dreams from My Father*, Barack Obama shares his experiences growing up as a black American and the struggles he faced as he traced his origins, something many readers can relate to. He tells his story through a series of anecdotes that read like a conversation, beginning with how he heard of his father's death. By beginning with such a universal situation and using an informal tone, Obama gets readers invested in his story.

**Rhetorical appeals: How do we use them to tell stories?**   Whether your favorite narrative genre is the Facebook status line or the memoir, you'll be most effective if you tap into the rhetorical appeals: ethos, logos, and pathos.

- *Ethos*—how you, as an author or composer, are perceived by your audience—is crucial when you tell a story. For example, if you write an autobiography, deliver a eulogy, or share an oral history, your readers and listeners assume that what you are telling them is true, that the stories have actually taken place. If you create a photo essay, your viewers assume that you have accurately depicted real events. If you create a work of fiction, your ethos as an author is also important. Readers want to trust that you're going to tell them an interesting, worthwhile story, perhaps with a solid, interesting plot and relatable characters they can care about.

- *Logos*—the logic you use as an author or composer—is also significant when you tell a story. For example, a short story, even if it is not told chronologically, usually follows a pattern in which the plot and characters unfold in a logical manner to the reader.

- *Pathos*—your appeal to readers' emotions—can go a long way in connecting readers with your story. For example, when you write a memoir, you identify a moment in your life that has emotional significance and convey it in a way that gets readers to identify emotionally with that experience.

## Persuading

Open your web browser, page through any magazine, scroll through Facebook, or take a walk to the coffee shop, and you will be barraged by texts and media created to persuade you—to think something, do something, like something, or buy something.

Online, advertisers individualize their messages to you. For example, when you log on to Amazon.com, you are greeted with a list of recommendations based on your previous purchases. On Facebook, the ads on your page are generated according to your likes and dislikes, as well as other information you provide in your profile and posts.

While advertising is probably the most pervasive attempt at influence, there are many other kinds of texts that we create at school, in the workplace, or for public audiences to convince others to see things our way. In fact, you could argue that almost every communication—a text message to a friend about what movie to see, a posting of a cute kitten or puppy, a dating profile, an editorial on Fox News, a joke made on *The Simpsons* about Fox News editorials, or even a chapter in a textbook—has persuasive elements built into it.

**Purpose: Why write to persuade?**   When we write to persuade, we do so because we want to convince our readers to do something—usually to agree with us about a topic, issue, or idea or to take a specific action. As a student, when you write a paper in which you take a stance on an issue or you give a speech in which you ask your audience to do something, you are writing to persuade. As a professional, when you apply for a job, you craft a résumé and cover letter and make a convincing case for yourself during your interview to persuade the person hiring that you are the best candidate. A persuasive text can also be as simple as a six-word slogan.

**Audience: How do we persuade others?**   As citizens of a democracy, we may read persuasive texts such as editorials to help us figure out our own positions on specific issues. As a writer, anytime you want to persuade your audience, you need to lay out your ideas, anticipate possible objections, and support your argument with relevant information. As with informing (see p. 34 of this chapter), accuracy is important when persuading others. Backing up your ideas and claims with correct information, gathered from reliable sources, will make your argument stronger.

**Rhetorical appeals: How do we use them to persuade?**   Whether you want to convince others to agree with you on an important issue, to date you, to vote for your candidate, or to buy your product, you will be most persuasive if you relate to your audience through the rhetorical appeals—ethos, logos, and pathos.

- *Ethos*—the authority and trustworthiness that you establish as a writer, composer, or speaker—is crucial when you want to persuade others. If your boss asks you to review several possible locations for an important fund-raising event and recommend one, you will want to establish yourself as dedicated to getting a high-quality venue for a reasonable price. To do this, you'll need to demonstrate that you've taken the assignment seriously, studied the options objectively, and weighed your company's needs and priorities carefully.

- *Logos*—the logical chain of reasoning that you provide for readers—is extremely important when you are making any kind of argument. Imagine you are taking a car for a test drive to decide whether you will buy it. You might mention to the salesperson that you are interested in a car that won't be too bad for the environment. The salesperson might then present you with some facts about the mileage the car gets, the measures the manufacturer has taken at the factory to protect the environment, and the paper-free policy the dealership has initiated by conducting as much business as possible electronically. By talking about these factors, the salesperson is creating a chain of reasoning that—she hopes—will lead you to conclude that the car you are driving is an environmentally responsible choice.

- *Pathos*—the appeal that you use when you want to evoke your readers' emotions—comes in handy when you are trying to persuade someone to do something. An appeal to pathos connects you with your audience, and vice versa. For example, when a salesperson asks you about yourself and then tells you a bit about himself and you find some commonalities, that salesperson is appealing to your pathos. When he later tells you that he loves the stereo you are looking at, you're more likely to buy it because you've already identified with him.

# Responding to One Event: Two Rhetorical Situations, Two Genres

## Arch Collapse at a National Park

In this case study, two writers report on a single event. One writes a press release, the other a blog post.

**The event.** In August 2008, a rock formation in Utah's famous Arches National Park collapsed.

**The writers.** Paul Henderson, a ranger at the park who also wrote press releases, and Shaan Hurley, a blogger and fan of the park who had hiked and photographed it.

**The compositions.** **Press Release:** "Wall Arch Collapses" (Henderson); **Blog Post:** "The Wall Arch Collapses in Arches National Park" (Hurley).

As you'll see, Henderson and Hurley provide much of the same information about the arch collapse, but they write in different genres and with different purposes and audiences in mind. The notes in the margins of each piece explain their rhetorical situations and how they work within the conventions of the press release and the blog post.

## Guided Reading | Press Release

At the time of the collapse, Paul Henderson was chief of Interpretation and Visitor Services for Arches National Park, which is managed by the National Park Service, part of the U.S. Department of the Interior. When the arch collapsed, Henderson was interviewed by news outlets, including MSNBC, which also quoted from the press release to the right.

# Paul Henderson, *Wall Arch Collapses*

## PURPOSE

Henderson, who works for the National Park Service, a government agency, writes to inform readers about the collapse. He reports that there were no injuries and that the area is temporarily closed. He reassures readers that the event is normal, that arches are temporary and "eventually succumb to the forces of gravity and erosion."

## AUDIENCE

Henderson's readers want an official statement from park management, rather than one by an outside observer. Readers are mainly members of news organization— but also park patrons, including hikers and nature photographers, looking for details.

## RHETORICAL APPEALS

For Henderson and other press release writers, ethos is crucial. Readers need to trust the authority of the writer and his information, especially because Henderson represents a government agency.

Henderson establishes logos by presenting information in a sensible order, beginning with the event and ending with its effects.

## MODES & MEDIA

**Mode:** Henderson uses text to inform and visuals to show the effect of the collapse.

**Media:** His press release was posted digitally on the National Park Service's site and was probably also distributed by e-mail to news organizations.

◄ What is the composer, Paul Henderson, doing?

How do I know this is a ► press release?

# Wall Arch Collapses

**Date:** August 8, 2008
**Contact:** Paul Henderson, 435-719-2140

Subscribe 🔊 | What is RSS

Wall Arch, located along the popular Devils Garden Trail at Arches National Park collapsed sometime during the night of August 4, 2008. Rock has continued to fall from the arms of the remaining portion of the arch necessitating the closure of the Devils Garden Trail just beyond Landscape Arch.

On August 7, 2008, representatives from both the National Park Service Geologic Resources Division and the Utah Geological Survey visited the site and noted obvious stress fractures in the remaining formation. Rock debris has completely blocked this section of the trail. The closure will remain in effect until visitor safety issues can be resolved.

First reported and named by Lewis T. McKinney in 1948, Wall Arch was a free standing arch in the Slickrock member of the Entrada sandstone. The opening beneath the span was 71-feet wide and 33-1/2 feet high. It ranked 12th in size among the over 2,000 known arches in the park.

All arches are but temporary features and all will eventually succumb to the forces of gravity and erosion. While the geologic forces that created the arches are still very much underway, in human terms it's rare to observe such dramatic changes.

No one has reported observing the arch collapse and there were no visitor injuries.

*Credit: Courtesy of National Park Service.*

## ELEMENTS OF THE GENRE

**Facts:** Henderson explains:
*Who* = people at the site of the collapse
*What* = the arch collapse
*When* = 8/4/08
*Where* = specific location of the collapse
*Why* = gravity and erosion
*How* = falling debris

**Brevity, timeliness:** Like most press releases, this is concisely worded, just a few paragraphs long. Henderson wrote it just four days after the event.

**Pointedness:** Henderson begins with the most crucial information and follows it with significant details.

**Contact information:** Henderson wants readers, especially the news media (the target audience for press releases), to be able to get in touch.

## STYLE

**Tone:** Henderson is objective in his writing. He doesn't give his opinion and writes in the neutral third person.

**Clarity, directness:** Henderson provides facts simply and details concisely (e.g., "Rock debris has completely blocked this section of the trail").

## DESIGN

**Simplicity:** Henderson uses a standard press release design, with a headline to summarize and get attention, a dateline, and contact information. There are just two images to support the text.

**Navigation:** The web page itself includes the name of the park, an image, and a menu bar for easy navigation.

## SOURCES

Draws on official information. Henderson uses facts from the National Park Service and from the Utah Geological Survey, which he credits in the body of his press release.

# Guided Reading | Blog Post

Blogger Shaan Hurley has a background in mechanical design and works in the field of technology. *Between the Lines* (autodesk.blogs.com) is Hurley's personal blog; he also posts on Twitter. He posted the following entry in August 2008.

## Shaan Hurley, *The Wall Arch Collapses in Arches National Park*

| RHETORICAL SITUATION & CHOICES | GENRE CONVENTIONS |
| --- | --- |

**PURPOSE**

Hurley has a few reasons for writing: to inform readers about the collapse, to share his own experiences and photos of the park, and to persuade readers to enjoy nature now, rather than later, when the opportunity may not exist. He writes: "Now I will not have the opportunity to photograph Wall Arch except the remnants on the ground. It is another example of how things you take for granted may disappear."

**AUDIENCE**

His readers are fans of the park, other hikers and photographers, and even potential park visitors. His readers are looking for a personal take (rather than an official statement) on the arch collapse.

◀ What is the composer, Shaan Hurley, doing?

How do I know this is a ▶ blog post?

# Between the Lines
Autodesk, Technology, Design & more
with Shaan Hurley

### The Wall Arch Collapses in Arches National Park

Almost one year ago to the week I was in the beautiful and world famous Arches National Park which is little more than 4 hours drive from my home in Utah. Just this week perhaps Tuesday one of the famous sandstone arches fell, Wall Arch is now Wall Pile. While Wall Arch was not the most spectacular or stunning, it was a beautiful arch.

Before          After
Photo by NPS

Arches are formed by an ever changing nature and erosion and leave us with only a small window of geological time in which to marvel at the arches before they succumb to gravity. Who knows, perhaps another arch was born that we have not seen in the past year as well. Last year while I was photographing many of the arches and absolutely enjoying the natural beauty and silence in between the tourist buses.

I hiked back to Landscape arch which itself had suffered a partial collapse in 1991. Since it was so hot that day and I figured I would get back there again soon I did not hike the remaining quarter mile to photograph Wall Arch by the Devils Garden. Now I will not have the opportunity to photograph Wall Arch except the remnants on the ground. It is another example of how things you take for granted may disappear.

If you ever have the chance to Visit the Moab Utah region or Southern Utah you should do so as it is beyond words and one of the reasons I know call this state home. This is photography heaven for color and so many varied landscape and rare geography. One of the other things I love about the area is the history of the Fremont people from thousands of years ago leaving their art on the rock walls and then last but not least Green River Utah having the worlds best watermelon when hiking in 100+ deg F. weather. If you are ever in Utah let me know as I am always happy to get an excuse to head to Moab and love showing the hidden gems beyond the tourist trails.

Here are a couple of my photos from the hike back on August 4th 2007 in Arches National Park. I still have hundreds of photos yet to publish. It may sound odd for someone to see some sense of loss in what to some may just be a sandstone structure born of erosion but if you have ever been there in the silence and the vibrant glow of red at twilight you would understand the magic of the area. This is natures art and landscape at it's finest.

Never take for granted who or what you can see today, you may not have the opportunity tomorrow.

Have a great weekend,

Shaan

*Credit: Courtesy of Shaan Hurley at Autodesk.*

**ELEMENTS OF THE GENRE**

**Brevity, visuals, hyperlinks:** Like most effective blog posts, Hurley's is just a few paragraphs long, visually interesting, and embedded with links that offer more information without adding length.

**Paragraphs:** Hurley's concise, chunked text keeps digital readers interested.

**Photos:** Hurley's images provide context, attract readers, and offer his perspective on the event.

**"About" page, comment option:** Hurley gives biographical information and a space for readers to offer feedback and share their own views on the park.

**RHETORICAL APPEALS**

Because Hurley's main goal is to urge readers to seize an opportunity, he relies largely on pathos to appeal to emotion. Notice how he describes the beauty and "magic" of the park.

He also establishes ethos, or his authority to write on this topic, by sharing his firsthand experiences and photos of the park.

**MODES & MEDIA**

**Mode:** Hurley uses text and visuals to inform.
**Media:** His blog is digital and embedded with hyperlinks that bring readers to additional information. Readers can also share the link so others can read Hurley's post.

**STYLE**

**Directness:** Hurley, like many bloggers, offers his own reflections and is present in his writing. He writes in the first person, addressing readers directly.

**DESIGN**

**Clarity, navigation:** Like other blogs, Hurley's is designed so users can easily find additional content; they can also access his page on flickr.com.

**SOURCES**

Draws on official and firsthand information. Hurley credits the National Park Service for some of the photos; he also draws on his own experience (his trip of 2007) and external sources such as *Wikipedia*.

# QUESTIONS | Analyzing the Guided Readings

## RHETORICAL SITUATION & CHOICES

1. **Purpose.** Reread Henderson's press release and Hurley's blog post. What are the writers' purposes? How can you tell? How do these purposes differ? How might they overlap?

2. **Audience.** Who do you imagine is the primary reader for Henderson's press release? For Hurley's blog post? Explain.

3. **Rhetorical appeals.** How effective are Henderson and Hurley in using ethos, pathos, or logos to reach their audiences? Which appeals do they rely on most effectively, and why?

4. **Rhetorical appeals.** Consider how hyperlinks, photos, and other information can contribute to a composer's ethos. Why do you think Hurley used the National Park Service as a source for information and images? How did this choice affect his ethos?

5. **Modes & media.** Both Henderson and Hurley use a combination of text and visuals. If you were to add audio or video to either piece, what would you add? What meaning or information would the audio or video add?

## GENRE CONVENTIONS

6. **Elements of the genre.** As a reader interested in the arch collapse, would you be likely to consult a press release? A blog? Both? Neither? Explain. To what extent is genre important? In what contexts? When might it not matter?

7. **Elements of the genre.** What are the most significant differences between the press release and blog post as genres? Based on these examples, what conventions of these genres can you identify? How do these conventions affect what the writers say and how they convey it?

8. **Style.** Analyze the language Henderson and Hurley use. What do their words and tone suggest about their different purposes and audiences?

9. **Design.** How does the design of each piece enable readers to quickly find information they want or need?

10. **Design.** Look again at the photos included in the blog post and press release. What purposes do they serve in each? How effectively do the authors use them?

11. **Sources.** How does Hurley use the National Park Service's press release as a source? How does that source contribute to his success in achieving his purpose and reaching his audience?

When you compose, you can refer to the checklist below as well as the blank guided reading grid provided earlier in this chapter.

## RHETORICAL SITUATION & CHOICES

☐ **Purpose.** Is my purpose to tell a story, inform, or persuade? Do I have several purposes, and if so, which is my primary purpose?

☐ **Audience.** How would I describe my primary audience? Whose attention do I want most? Who are the people I want to persuade? Do I have another, secondary audience? How will I entice this audience?

☐ **Rhetorical appeals.** How will I establish my credibility (ethos)? Will appealing to my audience's emotions help me persuade them (pathos)? How might logic (logos) help me convince others?

☐ **Modes & media.** Do I want to work with written words? Will I present my ideas in person, orally? Will I use visuals? How about audio? Does my idea lend itself to video? Do I want my piece to be available digitally or in print? Will I use some combination of these modes and media?

## GENRE CONVENTIONS

☐ **Elements of the genre.** How will I structure my composition? What is the best way to combine elements to convey my purpose—and make my case to my audience?

☐ **Style.** Whatever form my composition takes (visual, verbal, etc.), what is the best tone to use to reach my audience? What voice will I use? How present will I be in my composition? What kind of language will I use? What level of detail will I need to convey my purpose?

☐ **Design.** How do I want my composition to look? How will the layout help me achieve my purpose?

☐ **Sources.** What sources will I draw on for my composition? Do I need to conduct interviews? Do I need to research online or in the library? How will I attribute my sources?

---

**PRACTICE**

# Conducting a Rhetorical Analysis

Think of a current issue affecting your community and do some quick research to locate two responses to that issue. The responses should represent two different genres. For example, you might look at how the issue is covered in different genres such as a news report, editorial, documentary video, demonstration, or comic strip. Next, using the structure and categories of this book's guided readings (see the Arches texts earlier in this chapter), annotate both pieces. Then, write an analysis in which you focus on the rhetorical situations (purpose and audience) and some of the rhetorical choices (rhetorical appeals, modes/media) for both texts. How do the texts function as a social response to the rhetorical situations? What does comparing these two works teach you about genre?

**Note:** Although both pieces should respond to the same issue, they may not have identical rhetorical situations.

**Advanced move:** Want to take it a step further? Compose a response to the situation in a third genre.

# 4

# COMPOSING:
## DRAWING ON EXPERIENCE & EVIDENCE

# Responding to an Assignment

All composing takes place within a rhetorical situation. Remember that genre is a social response to a rhetorical situation. In this chapter, we will follow one of Amy's former students, Gwen Ganow, as she composes in response to the rhetorical situation of an assignment in her writing course. Here is the assignment she was given, along with her annotations. (Note: It's a good idea to annotate an assignment to make sure you understand it and to help you think through the different steps.)

**◄ STUDENT AUTHOR PHOTO**

**Gwen Ganow,** a graduate of Red Rocks Community College and Metropolitan State University of Denver, is now a Colorado State Parks Ranger.
*Credit: Courtesy Gwen Dalynn Ganow.*

**ATTENTION, COMPOSERS**

As we follow Gwen's process, and the processes of other composers in this book, keep in mind that there is no one correct or best way to respond to an assignment, do research, or revise your writing. We provide sample processes in order to offer various contexts that you can learn from, adapt, and if helpful, apply to your own processes.

## Annotated Example | Reading an Academic Text

ASSIGNMENT   **Amy Braziller,** *"Take a Position," with Notes by Gwen Ganow* (STUDENT)

### English 121
### English Composition

**Date:** November 1, 2019
**Assignment:** Take a Position

*Argue?*

Take a position on a topic you care about and have experience with. Then think about who you want to communicate your ideas to and compose in a genre that will allow you to do that.

*I get to pick the genre*

You may compose in any genre that seems appropriate for your purpose and audience. The length should be appropriate to the genre; in other words, a magazine article will have more words than a poster. Be sure to choose a genre that will allow you to communicate with the audience you have in mind.

*My experience. For this assignment, research is optional.*

For sources, you should primarily draw upon your own experience. If you wish, you can use other source material if it is appropriate to your genre choice and topic.

*Movies, video games, outdoors, comics, animals?*

1. Brainstorm potential topics you have experience with and could take a position on.

*(Continues on next page)*

2. Select the topic you are most excited about and take a position. You might find freewriting useful to help you articulate your position.

3. Consider your rhetorical situation. You know your purpose is to take a position and try to convince others of its merit. Who are the others you are convincing? That is your audience.

What do I want to say? Who do I want to say it to?

4. What genres might that audience encounter? List three of them that would allow you to achieve your purpose and reach your audience.

5. Analyze and annotate examples of the three different genres that you are considering composing in, identifying the genre conventions.

The genre I choose needs to respond to my purpose and audience. How will I figure this out?

6. Draft your genre piece.

7. Revise your genre piece.

Credit: Courtesy of the author and Gwen Dalynn Ganow.

## Getting Started

Whenever you write—as a student in a composition classroom or a professional in a workplace—you focus on a specific topic. In some instances, you may be asked to address a general theme or a specific topic or issue. For example, your instructor might ask you to respond to an essay you've read for class, or your manager at work might ask you to develop and share plans to improve business or increase sales. Other times, most often in the course of college work, you get to start from scratch and choose a topic purely out of your experience, interest, and curiosity.

So, how do you choose a topic? Where should you start? One place might be this book. The Index of Themes, page T-1, organizes every reading in the text by topic, and the Index of Genres, page G-1, will help you see the relationship between topic choice and genre choice.

The best way to get started on identifying a topic that is meaningful to you is to get your ideas flowing. Following are some ways to do that.

**Talk to people.**   Discuss your topic ideas and questions with classmates, friends, family, and coworkers to find out what others have to say about the topic you're considering. Often, explaining why you're interested in a topic can help you focus. When others ask you to clarify your ideas, you will often discover what you really want to say.

**Make a brainstorm list.**   What do you care most about? Begin by making a list of things you are passionate about, your pet peeves, things you are curious about, things you don't understand, or things you'd like to change about the world. From your initial list, force yourself to double or triple the size of the list. Often the best topic ideas are the less obvious ones—ideas that will come to you when you push yourself to keep listing.

**English 121**
English Composition

**Date:** October 21, 2019
**Name:** Gwen Ganow
**Brainstorm List:** Ideas for the "Take a Position" Assignment

What issues, ideas, or practices do I care about most? What topics would I want to take a position on?

**PASSIONS**

Movies
Comic books
Video games
Hiking
Dogs
Camping

**PET PEEVES/CURIOSITIES**

Why do people hate?
How to respond to hate?
Why do people drive slowly in the left lane?
Should I major in biology?
Why do people toss their beer cans on the ground at concerts?

**MORE IDEAS**

**Superheroes**
Good guys save the world
Gay rights
Winter hikes
How to stay safe on a mountain in bad weather
Summer hikes
Border collies
Animal rescue
Best training methods for dogs
Water conservation
Zombies
Simpsons
How bad are sugary cereals?
Batman and the remakes
Why is black associated with bad guys?
What is the most humane way to keep elk out of your yard if you live outside a city?
Adventure films
Bacteria: what jobs could I get that deal with bacteria?
What kind of training could police departments implement to improve public relations?

**Mind map.** Like list making, mind mapping gives you a creative format for sketching out your early ideas about a topic. To begin, write the topic or idea you are exploring in the middle of a blank piece of paper (alternatively, you can use mind-mapping software, some of which is available for free online). As you think of details and related ideas, write them around the central topic, connecting them with lines that indicate their relationships.

# Freewriting

If you've identified a general topic area, or some of the ideas you've generated in your conversations and brainstorm lists interest you, try freewriting. The goal is to get your ideas written down without judging what you're writing, editing yourself, or trying to write beautifully. Experiment by making yourself write nonstop for ten to thirty minutes. As you keep your fingers moving, don't worry about making sense or about readers being confused or impressed. No one will read this document but you. When you take away the pressure of producing smooth prose, you may be surprised to see the ideas you generate. We'd like to refer to this as a "shitty first draft" (see Anne Lamott's essay "Shitty First Drafts" in the Reader section of this book, on pp. 523–26).

## Advice for Freewriting

As you begin your rough or exploratory draft, remember that it is just for you. No one else ever needs to see it. Think of your draft not as an organized, perfect piece of writing with a clear purpose, but as a messy opportunity for creativity and experimentation.

Don't worry about a thesis or about being logical or eloquent. Instead, focus on quantity rather than quality. That's right: quantity, not quality. Think of words in the first draft as raw materials. You want as much raw material to work with as possible. Imagine an artist beginning a painting. Would she have only the exact amount of paint she needs to create her piece? What if she changes her mind midway through the painting and wants to use more yellow than red? Wouldn't it make sense for her to begin with extra paint in each color to allow her the flexibility to modify her ideas? Writing and other kinds of composing are similar. Beginning with more words than you need gives you more options. Here are some pointers for getting your first draft written:

1. Set a timer for thirty minutes and force yourself to write for the entire time. Do not stop for anything. That means no stopping to reread, correct, or to refer to sources or models, and definitely no stopping to check social media.

2. For real: Don't stop to correct or edit what is on the page.

3. Write until you have five thousand words or you run out of time.

Don't worry about grammar, punctuation, spelling, transitions, topic sentences, organization, titles, and so on. Don't even worry about genre or what the finished piece will look or sound like. Once you have your thoughts down, you can think logically about your purpose, audience, and the points you want to convey.

At this stage, if you're putting pressure on yourself to write flawless, beautiful prose, remind yourself of the term *freewrite*. Take a little more pressure off by thinking of Anne Lamott's phrase "shitty first draft." Everybody, including published authors, writes them. In nearly any genre, you will write them too.

Let's circle back to Amy's student Gwen. Earlier in this chapter, we looked at the "Take a Position" assignment that Gwen responded to, followed by her brainstorm. Her thoughts on the assignment and her brainstorm led her to focus on superheroes and social attitudes. What position could she take on the relationship between the heroes and the values and prejudices of the real world? She began with this question:

**TOPIC QUESTION FOR "TAKING A POSITION" ASSIGNMENT**
To what extent do superheroes reflect real-world values and attitudes?

Gwen then moved from that question to a freewrite.

# Guided Reading | Freewrite

Gwen began with some exploratory freewriting, a low-stakes method that allowed her to reflect on her experiences and solidify her thoughts about superheroes and social attitudes.

## Gwen Ganow (STUDENT), *Topic for the "Take a Position" Assignment: Superheroes and Social Attitudes*

| GWEN'S RHETORICAL SITUATION & CHOICES | | GENRE CONVENTIONS |
|---|---|---|

**AUDIENCE**
At this point, Gwen is writing for herself and her instructor, Amy. They'll go over this draft together to try to pin down a direction. Gwen will later identify her additional audiences—her classmates as well as public audiences.

**RHETORICAL APPEALS**
Gwen is in exploration mode so is not concerned right now about ethos, logos, and pathos.

**MODES & MEDIA**
Gwen e-mailed this Word document to her instructor.

◀ What is the author, Gwen Ganow, doing?

What characterizes a ▶ freewrite?

**ELEMENTS OF THE GENRE**
A freewrite is characterized by free-form thought and questions. It is a brainstorming tool to use to reflect on your experiences with your topic, to discover what you already know and think about your topic, and to consider what you want to say about it.

**STYLE**
Gwen is not worried about style, grammar, or how her freewrite reads. It's not meant to be perfect. Her writing is very casual, as if she's writing in a journal to herself.

**English 121**
English Composition

**Date:** November 1, 2019
**Name:** Gwen Ganow
**Freewrite:** Topic for the "Take a Position" Assignment: Superheroes and Social Attitudes

I've always been fascinated by superheroes. I remember sitting in my bedroom when I was in second grade and paging through a stack of comic books. I became obsessed with them. And my superhero posters, I could stare at them for hours. In a way, superheroes were my first loves.

Man, those superheroes—very, very cool. I loved the power they had.

What kind of power? They faced challenges and obstacles, evil men trying to destroy someone, usually evil men, seldom women. Why? Superheroes protect people. Innocent people

*(Continues on next page)*

**PURPOSE**

Gwen explores possible angles for her project. "To what extent do superheroes reflect real-world values and attitudes?"

She lets herself be unfocused as she writes about her fascination with superheroes. After her freewrite, she realizes that she wants to cover how superheroes fight intolerance.

Seems that the city was always the setting—not the suburbs. Why is that?

Regardless of challenges, superheroes win. Why can't they die? What would that mean? Losing hope, maybe. Okay, that's a downer. I need them to win.

Superheroes were giant protectors and a way for me to escape. I'd read at night, even after lights out, wanting to see how the superhero would save the day.

Subjected to prejudice or intolerance—superheroes are often seen as different, as outsiders. It causes social problems for them. They worry that their loved ones will be hurt—like Spider-Man and Mary Jane. The superhero is actually a victim of injustice. Many become superheroes because of injustice in their life, like Batman's parents being murdered.

Superheroes are champions fighting discrimination. They defeat evil powers. How do they do that? I'd like to explore that. Do they fight racial injustice? Are there other forms of intolerance? Other areas of intolerance in life: racism, sexism, prejudice against LGBT community?

**DESIGN**

A freewrite is not designed. It's typically a simple document without formatting.

**SOURCES**

Gwen does not discuss evidence in this draft, but she could have, depending on her rhetorical situation and whether source material was appropriate for the situation or assignment.

*Credit: By permission Gwen Dalynn Ganow.*

## CHECKLIST | Getting Started on Your Topic with a Freewrite

Keep the following questions in mind:

### RHETORICAL SITUATION & CHOICES

☐ **What is my purpose?** What do I want to say and how do I want to say it? What experiences have shaped my thoughts on this topic?

☐ **Who am I composing for?** Who will my audience ultimately be, beyond myself, my instructor, and maybe my classmates?

☐ **How will I connect with my audience?** How will I establish my authority as a composer (ethos) so that my readers will trust me? What is the most logical way for me to present what I have to say? To what extent do I want to appeal to my audience's emotions? For example, if I want to persuade people to take a certain action, how will I cultivate their enthusiasm?

### GENRE CONVENTIONS

☐ **As I freewrite, how can I take pressure off myself so I can generate my ideas freely?** I need to remember that freewriting is about quantity over quality. I can refine later.

☐ **What do I already know about my topic?** What intrigues me about this topic? What questions do I still have about it?

☐ **Based on my experience and thinking so far, what arguments am I familiar with about this topic?** Are there some that resonate for me more than others? Do I have an opinion on this topic?

☐ **Is there a way to narrow my topic by time, place, demographics, or something else?** For example, if I write about pets reducing anxiety, do I focus on therapy dogs (narrow by breed) or the acceptance of therapy animals in the workplace (narrow by place)?

# Choosing a Genre to Compose In

After reviewing your freewrite, you should have a better sense of what you want to say about your topic. Your next decision is to choose a genre. You may find the Choosing a Genre checklist on page 60 helpful.

## Steps for Choosing a Genre to Compose In

**Step 1. Revisit your topic & central idea.**  Remember that rough draft? Since you've done more reading and analyzed a variety of genres, what's changed for you? How might that affect your focus?

**Step 2. Revisit your rhetorical situation.**  Remember that the piece you are composing is a response to a situation. What has motivated you to communicate these ideas? What are you responding to? What's your stake in this? Why do you care about this?

- **Focus on your purpose.** Look over your initial freewrite and highlight some of the main ideas you want to explore. Make a list of four or five of them. Next, choose the idea you are most excited about. Then, decide on the primary purpose of the piece you are composing.
- **Really think about your audience.** Consider your audience. Keep in mind that aspects of your topic that are obvious to you may not be obvious to your audience.

**Step 3. Strategize on how you'll use rhetorical appeals.**  Start thinking about how to appeal to your audience's senses of ethos, logos, and pathos.

**Step 4. Consider your mode & medium.**  Once you have narrowed the scope of your purpose and audience, think about whether you want to work with text, visuals, video, audio, or some combination. Consider the advantages of each, as well as your skills and the tools available to you.

**Step 5. Narrow your choices down to three possible genres.**  Put together a short list of potential genres you want to consider. Remember that there is no perfect genre. Your goal at this point is to choose a genre that will best enable you to respond to your rhetorical situation.

**Step 6. Look at examples of the three genres you're interested in.**  There are many features to consider when looking at genre:

- **Is point of view important for your purpose and audience?** For example, if you need your piece to be first person so that it includes your perspective, make sure you choose a genre that accommodates this point of view.
- **What type of connection do you want to establish with your audience?** If you want to remain at a critical distance, consider choosing a genre that emphasizes ethos in its rhetorical appeal. To make a closer connection by appealing to readers' emotions regarding your topic, consider choosing a genre that emphasizes pathos.

Keep this in mind:
Genre decisions
at this point are
still tentative; as
you draft, you may
stumble upon a
completely different
genre idea that
fits your purpose,
audience, and other
aspects of your
rhetorical situation.
Keep an open
mind as you draft.
Remember that the
drafting process is a
process of discovery.

- **What tone do you want to use in order to achieve your purpose?** If you want your piece to have a certain level of formality (or informality), be sure to choose a genre that demonstrates that.

**Step 7. Zero in on how you'll use your experience & evidence.**   Finally, you'll need to think about how you will use sources in your piece and how the genre you're considering typically deals with sources. You may realize that you need to do research, talk to experts, or dig deeper. For more on help with research, see Part 4 of this book.

## Guided Process | Choosing a Genre

In the following pages, Gwen Ganow decides which genre she'd like to compose in by doing the following:

1. She considers her rhetorical situation and commits to a purpose and audience. Her purpose is to persuade her audience that superhero characters help to fight intolerance. Her audience is both academic and public, including her instructor and peers, as well as fans of comics and superheroes outside her course.

2. She looks at three examples of public and academic genres: an ad, a researched argument, and a film review.

3. She decides how she wants to use her own experience and evidence and which genre will work best overall. In this section, Gwen moves from brainstorming about a possible genre into making a final choice about which genre will be best for her project. (Spoiler alert: It's a film review.)

Even though Gwen has decided on her purpose and audience, she still needs to work out a few details to choose a genre that best responds to her rhetorical situation and allows her to achieve her purpose.

BRAINSTORM   **Gwen Ganow** (STUDENT), *Choosing a Genre for the "Take a Position" Assignment: Superheroes and Social Attitudes*

**English 121**

English Composition

**Date:** November 8, 2019
**Name:** Gwen Ganow
**Brainstorm:** Choosing a Genre for the "Take a Position"
**Assignment:** Superheroes and Social Attitudes

**RHETORICAL SITUATION & CHOICES**

**How can I achieve my purpose?**
Since I want to persuade my reader that there is a need for
superhero characters to fight intolerance, I might create a

fictional account that illustrates a superhero fighting some evil. I could also create an advertisement that shows a superhero in action fighting injustice.

### Who is my audience?
My academic audience already knows something about superheroes. And my public audience, comic book lovers and experts, will expect me to be very well-informed about superheroes. I'll need to draw on evidence and details from comics to support my points. Whatever genre I choose for my composition, something visual and narrative will most appeal to my readers.

### How can I connect with my audience rhetorically?
*Ethos.* As an author, if I want to persuade my audience it's going to be crucial to convince them that my information and argument are credible—and that I am qualified to make the argument. I've grown up with comics and have a good base of knowledge; I'll establish that in my composition.

*Logos.* I'll need to build a logical case for my audience. I'll need to be methodical and organized.

*Pathos.* Part of what makes me care about superheroes is my emotional connection to them as people who care—who put themselves "in harm's way" to help and rescue others.

### How will I reach my audience through mode and media?
*Mode.* My composition will probably have more text than visuals. My comics-fan audience may expect visuals, but I'm more comfortable working in text and presenting arguments that way. Also, I might be drawing on evidence. How would I do that in a nontextual medium? I'm a good writer, but I feel less comfortable as an artist. Maybe I can use existing images from comics in my work as evidence to support my points.

*Media.* If I create a written text for a digital environment, I can embed links. That might be an easy way to bring in my sources. I'd like to build into my work some existing clips from films and animations.

### POSSIBLE GENRES

### What are three genres that respond to my rhetorical situation?
1. *An advertisement?* I like that I could mix visuals with text if I made an ad. Where would I publish this ad? It would need to be somewhere that comic book fans would see it. If my ad is image centered, then I will be creating a type of visual argument. That may be a good way to reach comic book lovers, a public audience.
2. *A researched argument?* I wouldn't mind doing research and drawing on some evidence. If I choose this academic and

*(Continues on next page)*

public audience genre, I won't have to worry about length problems and could easily include visuals to make my case. I'm now thinking I could present this online in a magazine, journal, or blog.

3. *Film review?* As an avid film-viewer I do read a lot of film reviews. I could review a film that focuses on a superhero. I'm not sure if I could use visuals with this.

*Credit: By permission of Gwen Dalynn Ganow.*

Now that Gwen has narrowed her choice of genre down to three types—an ad, a researched argument, and a film review—she looks at an example of each. She annotates the examples, reading them not only for information about her topic but also to find out more about the genres and their conventions. For example, how did the composers of these works incorporate sources? As she reads these texts closely, she asks herself: Which of these genres should I ultimately choose for my composition?

Gwen analyzes and annotates each piece according to the composer's rhetorical situation and use of genre conventions. Below is her annotation of A. O. Scott's film review: "Iron Man: Heavy Suit, Light Touches" from *The New York Times* online.

## Guided Reading | Annotated Sample Film Review

**A. O. Scott,** *"Heavy Suit, Light Touches,"* with Notes by Gwen Ganow (STUDENT)

| RHETORICAL SITUATION & CHOICES | GENRE CONVENTIONS |
|---|---|

*Gwen's notes on Scott's review*

◀ **What is the composer, A. O. Scott, doing?**

**How do I know this is a film ▶ review? Do I want to write one?**

*Gwen's notes on Scott's review*

**PURPOSE**
Scott wants to persuade readers that *Iron Man* is a film to see. He shows readers that it's a "superhero movie that's good in unusual ways." I like that his purpose is extremely clear and that he draws on moments in the film as evidence for his claims.

The world at the moment does not suffer from a shortage of superheroes. And yet in some ways the glut of anti-evil crusaders with cool costumes and troubled souls takes the pressure off of *Iron Man*, which clanks into theaters today ahead of Hellboy, Batman, and the Incredible Hulk. This summer those guys are all in sequels or redos, so *Iron Man* (a Marvel property not to be confused with the Man of Steel, who belongs to DC and who's taking a break this year) has the advantage of novelty in addition to a seasonal head start.

And *Iron Man*, directed by Jon Favreau (*Elf, Zathura*), has the advantage of being an unusually good superhero picture. Or at least—since it certainly has its problems—a superhero movie that's good in unusual ways. The film benefits from a

**ELEMENTS OF THE GENRE**
In a film review, a writer takes a position about a movie and backs that up by drawing on moments from the film, and even from film history. Here, Scott's first paragraph gets my attention. He identifies the genre of the film and makes clear what he thinks of the film.

**AUDIENCE**

As a film critic for *The New York Times*, Scott writes for fellow film experts and anyone interested in movies. In this case, his audience also includes people familiar with comics, especially with Marvel's *Iron Man*. My audience is similar: beyond my academic audience, my public audience is made up of fans of comics and superheroes.

script (credited to Mark Fergus, Hawk Ostby, Art Marcum, and Matt Holloway) that generally chooses clever dialogue over manufactured catchphrases and lumbering exposition, and also from a crackerjack cast that accepts the filmmaker's invitation to do some real acting rather than just flex and glower and shriek for a paycheck.

There's some of that too, of course. The hero must flex and furrow his brow; the bad guy must glower and scheme; the girl must shriek and fret. There should also be a skeptical but supportive friend. Those are the rules of the genre, as unbreakable as the pseudoscientific principles that explain everything (An arc reactor! Of course!) and the Law of the Bald Villain. In *Iron Man* it all plays out more or less as expected, from the trial-and-error building of the costume to the climactic showdown, with lots of flying, chasing and noisemaking in between. (I note that there is one sharp, subversive surprise right at the very end.)

What is less expected is that Mr. Favreau, somewhat in the manner of those sly studio-era craftsmen who kept their artistry close to the vest so the bosses wouldn't confiscate it, wears the genre paradigm as a light cloak rather than a suit of iron. Instead of the tedious, moralizing, pop-Freudian origin story we often get in the first installments of comic-book-franchise movies—childhood trauma; identity crisis; longing for justice versus thirst for revenge; wake me up when the explosions start—*Iron Man* plunges us immediately into a world that crackles with character and incident.

**STYLE**

Scott writes in the third person. His tone is mostly formal but is sometimes informal, such as when he uses exclamation points and phrases such as: "Yeah, that guy." He even addresses the reader as "you." I like that informality.

*Credit: Everett Collection, Inc.*

(Continues on next page)

Choosing a Genre to Compose In     **57**

Scott uses logos by
referring to parts of
the plot to make his
case. He chooses
language that conveys
pathos and playfulness
("bon vivant"
and "incorrigible
playboy"). I like that
combination and
might try that.

It is not quite the real world, but it's a bit closer than
Gotham or Metropolis. We catch up with Tony Stark in dusty
Afghanistan, where he is enjoying a Scotch on the rocks in the
back of an armored American military vehicle. Tony is a media
celebrity, a former M.I.T. whiz kid and the scion of a family
whose company makes and sells high-tech weaponry. He's also a
bon vivant and an incorrigible playboy. On paper the character
is completely preposterous, but since Tony is played by
Robert Downey Jr., he's almost immediately as authentic and
familiar—as much fun, as much trouble—as your ex-boyfriend
or your old college roommate. Yeah, that guy.

Tony's skeptical friend (see above) is Rhodey, an Air
Force officer played with good-humored sidekick weariness
by Terrence Howard. The girl is one Pepper Potts (Gwyneth
Paltrow, also in evident good humor), Tony's smitten,
ultracompetent assistant. His partner and sort-of mentor in
Stark Enterprises is Obadiah Stane, played by Jeff Bridges with
wit and exuberance and—spoiler alert!—a shaved head.

These are all first-rate actors, and Mr. Downey's antic energy
and emotional unpredictability bring out their agility and
resourcefulness. Within the big, crowded movements of this
pop symphony is a series of brilliant duets that sometimes
seem to have the swing and spontaneity of jazz improvisation:
Mr. Downey and Ms. Paltrow on the dance floor; Mr. Downey
and Mr. Howard drinking sake on an airplane; Mr. Downey and
Shaun Toub working on blueprints in a cave; Mr. Downey and
Mr. Bridges sparring over a box of pizza.

Those moments are what you are likely to remember. The
plot is serviceable, which is to say that it's placed at the service
of the actors (and the special-effects artists), who deftly toss
it around and sometimes forget it's there. One important twist
seems glaringly arbitrary and unmotivated, but this lapse may
represent an act of carefree sabotage rather than carelessness.
You know this ostensibly shocking revelation is coming, and
the writers know you know it's coming, so why worry too
much about whether it makes sense? Similarly, the patina of
geopolitical relevance is worn thin and eventually discarded,
and Tony's crisis of conscience when he discovers what his
weapons are being used for is more of a narrative convenience
than a real moral theme.

The designers of the
*NYT* print paper and
news site present
content in columns
and with standard
headings. The writing
is broken into brief
paragraphs for easy
reading, and the
online version of
the review includes
hyperlinks that
enhance the content.

**MODES & MEDIA**
This film review is a text document with images. It's available in the *NYT* print and online editions. The digital version includes embedded links to sources and related materials. I also plan to publish my work online and am interested in embedding links.

All of which is to say that *Iron Man*, in spite of the heavy encumbrances Tony must wear when he turns into the title character, is distinguished by light touches and grace notes. The hardware is impressive, don't get me wrong, but at these prices it had better be. If you're throwing around a hundred million dollars and you have Batman and the Hulk on your tail, you had better be sure that the arc reactors are in good working order and that the gold-titanium alloy suit gleams like new and flies like a bird.

And everything works pretty well. But even dazzling, computer-aided visual effects, these days, are not so special. And who doesn't have superpowers? Actually, Iron Man doesn't; his heroism is all handicraft, elbow grease and applied intelligence. Those things account for the best parts of *Iron Man* as well.

*Iron Man* is rated PG-13 (Parents strongly cautioned). It has a lot of action violence, none of it is especially graphic or gruesome. Also, Iron Man has sex, and not with the suit on. But not completely naked either.

**Opens on Friday nationwide.**

Directed by Jon Favreau; written by Mark Fergus, Hawk Ostby, Art Marcum and Matt Holloway based on the character created by Stan Lee, Larry Lieber, Don Heck and Jack Kirby; director of photography, Matthew Libatique; edited by Dan Lebental; music by Ramin Djawadi; production designer, J. Michael Riva; visual effects by John Nelson; produced by Avi Arad and Kevin Feige; released by Paramount Pictures and Marvel Entertainment. Running time: 2 hours 6 minutes.

With: Robert Downey Jr. (Tony Stark), Terrence Howard (Rhodey), Jeff Bridges (Obadiah Stane), Shaun Toub (Yinsen) and Gwyneth Paltrow (Pepper Potts).

**SOURCES**
Scott's primary source is the movie *Iron Man*.

Note: The entire text of this review is available online.

Gwen has decided she wants to write a film review because it allows her to achieve her purpose and is a genre her audience is likely to read. She needs to figure out what movie to review and how that will allow her to make her argument.

Keep the following questions in mind:

**RHETORICAL SITUATION & CHOICES**

☐ **Purpose.** What is my purpose? Which genres respond to my rhetorical situation best? Which ones do I know the most about? Which ones do I want to try out? Which ones can I get help with? Among the sources I've drawn on in my research, which ones stood out? What are their genres?

☐ **Audience.** How familiar is my audience with my topic? What assumptions might my audience make about my topic? What expectations will my audience have about my piece?

☐ **Rhetorical appeals.** How will I connect with my audience? For example, if I create an ad or an editorial, how will I work within that genre to be as compelling and convincing as possible?

☐ **Modes & media.** What is the best mode for saying what I want to say? If I rely on text only, will anything be lost? Which medium would be best?

**GENRE CONVENTIONS**

☐ **Elements of the genres.** What features make a particular genre what it is? How would I use (or not use) those features?

☐ **Style.** What are my strengths as a writer or composer? What tone will be most appropriate for my composition, considering the genre I choose? What kind of vocabulary will I use? How much detail will be appropriate?

☐ **Design.** Once I choose the genre for my composition, how will it look or sound? Will I use a conventional design, or perhaps tailor a standard layout or structure to my own purposes?

☐ **Sources.** What do I already know about my topic? What experiences have I had? To what extent will I need to draw on sources? Will I need to quote from them? Document them?

# Composing Your Genre Piece

If you've followed Gwen to this point, we hope you have some solid ideas for your own composition, including a sense of your rhetorical situation and choices—and of the genre or genres that would work best in response.

## Steps for Composing

Once you're ready to move from your freewrite to creating a first draft, keep the following steps in mind. As we've mentioned elsewhere, there is not one process that will work for everyone, and your own processes will likely vary from project to project. These guidelines for composing are here for you to draw on as needed:

**Step 1. Write a solid draft.** Review the freewrite you created earlier in this process and begin fleshing it out so it has a beginning, middle, and end, or whatever elements are appropriate for your chosen genre. It should include, at least in rough form, the main points you want to make, as well as some examples or evidence you'll use to support your points.

Working from this draft, follow the steps below to evaluate and revise it.

**Step 2. Evaluate your use of experience & evidence.**  Look at a really good example of the genre you're working in and compare it to yours. How does that author support claims with evidence? Draw on experience? What kind of evidence will your audience expect and respond to? Will anecdotes and personal stories be convincing to your audience, or will they be more convinced by statistics and references to peer-reviewed studies?

Note: Refer to the sample of your genre as you complete steps 3–7.

**Step 3. Confirm the scope of information to provide.**  How much coverage of the topic is appropriate for the genre you've selected? Examine the sample of the genre you're comparing your draft to. Does it present an overview of the subject? What is the level of detail?

**Step 4. Consider your use of style.**  Think about voice, tone, language, and point of view. Is the genre you're composing in characterized by the use of first or third person? How explicit and present will your voice and experience be in the piece? Look at the example you're comparing your piece to. Does that composer use an objective, authoritative tone, or a personal, subjective tone, or something else?

ATTENTION, COMPOSERS

Wondering about media? What medium will best suit your genre and rhetorical situation? Will you reach your audiences best through a print or physical medium or in a digital environment? If you're composing online, will you use audio? How about video or animation? What medium will your primary audience respond to best?

**Step 5. Look at how you use rhetorical appeals.**  Look at your draft and the sample genre piece you're consulting. To what extent does the other author use ethos, pathos, and/or logos? How effective is his or her approach, and what might you want to adapt for your own work?

**Step 6. Look at your organization.**  How have you organized your content? Is this the best way, considering whom your audience is and what you're trying to achieve? Is it logical? Persuasive? Does the sample you're consulting have anything to offer you in terms of a model for improving your work?

**Step 7. Consider your mix of words & images.**  This is also a moment to think about design and medium. Are you being as effective as you could be? Again, consult your example.

**Step 8. Make a list of what you want to work on when you revise.**  Base your list on what you've determined in steps 2–7.

**Step 9. Revise your draft based on your revision list.**  After you've revised, reread your work and make notes to address things you want to improve for the next draft.

**Step 10. Revise a little more.**  Get your work in the best shape you can in the time you have.

## Guided Process | Composing a Film Review

At this point in her process, Gwen has a clear sense of her genre as well as her rhetorical situation. She now gets down to writing. In the following section, she writes a first draft of her film review. She then spends time evaluating it—reading it against a published film review—to see how she might improve her own. In this process, she reviews her work for how well she deals with purpose, audience, and other rhetorical concerns.

She also pays attention to how well she works within the genre of the film review itself. After this process, she revises her first draft, creating a second and third draft.

Gwen notes: "I decided to review the film *X-Men*. It's a significant film in the superhero genre that my audience will be familiar with. Following is my attempt at a first draft."

**DRAFT 1** **Gwen Ganow** (STUDENT), *"Take a Position" Assignment, Superheroes and Social Attitudes:* X-Men

**English 121**
English Composition

**Date:** November 11, 2019
**Name:** Gwen Ganow
**Assignment:** "Take a Position" Film Review
Superheroes and Social Attitudes: *X-Men*

The punctuated equilibrium concept of Niles Eldredge and Stephen Jay Gould states that evolution and speciation occur at a rapid rate followed by long periods of stasis. The film *X-Men* explores how a modern American society would react to its own punctuated equilibrium in which a new, superhuman species rises and suddenly integrates with "normal" humans. Through the events and emotions of the movie *X-Men*, our past and current social issues of prejudice and intolerance as an American society become exposed.

X-Men opens with a powerful image of prejudice and intolerance, a Nazi concentration camp. While unloading a new trainload of Jews, Nazi soldiers rip a young boy from the arms of his parents. He sits in the rain crying and watches helplessly as his parents are herded off to other buildings. His yellow Star of David, his label of difference, is the only color against the dismal backdrop of rain, mud, and hate. The young boy survives his Nazi captors and grows up to be a mutant with the power to move and control metal.

The movie leaves the scene of war and enters the chambers of Congress where a Senate committee hearing is taking place. Magneto attends this committee hearing of the Senate because he is curious about what the American government is doing about the so-called "mutant problem" in the United States. Senator Kelly, a staunch supporter of the Mutant Registration Act, is debated by Dr. Jean Grey (a mutant herself). Jean Grey argues against the Mutant Registration Act and says, "Mutants who have revealed themselves publicly have been met with fear, hostility, and violence." To this, Senator Kelly responds with the questions, "Are they dangerous? Do you want your children in school with mutants? Do you want your children to be taught by mutant teachers?"

To shield the younger generation from the violence created by the words of intolerance spoken by Senator Kelly, Charles Xavier (a mutant with powerful psychic abilities) creates Xavier's School for Gifted Youngsters and makes it a place for young mutants who have recently discovered that they are very different from their peers and have run away from home. Here he offers these young men and women a place of refuge and sense of inclusiveness. This is a safe environment where they can be taught how to control their developing minds and powers by some of Xavier's finest past students like Storm, Cyclops, and Jean Grey, who become mentors to a new generation of young mutants, afraid of the world around them. Charles Xavier never gives up hope that humanity will come to realize the error of their judgment. He teaches his students that intolerance should not be returned with even more intolerance.

Magneto's view of humanity is radically different from the views of Charles Xavier. Magneto sees nothing wrong with trying to solve the plight of mutants by using violence and fear against humans. He devises a plan using his own powers combined with a radiation-generating machine to change non-mutants into mutants. By doing this, he feels that vengeance will be carried out by putting would-be persecutors into the lives of the people they sought to persecute and chooses Senator Kelly as his first test subject. Magneto tells the senator: "Humankind has always feared what it doesn't understand. You have nothing to fear from God and nothing to fear from me. Not anymore."

The fear, intolerance, and violence toward mutants that is conveyed in *X-Men* closely ties in with the fear, intolerance, and violence endured by the GLBT community today. Sometimes, the reality of the comic book universe resembles our own reality more than we would like to admit. The movie *X-Men* questions whether we as Americans really believe in freedom for all or whether we really mean freedom for some.

Next, Gwen evaluates her film review by comparing it to an example of the genre: A. O. Scott's review "*Iron Man*: Heavy Suit, Light Touches," which she looked at earlier. She evaluates Scott's use of evidence and sources, his scope and use of rhetorical appeals, and his organization and use of visuals. Then she applies this lens to her own review.

**RHETORICAL SITUATION & CHOICES**  |  **GENRE CONVENTIONS**

*Gwen's notes on sample film review by A. O. Scott*

**USE OF EVIDENCE & SOURCES**
Scott puts *Iron Man* in context with other movies of the same genre. He refers to the director, his other films, and the scriptwriters.

Scott gives plot details but does not give the story away. He supports each claim with a brief snippet from the plot. Whenever he makes a point, he backs it with specific evidence and quotations from scenes.

**SCOPE**
His scope is in line with his purpose: to evaluate the film and make an argument in favor of it. Scott chooses key details about characters and from specific scenes to support his case.

He summarizes quite a bit: He gives just a snapshot of the plot by providing setting, character descriptions, and parts of the story.

**STYLE**
I like Scott's writing style. It's almost as if I can hear him speaking. He chooses each word carefully and keeps his language

Heavy Suit, Light Touches
By A. O. SCOTT

Movie review | 'iron man'
Iron Man (2008)

Credit: Everett Collection, Inc.

The world at the moment does not suffer from a shortage of superheroes. And yet in some ways the glut of anti-evil crusaders with cool costumes and troubled souls takes the pressure off of *Iron Man*, which clanks into theaters today ahead of Hellboy, Batman, and the Incredible Hulk. This summer those guys are all in sequels or redos, so Iron Man (a Marvel property not to be confused with the Man of Steel, who belongs to DC and who's taking a break this year) has the advantage of novelty in addition to a seasonal head start. . . .
**(For the full version of Scott's review, see p. 56.)**

(For the full version of Scott's review, see p. 56.)

---

**English 121**

English Composition

**Date:** November 12, 2019
**Name:** Gwen Ganow
**Assignment:** "Take a Position" Evaluation of Film Review: Superheroes and Social Attitudes *X-Men*

The punctuated equilibrium concept of Niles Eldredge and Stephen Jay Gould states that evolution and speciation occur at a rapid rate followed by long periods of stasis. The film *X-Men* explores how a modern American society would

*Gwen's notes on draft 1 of her film review*

**USE OF EVIDENCE & SOURCES**
In my review, I put the movie *X-Men* in context with the theory of "punctuated equilibrium," which I learned about in a biology class (and cite Eldredge and Gould as my source). I support my claims about the "powerful image of prejudice and intolerance" (paragraph 2) with plot details and specifics from a scene. Like Scott, the evidence I use to support my position includes details from the plot and other aspects of the film and its creators.

**SCOPE**
I go into way more detail than Scott does, maybe because I am retelling the plot chronologically. Is this a problem? Do I need to pull back from some of my details to give more summary?

**STYLE**
I'm not sure my voice comes through enough in my review. I think I sound knowledgeable, but I'm not so sure how present I am in the writing in terms of voice,

interesting. For example, he uses a variety of terms (film, picture) to refer to the movie. Scott writes in the third person, but I like how he sometimes invites the reader in by using the word "we."

**RHETORICAL APPEALS**
Scott builds his ethos by drawing on evidence and crediting the film's creators. He also appeals to readers through pathos: He entices readers to go see *Iron Man* through his language and tone.

**ORGANIZATION**
Scott begins with general comments about superheroes and the popularity of superhero movies before he moves on to Iron Man.

Next, he situates the film within its genre, hinting at his opinion of the movie. He outlines some of his expectations. He makes claims that he supports with details of the plot and characters; he closes with a final evaluation of the film.

**USE OF VISUALS**
Scott includes a few visuals. The large still featuring Robert Downey Jr., who plays the lead, is pretty striking. There is also a small picture further into the review.

react to its own punctuated equilibrium in which a new, superhuman species rises and suddenly integrates with "normal" humans. Through the events and emotions of the movie *X-Men*, our past and current social issues of prejudice and intolerance as an American society become exposed.

*X-Men* opens with a powerful image of prejudice and intolerance, a Nazi concentration camp. While unloading a new trainload of Jews, Nazi soldiers rip a young boy from the arms of his parents. He sits in the rain crying and watches helplessly as his parents are herded off to other buildings. His yellow Star of David, his label of difference, is the only color against the dismal backdrop of rain, mud, and hate. The young boy survives his Nazi captors and grows up to be a mutant with the power to move and control metal.

The movie leaves the scene of war and enters the chambers of Congress where a Senate committee hearing is taking place. Magneto attends this committee hearing of the Senate because he is curious about what the American government is doing about the so-called "mutant problem" in the United States. Senator Kelly, a staunch supporter of the Mutant Registration Act, is debated by Dr. Jean Grey (a mutant herself). Jean Grey argues against the Mutant Registration Act and says, "Mutants who have revealed themselves publicly have been met with fear, hostility, and violence." To this, Senator Kelly responds with the questions, "Are they dangerous? Do you want your children in school with mutants? Do you want your children to be taught by mutant teachers?" . . .

**(For a full version of Ganow's Film Review Draft 1, see p. 62.)**

personality, or humor. My review does not seem as personal or subjective as Scott's. I think my perspective is more objective. Is that a strong point? Or a problem?

**RHETORICAL APPEALS**
I want to establish myself as an expert on superheroes and film. I'm not sure how well I've conveyed my ethos. I also need to persuade my audience, so I need to appeal to pathos.

**MY ORGANIZATION**
I move through the plot, giving readers a general sense of the story. I don't discuss the film in terms of a broader context but I probably should. I need to state my position clearly and directly.

**MY USE OF VISUALS**
I haven't yet added any images/film stills into my review, but I need to. Which characters and key scenes do I want to show?

*(Continues on next page)*

**What to focus on when I revise? ▼**

1. **Reorganize my review so it isn't just a chronological plot summary.** I need to identify the points I want to make and then choose supporting details from the plot, much as Scott does.

2. **Establish a clearer sense of voice.** Make sure not to shift between third and first person. Add a little personality.

3. **Make my opinion of the film much clearer.** I need my position about the film to be stronger. Is it worth seeing? Why or why not? Also, I want readers to see the dilemma of the hero as related to that of the GLBT community.

4. **Do more to establish ethos and appeal to readers' emotions.**

5. **Pay more attention to language.** Incorporate visuals—also maybe embed video.

Based on her evaluation of her first draft (see above) and the items she's identified to revise (see list in right column), Gwen rewrites to create her second draft that she titles "*X-Men*: Mutants R Us."

**English 121**

English Composition

**Date:** November 14, 2019

**Name:** Gwen Ganow

**Assignment:** "Take a Position" Film Review

*X-Men*: Mutants R Us

As a "hard-core" comic book fan, I always considered the 2000 *X-Men* film the epitome of a true comic book movie. What sets the *X-Men* apart from other comic book films is that the story behind the *X-Men* is not overshadowed by special effects. In *X-Men*, equilibrium is punctured; humans face a sudden and dramatic evolutionary change, one that results in the existence of "mutants." The mutants are humans with superhuman powers, who look human enough to integrate invisibly into society. The movie explores how American society might react to the existence of these mutants, exposing our past and current social issues of prejudice and intolerance. Bryan Singer, best known for 1995's *The Usual Suspects*, directs from the screenplay written by David Hayter.

Created by Stan Lee and Jack Kirby in 1963, X-Men are children of parents who were exposed to atmospheric radiation and became genetically altered. The mutant kids are outsiders in the world, and are envied and feared by "normal" humans. The alienation of the X-Men is similar to that of other groups of people who have experienced prejudice, like African Americans, Jews, Japanese, and homosexuals. Singer makes this parallel explicit with the opening scene.

*X-Men* opens with a powerful image of prejudice and intolerance, a Nazi concentration camp. While unloading a new trainload of Jews, Nazi soldiers rip a young boy from the arms of his parents. He sits in the rain crying and watches helplessly as his parents are herded off to other buildings. His yellow Star of David is the only color against the dismal backdrop of rain, mud, and hate. The young boy survives his Nazi captors and grows up to be a mutant known as Magneto with the power to move and control metal.

The movie leaves the scene of war and enters the chambers of Congress where a Senate committee hearing is

*(Continues on next page)*

taking place on the Mutant Registration Act, which would require mutants to register with the government and list their special abilities, making it impossible for them to blend in unnoticed with the rest of society. Magneto, played by Ian McKellen, attends this committee hearing because he is curious about what the American government is doing about the so-called "mutant problem." Senator Kelly, played by Bruce Davison, a staunch supporter of the Mutant Registration Act, is debated by Dr. Jean Grey, a mutant herself, played by Famke Janssen. Kelly supports the Mutant Registration Act, believing that mutants are a danger to "normal" humans and should be locked away, while Grey argues that forcing mutants to register would create the potential for them to be treated as freaks.

The performers share good chemistry, with the one-upmanship between Hugh Jackman's Wolverine and James Marsden's Cyclops bringing humor to their scenes. Patrick Stewart's Charles Xavier seems both fatherly and professorial, and Anna Paquin as Rogue does a fine job conveying fear about her future as a mutant and lovesickness over Wolverine. Rebecca Romijn makes an impression in a role that relies more on physical presence than lines.

In *X-Men*, responses to prejudice by the victims of prejudice are explored through the actions of two important mutants, both leaders of mutant groups. Charles Xavier, a mutant with powerful psychic abilities, creates a school for the gifted for young runaway mutants. Here he offers these young men and women a place of refuge and a sense of inclusiveness. This is a safe environment where they can be taught how to control their developing minds and powers by some of Xavier's finest past students like Storm, Cyclops, and Jean Grey, who become mentors to a new generation of young mutants, afraid of the world around them. Xavier's "turn the other cheek" philosophy links him to the Jesus Christ of the Christian culture. The fact that Charles Xavier provides a safe house for people rejected by humanity also links him to our real-life organizations like NAACP, GLBT (gay, lesbian, bisexual, and transgender) resource centers, and some of our churches.

The other leader is Magneto, who fronts the Brotherhood of Mutants. Magneto's perspective on humanity stems from his experiences as a young boy at a WWII concentration camp, which was captured in the film's opening scene. This experience left Magneto distrustful of humanity and convinced that mutants are bound to suffer the same fate met by the inmates of the Nazi death camps. To preserve the survival of his mutant species, Magneto declares war on humankind. Magneto's view of humanity is radically different from the views of Charles Xavier. Magneto sees nothing wrong with trying to solve the plight of mutants by using violence and fear against humans.

Although the film is worth seeing for the performances and direction alone, the special effects, while relatively low-key for a superhero movie, are stunning. Magneto's spinning contraption, the fight scenes, and Storm's weather conjuring add to the fun. Finally, while there is seldom a clear right and wrong in real life, Singer's film makes it easy for us to take the right side. The heroes of the film are clearly Professor Xavier's X-Men. In this way, Singer allows us to imagine the consequences of violence and anger, as shown by Magneto's band of mutants, and ultimately root for Xavier's more tolerant gang.

*Credit: By permission Gwen Dalynn Ganow.*

Gwen evaluates her second draft and comes up with a list of items to focus on for her third and final draft. Gwen observes the following:

1. Overall, I've done a better job in Draft 2 in evaluating the film and taking a position about it. It's clear what I think of the movie and why.

2. Draft 2 is also more interesting and readable. I've done more to appeal to my audience of superhero/comic lovers. For example, my first sentence and paragraph are aimed at drawing them in.

3. My writing still seems stiff in places. I want to make the style and tone a little more casual; also, I want to tighten up the wording and do more to make this flow.

4. A final point: This doesn't look like a film review yet. I'll need to apply design principles and add an image from the film. I'd also like to embed links to other reviews and to interviews with the director and actors.

When she revises again, she addresses document design, images, and embedded links. She also polishes her writing and continues to evaluate her choice of mode and medium, with thoughts of future iterations of her project. Following is an excerpt from her final review.

**English 121**

English Composition

**Date:** November 21, 2019

**Name:** Gwen Ganow

**Assignment:** "Take a Position" Film Review

*X-Men*: Mutants R Us

As a "hard-core" comic book fan, I always considered the 2000 *X-Men* film the epitome of a true comic book movie. What sets the *X-Men* apart from other comic book films is that the story behind the X-Men is not overshadowed by special effects. In *X-Men*, it's the story that matters. In the world of this film, the equilibrium of existence has been punctured; humans face a sudden and dramatic evolutionary change, one that results in the existence of "mutants."

The mutants are humans with superhuman powers, who look human enough to integrate invisibly into society. The movie explores how American society might react to the existence of these mutants, exposing our past and current social issues of prejudice and intolerance.

Bryan Singer, best known for 1995's *The Usual Suspects*, directs from the screenplay written by David Hayter. . . .

The performers share good chemistry, with the one-upmanship between Hugh Jackman's Wolverine and James Marsden's Cyclops bringing humor to their scenes. Patrick Stewart's Charles Xavier seems both fatherly and professorial, and Anna Paquin as Rogue does a fine job.

Hugh Jackman as Wolverine, from *X-Men* (2000).

*Credit: Everett Collection, Inc.*

*Credit: By permission Gwen Dalynn Ganow.*

As you compose, keep the following in mind. (For help with composing from sources, see Chapter 14.)

**RHETORICAL SITUATION & CHOICES**

☐ **Purpose.** Why am I composing this piece? What do I hope it will achieve? How can I best convey my interest and passion to meet my purpose?

☐ **Audience.** Whom am I composing for? What will they already know about my topic? What will they need to know? What level of detail will my audience want and need? Do I need to consider a secondary audience?

☐ **Rhetorical appeals.** What experiences and evidence can I draw on to establish my credibility? Is it appropriate to emphasize pathos? How can I make the logic of my position or point clear?

☐ **Modes & media.** Should I mix words, audio, and/ or images to be most effective? Will my audience want something digital or a hard copy? What medium will my primary audience respond to best?

**GENRE CONVENTIONS**

☐ **Elements of the genre.** Am I using the conventions of the genre appropriately? Do I need to look at more examples of the genre?

☐ **Style.** Have I used a tone that is appropriate for my genre and will it achieve my purpose with my audience? What point of view (first person, second person, third person) will help me achieve my purpose? Have I chosen my words carefully?

☐ **Design.** How have I used design elements to direct my audience's attention? Have I designed my piece according to the design conventions of the genre? For example, if I'm writing a blog, does it look like a blog?

☐ **Sources.** Are the experiences and evidence that I draw on appropriate for my genre? Have I cited them according to the genre's conventions? Is there additional experience or evidence that I need to incorporate to achieve my purpose?

**PRACTICE**

# Taking a Position

Do the same assignment Gwen did: Take a position on a topic you care about and have experience with. Then think about whom you want to communicate your ideas to and compose in a genre that will allow you to do that.

You may compose in any genre that seems appropriate for your purpose and audience. The length should be appropriate to the genre; in other words, a magazine article will have more words than a poster. Be sure to choose a genre that will allow you to communicate with the audience you have in mind.

For sources, you should primarily draw upon your own experience. If you wish, you can use other source material, if it is appropriate to your genre choice and topic. Refer back to Gwen's process and try to mimic it as closely as possible.

# 5

# REVISING & REMIXING

While feedback can help during any stage of your composing process, once you have a solid draft of your work, it's an ideal time to get some advice on how to make it even better. In this chapter, we pick up where we left off with Gwen Ganow. She's finished her genre piece—a film review of the movie *X-Men*—and has a first draft of her accompanying Author's Statement (see Chapter 6), which still needs work. In the first part of this chapter, she revises two drafts and polishes her final Statement, working with her own ideas and those she gets from peer review.

Later, Gwen decides she wants to remix her genre project to repurpose her film review and create something entirely new. Later in this chapter, we provide guidelines for remixing any genre project—that is, advice for how to work with your topic, research, and any composing you've already done to make something totally different.

# Revising Your Work

Why revise, you ask? Because your first draft is geared toward getting your ideas out of your head and onto the page. Some people call this a writer-based draft. A writer-based draft usually has gaps in development and logic. The purpose and sense of audience are usually unclear. They become clear through revision and as you move toward a more audience-focused composition.

## Revising Based on Your Own Observations

Gwen has a solid first draft of her Author's Statement to accompany her film review. Now she wants some input from others—from her instructor and classmates—on how to revise her Statement so it's more analytical and persuasive. Gwen's Author's Statement gives her an opportunity to explain the choices she made in addressing her rhetorical situation and working with her genre. But it's also a document in which she can reflect on and learn from her own process.

**▲ STUDENT AUTHOR PHOTO**

**Gwen Ganow.**
*Credit: Gwen Dalynn Ganow.*

**◄ DRAFT AUTHOR'S STATEMENT & FILM REVIEW**

**Gwen Ganow.**
Draft 1 (left); Final draft (right)
(Gwen's film review appears in Chapter 4.)
*Credit: Gwen Dalynn Ganow; Everett Collection, Inc.*

**Who should respond to your drafts?**   Friends, family, and roommates may not be familiar with your topic, but they can tell you whether your argument is logical, for example, or whether your introductory paragraph is clear. They can point out spots in the draft where they got confused, found inconsistencies, or wanted more explanation or evidence.

That said, responses from your classmates, writing center tutor, instructor, or others in your target audience are probably going to be most helpful. We recommend that you ask at least one person from your intended primary audience to respond to your draft.

When you reflect on your writing and create an Author's or Artist's Statement, you develop skills that will transfer into other settings. You learn to reflect critically on your own work so that you can improve on it. This is a skill, a habit, even, that you (and all of us) can use in other coursework and outside of school—in future professions or when creating for any audience.

Need another reason why reflecting and revising—or re-seeing—your genre project is a good idea? Here's an example: In art school, students hardly ever create the "perfect" painting or sculpture or installation in one course or semester. Often, they'll sketch, paint drafts, or create models that they'll use later as maps or inspiration for when they can flesh out their vision for the composition in a different or fuller way. Drafting, thinking critically, and revising go a long way in making great authors and artists truly great. Why not be great?

## Revising Based on Peer Review

Let's say that, like Gwen, you've created your genre piece and/or your Author's or Artist's Statement. You've done some revising, and you feel that you've done the best you can. Maybe you can no longer review the content objectively because you've been working on it for a while. Asking others for feedback on your draft is an excellent way to find out how well you've met your purposes or reached your audience. Readers/viewers/listeners will experience your composition with fresh eyes and ears. They can help you figure out where you need to make connections more explicit, where you need to develop examples, and where the draft could be restructured, among other things.

Respondents to your work can be classmates, a teacher, a tutor, friends, parents, or coworkers. Ideally your respondents are from your intended primary audience. These individuals are most likely to give you solid advice on how well you're doing in terms of your rhetorical situation and chosen genre. The respondents you choose, even if they're not part of your primary audience, should be those whose opinions you value, people whom you can trust to respond constructively. They should be able to articulate clearly their reactions to your draft.

Ask for responses at any point in your composing process. For example, at the beginning, when you're brainstorming, you can ask others to talk with you about your ideas and approach to your topic. Once you have a rough draft or a first solid draft, you can ask others to respond to your focus, development, voice, and organization. Once you have completed your first or second draft, ask respondents to give you feedback on how clearly you convey your purpose, how well you're reaching your audience, and what you might do better or differently. Respondents can also help you see counter-arguments and other perspectives at this stage. Near the end of your composing process, ask respondents to take a finer focus: Ask whether your transitions between ideas are consistent, and whether you need to do any fine-tuning in regard to working in your genre, for example.

To get feedback that will be helpful, ask yourself: What do I want to know from my respondents? What would be most helpful to know at this stage? Here are some questions you might ask respondents:

- Would you take a look at my paper (or watch my video, or listen to my podcast, etc.) and tell me what you think? As someone who isn't (or is) familiar with my topic, how well do you think I am conveying my ideas? How persuasive do you find the writing? I'm looking for "big picture" comments right now.

- I'm really struggling with adding specific details (or some other issue). Can you read my draft and point out some places where I could add more detail?

- Other respondents have found some parts of my composition confusing (or identified some other specific problem). Could you take a look at this and let me know if you're sometimes confused, and at what point you start to feel that way?

Gathering responses doesn't mean you'll implement every change that your respondents suggest. You may ultimately decide not to make a particular recommended change, perhaps because you disagree with the suggestion or think the reader misunderstood your purpose. But even if you disagree with a reader comment, consider why the reader made it. And if more than one person makes the same recommendation, you might want to consider it more seriously.

ATTENTION, AUTHORS & ARTISTS

A word on using technology for peer review. If you are drafting your composition in a Microsoft Word or Apache OpenOffice document, there are features that allow you to track your changes so others can edit and add comments on your draft electronically. This might be handy if you can't arrange to meet with a reader in person. E-mail your draft to a reader, or share it in a space such as Google Drive (drive.google.com) or DropBox (dropbox.com).

## CHECKLIST | Questions to Ask People Responding to Your Draft

Wherever you are in your composing process, it can be helpful to get feedback. Here are some more questions you might want to ask your respondents:

☐ **What kind of genre does this piece appear to be? How can you tell?**

Possible follow-up questions:

☐ Can you suggest some ways to make it read more like an encyclopedia entry/photo essay/blog/other genre piece?

☐ Can you suggest any areas that are not consistent with the genre?

☐ **What would you say is the purpose of this document? How can you tell?**

Possible follow-up questions:

☐ Can you suggest some ways to make the purpose of the piece clearer?

☐ Can you point to some places where the purpose is not consistent?

- ☐ **How would you characterize the rhetorical appeals the genre piece uses?**

  Possible follow-up questions:

  - ☐ Can you suggest ways to make the appeal to my audience more defined?
  - ☐ Can you suggest some ways to emphasize ethos so that my reader accepts the piece's credibility?
  - ☐ Can you suggest some ways to emphasize pathos so that my reader understands the emotion behind the piece?

- ☐ **How would you characterize the writing style of this document?**

  Possible follow-up questions:

  - ☐ Can you point to some places where that style is particularly apparent?
  - ☐ Can you point to some places where that style is not apparent?
  - ☐ Can you point to some places where the style is inconsistent?
  - ☐ Can you suggest some ways to make the style more consistent with that of an encyclopedia entry/photo essay/blog/other genre piece?

- ☐ **How would you characterize the tone of this document?**

  Possible follow-up questions:

  - ☐ Can you point to some places where that tone is particularly apparent?
  - ☐ Can you point to some places where that tone is not apparent?
  - ☐ Can you point to some places where the tone is inconsistent?
  - ☐ Can you suggest some ways to make the tone more consistent with that of an encyclopedia entry/photo essay/blog/other genre piece?

- ☐ **How would you characterize the voice in this document?**

  Possible follow-up questions:

  - ☐ Can you point to some places where that voice is particularly strong?
  - ☐ Can you point to some places where that voice is not as strong?
  - ☐ Can you point to some places where the voice is inconsistent?
  - ☐ Can you suggest some ways to make the voice more consistent with that of an encyclopedia entry/photo essay/blog/other genre piece?

- ☐ **How do the design elements direct your attention?**

  Possible follow-up questions:

  - ☐ Can you suggest some ways I might better use design to help me get into my topic?
  - ☐ Can you suggest some ways to emphasize the visual elements?
  - ☐ Can you suggest some ways to help the text have more impact on the reader?
  - ☐ Can you suggest some ways design elements might clarify for readers that this is an encyclopedia entry/photo essay/blog/other genre piece?

- ☐ **How have experience and evidence informed the piece?**

  Possible follow-up questions:

  - ☐ Can you suggest some ways I might use experience and evidence to make the piece more credible?
  - ☐ Can you suggest some places where I need to add more evidence?

# Guided Process | Integrating Peer Feedback: Draft to Finished Composition

Let's circle back to Gwen Ganow and her draft of the Author's Statement that will accompany her film review.

**Draft 1**   Gwen asks a few of her classmates the following questions about her Author's Statement:

- Have I made my purpose in writing a film review clear?
- Have I clearly communicated the ways I used rhetorical appeals to reach my audience?
- Is my tone reflective and persuasive enough for an Author's Statement?

Her readers report back that they want more information about how Gwen thinks she demonstrated her passion for the subject. They also suggest that she clearly connect her research to what she incorporated into her review, to make her Statement more reflective and persuasive. Finally, one classmate recommends that Gwen rethink the organization of the second half of her Statement.

DRAFT 1   **Gwen Ganow** (STUDENT), *Superhero Project, Author's Statement*

### Author's Statement
### Why I Wrote a Film Review of *X-Men*

There are two reasons I chose to write a film review. As a "hard-core" comic book fan, I always considered *X-Men* (Singer) as a good example of what a true comic book movie should be. What sets the movie apart from other comic book movies is that the story behind *X-Men* is not overshadowed by special effects. The second reason I chose to do a film review was to show another perspective on how comic books are interrelated with our modern culture. Superheroes, heroes, antiheroes, and villains don't just come to us through the pop culture pages of a comic book. They have also expanded their influence to include the American silver screen. The stories of these comic book characters are now told by our Hollywood actors and actresses.

Created by Stan Lee and Jack Kirby in 1963, the X-Men are the children of humans who were exposed to atmospheric radiation and became genetically altered. These children

*(Continues on next page)*

are born with "differences" and become outsiders in a world that considers them mutants. Even though they do not show any outward signs of difference, their extrahuman powers evoke the envy and fear of ordinary people (Brewer 134). We can link the alienation of the X-Men to groups of people who have gone through their own form of prejudice in real life. African Americans, Jews, Japanese, and homosexuals have all endured the pain of living in an American society that is quick to respond in fear to someone who may be different from the norm.

In *X-Men*, solutions to the problems of prejudice are explored through the actions of two important mutants. Both of these men are leaders, one being the leader of the X-Men, the other the leader of the Brotherhood of Mutants. Charles Xavier creates a school for the gifted for young ostracized mutants. He teaches his mutant students to use their powers to benefit humanity, even if that same humanity hated and distrusted them (Brewer 142). Xavier's "turn the other cheek" philosophy links him to the Jesus Christ of Christian culture. The fact that Xavier provides a safe house for people rejected by humanity also links him to our real-life organizations like NAACP, GLBT resource centers, and some of our churches.

Magneto's perspective on humanity stems from his experiences as a young boy at a WWII concentration camp. This experience left Magneto distrustful of humanity, and he is convinced that mutants are bound to suffer the same fate met by the inmates of the Nazi death camps (Brewer 143). To preserve the survival of his mutant species, Magneto declares war on humankind. We can link the thoughts and actions of Magneto to our own real-world thoughts and actions. We, as humans, have always wanted to put our persecutors into the shoes and lives of the persecuted. If we were given the technology to right the wrongs against us, would we create a machine similar to Magneto's? As humans, why are we quick to return violence with more violence?

Overall, I wanted my readers to see my passion for the subject. I wanted to persuade them, using pathos, to understand that you could read the film as a larger statement on the intolerance GLBT people often face. One of the ways I achieved this was by relying on logos, helping my readers follow the film logically, using strategies employed in other film reviews, such as giving snippets of the plot and using some of the plot summary to highlight the film's strength.

I studied several film reviews to help me figure out how to best create my review. One of the things that was missing from my initial draft was placing the film in a broader context. Thus, in my revision I began the review by discussing my relationship to comics (even if briefly) and then moved on to the film itself. I also incorporated the theory of punctuated equilibrium to help establish my ethos; I know about the theory because of my zoology/biology major. Another thing I wanted to make sure to achieve in the film review was a clear evaluation of the film. My earlier draft did not really make this clear; it primarily consisted of a retelling of some of the plot. In the revision I made sure to include this, not only in the close of the review but with some word choices in the review, such as "powerful image," "good chemistry," and "fine job."

When comic book fans or superhero film fans finish reading my review, I hope that they will see that *X-Men* is definitely an appealing film. More importantly, though, I want my audience to realize that lessons about ourselves can be learned through the story of the X-Men. By witnessing and learning from the actions of a misguided mutant like Magneto, humankind can learn how to be more understanding and tolerant—like Charles Xavier.

## Works Cited

Brewer, H. Michael. *Who Needs a Superhero? Finding Virtue, Vice, and What's Holy in the Comics.* Baker Books, 2004, pp. 134–44.

Singer, Bryan, director. *X-Men.* Performances by Hugh Jackman, Ian McKellen, and Patrick Stewart, Marvel Studios, 2000. Film.

With her readers' comments in mind, Gwen creates a list of what to focus on in her next draft.

**Author's Statement**
**Revision List**

Based on my careful rereading of my draft—and comments from others who have read it—I need to do the following in my next draft:

- In general, use my Author's Statement to make a case for my film review. I need to do a better job of letting readers know what I set out to do, and why, and how.
- Explain how I use rhetorical appeals (or at least intended to use them). In my draft I've listed the appeals I worked with, but have not organized my ideas well enough for readers. Just stating my passion is not enough. I need to include an example or two to back up that claim.
- Connect my evidence to the choices and claims that I make in my review.
- Add signal phrases to clearly separate my research from my own ideas.

Gwen then implements these revisions in the following draft. The blue text in the body of the Statement indicates places where Gwen reworked her Statement.

Gwen's notes on draft 2 of her Author's Statement

**Author's Statement**
**Why I Wrote a Film Review of *X-Men***

There are several reasons I chose to write a film review. As a "hard-core" comic book fan, I always considered *X-Men* (Singer) as a good example of what a true comic book movie should be. What sets the movie apart from other comic book movies is that the story behind *X-Men* is not overshadowed by special effects. The second reason I chose to do a film review was to show another perspective on how comic books are interrelated with our modern culture. Superheroes, heroes, antiheroes, and villains don't just come to us through the pop culture pages of a comic book. They have also expanded their influence to include the American silver screen. The stories of these comic book characters are now told by our Hollywood actors and actresses. My final reason for writing a film review is that I wanted to choose a genre that I felt my peers would be interested in reading. Many of my classmates are moviegoers, and even if they are not comic book fans, they probably would be interested in an action film like *X-Men*.

Gwen's notes on draft 2 of her Author's Statement

I'm giving readers more context for why I chose to write my film review.

When writing the film review, I wanted to demonstrate I had a clear understanding of the role of the outsider in the film by using some of my research and my knowledge about the original comic book story. **Created by Stan Lee and Jack Kirby in 1963, the X-Men are the children of humans who were exposed to atmospheric radiation and became genetically altered.** H. Michael Brewer, in his book *Who Needs a Superhero?*, discusses how these children are born with "differences" and become outsiders in a world that considers them mutants. Even though they do not show any outward signs of difference, their extrahuman powers evoke the envy and fear of ordinary people (134). If we think about the movie in terms of a larger context, we can link the alienation of the X-Men to groups of people who have gone through their own form of prejudice in real life. **African Americans, Jews, Japanese, and homosexuals have all endured the pain of living in an American society that is quick to respond in fear to someone who may be different from the norm.**

Here I connect with my research—through citing a specific source.

Brewer also discusses how in *X-Men* solutions to the problems of prejudice are explored through the actions of two important mutants. Both of these men are leaders, one being the leader of the X-Men, the other the leader of the Brotherhood of Mutants. Charles Xavier creates a school for the gifted for young ostracized mutants. He teaches his mutant students to use their powers to benefit humanity, even if that same humanity hated and distrusted them (142). Xavier's "turn the other cheek" philosophy links him to the Jesus Christ of Christian culture. The fact that Xavier provides a safe house for people rejected by humanity also

(Continues on next page)

**Gwen's notes
on draft 2 of her
Author's Statement**

I've worked in signal
phrases to make
my research more
apparent and to make
my Statement more
readable.

links him to our real-life organizations like NAACP, GLBT
resource centers, and some of our churches.

In his book, Brewer also focuses on how Magneto's
perspective on humanity stems from his experiences as a
young boy at a WWII concentration camp. This experience
left Magneto distrustful of humanity, and he is convinced that
mutants are bound to suffer the same fate met by the inmates
of the Nazi death camps (143). To preserve the survival of
his mutant species, Magneto declares war on humankind.
We can link the thoughts and actions of Magneto to our own
real-world thoughts and actions. We, as humans, have always
wanted to put our persecutors into the shoes and lives of
the persecuted. If we were given the technology to right the
wrongs against us, would we create a machine similar to
Magneto's? As humans, why are we quick to return violence
with more violence?

Overall, I wanted my readers to see my passion for the
subject. One of the ways I did this was by opening with
the fact that I am a "hard-core" comic book fan. Besides
demonstrating my passion, I wanted to persuade my readers,
by using pathos, to understand that you could read the film
as a larger statement on the intolerance GLBT people often
face. One of the ways I achieved this was by relying on logos,
helping my readers follow the film logically, using strategies
employed in other film reviews, such as giving snippets of
the plot and using some of the plot summary to highlight the
film's strength. While both pathos and logos are important
for reaching my audience, I realized that if I did not establish
my ethos, people would not care about what I had to say.
By incorporating the theory of punctuated equilibrium,
which I know about because of my zoology/biology major,
and connecting it to the film, I help readers view me as a
knowledgeable and informed writer.

I've made it clearer
how I set out to use
ethos, pathos, and
logos, and backed
that up with details.

I studied several film reviews to help me figure out how
to best create my review. One of the things that was missing
from my initial draft was placing the film in a broader
context. Thus, in my revision I began the review by discussing
my relationship to comics (even if briefly) and then moved
on to the film itself. Another thing I wanted to make sure to
achieve in the film review was a clear evaluation of the film.

My earlier draft did not really make this clear; it primarily consisted of a retelling of some of the plot. In the revision I made sure to include this, not only in the close of the review but with some word choices in the review, such as "powerful image," "good chemistry," and "fine job."

When comic book fans or superhero film fans finish reading my review, I hope that they will see that *X-Men* is definitely an appealing film. More importantly, though, I want my audience to realize that lessons about ourselves can be learned through the story of the X-Men. By witnessing and learning from the actions of a misguided mutant like Magneto, humankind can learn how to be more understanding and tolerant—like Charles Xavier.

### Works Cited

Brewer, H. Michael. *Who Needs a Superhero? Finding Virtue, Vice, and What's Holy in the Comics*. Baker Books, 2004, pp. 134–44.

Singer, Bryan, director. *X-Men*. Performances by Hugh Jackman, Ian McKellen, and Patrick Stewart, Marvel Studios, 2000. Film.

At this point, Gwen asks her classmates to read the above draft with the following questions in mind:

- Is my tone persuasive enough?
- Have I said enough about the film reviews I studied as models?
- What is the single most important revision I can make to strengthen my Author's Statement?

Classmates suggest that Gwen:

- Improve her persuasiveness by looking carefully at the word choices in her Author's Statement.
- Make more specific comments about the film reviews she used as models for her own review.
- Refer to more than one outside source.

Gwen agrees with the first two suggestions, but feels that adding more sources is not necessary to achieve her purpose. With this feedback and her own ideas in mind, Gwen creates a quick revision list before moving on to her final draft.

**Author's Statement**
**Revision List**

I think I'm making a pretty good case for my review—and am specifically explaining my intentions to my readers. I've incorporated research successfully. Now I just have a little more to do:

- Back up my choices by referring specifically to the film reviews I used as models for my own composition.
- Fine-tune my writing to make it more persuasive overall; also, make sure I'm choosing the most persuasive words and phrasing.
- Check my Statement for mechanics, grammar, tense, spelling, and so on. Proofread.

With these points in mind, Gwen revises her Statement a final time. The document below (created in Microsoft Word) shows Gwen's edits as tracked changes.

FINAL   **Gwen Ganow** (STUDENT), *Superhero Project: Author's Statement* (shows edits)

**Author's Statement**
**Why I Wrote a Film Review of X-Men**

Why did I choose to write a film review—and to write one about *X-Men*? I have several reasons. ~~There are several reasons I chose to write a film review. As~~ First, as a "hardcore" comic book fan, I've always considered *X-Men* (Singer) to be a good example of what a true comic book movie should be. ~~What sets the movie apart from other comic book movies is that the story behind X-Men is not overshadowed by special effects.~~ *X-Men*, the film, inspired me to write a review because of what sets it apart from other comic book films: the *X-Men* story itself. The filmmaker clearly understood this, and did not clutter the story with over-the-top special effects. The second reason I chose to ~~do~~ write a film review is a little broader: I wanted to comment on ~~was to show another perspective on~~ how comic books are ~~interrelated~~ intertwined with ~~our~~ modern popular culture. Superheroes, heroes, antiheroes, and villains don't just come to us through ~~the pop culture pages of a~~ comic books anymore. They ~~have also~~ come to us through Hollywood, brought to life ~~expanded their influence to include the American silver screen. A~~ by the actors and actresses who portray the characters and stories of America's favorite superheroes. ~~The stories of these comic book characters are now told by our Hollywood actors and actresses.~~ My final reason for choosing to write a film review, rather than a researched journal article, for example, is that I wanted to choose a genre that I ~~felt~~ knew my peers would relate to. ~~be interested in reading.~~ Many of my classmates are moviegoers and readers of reviews: ~~, and e~~Even if they are not comic book fans, they are likely to ~~probably would~~ be interested in an action film like *X-Men*, and therefore in a review of the film.

~~When writing the~~ In my ~~film~~ review, I wanted to demonstrate ~~I had~~ a clear understanding of the role of the outsider in *X-Men*. ~~the film.~~ To do this, I drew on ~~by using some of my~~ research and my own knowledge ~~about~~ of the original *X-Men* comic book story. Created by Stan Lee and Jack Kirby in 1963, the X-Men are the children of humans who were exposed to atmospheric radiation and became genetically altered. H. Michael Brewer, in his book *Who Needs a Superhero?*, discusses how these children are born with "differences" and become outsiders in a world that considers them mutants. Even though they do not show any outward signs of difference, their extrahuman powers evoke the envy and fear of ordinary people (134). If we think about the movie in terms of a larger context, we can link the alienation of the X-Men to groups of people who have gone through their own form of prejudice in real life. African Americans, Jews, Japanese, and ~~homosexuals~~ gay men and lesbians have ~~all~~ endured the pain of living in an American society that is

*(Continues on next page)*

quick to respond in fear to someone who may be different from the norm.

Brewer also discusses how in *X-Men* authors Lee and Kirby explore solutions to the problems of prejudice ~~are explored~~ through ~~the actions of~~ two important mutants: Charles Xavier and Magneto. Both of these characters ~~men~~ are leaders; Xavier~~, one being the leader of~~ leads the X-Men, while Magneto ~~the other the leader of~~ leads the Brotherhood of Mutants. ~~Charles~~ Xavier creates a school for the gifted for young ~~ostracized~~ outcast mutants~~.~~, where he ~~He~~ teaches ~~his mutant students~~ them to use their powers to benefit humanity, even if that same humanity hate~~d~~s and distrust~~ed~~s them (142). Xavier's "turn the other cheek" philosophy links him to the Jesus Christ of Christian culture. The fact that Xavier provides a safe house for people rejected by humanity also links him to our real-life organizations ~~like~~ such as the NAACP, GLBT resource centers, and some of our churches.

In his book, Brewer also focuses on how Magneto's perspective on humanity stems from his experiences as a young boy at a WWII concentration camp. ~~This experience~~ Life in the camp left Magneto distrustful and despairing of humanity, and ~~he is~~ convinced that mutants are bound to suffer the same fate as Jews imprisoned and murdered in ~~met by the inmates of the~~ Nazi death camps (143). To preserve the survival of his mutant species, Magneto declares war on humankind. ~~We can link~~ I see Magneto's ~~the thoughts and actions~~ distrust and violence as related to contemporary life and the collective urge to "right wrongs," gain power, or find revenge through warfare. ~~of Magneto to our own real-world thoughts and actions. We, as humans, have always wanted to put our persecutors into the shoes and lives of the persecuted.~~ If we had the technology available to Magneto in *X-Men*, would we use it the same way? ~~were given the technology to right the wrongs against us, would we create a machine similar to Magneto's? As humans, why are we quick to~~ Would we return violence with more violence?

In my review, I consciously worked with rhetorical appeals. Overall, I wanted my readers to see my passion for my topic— toward superheroes, society, and the film *X-Men*. ~~the subject.~~ I worked to establish ethos ~~One of the ways I did this was opening with the fact that I am~~ by letting readers know I am ~~"hard-core"~~ a serious comic book fan and think of myself as somewhat of an expert on the genre. Besides demonstrating my passion, I wanted to persuade my readers~~,~~ by using pathos, by appealing to emotion to persuade them to ~~understand that you could~~ read the film as a larger statement—a statement on the intolerance that "outsiders," specifically GLBT people, often face. I supported my argument logically, with ~~One of the ways I achieved this was by relying on logos, helping my readers follow the film logically,~~ key points from the plot, ~~using~~ and used strategies I learned from other film reviewers, such as using summary and highlighting particular moments in a film. ~~employed in other film reviews, such as giving snippets of the plot and using some of the plot summary to highlight the film's strength.~~ While both pathos and logos ~~are~~ were important for reaching my audience, I realized that if I did not establish my ethos, people would not care about what I had to say. For example, I ~~By~~ incorporat~~ing~~ed the theory of punctuated equilibrium that I learned about in my studies as a~~, which I know about because of my~~ zoology/biology major, and used that as a lens for reading ~~and connecting it to~~ the film~~;~~. I believe this perspective, and the fact that I am a longtime and avid comics reader, helped my audience see ~~I help readers view~~ me as a knowledgeable and informed writer.

I studied several film reviews to help me figure out how to best create my own review. ~~One of the things~~ Something that I did not do in ~~was missing from~~ my initial draft was to place ~~placing~~ the film in a broader context. ~~Thus, in my revision~~ In my next draft, I began with a brief discussion of ~~the review by discussing~~ my relationship to comics ~~(even if briefly)~~ and then moved on to the film itself. Another thing I focused on in revisions was ~~wanted~~ to make sure

*(Continues on next page)*

~~to achieve in the film review was~~ I gave a clear opinion ~~a clear evaluation~~ of the film. I did not do this in ~~My~~ my earlier draft, ~~did not really make this clear; it primarily consisted of a~~ which was also too focused on retelling ~~of some of~~ the plot~~.~~—and not focused enough on evaluating it. In my revised review, ~~the revision~~ I made sure to be more straightforward in my opinion, and to choose words that supported my observations clearly. I sharpened up my language to make it more persuasive and precise, using phrases ~~include this, not only in the close of the review but with some word choices in the review,~~ such as "powerful image~~;~~" and "good chemistry~~,~~." ~~and "fine job."~~

When comic book fans ~~finish reading~~ or superhero film fans read my review, I want them to ~~hope that they will~~ see that *X-Men* is ~~definitely an appealing~~ a film worth seeing—and one that offers insight into human experience. ~~More importantly, though,~~ I want my audience to realize that—through the story of the X-Men—we can learn ~~lessons~~ about ourselves. ~~can be learned through the story of the X-Men.~~ Maybe we can learn something from ~~By witnessing and learning from the actions of a~~ the misguided mutant ~~like~~ Magneto~~, humankind can learn how to be more understanding~~ and his tolerant, loving counterpart, ~~—like~~Charles Xavier.

## Works Cited

Brewer, H. Michael. *Who Needs a Superhero? Finding Virtue, Vice, and What's Holy in the Comics*. Baker Books, 2004, pp. 134–44.

Singer, Bryan, director. *X-Men*. Performances by Hugh Jackman, Ian McKellen, and Patrick Stewart, Marvel Studios, 2000. Film.

The following document shows Gwen's work with her edits accepted.

**FINAL**    **Gwen Ganow** (STUDENT), *Superhero Project*
*(edits incorporated)*

**Author's Statement**
**Why I Wrote a Film Review of *X-Men***

Why did I choose to write a film review—and to write one about *X-Men*? I have several reasons. First, as a "hard-core" comic book fan, I've always considered *X-Men* (Singer) to be a good example of what a true comic book movie should be. *X-Men*, the film, inspired me to write a review because of what sets it apart from other comic book films: the *X-Men* story itself. The filmmaker clearly understood this, and did not clutter the story with over-the-top special effects. The second reason I chose to write a film review is a little broader: I wanted to comment on how comic books are intertwined with modern popular culture. Superheroes, heroes, antiheroes, and villains don't just come to us through comic books anymore. They come to us through Hollywood, brought to life by the actors and actresses who portray the characters and stories of America's favorite superheroes. My final reason for choosing to write a film review, rather than a researched journal article, for example, is that I wanted to choose a genre that I knew my peers would relate to. Many of my classmates are moviegoers and readers of reviews: Even if they are not comic book fans, they are likely to be interested in an action film like *X-Men*, and therefore in a review of the film.

In my review, I wanted to demonstrate a clear understanding of the role of the outsider in *X-Men*. To do this, I drew on research and my own knowledge of the original *X-Men* comic book story. Created by Stan Lee and Jack Kirby in 1963, the X-Men are the children of humans who were exposed to atmospheric radiation and became genetically altered. H. Michael Brewer, in his book *Who Needs a Superhero?*, discusses how these children are born with "differences" and become outsiders in a world that considers them mutants. Even though they do not show any outward signs of difference, their extrahuman powers evoke the envy and fear of ordinary people (134). If we think about the

*(Continues on next page)*

movie in terms of a larger context, we can link the alienation of the X-Men to groups of people who have gone through their own form of prejudice in real life. African Americans, Jews, Japanese, and gay men and lesbians have endured the pain of living in an American society that is quick to respond in fear to someone who may be different from the norm.

Brewer also discusses how in *X-Men* authors Lee and Kirby explore solutions to the problem of prejudice through two important mutants: Charles Xavier and Magneto. Both of these characters are leaders; Xavier leads the X-Men, while Magneto leads the Brotherhood of Mutants. Xavier creates a school for the gifted for young outcast mutants, where he teaches them to use their powers to benefit humanity, even if that same humanity hates and distrusts them (142). Xavier's "turn the other cheek" philosophy links him to the Jesus Christ of Christian culture. The fact that Xavier provides a safe house for people rejected by humanity also links him to our real-life organizations such as the NAACP, GLBT resource centers, and some of our churches.

In his book, Brewer also focuses on how Magneto's perspective on humanity stems from his experiences as a young boy at a WWII concentration camp. Life in the camp left Magneto distrustful and despairing of humanity, and convinced that mutants are bound to suffer the same fate as Jews imprisoned and murdered in Nazi death camps (143). To preserve the survival of his mutant species, Magneto declares war on humankind. I see Magneto's distrust and violence as related to contemporary life and the collective urge to "right wrongs," gain power, or find revenge through warfare. If we had the technology available to Magneto in *X-Men*, would we use it the same way? Would we return violence with more violence?

In my review, I consciously worked with rhetorical appeals. Overall, I wanted my readers to see my passion for my topic— toward superheroes, society, and the film *X-Men*. I worked to establish ethos by letting readers know I am a serious comic book fan and think of myself as somewhat of an expert on the genre. Besides demonstrating my passion, I wanted to persuade my readers by using pathos, by appealing to emotion to persuade them to read the film as a larger statement—a statement on the intolerance that "outsiders," specifically

GLBT people, often face. I supported my argument logically, with key points from the plot, and used strategies I learned from other film reviewers, such as using summary and highlighting particular moments in a film. While both pathos and logos were important for reaching my audience, I realized that if I did not establish my ethos, people would not care about what I had to say. For example, I incorporated the theory of punctuated equilibrium that I learned about in my studies as a zoology/biology major, and used that as a lens for reading the film. I believe this perspective, and the fact that I am a longtime and avid comics reader, helped my audience see me as a knowledgeable and informed writer.

I studied several film reviews to help me figure out how to best create my own review. Something that I did not do in my initial draft was to place the film in a broader context. In my next draft, I began with a brief discussion of my relationship to comics and then moved on to the film itself. Another thing I focused on in revisions was to make sure I gave a clear opinion of the film. I did not do this in my earlier draft, which was also too focused on retelling the plot—and not focused enough on evaluating it. In my revised review, I made sure to be more straightforward in my opinion, and to choose words that supported my observations clearly. I sharpened up my language to make it more persuasive and precise, using phrases such as "powerful image" and "good chemistry."

When comic book fans or superhero film fans read my review, I want them to see that *X-Men* is a film worth seeing— and one that offers insight into human experience. I want my audience to realize that—through the story of the X-Men—we can learn about ourselves. Maybe we can learn something from the misguided mutant Magneto and his tolerant, loving counterpart, Charles Xavier.

## Works Cited

Brewer, H. Michael. *Who Needs a Superhero? Finding Virtue, Vice, and What's Holy in the Comics.* Baker Books, 2004, pp. 134–44.

Singer, Bryan, director. *X-Men.* Performances by Hugh Jackman, Ian McKellen, and Patrick Stewart, Marvel Studios, 2000. Film.

# Remixing Your Work into Different Genres

Sometimes we ask our students to remix their finished genre piece into a different genre. For example, Gwen, who composed a film review on superheroes and justice, thought at one point that she'd create a presentation, animation, or advertisement. Remixing her film review would be an opportunity to work in a different genre on a topic she had already researched and written about—and to think about the different ways of reaching an audience that other genres allow.

## Guided Process | Remixing a Genre Project

Gwen wants to shape her film review into something new. When our students create remixes, we ask them to think their projects through as shown in the following assignment.

REMIX **Gwen Ganow** (STUDENT), *Film Review PowerPoint: "We Are All Mutants"*

---

**English 101**
**Professor Braziller**

**Assignment: Remix Your Genre Project**

**What is a remix?** When you remix an object or composition, you repurpose it. For example, Martha Stewart might repurpose flowerpots to be utensil holders in her kitchen. Originally intended for outdoor use to hold soil and plants, the pots will need to be overhauled for indoor kitchen use. Stewart would probably wash them, apply a nontoxic sealant, and paint them or decorate them in some way. The finished product—the utensil holder that was formerly a flowerpot—is a remix.

   **How will you create a remix?** Your assignment is to remix one of the genre pieces you've already composed. You will repurpose your creation for a different context. This may involve changing the purpose, audience, and/or message of your original piece. Your energy should go toward revising your original material to fit into a new mode and/or genre appropriate to your new context.

   For example, you might remix an editorial you wrote about school funding into a short YouTube video. The editorial was

---

originally geared toward politicians or taxpayers, but you now imagine an audience of college students. Thus, you need to make the editorial interesting and palatable to college students. You also need to take into account the conventions of the new genre.

You might also consider taking parts from other assignments and weaving them together into a new work. Quilters do this when they take scraps of fabric from outgrown clothing and sew them together into a new item: a quilt.

Gwen repurposes her film review to create a PowerPoint presentation that begins with a top 10 list. In this case, her purpose is to persuade an audience of fans who watched the film when it came out in the year 2000 to watch it again. She chooses the genre of the top 10 list because it gives her the opportunity to use humor to persuade. Her plan is to share her list with friends and fans on social media sites, and to ask them to contribute their own lists of reasons for watching the *X-Men* movie again.

Following are her first three slides.

▶ POWERPOINT SLIDE

**Gwen Ganow,** Remix of film review.

*Credits: Gwen Dalynn Ganow; Everett Collection, Inc.*

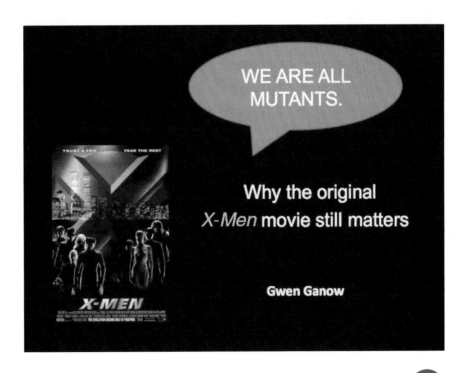

◀ POWERPOINT
SLIDES
Gwen Ganow, "We
Are All Mutants."
Credit: Gwen Dalynn Ganow.

## CHECKLIST | Remixing a Genre Piece?

Keep the following questions in mind:

### RHETORICAL SITUATION & CHOICES

☐ **Purpose.** What is the purpose of my new, remixed composition? How can I make that purpose clear?

☐ **Audience.** Who is the targeted audience for my remix? How can I take my new audience's expectations, values, and concerns into account? What kind of vocabulary, examples and details, organization, and other elements should I use to appeal to my new audience?

☐ **Rhetorical appeals.** How can I use rhetorical appeals to connect with my new audience?

☐ **Modes & media.** What mode and medium will be most likely to engage my new audience?

### GENRE CONVENTIONS

☐ **Elements of the genre.** How can I use the elements of my new genre to guide my new audience's experience?

☐ **Style.** How can I use word choice, sentence structure, literary devices (like metaphor), and other stylistic techniques to keep my new audience engaged?

☐ **Design.** How can I use design elements, such as color, images, and font, to emphasize my purpose and main point?

☐ **Sources.** What kinds of sources should I use to convince my new audience of my point? How should I cite these sources appropriately in my new genre?

# 6

# REFLECTION:
## THE AUTHOR'S/ARTIST'S STATEMENT

Reflection happens periodically throughout the writing process. After you get feedback from a peer or put a draft away for a day, considering what's working or not working helps you make decisions about what you want to revise. You might do this by talking with a classmate, jotting some notes on your phone, or writing ideas down on scraps of paper. During the writing process is not the only time you might want to reflect. In fact, reflection at the end of the writing process can be particularly helpful.

We know what you're thinking. You've finished your composition, submitted it, and high-fived your friend. You just want to be done. This is actually a perfect time to reflect on the decisions you made as you were composing. Reflecting at the end helps you see what you might do differently next time. For example, perhaps you learn that starting with more freewriting minimizes the amount of time you stare at the computer. Or, maybe you realize that seeking out your instructor during office hours or a writing center tutor helps you see potential areas to sharpen. You might also notice your strengths so that you can draw on them in your next composition.

## Genres for Reflection

Explaining the rationale behind our actions and decisions is an important kind of reflective writing because it makes visible what is otherwise invisible. Amy can see that Elizabeth may have chosen to write an e-mail in Comic Sans font, but unless Elizabeth explains why, the choice may seem mysterious and odd to Amy. Composers and artists of all sorts often write a statement for their audience that explains their inspirations, intentions, and choices in their creative and critical processes. Annotations by musicians found on a website such as Genius.com, the program you receive at the theater or symphony, the director's commentary often found when streaming the Director's Cut, the Artist's Statement pinned to the wall at an art gallery—these are all forms of Authors' or Artists' Statements. We write explanations of our decisions to support many academic, workplace, and public genres. Below, we discuss an academic example and an example from a public setting; a workplace example might be a self-review or part of an organization's annual report.

On page 98, there is an example of a reflective statement written by a chef for the magazine *Cook's Illustrated*. The point of the discussion— or what you could call an Author's Statement, as the chef is the author of the recipe he is explaining—is to explain and discuss what went into the creation of the recipe, what went well, and what could have gone better, as well as to discuss the cooking process. The Author's

WRITE

What are some examples of Authors'/Artists' Statements that you've seen lately? How does understanding a composer's perspective and intent contribute to how you relate to the composer's work? Write a quick list of movie scenes, lyrics, art pieces, and other creative works you've understood differently once you read or heard about the composer's rationale.

▲ CHEF PHOTO
Andrew Janjigian.
*Credit: America's Test Kitchen.*

Statement articulates the different, otherwise invisible, choices and decisions the chef made in the creation of the recipe, from the selection of one ingredient over another to the order in which ingredients are combined and why. The Author's Statement discusses not just what ended up in the final recipe, but what was tried but didn't work, and why it didn't work. In this way, the statement helps readers understand the invisible logic behind the finished product, the recipe.

You may wonder why a cook would go to all this trouble—not just to develop a recipe but then to put energy into articulating in writing the process of developing that recipe.

# Thai Grilled-Beef Salad

Our goal was to look no further than the supermarket to replicate this salad's complex range of flavors and textures. Along the way, we learned a neat trick for grilling meat.

∋ BY ANDREW JANJIGIAN ∈

In winter when I crave Thai food, it's often a rich, coconut milk–based curry or a wok-charred noodle dish. But in the summer months, I'm more tempted by the country's famous salads, particularly the grilled-beef rendition known as *nam tok*. Served warm or at room temperature, this preparation features slices of deeply charred steak tossed with thinly sliced shallots and handfuls of torn mint and cilantro in a bright, bracing dressing. In the best versions, the cuisine's five signature flavor elements—hot, sour, salty, sweet, and bitter—come into balance, making for a light but satisfying dish that's traditionally served with steamed jasmine rice.

I paged through the test kitchen's stack of Thai cookbooks for some nam tok recipes to try and was pleased to find that both the shopping list and the cooking time—about half an hour from start to finish—were very manageable. The most unusual ingredient was toasted rice powder, which I knew would be easy enough to make at home. Still, the salads that I produced in the test kitchen, while not bad, fell short of the versions that I've eaten in good Thai restaurants. Either the dressing's flavors were unbalanced—too sweet, too salty, too sour—or the beef itself didn't boast enough char to give the salad its hallmark smoky, faintly bitter edge. Clearly, I had some tinkering to do.

**High-Steaks Decisions**

The obvious place to start my testing was with the beef. Surprisingly, the recipes that I consulted were all over the map. Some specified lean cuts like tenderloin, others more marbled choices like skirt

A scoop of rice turns this steak salad into a meal.

steak or New York strip steak. A few recipes called for marinating the meat before grilling; others suggested simply seasoning it with salt and white pepper (a staple ingredient in Thai cuisine). Most of them didn't even specify a grilling method. As a starting point, I built a standard single-level fire—a full chimney's worth of coals spread in an even layer over the kettle—and seared a variety of beef cuts: New York

strip steak, boneless short ribs, tenderloin, and flank steak, each one sprinkled with salt and white pepper. Once each piece had developed a thick, dark crust, I pulled it off the fire, let it rest briefly (to allow the interior juices to be reabsorbed), cut thin slices, and tossed them in a standard dressing of equal parts fresh lime juice and fish sauce, a little sugar, and a thinly sliced Thai chile.

Just as I had expected, the more marbled pieces of beef fared better than the lean tenderloin, which started out woefully bland and ended up overcooked by the time it developed even the barest crust. Flavorwise, any of these fattier cuts would have been a fine choice, but two came with a caveat. Boneless short ribs vary in quality: Some are evenly marbled and ideally shaped, almost like small strip steaks, while others are misshapen and full of interior fat and connective tissue that requires trimming. Meanwhile, New York strip steaks boast good flavor and pleasantly tender chew but don't come cheap. I settled on flank steak. The uniformly shaped, moderately priced slab was also beefy, juicy, and sliced neatly.

Next decision: whether or not to marinate the meat in a mixture of the dressing ingredients. A quick side-by-side test made my decision easy. Since moisture thwarts browning, the crust on the marinated flank steak was markedly thin and pale compared with that on the nonmarinated sample. Besides, once the slices of grilled steak were tossed with the dressing, they were plenty flavorful.

**Five Tastes of Thai Grilled-Beef Salad—and One More**

One of the keys to this salad is balancing the signature flavor elements of Thai cuisine. In addition to achieving this, we added one more complementary flavor: the earthiness of toasted cayenne and sweet paprika.

| HOT | SOUR | SALTY | SWEET | BITTER | EARTHY |
|---|---|---|---|---|---|
| A fresh Thai bird chile creates bright, fruity heat in the dressing. | A generous 3 tablespoons of fresh lime juice adds bracing acidity. | Derived from salted, fermented fish, pungent fish sauce acts as a rich flavor enhancer. | A half teaspoon of sugar tames the dressing's salty-sour flavors without becoming cloying. | Thoroughly charred steak adds both a pleasing textural contrast and a subtle bitter edge. | Though nontraditional, ground cayenne and sweet paprika add earthy flavor without too much heat. |

COOK'S ILLUSTRATED

12

▲ AUTHOR'S STATEMENT

The rhetorical situation of writing for *Cook's Illustrated* is that readers are not your typical home cooks who just want to get a meal on the table fast. *Cook's Illustrated* readers are serious foodies who don't mind spending hours on a recipe and they want to understand every decision the chef made so they can learn from the chef's mistakes or maybe even use the recipe as inspiration for their own creation.

In the following discussion of the recipe for Thai Grilled-Beef Salad, recipe writer Andrew Janjigian explains what his goals were and the thought processes behind the decisions he made as he tinkered with the recipe. Janjigian is an associate editor for *Cook's Illustrated* and also works for *America's Test Kitchen*.

## Falling Water

With the cut of meat decided, I could now focus my attention on the grilling method. The single-level fire had produced decently charred results, but for this salad, the contrast of a crisp, smoky, faintly bitter crust and a juicy center was a must, and I knew I could do better. To get a true blaze going, I turned to the test kitchen's favorite high-heat grill method: a modified two-level fire, in which all the coals are concentrated in an even layer over half of the grill. This way, the meat's exterior would caramelize almost on contact and would cook more rapidly, ensuring that the interior would stay medium-rare.

The recipes that I consulted may have been vague about the fire setup, but they did offer one grilling pointer: As the steak cooks, beads of moisture will appear on its surface—an indication that the meat is ready to be flipped. In fact, the dish is named for this visual cue; "nam tok" translates as "water falling." Grateful for the cue, I flipped the meat as soon as beads of moisture showed up, let it sear another five minutes on the second side, and pulled it off the grill. To my delight, this steak was not only perfectly charred on the exterior, but also spot-on medium-rare within. (For more information on the topic, see "Unbeadable Thai Trick: Knowing When to Flip.")

## Well Dressed

With perfectly grilled and subtly, satisfyingly bitter meat in hand, I moved back indoors to address the other four flavor elements: hot, sour, salty, and sweet. Everyone agreed that my initial dressing needed some tweaking—a bit more sweetness, a more balanced (and less heady) salty-sour punch, and more complex heat. The first two requests were easy to fix: I quickly landed on a 2:3 ratio of fish sauce to lime juice, plus ½ teaspoon of sugar and 2 tablespoons of water to tone it all down a touch. But the chile situation required a bit more attention. A fresh chile was a given, and I'd been using a Thai bird chile; when sliced thin and tossed with the other vegetable components, it adds a fruity, fiery blaze to each bite. So why did something still seem to be missing? I found the answer in a recipe from Thai cuisine guru David Thompson: His grilled-beef salad calls for not only fresh Thai bird chile, but also a toasted powder made from the dried pods.

Hoping that regular old cayenne powder toasted in a skillet would suffice, I compared its effects on the salad with that of a powder made with dried, toasted chiles following Thompson's instructions. The consensus was unanimous: The powder made from the dried Thai bird chiles added a deeper, earthier complexity than the hotter, more one-dimensional cayenne. Just ½ teaspoon of cayenne, in fact, overpowered the meat's smoky char. I was about to resign myself to the extra step of grinding my own powder when I spied a jar of sweet paprika in the spice cabinet. Could this give me the earthy, fruity red pepper flavor that was missing from the cayenne? As it turned out, a 50-50 mix of cayenne

and paprika did the trick. I added just a dash of the toasted spice mixture to the dressing and put the rest aside as a seasoning for those who wanted to kick up the heat another notch.

The other condiment that I had to address was the *kao kua*, or toasted rice powder. These days most Thai recipes call for the commercially made product, but it can be hard to find. It was simple enough to make my own by toasting rice in a dry skillet and pulverizing it in a spice grinder. Tossing half of the powder with the salad components gave the dressing fuller body, while sprinkling on the rest at the table added faint but satisfying crunch.

As for the vegetable components, it was really a matter of personal taste. Some salads called for incorporating only the requisite sliced shallots and torn mint leaves and cilantro, while others required adding green beans, cabbage, cucumbers, and lettuce. My tasters and I agreed that any accoutrements should complement—not compete with—the grilled beef. We settled on just one extra: a thin-sliced cucumber, which contributed a cool crispness to this nicely balanced, complexly flavored Thai classic.

### THAI GRILLED-BEEF SALAD
SERVES 4 TO 6

Serve with steamed jasmine rice, if desired, although any style of white rice can be used. Don't skip the toasted rice; it's integral to the texture and flavor of the dish. If a fresh Thai chile is unavailable, substitute half of a serrano chile.

| | |
|---|---|
| 1 | teaspoon sweet paprika |
| 1 | teaspoon cayenne pepper |
| 1 | tablespoon white rice |
| 3 | tablespoons lime juice (2 limes) |
| 2 | tablespoons fish sauce |
| 2 | tablespoons water |
| ½ | teaspoon sugar |
| 1 | (1½-pound) flank steak, trimmed |
| | Salt and white pepper, coarsely ground |
| 4 | shallots, sliced thin |
| 1½ | cups fresh mint leaves, torn |
| 1½ | cups fresh cilantro leaves |
| 1 | Thai chile, stemmed and sliced thin into rounds |
| 1 | seedless English cucumber, sliced ¼ inch thick on bias |

1. Heat paprika and cayenne in 8-inch skillet over medium heat; cook, shaking pan, until fragrant, about 1 minute. Transfer to small bowl. Return now-empty skillet to medium-high heat, add rice, and toast, stirring frequently, until deep golden brown, about 5 minutes. Transfer to second small bowl and cool for 5 minutes. Grind rice with spice grinder, mini food processor, or mortar and pestle until it resembles fine meal, 10 to 30 seconds (you should have about 1 tablespoon rice powder).

2. Whisk lime juice, fish sauce, water, sugar, and ¼ teaspoon toasted paprika mixture in large bowl and set aside.

## Unbeadable Thai Trick: Knowing When to Flip

This salad's Thai name, *nam tok* (literally "water falling"), refers to the beads of moisture that form on the surface of the steak as it cooks—an age-old Thai cookery clue that the meat is ready to be flipped. While this method sounded imprecise, during testing I found it to be a surprisingly accurate gauge of when the flank steak is halfway done. Here's why: As this steak's interior gets hotter, its tightly packed fibers contract and release some of their interior moisture, which the fire's heat then pushes to the meat's surface. When turned at this point and cooked for an equal amount of time on the second side, the steak emerged deeply charred on the outside and medium-rare within. (Note: We do not recommend this technique across the board for steaks; since the thickness and density of the meat fibers vary from cut to cut, the time it takes for heat to penetrate and for beads of moisture to be pushed to the meat's surface differs.) —A.J.

**TIME TO FLIP**
For perfectly cooked meat, flip the steak when beads of moisture appear on its surface.

**3A. FOR A CHARCOAL GRILL:** Open bottom vent completely. Light large chimney starter filled with charcoal briquettes (6 quarts). When top coals are partially covered with ash, pour evenly over half of grill. Set cooking grate in place, cover, and open lid vent completely. Heat grill until hot, about 5 minutes.

**3B. FOR A GAS GRILL:** Turn all burners to high, cover, and heat grill until hot, about 15 minutes. Leave primary burner on high and turn off other burner(s).

4. Clean and oil cooking grate. Season steak with salt and white pepper. Place steak over hot part of grill and cook until beginning to char and beads of moisture appear on outer edges of meat, 5 to 6 minutes. Flip steak and continue to cook on second side until charred and center registers 125 degrees, about 5 minutes longer. Transfer to plate, tent loosely with aluminum foil, and let rest for 5 to 10 minutes (or allow to cool to room temperature, about 1 hour).

5. Slice meat, against grain, on bias into ¼-inch-thick slices. Transfer sliced steak to bowl with fish sauce mixture. Add shallots, mint, cilantro, chile, and half of rice powder; toss to combine. Transfer to platter lined with cucumber slices. Serve, passing remaining rice powder and toasted paprika mixture separately.

**Look: The Moisture Beads**
Video available FREE for 4 months at www.CooksIllustrated.com/aug11

## ▲ RECIPE

**Andrew Janjigian.** In his article "Thai Grilled-Beef Salad," from *Cook's Illustrated*, July/August 2011, the chef reflects on one of his creations.

*Credit: America's Test Kitchen.*

An Author's/Artist's Statement helps the reader understand the process that led to the product. If you've streamed a movie recently, you may have found a behind the scenes feature available. In this feature, the director—or an actor, choreographer, or other person associated with the film—talks about the considerations that went into making the film, such as casting, lighting, music, and blocking. These commentaries, like an Author's Statement, make visible, to some extent, the behind-the-scenes work that is invisible in the final product.

When our students create assignments—whatever genre or media they create in—we ask them to write an accompanying Author's/Artist's Statement that can give us insight into what they set out to do, how they did it, and what they might do to further improve the piece.

# Analyzing Authors'/Artists' Statements

## Purpose

The purpose of an Author's/Artist's Statement is for an author (or artist or other composer) to discuss the decisions and choices he or she made in composing a specific text or other work. Let's say you've created an ad or a documentary film for your course. By writing an accompanying Statement, you can persuade your readers to see your finished piece in a particular way. A successful Statement reflects your understanding of your chosen genre (and the elements, style, design, and use of sources that characterize it)—and of your specific rhetorical situation (your reasons for composing, your audience, how you use rhetorical appeals, and your choice of mode and medium).

If you're writing an Author's Statement in an academic setting, your main purpose is to inform and persuade readers—your peers, your instructor, your audience—of the critical and creative thought you put into your composition. For example, Michael Kipp explains on p. 106 that he "used striking contrast and positioned the objects in ways the viewers might not expect, thereby drawing attention to them." Knowing that the "striking contrast" in the collage is deliberate and not merely a happy accident helps the reader understand the thought process that went into arranging the images.

## Audience

The audience for an Author's/Artist's Statement is usually a particularly engaged and interested reader or viewer. In an academic setting, your audience is made up of invested and critical readers and viewers, such as your professor and peers, who want to confirm that you've made deliberate choices throughout your composing process. In Kipp's statement, he notes his audience as "those who want to be happier and . . . are open to developing a different mindset." In addition to an external audience, you may also be the audience for this piece. Your reflections help you see what you achieved and inform your next compositions.

# Rhetorical Appeals

In an Author's/Artist's Statement, writers persuade readers by appealing mainly to ethos and logos. Depending on the work, a writer might also use pathos.

- *Ethos* The author's credibility (ethos) is particularly important because, as with most persuasive pieces, the writer needs to come across as honest and thoughtful.
- *Logos* Authors can establish ethos through the reasoning (logos) they present in their Authors' Statements. When writers logically present evidence to readers about the choices they made in organizing and presenting their work, readers are more likely to accept the claims they make.
- *Pathos* To persuade, composers may sometimes appeal to their audience's emotions. For example, if a composer wrote a piece of music as a memorial and wanted it performed a certain way, that message would appear in the program.

# Modes & Media

Authors choose modes and media for their Statements that are appropriate for those of the work they're discussing. An artist showing work online would probably create a digital Artist's Statement, whereas an artist showing work in a brick-and-mortar gallery would probably print out a text-based statement to hang next to his or her masterpieces.

# Elements of the Genre

In their Authors'/Artists' Statements, writers do the following:

- *Discuss a specific composition and make an argument.* In an Author's/Artist's Statement, writers discuss a particular composition—such as an essay, painting, photo, documentary, ad, or other work. They refer directly to that work and provide specific details as they explain the "what, why, and how" of their creation. For example, in the Author's Statement example from *Cook's Illustrated*, Andrew Janjigian explains that he set out to create a dressing that would successfully blend "the four [Thai] flavor elements: hot, sour, salty, and sweet." He then explains how he did that.

  Writers also make a case for their compositions in order to persuade readers to see their work in a particular way. For example, Andrew Janjigian wants us to see that his beef salad recipe succeeds in blending desired flavors.

- *Discuss their specific rhetorical situation and related choices.* The Author's/Artist's Statement gives you, as a composer, an opportunity to explain to audiences:
  - » **Your purpose:** why you composed the work on that specific topic, in that specific way
  - » **Your audience and use of rhetorical appeals:** what you understand about your readers and how you connected with them through choices regarding ethos, pathos, and logos
  - » **Your mode and medium:** why you chose them and how they benefit your work overall

For example, if you created a collage—perhaps on the topic of body art and identity—in your Artist's Statement, you could explain to viewers:

» Your purpose or main point in creating a collage on the relationship between body art and identity—and what the relationship is

» Why you chose specific central images, how they contribute to your message, and how you hope your viewers will read them and relate to the overall collage

» How you wanted to connect with your viewers through pathos, logos, and ethos (for example, your arrangement of images might appeal to their logic or emotions)

» Why you decided to create the collage, say, in a digital format

- *Answer the question "why."* Readers of Author's or Artist's Statements want to understand all the thinking that went into the creation of the final product. While that thinking is obvious to you, it is invisible to readers. The point of the Author's or Artist's Statements is to make it visible, and that can only be done by providing many specific details about the "why" of decisions that were made. If you write "I decided to create an advertisement," you should follow it up with an explanation of why you decided to create an advertisement.

- *Address readers directly.* Writers use the "I" construction, which allows them to speak plainly to readers about their choices. They also refer to the works they're discussing in the Statement as "my essay" (or "my painting," "my photograph," etc.), indicating their ownership of the composition and the choices they made.

- *Explain their choice of genre and how they worked with its conventions.* The Author's/Artist's Statement is a place for a composer to explain why he or she chose to work in a particular genre. For example, let's say that for your composition course you chose to write an opinion piece on gun control. In a separate statement, submitted with your opinion piece, you might explain to your instructor and classmates why you chose this genre. Pointing out your specific choices builds your ethos and persuasiveness. You might note, for example, that the opinion piece was the best choice of genre because it allowed you to:

» Clearly present your opinion on the topic of gun control (and write in the first person)

» Be brief (just a few paragraphs) and lively

» Deal with potential objections and offer potential solutions

» Invite readers to respond

Alternatively, maybe you created a photo essay for your class or a wider audience. An accompanying statement—in which you explain why you found the photo essay to be the best way to communicate your ideas about gun control—would go a long way toward helping your viewers get the most out of your work.

- *Reflect on their compositions, discussing successes and limitations.* Writers use Authors' Statements as an opportunity to look back at a composition and evaluate the extent of their achievement; they might also note what they would have done differently or better. For example, if you created an advertisement showing how marines achieve strength without steroids, you might note in an accompanying Author's Statement that you felt you'd succeeded in providing a captivating visual, an original slogan, and an emotional appeal. On the other hand, don't hesitate to mention places where you could improve your work editorially or technically. Doing your best, reflecting on what you did well, and talking about what you'd like to improve adds to your ethos as a composer and to the persuasiveness of your work.

- *Provide context.* In the Author's/Artist's Statement, it's useful for writers/artists to give some background on their composition, such as how they became interested in the topic, what their inspirations were, or, if they've created a series of related works, how the piece fits in with other pieces. Andrew Janjigian explains in his Author's Statement that he decided to create his own beef salad recipe because he hadn't found one that came close to achieving the quality of beef salads he'd eaten in Thai restaurants.

## Style

Statement authors do the following:

- *Use detail.* The persuasive and critical nature of the Statement depends on the use of specific detail. Janjigian, for example, names particular ingredients that he tried and describes the exact result he got, such as in his discussion of what happened when he used cayenne pepper instead of powdered Thai bird chiles: "Just ½ teaspoon of cayenne, in fact, overpowered the meat's smoky char."
- *Write in a tone that builds ethos.* In their Statements, authors use critical, analytical language to make their points. They choose words related to their subject of inquiry to establish themselves as experts. When you write such a Statement, even though you're writing in the first person (I), use a serious, straightforward tone to emphasize that you have made deliberate, thoughtful choices. Kipp establishes himself as an expert on gratitude when he says "the landscape refers to the fact that grateful people experience a positive memory bias," showing that he is familiar with the research on his subject and fluent with the terms.

## Design

Authors'/Artists' Statements can often look like an academic essay, with indented paragraphs and little or no decoration except for subheadings that offer structure and organization. However, a writer might choose to design a Statement to reflect the genre of the composition. For example, the Statement might take the form of a letter written to a professor, a Director's Statement, or a one-page Artist's Statement.

## Sources

The most persuasive authors discuss the sources that informed their composing process. For example, in his Statement, student Michael Kipp mentions specific sources by title or author's name, including page numbers. Depending on the audience, sources may be cited according to MLA or APA or other academic formats, as in Michael Kipp's Statement on page 106. An artist who is inspired by another artist usually names his or her inspiration and cites specific works by that artist.

## Academic Reflective Genres

When you reflect in your journal, you are writing just for yourself. Unless your journal is meant for consumption by others, you are writing *only* for yourself. In that case, your writing scenario is not a social situation (even if someone snoops in your desk to find your writing). In this section we focus on genres that allow writers to reflect but that are also intended to be shared with an audience.

Reflective genres allow you to contemplate what you think and why, what you did and why, or what you could do and why. Other times, reflective genres are used to describe and reflect upon challenges. Reflective genres depend upon describing thoughts or actions but also move beyond description to analysis.

What are some of the reflective genres you might encounter in college? Your professor might ask you to write a reflection on your writing process and turn it in alongside a research report, or you might be asked to write a reflection on a field experience for your geology class. You will also encounter reflective genres in the workplace; for example, an organization's employee evaluation and review process might involve having employees write self-evaluations.

In public life, reflective speaking is often used in self-help groups (e.g., Alcoholics Anonymous, Narcotics Anonymous), such as when a participant stands up and tells his story and reflects on his experience. Another example of reflection in a public setting is when a musician is asked by an interviewer to reflect on his or her influences. However, the stand-alone reflection is usually only seen in academia or the workplace.

The audience for reflective genres is usually either a professor (in academic settings) or a supervisor (in workplace settings). Readers want to gain insight into what you did and why. In the case of someone in a self-help group, the audience is other members of the group and possibly a facilitator, who can respond to the reflection in helpful ways.

Reflective genres also respond to a rhetorical situation. For example, if you have to write a reflective essay to accompany a visual argument you created, your purpose might be to help your professor (your audience) understand why you made particular choices in composing the visual and what overall effect you want the visual to have on its audience.

Some typical genres for reflective writing are portfolio cover letters, in which you describe and reflect on items in a portfolio of writing or artwork; progress reports, in which you describe and analyze the progress you've made toward achieving a particular task or outcome; and self-evaluations, in which you discuss some of your successes and challenges on the job.

WRITE

Make a list of all the genres you remember writing in when you were in high school or in your most recent education experience. Which ones did you enjoy the most and why? Which ones did you find most challenging and why? Which ones do you think helped you grow the most as a writer and why?

The following is an example of an Artist's Statement, an assignment we like to give students in our classes that prompts them to discuss and reflect on the composing choices they've made. Shown here is an excerpt.

## Guided Reading | Artist's Statement

As a student at Red Rocks Community College, Michael Kipp became interested in the concept of gratitude and happiness when he took a psychology course and studied positive psychology. In his second-semester research-based composition class, Kipp decided to focus his semester-long multigenre project on the idea of gratitude, looking at research in the field and reflecting on his own experience with feeling gratitude. One of the pieces that Kipp created for the project was a collage illustrating gratitude. Accompanying the collage was his Artist's Statement, which analyzed the choices he made in creating the collage, such as design and organization, and illustrated how his collage achieved his purpose and used rhetorical appeals to persuade his audience.

▲ **STUDENT AUTHOR PHOTO
& COLLAGE**

**Michael Kipp** and his composition, *Thank You*, the subject of his Artist's Statement on page 106.
*Credit: Michael Kipp.*

# Michael Kipp (STUDENT), *On Composing Happiness: How and Why I Created My Collage* Thank You

## RHETORICAL SITUATION & CHOICES

**PURPOSE**

Kipp's purpose is to persuade readers that "practicing gratitude can make us happier" and that his collage furthers that goal. He wants readers to know that he made thoughtful decisions when composing the collage.

**AUDIENCE**

His readers are his instructor and fellow students. They want to know why he created a collage and what research informed it.

◀ What is the composer, Michael Kipp, doing?

## GENRE CONVENTIONS

Michael Kipp created an ▶ Artist's Statement to accompany his collage. What are the conventions of the genre? To what extent does he adhere to them?

**ELEMENTS OF THE GENRE**

Kipp discusses a specific composition and makes an argument about it. He supports claims. Kipp addresses readers directly. Kipp talks about his rhetorical situation and specific related choices. Kipp reflects on his successes and limitations.

**STYLE**

Kipp uses specific details.

"Psychologists have repeatedly shown that perceptions are more important than objective reality" ("Positive Thinking"). That statement embodies the message behind my collage. It ties in with messages from other research I've done on the science of happiness, including my reading of the article "Psychological Research: Gratitude," by Jerry Lopper. In that piece, Lopper quotes psychologist and researcher Dr. Alex Wood as saying: "Gratitude is a life orientation towards noticing and appreciating the positive in the world." What Wood suggests is that feeling grateful requires mental work (Emmons, *Thanks!* 6). Gratitude is a part of our perception, a "life orientation," and without effort that perception will not arise or be maintained. Thus, to have an attitude of gratefulness, we must change our outlook on life. My purpose in creating this collage is to promote the idea that we make choices about how we perceive experience, and that practicing gratitude can make us happier.

My intended audience for my collage is made up of people who like art, psychology, and philosophy, who appreciate the abstract expression of concepts, and who may be persuaded to think about how a grateful attitude could be more important than one's objective reality—and how they may practice that in their own life to be happier.

In my collage I used *pathos* to convey these ideas—I wanted to sway my viewers emotionally, to cause them to feel curious and inspired when looking at the collage. I did this through my choices of composition, colors, and subjects, which are discussed in depth below. I used striking contrast and positioned the objects in ways the viewer might not expect, thereby drawing attention to them. I also used *logos* by putting the piece together in a logical manner, and by grounding my concept in positive psychology research. Furthermore, by connecting my audience with research on the power of the perception (in para. 1), I ask viewers to think about how the collage illustrates that concept. My goal is

**RHETORICAL APPEALS**
Kipp establishes his credibility, or ethos, in paragraph 1 by including quotes from experts to show he's done research on positive psychology. Kipp appeals to logos by explaining his choices logically.

**MODES & MEDIA**
Mode = written
Medium = print

that my audience will ponder what each part of the collage represents and come to logical conclusions about . . .

*Note from editors: This marks the end of the excerpt of Kipp's Statement.*

---

## Works Cited

Emmons, Robert A. *Thanks! How the New Science of Gratitude Can Make You Happier*. Houghton Mifflin Harcourt, 2007. Google Books, books.google.com/books?id=tGCcH2l4jUUC.

Emmons, Robert A., and Charles M. Shelton. "Gratitude and the Science of Positive Psychology." *Handbook of Positive Psychology*, edited by C. R. Snyder and Shane J. Lopez, Oxford UP, 2002, pp. 459–71.

Lopper, Jerry. "Psychological Research: Gratitude." *Suite101*, 19 May 2008, www.suite101.com/content/psychological -research-gratitude-a54399.

Martinez-Marti, et al. "The Effects of Counting Blessings on Subjective Well-Being: A Gratitude Intervention in a Spanish Sample." *Spanish Journal of Psychology*, vol. 13, no. 2, 2010, pp. 886–96, www.ucm.es/info/psi/docs/journal/ v13_n2_2010/art886.pdf.

Pursuit of Happiness. "Positive Thinking: Optimism and Gratitude." *The Pursuit of Happiness*, www.pursuit-of -happiness.org/science-of-happiness/positive-thinking/. Accessed 26 Nov. 2012.

Rodin, Auguste. *The Thinker*. 1880–81, Cleveland Museum of Art, Cleveland. Bronze sculpture.

Tsang, Jo-Ann. "Gratitude and Prosocial Behaviour: An Experimental Test of Gratitude." *Cognition and Emotion*, vol. 20, no. 1, 2006, pp. 138–148, www.academia.edu/365898/ Gratitude_and_prosocial_behavior_An_experimental_test _of_gratitude.

Watkins, Philip C., et al. "Counting Your Blessings: Positive Memories among Grateful People." *Current Psychology*, vol. 23, no. 1, 2004, pp. 52–67. JSTOR, doi: 10.1007/512144-004-1008-2.

**DESIGN**
Kipp structures his statement as a traditional researched essay.

**SOURCES**
Kipp's sources for his statement include the collage itself and the research he conducted on gratitude. He cites his sources per MLA style.

*Credit: Artist's Statement: Why and How I Created My Collage Thank You. Reprinted courtesy of Michael Kipp.*

**RHETORICAL SITUATION & CHOICES**

1. **Purpose.** How does Kipp convince you that his collage illustrates that "practicing gratitude can make us happier"?

2. **Audience.** Although the primary audience for the piece is Kipp's instructor, are there other audiences that might be interested in reading the piece? If so, who? Why?

3. **Rhetorical appeals.** One of the ways Kipp establishes his ethos is by including research. How else does he establish his ethos?

4. **Rhetorical appeals.** Why would it be inappropriate for Kipp to use pathos in an Artist's Statement? Are there any circumstances where pathos might be appropriate for an Artist's Statement? What circumstances? Why?

5. **Modes & media.** How would including visuals enhance Kipp's Artist's Statement? Where might he incorporate visuals?

**GENRE CONVENTIONS**

6. **Elements of the genre.** What types of evidence does Kipp use to support his claims? How effective is the evidence? Are there places where he might have included different evidence? If so, where and what?

7. **Elements of the genre.** Throughout the statement, Kipp shows how research influences his choices and motivations. Do you learn anything about Kipp's own personal motivation for exploring this subject? If so, how? If not, what would this add to the Artist's Statement?

8. **Style.** How does Kipp use language to establish his credibility?

9. **Design.** Kipp chose to submit his Artist's Statement in a traditional academic essay form. Would the piece be strengthened if he had used subheads and divided the Artist's Statement into sections? If so, what would be the different sections?

10. **Sources.** What are the different purposes the research serves in Kipp's Artist's Statement?

## CHECKLIST | Drafting an Author's/Artist's Statement

Thinking of drafting an Author's/Artist's Statement? Ask yourself the following questions.

**RHETORICAL SITUATION & CHOICES**

☐ **Purpose.** What is the central claim I want to make about my piece? What particular elements do I need to justify? What choices did I make as I created the piece? What motivated me to create the piece?

☐ **Audience.** Am I writing this Statement for my instructor? For fellow students? Will my Statement be read by people outside the academic setting? If so, how will this affect what I write?

**GENRE CONVENTIONS**

☐ **Elements of the genre.** What persuasive point do I want to make about my piece? How can I support that point with specific examples and details from my composition and process? Are there aspects of the context that readers should know to fully understand and appreciate my work?

☐ **Style.** How can I use my tone to convey the seriousness with which I view my work? What details can I use to support the generalizations I make?

☐ **Rhetorical appeals.** What makes me a credible writer on this subject? How will I show readers my credibility? How will I organize my information to support my claims?

☐ **Modes & media.** Will I present my Statement only in written form? Is it appropriate to incorporate visuals? If so, what types of visuals? How would the inclusion of audio enhance my Statement? Would it be appropriate to just use audio? Do I want to present my work in print or digital form?

☐ **Design.** How will I organize my Statement? What visuals should I include? Should I use subheadings, or is my Statement short enough that subheadings aren't necessary?

☐ **Sources.** Is the piece I composed informed by source material? What inspired me? Where did I get the facts and information that I used? Will my audience expect formal citations?

## Reflecting on a Composition

Look at a composition that you completed earlier in the semester or for another class. It can be any kind of composition: a report, an object, a video, and so on. Reflect on the choices you made as you thought through and created the piece. Where did you put most of your energy, and why? Where did you get your ideas? What did you tinker with? Imagine that your instructor had asked you for permission to use your composition as an example for future students and wants you to write a letter to the students in which you articulate some of the more important choices you made. Then draft a brief statement in which you discuss your process and thoughts.

# 7 ACADEMIC GENRES

# Academic Genres & Assignments

Any writing you do for the classes you take in college is considered academic writing. Most of this writing is done on demand, meaning you are not writing because the muse inspired you, but rather because your professor told you to. Most academic writing begins when an assignment is given.

Some of the typical purposes of academic writing are to demonstrate that you can think in ways appropriate for the discipline, to give you practice with writing skills you'll need for other classes, to give instructors an opportunity to guide you as a writer and learner in a fairly personalized way through their feedback, and to give your instructors a chance to assess how well you have grasped the concepts and skills the course focuses on. You may have other purposes as well, such as learning about the topic you are writing about and sharing what you've learned with your reader(s).

In most academic writing, your audience will be your professor and sometimes your classmates. Sometimes your professor might tell you to write for another audience, such as the board of regents, the city council, community leaders, or local business owners. In some cases, your audience might be a wider one. For example, some instructors ask students to create or edit *Wikipedia* entries or to do other composing that will be published online for a public audience. If your assignment doesn't specify whom you are writing for, you should ask.

Genre is often dictated by the assignment itself. For example, academic assignments include the lab report, the annotated bibliography, and the film analysis essay. In these situations, you do not get to choose the genre you want to write in. You might be wondering now if this means that genre is not always a response to a rhetorical situation. It still is: Genre is *always* a response to a rhetorical situation. For example, if your biology professor asks you to write a lab report, that's because when someone in biology finds herself in a rhetorical situation in which the purpose is to report the results of an experiment, and the audience is the professor or another biologist, the common social response is to write a lab report. You could write a lyrical poem instead, and frankly, nothing is stopping you from doing so. However, when a composer gives an audience something very different from what they were expecting, there are consequences. In this particular rhetorical situation, the consequence could be an F on the assignment. (It's always a good idea if you want to deviate from the assigned genre to talk to your professor first.)

Some typical assignments you might encounter include a position paper in which you take and defend a position on an issue, an analysis of a film or art piece in which you discuss the choices the filmmaker or artist made, a literacy narrative in which you discuss an aspect of yourself as a reader and writer, a research report in which you share what you learned through research about a particular topic, a proposal to conduct research on a particular topic, a presentation to your classmates in which you share your research on a particular topic, and an annotated bibliography in which you summarize and analyze source material you have read in your research. You will find examples of some of these genres throughout the book. (For a list, see the Index of Genres, p. G–1.)

On the pages that follow are examples of a variety of academic genres, including some—like the academic research paper—that are probably already familiar.

# Researched Arguments

A researched argument is any work in which a writer presents an argument and backs it up with solid sources. Most academic research papers are researched arguments (see also Peer-Reviewed Journal Articles discussed on p. 123). Writers of researched arguments do the following:

- Investigate a topic and work with sources
- Make a specific and persuasive case about that topic
- Incorporate in their writing the voices of their sources through summary, paraphrase, and quotation
- Cite those sources in the body of the composition
- List the sources at the end

The main purpose of writing a researched argument is to persuade your readers of the merits of your argument. Drawing on and citing your sources builds a case for your argument.

In academic settings, researched arguments appear in the classroom and in peer-reviewed journals. Researched arguments appear beyond academia too—in magazines and on the internet in the form of blog entries and other argumentative pieces. Depending on the level of research they've conducted and where they publish their work, authors of this genre may be scholars who are recognized by other scholars as experts on the subject they are writing about, or they may be reporters, bloggers, or other types of experts on their subject. For example, an experienced snowboarder who researches different snowboarding designs and blogs in favor of one would be considered an expert on the subject she's writing about.

In the workplace, researched arguments often take the form of reports or memos. When an employee wants to persuade an organization to change a policy or procedure, they may write a memo or report in which they refer to specific research or to policies at similar organizations.

## Analyzing Researched Arguments

**Purpose**   We write researched arguments because we want to persuade others to share our point of view on a topic. We may be looking for readers to simply agree, or maybe to take a specific action. When you write a researched argument, you begin by conducting research in hopes that the quality and quantity of the data you present will convince readers.

**Audience** Authors of researched arguments usually write in response to an assignment for a class. This might be for an English, psychology, biology, or business class. The initial audience for the assignment is your instructor, while the secondary audience might be your peers, if they are going to read your paper. Readers may or may not agree with the argument the writer proposes, but they're generally curious enough to read about others' perspectives. If you're an expert writing a researched argument for a peer-reviewed journal, then your audience is other experts.

**Rhetorical appeals** When writing a researched argument, authors can establish *ethos* when they do the following:

- Describe their research methods
- Explain the data they collected and how they analyzed it
- Discuss their findings and conclusions in detail
- Cite their sources appropriately
- Write as directly and persuasively as possible

Writers can establish *logos* when they:

- State their position clearly
- State each aspect of their argument clearly and in an order that makes logical sense
- Anticipate and address objections
- Support their claims with evidence, including the views of others, drawn from their sources

**Modes & media** Researched arguments are primarily text-based and may include visuals such as charts, graphs, and images to support and illustrate points. These types of pieces can be available in print or online.

**Elements of the genre** To compose a successful researched argument, writers do the following:

- *State a thesis or make a clear claim.* To make a position clear, a writer can (1) indicate the topic at hand and his or her position on it right in the title; (2) provide a clear thesis, doing so right at the beginning; or (3) combine both.
- *Present an argument.* The reasons for the position the author takes need to be clearly stated and explained.
- *Base their arguments on solid research.* All researched writing relies on research of some kind. Most writers support their ideas by drawing on the research of others— of experts and leaders in the field. As a student, unless you do primary research (such as conducting interviews), you most likely draw on the research of others in your researched writing. Some authors—mainly academics writing for peer-reviewed journals—draw on their own research, particularly if they've conducted a study or survey of some kind that brings in data. When Elizabeth and Amy present

ATTENTION, RESEARCHERS & WRITERS

Poorly integrated and cited research casts doubt on you as an author and seriously compromises your ethos, while a smart use of sources does a lot to build it. See Chapter 13 for more on integrating and citing sources.

papers at conferences, they draw on and cite specific research done by academic experts and colleagues to support their arguments. Arguments for peer-reviewed journals are usually written in a formal style using precise language and are reviewed by others in the field for accuracy and reliability. (For more, see Peer-Reviewed Journal Articles on p. 123 of this chapter.)

- *Address counterarguments.* To build ethos and logos, writers need to acknowledge contrasting or opposing arguments and either (1) refute them by exposing their holes or presenting evidence that outweighs them, or (2) concede that they are legitimate and then explain why, despite this legitimacy, the audience should take the author's position.

- *Synthesize and attribute the work of others.* As noted above, citing sources and specific examples builds ethos. It's also a good idea to pull information from multiple sources and to synthesize it by showing readers how these sources align and differ. When a writer relies on only one source, the argument looks weak and is therefore much less persuasive. (For more on synthesizing sources, see Chapter 13.)

**Style**   Authors use style in the following ways to present their researched arguments:

- *They title their work to make their position clear.* Readers need a clear sense of the writer's topic and perspective on that topic.

- *They write with authority.* Writers use a strong voice and tone to convey expertise on a topic, support their ethos, and persuade their readers.

- *They gain readers' attention with simple but memorable introductions and closing statements.* For example, a writer may begin with an anecdote or statistic that demonstrates the importance of the topic.

- *They use detail.* The more specific writers are, in terms of both the main point and the research they're drawing on, the better and more persuasive the argument.

**Design**   Writers of researched arguments design their documents with their readers in mind by doing the following:

- *They provide subheadings.* Dividing a researched argument into sections with subheadings makes a long, complex piece easier to navigate. Subheadings also signal readers that an author is shifting his or her focus.

- *They support their arguments with images.* Photos, charts, and illustrations convey complex information visually and can serve as sources.

**Sources**   Because a successful researched argument draws on solid research, authors do the following:

- *Curate sources carefully.* Authors use credible sources that their readers will respect.

- *Cite sources according to genre conventions.* If you've been asked to compose a researched argument in response to an academic assignment, your instructor will most likely require a particular citation system, such as MLA, APA, or *Chicago* style. You would include a bibliographic list at the end of the article and use parenthetical citations throughout.

# Guided Reading | Researched Argument

Chase Dickinson, a former student from Herriman, Utah, wrote the following researched argument when he was a freshman at Weber State University, where he studied geoscience. As he mentions in the following essay, Dickinson worked for a video game vendor called Play N Trade, a fact that influences his argument about video games in "Are Kids on a One-Way Path to Violence?" The essay, which he wrote for his English composition course, was also published in Weber State's journal of student work, called *Weber Writes*, edited in 2010 by Scott Rogers and Sylvia Newman.

**◄ STUDENT AUTHOR PHOTO, JOURNAL COVER, WEBSITE**

**Chase Dickinson;** *Weber Writes*, the student journal that published Dickinson's researched essay; and Weber State University's site.

*Credits: (top left) Chase Dickinson. (top right and bottom) Weber State University.*

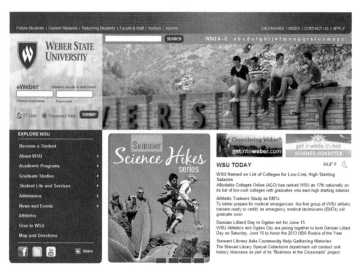

# Chase Dickinson, *Are Kids on a One-Way Path to Violence?*

| RHETORICAL SITUATION & CHOICES | | GENRE CONVENTIONS |
|---|---|---|

**PURPOSE**
Dickinson wants to persuade readers that video games do not cause violent behavior in mentally healthy children.

**AUDIENCE**
His readers are his instructor, his classmates, and the students at Weber State University who read the journal *Weber Writes.*

**RHETORICAL APPEALS**
Dickinson develops his ethos by stating that he is a gamer himself and that he's even worked in the industry.

By noting that the DC Sniper trained at a shooting range, Dickinson appeals to readers' sense of logos to question the connection between the DC Sniper and his video game experience.

**MODES & MEDIA**
Mode = written: Dickinson's assignment specified that he write an essay; however, sometimes assignments allow students the latitude to choose another mode, such as a video or audio essay. Dickinson could have included visuals with his essay, perhaps screenshots

◄ **What is the composer, Chase Dickinson, doing?**

**How do I know that this is a researched argument?** ►

In the popular video game *Grand Theft Auto* (GTA), players are thrust into a world without laws, free to do just about anything they want. Stealing cars, killing civilians, and causing general mayhem are common occurrences in the fictitious world of Liberty City (Rockstar Leeds). In fact, GTA is about as lawless as games get. But can a game such as *Grand Theft Auto* actually fuel real-world violence? There are many who believe so, and violent video games have therefore become a hotly debated topic in today's headlines.

If you were to listen to politicians and critics, the relationship between video games and crime is blatantly clear: children who play video games will either become more aggressive or actually commit real-world acts of violence. According to the lawyers of Lee Malvo, the young "DC Sniper," Malvo learned to shoot by playing "very realistic and gory" video games. These games were also said to have "desensitized (him) . . . to train him to shoot human forms over and over" (qtd. in Provan). Another popular argument against violent video games comes in the form of the infamous Columbine shootings in which Dylan Klebold and Eric Harris killed thirteen students and injured twenty-three more before killing themselves. During the investigation that followed, it was discovered that both teenagers enjoyed playing the bloody first-person shooter *Doom*, and that they went on the rampage shortly after their parents took the game away from them. It has also been speculated that the pair created a level in *Doom* with the same layout as their school in order to plan out their attack (Mikkelson). Yet another argument finds Jack Thompson, a leader in the fight against violent video games, blaming the Virginia Tech shooting on the first-person shooter *Counter-Strike*, saying that once again the shooter trained for his crime by playing the popular first-person shooter (qtd. in Benedetti).

With video games rapidly gaining popularity, we have to ask ourselves if these crimes are actually caused by the increasing violence in games. While there are many who tend to think so, I believe that it is not the fault of the games themselves, but the lack of parental supervision and interaction with today's youth. Also, preexisting mental

**ELEMENTS OF THE GENRE**
**States a thesis or makes a clear claim:** Dickinson's thesis is "I believe that [violent behavior in people who play video games] is not the fault of the games themselves, but the lack of parental supervision and interaction with today's youth."

**Presents an argument based on research:** He presents his argument in paragraph 3 and develops it in subsequent paragraphs—reasoning that the DC Sniper, Columbine shooters, and Virginia Tech shooter had histories of mental illness, and that is what the crimes should be attributed to. He argues that parents should monitor children's use of games and take mental health into account when deciding what their children can handle.

**Acknowledges counterarguments:** For example, in paragraph 2, the author mentions that lawyers claimed there were connections between their clients' violence and use of video games.

of the video games mentioned in the essay or mug shots of the DC Sniper.

**Medium = print:** Again, Dickinson was required by his assignment to produce an essay in print form, but researched arguments often appear digitally, on blogs, for example.

disorders have been found to play a huge role in how different people will react to video games.

Take, for example, the DC sniper shootings. *Halo*, the game that Malvo supposedly used to prepare for his crimes, employs the use of unrealistic guns to shoot giant alien bugs (Bungie). Such actions are hardly effective ways to learn how to shoot a sniper rifle at human beings. Malvo even admitted that he trained by shooting a real gun at makeshift targets with paper plates for heads (Provan). Similarly, the claims that the Columbine shooters created a level with their school's layout were never found to be true. In fact, all of the levels they made were later found on their website, and all of them were based on fictitious locations on alien planets (Mikkelson). Lastly, no one was ever reported to have seen Seung-Hui Cho, the Virginia Tech shooter, playing any video games. His roommate told *The New York Times* that he would sometimes enter Cho's room and find Cho sitting at his desk, staring into nothingness (Biggs). He wasn't staring at a computer and playing *Counter-Strike*, but was rather staring at nothing at all.

In addition, Seung-Hui Cho had been diagnosed with selective mutism, a severe anxiety disorder, as well as major depressive disorder (Adams). The DC shooter had a long history of antisocial and criminal behavior, including the torturing of small animals (Kutner 8). Similarly, FBI investigations were able to conclude that Klebold was significantly depressed and suicidal, and Harris was a sociopath (Kutner 8).

Ultimately, it falls upon the parents to filter what gets to their kids, and, when a known mental problem exists, parents should be that much more strict on what their kids play. As an avid gamer myself, and as someone who has worked in the industry, I understand the sense of accomplishment received from a well placed shot in *Modern Warfare* just as much as I understand that video games are not real. I was personally raised buying and playing games under the supervision of my parents, and am a strong supporter of such supervision. Even so, according to the anti-video game activist Jack Thompson and others with his mindset, I should be a ball of boiling hatred ready to explode at the slightest provocation (Musgrove).

Contrary to the claims of many naysayers, it is becoming easier to filter what a child does and does not play. A rating system implemented by the Entertainment Software Rating Board (ESRB) provides a fantastic way for parents to monitor what their kids are playing. This rating system issues an age range for each game, disclosing the full contents of the game. The most common ratings include E (Everyone, suitable for everyone age six and older), T (Teen, suitable for ages thirteen

**Refutes or concedes counterarguments:** For example, in paragraphs 4 and 5, the author discredits the links others have made between specific criminals and video game habits.

**Cites specific examples, synthesizing them into his main argument.** Rather than being general, the author specifies shooters (DC Sniper, Columbine, and Virginia Tech) and particular games (*Grand Theft Auto*, *Doom*, *Halo*, and *Counter-Strike*).

**STYLE**
**Descriptive title:** Dickinson's title makes it clear that his essay deals with kids and violence.

**Gets readers' attention in the introduction:** Dickinson accomplishes this by stating that players are "free to do just about anything they want" in the game *Grand Theft Auto*.

**Closes with a simple, memorable statement:** His final sentence reads: "Rather than focusing on trying to ban video games for their so-called influence on violent crime, an emphasis on parental supervision should be implemented in the fight against modern-day crime."

*(Continues on next page)*

and older), and M (Mature, suitable for ages seventeen and older). The AO rating (Adult Only) is the only one higher than the M rating, and is actually considered to be a death sentence for games because brick-and-mortar stores will not sell them. AO- and M-rated games are the ones that come under the most fire from the media because they contain the most violent and bloody content. However, many people don't realize that in order to purchase an M-rated game from any major retailer, the customer must be at least seventeen years of age. Because of this age restriction, it is harder for young children to get their hands on violent content without parental approval (Entertainment Software Assoc.).

There is no denying that video games have matured since their introduction in the '70s. Back then, games meant playing *Pong* or *Space Invaders* with friends and family. Today, games are becoming more and more complex, with violence playing a large role in almost all modern titles. Still, with parents staying involved in their kids' lives, it is possible to filter violent content and keep it to a minimum, which can prevent any type of aggressive behavior from developing. And with resources such as ESRB, it is becoming easier and easier to keep children from playing games that are not age appropriate. Rather than focusing on trying to ban video games for their so-called influence on violent crime, an emphasis on parental supervision should be implemented in the fight against modern-day crime.

---

### Works Cited

Adams, Duncan. "The Alienation and Anger of Seung-Hui Cho." *The Roanoke Times*, 31 Aug. 2007, www.roanoke.com/vtinvestigation/wb/130177.

Benedetti, Winda. "Were Video Games to Blame for Massacre?" *MSNBC.com*, 20 Apr. 2007, http://www.nbcnews.com/id/18220228/ns/technology_and_science-games/t/were-video-games-blame-massacre/#.Xi853BNKh24.

Biggs, John. "Why Video Games Don't Cause Violence." *CrunchGear.com*, 18 Apr. 2007, techcrunch.com/2007/04/18/why-video-games-dont-cause-violence/.

Bungie, developer. *Halo: Combat Evolved.* Microsoft Studios, 15 Nov. 2001, www.halowaypoint.com/en-us.

Entertainment Software Association. *Entertainment Software Rating Board*, www.esrb.org. Accessed 27 Jan. 2001.

Kutner, Lawrence, and Cheryl Olson. *Grand Theft Childhood: The Surprising Truth About Violent Video Games and What Parents Can Do.* Simon & Schuster, 2008, p. 8.

**Strong authoritative voice and tone:** The author chooses to avoid phrases such as "I think" and "in my opinion" but is still present in the essay.

**Uses detail:** For example, he names violent criminals and identifies the games they're associated with.

**DESIGN**
For this brief essay, the author decided that subheadings and explanatory notes would be inappropriate. When he submitted it for class, it was double-spaced. For use in *Weber Writes*, it was single-spaced to conform to that journal's design.

**SOURCES**
Using the MLA style of documentation, the author cites sources in the body of the text and at the end in a Works Cited list. His sources are varied and include video games, works by scholars and journalists, and the fact-checking site Snopes.com. For help with documenting sources, see Chapter 13.

Mikkelson, Barbara. "Columbine Doom Levels." *Snopes.com*, 1 Jan. 2005, www.snopes.com/horrors/madmen/doom.asp.

Musgrove, Mike. "Va. Tech: Dr. Phil and Jack Thompson Blame Video Games." *The Washington Post*, 17 Apr. 2007, Voices .washingtonpost.com/posttech/2007/04/va_tech_dr_phil_ jack_thompson.html.

Provan, Alexander. "The Education of Lee Boyd Malvo." *Bidouan*, 13 Jan. 2009, www.bidoun.org/magazine/16-kids/ the-education-of-lee-boyd-malvo-by-alexander-provan/.

Rockstar Leeds and Rockstar North, developers. *Grand Theft Auto: Liberty City Stories*. Rockstar Games, Capcom, 24 Oct. 2005, www.rockstargames.com/libertycitystories.

*Credit: By permission of Chase Dickinson.*

## QUESTIONS | Analyzing Dickinson's Researched Argument

**RHETORICAL SITUATION & CHOICES**

1. **Purpose.** Has Dickinson persuaded you that video games cannot be conclusively linked to violent behavior in players? Why or why not?

2. **Audience.** Besides Dickinson's professor and classmates, who else might be an appropriate audience for this essay? Would Dickinson need to revise his essay to make it accessible for other audiences?

3. **Rhetorical appeals.** What are two techniques Dickinson uses to develop his ethos?

4. **Rhetorical appeals.** Dickinson's appeals to ethos and logos are discussed in the annotations. Can you find any appeals to pathos in the essay?

5. **Modes & media.** How would the inclusion of screen shots of the video games mentioned add to or detract from the essay?

**GENRE CONVENTIONS**

6. **Elements of the genre.** How effective do you think Dickinson's refutation of the counterarguments is? What other refutations could he have used?

7. **Style.** Dickinson begins his essay by stating that players are "free to do just about anything they want" in *Grand Theft Auto*. What are some other ways Dickinson could have gained readers' attention at the beginning? For example, how could a reference to one of the criminals mentioned in the essay be used in the introduction?

8. **Style.** Dickinson writes in a strong, declarative voice rather than in a tentative "I'm just a student" voice. Find two or three sentences that are particularly strong and analyze the techniques Dickinson uses to come across as authoritative.

9. **Design.** Because this is a short essay, Dickinson opted against using subheadings. If the essay were developed into a longer one, say, fifteen pages, what are some subheadings he might use?

10. **Sources.** Look over Dickinson's Works Cited list. Do some sources appear more reliable than others?

## CHECKLIST | Drafting a Researched Argument

Are you thinking of writing a researched argument? Ask yourself the following questions:

### RHETORICAL SITUATION & CHOICES

☐ **Purpose.** What topic am I researching that might lend itself to an argument? What are some potential persuasive claims I could make about that topic? Have I discovered something about the topic that would contribute to other scholarly research?

☐ **Audience.** Assuming my readers are my classmates and professor, I need to think about how much they already know about my topic. How much background information will they need? What kind of terminology will they expect? How will they use the information I present?

☐ **Rhetorical appeals.** How will I establish my authority as a writer? How will I build a case for my conclusions using logic? What kinds of sources establish me as an expert and work to build my case?

☐ **Modes & media.** Can some of the information I present be shown with a chart or graphic? Do I want readers to access my article in print or digitally? Or do I want to make both options available?

### GENRE CONVENTIONS

☐ **Elements of the genre.** How will I make my thesis clear and declarative? How will I refer to my sources? How can I synthesize my sources to show readers that my sources are in conversation with each other?

☐ **Style.** How can I project an authoritative voice? How much detail will I need to provide so that readers understand the complexity and validity of my research?

☐ **Design.** How will I use design elements to my advantage? Will I use subheadings to organize and chunk information? Will I use images to illustrate points?

☐ **Sources.** Will my readers expect me to cite my sources in MLA, APA, or another format? Will my readers respect the types of sources I've referred to?

---

**PRACTICE**

# Researching & Making an Argument

Think of a controversial topic you are curious about, even one that you don't feel informed about. Some topics might be the environment, the right to clean water, the future of AIDS research, or perhaps a topic drawn from ideas represented in the Reader section of this book (see Chapters 15 through 18). Ask your instructor, librarian, or another expert to help you find three reliable sources on the subject. Read the sources and then draft an argumentative thesis statement in which you take a position on the topic. Sketch out at least two counterarguments and your refutations of them. Consider how you might integrate your sources. As you sketch out the counterarguments and refutations, indicate what information came from your sources.

# Peer-Reviewed Journal Articles

The research paper we have just discussed is a common assignment that often introduces you to the next genre: peer-reviewed journal articles. As you investigate a specific topic—let's say, feral (wild) domestic cats—you can gather information from primary sources or secondary sources, and sometimes both. A primary source would be your own observations of feral cats; a secondary source would be someone else's thoughts and observations about feral cats. If the results of your research produce a paper that you think is good enough to publish in a journal, you will send it to a journal, and it will be reviewed by certain other scholars on the topic of feral cats and either rejected or accepted for publication. This is the "peer-reviewed journal article."

This section will help you analyze scholarly articles and perhaps give you ideas about writing an article of your own. Authors of peer-reviewed articles are scholars who are recognized as such by fellow experts. Many scholars are college professors; some work in research laboratories. Research labs can be associated with universities, medical facilities (such as the Mayo Clinic), the government (such as the U.S. Naval Research Laboratory), for-profit organizations (such as Pfizer and other pharmaceutical companies), or nonprofit organizations (such as the Pew Research Center). Research labs are sometimes referred to as "think tanks."

Publishers of peer-reviewed journal articles, such as the science journal *Nature*, present the latest research in a given field to a specialized audience. The scholarly authors of these articles might also present them as papers or talks at academic conferences to audiences of fellow experts. They must cite their sources rigorously; a charge of plagiarism can easily end an academic career. As noted, readers of these articles are usually experts, but general readers, such as students or other nonexperts, might read them sometimes because they are interested in learning more about the topic covered.

Most of the time, you will use peer-reviewed journal articles to support some research paper you are writing for class, so you will use them as secondary sources. After you locate a source, you don't merely report what you've found: You also synthesize, compare, and analyze what has been said. You incorporate the voices of your sources in a systematic way, using quotations, citing sources in the body of your paper or other composition, and listing your sources at the end. For some assignments, you might also respond to the work of others by presenting and supporting your own argument. (For more on researched writing, see Researched Poster Presentations pp. 141–47 of this chapter.)

## Analyzing Peer-Reviewed Journal Articles

**Purpose**  Scholars write articles for peer-reviewed journals in order to share their research results with others in the same field. Sometimes scholarly writers present groundbreaking new research, such as a new drug or an alternative energy source. Other times, they present more subtle findings, such as a different way of looking at existing data.

Another purpose of scholarly writers is to persuade readers to see things the way they do. For example, when presenting data, a scholar may want to argue for his or her own particular interpretation of the data. Most scholarly articles are meant to both inform and persuade.

**Audience**   Authors of scholarly articles usually write for a fairly narrow primary audience that includes researchers, professors, and other scholars who want to stay up-to-date in their fields. However, they also have secondary audiences in mind. As a student, for instance, you might refer to a scholarly journal article as a source for a research paper. Peer-reviewed journals exist in every academic field, including the sciences, humanities, and social sciences. For example, Amy and Elizabeth both read academic journals such as *College Composition and Communication* (*CCC*), which focuses on teaching and composition; they use *CCC*'s journal articles to deepen their own understanding of writing and teaching research.

WRITE

Which scholarly journals are related to your major? To what extent do you relate to them as a reader? Make a list of all the scholarly journals and next to each, indicate how you might relate to it as a reader.

**Rhetorical appeals**   Scholars who write articles for peer-reviewed journals need to establish ethos by describing their research methods, explaining the data they collected, and how they analyzed that information, and discussing their findings and conclusions in detail. They must also cite sources appropriately, taking into account the findings of others. And, because logic is important to scholarship and the writers' audience, writers must appeal to logos by building arguments that rest on tightly organized pieces of evidence and scrupulously researched data. Scholars must keep in mind that their readers need to be convinced of the legitimacy of their research methods, the accuracy of their data collection, and the logic of their data analysis.

**Modes & media**   Scholarly articles are text based and may include visuals, such as charts, graphs, and images to support and illustrate points. Journals are available in print and, increasingly, online. Many articles that originate in print-based journals are available through subscription databases, such as *EBSCOhost*, *JSTOR*, and *Project MUSE*. There are also a few scholarly journals that are only available digitally.

**Elements of the genre**   Peer-reviewed articles are:

- *Based on original research or research of another expert or peer*. In a peer-reviewed journal article, scholars usually write about their own original research.
  - » First, they identify a question that needs to be answered, such as "How does living near a nuclear reactor affect birthrates?"
  - » Next, they design an experiment or research plan that will allow that question to be studied; for example, identifying nuclear reactors, collecting data on birthrates in the surrounding communities over time, interviewing obstetricians who practice in the area, and so on.
  - » Then they perform the research, analyze the data they've gathered, and offer their interpretations in writing. Authors usually refer to related research by other scholars to contextualize their own work.

- *Reviewed by others in the field for accuracy and reliability.* Scholars write scholarly articles for other scholars. During the peer review process, other experts in the field review the article to check for clarity and style, but even more important, to make sure the research conducted is a legitimate means of measuring or studying the subject of the article. Peer reviewers might question, for instance, the validity of studying birthrates near nuclear reactors by merely interviewing people who live in the community. They would probably want more rigorous, objective data, such as hospital records documenting pregnancies, fertility rates, and births.

- *Organized around a thesis.* Scholarly authors write to make a point about the research they've conducted—a point that usually has both informative and persuasive elements. For example, if an author's point is "drugs X, Y, and Z alleviate symptoms of condition A," she will go on to inform readers of how she drew that conclusion (how she conducted the research and analyzed the data) and will also—if the article is well researched and written—persuade readers that the drugs discussed in the article should be prescribed more often.

- *Based on sources or works of others.* Scholars who write articles for peer-reviewed journals summarize, paraphrase, and quote from their sources. When writers use other sources (outside of their own original research), they properly document the work of others through in-text citations and Works Cited lists.

- *Syntheses of multiple sources.* Like a student writing a research paper, scholars must synthesize their sources in journal articles. That is, they pull together information across multiple sources to make their points.

- *Formal and precise in their use of language.* Scholarly writers use formal language to convey the seriousness of their ideas and research. They also use precise language to communicate complex information accurately and in detail. In a scientific research study, the difference between .1 and .01 can be crucial.

**Style**   Peer-reviewed journal articles are characterized by the following stylistic elements:

- *Descriptive title.* In scientific fields, the more descriptive the title is, the better, such as "Hospital Mortality, Length of Stay, and Preventable Complications Among Critically Ill Patients Before and After Tele-ICU Reengineering of Critical Care Processes" (from *JAMA*). In the humanities, titles often have two parts: an imaginative or creative phrase, followed by a colon, and then a more descriptive phrase, such as "Black, White, and Blue: Racial Politics in B. B. King's Music from the 1960s" (an article by Ulrich Adelt, from *The Journal of Popular Culture*).

- *Strong, authoritative voice and tone.* Authors use voice and tone to establish their ethos. For example, in "Status Struggles: Network Centrality and Gender Segregation in Same- and Cross-Gender Aggression," an article in *American Sociological Review,* authors Robert Faris and Diane Felmlee begin their article in a way that reinforces their expertise and authority:

WRITE

Why do authors of scholarly articles tend to use long, descriptive titles? What are the benefits and drawbacks of such titles? Use these questions to begin a freewrite. Write for at least five minutes.

Aggression is commonplace in U.S. schools: bullying and other forms of proactive aggression adversely affect 30 percent, or 5.7 million, American youth each school year (Nansel et al. 2001). The National Education Association (1995) estimates that each weekday, 160,000 students skip school to avoid being bullied. This aggression has important consequences. Being victimized by bullies positively relates to a host of mental health problems, including depression (Baldry 2004), anxiety (Sharp, Thompson, and Arora 2000), and suicidal ideation (Carney 2000).

**Robert Faris and Diane Felmlee,** from "Status Struggles: Network Centrality and Gender Segregation in Same- and Cross-Gender Aggression," *American Sociological Review,* February 2011

- *Use of detail*. Authors of scholarly articles use specific details to develop complex ideas. They also use details as evidence to back up their assertions. For example, in the article discussed above, Faris and Felmlee support general statements ("Aggression is commonplace in U.S. schools") with examples and evidence (bullying "affect[s] 30 percent, or 5.7 million, American youth each school year").

**Design**   Peer-reviewed journal articles feature the following design elements:

- *Subheadings*. Many peer-reviewed articles are divided into sections by subheadings that make a long, complex article accessible. Subheadings also signal to the reader when the writer is about to turn his or her focus to another example or another aspect of the topic.

- *Images*. Many scholarly articles include images, such as photos, charts, and illustrations, to convey complex information visually. Those that are published digitally can include hyperlinks to sources and other materials.

**Sources**   Scholarly writers must use sources that are authoritative and are appropriate to their topic and approach. Of particular importance are the following:

- *Types of sources used*. Authors must choose sources carefully. For example, in the peer-reviewed article that follows on the next page, the authors draw on scholarly research, but also quite heavily on cultural artifacts. This is appropriate because they discuss a graphic novel and its cultural impact. Graphic novels would not be used as sources for an article on molecular science, unless, for instance, the essay focuses on how molecular science is portrayed in media.

- *Works Cited list*. Scholarly writers include a bibliography at the end of their articles. They list sources in the format dictated by the journal they're publishing in, or according to the format favored in their discipline's professional organization, such as the Modern Language Association (MLA style) or the American Psychological Association (APA style). For more on documentation, see Chapter 13.

# Guided Reading | Peer-Reviewed Journal Article

Mario Worlds and Henry "Cody" Miller are both graduate students at the University of Florida, pursuing their PhDs in English Education. Worlds's research focuses on the educational experiences of minority students, especially as they relate to literacy. Miller's research examines how young adult literature helps shape a student's worldview. Their article, "Miles Morales: Spider-Man and Reimagining the Canon for Racial Justice," first appeared in 2019 in an "Exploring Colored Hierarchies"-themed issue of *English Journal*, a scholarly, peer-reviewed journal. The journal, published by the National Council of Teachers of English, presents the works of English scholars focused on English language arts in high school and middle school.

▲ PEER-REVIEWED JOURNAL COVER

The "Exploring Colored Hierarchies" edition of *English Journal*, which published Worlds's and Miller's article.

Credit: Copyright 2019 by the National Council of Teachers of English. Reprinted with Permissions. Artwork ("Twelve Manos") by Hannah Simone Smith.

## Mario Worlds and Henry "Cody" Miller, *Miles Morales: Spider-Man and Reimagining the Canon for Racial Justice*

| RHETORICAL SITUATION & CHOICES | GENRE CONVENTIONS |
|---|---|

**PURPOSE**
As authors of a peer-reviewed journal article, Worlds and Miller aim to show their readers why the literary canon needs to be reimagined in order to disrupt systems of racism. They make an argument that teaching the text *Miles Morales: Spider-Man* and other young adult texts representative of a minority experience from a non-white perspective is a needed change.

◄ What are the composers, Mario Worlds and Henry "Cody" Miller, doing?

How do I know that this is a ► peer-reviewed journal article?

Racial hierarchies within English courses are perpetuated by the reverence for the literary canon. When left unchallenged, the canon is a weapon of the colonial project, which perpetuates Eurocentrism and violence against people of color (Durand and Jiménez-García). Often, canonical texts that are used to discuss racism, such as *To Kill a Mockingbird* and *Adventures of Huckleberry Finn*, are centered on White characters' experiences learning about racism and/or take place in the past: *Invisible Man* and *Black Boy* are examples. While texts associated with the canon certainly have a place in English classrooms, we worry that neglecting contemporary texts that address racism results in students associating racism with the past. Legislation and policy have added to this concern.

**ELEMENTS OF THE GENRE**
Is based on original research and research by other scholars: Worlds and Miller examine the ways the novel helps disrupt racial hierarchies. They reference scholars throughout the article who have explored racist implications of the literary canon and scholars who have examined issues of the school-to-prison.

*(Continues on next page)*

**RHETORICAL SITUATION & CHOICES**  |  **GENRE CONVENTIONS**

**AUDIENCE**
Readers are most likely to be educators, scholars, and/or researchers interested in race, literacy, and English education. As readers of *the English Journal*, they are already interested in language arts and issues related to the classroom.

For instance, the Common Core State Standards draw from canonical texts and Newbery Award winners that are overwhelmingly historical narratives, which can lead students and teachers to believe racism is a relic of the past (Thein and Beach). Meredith Sinclair criticized the exemplary texts set that accompanies the Common Core as being "colonized by whiteness" for centering White authors as being "worthy of study" while largely omitting or marginalizing authors of color (90). Subsequently, teachers' inability to challenge the status and content of the canon emboldens a hierarchy that places White characters *learning* about racism over characters of color *experiencing* racism. In short, an uncritical acceptance of the canon prevents students from addressing racism in its contemporary contexts.

As educators and researchers—Mario is a Black cisgender straight male, and Cody is a White cisgender gay male—it is our belief that English language arts classrooms must be sites to name, challenge, and ultimately dismantle oppressive systems. Traditional canonical curriculum and pedagogy will only reinforce the systems we seek to disrupt. Young adult literature, when paired with intentional pedagogical choices, is a powerful tool to fulfill our aims. E. Sybil Durand and Marilisa Jiménez-García argue that young adult literature allows students to "engage social issues that the established canon obscures" (16). Jason Reynolds's *Miles Morales: Spider-Man* is a text that opens conversations about contemporary manifestations of racism. Reynolds's novel can be part of a larger effort to reimagine the canon. In an exchange with Trevor Noah, Reynolds vocalizes what that effort entails:

> We have to rethink what the literary canon is and whether or not it should remain fossilized and concrete as it is today. It's stagnant. It's static, right? Why not figure out how to expand the canon? To be diverse. To be young. To be old. To have like, poetry, poetry should be, Shakespeare's sonnets and it should be by Queen Latifah. Teach comparative literature where you take Queen Latifah's "Ladies First" and Maya Angelou's "Phenomenal Woman" and you show young people that nothing is new. This is all a continuum. We are working with tradition. Then they can start to see their place in the things that they're reading.

**Has been reviewed by peers:** *The English Journal*, where the article was published, is a scholarly, peer-reviewed journal produced by the National Council of Teachers of English.

**Is thesis-driven:** Worlds and Miller begin by stating the central issue they will address. Their thesis (spread over several sentences) provides their main argument and its consequences.

**RHETORICAL APPEALS**
One way the authors establish their ethos is by providing a careful analysis of the Jason Reynolds's young adult novel *Miles Morales: Spider Man*. Worlds and Miller appeals to readers' logos by building their argument from an examination of the problem (white supremacy/ the canon/school to prison pipeline) to an analysis of the novel to a connection between the novel and the problem.

We agree with Reynolds's call and want to place his young adult novel, *Miles Morales: Spider-Man,* in the reimagining of the literary canon to discuss the racist policy structure that is conceptualized as the "school-to-prison pipeline."

We work to illustrate how *Miles Morales,* along with a variety of other texts, can constitute a new type of canon that foregrounds addressing contemporary issues of racism. First, we outline the key concepts of "White supremacy" and the "school-to-prison pipeline" before providing a brief overview of the book *Miles Morales: Spider-Man.* We end our article with additional suggestions for classroom teachers.

## WHITE SUPREMACY, THE CANON, AND THE SCHOOL-TO-PRISON PIPELINE

Like education professor Sabina Vaught, we draw on legal scholar Cheryl Harris's definition of White supremacy as a

> political, economic, and cultural system in which Whites overwhelmingly control power and material resources, conscious and unconscious ideas of White superiority and entitlement are widespread, and relations of White dominant and non-White subordination are daily reenacted across a broad array of institutions and social settings. (1714)

In *Racism, Public Schooling, and the Entrenchment of White Supremacy: A Critical Race Ethnography,* Vaught outlines how schools are rooted in and sustain White supremacy through a number of methods including policy, procedures, structures, and curriculum. For the purpose of this article, we will examine how curricular considerations such as a devotion to the literary canon and school policies and procedures relating to discipline uphold White supremacy.

The literary canon perpetuates White supremacy by positioning White authors as essential to cultural knowledge through descriptors such as "classic" and "foundational." Defenders of the literary canon position the themes of canonical texts as "objective knowledge" and "universal in nature" despite the reality that the construction of the canon reflects "values, ideologies, political positions, and human interests" of Western imperialism (Banks 5–8). The canon submerges knowledge in an unnamed Whiteness that masquerades under labels such as "universal" and "timeless." Vaught reminds us that labels act as "ideological and structural gateways to the effective maintenance of racial hegemony" (148). When left unquestioned, the construction and continual credence of the literary

**Identifies and synthesizes sources:** The authors go beyond summarizing, paraphrasing, and quoting from sources; they synthesize them to make a point. For example, when discussing the concept of race-bending, they pull together several sources to make their point.

*(Continues on next page)*

**RHETORICAL SITUATION & CHOICES**  **GENRE CONVENTIONS**

**MODES & MEDIA**
**Mode = written:** The authors' scholarly article is text based (it appears in print and as a PDF online) and includes no images or graphics. Some journals encourage authors to use images and graphics; this is especially true for business and economics journals that publish articles that analyze relationships among factors, and as you might expect, art journals make heavy use of images of the art being discussed. (See "Infographics" on p. 198.)

canon acts as a "structural message" that teaches "consistent racial grammar" within English classrooms and schools (155). This structural message affects both students and teachers. Scholars H. Richard Milner and Jane Murray Agee have demonstrated how a department's or school's strict reverence of teaching canonical literature marginalizes teachers of color. The canon is not merely a collection of texts. Rather, the canon represents a cultural construction of knowledge centered in Whiteness that institutions deem superior and essential.

Similarly, schools can uphold White supremacy through policies and discipline procedures by implicitly demanding compliance to White, middle-class norms of dress, speech, and classroom engagement (Hatt-Echeverria and Jo). Black and Latinx students are disproportionately punished within schools when they fail to succumb to those norms by teachers who have not critically examined their own cultural biases. Punishments, as a result of "zero tolerance" policies, often include suspension and expulsion. These punitive punishments frequently occur at schools with heavy police presence, which statistically are schools that are underfunded and serve predominantly Black and Latinx students. The multiple and interconnected factors of underfunded schools, police presence, centering of White norms, and harsh punishment result in Black and Latinx students being forced out of schools and into prison systems, whether directly or indirectly. This reality has been conceptualized as the "school-to-prison pipeline" to make the implicit threads between White supremacist school policies and the prison system explicit (Kim et al.).

The literary canon and the school-to-prison pipeline are different in form but manifest from the same White supremacist ideology. The canon positions White authors' experiences and language as aspirational and superior while the school-to-prison pipeline codes White cultural norms as essential for academic success. Both the canon and the school-to-prison pipeline are upheld, perpetuated, and even strengthened through the institution of school. Fortunately, schools, especially English classrooms, can be spaces to challenge these manifestations of White supremacy. Teaching Reynolds's *Miles Morales: Spider-Man* disrupts canonical wisdom about what "counts" as a valuable text.

### MILES MORALES: SPIDER-MAN

The titular character in Reynolds's text is described as "Baby Einstein" and "Smarty Arty" (Reynolds 43). Miles is the son of Rio Morales, a Puerto Rican woman, and Jefferson Davis, an African American man. Miles prefers to use his mother's

**Documents sources:** The authors provide in-text citations when drawing on outside sources.

**Uses formal language:** The authors' choice of terms such as *positions*, *problematizes*, and *critically compare* adds to the serious tone of the writing.

**Uses precise language:** For example, Worlds and Miller specify that *Miles Morales* "challenges existing notions about who can and should be a hero," showing that they see this novel as pivotal in questioning literary expectations.

**Medium = print and digital:** This piece originally appeared in both the print and digital versions of *the English Journal.* Subscribers to the print journal automatically get online access to the digital version of the journal, enabling readers to choose which medium they'd prefer to read an article in (there are no content differences between the versions). Some journals have developed apps for iPads and other mobile devices that allow readers to access the online version of an article on the go.

last name to avoid jokes about the musician Miles Davis and, more seriously, to avoid the "dirt" his father's last name carries in the neighborhood (20–21). Ganke, Miles's best friend, is Korean American. *Miles Morales: Spider-Man* features a multicultural cast that is significantly different from the nearly racially homogenous cast of the original series. Most notable is the fact that Spider-Man is no longer Peter Parker, the White hero audiences have known for decades.

In recasting Spider-Man as Miles Morales, an Afro-Latino male, Marvel comics engaged in a process known as "racebending." Bryan Cooper Owens defines racebending as the "practice in comic books (and other media) of taking an established character and rebooting them as another ethnicity." Racebending is far more than casting choices and fan art. Ebony Elizabeth Thomas and Amy Stornaiuolo argue that racebending is a form of restorying, a "process by which people reshape narratives to represent a diversity of perspectives and experiences that are often missing or silenced in mainstream texts, media, and popular discourse" (313).

The racebending of Spider-Man, a story with a traditionally White male hero, is especially difficult for some to fathom because it challenges existing notions about who can and should be a hero. By reimagining Spider-Man as an Afro-Latino boy from an urban environment, Reynolds problematizes the belief that heroes must be White males. Visions of who villains are and what they look like, largely perpetuated by racist stereotyping and media representation, are challenged when the hero looks like someone society has historically villainized. The presence of Black superheroes destroys illusions of who commits crime (Black males) and the heroes who save society from them (White police officers).

Racebending is also important because (re)casting characters using alternative race and ethnicities creates possibilities for popular comics and other "classics" to be told from underrepresented perspectives rarely seen in literature. In an interview about his novel, *Shadowshaper*, Daniel José Older explains that diversity is needed in literature because "there are other ways of thinking about time, there are other ways of thinking about place and community, what it means to win, be a hero, or save the world" (qtd. in Gonzalez).

Miles attends Brooklyn Visions Academy, which he describes as a "bougie boarding school" with "a lot of rich kids acting like rich kids" (Reynolds 92). He relies on a scholarship for tuition and works a job at the campus store to waive room and board fees. Most teachers are described as wearing blazers, "over-starched button up" shirts, khakis,

**STYLE**
**Descriptive title:** The authors use their title to grab attention and present the gist of their argument.

**Strong author's voice:** Worlds and Miller refer to many sources, but their voice stays in control; their voice doesn't get lost in the midst of quotations.

**Authoritative and declarative tone:** The authors state their case with confidence. They sometimes use the first person (*we*) to present their ideas as researchers and scholars.

*(Continues on next page)*

and "sensible shoes" (52–53). Miles is aware that his race and economic status mark him as an outsider within Brooklyn Visions Academy, noting that he is from the "part of Brooklyn that Brooklyn Visions Academy didn't have much vision for at all" (259). Like its real-life counterparts in many urban areas, Brooklyn Visions Academy relies on a dress code that makes White, upper-middle-class culture, attitude, and beliefs aspirational (Hatt-Echeverria and Jo).

*Miles Morales: Spider-Man* follows the eponymous character throughout one year in high school. The plot revolves primarily around the fact that Miles's powers are acting strangely while he is antagonized by his history teacher, Mr. Chamberlain. The racebending in *Miles Morales: Spider-Man* not only recasts the superhero but also recasts the villain, Mr. Chamberlain, a White male. Through Mr. Chamberlain's actions, the audience is able to see a reconceptualization of teachers and the negative impact their teaching can have on students when their instruction reflects racist beliefs. By offering alternative representations of both the hero and the villain, Reynolds's text actively works to dismantle racial hierarchies.

### THE SCHOOL-TO-PRISON PIPELINE AND *MILES MORALES*

The school-to-prison pipeline is a concept used to illustrate how schools employ "discipline policies that push students out of the classroom and into the criminal justice system at alarming rates," especially Black and Latinx students (Elias). English classrooms have been seen as sites to resist the school-to-prison pipeline (Rubin). Indeed, the racial categorizing that determines which piece of literature is deserving to be part of the canon is the same system of White supremacy that dictates who will be part of the school-to-prison pipeline. The school-to-prison pipeline acts as the central antagonist in *Miles Morales: Spider-Man*. Thus, Reynolds's book offers an opportunity to examine the school-to-prison pipeline and deepen students' understanding of slavery in America's history.

### Teacher as Villain

Miles's history teacher, Mr. Chamberlain, is the primary antagonist for Miles throughout the book. Mr. Chamberlain talks about the Civil War "like this beautiful, romantic thing" and defends slavery as "kind of good for the country" (Reynolds 40). Miles notes that Mr. Chamberlain's defense of slavery is dead wrong, but he keeps his thoughts to himself initially; Miles even wonders if Mr. Chamberlain is trying to anger students so they'll engage in the curriculum (61). As a history teacher, Mr. Chamberlain uses his classroom as a site to replicate White supremacist myths about the purpose and morality of the Civil War. He compares enslaved people to dogs, suggests enslaved people should be "grateful" to their masters, and informs students he will bring in images of enslaved people to confirm that "many slaves were comfortable with being enslaved. Happy even" (115). Mr. Chamberlain even dresses as a Confederate soldier for a Halloween school party.

Miles has an emotional reaction when he eventually challenges Mr. Chamberlain's assertion that enslaved people should be "grateful" to their masters, which causes Mr. Chamberlain to tell Miles to "put a muzzle on . . . this anger of yours" (117). Mr. Chamberlain's response reflects dangerous and unexamined views White teachers hold about Black youth that lead to higher rates of disciplinary action taken against Black students (Morris).

Sip, one of Miles's father's friends, argues that educators can cause even greater harm to already marginalized youth: "school is like a tree we get to hide in. And at the bottom of it is a bunch of dogs. Them dogs are bad decisions. So when people shake us out of that tree for no reason, it becomes a lot easier to get bit" (Reynolds 207). Educators shaking students out of the metaphorical tree include an English teacher who picked on a student who couldn't read well, a principal who had no concern for the well-being of students, and a dean who would "pop into classrooms and pick out students he felt needed to be chastised" (204–06). Each of these figures, all named Chamberlain, are later revealed to be a group being led by a Confederate zombie named the Warden who works in schools to punish young students of color until the students are sent to prison, where they work as indentured servants and are enslaved. The history teacher Mr. Chamberlain foreshadows this plot when he muses that the "South rose up again, by a new, much smarter form of slavery. Prison" (155). The Chamberlains literally represent the school-to-prison pipeline as they use racist discipline policies to funnel students of color into the prison system.

## Nonfiction Texts as Pairings

We offer a list of nonfiction texts that can be paired with *Miles Morales: Spider-Man* to further the discussion of the school-to-prison pipeline within secondary English language arts classrooms (see Table 1). These texts, which vary in format and genre, can deepen students' historical understanding of the school-to-prison pipeline and its connections to American slavery.

Ava DuVernay's documentary, *13th*, offers a historical context of Black and Latinx imprisonment and outlines the

**Use of detail:** The authors follow their generalizations with specific examples to back up their claims. For example, they state, "Miles's history teacher, Mr. Chamberlain, is the primary antagonist for Miles throughout the book," and then provide evidence: "Mr. Chamberlain uses his classroom as a site to replicate White supremacist myths," "He compares enslaved people to dogs," and he "dresses as a Confederate soldier for a Halloween school party." Details help readers understand their research and evaluate the validity of their conclusions.

*(Continues on next page)*

**TABLE 1.**

Nonfiction Pairings to Teach About the School-to-Prison Pipeline

| Author and Title | Description |
|---|---|
| *13th.* Directed by Ava DuVernay, Kandoo Films, 2016. | Documentary detailing the historical nature of modern-day slavery, including the school-to-prison pipeline |
| Alexander, Michelle. *The New Jim Crow: Mass Incarceration in the Age of Colorblindness.* New Press, 2012. | Book detailing the history of mass incarceration through policy analysis |
| Elias, Marilyn. "The School-to-Prison Pipeline." *Teaching Tolerance,* vol. 14, 2013. | News article detailing the history of the school-to-prison pipeline and contemporary legislative attempts to counter it |
| Lopez, German. "How Schools Push Black Students to the Criminal Justice System." *Vox,* 30 July 2015, www.vox .com/2015/7/30/9075065/ school-to-prison-pipeline-study. | Explainer article detailing the statistics and research associated with the school-to-prison pipeline |
| Morris, Monique. *Pushout: The Criminalization of Black Girls in Schools.* New Press, 2016. | Book detailing how racist and sexist structures in schools push Black female students out of school and into prison |
| Teaching Tolerance. *Teaching "The New Jim Crow."* Southern Poverty Law Center, 2014. | Curricular resources for teaching *The New Jim Crow* in secondary classrooms |
| TED. "The Urgency of Intersectionality: Kimberlé Crenshaw." *YouTube,* 7 Dec. 2016, youtu.be/akOe5-UsQ2o. | TED Talk video detailing why we need to address gender in our analysis of racist policies |
| Vox. "The School-to-Prison Pipeline, Explained." *YouTube,* 11 Jan. 2016, youtu.be/HoKkasEyDOI. | Explainer video briefly detailing the history of the school-to-prison pipeline |

progression of incarceration from slavery to prison. The film gives historical background knowledge that can be used as a framework through which the text, *Miles Morales: Spider-Man*, can be read. The film explores the loophole in the Thirteenth

Amendment that made modern-day slavery possible. The amendment states that slavery is illegal in the United States, "except as a punishment for crime whereof the party shall have been duly convicted." The film notes criminal offenses that people of color are routinely convicted of often stem from policies that specifically target Black and Latinx students.

While *Miles Morales: Spider-Man* focuses primarily on male characters such as Miles and makes analysis of the school-to-prison pipeline more easily viewed as a phenomenon affecting mostly young Black and Latinx boys, the text also demonstrates how young girls of color, too, are victims of school systems that usher girls into the school-to-prison pipeline. In her TED Talk, "The Urgency of Intersectionality," Kimberlé Crenshaw challenges audience members to recognize the number of Black women who have been victims of police brutality. In doing so, she encourages the larger society to #SayHerName and brings awareness to forgotten or ignored stories of women of color who suffer, often silently, within systems of oppression.

Being sure to consider the ways in which women of color are marginalized because of the intersection of both their race and gender, Reynolds answers Crenshaw's call to #SayHerName through the character Alicia. In class, Alicia challenges Mr. Chamberlain's interpretation of the Civil War and his racist teaching philosophies and is consequently punished. *Pushout: The Criminalization of Black Girls in School* represents a foundational text that can be used to understand Alicia's experiences and make room for discussions about young girls and the school-to-prison pipeline. This text looks at disciplinary practices and school policies that punish Black girls at alarming rates, creating gateways for them to be forced into the pipeline. This text can help students make sense of Alicia's experience from a feminist perspective that offers opportunities to understand how Alicia is uniquely gendered and racialized in ways that characterize her as insubordinate or criminal.

Michelle Alexander's work, *The New Jim Crow: Mass Incarceration in the Age of Colorblindness*, is an important pairing that explores the historical, sociological, and political contexts that situate the school-to-prison pipeline in a broader scope of White supremacist policies. Miles's school and the school-to-prison pipeline concept inevitably reflect a microcosmic representation of how White supremacy evolves and is enacted in different policies across various US institutions like schools. *The New Jim Crow* allows students ample

*(Continues on next page)*

chances to draw connections from *Miles Morales: Spider-Man*
to larger social issues and offer critiques of policies
that unfairly target and punish already marginalized
students.

## OTHER CLASSROOM SUGGESTIONS

This article suggests one way in which the canon can be
reimagined to address contemporary sociopolitical issues.
Specifically, we examined how *Miles Morales: Spider-Man* can
be used to address the school-to-prison pipeline. This is just
one text and one racist policy. We must reimagine the canon
to address how racism embedded in political systems perpetuates racial hierarchies within our societies and schools. Fortunately, we are not alone.

#DisruptTexts is a "crowdsourced, grass roots effort by
teachers for teachers" meant to "challenge the traditional
canon in order to create a more inclusive, representative,
and equitable language arts curriculum that our students
deserve." Developed by English teachers Tricia Ebarvia,
Lorena Germán, Kim Parker, and Julia Torres, #DisruptText
is determined to "aid and develop teachers committed to
anti-racist/anti-bias teaching pedagogy and practices." The
movement works through Twitter participation. A Twitter chat
that takes place over a week is dedicated to a canonical text.
Teachers are invited to discuss the values of teaching the
canonical piece, the problematic nature of the canonical text,
how the canonical text can be used to discuss contemporary
political issues, and what additional texts can be used to "disrupt" the perspectives and ideologies in the canonical text.
#DisruptTexts is an invaluable source for any teachers seek-
ing to speak against the White supremacy inherent in
the canon.

*Miles Morales: Spider-Man* can enter dialogue with other
texts, even canonical ones, in thematic units. This approach
may be especially valuable for teachers who are institution-
ally obligated to teach canonical texts. For instance, *Miles
Morales* can be taught with *Beowulf* in a unit focusing on hero
narratives. Students can be asked to analyze what makes a
hero, who has historically been considered a hero, and how
unequal power dynamics shape our understanding of heroes
and villains. Teachers can pair *Miles Morales* with *The Catcher
in the Rye* to critically examine how youth, as a concept, has
been socially constructed over time. Students can be asked to
tackle the question of how race and class shape experiences
youth face, and whose youth gets positioned as universal.

**DESIGN**
The authors use
subheadings to
organize their article
into digestible chunks.
They provide a Works
Cited list at the end
of their article.

Finally, Miles's schooling experiences can be compared with Scout's in *To Kill a Mockingbird*.

Teachers could ask students to critically compare how Scout and Miles are positioned in their respective schools and how their actions are interpreted and reacted to by teachers. In each of these examples, *Miles Morales: Spider-Man* acts as a counter to canonical texts to provide students with an opportunity to challenge assumptions about heroes, youth, and schooling experiences.

## CONCLUSION

Jason Reynolds's novel adaptation of the beloved superhero can be used in classrooms to teach about "forms of racism and colonialism that persist for youth of color today, particularly African American and Native American youth, who continue to be located in the margins of society" (Durand and Jiménez-García 12). Incorporating *Miles Morales: Spider-Man* offers opportunities to address and challenge the school-to-prison pipeline within secondary English language arts classrooms. Including Reynolds's racebending Spider-Man in classrooms and reading lists pushes against literary hierarchies that place whiteness as aspirational.

Not challenging canonical wisdom and avoiding important conversations about race and racism in our contemporary society creates classroom conditions similar to those Miles has to survive in the novel. Just as Miles Morales's actions set in motion the toppling of Mr. Chamberlain's attempt to preserve a racial hierarchy, reimagining the canon with books like *Miles Morales: Spider-Man* can begin to splinter the racial hierarchy that reigns over English curricula.

**SOURCES**
Worlds and Miller use sources appropriate to their topic and audience, including an interview between the talk-show host Trevor Noah and Jason Reynolds, the author of *Miles Morales*, because it illustrates how the novel and other pieces can work alongside the literary canon. They cite sources as in-text citations in the body of the paper and list these sources in the Works Cited list at the end. They use MLA documentation style, which is the style favored by the *English Journal*, where their article appears.

Works Cited

*13th*. Directed by Ava DuVernay, Kandoo Films, 2016.

Agee, Jane Murray. "Negotiating a Teaching Identity: An African American Teacher's Struggle to Teach in Test-Driven Contexts." *Teachers College Record*, vol. 106, no. 4, 2004, pp. 747–74.

Banks, James. "The Canon Debate, Knowledge Construction, and Multicultural Education." *Educational Researcher,* vol. 22, no. 5, 1993, pp. 4–14.

Durand, E. Sybil, and Marilisa Jiménez-García. "Unsettling Representations of Identities: A Critical Review of Diverse Youth Literature." *Research on Diversity in Youth Literature*, vol. 1, no. 1, 2018, sophia.stkate.edu/rdyl.

*(Continues on next page)*

Ebarvia, Tricia, Lorena Germán, Kimberly Parker, and Julia Torres. "What Is #DisruptTexts?" *#DisruptTexts,* disrupttexts.org/lets-get-to-work/.

Elias, Marilyn. "The School-to-Prison Pipeline." *Teaching Tolerance,* vol. 43, 2013, pp. 39–40.

Gonzalez, Barbara. "Daniel José Older Talks Diversity in Young Adult Novels and New Project *Dead Light March.*" *Cassius,* 6 July 2017, cassiuslife.com/5873/daniel-jose-older-dead-light-march/.

Harris, Cheryl. "Whiteness as Property." *Harvard Law Review,* vol. 106, no. 8, 1993, pp. 1709–91.

Hatt-Echeverria, Beth, and Ji-Yeon Jo. "Understanding the 'New' Racism Through an Urban Charter School." *Educational Foundations,* vol. 19, no. 1–2, 2005, pp. 51–65.

Kim, Catherine, et al. *The School-to-Prison Pipeline: Structuring Legal Reform.* NYU P, 2012.

Milner, H. Richard. "Developing a Multicultural Curriculum in a Predominantly White Teaching Context: Lessons from an African American Teacher in a Suburban English Classroom." *Culture, Curriculum, and Identity in Education,* edited by H. Richard Milner, Palgrave Macmillan, 2010, pp. 37–76.

Morris, Monique. *Pushout: The Criminalization of Black Girls in School.* New Press, 2016.

Owens, Bryan Cooper. "Racebending and Representation in Comic Books." *African American Intellectual History Society,* 6 Feb. 2017, www.aaihs.org/racebending-and-representation-in-comic-books/.

Reynolds, Jason. Interview by Trevor Noah. *The Daily Show.* Comedy Central. 23 Jan. 2018, www.cc.com/video-clips/avk8pe/the-daily-show-with-trevor-noah-jason-reynolds-serving-young-readers-with-long-way-down-.

———. *Miles Morales: Spider-Man.* Marvel, 2017.

Rubin, Daniel Ian. "Engaging Latino/a Students in the Secondary English Classroom: A Step Toward Breaking the School-to-Prison Pipeline." *Journal of Latinos and Education,* vol. 13, no. 3, 2014, pp. 222–30.

Sinclair, Meredith. "Decolonizing ELA: Confronting Privilege and Oppression in Textual Spaces." *English Journal,* vol. 107, no. 6, 2018, pp. 89–94.

Teaching Tolerance. *Teaching Hard History: American Slavery.* Southern Poverty Law Center, 2018, www.tolerance.org/sites/default/files/2018-02/TT-Teaching-Hard-History-American-Slavery-Report-WEB-February2018.pdf.

Thein, Amanda, and Richard Beach. "Critiquing and Constructing Canons in Middle Grade English and Language Arts Classrooms." *Voices from the Middle,* vol. 21, no. 1, 2013, pp. 10–14.

Thomas, Ebony Elizabeth, and Amy Stornaiuolo. "Restorying the Self: Bending Toward Textual Justice." *Harvard Educational Review,* vol. 86, no. 3, 2016, pp. 313–38.

Vaught, Sabina. *Racism, Public Schooling, and the Entrenchment of White Supremacy: A Critical Race Ethnography.* SUNY P, 2011.

## QUESTIONS | Analyzing Worlds's and Miller's Article

### RHETORICAL SITUATION & CHOICES

1. **Purpose.** Worlds and Miller discuss the novel *Miles Morales: Spider-Man,* but how do they make it clear from the beginning that they're not just writing about this novel? What seems to be their main purpose? Do they seem to have secondary purposes?

2. **Audience.** What features of this article make it clear that they're writing for other scholars, rather than, say, general readers of book reviews, who might also be interested in reading about the role of this novel? How would the authors need to revise their article to appeal to a more general book review audience?

3. **Rhetorical appeals.** How do Worlds and Miller establish their authority on the topic they write about?

4. **Rhetorical appeals.** How do the authors appeal to your sense of logic in presenting examples and details to support their points? What specific details appeal to your sense of logos?

5. **Modes & media.** This particular article does not include any images, although there are many images of Spider Man. Why do you think the authors opted not to integrate images into their article?

### GENRE CONVENTIONS

6. **Elements of the genre.** What is the authors' thesis? How easy was it for you to locate their thesis? What cues do they use in their introduction to indicate that the thesis is there or coming?

7. **Elements of the genre.** Do you have to be familiar with the authors' sources to understand their point? Explain.

8. **Style.** How do the authors use details to explain complex ideas? Are there areas where this is particularly effective?

9. **Design.** Worlds and Miller use subheadings to break the article into chunks. Did you find these helpful? Did you want fewer or more of them? Why or why not? How did these subheadings work on you as a reader? Did they make you want to keep reading? Explain.

10. **Sources.** Note the extensive Works Cited list. Glance through the list of sources and note how many seem to be scholarly sources and how many seem to be other types of sources. Does the use of nonscholarly sources seem appropriate or inappropriate for this article?

# CHECKLIST | Drafting a Peer-Reviewed Journal Article

Are you thinking of drafting a peer-reviewed journal article? Ask yourself the following questions:

## RHETORICAL SITUATION & CHOICES

☐ **Purpose.** What topic have I researched that I could inform other experts about? Have I discovered something about the topic that others like me might find interesting or conducive to their own research? Do I want to persuade readers of something? To effectively persuade readers, what will I need to inform them about?

☐ **Audience.** My readers will be experts on my general topic, but they won't know as much as I do about the aspect I'm writing about. How much background information will they need? What kind of terminology will they expect? How will my readers use the information I present?

☐ **Rhetorical appeals.** How will I establish my authority as a writer? How will I build a case for my conclusions using logic? Will I need to cite sources to establish myself as an expert? What kinds of sources will help me build my case?

☐ **Modes & media.** Can some of the information I present be shown with a chart or graphic? Do I want readers to access my article in print or digitally? Or do I want to make both options available?

## GENRE CONVENTIONS

☐ **Elements of the genre.** How can I make sure my thesis is clear and declarative? How will I refer to my sources? How can I synthesize my sources to show readers how they are in conversation with each other?

☐ **Style.** How can I project an authoritative voice? How much detail will I need to provide so that readers will understand the complexity and validity of my research?

☐ **Design.** How will I use subheadings to present my information in chunks? Will I use images to illustrate points?

☐ **Sources.** Will my readers expect sources to be cited in MLA style, APA style, or another format? Will my readers respect the types of sources I've referred to?

---

## PRACTICE

# Analyzing a Peer-Reviewed Article

Think about a topic you are researching or have already researched for one of your courses. Then find a peer-reviewed article related to that topic. If you need help locating a peer-reviewed article, please refer to Chapter 12, or ask your instructor or librarian for help. Once you've found the article, read through it carefully, considering the rhetorical choices and genre conventions. Then create your own close reading or chart using the article on Miles Morales as a model. After you finish, write a one-page reflection that conveys how the close reading either helped or didn't help you understand the peer-reviewed article.

# Researched Poster Presentations

Many scholarly articles are science reports, and they are usually submitted as written papers. Sometimes, however, they take different forms. In the following section, we will discuss and present a researched poster presentation. But first, here is some background on why and where this kind of scholarly work would be presented.

An academic or scholarly conference is an event in which faculty, scholars, and/or researchers formally gather to share and discuss their research. Usually three or four scholars each get fifteen to thirty minutes to present their research orally in what is called a panel presentation. Many conferences, however, include sessions called "poster sessions," where researchers present their research in the form of a poster rather than by doing an oral presentation. Ten to several hundred scholars set up their posters in a large room, and conference attendees walk around the room, stopping to view and read the posters they are interested in. Researchers usually stand by their poster so they can answer questions. Poster sessions are less formal than panel presentations and give attendees the opportunity to spend as much or as little time as they want lingering over a poster and talking with its creator.

**WRITE**

Would you rather read scholars' work in detail in a peer-reviewed journal article or read and view their poster and ask them questions about it? Why? Can you think of a situation in which your answer might be different? Jot some notes down as an answer to these questions. Then share your answers with a classmate.

Academic or scholarly conferences are organized and hosted by scholarly organizations. Sometimes conferences are organized around a discipline, such as the American Psychological Association's annual convention; other times, conferences attract researchers from a variety of different disciplines who are interested in a particular topic, such as the League for Innovation in the Community College's annual conference on STEM (science, technology, engineering, and math) technology. Many universities have student research conferences on campus that include poster sessions. Scholars who want to present their work, whether as part of a panel or in poster form, must submit a proposal that is peer-reviewed.

## Analyzing Researched Poster Presentations

**Purpose**   Scholars create researched posters to share their research and findings with other scholars and experts and to engage in conversation with others who are doing research in the same field. As with peer-reviewed journal articles, poster creators may be sharing work that is highly original and groundbreaking, or they may be sharing work that is a replication or extension of another researcher's work.

Creators of researched posters aim to inform other researchers about their work and also to persuade others of the value or significance of their research.

Because poster sessions allow attendees to interact with the poster creator, poster creators often have several purposes: to discuss their research with others, hear feedback from other researchers on their methods or findings, or to meet potential collaborators for related projects.

**Audience**   The audience is conference attendees. Generally scholars attend conferences in their discipline or related ones to find out what other researchers are doing. A physicist, for example, would likely attend physics conferences, but may also attend conferences on astronomy or engineering or education, depending on her research interests and employment.

**Rhetorical appeals**   For a scholarly poster, the most significant appeals are ethos and logos. Like authors of peer-reviewed journal articles, poster makers need to establish their credibility by carefully describing their research methods, data collection, analysis strategies, and findings. They must cite sources scrupulously. Logos is important because audiences need to understand the logic of the particular research method that was used and see how the conclusions or findings flow logically from the data analysis.

**Modes & media**   Researched posters use both text and images to present information. Most posters are created on poster board, but depending upon the conference, posters may also be accompanied by sounds, projected images, or other items. A poster displayed at an archaeology conference, for example, could be accompanied by a vase that was excavated at the site discussed on the poster. A poster can also be presented digitally at a conference. Digital posters allow for the inclusion of both audio and video files and can be viewed by people who are not able to attend the conference.

**Elements of the genre**   Researched, scholarly posters are characterized by the following:

- *They are based on original research.* Poster makers usually present their own original research. Their posters convey information about the research question or topic they studied, the research methods they used, the data they collected, how they analyzed that data, and the conclusions they drew from the data.

- *They are peer-reviewed at the proposal level.* Conferences typically require poster presenters to submit a proposal in which they summarize the research for their poster. Scholars determine whether the proposed poster is relevant to the conference and whether the research described is ethical, in line with the scientific method, and significant.

- *They are concise.* Because all the information must be contained on the poster and easily read by people standing several feet away, text must be concise and to the point.

- *They are informative and eye-catching.* To attract attention from attendees who might be wandering around the room, posters usually include color and visuals, including charts and graphs, which can be easily viewed from several feet away.

- *They are visually organized.* Information is presented in chunks, such as "methods" and "discussion," set off from other chunks with a combination of white space, headings, boxes, borders, and color.

**Style**  Following are some stylistic elements of researched, scholarly posters:

- *They feature a descriptive title.* The title needs to immediately convey the topic and significance of the research presented in the poster.
- *They present concise and precise data.* Research and scholarship rely on precision, so posters give specific amounts, durations, chemical names, and so forth, rather than generalizations and abstractions.
- *They use simple, clear language.* Posters must clearly convey precise and accurate information, so they do not use figurative language.

**Design**  Scholarly posters presented at conferences are characterized by the following:

- *They are large.* Some posters are sturdy trifold objects that can stand on a table, if the conference provides one. Some conferences provide hanging space for posters that are flat. In either case, posters are large, usually between two to three feet by five to eight feet.
- *They include text and images.* Posters historically featured computer-printed text and images glued onto poster board; more commonly these days, the text and images are created using a template and then printed on paper the size of the finished poster.
- *They are made to be viewed from a distance.* Because posters are meant to be seen from several feet away, they usually involve large text, images, and colors that contrast for easy reading.

**Sources**  Creators of researched, scholarly posters cite their sources carefully, providing bibliographies of sources cited. Sometimes sources are cited directly in the text of the poster or listed at the bottom of the poster. Other times, an accompanying bibliography might be handed out at the session.

# Guided Reading | Researched Poster Presentation

Ricky Martinez, Vinson Turco, and Ashleigh Nakata are students at Metropolitan State University of Denver. MSU holds an annual undergraduate research conference in which Martinez, Turco, and Nakata participated in a poster session. This poster represents research that they conducted on bird habitats.

## Ricky Martinez, Vinson Turco, and Ashleigh Nakata (STUDENTS),
*Reforested Pastures and Plantations as Valuable Habitat for Birds in Costa Rica*

---

### RHETORICAL SITUATION & CHOICES

**What are the ▶ composers, students Ricky Martinez et al., doing?**

Credit: Christy Carello.

### GENRE CONVENTIONS

**How do I know ▶ that this is a researched science report?**

**ELEMENTS OF THE GENRE**

**Based on original research:** The poster presents original research the creators conducted.

**Peer-reviewed at the proposal level:** The MSU Denver Undergraduate Research Conference requires that all presenters submit an abstract several months before the conference; abstracts are peer-reviewed by a committee.

**Concise:** Information is conveyed directly, without any extraneous detail. For instance, the poster says, "Surveys conducted of breeding bird populations have shown significant declines in the abundance of migratory song birds."

## RHETORICAL SITUATION & CHOICES

### PURPOSE
The main purpose of the poster creators is to share what happened when they tested their hypothesis about bird populations in different climates.

### AUDIENCE
The poster creators presented their poster at Metropolitan State University of Denver's Undergraduate Research Conference, so their audience was undergraduate researchers, mostly in the sciences but some from other disciplines.

### RHETORICAL APPEALS
The poster creators carefully articulated their methods and results to come across as credible and develop their **ethos.** The discussion relies on logic to explain their results, appealing to **logos.**

### MODES & MEDIA
**Mode = written and visual:** The poster includes both text and images.

**Medium = print:** The poster was displayed as a professionally printed object that was 36" high and 48" wide.

## GENRE CONVENTIONS

### STYLE
The poster's title clearly indicates the research the poster reports. The poster uses precise language, such as "There were significantly more resident birds (3.365 +/− 1.727) than migratory birds (1.471 +/− 0.943) for species richness for all three treatment groups ($F = 23.686$, $df = 1$, $p = 7.94e{-}06$)."

**Visually organized:** The poster uses color, image, and white space to capture viewers' attention and help them understand how information is organized.

### DESIGN
The poster is carefully designed to be readable from several feet away. The poster's creators used a PowerPoint template to create the poster. Chunks of information are clearly defined through the use of boxes and headings.

### SOURCES
The poster includes citations.

**RHETORICAL SITUATION & CHOICES**

1. **Purpose.** Does the title of the poster make you aware of the purpose of the research that was conducted? If so, how? If not, why not?

2. **Purpose.** One purpose of the poster is to inform viewers/readers about the research the creators did on bird habits. What do you think they are trying to persuade you of?

3. **Audience.** What features of the poster make it clear that the authors anticipated an audience of scientists?

4. **Rhetorical appeals.** How do the poster creators establish their credibility?

5. **Modes & media.** If this poster presentation were being revised into a peer-reviewed journal article, which of the images would you recommend including in the article and why?

**GENRES CONVENTIONS**

6. **Elements of the genre.** Imagine this poster being 36 inches tall by 48 inches wide and seeing it from several feet away. Would the layout, color, and images catch your attention? How is the color scheme of the poster appropriate or inappropriate for the subject of the poster?

7. **Style.** How specific and precise is the "methods" section of the poster? Based on the description of the methods used, do you get a clear sense of what the researchers actually did?

8. **Style.** Can you find any text in the poster that could have been expressed more concisely?

9. **Design.** How do the images in the poster help you understand the information?

10. **Sources.** How do the sources cited add to or detract from the creators' ethos?

# CHECKLIST | Drafting a Researched Poster Presentation

Are you thinking of composing a researched science report in poster form? Ask yourself the following questions:

**RHETORICAL SITUATION & CHOICES**

☐ **Purpose.** What topic have I researched that I could tell others about? How can I persuade others of the significance of my research?

☐ **Audience.** Considering that I have limited words and space on a poster, what are the key ideas I need to communicate to my audience in order to capture their interest? What will they already know about my topic? What will I need to explain to them?

**GENRE CONVENTIONS**

☐ **Elements of the genre.** How can I present my research concisely without leaving out important details? How can I title my poster to efficiently convey its topic? How can I visually organize the information on my poster?

☐ **Style.** How can I make my title descriptive and specific? How can I express the information I want to share as accurately as possible? How can I be as concise as possible?

- ☐ **Rhetorical appeals.** How can I establish myself as a credible researcher? How can I make the logical connections between my research and findings clear?
- ☐ **Modes & media.** What kinds of images can I use? How can I present some of my information through charts and graphs?
- ☐ **Design.** What images can I use to help readers/viewers understand the information I am presenting? How can I use color to catch readers'/viewers' attention and help them make sense of the information I am presenting? Which information can I present with charts and graphs?
- ☐ **Sources.** What sources did I use? Will my readers expect sources to be cited in MLA style, APA style, or another format? Will my readers respect the types of sources I've referred to?

---

**PRACTICE**

## Remixing Your Research

Think about a research project you recently completed. If you don't have one handy, then find a friend's project or find something on the web. Consider how you might remix this project into a poster. What kinds of images would you include? What might you use for a descriptive and attention-getting title? Sketch out on paper or on the computer a layout for a poster that would present the information in the original project. Show this to a classmate and get feedback on your concept. Incorporate that feedback as you create the actual poster. Your finished poster can be digital or print.

---

# Rhetorical Analyses

A rhetorical analysis is an evaluation of a particular work. This work might be a piece of literature, a film, an essay, an advertisement, a symphony, or a sculpture. Essentially, the writer does a close reading of the piece and then breaks it down to more fully understand what is being communicated and how. The writer then explains the composer's central points and provides their own evaluation of whether the composer's argument was or was not successful.

Rhetorical analyses are commonly assigned in academia. In literature classes, you often undertake a literary analysis to gain a deeper understanding of literary elements.

In a composition class, you might be assigned to read an argumentative essay and then analyze how the writer supports their position in order to help you make your own arguments. In a film studies class, you might be assigned to write a critical analysis of a documentary film to see how a director mediates truth.

The ultimate purpose of a rhetorical analysis is to evaluate and understand how another writer/artist/composer created meaning.

## Analyzing Rhetorical Analyses

WRITE
—————
What types of rhetorical analyses do you enjoy reading, viewing, or listening to? Have you ever composed one outside the classroom (for example, have you posted a review of a business on a website like Yelp)? If so, what was it, and what was your purpose? Make a two columned list. In one column, include the types of analyses you enjoy reading, viewing, or listening to, and in the other column, include all the analyses you've composed.

**Purpose**   Writers critique a work to provide a deeper understanding of how a piece works and to evaluate it. Their purpose is to take a stance on the work and provide evidence from the work to support that stance.

**Audience**   When a rhetorical analysis is written for a school assignment, the audience is usually the teacher and the secondary audience might be peers in the class if they are going to read or peer-review the piece. A rhetorical analysis of a literary work published in a literary journal is written for an audience of scholars who want to understand more about that particular work.

**Rhetorical appeals**   Writers of rhetorical analyses rely on ethos and logos to make their points. Since a rhetorical analysis is essentially an argument, writers must first establish ethos to gain the reader's trust. For example, to indicate their expertise, they would use terminology associated with the genre they're evaluating. Someone analyzing a poem would use terms such as *meter* and *tone*, while someone analyzing a scientific report might use terms such as *methodology* and *materials*. Writers also rely on logos, supporting their claims with evidence from the text they're analyzing.

**Modes & media**   Rhetorical analyses are most often published as text. When they're part of an academic assignment, they usually must be submitted as written words. They might have visual elements combined with the text if appropriate. For example, if you were analyzing a painting, you might include small visuals that illustrate the part of the painting you are discussing. A rhetorical analysis could also use the mode of audio. The evaluation and analysis could be delivered on the radio as part of a news program or a podcast. Rhetorical analyses are available in both print and digital formats.

**Elements of the genre**   Rhetorical analyses use the following conventions:

- *Composers introduce the work they're analyzing.* Since a rhetorical analysis focuses on a particular piece of literature, a film, or something else, the writer always introduces that work to the reader. Sometimes this can be done through the title of the analysis. In addition, an introductory paragraph usually provides the reader with information about the work. If the rhetorical analysis is about a work of art, the writer would provide the reader with the title of the artwork, the name of the artist, the year it was created, and its medium.

- *Composers provide a summary or description of the work.* The summary is usually brief and provides only the necessary information a reader needs to understand the evaluation.

- *Composers identify the work's central point or thesis.* What is the central point that the artist, writer, or composer of the piece being analyzed makes? Since an analysis evaluates the success of the piece's argument, it's important to clearly state what the writer believes the composer is attempting to achieve. Besides identifying a central claim, the writer also examines the evidence provided to support this claim.

- *Composers make a clear evaluative claim.* The writer takes a position about they work being analyzed. It's clear what the writer thinks about the work that is being analyzed. The writer doesn't just restate the work's central point, but judges or evaluates it.

- *Composers provide evidence from the work to support claims.* Assertions are supported by specific evidence from the text, artwork, or piece being examined.

**Style**   Authors of rhetorical analyses choose titles for their work that make their position clear for readers right away. They also use language that shows their perspective on the piece they are evaluating.

**Design**   Rhetorical analysis papers are formatted like most other academic papers, as text-based essays or researched arguments that follow a specific documentation style, such as MLA, APA, or *Chicago Manual of Style*. Usually these papers have one-inch margins, an introductory paragraph, supporting body paragraphs, a concluding paragraph, and a list of citations because an analysis always draws on at least one other work (the piece being analyzed) and often other sources as well.

**Sources**   Writers of rhetorical analyses provide the following for their readers:

- *Specific examples from the text.* The main source of a rhetorical analysis is the text being analyzed. Sometimes writers include outside research, if appropriate, to help support their claims. For example, in doing a literary analysis, writers might include some analyses by other literary critics that help support their claims about the work.

- *Documentation of the piece they're analyzing.* The piece being analyzed, plus any outside sources, are included in a Works Cited list at the end of the analysis as well as in parenthetical citations in the body of the essay.

## Guided Reading | Rhetorical Analysis

Student Ren Yoshida was given an assignment to find an advertisement on a topic that interests him. He was asked to then compose a rhetorical analysis of that ad. In his analysis, Yoshida responds to a coffee ad created for a company called Equal Exchange. Before he wrote his analysis, he did a close reading of the ad and annotated it. Take a look at the annotated version of the ad below before you read Yoshida's analysis.

▶ **ANNOTATED ADVERTISEMENT**

**Equal Exchange, "Empowering Farmers."** Annotations by Ren Yoshida, student.

What does "Equal Exchange" mean? What is being exchanged? Is the exchange truly "equal"?

Who is "Empowering Farmers"? Why is "Empowering" presented in a cursive font? Maybe to contrast the "FARMERS," in sturdy all capital letters?

Straightforward design and not much text.

The central image is outstretched hands. Is she giving a gift? Inviting a partnership?

Model's hands held in a heart shape, filled with coffee beans. Angle makes her hands large.

Coffee beans are red, earthy.

Ad text has positive words: consumers choose, join, empower, farmers stay, care, farm, support, plan.

What is the "network"?

How would I know whether buying this coffee will help farmers stay on their land?

# Ren Yoshida (STUDENT), *Sometimes a Cup of Coffee Is Just a Cup of Coffee*

**RHETORICAL SITUATION & CHOICES**

**GENRE CONVENTIONS**

## PURPOSE
Yoshida takes an evaluative stance regarding the advertisement. He wants to show readers that while the ad succeeds on an emotional level, it fails on a logical level.

## AUDIENCE
Since the rhetorical analysis was a response to an assignment in class (to analyze an advertisement), Yoshida's audience is his instructor and peers (unless he chooses to share his work outside the classroom).

## RHETORICAL APPEALS
Yoshida establishes his ethos by using specific elements found in advertising. This shows that he is familiar with the genre's conventions, such as by discussing the ad's design elements. He also relies on logos to make his case, providing specific examples from the ad as support for his assertions.

◀ What is the composer, Ren Yoshida, doing?

How do I know that this ▶ is a rhetorical analysis?

**English 101**

Ren Yoshida
Professor Marcotte
4 November 2019

### Sometimes a Cup of Coffee Is Just a Cup of Coffee

A farmer, her hardworking hands full of coffee beans, reaches out from an Equal Exchange advertisement (Equal Exchange). The hands, in the shape of a heart, offer to consumers the fruit of the farmer's labor. The ad's message is straightforward: in choosing Equal Exchange, consumers become global citizens, partnering with farmers to help save the planet. Suddenly, a cup of coffee is more than just a morning ritual; a cup of coffee is a moral choice that empowers both consumers and farmers. This simple exchange appeals to a consumer's desire to be a good person—to protect the environment and do the right thing. Yet the ad is more complicated than it first seems, and its design raises some logical questions about such an exchange. Although the ad works successfully on an emotional level, it is less successful on a logical level because of its promise for an equal exchange between consumers and farmers.

The focus of the ad is a farmer, Jesus Choqueheranca de Quevero, and, more specifically, her outstretched, cupped hands. Her hands are full of red, raw coffee, her life's work. The ad successfully appeals to consumers' emotions, assuming they will find the farmer's welcoming face and hands, caked with dirt, more appealing than startling statistics about the state of the environment or the number of farmers who lose their land each year. It seems almost rude not to accept the farmer's generous offering since we know her name and, as the ad implies, have the choice to "empower" her. In fact, how can a consumer resist helping the farmer "[c]are for the environment" and "[p]lan for the future," when it is a simple matter of choosing the right coffee? The ad sends the message that our future is a global future in which producers and consumers are bound together.

First impressions play a major role in the success of an advertisement. Consumers are pulled toward a product, or pushed away, by an ad's initial visual and emotional appeal.

## ELEMENTS OF THE GENRE
- In the opening sentence, Yoshida **introduces the advertisement** and its creator, The Equal Exchange.
- Yoshida's opening paragraph **provides a summary and description** of the advertisement. He gives us details about the ad, such as the hands being "in the shape of a heart."
- At the end of his opening paragraph, Yoshida **makes a clear evaluative claim:** "Although the ad works successfully on an emotional level, it is less successful on a logical level because of its promise for an equal exchange between consumers and farmers."
- Throughout the analysis, Yoshida **provides evidence to support his claims.** He discusses the farmer's hands, uses pieces of text from the ad, and incorporates elements of the ad's design.

*(Continues on next page)*

**Mode = text:** While Yoshida might have included some specific screenshots from the ad to illustrate his point visually, he instead relies on just text to make his points.
**Medium = print:** This assignment was submitted in print form.

Here, the intended audience is busy people, so the ad tries to catch viewers' attention and make a strong impression immediately. Yet with a second or third viewing, consumers might start to ask some logical questions about Equal Exchange before buying their morning coffee. Although the farmer extends her heart-shaped hands to consumers, they are not actually buying a cup of coffee or the raw coffee directly from her. In reality, consumers are buying from Equal Exchange, even if the ad substitutes the more positive word *choose* for *buy*. Furthermore, consumers aren't actually empowering the farmer; they are joining "a network that empowers farmers." The idea of a network makes a simple transaction more complicated. How do consumers know their money helps farmers "[s]tay on their land" and "[p]lan for the future" as the ad promises? They don't.

The ad's design elements raise questions about the use of the key terms *equal exchange* and *empowering farmers*. The Equal Exchange logo suggests symmetry and equality, with two red arrows facing each other, but the words of the logo appear almost like an eye exam poster, with each line decreasing in font size and clarity. The words *fairly traded* are tiny. Below the logo, the words *empowering farmers* are presented in contradictory fonts. *Empowering* is written in a flowing, cursive font, almost the opposite of what might be considered empowering, whereas *farmers* is written in a plain, sturdy font.

The ad's varying fonts communicate differently and make it hard to know exactly what is being exchanged and who is becoming empowered.

What is being exchanged? The logic of the ad suggests that consumers will improve the future by choosing Equal Exchange. The first exchange is economic: consumers give one thing—dollars—and receive something in return—a cup of coffee—and the farmer stays on her land. The second exchange is more complicated because it involves a moral exchange. The ad suggests that if consumers don't choose "fairly traded" products, farmers will be forced off their land and the environment destroyed. This exchange, when put into motion by consumers choosing to purchase products not "fairly traded," has negative consequences for both consumers and farmers. The message of the ad is that the actual exchange taking place is not economic but moral; after all, nothing is being bought, only chosen. Yet the logic of this exchange quickly falls apart. Consumers aren't empowered to become global citizens simply by choosing Equal Exchange, and farmers aren't empowered to plan for the future by consumers' choices. And even if all this empowerment magically happened, there is nothing equal about such an exchange.

Yoshida's title "Sometimes a Cup of Coffee Is Just a Cup of Coffee" indicates **his position.** Yoshida uses **language that illustrates judgment.** He uses words like *successful* and *suggests.*

Straightforward academic essay and research paper format: text organized into paragraphs with source citations.

Advertisements are themselves about empowerment—encouraging viewers to believe they can become someone or do something by identifying, emotionally or logically, with a product. In the Equal Exchange ad, consumers are emotionally persuaded to identify with a farmer whose face is not easily forgotten and whose heart-shaped hands hold a collective future. On a logical level, though, the ad raises questions because empowerment, although a good concept to choose, is not easily or equally exchanged. Sometimes a cup of coffee is just a cup of coffee.

————

Work Cited

Equal Exchange. Advertisement. Equal Exchange. Viroqua
   Food Co-Op, www.viroquafood.coop/hs-fs/hub/62289/file
   -14957146-jpg/images/fair_trade.jpg?width=320&height=
   312&name=fair_trade.jpg, n.d. Web. 14 Oct. 2019.

**SOURCES**
Using the MLA style of documentation, the author cites his source in the body of the text and at the end under a Work Cited heading.

## QUESTIONS | Analyzing Yoshida's Rhetorical Analysis

**RHETORICAL SITUATION & CHOICES**

1. **Purpose.** What stance does Yoshida take regarding the advertisement? Is his claim evaluative? Why or why not?

2. **Purpose.** How does Yoshida provide his audience with a deeper understanding of how the advertisement is constructed and its effectiveness?

3. **Audience.** Even though this piece was written for a class assignment, and thus his audience are his teacher and peers, this analysis might have other audiences. Who might they be? Why?

4. **Rhetorical appeals.** How does Yoshida establish his ethos? Do you find him to be a credible writer? Why or why not?

5. **Modes & media.** How would the piece be stronger if Yoshida had included visuals of the ad throughout? Which visuals might he have included?

**GENRE CONVENTIONS**

6. **Elements of the genre.** How effective is Yoshida in presenting a balance of summary and evaluation? Are there places where you wanted more summary? More evaluation?

7. **Style.** How does Yoshida use diction to show that his writing is evaluative? Use specific examples from the analysis.

8. **Style.** How does Yoshida's title prepare you for his analysis? Is the title aligned with his purpose? Why or why not?

9. **Design.** Yoshida has clearly designed this piece as an essay for a class assignment. Consider your response to question 3 on audience. How would he need to alter the design to address a different audience?

10. **Sources.** How effective is Yoshida in providing evidence from the text? Are there places where he might have used more evidence? If so, where? What types of evidence?

## CHECKLIST | Drafting a Rhetorical Analysis

Are you thinking of writing a rhetorical analysis? Ask yourself the following questions:

### RHETORICAL SITUATION & CHOICES

☐ **Purpose.** What is my central evaluative claim I want to make? What is it that I want to understand about the piece I'm analyzing?

☐ **Audience.** What do I hope my audience learns from this piece? Have I described the piece enough for an audience that is unfamiliar with what I'm analyzing?

☐ **Rhetorical appeals.** Have I established my ethos so that my reader trusts my judgments? Have I used terminology that shows I'm familiar with the genre I'm analyzing? Is my use of logos evident? Have I used enough evidence to build my case?

☐ **Modes & media.** Is text the only way to present my analysis? How would it be strengthened by including audio? Visuals? Are there advantages to presenting this digitally? Print?

### GENRE CONVENTIONS

☐ **Elements of the genre.** Have I properly introduced the work being analyzed? Have I provided a brief summary? Have I examined the writer/composer's central claim? Have I presented my own clear evaluative claim?

☐ **Style.** Does my title indicate the position I'm taking? Am I using language throughout that indicates how I feel about the work I'm evaluating?

☐ **Design.** Have I formatted this to meet the assignment? Have I used proper essay structure? Do I have a clear introductory and concluding paragraph?

☐ **Sources.** Have I included enough evidence from the work to support my claims? Have I properly cited my information? Have I included a Works Cited page for any of the sources used?

---

### PRACTICE

# Analyzing the Work of Others

Is there a film you watched recently that was particularly interesting or memorable? Or perhaps a new album has come out by your favorite artist? Maybe you are mesmerized by a particular ad or a series of tweets? Choose something that captivates you and read/watch/listen to it several times very closely. What do you notice about the work upon close examination? Take notes about what the composer's central point is and how they achieve it, perhaps breaking the piece into its parts. Then draft a rhetorical analysis in which you take a clear stance about the work you're evaluating. Be sure to include specific evidence from the original work.

# Literacy Narratives

A literacy narrative tells a story of remembering. In this sense, it is similar to a memoir. Like memoirists, when the writers of literacy narratives tell their own stories, they relate events and also analyze how these events have shaped their identities. However, there is an important difference between the memoir and the literacy narrative: The writers of literacy narratives tell a story specifically about how they learned to read and/or write.

You may be familiar with literacy narratives already; many memoirs include sections about how the authors learned to read or write or important moments in the development of their literacy. Examples include Jimmy Santiago Baca's *Working in the Dark* and Eudora Welty's *One Writer's Beginnings*. Other memoirs focus more on the development of the author's literacy, such as Stephen King's *On Writing* and Anne Lamott's *Bird by Bird*. Sometimes memoirists will use the story of the development of their reading and writing as a context in which other stories are woven, as Azar Nafisi does in *Reading Lolita in Tehran: A Memoir in Books*, in which she tells the story of a secret women's book group in Iran and how the books they read reflected and affected the lives of the women in the group.

**WRITE**

What was the first book (or sentence or word) you read? What was the context? Where were you, and who was present? What was the experience like for you? Put your pen to paper and freewrite for ten minutes about this experience.

## Analyzing Literacy Narratives

**Purpose**   People write literacy narratives because their formative experiences with reading and writing are important to them; they want to share their stories with others, especially if their literacy histories involve obstacles or challenges. Some may also want to make an argument about the importance of literacy.

**Audience**   Literacy narratives are often written in composition classes and other college courses. Instructors assign this genre to help students understand what influences their speaking, reading, and writing. In this case, a writer's main audience is their instructor and classmates. Outside the classroom, writers create literacy narratives to help educators, librarians, and other people involved in literacy fields better understand how literacy practices and histories manifest themselves in people's lives. (For examples of narratives in various media—text, audio, and video—see the Digital Archive of Literacy Narratives at Ohio State University.)

Literacy narratives are often published for a wider, popular audience; they may appear in a magazine or journal, or as part of a larger collection of essays, as is the case for the narrative that appears later in this section (the excerpt from Richard Rodriguez's *Hunger of Memory* on p. 158).

**Rhetorical appeals**   Writers of literacy narratives use direct language and real details from their lives to establish credibility (ethos). They also make logical connections (logos) between their narratives and the larger issues of literacy; often these authors write to emphasize and argue about the importance of literacy, which makes the use of logos especially important.

**Modes & media**   Many writers of literacy narratives use the traditional essay or book form; for example, Helen Keller includes her memoir of learning to understand Braille in her autobiography, *The Story of My Life*. Other literacy narratives appear on the internet as blog entries or YouTube videos, or are presented in online archives.

**Elements of the genre**   Literacy narratives can take the form of memoirs, in which writers reflect on moments in their lives that show how reading and writing have affected their experiences and sense of self. Authors of literacy narratives convey their experiences, framing their interactions with the world in terms of reading and writing. They also use personal anecdotes and autobiographical details to re-create their experiences for the reader.

Like memoirs, most literacy narratives are written in the first person. Authors of literacy narratives tell stories not just for the sake of recounting events; rather, their goal is for the narrative to culminate in a larger idea or theme. Writers also use literary elements such as setting, character development, dialogue, vivid descriptions and details, symbols, and metaphors.

**Style**   Authors use detail to re-create their literacy experiences for readers. For example, in her literacy narrative, Helen Keller shows readers through specific examples what it was like to be a blind and deaf child.

> **EXCERPT FROM A LITERACY NARRATIVE**
>
> My aunt made me a big doll out of towels. It was the most comical, shapeless thing, this improvised doll, with no nose, mouth, ears or eyes—nothing that even the imagination of a child could convert into a face. Curiously enough, the absence of eyes struck me more than all the other defects put together. I pointed this out to everybody with provoking persistency, but no one seemed equal to the task of providing the doll with eyes. A bright idea, however, shot into my mind, and the problem was solved. I tumbled off the seat and searched under it until I found my aunt's cape, which was trimmed with large beads. I pulled two beads off and indicated to her that I wanted her to sew them on my doll. She raised my hand to her eyes in a questioning way, and I nodded energetically. The beads were sewed in the right place and I could not contain myself for joy.
>
> **Helen Keller,** from *The Story of My Life*

Most authors of this genre take literacy seriously, which is why they want to write about it and share their experiences with readers; however, each author of a literacy narrative conveys their story in a unique voice. Keller's voice emphasizes that, in many ways, she was just like any other child, playing with dolls. Her matter-of-fact tone helps readers identify with and understand her childhood experiences.

**Design**   The literacy narrative usually takes an essay format: It has an introduction, body paragraphs, and a conclusion. However, literacy narratives can take different forms, including audio essay and documentary. In their written form, literacy narratives use typography to emphasize certain points or language. For example, in Rodriguez's excerpt, Spanish words are in italics to call attention to them.

**Sources**   Like print and graphic memoirs, literacy narratives seldom cite outside sources because the source of information is almost always just the writer's memories of their own life.

## Guided Reading  |  Literacy Narrative

Richard Rodriguez's *Hunger of Memory* is a collection of autobiographical essays. In the following excerpt, which he calls a memoir and which is also a literacy narrative (genres sometimes overlap), Rodriguez focuses on the power of language as he explores his childhood experiences in a bilingual world. He relates the struggles he faced living in between a Spanish-speaking world and an English-speaking world.

The notes in the margins point out Rodriguez's goals as a writer and his strategies for connecting with his readers. They also show how he works with the genre's conventions to tell a compelling story about literacy.

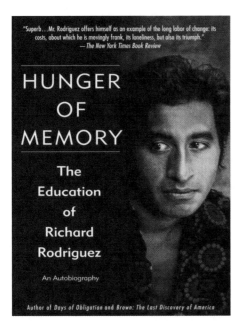

◄ **BOOK COVER**
Richard Rodriguez on the cover of his autobiography.

# Richard Rodriguez, From *Hunger of Memory: The Education of Richard Rodriguez*

| RHETORICAL SITUATION & CHOICES | | GENRE CONVENTIONS | |
|---|---|---|---|

**◄ What is the composer, Richard Rodriguez, doing?**

**How do I know that this ► is a literacy narrative?**

## PURPOSE
Rodriguez aims to share the story of how he came to speak both English and Spanish.

## AUDIENCE
The author knows his primary readers care about language and identity. They are bilingual or native English speakers interested in themes of education, family, and coming-of-age.

## RHETORICAL APPEALS
Rodriguez begins with a brief story about his parents being willing to do anything for their children, an appeal to pathos. The teachers' connecting of Rodriguez's behavior to his lack of English is an example of logos.

## MODES & MEDIA
**Mode = written:**
This literacy narrative is written. Because Rodriguez's topic is language, his choice to convey his story in written words makes sense. If he were to adapt this narrative using digital technology, he might embed audio so his readers could hear what he experienced.

**Medium = print:**
Rodriguez's book is intended to be read in hard-copy format or as an e-book. In either case, it's intended

Three months. Five. Half a year passed. Unsmiling, ever watchful, my teachers noted my silence. They began to connect my behavior with the difficult progress my older sister and brother were making. Until one Saturday morning three nuns arrived at the house to talk to our parents. Stiffly, they sat on the blue living room sofa. From the doorway of another room, spying the visitors, I noted the incongruity— the clash of two worlds, the faces and voices of school intruding upon the familiar setting of home. I overheard one voice gently wondering, "Do your children speak only Spanish at home, Mrs. Rodriguez?" While another voice added, "That Richard especially seems so timid and shy."

*That Rich-heard!*

With great tact the visitors continued, "Is it possible for you and your husband to encourage your children to practice their English when they are home?" Of course, my parents complied. What would they not do for their children's well-being? And how could they have questioned the Church's authority which those women represented? In an instant, they agreed to give up the language (the sounds) that had revealed and accentuated our family's closeness.

The moment after the visitors left, the change was observed. "*Ahora*, speak to us *en inglés*," my father and mother united to tell us.

At first, it seemed a kind of game. After dinner each night, the family gathered to practice "our" English. (It was still then *inglés*, a language foreign to us, so we felt drawn as strangers to it.) Laughing, we would try to define words we could not pronounce. We played with strange English sounds, often over-anglicizing our pronunciations. And we filled the smiling gaps of our sentences with familiar Spanish sounds. But that was cheating, somebody shouted. Everyone laughed. In school, meanwhile, like my brother and sister, I was required to attend a daily tutoring session. I needed a full year of special attention. I also needed my teachers to keep my attention from straying in class by calling out, Rich-heard— their English voices slowly prying loose my ties to my other name, its three notes, Ri-car-do. Most of all I needed to hear my mother and father speak to me in a moment of seriousness in broken—suddenly heartbreaking—English. The scene was

## ELEMENTS OF THE GENRE
This is an **autobiographical account about literacy**. Rodriguez shares childhood experiences of learning to speak, read, and write.

He uses **anecdotes** to advance a central idea; for example, with the brief, personal story in paragraph 1, Rodriguez prepares readers for his ideas about language and identity and for his argument about bilingual education.

He writes in the **first person** and **describes settings** to connect readers with his experience. He contrasts his home setting with his classroom (where he is an outsider) to emphasize the difference in his private and public encounters with literacy.

## STYLE
Rodriguez **uses rich detail** to re-create his experience for readers. Because his essay centers on how he hears language, he focuses on bringing the **dialogue** alive and uses phonetic spelling so that readers hear exactly what he hears.

His **tone and voice reflect his personality**

to be read from beginning to end, one page at a time, unlike online literacy narratives, which can be read in a nonlinear fashion.

inevitable: One Saturday morning I entered the kitchen where my parents were talking in Spanish. I did not realize that they were talking in Spanish, however, until at the moment they saw me, I heard their voices change to speak English. Those gringo sounds they uttered startled me. Pushed me away. In that moment of trivial misunderstanding and profound insight, I felt my throat twisted by unsounded grief. I turned quickly and left the room. But I had no place to escape to with Spanish. (The spell was broken.) My brother and sisters were speaking English in another part of the house.

Again and again in the days following, increasingly angry, I was obliged to hear my mother and father: "*Speak to us en inglés*" (Speak). Only then did I determine to learn classroom English. Weeks afterward, it happened: One day in school I raised my hand to volunteer an answer. I spoke out in a loud voice. And I did not think it remarkable when the entire class understood. That day, I moved very far from the disadvantaged child I had been only days earlier. The belief, the calming assurance that I belonged in public, had at last taken hold.

and speech. He quotes the nuns to emphasize how they enunciate and "Americanize" words.

**DESIGN**
Rodriguez uses italics to highlight Spanish and English words, and also to emphasize certain passages and sounds ("*That Rich-heard!*").

**SOURCES**
Rodriguez does not cite outside sources because he is the source of his story.

Credit: From Hunger of Memory: The Education of Richard Rodriguez by Richard Rodriguez.
Reprinted by permission of David R. Godine, Publisher, Inc.
Copyright © 1982 by Richard Rodriguez.

## QUESTIONS | Analyzing Rodriguez's Literacy Narrative

### RHETORICAL SITUATION & CHOICES

1. **Purpose.** Rodriguez not only tells a story about his experiences with language but also makes an argument regarding bilingual education. What is his argument? How persuasive is he?

2. **Purpose.** Reread the final paragraph of the essay. Why do you think Rodriguez chose to conclude this way?

3. **Audience.** What techniques does Rodriguez use to connect with his audience? Is an audience that has experienced bilingual education his target audience? Why or why not?

4. **Rhetorical appeals.** How does Rodriguez develop his ethos as someone who speaks about education with authority? How does his phonetic spelling of "Rich-heard" contribute to the pathos of the piece?

### GENRE CONVENTIONS

6. **Elements of the genre.** What are some similarities between Rodriguez's literacy narrative and memoirs that you may be familiar with (e.g., see Alison Bechdel's graphic memoir on p. 268)?

7. **Style.** Given that writers of literacy narratives tell stories about how they learned to speak, read, or write, why might many of them include dialogue? What role does dialogue play in Rodriguez's literacy narrative?

8. **Style.** Rodriguez includes some Spanish words in his narrative. How do the Spanish words contribute to the essay's effect?

9. **Design.** Rodriguez italicizes bits of dialogue. What do you think is his purpose for doing so?

**RHETORICAL SITUATION & CHOICES**

5. **Modes & media.** Imagine Rodriguez's literacy narrative as a digital text online. Which words of the excerpt could be linked to other websites? For example, perhaps the word "Rich-heard" could be linked to a YouTube video in which someone says the name as Rodriguez's family would say it; this might emphasize how strange the Americanized pronunciation sounded to Rodriguez.

**GENRE CONVENTIONS**

10. **Sources.** The source for this literacy narrative excerpt is Rodriguez's own memory. Do you think a narrative written by one of the nuns would differ significantly from Rodriguez's? Why or why not?

## CHECKLIST | Drafting a Literacy Narrative

Are you thinking of writing about how you learned to speak, read, and write? Ask yourself the following questions:

**RHETORICAL SITUATION & CHOICES**

☐ **Purpose.** What specific moment in my life as a reader or writer do I want to write about? Why? What questions do I have about that moment? How might I interpret that moment? What insights do I want to share with others? How did that moment shape me as a reader or writer?

☐ **Audience.** How would I describe my readers? Why will my experience with reading or writing matter to my readers? What do I want them to get out of my story? How will I reach them?

☐ **Rhetorical appeals.** How will I establish my authority as a writer? How reliable will I be as a narrator? To what extent will I appeal to my readers' emotions? To what extent will I rely on logic to support my interpretations of my experiences?

☐ **Modes & media.** Do I want readers to experience my story in written, audio, or visual form? Do I want my literacy narrative to be print, electronic, or presented face-to-face?

**GENRE CONVENTIONS**

☐ **Elements of the genre.** I'm writing about my own life: How will I keep my writing true and accurate? How much will I disclose about myself (and others) in my literacy memoir? Will I write in the first person? What anecdotes will I use to tell the story of myself as a reader or writer, and why? Also, what literary elements might I use? For example, will I use dialogue (as Rodriguez does) or a metaphor to help readers compare my experience to something else?

☐ **Style.** What tone will I take in my writing? Will my literacy narrative be serious or funny? Academic or down-to-earth? What kind of language will I use? How much detail will I include?

☐ **Design.** What format will my literacy narrative take? Do I want to compose a standard literacy narrative, focusing on words, or do I want to create a graphic literacy narrative that includes illustrations?

☐ **Sources.** What memories will I draw on? Will I need to check my story with others from my life, or will I rely on my own recollections and interpretations?

# Drawing on Memory & Experience

Think of a single moment from your early life, one that has to do with how you read, see, and experience the world through language. Or perhaps you want to draw on a recent experience that has shaped you in terms of language, reading, and writing. Freewrite about the experience and how it has shaped your attitudes toward language. Draft a narrative in which you tell the story of your experience; be sure to make specific points about how it shaped you as a reader, writer, and/or speaker. Include anecdotes, details, and quotations from conversations, as Rodriguez does.

# Digital Stories

Digital stories are short narratives composed with digital tools. They usually include a combination of digital images, recorded narration, video clips, text, and/or music. Much like other types of stories, digital stories tend to focus on a particular topic and are told from a specific point of view. These finished stories are often shared on the internet, hosted on such sites as YouTube or Vimeo, or published on digital storytelling sites such as StoryCenter. They can also be shared in the classroom as a culminating presentation of an assignment.

One of the early pioneers of digital storytelling is the documentary filmmaker Ken Burns. In his documentary *The Civil War*, he combined first-person accounts of events with narration, music, and photographs. In the 1990s, digital stories began to be integrated into academia. They are used in a variety of subject areas, such as humanities, science, sociology, and composition.

**WRITE**

What are some stories you might tell that would be enhanced by using pictures and music? Make a list of those stories and next to each story, jot down what types of pictures and/or music might enhance the story.

## Analyzing Digital Stories

**Purpose**   Writers often compose digital stories to share an experience with their audience. Like a memoirist, digital story composers believe that their insights might help others who have found themselves in similar situations. Sometimes digital storytellers want to share a piece of their family history or help others travel to distant lands in order to experience the wonder and discoveries of their journey. Other times, a digital story might be told to help someone care about or understand an issue, as when a person who has struggled with depression tells his story, hoping to help people who have never experienced depression understand the illness.

**Audience**   Digital storytellers often compose for a wide audience. However, some might imagine that their audience will be someone who has shared a similar experience. If a digital story is related to a particular cause, then the audience might be someone who wants to learn about that issue or is already involved in the movement. When a digital story is part of an academic class, the audience is your classmates and professor.

**Rhetorical appeals**   In order for their story to be believed, digital storytellers need to be reliable narrators. They develop ethos through the anecdotes they share from their own experience. Photographs from the narrator's archives also help convey the truth of the story. Pathos is also central in a digital story, since most digital stories have an emotional layer to help the audience connect with the experience.

**Modes & media**   Digital stories combine audio and visuals. The audio almost always includes the story's narration. Other audio elements commonly included in a digital story are a soundtrack and sound from any included video. The visuals are usually a series of photographs. Sometimes a digital story might also include some video. Although text is often a part of the story, usually it is only a minor part, in the form of captions or as a title or closing screen. Digital stories are always presented through a digital medium.

**Elements of the genre**   Following are some of the most common elements of the digital story. Composers of this genre provide:

- *A central, dramatic question.* The story has at its core a particular question that is ultimately answered by the end of the story. This is not always an actual question, but rather a statement that provides the arc for the story.

- *A point of view.* Every story has a particular point of view. This is the vantage point of the narrator. Digital stories use first-person narration (*I did this*) to help the audience connect with the narrative.

- *Emotional content.* Since digital stories tend to use pathos to connect with their audience, the content of the story usually has some type of emotional pull. Content might elicit laughter, tears, shock, or sympathy.

- *Economy.* Digital stories are usually two to five minutes long. The focus should be limited in scope, using just enough detail to get the central point across.

- *Voice.* Since digital stories are usually narrated by the story's writer, the voice can help deliver emotional meaning. By changing the pitch, the narrator can illustrate emotions such as curiosity or anger.

- *Pacing.* A digital story is neither rushed nor told at a crawling pace. Instead, it tends to vary, speeding up to help build tension and slowing down for emphasis (such as by lingering on a particular visual). Varying the pacing helps hold the audience's attention.

- *Soundtrack.* Music and other sounds are often included to help build the story. Music can help establish the mood. It's important that the music doesn't compete with the story by being too loud or having lyrics run over the narration. Also, any music that is added needs to adhere to copyright laws.

**Style**  Composers of digital stories make stylistic choices based on the following:

- *Detail.* Digital stories usually provide details through narrated anecdotes and visuals. The details help develop the central character (usually the narrator) and her situation. Since economy is a key element of a digital story, details are kept to a minimum—just enough to convey the central point.

- *Tone.* The overall tone of the story is usually informal. It contains language that is natural to the speaker, rather than the elevated diction that might characterize a peer-reviewed journal article. It may include colloquialisms, such as "y'all."

- *Organization.* A digital story is usually organized around a sequence of events that are ordered in a way that helps build tension and that illustrates the experience of the narrator.

**Design**  When designing their digital stories, composers consider the following:

- *Framing.* Much like films, a digital story uses framing to help a viewer see what to focus on. Zooming can be used to highlight a particular aspect of a photograph, such as a face. Panning from one side of the visual can simulate the reading of a storyboard, revealing pieces of the photograph slowly to the viewer.

- *Duration of images.* When a digital story is assembled, the creator decides how much time a visual should be on-screen. The amount of time is usually varied throughout so that the pacing of the visuals is not monotonous.

- *Transitions between images.* Composers need to decide how to transition between different visuals. Sometimes there is a fade-in, while at other times there might be a dissolve of one photo before the next one appears. Whatever transitions are chosen, it's important to avoid distracting the viewer with techniques such as swirling, where a visual spins around into focus.

**Sources**  The primary source of information for a digital story is usually the composer's life. Any other material that is included is usually attributed in the closing credits with a list of where the visuals/audio were found (while paying close attention to copyright laws).

## Guided Reading | Digital Story

In her digital story *Writing the Music Train*, Amy documents her days as a punk rocker. She presents herself as a writer who was stunted by a teacher's comments on her early writing; she tells how she succeeded as a writer by composing songs and lyrics in a punk rock band. Here, Amy establishes her ethos as a memoirist by presenting original lyrics, a piece of writing corrected by her teacher, and a series of punk-inspired self-portraits.

# Amy Braziller, *Writing the Music Train*

## PURPOSE

Amy shares a story of how she triumphed over an early writing injury. She uses her musical journey to show how she never stopped writing. Besides telling the story, she hopes that viewers can relate to her journey and find ways to overcome their own perceived failures.

◄ What is the composer, Amy Braziller, doing?

How do I know that this is ► a digital story?

## ELEMENTS OF THE GENRE

**Central, dramatic question:** Amy's central question revolves around how one overcomes being told that you cannot be a writer. The story moves from her beginnings as a writer, hearing that perhaps she is not a writer, and then ultimately reclaiming her writing voice through playing music in a band.

The one thing I always wanted to be was a writer. In first grade, Mrs. Kaylor would brag to my parents about my stories. When cousins would come to town, I was the playwright, assigning roles.

My brother was always the dog. I'd summon all the adults to take their seats in the den, thrilled by the applause.

**AUDIENCE**
Amy creates the digital story primarily for other writers who might have had an experience that made them question their ability to write. She also hopes that other artists might view this and be able to relate.

In the dark of my teen years, I wrote my way through anger.

When I was a sophomore creative writing major, the response to my final portfolio, uttered by the almighty program director, was: "You can't write."

I don't know what his last name was, but his first name was Stuart.

What I do remember, though, was sitting in a laundromat, clothes spinning, me strumming, composing on the guitar, deciding that I would trade college for the music scene in New York City.

**Point of view:** Amy uses first person throughout. She tells the story from her own experiences. Many of the visuals included feature Amy in the picture to help emphasize that this is her story.

**Economy:** The digital story is just a little over 4 minutes. Details included relate specifically to her dramatic question rather than showing the entire evolution of her band.

*(Continues on next page)*

**RHETORICAL APPEALS**
Amy establishes her ethos by conveying specifics about her experience. Including visuals, such as comments on her writing and footage from her band, she establishes her credibility as the narrator of this event. She appeals to her audience's emotions (pathos) throughout the story, hoping that they can empathize with her challenges and ultimate triumph. She also includes a blank screen to show the darkness of her experience.

At the close of the semester, I packed a car, tossing the isolation of Oberlin aside for a straight shot on I-80 to the city.

I traded the guitar for the steady beat of a bass, spending hours teaching myself to play.

With three other women, we formed The Sirens, playing music with an edge of punk-meets-new-wave.

I spent my nights writing music and lyrics, putting voice to ideas I couldn't abandon.

**Soundtrack:** Since the story illustrates how Amy's musical career helped her feel more secure as a writer, she includes some of the songs so that the audience can hear her lyrics. She includes several different pieces of music to help show that it wasn't just one song that helped her transform.

**MODES & MEDIA**
**Mode = visual, audio, text:** Visuals are a combination of photos taken from Amy's life, along with video footage from her time playing in a band. Audio includes not only the narration of the story, but also music from her band that she helped compose. Text is used to provide opening titles and attribute her sources at the end.

There were no longer comments on the page asking me "what the point" was. "Whose ideas are these? Why is the voice changing here?"

Instead, there were thrashing guitars and a steady beat behind lyrics.

"Your daddy was a 44 magnum" would seg[ue] into "Lisa wanted Robin, but Robin wanted Billy. But Billy wanted somebody else."

With the help of a well-connected CBGB soundman, who became our manager, we got our "fifteen minutes" of Andy Warhol fame opening for The Clash in May of 1981 at Bond's. We were told to play our songs without any chitchat. Get on and get off. So with the crowd screaming: "We want The Clash," I played it loud, thrilled in the moment of performing.

It didn't matter if my words weren't heard. They were sung. For the next eight years, I played in different bands, traveled in and out of different music circles, always composing. Still writing.

**STYLE**
**Tone:** Amy uses an informal tone to tell her story. She tells it as if she was sitting down with you and relating a bit of her past.

**Organization:** The events in the story are presented chronologically since Amy wants to illustrate how one event led to the next and to the next.

**DESIGN**
Throughout the digital story, Amy **zooms** in to help the reader focus on a particular aspect of the visual. The **duration of visuals** is varied throughout. The video of her performance is on-screen for the longest amount of time.

(Continues on next page)

**Media = digital:**
*Writing the Music Train* was composed to be seen in a digital form. Even though screenshots are here in print, the original story resides on Amy's YouTube channel at: https://www.youtube.com/watch?v=yic7z84YDBk.

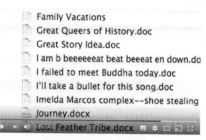

Big sheets of yellow paper found their way back into my college typewriter, spilling lyrics, spilling characters, spilling images. All mine.

**SOURCES**
The visuals come from Amy's own life, and she includes photos of her writing and band days. in the closing title, she lists the songs played in the video, attributing them to their composers.

*Credit: Amy Braziller.*

**RHETORICAL SITUATION & CHOICES**

1. **Purpose.** What do you think Amy's main purpose is in telling this story? To simply share an experience? To help others understand an issue? Or something else?

2. **Purpose.** Are there particular images or sounds that help convey Amy's purpose? Are there any that distract from her purpose?

3. **Audience.** Do you feel like you are part of Amy's intended audience? Why or why not?

4. **Rhetorical appeals.** How do the images help convey Amy's credibility as a writer of different kinds of texts?

5. **Modes & media.** Imagine Amy had decided to tell this story only in written form. What might she have to do to make up for the lack of images and sound?

**GENRE CONVENTIONS**

6. **Elements of the genre.** Because this is Amy's story, it is told from her point of view. Can you imagine how the story might differ if told from someone else's point of view, such as perhaps her sophomore creative writing teacher, Stuart? Or her first-grade teacher, Mrs. Kaylor? Or one of her bandmates?

7. **Style.** How consistent are the images with the tone of Amy's narration? Are there some images that seem more consistent than others?

8. **Style.** Amy chose to tell her story chronologically, beginning with her in the first grade. How might her story have come across differently if she had chosen to begin with herself as a textbook author and then told about her past experiences as flashbacks?

9. **Design.** How do framing, duration of images, and transitions between images heighten the drama of the story Amy tells?

10. **Sources.** Luckily, Amy had kept old papers, photos, and videos from her past. Can you think of sources she might have used for visuals if she hadn't kept those artifacts from her past?

# CHECKLIST | Drafting a Digital Story

Are you thinking of writing a story about an important aspect of your life? Ask yourself the following questions:

**RHETORICAL SITUATION & CHOICES**

☐ **Purpose.** What is my purpose in telling my story? Do I want to share an experience I had? Help people understand something I have struggled with?

**GENRE CONVENTIONS**

☐ **Elements of the genre.** What is my dramatic question? What is the heart of my story? Have I kept the story between two to five minutes? What types of music do I want to include? Have I made sure I'm not breaking any copyright laws? Is the pacing of the narration appropriate for my purpose? Have I used tone to help my viewer feel the emotion?

## RHETORICAL SITUATION & CHOICES

☐ **Audience.** Who do I want to tell my story to? Which details of my story will appeal to them the most? Are there details of the story I might leave out because they will confuse my audience?

☐ **Rhetorical appeals.** How will I establish my credibility? What are some ways I can appeal to my viewers' emotions? Do I want to include humor? Do I want my viewer to feel sad?

☐ **Modes & media.** Do I want to use just photographs, or are there video pieces that make sense to include? What types of audio do I want to include? Does it make sense to include sounds and/or music? Do I want to use any text captioning throughout?

## GENRE CONVENTIONS

☐ **Style.** How do I want to organize my story? Do I want to tell the events chronologically? Is there a reason to tell it out of sequence, such as starting from the end and moving to the beginning? Or perhaps starting in the middle? What are the details I want to include? Which details should I omit? How do I want to convey my own personal tone? How can I help the reader feel as though she were sitting with me and listening to my story?

☐ **Design.** How do I want to transition between images? Do I want particular images to fade into another? Are there any images I want to linger on-screen for longer than others? Are there any places where I want a blank screen to emphasize a particular emotion? What aspects of photographs do I want to zoom into? Are there places in the story where panning from one part of a photo to another makes sense?

☐ **Sources.** What personal photos will I use for my digital story? Do I have any video I want to include? Would interviews help with my story? What sources am I using that aren't my own? How will I cite those sources at the end of my digital story?

---

**PRACTICE**

# Telling a Digital Story

Create a three- to five-minute digital story that recounts an event or tale from your life. Alternatively, you could create a story that tells about a historical moment, and why it matters to you, or reflects on a hero in your life. Before you begin drafting your story, view some digital stories on the web to get an idea of the scope that writers cover in their story. Then draft a written script that tells your story. Consider what your main dramatic question is and who your audience is to help you focus your ideas. Read this script aloud to others to get feedback about where you need to add or delete details. Once your script is finalized, record it, making sure to pause in places where you want your viewers and listeners to rest on an idea. Gather photos and other visuals that will help tell your story. Put it all together using movie-making software, such as iMovie, or online software, such as YouTube video editor.

# ACADEMIC GENRES

Now that you have considered a variety of different academic genres, noticing what they have in common and how they diverge, and practiced a few of the key moves made in academic genres, you should feel ready to tackle something meatier. Here we offer two extended project ideas for you to play with. The first invites you to do an extended rhetorical analysis of how a particular topic is treated in multiple genres and present your findings in both written and poster form. The second offers you an opportunity to share your experiences with writing/reading in a literacy narrative and digital story.

## IN PRACTICE   Academic Writing Projects

### Extended Rhetorical Analysis

1. **Investigate how a particular topic is rhetorically framed.** Identify a topic you are interested in exploring further, such as anxiety, standardized testing, fracking, gluten intolerance, or heavy metal music. Then gather a variety of different types of source material on that topic. For example, if you are focusing on gluten intolerance, you might collect a few news stories about the prevalence of gluten intolerance, an advertisement for gluten-free bread, a peer-reviewed journal article about gluten sensitivity and the brain, and a couple of blog entries about switching to a gluten-free diet. Aim to collect between five and ten sources.

    a. Read each source carefully, noting in particular how each source talks about the topic.
      - What kinds of words are used? For the gluten intolerance example, you might note whether gluten intolerance is described as a condition, a diagnosis, a syndrome, or something else. Then consider the connotations of the words used and how those words connect to pathos, logos, and ethos.
      - What attitude is conveyed toward the topic? Do authors seem skeptical, supportive, angry, optimistic?
      - What type of rhetorical appeals—pathos, logos, and ethos—are made?
      - How does each author position themselves in relation to the topic? Do they position themselves as directly affected, neutral observers, something else?
      - What kind of source material is referenced?

    b. After you've read all the sources you collected, look through your notes to find patterns in the language and rhetorical approaches to the topic. You might find, for instance, that almost all of your sources rely on appeals to pathos to make their points. Or perhaps the majority of your sources imply that the research done on this topic is not reliable enough to draw conclusions.

    c. Compose a rhetorical analysis essay that presents your findings about how the topic you researched is rhetorically framed in the sources you studied.
      - Begin by introducing the topic you investigated, briefly describing and summarizing the sources you examined.
      - Discuss the patterns you noticed in how the sources talk about the topic. Give specific examples from the sources to support your observations.
      - Explain how the patterns you identified shape the attitude toward the topic that is projected by the sources. An essay

about how gluten intolerance is rhetorically framed might talk about how word choices such as "purport," "no official diagnosis," and "claim" cast doubt on people who identify as having an intolerance to gluten.

- Include a Works Cited list of the sources you examined.

d. Create a researched poster presentation that highlights your most interesting findings in a visual way. Keep in mind that a researched poster presentation needs to be visually appealing to attract the attention of audience members, so you'll want to use color, infographics, and other visual elements. You should also come up with a descriptive title for your poster, such as "Implied Suspicion of Gluten Intolerance."

## Multigenre/Multimodal Literacy Narrative

1. **Literacy Narrative**

   a. Freewrite on how you feel about yourself as a writer and/or reader. Don't worry about structure, whether you have memories around any of your feelings, or whether any of your ideas make sense. Just write for twenty minutes about your attitudes and beliefs related to your own writing and reading. When you are finished, go through the freewrite and circle or underline any points that are particularly interesting or seem especially important to you.

   b. Brainstorm a list of events that influenced those interesting or important points you noted. For example, maybe you indicated that you hate writing. You might then list times when something occurred that made you hate writing. Perhaps a teacher made fun of the way you expressed something. Or maybe a classmate laughed at something you wrote that wasn't meant to be funny. Think about all the events that might have shaped your beliefs about yourself as a writer.

   c. Once you have a list of the events, do some writing about each event. Try to use concrete details to bring the event to life. Help your readers feel as if they are experiencing things with you. You might reread the excerpt from Richard Rodriguez's literacy narrative and see how he re-creates scenes for you.

   d. Read through the mini-narratives you've written about the events that contributed to your belief about yourself as a writer to identify a theme or pattern that comes through. Use that theme or pattern to create sentences to connect the mini-narratives together into a whole. For instance, if you find that all of your mini-narratives are about events involving authority figures, you might transition between mini-narratives with references to rebelling against authority, questioning authority, and feeling oppressed by authority.

   e. Finally, reread the entire piece. When you are done, what idea or image sticks with you? Use that to create a title for the piece.

2. **Digital Story**

   a. Read over your literacy narrative and make a list of objects that relate to your story. Consider photos, videos, and memorabilia. Perhaps one of your memories related to writing is a graded story that your teacher bled red pen over. You might gather that to help tell your story. You want objects that not only convey the ideas/experiences in the story, but objects that perhaps help convey the mood/how you experienced things.

   b. Write a script. This simply means to write down what you will say while the images of the items you collected are on the screen. Keep in mind that you are not going to read the literacy narrative you wrote above because the photos, videos, and memorabilia will take the place of some of the words. Think about sitting down with someone and telling them a story about how you came to your belief/attitude. A digital story is only three to five minutes long. As you write, think about the narrative arc—you need a beginning, middle, and end. The beginning of the story gives the basic context and sets up the tension for your reader. In the middle, you want your conflict/what you wrestle with to be present. The end of the story is where you reveal your insight/show your reader how you have changed from the beginning.

c. Read your script aloud several times to notice any words or phrasing that doesn't sound natural to you. You want to avoid any fancy words or long phrases that don't sound conversational. Listen for pacing and note in the script places where you take a breath. You might even want to allow longer pauses to let the information linger and make an impact. Note places in the script where you pause, or where your voice gets louder or softer.

d. Once you are happy with your script, find someone to read it to. Ask them to note places that don't sound authentic. Have them indicate places that seem too wordy.

e. Next record the audio. Then gather all your photos and visuals that help your reader see your story. Put them all together using digital story software/movie making software.

# 8 WORKPLACE GENRES

# Workplace Genres & Projects

Workplace writing is any kind of writing or composing you do in a business or professional setting. Sometimes this is referred to as business writing. Much like academic writing, workplace writing is also produced on demand. You are usually asked by your manager to compose something specific because of the particular job you are doing.

Workplace writing usually responds to a need someone has. For example, you write a résumé and cover letter in response to a job opening because you need a job and your potential employer needs an employee, or you create a presentation to help pitch a solution for a client's problem. Other typical purposes of workplace genres are to communicate ideas to internal or external audiences, to analyze situations so that you and your colleagues can make informed decisions, to report on the progress of a project, or to persuade your reader to take a certain action.

The readers of workplace genres can be divided into internal or external audiences. Often you create something that is distributed within a company, such as a memo written to members of your team that captures the salient points discussed for an upcoming sales meeting. At other times, you direct your message outside the workplace; for example, you might deliver a proposal for a new medical records system to a local hospital.

The situation, the task, and the audience usually dictate the types of genres chosen. If you wanted to quickly communicate something to a few coworkers, such as a follow-up communication after a meeting, you would send an e-mail. However, if you needed to communicate something more formally, such as a serious safety concern or another issue you discovered, you might choose a report to your supervisor that would be delivered in hard copy to emphasize the seriousness of the matter at hand.

Your choice of workplace genres, just like other genres, is always based on the rhetorical situation. You want to determine your purpose and audience, and then choose the best ways to approach and reach that audience. For example, if you were searching for a job on campus and you saw a notice for an open position for a student worker to assist people at the Student Life Desk, you would most likely submit your résumé and a cover letter to the person who oversees the desk. Your purpose would be to get the job, and your audience would be the person who is doing the hiring.

Some typical workplace genres are memos, which are internal and generally fairly short informational updates; reports, which can be internal or external and are generally long and complex, giving a rich analysis of a situation, often with recommendations; proposals, which usually outline costs and plans associated with taking a particular course of action; and presentations, in which someone shares information live with an audience, often accompanied by PowerPoint slides or other visuals.

**WRITE**

You may or may not have experience writing in workplace genres, but you certainly have experience writing in academic genres. How do you think writing in academic genres might help prepare you to write in workplace genres? Imagine you are in an elevator on your way up to a job interview. To your surprise, the person in the elevator with you is your interviewer. She asks you to explain how your experience writing as a student might make you a good on-the-job writer. Turn to a classmate, and answer the question.

Workplace genres often depend to some degree on templates, which provide a standard structure to documents. For example, some companies have templates for trip reports, so that when an employee returns from a business trip, they can simply plug in information about where they went, what purpose the trip had, and what the outcome was.

# Cover Letters & Résumés

WRITE

When did you last write a cover letter to apply for a job? What was the job? What did you emphasize in the letter? How persuasive was it? Ultimately, was it successful? Why or why not? Write for five minutes about these questions. Include details in your answers.

A cover letter, sometimes called a job application letter, is a persuasive piece of business writing that accompanies a résumé (and sometimes other documents). When you're applying for a job, always send your résumé—the document that outlines your skills, education, and experience—with a cover letter tailored to the job you're interested in.

At just a page or less, a cover letter is a tool that allows you to introduce yourself, identify the job you'd like to interview for, and make a case for why you are a great candidate. Unless you've exchanged some preliminary e-mails, your cover letter is usually your first written communication with a potential employer. This means you need to make a good impression.

When organizations advertise available positions, they may receive applications from many more people than they could possibly interview. That's why the persuasive aspect of the cover letter is so important.

Imagine a hiring manager faced with a stack of thirty résumés to read. They are probably very busy and need a clean, simple way to turn that stack of thirty résumés into a more manageable pile of five or six. Skimming cover letters is a good way to do that. So keep in mind that when you write a cover letter, your main goal is to persuade readers to invite you in for an interview.

ATTENTION, JOB APPLICANTS

*Always* send a thank-you note, card, or e-mail after any interview and as soon as possible. In this correspondence, you should point out a few specific details from the interview to reinforce your professionalism, your interest in the job, and your potential as the candidate for the job. This letter is not only another tool for being persuasive—it's a great opportunity to ask any questions you wish you'd asked when you were face-to-face with your interviewer.

A résumé is a document that lists and highlights a person's credentials for a job. When you write a résumé, you're writing to convince a potential employer that you have the right education, experience, and skills to succeed in the job you're applying for. A résumé typically begins with the writer's name and contact information and a statement about the kind of position they are looking for, followed by specific academic and employment information relevant to the particular job they're seeking. It's crucial for applicants to portray their qualifications accurately and to keep all résumé information up-to-date.

Like cover letters, résumés are usually very brief. A good practice is to limit your résumé to one page until you have at least ten years of experience in the field in which you're applying for a job. Résumés, as with cover letters, are read quickly by busy people, so they need to be extremely clear and match your experiences precisely with the qualifications listed in the job posting. Be sure to carefully tailor your résumé to each job you apply for, paying particular attention to the section that states the kind of job you're looking for. It would be embarrassing, for example, to send out a résumé that focuses on how you are a "people person" and thrive in team environments when you're applying for a job that requires you to work alone. Additionally, résumés focus on the positive only—projects managed successfully, sales goals met, increased responsibility, and the like.

# Analyzing Cover Letters & Résumés

## Purpose

- *Cover letters.* People write cover letters, or job application letters, to persuade potential employers to read their résumés and contact them for an interview for the job they want. Employers use résumés and cover letters in part as screening devices, to help them sift through a large number of applications to a smaller, more manageable number. A cover letter must capture the attention of the person reading it.

- *Résumés.* Résumé writers need to demonstrate to potential employers that their experience and skills align with the employer's needs. The résumé needs to be organized and worded in a way that persuades an employer to consider the applicant seriously.

## Audience

- *Cover letters.* Writers need to take into account several potential readers: the person who will supervise the new hire, a human resources employee, and members of a screening committee made up of supervisors and employees at the hiring organization. Successful cover letters:

  - » *Convey personality.* Readers want to get a sense of the person they may work with. They'll want to know: Will they be interesting as a colleague?

  - » *Communicate a strong work ethic.* Readers want to know: Will this person do their share of the work?

  - » *Highlight qualifications.* Readers want a quick sense of what the applicant has done that makes him or her a good candidate for the job. What specific experiences connect up with the job in question? What stands out about this person and their experience?

  - » *Get to the point.* Writers should keep in mind that their potential employers usually read cover letters *in addition to* their usual workload. That means readers are moving fast; they want to get an immediate sense of whether the applicant may be a good fit.

- *Résumés.* When composing a résumé, writers need to keep the same factors in mind as when they write a cover letter (see Purpose above). Their readers are busy and want a quick and clear case for how fit the applicant is for the position.

## Rhetorical Appeals

- *Cover letters.* Writers need to establish ethos by conveying their ethics and professionalism, noting related past successes, experiences, and aptitudes that qualify them for the job, and showing that they're genuinely interested in working for

WRITE

Have you ever created different versions of your résumé for different jobs? If so, what types of edits did you make? What did you do to tailor your message to a specific audience? Jot down the answers to these questions and then share your responses with a classmate.

the organization, perhaps by mentioning something specific about it that they especially like. Writers also need to appeal to readers' sense of logos by making logical connections between their résumé and the organization's values and the requirements of the position.

- *Résumés.* Résumé writers need to develop ethos too. They need to be accurate and ethical in everything listed on their résumés. The stakes are high: You've probably seen news stories about people being fired for lying on their résumés, such as Yahoo! CEO Scott Thompson, who was fired for listing a degree on his résumé that he didn't actually hold.

### Modes & media

- *Cover letters.* Cover letters can be sent by e-mail, uploaded to an employment site, or printed and delivered in person. Traditional cover letters are written documents and rarely contain any visual elements. However, LinkedIn and other career-related

▼ VISUAL RÉSUMÉ

**Kevin Burton,** disaster recovery professional.

*Credit: By permission of Kevin Burton.*

networking options are causing standards to change. Talk to people in the industry you're interested in to find out what the standard is for that audience. Creative industries, such as publishing and advertising, may allow more flexibility, while other industries may want a text-only cover letter.

- *Résumés.* As with cover letters, résumé standards vary from industry to industry. Social networking sites have made digital résumés that incorporate visuals much more acceptable in some industries. For example, Kevin Burton, who works in disaster recovery, created the visual résumé on page 178 for the internet.

**Elements of the Genre** In their résumés and cover letters, job seekers do the following:

- *Introduce themselves as applicants.*
  - » *Cover letters.* This is usually the first communication a job applicant will have with a potential employer, so it's important for writers to present themselves as competent and engaged. See the letter by Julia Nollen on page 185 for an example. Nollen provides context for why she's applying for the job she's writing about.
  - » *Résumés.* Writers provide their names and objectives at or near the top of their résumés, highlighting the details that would be highlighted in a traditional, face-to-face introduction. Think about how you normally introduce yourself to people; you probably say something like, "Hi, my name is John. I'm a student at XYZ College." A résumé communicates the same information.

- *Refer specifically to the position they're applying to.*
  - » *Cover letters.* So that readers can instantly identify which position the writer is applying for, writers need to state the specific job title and reference number (if applicable) near the beginning of the letter.
  - » *Résumés.* Writers need to tailor their objectives to the position they are applying for. This is probably the most important thing to keep in mind each time you apply for a job. Your résumé should be a flexible document that you revise as needed for different audiences.

- *Explain why the job and organization are appealing.* The cover letter should be personalized for the specific job and organization being applied to. Candidates applying for a position with Red Rocks Community College, where Amy teaches, would do well to mention something in their cover letter about their experience with or appreciation of the community college mission. This shows that they share values with the organization.

- *Organize content so it's persuasive and reader-friendly.*
  - » *Cover letters.* Cover letters usually begin with a reference to the position being applied for and a brief summary of the writer's qualifications. One to three

**WRITE**

When you are interested in a job, do you research it before applying for it? If so, what things do you look for? Have you ever included any of that information in your cover letter? What are some ways that including these specifics could assist you in your job search? Answer these questions on paper.

paragraphs elaborating on qualifications follow, and then the letter closes with a request for an interview.

> » *Résumés.* Job seekers typically organize their experiences either chronologically, working backward from their most recent employment experiences, or according to skill sets, such as by listing all their project management experience under one heading and then all their budget management experience under another. Writers should think about the job they are applying for and which organizational pattern will best highlight their qualifications.

- *Present a clear argument about their qualifications.*

  > » *Cover letters.* Writers summarize their qualifications in one or two sentences near the beginning of the letter. They specify the experiences that make them ideal candidates for the job.

  > » *Résumés.* Résumé writers continue building their arguments by listing specific experiences that illustrate how qualified they are for the position. A student applying for a position might list relevant classes they have taken.

- *Make connections between the cover letter and résumé and between different personal experiences.* In their cover letters, applicants refer to the specific experiences listed in their résumés. They draw connections between those experiences and the qualifications that the employer has noted in the job listing. If the job listing states that candidates need to have strong customer service skills, the applicant should address that in their letter. A cover letter is also a good tool for showing relationships between seemingly unrelated experiences or tasks. If an applicant has worked as a swim coach and a café manager, they might say that these jobs tied together because they allowed them to develop as a communicator and a leader.

- *Use concise language.* A cover letter should be no more than one page long. The purpose of the cover letter is not to tell the entire story of the writer, but to whet the appetite of the reader. A résumé should also be limited to one page until the applicant has at least ten years' experience in a particular field. You can provide your list of references, writing samples, or other portfolio of work separately from the résumé.

- *Request an interview.* Cover letters should end with a polite direct request for an interview, such as "I would welcome the opportunity for an interview and hope to hear from you."

**Style**   When creating a résumé and cover letter, writers do the following:

- *Use professional language.* Just as applicants dress formally for a job interview, they also write their cover letters using business- and workplace-appropriate language.

That said, because writers are writing about themselves, the use of the first person (I) is appropriate. Use language that is formal enough to be respectful but that is not stilted or boring. In your résumé, use professional, specific language to describe your accomplishments.

- *Give a sense of their personalities.*
  - » *Cover letters.* Just because this is formal correspondence doesn't mean it has to be lackluster. It's okay for a writer to use a voice and tone that let readers know something about who the writer is and why they are special. Use the active voice and verb construction. For example, "A degree was earned in history from XYZ University" could be written in the active voice this way: "I earned a degree in history from XYZ University."
  - » *Résumés.* Writers need to convey attributes of their personality and work ethic through the details they provide in their résumés. The voice and tone of a résumé, regardless of the voice and tone in the cover letter, need to be professional and businesslike.

- *Provide specific relevant details.* Specific statements in cover letters ("I exceeded sales goals by 15 percent at the Limited") do a better job of persuading readers than *generalizations* ("I am a good salesperson"). Résumés should be precise.

- *Proofread and make sure their documents are error-free.*
  - » *Cover letters.* While proofreading is important for all compositions, it is particularly important when you're reviewing a cover letter; even one typo can cause a reader to dismiss you completely as a job applicant. Recently, Elizabeth received a cover letter and résumé from someone who wanted to work in the writing center she directs on campus. One sentence in the cover letter read, "I kept my death clean." The word *death* was probably a simple typo, but Elizabeth could not bring herself to schedule an interview with the writer.
  - » *Résumés.* As with cover letters, it's crucial to proofread your résumé so readers will see you as professional. Make sure to keep tenses consistent, place periods at the end of sentences, and carefully check for any misuse of words. Always have someone else proofread your résumé to be sure you haven't overlooked anything. Make sure your verbs are parallel in construction in all sections of your résumé, including your lists of tasks.

**Design** Writers of cover letters and résumés:

- *Use standard business formatting and personalized headings.*
  - » *Cover letters.* Like any other business letter, a cover letter includes the complete contact information of both the recipient and the sender. It also includes a date, a salutation, and a signature. With word processors and online cover letter templates, writers can easily create personalized letterhead that

WRITE

What are some ways you can personalize your cover letter to reflect your personality? How about your résumé? Write a list of the different ways you might do this.

Standard letter templates are available on the internet and as part of Microsoft Office. Shown here is the typical styling that precedes the message of a business letter.

1936 Elm St.
Atlanta, GA  30098

July 9, 2019

Amy Downs
PricewaterhouseCoopers
1 Park Place
Atlanta, GA 30303

Dear Ms. Downs:

includes their name and contact information at the top or bottom of the page.

» *Résumés.* Job seekers place their contact information at the top of their résumés. They also include standard sections such as "Objective," "Education," and "Experience."

• *Use standard spacing and plenty of white space.*

» *Cover letters.* Writers single-space their cover letters but insert an extra space between paragraphs. They do not use indentation.

» *Résumés.* Within each section, writers use single spacing. Between sections, they add an extra space. Margins are usually one inch. Make sure to use some white space to separate different areas of the résumé in order to keep it from appearing too cluttered. In the sample on page 183, the writer uses white space by indenting the copy.

• *Choose simple, classic fonts.*

» *Cover letter.* In keeping with the formality of a cover letter, the font should be a simple, classic one like Arial, Calibri, or Times New Roman in 11 or 12 point. This makes the cover letter easy for most readers to read.

» *Résumés.* Use fonts consistently throughout your résumé. Sans serif fonts (such as Arial) are typically used for headings, while serif fonts (such as Times New Roman) are typically used for the text. If you use more than two fonts, you run the risk of distracting your reader.

• *Adhere to any design specifications given by employers or online resources.* When creating a cover letter, follow any specifications supplied by the potential employer, especially the file formats requested. As for your résumé, see how others in your industry present their résumés. For example, a visual résumé can work for some industries; see Kevin Burton's résumé on page 178.

**Sources** The main source of a cover letter is the résumé, which is referred to throughout, and the writer's experiences. The main source of a résumé is the applicant's own experiences. When you create a résumé, you may want to use other résumés as models for your own.

ATTENTION, OVERACHIEVERS

Wondering how you can get ahead in the job search? Gather some letters of recommendation from former employers, professors, and colleagues. You can submit these shining references— along with writing or other portfolio samples tailored to the position—to a future employer and distinguish yourself from the throng.

**William Watson**
4460 Main St., Sacramento, CA 95818
(916) 555-0684
williamwatson@email.com

| | |
|---|---|
| **Objective** | A full-time position in youth counseling. |
| **Education** | **California State University**, Sacramento<br>B.A., **Psychology.** May 2017.<br>GPA: 3.4 |
| **Related Experience** | Volunteer, Sacramento Community Mental Health Center<br>July 2015–present<br>• Organize mentoring events with local schools and organizations.<br>• Hold regular tutoring sessions.<br>• Lead monthly group discussions with teens, under supervision of staff psychologist. |

# Guided Reading | Cover Letter & Résumé

Julia Nollen is a graduate of the University of Delaware, where she studied English, film, art, and web design. She then completed a Certificate in Publishing program at New York University. Nollen wrote a cover letter to accompany her résumé when she applied for a marketing assistant position at Bedford/St. Martin's, the publisher of this textbook. After introducing herself and naming the position she is applying for, she summarizes her qualifications and her reasons for wanting to work for Bedford/ St. Martin's. As you read, notice how Nollen tailors her letter for the specific position and employer. Why do you think she's chosen to mention the name of an executive editor? How does her description of projects she's worked on shape your impression of her?

**▶ APPLICANT PHOTO &
JOB DESCRIPTION**

**Julia Nollen** submitted a
cover letter and résumé for
a marketing assistant job
with Bedford/St. Martin's, an
imprint of Macmillan Learning.
**Macmillan Learning** posted the
job description shown here, the
one that Nollen responded to.

*Credit: Photo, by courtesy of Julia Nollen.
Screenshot of job description by courtesy
of Macmillan Learning.*

# Julia Nollen, *Application for Marketing Assistant Job*

## RHETORICAL SITUATION & CHOICES

## GENRE CONVENTIONS

**PURPOSE**
Nollen writes her cover letter to persuade the director of marketing that her background makes her an ideal fit for a marketing assistant position.

**AUDIENCE**
Nollen's primary audience is Karen Soeltz, the director of marketing. Secondary readers might be other supervisors and employees who work with the marketing department.

**RHETORICAL APPEALS**
Nollen establishes her ethos by describing the variety of her work experience in the publishing industry, such as writing and designing press releases. Nollen appeals to logos by making logical connections between experience mentioned on her résumé and her desired place of employment, Bedford. She connects digital publishing trends with part of Bedford's mission statement.

**MODES & MEDIA**
Mode = written:
Nollen relies on text for her cover letter. She does mention a visual in her ending summary of samples included, but the

◄ **What is the composer, Julia Nollen, doing?**

**How do I know this is a ►
cover letter?**

October 6, 2019

Karen Soeltz
Director of Marketing
Bedford/St. Martin's
75 Arlington St.
Boston, MA 02116

Dear Ms. Soeltz:

My name is Julia Nollen, and I am writing at the suggestion of Executive Editor Ellen Thibault, who recommended I apply for the open Marketing Assistant position at Bedford/St. Martin's. I am currently attending New York University's Summer Publishing Institute until July 16 but am available to interview in Boston at your convenience. I've been a longtime fan of Bedford's titles and have even contributed to one of your books. Further, during a recent informational interview at your Boston office, I was impressed by the creative energy and commitment of the people working there. I'd love to be a part of that.

What interests me most about Bedford is its mission to publish educational products across several platforms. At NYU I've studied the publishing industry and confirmed that I want to work for a company that blends established practices and innovative technology to create the best educational tools. I've learned that a firm understanding of both digital and print publishing best addresses the changing currents in pedagogy; Bedford reflects this hybrid approach to content development in its mission to publish texts that stem from "where our disciplines are, where they're going, and what they need," as your website states.

While at the University of Delaware, I contributed four student essays to Bedford's textbook *Mirror on America: Essays and Images from Popular Culture*. I was also lucky enough to gain practical editorial and marketing experience for both print and web products by interning for three very

**ELEMENTS OF
THE GENRE**

**Introduces herself as an applicant:** Nollen names the position she's interested in and mentions that she is currently attending NYU's Summer Publishing Institute, which indicates engagement.

**Uses standard business letter formatting:** Nollen includes the address and name of the recipient, the date, a salutation, and a signature.

**Refers specifically to the position:** Nollen mentions the position, marketing assistant, in the opening sentence of her cover letter.

**Explains why this job and organization are appealing:** In the opening of the letter, and throughout, Nollen discusses Bedford, making the reader aware that she has not only researched the company, but also sees how she fits as a potential employee.

**Refers to the résumé:** On Nollen's résumé, she lists the different internships she has had. By explaining some of the work she did during the internship, she gives the reader detailed information that is not available on

*(Continues on next page)*

visuals are not an actual part of her cover letter.

**Medium = digital:** This cover letter was sent digitally, by e-mail.

different companies: a web design studio (Bright Orange Thread), a freelance columnist (MSNBC.com's Eve Tahmincioglu), and a niche publishing house (Oak Knoll Press). At all three companies, I designed press releases using Adobe InDesign; wrote persuasive copy for mailers, flyers, blog posts, and articles; and posted these materials online. My recent experience at NYU has been even more multifaceted. For the first half of the program, I was appointed Art Director of my group's magazine and won the "Best Art Director" award by professionals, including the Editor in Chief of *People*. In my current appointed role as Marketing Director, my job is to develop a marketing strategy for a mock book imprint and its digital extension, including a pre- and post-publication campaign for each of our first three titles. After presenting my campaign to the VP Associate Publisher of Simon & Schuster, later today, I will devise a budget to present to a panel of marketing experts next week. From writing and designing press releases to updating book and social media sites, I want to learn as much as I can about the present publishing industry, as well as where it's going in the future.

Whether by e-mail, by phone, or in person, I would love to find out more about the open Marketing Assistant position at Bedford and the responsibilities it entails. I've included my contact information at the bottom of this e-mail and attached my résumé and writing samples to this e-mail. Thank you for your time and consideration, and I look forward to hearing from you.

Sincerely,


Julia Nollen

0000 Newark Drive
Newark, DE 19711
19711julianollen@000.com
(C) 302.555.0000
(H) 302.555.0000


Enclosed are the following writing samples.

1. Cover for *Expresión* magazine, a bimonthly arts and culture magazine that targets young Latin Americans living in the United States. My cover was awarded "Best Art Design" at New York University's Summer Publishing

the résumé, such as mentioning that she wrote "persuasive copy for mailers," something she might do as a marketing assistant.

**Is brief:** Nollen's cover letter gives enough details to expand on the résumé, yet doesn't give so many extraneous details that the reader is bogged down with a long letter.

**Closes with a request for an interview:** Nollen's final paragraph discusses her availability and desire to meet for an interview.

**STYLE**
**Technique:** Nollen uses the first person throughout. For example, she writes, "I want to learn as much as I can about the present publishing industry. . . ."

**Voice and tone:** While Nollen keeps the tone professional, detailing her accomplishments and fit for the job, she also infuses the letter with part of her personality, such as when she says, "I'd love to be a part of that."

**Detail:** Nollen uses specific details throughout. Rather than just mentioning that she is a marketing director for a project in the NYU publishing program, she details what that position entails.

Institute and was designed using Adobe Photoshop and InDesign.

2. Research paper written for a film class at the University of Delaware, titled "Reflecting on Manufactured Masculinity and Motherhood in Brett Ratner's *Red Dragon*."

3. Book review on Shawn Achor's *The Happiness Advantage*, as published on careerdiva.net, which has up to 20,000 unique visits monthly.

**DESIGN**
Nollen follows cover letter design conventions by using single-spaced paragraphs with spaces between each paragraph.

**SOURCES**
Nollen draws on her own experiences throughout the cover letter.

**◄ RÉSUMÉ**
**Julia Nollen**
submitted this résumé along with the cover letter shown on the previous page when she applied for a job with Bedford/ St. Martin's as a marketing assistant.
*Credit: Used with permission of Julia Nollen.*

## JULIA NOLLEN
julianollen@000.com • 0000 Newark Drive, Newark, DE 19711 •
(C) 302.555.0000 • (H) 302.555.0000

**EDUCATION**
Certificate in Publishing, New York University, July 2019

BA of English and Film, Interactive Media minor, University of Delaware, May 2019

Study Abroad Programs:

- London—literature, film, political science and theater (Fall 2017)
- Athens—art history, Greek language and literature (Summer 2016)
- Caen—contemporary and conversational French (Winter 2016)

**RELATED EXPERIENCE**

Intern, Oak Knoll Press & Books, New Castle, DE (Winter, Spring 2019)

Proofread manuscripts, designed press releases using Adobe InDesign, wrote and edited book descriptions, and cataloged rare books for sale on the Web. 360+ hours.

Intern, **MSNBC.com** columnist Eve Tahmincioglu, Wilmington, DE (Fall 2018)

Wrote, researched, and edited articles and videos for **CareerDiva.net**. Also featured on **MSNBC.com, Excelle.monster.com, thedailybrainstorm.com**, and others. 180+ hours.

Intern, Bright Orange Thread Web Design Studio, Lincoln University, PA (Summer 2018)

Wrote and published articles and coupons for the website and blog. Used Basecamp daily, wrote and posted tweets, and helped design a wireframe. 180+ hours.

*(Continues on next page)*

Student Writer, Bedford/St. Martin's, Boston, MA (2012–Present)

Research material for upcoming editions of *Mirror on America: Essays and Images from Popular Culture*, attend meetings with the editor, and write and edit student essays (four published so far). 100+ hours.

Nonfiction Editor, *Caesura Literary Magazine*, University of Delaware (Fall 2017–May 2018)

Edit submissions, design cover and layout, advertise, and update social media sites. 30 hours.

### SKILLS

- Adobe Creative Suite 5 and 6 (Dreamweaver, Photoshop, InDesign, and Bridge)
- Working knowledge of HTML
- Practiced photographer (Nikon D5100, EOS Rebel) and published video editor (Final Cut Pro X, iMovie '11)

### ACCOMPLISHMENTS

Published in *Mirror on America: Essays and Images from Popular Culture*, Bedford/St. Martin's

Published four essays on popular culture in the third, fourth, and fifth editions (2011, 2014, and 2016).

Presented research at the English Association of Pennsylvania Undergraduate Conference, West Chester (2014)

Presented "The Best of Both Worlds: Ofelia as Gender Role Revisionary in del Toro's *Pan's Labyrinth*."

Presented research at the National Popular Culture Association Conference (St. Louis 2015, New Orleans 2014)

Presented "One Last 'Memo from Turner': Gender Roles Revisioned in Performance."

## RHETORICAL SITUATION & CHOICES

1. **Purpose.** Nollen mentions her familiarity with Bedford several times in the letter. Is this an effective strategy for persuading her reader to interview her for the position? Why or why not?

2. **Audience.** Is the letter appropriately tailored to the director of marketing? What information does Nollen include that shows she realizes this is her audience?

3. **Rhetorical appeals.** How does the cover letter demonstrate that the writer would make a desirable employee? How does the résumé do this?

4. **Rhetorical appeals.** How does the cover letter use ethos and logos to persuade the recipient to schedule an interview?

5. **Modes & media.** Read Nollen's cover letter out loud and notice how well it flows as a kind of audio essay. What might be some of the benefits—and drawbacks—of reaching an audience through an audio cover letter?

## GENRES CONVENTIONS

6. **Elements of the genre.** Are there items on Nollen's résumé that she should have elaborated on in the cover letter? If so, which items and why?

7. **Elements of the genre.** Nollen includes a summarized list of her writing samples at the end of her cover letter. Is this necessary? Why or why not?

8. **Style.** How does the author convey her personality while still maintaining a formal tone?

9. **Design.** How does the cover letter's design make it easily and quickly readable?

10. **Sources.** How does Nollen draw on her résumé as a source for the cover letter?

## CHECKLIST | Drafting a Cover Letter & Résumé

Are you thinking of drafting a cover letter and résumé? Ask yourself the following questions:

### RHETORICAL SITUATION & CHOICES

☐ **Purpose.** I need to remember that the main purpose of my cover letter is to persuade the reader to schedule an interview with me. How can I draw on my experiences to best position myself as a good candidate for an interview? Does my résumé illustrate how my experiences and skills align with my potential employer?

☐ **Audience.** When I sit down to write my cover letter, I need to think about what my reader's concerns are. How can I appeal to those concerns in my letter and résumé? To what extent does my

### GENRE CONVENTIONS

☐ **Elements of the genre.** In my cover letter, what aspects of my résumé will I want to elaborate on to highlight my qualifications for the specific job I'm applying for? What makes this particular position and organization appealing to me? How do my experiences correspond with what the employer is looking for?

☐ **Style.** In my cover letter, how can I use specific details to support and develop generalizations that I make about myself? Does my résumé support the case I make for myself in my letter? And for both documents, is my tone inviting yet professional?

| | |
|---|---|
| résumé provide a quick snapshot of my skills for my reader? | Is my language formal enough? Did I proofread carefully? |
| ☐ **Rhetorical appeals.** How can I establish myself as reliable and responsible? How can I logically connect my experiences and skills with the reader's needs and the position's requirements? | ☐ **Design.** Will I create personalized letterhead for my letter? And how will I lay out my résumé? Is it consistent in design? Am I using no more than two fonts? Am I using headings and white space to direct my reader's attention to certain parts of the résumé? |
| ☐ **Modes & media.** Will my cover letter and résumé be delivered in print form or digitally? Would it be appropriate for me to include one or more visuals? | ☐ **Sources.** Did I remember to use my résumé as a source for the details and anecdotes in my cover letter? |

---

**PRACTICE**

## Responding to a Specific Job Description

Want to experiment? Draft your own cover letter and résumé.

Locate a description for a job in your field that you are interested in. Working with that job description and your own experience, respond to the individual qualifications in both your résumé and cover letter. Create a new résumé or revise an existing one using the advice and models in this chapter. Draft a cover letter that expresses your interest in the job and that makes explicit connections between what the employer's stated needs are and what you have to offer. Remember to close with a request for an interview. Be sure that your cover letter expands on the details in your résumé that show how you are an excellent fit for the job.

## Business Memos

The word *memo* is short for *memorandum*, a document used for communicating within a business or organization, so the authors of and audience for memos are colleagues in a workplace. Memos are generally brief, seldom running more than a few pages long when printed out. Some memos are formatted as the document on page 191: The "professional design" memo template offered by Microsoft Office. Others are sent as e-mails or attachments to e-mails. (See Microsoft Office for templates for memos, e-mails, and more.)

In the workplace, we write and read memos for a variety of reasons, such as:

- To provide (or receive) information for specific plans, meetings, events, policies, and so on
- To provide (or receive) instructions for specific tasks
- To persuade others (or be persuaded) to take a specific action or make a decision

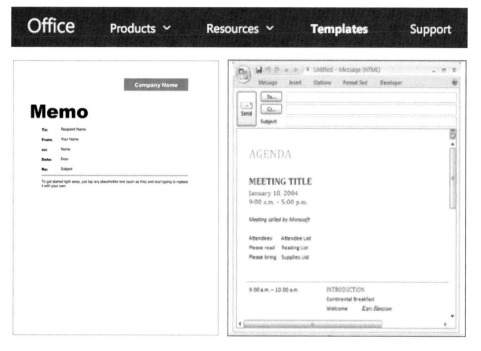

**Microsoft Office**
offers templates
for business
memos, agendas,
e-mails, and other
common workplace
documents.

The information in memos is often time sensitive and related to specific tasks or events, so people usually read them when they receive them or in preparation for a specific meeting, discussion, or decision. For example, a company president trying to decide whether to create a new position for a director of sales and marketing might read the company's year-end report and the memos about sales, competition, and the larger marketplace as part of their decision-making process.

## Analyzing Business Memos

**Purpose**  We write memos to share data, summarize events, give instructions, lay out a plan, and explain and get buy-in for our ideas. In some cases, a colleague or manager may ask you to write a memo that provides an update on a project you're working on, a problem you're solving, or a schedule you're planning. Other times, you may decide to write a memo to a specific reader (or readers) with a proposal for getting something done or a plan for making an improvement to a process or product. Often our memos have multiple purposes—not just to inform, but also to convince our readers to agree with something or to do something specific.

Memos are often written collaboratively by a group of people who worked on a project together. For instance, a college committee charged with exploring ways to better serve alumni might write a memo to the administrator responsible for alumni communications with its recommendations.

**Audience**   In the workplace, memo writers know that their readers need information in order to take specific actions or make decisions. Readers of instructional memos—or any correspondence that provides instruction—want to learn quickly what needs to be done—and why, when, how, and in what order.

Workplace writers need to keep in mind that they always have multiple audiences. Their primary readers are the people they've addressed the memo to; they are the ones who will use the information and/or take action based on the content of the memo. Writers' secondary audiences might include the supervisor(s) of the primary audience. Finally, memos and e-mails can have unforeseen audiences, as is the case when an e-mail is accidentally sent to the wrong person or forwarded by the recipient to people the author may not have intended as readers.

Sometimes a memo or e-mail is leaked to the press, as happens with company or government scandals. Internal memos are often presented as evidence in court when companies are charged with crimes. Amid the 2015 Volkswagon emissions scandal, internal memos came to light revealing that the company's CEO knew that the vehicles were equipped with devices that allowed them to cheat on emissions tests.

**Rhetorical appeals**   Memo writers appeal most often to readers' senses of ethos and logos, and sometimes to pathos. Because readers will use the information in the memo to formulate plans, make decisions, and take action, it's important that they feel that the information contained in the memo is accurate and true. Sometimes an appeal to pathos can help you develop a rapport with your readers.

**Modes & media**   Memos are text based, and writers sometimes include images. For example, if you need to discuss sales figures, you might present them in a chart. Memos can be in print or digital format. Many organizations ask their employees to send memos as e-mails to reduce paper usage. Sending memos digitally also allows readers to archive memos, which saves space and makes it easier to search for particular memos.

**Elements of the genre**   Business memos are characterized by the following qualities:

- *They are written to specific recipients.* As discussed above, memos always have multiple audiences. When writing a memo, identify your primary and secondary audiences. To determine if a person is part of your secondary audience, think about (1) to what degree that person will be interested in the information you're presenting, and (2) what their connection is to your primary audience.

- *They answer the questions who, what, when, where, why, and how.* Be sure to provide recipients with the information they'll need to understand your context and purpose. If you're reporting on a client visit, for example, include the name of the client and their company; the date of the visit; a clear statement about the purpose of the visit; a summary of the visit; an explanation of whether or to what extent the purpose of the visit was achieved; how the purpose was achieved; and an explanation of the next steps. If any of this information is missing, the reader will need to contact the author for more information.

- *They include important information in subject line and first paragraph.* Use your memo's subject line to concisely and specifically state what the e-mail is about. "Client visit" is too vague in a company that might make hundreds of client visits every month; "Simpson follow-up visit, June 2020" gives more information for the reader who wants to quickly determine what the memo is about. Use your first paragraph to convey the most important points; many readers will only have time to read the first paragraph carefully and will then skim the rest of the memo.

**Style**   Business writers make sure that their memos are:

- *Accurate and clear.* Whether you are writing to inform, instruct, or persuade, the information in your memo must be correct and easy to understand. This is crucial when providing instructions to a colleague or when supplying information that will be used as the basis for plans and decisions.

- *Concise and precise.* Readers want data, steps to specific tasks, and any arguments for taking action presented succinctly; they also need to be able to skim your memo or e-mail quickly to find what they need. Information must be precise. For example, telling a company president that "sales are up" may not be enough information for them to make an informed decision; the president needs to know that sales are up by 0.5 percent or 3 percent.

- *As brief as possible.* Writers of memos and e-mails strive to be as brief as their subject allows, especially in a busy workplace.

- *Informal yet professional in tone and voice.* Memos are internal business documents; colleagues write them to each other. This allows for a certain level of informality; the writing can be friendly yet professional.

- *As detailed as required for the situation.* Use details to help your readers understand your purpose. Stating that there "were problems" at a client site won't be particularly illuminating to your audience. However, if you write, "I encountered problem X. I resolved problem X by doing A, B, and C," you give readers enough detail to understand the situation.

**Design**   Business writers use the following design elements:

- *Headings.* Memo headings include the date, recipients' names, sender's name, and a descriptive subject line. The names of anyone receiving a copy of the memo (secondary readers) are listed after "CC." ("CC" stands for "carbon copy," an old-fashioned way of producing an instant copy by using carbon paper between two

Review a piece of workplace writing that you or someone else composed. Does it include detailed paragraphs that you wish were in list form? If so, revise the memo or e-mail so that the details or steps are presented in a succinct bulleted list. Is it easier to read? How might you apply this practice to future business correspondence?

sheets of regular paper.) In e-mailed memos, the e-mail's "To," "CC," "From," and subject lines serve the purpose of a heading. E-mail also makes possible blind CCing, in which an e-mail is CCed to someone who is not listed in the heading. However, blind CCing can be seen as unfair or deceptive, so it's best to avoid this practice.

- *Spacing.* Memos are usually single-spaced within paragraphs, with an extra line break between paragraphs (rather than indenting paragraphs). This extra white space between paragraphs makes it easier for memos to be read quickly, which is often necessary in a business or organizational setting. E-mailed memos are generally formatted in the same way.

- *Numbered and bulleted lists.* Because memos are usually read very quickly (or skimmed), format important information so that readers can grasp it quickly. Use numbered and bulleted lists to present brief points of information: A numbered list indicates that order matters; a bulleted list indicates that order is not as important. In a memo about steps taken to solve a client's printer issues, for example, a numbered list would give which steps were taken and in what order.

**Sources**   Include sources as needed to back up and support your points and to credit others who have contributed to the ideas you're presenting. If you're sending a memo about sales figures to your company's president, you might refer to a recent sales report. You wouldn't include a Works Cited page as you would for a research or scholarly article; instead, you might refer to the specific report in the body of the memo and attach the report as a separate document. Alternatively, you could copy and paste it directly into your memo.

# Guided Reading | Business Memo

The memo below was written by Sherry Mooney, the editor for the 3rd ed. of this book at Bedford/St. Martin's, an imprint of Macmillan Learning. In it, Mooney asks for feedback on some technical specifications before she and another colleague begin work on a project. She sent the memo as an e-mail and copied everyone who needed to see the response.

## Sherry Mooney, *Hiring a Vendor*

| RHETORICAL SITUATION & CHOICES | | GENRE CONVENTIONS | |
|---|---|---|---|

**PURPOSE**
Mooney's purpose is to get feedback on technical specifications so that she can move forward on a video project.

**AUDIENCE**
The primary audience is Emily, a media producer. She needs to weigh in on the technical specifications of the videos. Julia, a media editor, is the secondary audience.

**RHETORICAL APPEALS**
Mooney appeals to Emily's sense of logos by listing the questions in priority order. Mooney develops her ethos by indicating that she is well informed about the project she's working on and has a clear and systematic approach to the project in mind.

**MODES & MEDIA**
Mode = written: The memo is text based and does not include images, though some memos benefit from images. Because the document is a written text (and not, say, a voice mail), the recipient, Brower, will

◄ **What is the composer, Sherry Mooney, doing?**

**How do I know this is a ►
business memo?**

From:      Mooney, Sherry
Sent:      Monday, July 1, 2019      3:07 PM
To:        Emily Brower
CC:        Julia Domenicucci

Subject:   Hiring a Vendor: Video Scripts

Emily,

I'm reaching out so that we can get an early start on finding a vendor for an upcoming project. We have been working with samples generated in-house for the past several months, soliciting feedback from the market, and I believe we're ready to move forward in drafting the individual video scripts. Below are the remaining open questions. When you have a moment, please do weigh in on the below and then I will ask Julia to begin the search based on the below criteria:

1. We need to request samples and quotes from between three and five potential vendors. We already have TStop as one potential option, as we have worked with them in the past, so we will need two to four more.
2. The project start date is negotiable, but should not be later than September 20. (Does this work with your schedule?)
3. The project end date is not negotiable—we need all fully completed and approved files by December 31. (Is there any cushion here, in case we need it?)
4. What are the technical specifications needed on your end? We will be using the scripts as the basis for the transcripts, so let me know if we need to include any details (descriptions of the characters, etc.) to maintain our accessibility standards.

**ELEMENTS OF THE GENRE**
**Important information is given up front:** The subject line tells the topic of the memo and the first paragraph gives context for the questions that need to be answered.

**Writing is clear, precise, and directive:** Mooney states clearly what she would like Brower to do. She doesn't provide her opinions or say more than she needs to: She sticks to the information relevant to the tasks at hand.

**Brief:** This memo is primarily composed of bulleted and numbered lists but conveys enough instruction and information for Brower to take action. Mooney does not include irrelevant detail; she sticks to the point.

**STYLE**
**Detail:** Mooney gives precise technical specifications for the video scripts.

*(Continues on next page)*

be able to reread the memo (even print it out as a to-do list) as she responds to the items needing feedback to make sure she has done everything asked of her.

**Medium = Digital:** Mooney and Brower's company, Bedford/ St. Martin's, like most companies in the twenty-first century, encourages employees to use e-mail to send memos. E-mails allow colleagues to communicate quickly— and also allow for easy tracking of the memo. If Mooney wants to double-check when she sent the memo, she can simply check her "sent" or "Browser" folder and look at the time stamp on the e-mail. She could even enable her e-mail to request a "read receipt," which is an automatically generated e-mail from the recipient to the sender confirming that the e-mail has been received and opened.

### Technical Specifications for the Video Scripts

- Two-column **action/audio format**. Let's have the action on the left, audio on the right, so that the script is broken down screen-by-screen/visual-by-visual (so these will be broken down more finely than all existing scripts). Action descriptions include anything appearing on screen and should be very detailed. As a general rule of thumb, any static visual should be present for no more than five seconds. (Each visual description should be in its own row with accompanying audio on the same row in the right column.) If the visual is a chunk of text that needs to be on screen for a longer period of time, describe animations like highlighting, on-screen notes, or callouts that can help keep visuals lively.
- Videos should be **one to three minutes** long, so reading a script aloud should take roughly that long.
- Scripts should include **three key sections**: Adult narrator introduction, student narration and action, adult narrator conclusion. The introduction should set the scene and establish goals. The conclusion should provide takeaways and clearly tie the video to the chapter content. Both the intro and conclusion should be very brief.

Thanks so much for your help!

— Sherry

Sherry Mooney | Senior Editor | she/her/hers

bedford/st.martin's
Macmillan Learning

**Informal yet professional tone and voice:** Although Mooney comes across as approachable ("when you have a moment") and polite, she takes a very professional tone in the memo, explaining the feedback that is needed in an organized and methodical way.

**DESIGN**

**Lists:** Mooney provides a numbered list of items for feedback and a bulleted list of technical specifications.

**SOURCES**

Mooney's memo doesn't require sources because Mooney herself is the source of the information.

---

## QUESTIONS | Analyzing Mooney's Business Memo

### RHETORICAL SITUATION & CHOICES

1. **Purpose.** What is the main purpose of Mooney's memo? To inform? To persuade? To move to action?

2. **Audience.** To what degree does Mooney's memo anticipate her reader's questions about who, what, when, where, why, and how?

### GENRE CONVENTIONS

5. **Elements of the genre.** How does the subject line "Hiring a Vendor: Video Scripts" give the memo a context and describe the tasks for the reader? What purpose does the first paragraph of the memo serve? Would the memo be more or less effective without the first paragraph? Why?

3. **Rhetorical appeals.** What does Mooney do to develop her ethos? How does she come across?

4. **Modes & media.** Smartphones and computer programs often offer voice memos as an option. Do you think Mooney's memo would be more or less effective if recorded as a voice memo? Why?

6. **Elements of the genre.** Notice how specific Mooney is about the information she needs Brower to provide. Does the order in which items are presented make sense? Is there another order or organization that might make more sense?

7. **Style.** How would you characterize the tone of the memo? Which words and phrases contribute to the tone? How does the tone contribute to the development of Mooney's ethos?

8. **Design.** Mooney uses two different types of lists in the memo: numbered and bulleted. How do the different types of lists organize the material?

9. **Sources.** This particular memo does not use sources. Can you think of sources that could have been mentioned to make the memo more effective?

## CHECKLIST | Drafting a Business Memo

Are you thinking of drafting a business memo or e-mail? Ask yourself the following questions:

### RHETORICAL SITUATION & CHOICES

☐ **Purpose.** What is the purpose of the memo I am writing? What kind of information do I need to provide? Will the information be used to inform a decision or action? Do I want to persuade my reader to take action? Am I collaborating with others? If so, do we all have a similar purpose in writing the memo?

☐ **Audience.** Who will use the information in my memo, and how will they use the information? Is there anyone else who needs to be in the loop? How would the organization or company I represent look if the memo were leaked or blind copied to unintended readers?

☐ **Rhetorical appeals.** How will I establish my credibility as a writer? How can I organize my information and use lists to appeal to readers' sense of logos? If appropriate to the context of the memo, how will I appeal to my readers based

### GENRE CONVENTIONS

☐ **Elements of the genre.** How will I convey information about who, what, when, where, why, and how? How will my subject line indicate as precisely as possible my purpose in writing the memo? How will my first paragraph neatly summarize my most important points? How can I convey information precisely, accurately, and clearly, while still being brief?

☐ **Style.** How much detail will I need to include to allow readers to fully understand and contextualize the information in the memo? How can I come across as friendly yet professional?

☐ **Design.** How will I use lists to make my information clear and easy to understand? Would numbered lists, which indicate order, make more sense, or would bulleted lists work better?

on pathos? Will an emotional appeal give me a rapport with my readers?

☐ **Modes & media.** Will my text-based memo benefit from images to convey my point(s) quickly and clearly? Will my memo be more effective in print or digital form? What is the best way to reach my readers? Are they working in the office with me, or are they working remotely?

☐ **Sources.** Will I need to cite sources to back up the information in my memo? Are there attachments I might include to assist readers in understanding the memo better?

---

**PRACTICE**

## Communicating in the Workplace

Think about where you currently work or where you worked most recently. Make a list of the different policies/practices that employees had to follow. Look over your list and underline those that were perhaps controversial or were ones employees often disregarded. Choose one of those policies, and brainstorm a list of reasons why that policy/practice needs to be eliminated. Then draft a memo to your boss addressing that policy. In your memo, be sure to include a heading with the date, your recipient's name, your name, and a descriptive subject line. Organize your memo logically and be as specific and precise as you can.

# Infographics: Visual Instructions

Infographics, like charts, are visual representations of information. Infographics can help you simplify complicated information by providing graphics that consolidate the information into several captivating visuals. In the workplace, infographics can be used to help convey material prior to a training session, to illustrate results of a campaign, to reinforce a company's message, and to illustrate the features of a new product.

## Analyzing Infographics

**Purpose**   Composers create infographics to explain complex information concisely by using engaging visuals. When people view an infographic, they should be able to understand the information presented with a simple glance. Infographics can be designed to communicate messages, show relationships between things, and/or clarify complex processes.

**Audience**   Composers of infographics know that their readers want information in a concise, easy-to-read format. They know readers might consult their infographic for data that will help them make a decision.

**Rhetorical appeals**   To gain readers' confidence in the content and establish ethos, composers of infographics need to conduct research and present correct information. They can also appeal to audiences through logos by using logical organization and smart, digestible design.

**Modes & media**   Infographics use visuals and text to convey information. Often the visual content dominates and text is used mainly for labels. Infographics can be communicated in print and digitally, although most are distributed digitally.

**Elements of the genre**   Infographics are:

- *Based on facts and data.* The information presented in infographics is based on research that others have done (such as existing statistics) or that the composer has collected personally (through primary research, such as interviews).
- *Precise and clearly labeled and titled.* The elements in infographics are labeled so that readers know what they represent.
- *Illustrated with symbols that convey information.* Visual devices, such as icons, represent ideas.
- *Focused on relevant data.* Only data that is relevant to the information being presented is included.

**Style**   Creators of infographics make the following stylistic choices:

- *What details to present.* Infographics only include the details necessary to convey the message. Since the goal of an infographic is to make it easy for readers to absorb data quickly, too much detail might make it difficult for readers to see what's most important.
- *What techniques, tone, and voice to use.* The best infographics use simple, direct language. Text is used judiciously, providing just enough information to clarify the visuals. Tone is neutral and objective.

**Design**   When designing an infographic, remember the following:

- *Simple is best.* Infographics make information accessible and digestible.
- *Color is key.* Colors are used to help separate and highlight different pieces of information. However, too many colors can be distracting.
- *The parts need to be arranged logically and spatially.* Infographics lay out information and visuals in a way that shows readers what is most important. When there are multiple visuals, designers add white space between the elements to show separation or place the elements near each other to show connections.

**Sources**   Infographics are based on composers' knowledge or research. Readers assume that the infographic is presenting reliable data based on specific sources. Many infographics include a source or list of sources, which adds to their credibility and authority.

# Guided Reading | Infographic

Jennifer Ackerman, who wrote the text, is a writer who focuses on science, nature, and human biology. Javier Zarracina, who designed the graphics, is the graphics director at *USA Today*. The infographic explains what a nap is, why we should do more of it, and how to do it well. Ackerman and Zarracina created it as a part of their work as content creators for new outlets.

## The Boston Globe, *What's the Best Way to Nap?*

**RHETORICAL SITUATION & CHOICES**

What are the ▶ composers, Ackerman and Zarracina, doing?

**GENRE CONVENTIONS**

How do I know this ▶ is an instructional infographic?

**BORN TO NAP**
Most mammals sleep for short periods throughout the day. We have consolidated sleep into one long period, but the biological vestige remains. Our bodies are programmed for two periods of intense sleepiness: in the early morning, from about 2 to 4 a.m., and in the afternoon, between 1 and 3 p.m. This midday wave of drowsiness is not due to heat or too many fries at lunch (it occurs even if we skip eating). Rather, it arises from an afternoon quiescent phase in our physiology, which diminishes our reaction time, memory, coordination, mood, and alertness.

**ARE YOU A LARK OR AN OWL?**
To determine the best time to nap, it helps to know your "chronotype." What time you would get up and go to sleep if you were entirely free to plan your day? If you're a lark, apt to wake as early as 6 a.m. and go to sleep around 9 or 10 p.m., you're going to feel your nap need around 1 or 1:30 p.m. If you're an owl, preferring to go to bed after midnight or 1 a.m., and to wake around 8 or 9 a.m., your afternoon "sleep gate" will open later, closer to 2:30 or 3 p.m.

**WHAT'S IN A NAP?**
In designing the optimal nap you need to grasp its potential components. During sleep, your brain's electrical activity goes through a five-phase cycle:

**STAGE 1:** *Falling asleep*    **STAGE 2:** *Light sleep.*    **STAGES 3 AND 4:** *Deep, slow-wave sleep.*    **REM:** *Dreaming stage.*    *A whole cycle lasts about an hour and a half (and repeats during nighttime sleep).*

20 min    45 min    60 min    90 min

**A short afternoon catnap of 20 minutes** yields mostly Stage 2 sleep, which enhances alertness and concentration, elevates mood, and sharpens motor skills. To boost alertness on waking, you can drink a cup of coffee before you nap. Caffeine requires 20 or 30 minutes to take effect, so it will kick in just as you're waking. Naps of up to 45 minutes may also include rapid eye movement (REM) sleep, which enhances creative thinking and boosts sensory processing.

**Limit your nap to 45 minutes or less,** if you need to spring into action after dozing. Otherwise, you may drift into slow-wave sleep. Waking from this stage results in serious sleep inertia, that feeling of grogginess and disorientation that can last for a half hour or more.

But you might want to take a long nap, **at least 90 minutes.** Many of us get about an hour to an hour and a half less sleep per night than we need. A new study shows that the sleep-deprived brain toggles between normal activity and complete lapses, or failures, a dangerous state of slowed responses and foggy inattention. Sound familiar?

**Naps of 90 to 120 minutes** usually comprise all stages, including REM and deep slow-wave sleep, which helps to clear your mind, improve memory recall, and recoup lost sleep. Longer naps in the morning yield more REM sleep, while those in the afternoon offer more slow-wave sleep. A nap that is long enough to include a full sleep cycle, at least 90 minutes, will limit sleep inertia by allowing you to wake from REM sleep.

**THE PERFECT SIESTA**
Once nap time and length are settled, you need some preparations for the rest:

Find a safe, quiet, comfortable place, preferably one where you can lie down. (It takes about 50 percent longer to fall asleep sitting upright.)

Have a light blanket handy in case you get chilly, but nothing too heavy (excess warmth can make you oversleep).

Set an alarm.

Darken the room or use eye shades.

Calm your body by breathing slowly and deeply. Concentrate on relaxing your muscles one group at a time.

If noise is an issue, put in earplugs or turn on some white noise.

Quiet your mind by repeating a mantra, taking a mental walk at a relaxing place like the beach, or counting sheep or floating z's.

**ENJOY**
Relish the benefits of a sharper mind, improved accuracy and perception, quicker motor skills, keener coordination, and enhanced mood and memory. Getting even the briefest nap is better than nothing. A 2008 study at the University of Düsseldorf showed that the mere onset of sleep may trigger active memory processes that remain effective even if sleep is limited to only a few minutes. And last year, a British study suggested that just knowing a nap was coming was enough to lower blood pressure.

So heed the wake-up call: If you want to be your best all day long, at least *plan* on napping.

Credit: Boston Globe/Getty Images.

## RHETORICAL SITUATION & CHOICES

### PURPOSE
Their purpose is to remove the stigma around napping and help people nap better.

### AUDIENCE
Readers of this infographic are most likely people who feel guilty or embarrassed about napping. Another audience might be experienced nappers.

### RHETORICAL APPEALS
The composers establish their ethos by showing that their ideas are based on scientific evidence, such as the Harvard study. The composers use logic (logos) by organizing the information into concrete steps readers can take to improve their naps.

### MODES & MEDIA
**Mode = written and visual:** The composers use a combination of visuals and text to convey information about napping. They use clocklike visuals to illustrate the optimal times to nap.

**Medium = digital:** This information is published online.

## GENRE CONVENTIONS

### ELEMENTS OF THE GENRE
**Based on data:** The composers draw on various studies: Harvard, NASA, and University of Dusseldorf.

**Precise:** The sleep cycle is illustrated with numbered stages and a clear breakdown of minutes.

**Clearly titled:** The words in the title convey the main point of the infographic: How to Nap.

### STYLE
**Detail:** Just enough detail is used to make the information clear and authoritative. The upper portion of the infographic illustrates the difference between being a morning lark and a night owl, while the lower part gives pointers for napping well.

**Objective tone:** All information is presented as fact.

### DESIGN
The graphic at the bottom illustrates two people practicing the pointers that have been offered in the text. The predominant color is a soothing, calm blue.

### SOURCES
Ackerman and Zarracina reference sources throughout, such as various studies used.

## QUESTIONS | Analyzing *The Boston Globe*'s Infographic

**RHETORICAL SITUATION & CHOICES**

1. **Purpose.** How does the infographic convey information about ways to nap? To what extent does the infographic present its information as an argument?

2. **Audience.** If the infographic were designed primarily for experienced nappers, how would the information need to change?

3. **Rhetorical appeals.** Sources are mentioned sporadically. Is this enough to establish ethos? How else might the creators of the infographic convey their credibility?

4. **Modes & media.** What are the advantages of making the infographic available digitally? How could the infographic be revised to take better advantage of a digital medium?

5. **Elements of the genre.** How do the graphics add to the infographic? Which graphics would you change? How would you change them?

**GENRE CONVENTIONS**

6. **Elements of the genre.** How does the infographic show how ideas are related? What could be changed to make the relationships clearer?

7. **Style.** Describe the level of detail in the infographic. Why do you think the composers included the napping pointers at the bottom of the infographic? Is there too much text? Would there be a better way to represent the ideas?

8. **Design.** How does the use of color relate to the information presented in the infographic?

9. **Design.** The infographic includes a lot of information, separated with some subheads. What are some other ways the designers might have separated sections?

10. **Sources.** What kinds of additional research and sources would strengthen the infographic?

## CHECKLIST | Drafting an Infographic

Are you thinking of creating an infographic? Ask yourself the following questions:

**RHETORICAL SITUATION & CHOICES**

☐ **Purpose.** What complex information might be explained more easily by using engaging visuals? Is there a complex process I want to illustrate visually? How can I make sure the information presented is easily digestible? What message do I want to communicate?

☐ **Audience.** Who are my readers? Why should/will my infographic matter to them? What do I want them to get out of it? Does my audience consist of specialists or general readers? What level of visual detail will my infographic need to communicate my message to my readers?

**GENRE CONVENTIONS**

☐ **Elements of the genre.** What types of data will I use to create my infographic? Is my data focused? Do I want to include symbols? Do I want my title to indicate my ultimate findings or present a question?

☐ **Style.** How will I keep my tone objective? What level of detail will I include in the infographic?

☐ **Design.** How do I want to organize my infographic spatially? Are there multiple visuals I need to include? Does each visual have

□ **Rhetorical appeals.** How will I establish my authority and reliability? How will I convey my information so my readers believe my data? To what extent will I rely on logic to support my interpretations? How will I organize the information to convey this logic?

□ **Modes & media.** What balance of visuals and text do I want to use? Do I want readers to access my infographic digitally or in print? If digitally, how can I make use of the digital environment? Should I have links to other digital material?

accompanying text? How will I use colors in the infographic? What colors will help me convey my information?

□ **Sources.** Is the infographic based on my own knowledge, or do I need to do research to gather data and statistics? How many sources do I need to draw on in order to present the information effectively?

**PRACTICE**

## Conveying Information Visually

Think about a habit you have that may not be appreciated by others. Perhaps you play with a fidget toy to relieve stress. Maybe you drum your fingers on a tabletop when you are bored. Find out the science behind your unappreciated habit. Come up with a list of best practices for people who want to adopt this habit. How might you visually represent this information in an infographic? Using the infographic about how to nap as your model, create an infographic entitled "How to X." As you create your infographic, consider what you want to convey and why, how you can best establish your ethos, and how to best use images, text, color, and design.

# Proposals

A proposal is a persuasive document that suggests a plan or purchase. As with memos, proposals are often written collaboratively by a group of people. For example, a group of people who manage purchases for a company might collaborate to propose a new purchasing system that will save time and money.

## Analyzing Proposals

**Purpose**   We write proposals to suggest that something be purchased or an action be taken in the workplace. A proposal clearly states what is being proposed, why it is being proposed, what actions need to be taken and by whom to achieve the proposed idea, and how much the proposed item or plan will cost.

**Audience**   Proposals are usually written to the person who can make the decision to adopt the proposed plan. Proposal readers will reach a decision based entirely on the information included in the proposal, so it is important to anticipate exactly what they will need to know to make that decision. Secondary readers might include people who will be affected by the proposed plan or who might be consulted by the decision maker.

**Rhetorical appeals**   Proposal writers need to appeal primarily to readers' senses of ethos and logos. Because proposal readers make decisions based on proposals, the proposal writer must come across as ethical and trustworthy, and the plan proposed must logically grow out of a need (to save money, to make things more efficient, to improve quality, or the like).

**Modes & media**   Proposals are text based and may include images that help build the case for the proposed plan, such as a chart that compares the current cost of making copies with the cost of making copies with the fancy new copy machine the proposal suggests purchasing. Proposals can be in print or digital format; they are often sent out as e-mail attachments.

**Elements of the genre**   Proposals are characterized by the following:

- *They are written to specific recipients.* Like a memo, a proposal usually begins with the specific recipient(s) listed.

- *They provide context.* The proposal must establish that there is a need for the proposed plan, either a problem that the proposed plan will solve or another need, such as improving quality or cutting costs.

- *They make a clear statement of what is being proposed.* The proposal must precisely state what is being proposed so decision makers know exactly what they are saying yes or no to, such as the purchase of a new copy machine, a new policy on who can use the copy machine, or a new plan for training employees in using the copy machine.

- *They give information about the advantages of adopting the proposed plan and possible obstacles.* A proposal should explain what will be gained by adopting the proposed plan or acknowledge that there are obstacles to adopting it. For example, if use of the copy machine will be restricted, people who are accustomed to being able to make copies whenever they want may become disgruntled; the proposal should explain how to mitigate that disgruntlement.

- *They provide an implementation plan, including the costs of adopting the proposed plan.* The steps that need to be taken to implement the plan should be defined. If there are costs associated with it, those should be clearly spelled out in the proposal.

**Style**   Proposal writers make the following stylistic choices. Their work is:

- *Accurate and clear.* To enable the decision maker to make a good decision, the proposal must include accurate and clear information.

- *Detailed.* Details are important to help the reader understand exactly what is being proposed. Outlining a problem and then saying, "Something has to change" isn't helpful to the reader, but "We can mitigate this problem with a new three-step procedure," and then outlining the three steps is helpful.

**Design**   When designing a proposal, you will make choices about the following:

- *Headings.* Proposals are organized with headings for the different sections, such as "Background," "Plan," and "Budget." This allows busy readers to quickly identify what kind of information will be discussed in the section. It also helps a reader returning to the document to quickly find the information he or she needs; for example, if the decision maker has decided to green light a proposed plan, they may need to quickly flip to the budget section while on a phone call with the company financial manager.

- *Numbered and bulleted lists.* Like memos, proposals are often read very quickly, so the use of numbered and bulleted lists helps readers absorb important points.

**Sources**   Proposals may cite sources that support the proposed plan or help build the argument for the existence of a problem. A source that explains how older copy machines contribute to workplace toxins may help convince readers to consider replacing a machine that seems to be working just fine.

# Guided Reading | Proposal

## Kelly Ratajczak, *Proposal to Add a Wellness Program*

### PURPOSE
Ratajczak's purpose is to convince the head of Human Resources to implement a wellness program at their organization.

### AUDIENCE
As the head of Human Resources, the reader is the person who will make the decision on whether to implement the wellness plan Ratajczak proposes.

### RHETORICAL APPEALS
By citing reputable sources, Ratajczak appeals to ethos. Those sources help create the logical chain that supports her proposal to create a wellness program (logos).

### MODES & MEDIA
Mode = written: Ratajczak opted not to include any visuals and relied solely on words to make her argument.

Medium = digital: The proposal was e-mailed to the decision maker as an attachment.

◄ What is the composer, Kelly Ratajczak, doing?

How do I know this is ► a proposal?

To:  Jay Crosson, Senior Vice President, Human Resources
From:  Kelly Ratajczak, Intern, Purchasing Department
Subject:  Proposal to Add a Wellness Program
Date:  April 24, 2019

Health care costs are rising. In the long run, implementing a wellness program in our corporate culture will decrease the company's health care costs.

Research indicates that nearly 70% of health care costs are from common illnesses related to high blood pressure, overweight, lack of exercise, high cholesterol, stress, poor nutrition, and other preventable health issues (Hall, 2006). Health care costs are a major expense for most businesses, and they do not reflect costs due to the loss of productivity or absenteeism. A wellness program would address most, if not all, of these health care issues and related costs.

### BENEFITS OF HEALTHIER EMPLOYEES

A wellness program would substantially reduce costs associated with employee health care, and in addition our company would prosper through many other benefits. Businesses that have wellness programs show a lower cost in production, fewer sick days, and healthier employees ("Workplace Health," 2006). Our healthier employees will help to cut not only our production and absenteeism costs but also potential costs such as higher turnover because of low employee morale.

### IMPLEMENTING THE PROGRAM

Implementing a good wellness program means making small changes to the work environment, starting with a series of information sessions. Simple changes to our work environment should include healthier food selections in vending machines and in the employee cafeteria. A smoke-free environment, inside and outside the building, could be a new company policy. An important step is to educate our

### ELEMENTS OF THE GENRE
Specific audience: The proposal is addressed specifically to the head of Human Resources.

Context for the proposal: The proposal opens with information about how a wellness program could help reduce healthcare costs.

A clear statement of what is being proposed: The subject line is "Proposal to Add a Wellness Program."

Information about advantages of the plan and obstacles to adopting it. The proposal discusses both individual and financial obstacles to implementing a wellness program.

Implementation plan: The implementation plan is loosely described because several types of plans could be adopted. Ratajczak assumes her audience will decide what kind of plan to implement and that will then dictate the costs.

employees through information seminars and provide health care guides and pamphlets for work and home. In addition, the human resources department could expand the current employee assistance program by developing online materials that help employees and their families to assess their individual health goals.

Each health program is different in its own way, and there are a number of programs that can be designed to meet the needs of our individual employees. Some programs that are becoming increasingly popular in the workplace are the following ("Workplace Health," 2006):

- health promotion program
- subsidized health club membership
- return-to-work programs
- health-risk appraisals and screenings

## OBSTACLES: INDIVIDUAL AND FINANCIAL

The largest barrier in a wellness program is changing the habits and behaviors of our employees. Various incentives such as monetary bonuses, vacation days, merchandise rewards, recognition, and appreciation help to instill new habits and attitudes. Providing a healthy environment and including family in certain programs also help to encourage healthier choices and behaviors (Hall, 2006).

In the long run, the costs of incorporating a wellness program will be far less than rising costs associated with health care. An employee's sense of recognition, appreciation, or accomplishment is an incentive that has relatively low or no costs. The owner of Natural Ovens Bakery, Paul Sitt, has stated that his company gained financially after providing programs including free healthy lunches for employees (Springer, 2005). Sitt said he believes that higher morale and keeping valuable employees have helped his business tremendously.

It is important that our company be healthy in every way possible. Research shows that 41% of businesses already have some type of wellness program in progress and that 32% will incorporate programs within the next year ("Workplace Health," 2006). Our company should always be ahead of our competitors. I want to thank you for your time, and I look forward to discussing this proposal with you further next week.

**STYLE**

**Accurate and clear:** Ratajczak carefully refers to specific research studies that support her argument that the company would benefit from a wellness program.

**Detailed:** Ratajczak names specific benefits of an employee wellness program and gives the percentage of companies that already have wellness programs.

**DESIGN**

**Headings:** Each section ("Benefits," "Obstacles," etc.) begins with a heading.

**Numbered and bulleted lists:** The implementation section includes a bulleted list of the types of wellness programs.

*(Continues on next page)*

References

Hall, B. (2006). Good health pays off! Fundamentals of health promotion incentives. *Journal of Deferred Compensation 11*(2), 16–26. Retrieved from http://www.aspenpublishers.com/

Springer, D. (2005, October 28). Key to business success? *La Crosse Tribune*. Retrieved from http://lacrossetribune.com/

Workplace health and productivity programs lower absenteeism, costs. (2006). *Managing Benefit Plans 6*(2), 1–4. Retrieved from http://www.ioma.com/

**SOURCES**
Sources are cited throughout the text and in the references list in APA format.

## QUESTIONS | Analyzing Ratajczak's Proposal

### RHETORICAL SITUATION & CHOICES

1. **Purpose.** Aside from the fact that Ratajczak's text has the word "proposal" in the subject line, how can you identify this document quickly as a proposal?

2. **Audience.** Is the proposal appropriately tailored to the head of Human Resources? What information does Ratajczak include that shows she knows the organization's culture?

3. **Rhetorical appeals.** How does Ratajczak establish her ethos as a concerned employee? Can you think of additional ways Ratajczak could have developed her ethos?

4. **Rhetorical appeals.** How does the proposal logically connect the proposed wellness program to an existing problem?

5. **Elements of the genre.** Are you convinced by the first two paragraphs of the proposal that the organization would benefit from a wellness program? Why or why not? If not, is there a point later in the proposal that convinces you that the organization would benefit from a wellness program?

### GENRE CONVENTIONS

6. **Elements of the genre.** Do you think Ratajczak adequately deals with the obstacles to implementing a wellness program? Why or why not?

7. **Modes & media.** Ratajczak did not include any visuals in this proposal. Can you think of a chart or infographic that might have been helpful?

8. **Style.** Is one section of the proposal more or less accurate and clear than other sections? What advice would you give Ratajczak about making the proposal more accurate and clear?

9. **Design.** How does the proposal's design make it easily and quickly readable?

10. **Sources.** How do the sources used reflect upon Ratajczak?

## CHECKLIST | Drafting a Proposal

Are you thinking of drafting a proposal? Ask yourself the following questions:

**RHETORICAL SITUATION & CHOICES**

☐ **Purpose.** How can I convince the decision maker that there is a problem that my proposal will address? How can I persuade the decision maker that my proposed plan will address the problem?

☐ **Audience.** Who is the person who will make a decision about my proposal? How can I show the decision maker that my proposed plan will address his or her priorities?

☐ **Rhetorical appeals.** How can I establish myself as reliable and responsible? How can I logically connect my proposed plan with a problem that exists?

☐ **Modes & media.** Will my proposal be delivered in print form or digitally? Would it be appropriate for me to include a visual(s)?

**GENRE CONVENTIONS**

☐ **Elements of the genre.** Have I clearly explained the context for my proposal? Have I expressed my proposed plan clearly and succinctly? Have I provided information about advantages and/or obstacles to implementing my proposed plan? Have I suggested a plan for implementation?

☐ **Style.** How can I use specific details to support and develop generalizations that I make? Does my proposal state clearly exactly what I am proposing? Does my proposal clearly explain what it would take to implement my plan?

☐ **Design.** How can I use headings to organize the material in my proposal? How can I use bulleted or numbered lists to organize my material? How can I ensure that someone who reads my proposal quickly will understand what I am proposing and how it will address a problem?

☐ **Sources.** What sources can I use to establish myself as professional and knowledgeable? Have I properly cited any sources I do use both in the text and in a Works Cited list?

---

**PRACTICE**

# Proposing Ideas & Solutions in the Workplace

Think about a current or former job. Brainstorm a list of all the current problems you face or others face at that job. For each problem, generate potential solutions. For example, perhaps the cafeteria is too crowded at lunchtime. A possible solution might be to have staggered lunch hours. Look over your list and choose the problem you find most important/compelling. Who would be the person who could affect change? Draft a proposal to that person that establishes the problem, describes the need for change, makes an argument for a solution, acknowledges any obstacles, and includes an implementation plan. Make sure to include specific details/evidence to support your ideas.

# WORKPLACE GENRES

Now that you have reviewed a variety of different workplace genres, noticing their commonalities and differences, and practiced a few of the key moves made in workplace genres, you should feel ready to tackle some larger projects. Here we offer two extended project ideas for you to play with. The first invites you to write your school's administration a proposal for a new program, event, or process. The second offers you an opportunity to create a résumé and cover letter for your future self.

## IN PRACTICE Workplace Writing Projects

### Proposal & Infographic

1. **Identify a need in your institution.** Brainstorm a list of some of the problems you see in your institution. You can think of a "problem" as a broad category that includes obstacles to efficiency and small annoyances as well as larger issues. For example, you might consider it a problem that a particular department doesn't have advisers available during the hours that are convenient for you, or that some of the information about classes on the department website isn't updated regularly. You may notice other issues that affect more of the campus, such as a lack of compost bins in and near the residence halls. Or you may be more interested in problems you see on campus that mirror larger, societal issues, such as racism or poverty. For this project, you can tackle a problem large or small, located in a particular department or beyond.

   a. For each problem you've identified, brainstorm some potential solutions.

   b. Look over your list of problems and solutions and select one that you are interested in developing further.

   c. Determine whether the problem you've decided to focus on is departmental or institution-wide. This will help you figure out who to address your proposal to. A proposal related to a department problem will probably be addressed to the department chairperson. A proposal related to an institutional issue will probably go to a dean or another administrator. Your professor or student government officer can help you determine exactly who is the best person to receive your proposal.

   d. Do some research to determine how your proposed solution could be carried out. What are the costs associated with your solution? Think about material or equipment that would need to be purchased or construction that would need to be done. Would someone need to be hired? What else would need to be done, and who would do it? For example, would a guidebook or instruction manual need to be created? Would marketing need to happen?

   e. Draft a proposal that clearly states what is being proposed, why, and how much the proposed plan will cost to implement.

   f. Be sure to acknowledge any obstacles to adopting your proposed plan. For example, if three new positions would need to be created in the department to implement your plan, and you know the department's budget is tight, you could acknowledge that, and suggest a way to implement the plan over time, adding one new position a year for three years.

   g. Use headings to help your reader quickly identify sections.

2. Create an infographic that helps establish that the problem you identified is serious enough to warrant the time and energy of the person you've identified. Ultimately, your infographic should become part of the proposal.

a. Identify an aspect of the problem you are seeking to address that can be represented visually. For example, if you need to convey information about numbers of students affected, time lost, enrollment numbers, or other numerical data, infographics can be very helpful. Infographics can also be used to illustrate processes or show relationships between things.

b. Create an infographic that is clearly labeled and uses visual devices such as icons and color to convey information.

## Résumé & Cover Letter

1. Imagine you have just graduated and received an AA, BS, MBA, PhD, a certificate in a field, or finished your residency in a medical field. Imagine where you are at the end of your educational journey. Brainstorm a list of potential jobs you might seek after your education is complete. Just make a quick list of all the jobs you might be qualified for. Don't worry about whether someone will hire you, about whether you can afford that job, about whether it's realistic. If you want to be hired as a star in a Hollywood film, go for it. It is fine to fantasize.

2. After you have a list of potential jobs, choose the one that is most appealing. Then freewrite for twenty minutes about what skills you have gained through your education that makes you a good fit for this career. If you get stuck, write, "I'm a good fit for this job because . . ." and see where that goes. Keep writing that line, and eventually something will surface. Read over your freewrite and make a list of all the skills you noted. Remember to imagine the skills you will have developed throughout your time in college, not just the ones you have already developed.

3. Research the skills needed for the job you identified in step 2. What are some of the skills an employer might be seeking? Look over your freewrite and see if there are any skills you discovered in your research that you need to add to your list.

4. Now that you have a list of all the skills you have gained, write a list of all the jobs you imagine you might have had before graduation that might relate to the position you identified in step 2. For example, if you imagine your future graduated self as a pediatrician, perhaps one of the jobs you had was a volunteer in a hospital. Maybe you also did a stint as an EMT. Remember, this can be fantasy, so feel free to imagine you've had some pretty amazing jobs.

5. It's now time for your future, graduated self to apply for the job you identified in step 2. Find a real job description or posting for that job. Working with that job description and your list of future experience, create a résumé that highlights the skills, experiences, and jobs that would qualify you for this position. Use the models in Chapter 8 as you draft.

6. Draft a cover letter that addresses this position. Your cover letter should reflect your desire for the job and help your reader see why you are a good fit for the job.

7. Celebrate your new career!

# 9

# PUBLIC GENRES

# Public Genres & Projects

When you write for public audiences, consider that there are different degrees of publicness. When you post on Instagram, for example, you might consider yourself to be writing for your followers, but if you don't have your privacy settings configured to keep strangers from seeing your posts, you are actually composing for everyone on Instagram—over a billion users. In general, you are writing for a public audience any time you expect people you don't know personally to encounter your writing. Composing for public audiences can take many forms, from creating an art exhibit to writing a letter to the editor to posting a flyer on campus or an image on Instagram. Most composing for public audiences is initiated when a composer is moved to share a message with a public group.

Some of the typical purposes of composing for public audiences are to argue for a position on an issue, to share an idea, and to join an ongoing conversation. For example, you might decide to post a tweet that includes a link to an article about a topical issue to show that you agree with the sentiments presented. You are hoping that anyone who reads your tweet will then also read the article and see your viewpoint.

If your piece is created for a public audience, you don't necessarily have control over who that audience is. For example, while an initial tweet might only have the audience of your followers, one of your followers might decide to retweet you, and your tweet would then be received by a group of people you've never encountered. Additionally, this same tweet might be randomly found through a search for a hashtag you used. If we look at audience in relationship to visual art, the viewers might be people literally passing by (if the art is a mural painted on the side of a building), people who specifically went to the art gallery because they know the artist, or people who were visiting the museum and were intrigued by a poster they saw for the exhibit.

Genres for public audiences, just like the other genres previously discussed, respond to a rhetorical situation. Consider how many times you learn about something newsworthy via Facebook or Twitter. The composer of the post has chosen one of these genres because they can reach a wide audience immediately. It is then easy for anyone receiving the information to share that information with others. Another example to consider is a TED talk. When a colleague of Amy's shared his approach to a business class that integrated running a marathon during his TEDxYouth presentation, his purpose was to inspire a public audience to be challenged to change their habits by training for a marathon.

Some typical genres for public audiences are posts on social media sites (such as Facebook, Twitter, and Instagram), blog posts, art exhibits, music and theater performances, and presentations designed for a public audience (such as a TED talk).

Another purpose for public genres is activism. When considering the concept of genres used for activism, perhaps you first think of protests—people carrying signs with their

**WRITE**

As the discussion makes clear, you are part of a public audience. Have you ever considered yourself a public audience? If so, in what situations? If not, how does thinking about yourself as part of a public audience change the way you think about genres such as editorials and letters to the editor? Jot down your ideas and share with a classmate.

messages. Maybe you think about famous speeches, such as Martin Luther King Jr.'s 1963 "I Have a Dream" speech delivered at the National March on Washington. Have you ever received an e-mail from an organization encouraging you to vote a particular way? Perhaps someone with a clipboard has greeted you on the street, asking you to sign your name to bring a particular issue to the ballot. All of these situations involve genres used to effect change.

The purpose of composing a genre for activism is usually to encourage change or action. For example, if you posted a tweet after the August 2019 El Paso shooting and used the hashtag #ThisIsAmerica, your purpose might be to highlight how mass shootings have become commonplace in the United States. Sometimes it is to bring an issue into focus. For example, you might decide to hold up a sign at a rally for raising the minimum wage that says, "How about a maximum wage?" Here, you would want your viewer to understand that you are concerned about the 1 percent having too much wealth.

The audience for these genres is similar to those we discussed under "Public Genres." If you are standing at a rally, you might not know all the people who end up viewing your sign. While most of the viewers are others who share a similar opinion since they are attending the same rally, people who do not agree with you might also see your sign, such as when there are counterprotesters across the street. You might also be captured on the news, and then anyone who turns on that night's news sees you and your message. You might also hope that voters or lawmakers will hear about the rally, perhaps on TV or the internet, and see your sign.

**WRITE**

Make a list of all the genres you can think of in which you've seen appeals for public action, such as Twitter, GoFundMe, and signs. Which ones are you most likely to notice? Which ones have you used for composing messages geared toward social activism and change?

With the rise in social media use and the proliferation of digital devices, participatory or citizen journalism has also become a major player when it comes to activism and change. Basically, this means that a public citizen, you, distributes news to an audience. Most often, these acts of individual journalism are designed to highlight an injustice, such as when acts of brutality are videotaped, or to illustrate to a wide audience an event going on, such as the Climate Change protests of 2019.

Some typical genres for activism and change are similar to those for public audiences, such as posts on social media sites (Facebook, Twitter, Instagram) and blog postings. In addition, genres such as political speeches, protest signs, and petitions are commonly used to call for an action. Although flash mobs were originally created for entertainment, such as when a group of people gather in an airport and break into dance and song to entertain bored travelers, they can also be designed to effect change. In 2019, a flash mob gathered in Hong Kong on their lunch break to protest for Hong Kong's autonomy from China.

Following is an annotated example of a protest poster.

# Guided Reading | Poster

## Norma Jean Gargasz, *Give Bees a Chance*

| RHETORICAL SITUATION & CHOICES | GENRE CONVENTIONS |
|---|---|

**PURPOSE**
The composer of this protest sign likely wants to show support for restricting or labeling genetically modified foods.

**AUDIENCE**
The composer of this protest sign probably has multiple audiences. One is the public who will see the sign and perhaps be persuaded to share the same position. Another is voters or lawmakers who will vote on ballot measures or legislation regarding genetically modified foods.

**RHETORICAL APPEALS**
The protester's sign appeals to the viewer's sense of pathos. "Give bees a chance" implies that there are environmentally hazardous things in our food that we may not know about.

**MODES & MEDIA**
**Mode = text + art:** The sign's composer has chosen to convey the message with text and a visual only at the top, which allows for very large letters on the sign so the words are easily read from a distance.
**Media = print:** Protest signs must be print because a digital sign would require the protester to carry an open laptop or tablet, which is not practical and would be hard for anyone to view.

◄ **What is the composer of the poster, doing, rhetorically speaking?**

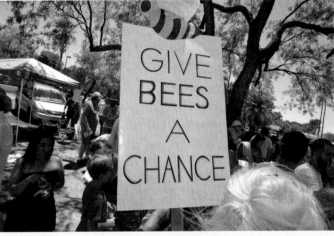

Credit: Norma Jean Gargasz/Alamy Stock Photo.

**What are some conventions ► of the protest poster, as a genre? To what extent does the poster adhere to those conventions?**

**ELEMENTS OF THE GENRE**
**A short, direct message:**
You can read the entire text in just a moment and know immediately which side of the issue the protester is on.

**Homemade:** The sign is clearly made by a person with magic markers rather than by a professional sign maker.

**Easy to read from a distance:** The letters are very large and take up most of the space on the sign.

**STYLE**
Because composers of protest signs need to convey their messages quickly, they often write in phrases or pithy sentences. If they can introduce cleverness into the sayings on their signs, viewers may remember them better. In the case of this sign, the slogan is a reference to the Plastic Ono Band's famous 1969 song "Give Peace a Chance."

**DESIGN**
Because protest signs must be easily read from a distance, composers of protest signs usually keep design very simple so there are minimum distractions from their message. Color is usually high-contrast, again to help with readability.

**SOURCES**
Protest signs may refer to statistics or facts that quickly convey their message. For example, a sign about fracking could cite a statistic on levels of contamination in water in areas where fracking takes place.

# Presentations

Most presentations are brief talks about a particular topic delivered by a knowledgeable speaker to a specific public audience, such as neighborhood associations and school boards. Often they are persuasive—aimed at getting audience members to agree with the speaker about something or to take action. For example, a speaker at a TED event might give a presentation to try to convince the audience to understand an aspect of human nature differently. Even though presentations usually occur in public spaces, they also are a part of academia and the workplace. You might give a presentation to persuade your classmates to agree with you about a specific topic or issue.

With software available online, you can reach more viewers and listeners and also make your presentation more visual and multimodal. For example, you might use online products such as Skype, WebEx, Microsoft Live Meeting, or Zoom to reach people at other locations. You can also record a presentation and then post it online for future viewing.

To put a presentation together, you can use software to organize your ideas. For years, PowerPoint, part of Microsoft Office, was the standard in many workplaces and classrooms. However, some presenters are now turning to more visually engaging tools, such as Prezi and Haiku Deck.

## Analyzing Presentations

**Purpose**    Presenters always have a goal for their presentations. In a neighborhood meeting, you might give a presentation about a problem to persuade your audience that your solutions are the best route to take. Over the last several years, a presentation series called Ignite talks has sprung up in cities around the world. The tagline for Ignite is "Enlighten us, but make it quick." Presenters persuade public audiences about their ideas and passions within a very small time frame. They can use only twenty slides that automatically advance every fifteen seconds. A similar phenomenon is the PechaKucha, which involves twenty slides that show for twenty seconds each.

**Audience**    Presenters know their audiences; they know what kind of background information they'll need to present, what terminology is useful, and what cultural references their listeners will connect with. For example, writer and professional speaker Scott Berkun gave a talk "How and Why to Give an Ignite Talk." He knew that his audience would be potential Ignite performers, so he geared his talk to persuade them that they all have a story to tell, something worth sharing on the Ignite stage.

**Rhetorical appeals**    Any time you want to persuade you need to establish your ethos in order to get your audience to embrace your ideas. Berkun establishes his ethos by showing he knows how to present within the constraints of Ignite—he uses twenty self advancing slides within five minutes. If you are giving a persuasive talk, some ways to build ethos are to state your argument clearly and to support it with accurate data and appropriate evidence. If you're working with slides, provide well-designed slides that are free of spelling and grammatical errors. When presenting, you can boost your

◄ PRESENTATION

**Ignite,** "How to Produce an Ignite Event."

*Credit: Courtesy of igniteshow.com/howto.*

ethos through good posture and eye contact. To be persuasive you'll also need to appeal to your audience's sense of logic. If you want to convince a client to purchase a product, then you need to provide the reasons and benefits in a logical order. You might also appeal to pathos by being funny or surprising. The humorous and unexpected can work well, depending on your audience.

**Modes & media** Presenters use a combination of audio, visual, and text. If slides are involved, they may include text, visuals, and even hyperlinks to multimedia, such as web pages, animated visuals, movie clips, music, and audio clips. Some speakers use physical props (for example, in the guided reading/viewing in this chapter, the speaker holds up a doll). Some provide their listeners with printouts of their slides. Some deliver their presentations face-to-face or in a digital environment (such as WebEx) where the talk can be replayed anytime, anywhere. Scott Berkun gave his presentation live at a conference; it was recorded and is now available on YouTube.

**Elements of the genre**    Effective presenters do the following:

- *Give a bold introduction to capture their audience's attention.* For example, Scott Berkun opens with "I think storytelling is everything," which prepares his audience for the persuasive claims he will make later in the presentation. Presenters also do the following:

  » Introduce themselves

  » Establish credibility and their relationship to the topic

  » Preview what they will cover during their talk

- The introduction is where speakers make a first impression on their audience and also where they need to persuade the audience that the presentation is worth listening to.

- *Provide enough background so that the audience can understand the content of the presentation.* Presenters must clarify acronyms and define unfamiliar terminology.

- *Present their information and arguments in the body of their talks.* This is where speakers make claims and back them up with facts, data, personal stories, and quotes from experts.

- *Address objections and counterarguments to make the best case possible.*

- *Conclude with a summary and solid message.* This ensures that the audiences have understood the argument presented, have gotten a clear message, and know what the speaker is asking of them in terms of agreeing and/or taking action (for example, against a particular injustice). Many speakers end by inviting the audience to ask questions.

- *Use visuals, video, audio, and other media to support their arguments.* Most presenters use slides as a way to present key points, infographics, photos, and links to various multimedia and to provide context and support for their arguments. For example, if a presenter wants to persuade listeners of the need for a program to reduce childhood obesity, they might include an image of obese children, or a chart showing the relationship between childhood weight and diabetes. To take another example, when Berkun mentions famous people who were "lousy speakers," he backs this up with a visual of Abraham Lincoln. However, visuals and other media should not distract the audience. It's a good idea to bring handouts of slides so audiences have something to refer to.

- *Make transitions to move the audience from one point to the next.* Presenters can do this by advancing slides or by cuing listeners through speech (for example, "This brings me to my second point . . .").

**Style**    Effective presenters do the following:

- *Organize their material so that it's clear and persuasive.* Presenters must make it easy for audiences to follow what they're saying and to accept their claims and arguments. Some speakers may arrange their talks into three or more main parts built around separate but related concepts. Others might use a chronological organization, which is especially useful for laying out the history of an idea or movement. A speaker arguing about the factors that led to the AIDS crisis might organize his talk chronologically, while a speaker arguing about possible ways to curb the spread of the disease might organize their talk by first focusing on the problem and then by focusing on potential solutions and actions.

- *Tailor their level of detail.* Presenters consider their subjects and audiences when deciding on the level of information to share. For an introduction to a topic, a speaker doesn't need to provide as much complex detail as they would for a more advanced approach to a subject. Similarly, for an audience of experts, a presenter would provide more depth and detail, such as a speaker talking about climate change and shifting geologic formations to a group of geologists.

- *Make eye contact with the whole room and stand tall.* These nonverbal cues connect speakers with audiences and convey their confidence, knowledge, and persuasiveness.

- *Vary their delivery and show emotion.* Speakers vary the volume of their voices, speaking softly at some points and loudly at others to stress certain aspects of what they have to say. For example, a speaker may raise their voice to show anger at a situation or excitement about a future possibility. Speakers also vary their pacing between speaking slowly and more quickly, depending on their content and what they want to stress. However, it's important to not speak too quickly, as Scott Berkun demonstrates, and to pause so that audiences can digest information. Many speakers work in a few funny stories or anecdotes: Humor can connect them with the audiences they want to persuade.

**Design**   For presenters creating slides, a smart, clean, non-distracting design will persuade audiences by allowing them to focus on content. Most successful slides reflect the following design features:

- Fonts are usually sans serif—at 20 points or larger for easy reading.

- There is contrast between backgrounds and text. Light-colored text on dark backgrounds or dark-colored text on light backgrounds works best. It's best to avoid clashing colors, such as pink text on an orange background.

- Slides are not crowded with too many ideas and images. Each slide should have only one main point with a few supporting points.

**Sources**   To persuade their listeners, presenters, like anyone building an argument, may do the following:

- Draw on their own expertise of a subject
- Confer with others who are knowledgeable in the field or subject

- Read articles, reports, books, or other reference material
- Provide a Works Cited list on a slide at the end of the presentation (and/or provide brief citations throughout the slides)
- Credit charts, photos, or any other graphics, usually on the slide where the visual appears, underneath the visual

## Guided Reading | Presentation

Sunni Brown is a visual thinker, researcher, and self-described "large-scale Info-doodler and Leader of the Doodle Revolution" who believes in the power of doodling. She argues that focused doodling, in any scenario, gets our minds and memories working better. Brown's academic background is in journalism and linguistics, and she holds a master's degree in public affairs. She lives in Austin, Texas, owns a design company, works as a consultant and creative director, and is the coauthor of *Gamestorming*, a book on innovation and visual thinking.

Brown gave a talk at an Ignite event in which she makes her case for the Doodle Revolution. Ignite hosts events around the country where speakers talk about things (in their lives, in their work, etc.) that they care about most. An Ignite talk can be no longer than five minutes. In her presentation, Brown uses images and statistics to support her points on the value of doodling.

▶ **PRESENTATION**

**Ignite,** *The Doodle Revolution,* introductory page for Sunni Brown's presentation.

*Credit: Courtesy of igniteshow.com/howto.*

# Sunni Brown, *Ignite Talk: "The Doodle Revolution"*

## PURPOSE
Sunni Brown wants to persuade her audience that doodling, though considered socially unacceptable in many settings, is actually a very effective tool for recording, absorbing, and retaining information. As she seeks to persuade, she also seeks to entertain her audience and hold their interest with visuals, humor, focused statements, and brisk pacing.

## AUDIENCE
Brown's audience is composed of information geeks, designers, writers, and doodle enthusiasts who appreciate irony, comedy, comics, and pop culture.

◀ What is the composer/ presenter, Sunni Brown, doing?

How do I know this is ▶ a presentation?

"I am what I refer to as a large-scale strategic doodler. So people pay me to track auditory content and display it to them in a visual language format. And I have a series of 'whoa' moments when I do this."

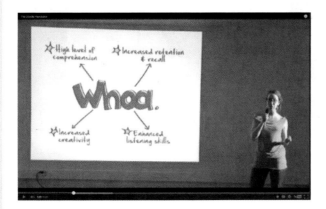

"I have a significantly high level of comprehension of the information that I doodle. I also have increased attention and recall of that content, weeks and months later, and I can easily immerse myself back into it. Additionally, I've noticed that when I do strategic doodling, I have increased creativity

## ELEMENTS OF THE GENRE
**Ethos-building introduction to her argument:** Brown establishes her ethos by explaining that people pay her to doodle, and she makes clear that she will argue for a "Doodle Revolution" and lay out the reasons that focused doodling should be taken seriously. Brown sets a tone that indicates she's knowledgeable; at the same time she uses humor, even before the presentation officially begins, that has her audience listening and laughing.

**Delivery technique:** Throughout her talk, Brown faces the audience comfortably (she does not fidget). Her facial expression and hand gestures are not distracting, but rather make the audience feel as though she is just having a casual (and funny) chat with them.

*(Continues on next page)*

**RHETORICAL APPEALS**
Brown builds **ethos** as a creator of doodles and expert on visual thinking. As a professional, scholar, and coauthor of a book on innovation and visual thinking, she is recognized by her viewers as an authority on her topic.

Brown appeals to her audience using **logos** by presenting specific examples in an orderly way.

She connects with viewers' sense of **pathos** through her use of humor—both in what she's saying and what she's showing.

and I can make solutions to problems that are even surprising to me. And finally, my listening skills are like, ninja-like. I can discern immediately what's relevant and what's not relevant."

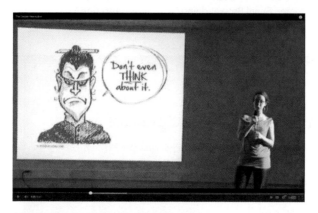

"So I have this series of 'whoa' moments, and simultaneously I notice that our society frowns on doodling in learning environments. In the boardroom, in the situation room, and in the classroom. So, I find that problematic. . . ."

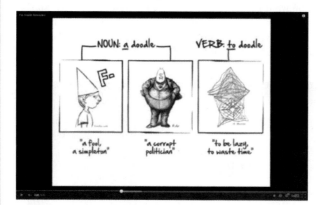

"I discovered five interesting things. One of them is that there is no flattering definition of a doodle. In the seventeenth century, a 'doodle' was a fool; in the eighteenth century, a 'doodle' was a corrupt politician; and in the modern-day society, in the 1930s we see the emergence of our verb 'to doodle,' and it means to be lazy or waste time. . . . [Later] there was a period in time when the ballpoint pen came into play, and people had access to mass-produced pulp paper. So they actually were kind of like flipping around, just like, 'wee, look at these tools we have!' But [doodling] wasn't necessarily meaningful at that point in time."

**Interesting visuals:**
Each of Brown's slides relates to a specific part of her argument for doodling. Her visuals include hand-drawn text, cartoons, the doodles of other people (including Ronald Reagan and Alexander Graham Bell), as well as statistical information. The slides are designed for readability and for persuasive and humorous impact.

**Clear transitions:**
Brown uses the slides themselves to advance the points of her talk. She also uses verbal cues to lay out the structure of her ideas and to transition from one idea to the next ("I discovered five interesting things. One of them . . ." and "finally").

**MODES & MEDIA**
**Mode = audio and visual:** Brown uses a combination of audio and visuals throughout her presentation. The audio is her voice presenting ideas, along with laughter from the audience. Her visuals are the images on her slides, which include doodles, comics, and hand-drawn infographics.

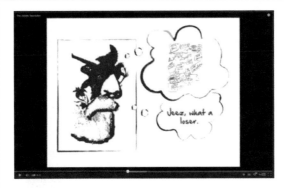

"In the 1930s, Freudianism was at its height, and people believed that you could actually psychoanalyze someone based on their doodles, and dig into the recesses of their freaky psyches. And naturally, people have an aversion to that." [laughter]

"And finally . . . the physical gesture of doodling gives people the impression that you're not present, right? So, whenever there's a speaker, um, not me, but if there were another speaker [up here] they would think that it was rude and that you're not paying attention."

*(Continues on next page)*

**Medium = face-to-face and video:** This talk was originally delivered before a live audience. In the example given, the presentation is digital, since it is a recording of the original talk that can be found on the Ignite website.

"... Also, in our society, we don't think that national leaders doodle. We don't think it's appropriate. But that's patently false. These are Ronald Reagan's doodles.... Every president, ever, in our history has been a doodler. Republicans are actually more prolific doodlers than Democrats, which I find interesting."

"Here's a better definition of 'doodle,' which is: scribblings to help a person think. And that definition came out of a 1936 movie called *Mr. Deeds Goes to Town*.... So what do we know about the doodle? We know that doodlers retain 30% more information than non-doodlers."

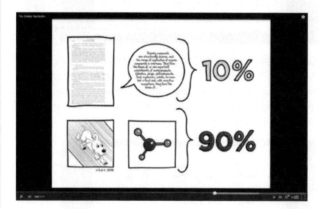

"We also know that there's a phenomenon called the 'picture superiority effect,' which means that after this event is over, you're only going to remember 10% of what I say, but you're going to remember 90% of what I showed you. And so when you're doodling and you're creating pictures that you

**Use of supporting examples:** Throughout the presentation, Brown shows an example to support her pro-doodle argument. In fact, she uses twenty examples (each slide is one idea).

get to reflect back on, it actually is a way of processing and retaining information. . . . So the doodle's not a joke, okay? Ya get it?" [laughter]

"We also know that almost every genius inventor and innovator and scientist and screenwriter and poet, they all use sketches and doodles in order to get to a solution they wouldn't otherwise have gotten to. This is Alexander Graham Bell's sketches of the telephone."

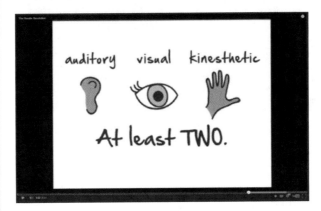

"There are three learning pathways, primarily, that we all have. . . . In order to lock in information, you have to engage at least two. . . . Or, you have to have an emotional experience coupled with one of those things."

## STYLE
**Smart use of detail:**
Brown offers just enough detail to illustrate her ideas. She chooses specific images, each for a reason. For example, to support her claim that scientists use doodles to work out solutions to complex problems, she shows a doodle by Alexander Graham Bell and moves on.

**Persuasive, friendly voice and tone:**
Brown speaks with an even pace throughout, never rushing through any parts of the talk. Her pacing works with her humor; for example, after she's laid out considerable evidence supporting her claims that doodling should be taken seriously, she says, "So doodling isn't a joke. Okay?" The audience laughs as she reinforces her points.

## DESIGN
The speaker does not use traditional slides with text; rather, she uses specific visuals to support the points she's making.

*(Continues on next page)*

**SOURCES**
Brown's sources for her presentation are her own experience and background, as well as information that she's gathered as a researcher on doodling, visual thinking, and memory. If this were a research paper and not a presentation, she would have a References list or Works Cited page that would include, for example, a source for her information on the phenomenon of "picture superiority effect," and the film *Mr. Deeds Goes to Town*, which she mentions in her talk.

"...These are the three things that you have to do in order to engage the pathways. And I think the reason why the doodle is so powerful for so many people around the world and throughout time is that it actually employs all three of your learning pathways simultaneously."

**Thoughtful conclusion:** Her ending sums up the essence of her presentation—and the humor of her delivery, her slides, and the statistics she shares—with clear statements on why and how doodling should be used.

"...I think that the doodle is actually most appropriate in those situations where society actually believes it to be the least appropriate, which is where you have an informationally dense situation, and people are accountable for learning that information. So I say bring on the freaking doodle revolution." [laughter, applause].

*Note from editors: The annotations in the Guided Reading above refer to the full video, available at igniteshow.com.*

*Credit: Sunni Bown, Infodoodler-in-Chief, Author and Leader of the Doodle Revolution.*

**RHETORICAL SITUATION & CHOICES**

1. **Purpose.** How does Brown use examples to support her central argument and purpose? Why does she choose to incorporate these specific examples in her talk, "Doodle Revolution"?

2. **Audience.** What assumptions do you think Brown holds about her audience at Ignite? Why do you think that?

3. **Rhetorical appeals.** One way in which Brown establishes her ethos is through her demeanor. How else does she establish ethos throughout the presentation?

4. **Rhetorical appeals.** What does Brown's appeal to pathos and use of humor add to the presentation? To what extent does it make it more (or less) persuasive?

5. **Modes & media.** What effect would it have had on the presentation if, rather than using illustrations, doodles, and infographics, Brown had used traditional slides with headings and explanatory text? Also, how is the experience of watching the talk digitally different from experiencing it as a live audience?

**GENRE CONVENTIONS**

6. **Elements of the genre.** At the start of the presentation, Brown mentions that as a professional strategic doodler she has lots of "whoa moments," and that thanks to strategic doodling, she has "ninja-like" listening skills. What effects do you think these statements have on her audience? Is this a good strategy for beginning her talk? Why or why not?

7. **Elements of the genre.** What are some of the choices that Brown makes to present her argument? Why does she make those choices, and which parts of her talk are most convincing? To what extent does she persuade you that a "Doodle Revolution" would be a good idea?

8. **Style.** How does Brown create a sense of a personal conversation throughout the talk? How do her delivery, tone, and pacing foster this sense?

9. **Design.** Brown says that most people remember 10 percent of what they hear and 90 percent of what they see or are shown in a presentation. Does this seem right to you? How does this apply to your experience of her talk?

10. **Sources.** Why do you think Brown chose the specific evidence (and visuals) that she uses in her talk (aside from Ignite's parameters of twenty slides)? Do the slides work? Why or why not?

# CHECKLIST | Drafting a Presentation

Thinking of drafting a presentation? Ask yourself the following questions:

## RHETORICAL SITUATION & CHOICES

☐ **Purpose.** What subjects am I passionate about? What current issues are most important to me? Do I want to motivate my audience to action? Do I want to persuade them to think differently about an idea? Do I want them to see things from a different perspective?

☐ **Audience.** When I deliver my presentation, will I be speaking to experts in the field? Or will I want to persuade a more general audience? What do I expect is my audience's attitude toward my topic? How will I inspire and persuade my audience? Will I post my presentation online to attract a wider audience?

☐ **Rhetorical appeals.** How will I establish my ethos? Do I want to use emotion to appeal to my audience? If so, how will I make sure my audience continues to see my approach to the subject as reasonable? Will I use logic in my appeal? How can I use logic to persuade my audience to accept my claim?

☐ **Modes & media.** Will I prepare slides with text to accompany my presentation? What visuals might I add to the slides? Should I embed video clips from YouTube? Should I provide handouts? Would audio enhance my presentation? Do I want my presentation to be viewed live (face-to-face)? Do I want it available for future viewing online?

## GENRE CONVENTIONS

☐ **Elements of the genre.** How will I grab my audience's attention at the start of my presentation? What background information or terminology do I need to cover first in my presentation? How will I anticipate and address my audience's opposition to any of my persuasive claims? How could slides and visuals enhance my presentation? Will they clarify concepts? Expand ideas? Persuade?

☐ **Style.** What organization is best for my presentation? Do I want to examine a problem and persuade my audience to adopt a solution? To what extent do I need to examine causes and effects? How much time have I allotted to practicing my delivery? What strategies can I use to make sure I stay composed while presenting? Do I want to incorporate humor? Shock?

☐ **Design.** Are my slides simple, uncluttered, and readable? Is my font size large enough for the room and screen? Do I have enough contrast between my font and the background? Is each slide focused around one main point?

☐ **Style.** What organization is best for my presentation? Do I want to examine a problem and persuade my audience to adopt a solution? To what extent do I need to examine causes and effects? How much time have I allotted to practicing my delivery? What strategies can I use to make sure I stay composed while presenting? Do I want to incorporate humor? Shock?

☐ **Sources.** Will my sources help me develop my ethos? Are my sources cited properly?

# Presenting Ideas to Boost Creativity

In the presentation featured in this unit, Sunni Brown argues that visualizing ideas—in a variety of contexts, including the workplace—boosts creativity and memory. What ideas do you have about boosting creativity and memory or for improving a process or learning environment? Plan out your argument and gather supporting evidence, and then put together an Ignite-style talk that:

- Is no longer than five minutes
- Is supported by twenty slides (that will advance every fifteen seconds)

As you plan your presentation, review the annotations provided in the Guided Reading of Sunni Brown's talk and keep the following in mind:

- Think about your rhetorical situation—your purpose, audience, and how you will use rhetorical appeals and media. For example, will you be most persuasive if you are also funny?

- Think about the genre's conventions—the elements of a presentation such as a strong introduction and conclusion, interesting visuals, and clear transitions, as well as appropriate style, design, and use of sources. For a five-minute talk, you'll want to streamline your major points, perhaps sticking to only three or so, and be sure to support each one.

- Ask yourself: What do I most want my audience to remember about my presentation?

# News Articles

The first newspapers were handwritten pages that reported on economic and social issues in Europe in the 1400s. The first successful English-language paper was *The Weekly Newes*, established in the 1620s; a little later, *The London Gazette* became the official newspaper of Great Britain (1666). In 1704, a bookseller and postmaster named John Campbell kicked off newspapers in America with *The Boston News-Letter*, an effort that was followed up more successfully in 1728 by Benjamin Franklin, who published *The Pennsylvania Gazette*, a paper considered to be *The New York Times* of the eighteenth century.

Today, most cities have at least one local daily newspaper; Chicago, for example, has the *Chicago Sun-Times* and the *Chicago Tribune*. Daily newspapers are divided into sections on world, domestic, and local news; sports; business; science; health; obituaries;

and weather. Many have sections dedicated to editorials/opinions, food, travel, education, entertainment, and fashion, along with advice columns, comics, puzzles, and horoscopes. Smaller communities and colleges also publish newspapers on topics of interest to more specific audiences. Many publications are available online and include links to related stories and topics, as well as social media features that allow readers to post reactions to published stories.

Before the internet, major newspapers were published once or twice a day. However, now that readers can check news headlines and follow stories online throughout the day, they expect constant updates. News reporting and publishing is now a 24/7 occupation.

While newspapers publish many kinds of writing—persuasive editorials, letters to the editor, advice columns, ads—at their core are factual news articles written by reporters. Reporters research their writing: They gather information for a story by conducting interviews, serving as eyewitnesses (reporting from the scene, for example), checking public records, and working with library and online sources. News journalists need to be able to back up the accuracy of their writing with facts from several reliable sources.

## Analyzing New Articles

**Purpose**  Journalists research and write news articles to inform readers of facts and events. Their purpose is to present true and fair accounts of issues and happenings, and to do so while adhering to ethical standards, such as those outlined by the Society of Professional Journalists. Like any organization, each news provider has its own policies, agenda, and built-in biases. That said, the news articles that providers publish or air should be as fact based and objective as possible.

**Audience**  Journalists who write news articles know that readers want to be informed about world events and issues and to be kept up-to-date, especially online. They know that some readers will scan the first few paragraphs to get the main idea, so they need to include the most important material up front. Some readers who are especially interested—personally or professionally—in a given topic, however, will read for depth. They will read the entire article and also turn to related articles. Journalists keep that audience in mind as well.

**Rhetorical appeals**  Journalists use ethos and logos to reach their audiences. A news publisher's reputation for "getting the story right" is crucial, as are the reputations of reporters associated with the publisher. If a reporter's credibility is seriously tarnished, his or her career in journalism will quickly end. In 2003, for example, promising *The New York Times* reporter Jayson Blair was fired for plagiarizing parts of several news reports he had written. The *Times* called it "a low point in the 152-year history of the newspaper" and apologized profusely to its readers. In 2016, the *Guardian* dismissed reporter Joseph Mayton for fabricating stories.

**Modes & media**   News articles can take many forms. Here, we're highlighting written news articles because text can appear in print or digital formats. With the rise of digital news sites such as *The Huffington Post*, many print newspapers have moved online (see also "Purpose" on p. 230). The advantages of the online news article are that it can be updated instantly, can link to related articles and sources, and can be accompanied by video. Online publications also allow readers to post comments, making these sources much more interactive than print newspapers.

In addition to appearing in print and in digital formats, news stories can take the form of audio and video reports. National Public Radio covers all the top stories that print and digital news outlets cover, but in audio form. Many digital news outlets, such as MSNBC, also make videos of news coverage available online.

**Elements of the genre**   Following are some of features that define news articles:

- *They are well researched and fact-checked.* As previously discussed, the authority (or ethos) of the reporter, publisher, and content is crucial. Writers must be scrupulous in their research and fact checking. A rule of thumb in journalism is to verify a report with at least three reliable sources. When an error is discovered in an article, journalists and publishers are usually quick to make a correction and apologize.

- *They usually aim at a broad audience.* Most newspapers, news magazines, and news sites have a very broad readership with varying degrees of education, so the level of vocabulary in a news article must be appropriate for all. Most are written with a ninth- or tenth-grade vocabulary. *The New York Times*, however, is written at a twelfth-grade level of vocabulary and comprehension.

- *They open with a concise summary in a lead (or lede) paragraph.* Most journalists begin their news articles with a paragraph that states the most important aspects of their story and grabs the reader's attention. In the rest of the article, reporters elaborate on what was presented in the opening paragraph. Because many readers skim rather than read a full article, the content of the lead paragraph is especially important.

- *They present information in order of importance.* Paragraphs that follow the lead and make up the body of the article provide details and supporting evidence from sources. Paragraphs closer to the beginning of the story provide details that are more important in understanding the essence of the story; those closer to the end, however, provide information that is less essential, given that some readers may not read the whole article to the end. As explained in the "Style" section on page 232, news journalists tend to structure their articles with an overview of the important information at the beginning so that readers can get information quickly.

- *They include quotations.* Journalists often quote sources directly to add flavor to their articles and to maintain the feel of "just the facts, ma'am." No one can accuse a reporter of misinterpreting what someone said if the reporter includes complete direct quotations.

- *They are written in short paragraphs.* Journalists often write in short paragraphs because they're easier to read than long ones. They're also easier on the eyes, especially considering the formats news articles are generally published in—either in narrow columns in print newspapers or online.

**Style**   News articles are characterized by the following stylistic features. They demonstrate:

- *A neutral tone and absence of personal opinion.* The goal of writing a news article is to report information. It's appropriate for news journalists to use a serious and fairly formal tone in their writing; of course, *formal* doesn't have to mean dry. It's also appropriate for journalists to refrain from editorializing, unless they are writing an editorial or hosting an opinion column, for example.

- *An objective, third-person voice.* An objective stance conveys the cut-and-dry, fact-based nature of news articles. News journalists also use precise language to clearly communicate facts and details, and they use the third person (*he/she/they*) rather than the first person (*I/we/they*).

- *Just enough detail for the general reader.* In the annotated article by Stephanie Pappas (p. 234), you'll notice that the writer is very specific about her subject: the structure of life on other planets. However, Pappas doesn't offer the level of detail that a specialist such as a scientist or researcher might want.

**Design**   News articles feature the following design elements, which also have editorial functions, including:

- *An attention-grabbing title or headline.* The title of a news article is called a headline. It is usually presented in much larger or bolder type than the story itself and is brief and descriptive. Headlines are used to attract readers and are sometimes provocative.

- *A byline.* A byline is the presentation of the author's name, usually below the headline and above the text of the article.

- *A serif typeface.* A serif font has a very small flare at the stroke ends and corners of letters, while a sans serif font lacks these strokes. Print articles are often presented in serif fonts (such as in the print edition of *The New York Times*), while sans serif fonts (such as those used by BBC News) are a good choice for the readability of digital content. Compare a serif **A** to a sans serif **A**.

- *Use of columns or chunking.* News sites such as the BBC's present articles in chunked sections that have their own headings. Digital content may be presented in multiple columns or on different sections of the grid with various ways to navigate the content. Print newspapers are limited to columns of no more than fifty-two characters wide.

- *Images: photos, charts, and multimedia components.* Many news articles, especially breaking news on a website or a front-page story in a print paper, are contextualized with photos, charts, and graphs, and when published online, they can include video and other multimedia. A piece with a video or audio component usually includes an arrow icon or other visual element to indicate this; sometimes the video or audio itself is the news story. News publishers use visual and multimedia to grab readers' attention, provide context, and enrich the content of print articles.

- *Headers, footers, and tabs.* Designers of online news sites provide tabs and navigational menus and search boxes to keep readers oriented. The designers use repeated design features to reinforce the agency's identity. For example, a print newspaper's title appears on every page and in other elements, and titles, headers, and footers (which include the date and section, for example) help readers find what they need on the page.

- *Use of color.* Online news sites include color images and video. Designers also use color typographically to direct attention toward particular content. Blue is sometimes used for hyperlinks (which turn a different color once you select them), red is sometimes used for breaking news headlines, and gray shading is sometimes used to orient readers as to their location within the content. Images and videos are shown in full color. Print newspapers, which are published on a thin paper called newsprint, are printed in black ink (such as in *The New York Times*) or in color (such as in *USA Today*).

**Sources**   News reports are based on eyewitness accounts, authoritative published documents, interviews, and records. Most journalists indicate their sources within their news articles, using attribution phrases such as "according to" and linking directly to their sources. Some online journalists indicate their sources by using hyperlinks.

Journalists, unlike the authors of peer-reviewed journal articles (see Chapter 7, "Academic Genres" p. 112), do not use academic documentation styles such as MLA or APA. Because news journalism is a popular genre and not a scholarly genre, it has a different set of conventions for documenting sources, such as the phrasing that Pappas uses on page 234. In news journalism, the thinking is that the reader doesn't need the same level of detail about sources that scholarly audiences need. That said, online news providers and journalists can boost their ethos by linking to their sources.

## Guided Reading | News Article

*Live Science* is a web-based newsmagazine focusing on scientific breakthroughs and odd scientific facts. Many of its articles are syndicated to news outlets such as MSNBC and Fox News. Stephanie Pappas is a freelance science writer who has contributed several articles to *Live Science*. Her writing often focuses on neuroscience and psychology. The following article appeared on *Live Science* in 2019.

# Stephanie Pappas, *Little Green Men? Nope, Extraterrestrial Life May Look More Like Pasta*

| RHETORICAL SITUATION & CHOICES | GENRE CONVENTIONS |
|---|---|

**PURPOSE**

As a science news reporter, Pappas aims to explain recent findings about how pasta-shaped rock formations might provide clues to extraterrestrial life.

**AUDIENCE**

Pappas's audience includes general science news readers, online readers, *and* fans of quirky science news. Also, as a freelance science journalist, Pappas may have her own following, so some readers may be her fans.

**RHETORICAL APPEALS**

Pappas appeals to readers' sense of **ethos** through specific references to the work of Bruce Fouke, a geobiologist and coauthor of a research study funded by NASA. She appeals to a readers' sense of logic (**logos**) by beginning with a general description of the pasta-like rock formations, and then continuing with details and analysis from the study. Even though it is not prevalent throughout, Pappas does appeal to **pathos** by using humor in her subheadings: "Hot pasta" and "Sulfuri on the edge."

◀ What is the composer, Stephanie Pappas, doing?

How do I know this is a ▶ news article?

To find life on Mars, scientists should keep their eyes peeled for pasta.

Hot-spring-loving microbes create rock formations that look like fettuccini or capellini, according to a new NASA-funded study published online April 30 in the journal *Astrobiology*. Such pasta-shaped formations could be the first clues to life on other planets, said study author Bruce Fouke, a geobiologist at the University of Illinois at Urbana-Champaign.

"If we go to another planet with a rover, we would love to see living microbes or we'd love to see little green women and men in spacecraft," Fouke told Live Science. "But the reality is we're going to be looking for life that was probably growing in a hot spring, life that was fossilized." [9 Strange, Scientific Excuses for Why Humans Haven't Found Aliens Yet]

**HOT PASTA**

To investigate what this extraterrestrial life might look like, Fouke and his team started at Mammoth Hot Springs in Yellowstone National Park. At this popular tourist spot, hot geothermal water rich in minerals flows from the ground. The minerals precipitate out of the water, creating striking formations made of calcium carbonate, also known as travertine.

But these formations don't get their shape in a vacuum, Fouke said. They're built, in part, by microbes. In the new study, the researchers focused on the fast-flowing, particularly hot water at the head of the mineral springs. Here, the water ranges in temperature from 149 degrees to 162 degrees Fahrenheit (65 to 72 degrees Celsius) and has a low pH of 6.2 to 6.8, meaning it's more acidic than basic.

The researchers worked in careful conjunction with the National Parks Service, to avoid damaging the rock formations, taking samples of filamentous microbe mats that thrive in these waters. The mats look like long, mucus-y pasta strands. This is an adaptation, Fouke said. In calm waters, microbes settle out in slimy, unconsolidated mats. But in rushing water, the organisms have to cling to one another to survive. Each

**ELEMENTS OF THE GENRE**

**Is well researched and accurate:** Pappas uses a published NASA-funded research study and talked to both Fouke and Sivaguru, coauthors of the study. The quotes from Fouke show the importance of his findings. Additionally, Pappas provides a link to Fouke's digital book so a reader might dig into the actual research described in her article.

**Opens with a lead paragraph:** This paragraph sets up the article's subject: "To find life on Mars, scientists should keep their eyes peeled for pasta."

**Presents information in order of importance:** Pappas begins with an overview of the research findings: "Hot-spring-loving microbes" created pasta-shaped rock formations. She then goes on to state how these formations "could be the first clues to life on other planets." Pappas ends the article with quotes by Fouke showing why this research and findings are important to future research related to life on planets such as Mars.

**MODES & MEDIA**

**Mode = written and visual:** Pappas shares most information in words, but photos of pasta-looking formations from Yellowstone help illustrate the basis of her article. Many news sites, such as *Science News*, accompany text with visuals.

**Medium = digital:** Pappas's article was published online at *Live Science*. Since it is published digitally, hyperlinks throughout the article can take readers to other information, such as the journal *Astrobiology*, where the Fouke study was originally published.

thread consists of trillions of microbes hanging on to each other for dear life. [The 7 Harshest Environments on Earth]

The researchers studied the genomes and protein production of their microbe samples. They discovered that 98 percent of the microbes living in these hot, fast-moving waters belong to a species called *Sulfurihydrogenibium yellowstonense*, or "sulfuri" for short.

**SULFURI ON THE EDGE**

Sulfuri is found in hot springs around the world, Fouke said, and lives by breaking down sulfur and using the resulting energy. The species evolved 2.5 billion years ago, when Earth's atmosphere contained barely any oxygen. That makes sulfuri likely very similar to any life that might have existed on ancient Mars, said Mayandi Sivaguru, a biologist at the University of Illinois at Urbana-Champaign and a co-author of the study.

If something like sulfuri did exist on another planet, it would have left fingerprints. In hot springs, change is a constant, Sivaguru told Live Science. Cooling geothermal waters constantly deposit minerals. But sulfuri, the researchers discovered, actively encourages this change. Proteins on the microbes' surfaces encourage the growth of calcium-carbonate crystals. Thus, the travertine that forms in the presence of sulfuri at Mammoth Hot Springs grows a billion times faster than travertine in other environments, Fouke said.

"It's an instant microbial fossil factory," he said.

Sulfuri survives by growing just a little bit faster than the minerals that get deposited around it, the researchers said. What's more, it uses the pasta-shaped rock to survive. Filaments of the microbes attach to the ridges formed by their fossilized compatriots, which boosts the microbes into very shallow water that contains the low levels of oxygen the microbes need to survive. (They die without oxygen, Fouke said, but they also die if exposed to the level of oxygen in air.)

Though any extraterrestrial microbe living in hot springs on another world would be a different species than sulfuri, it would probably have a similar lifestyle, Fouke said—it would have to, given the limited number of ways to make life work in such an extreme environment. Thus, the protein and genetic analyses done by the team would provide a benchmark for an alien comparison, should some future rover pick up a pasta-looking rock on a far-flung planet.

Uses short paragraphs to hold readers' attention.

**STYLE**

**Neutral perspective, no opinions:** Pappas doesn't indicate her personal opinion about whether these rock formations can help indicate life on Mars.

**Objective, third-person voice:** Pappas reports what researchers discovered, leaving herself out of the article.

**Just enough detail for the general reader:** Pappas relates relevant details precisely, such as the temperature and pH of the water in the hot springs: "the water ranges in temperature from 149 degrees to 162 degrees Fahrenheit . . . and has a low pH of 6.2 to 6.8."

**DESIGN**

**Appealing headline:** The title interests readers and conveys the gist of the article in a few words. Also, the page presents the news magazine's title, the name of the section, and the date of publication.

**Byline:** Pappas's name (rather than "staff writer") appears under the headline, which adds to her **ethos**.

**Images:** Two photos of rock formations give the reader a visual of the pasta-looking shape that inspired the research.

*(Continues on next page)*

News Articles

"It's the first study to ever have this kind of in-depth analysis of the environment, the rock deposits and also the omics," Fouke said, referring to the proteomics, transcriptomics and genomics that the researchers used to delve into the microbes' genetics, protein production and other biological processes. "That means now, for the first time, when we have a rock that is fettuccini-looking travertine, if that rock is collected and analyzed on Mars, we have the full suite of these extremely cutting-edge analyses for the microbes."

More information on the research is available in the digital book "The Art of Yellowstone Science—Mammoth Hot Springs as a Window on the Universe," by Fouke and colleagues.

**SOURCES**
Sources are acknowledged. Pappas and *Live Science* use hyperlinks to acknowledge sources. The journal where the study was published online is linked so readers can learn more. Additionally, a link to a digital book by Fouke and colleagues with additional information about the research is provided.

## QUESTIONS | Analyzing Pappas's News Article

### RHETORICAL SITUATION & CHOICES

1. **Purpose.** What is Pappas's main purpose in writing this article? What are some of her secondary purposes? Identify passages in the article where these purposes are apparent.

2. **Purpose.** Notice how Pappas uses a slightly humorous title for her science- and research-based article. Why does she do this?

3. **Audience.** How does Pappas appeal to people who are not research scientists?

4. **Rhetorical appeals.** The article includes hyperlinks that connect readers with additional information. How else does Pappas convey a sense of ethos?

5. **Rhetorical appeals.** Most of the article is written with scientific facts and research findings. Why does Pappas use bits of humor, such as in the opening line and subheadings?

### GENRE CONVENTIONS

6. **Modes & media.** Where do you read/learn about science news? Reading articles online? Listening to podcasts? Why?

7. **Elements of the genre.** How does the lead paragraph set the stage for the rest of the article?

8. **Style.** How does Pappas convey scientific information in a way that a general audience can understand? Are there areas in the article that might have been simplified for a general reader? Why?

9. **Design.** Notice that links to social media sites are at the top of the article, right under the byline, rather than at the end of the article or on the side of the article. Why did the designers at *Live Science* lay them out this way?

10. **Sources.** Make a list of all the sources Stephanie Pappas consulted while writing this article. Are there any sources that surprise you? How can you categorize the sources? Are they primary? Secondary? Tertiary? (See Part 4 for support with sources.)

## CHECKLIST | Drafting a News Article

Are you thinking of drafting a news article? Ask yourself the following questions:

### RHETORICAL SITUATION & CHOICES

☐ **Purpose.** What newsworthy event or issue do I want to report? Of all the people involved with the story, which person will be my focus? How can I bring the story and people to life for my readers?

☐ **Audience.** Who will read my article? How carefully will they read it? Why will they read it? What will they do with the information?

☐ **Rhetorical appeals.** How will I establish my authority as a writer? How will I logically connect ideas and details? How will I make sure that my use of pathos does not undercut my ethos?

☐ **Modes & media.** Will readers experience my article in print form or online? Do I want to include images or videos?

### GENRE CONVENTIONS

☐ **Elements of the genre.** Which information is important enough to my readers that I should present it first? Which information is interesting, but not as important?

☐ **Style.** How will I keep my tone objective and neutral? What level of detail will I include in my article?

☐ **Design.** How will I use headers and footers, titles, headlines, tabs, and other design features to keep my readers oriented? Will my article appear online? If so, what information will I hyperlink? How might I embed photos or videos into the layout?

☐ **Sources.** How much research will I need to do to compose this article? Are there people I'll need to talk to? Where will I need to go? Will I need to locate documents or records in a library or online?

---

**PRACTICE**

# Writing to Inform General Readers

Think of something you are curious about—for example, you might wonder why bees sting, why you yawn after seeing someone else yawn, or why dogs assume certain distinct postures (like the play bow). Search YouTube for videos that explore the behavior in depth. Find out if there is a faculty expert on that behavior on your campus, and if so, arrange to interview them. Then think about how to convey what you've learned to a general audience. Which quotations from the videos and/or interview will do the most to bring your article to life? Next, draft a short article for an online newspaper that conveys the big picture of the topic, as well as relevant details that will interest your readers. Be sure to create a catchy headline and to hyperlink to any sources you use (including the people you interview and the videos you reference).

# Editorials & Opinion Pieces

Editorials and other opinion pieces are texts that convey a writer's views on a particular topic, sometimes a controversial topic. This type of writing can be called by different names, such as *opinions, perspectives, commentaries,* and *viewpoints,* and can take the form of a letter to the editor or an online comment in response to an issue or other piece of writing.

Editorials and opinion pieces appear in newspapers and magazines, on TV and radio, and in blogs and other online publications. Editorials also include editorial cartoons. An editorial represents the opinion of a news agency's editorial board, and therefore represents the opinion of the publisher. An opinion piece, on the other hand, could take the form of opinion columns by regular featured writers, and letters from readers in which they share their views. If your school publishes a newspaper, it probably also includes a section dedicated to editorials or opinions.

## Analyzing Editorials & Opinion Pieces

**Purpose**   The purpose may vary depending on whether the writer is an individual or an editorial board writer.

- *Individual writers.* An average citizen or student who writes an opinion piece or letter to the editor does so to convey his or her view on a specific issue, with the intent of persuading other readers. For example, in one issue of the *Oregon Daily Emerald,* a University of Oregon student wrote a column titled "Students Should Have Wider Gun Liberties" in response to an article discussing how the university campus prepares for a campus shooting. The student's purpose is clear, as is his opinion.

- *The same is true for an individual columnist*—a staff or syndicated writer for a specific newspaper, magazine, or other news organization; that is, the columnist conveys their own opinion in the editorial and not the opinion of a publisher, though there is some gray area there, because the writers are usually employed by the publisher.

- *Editorial board writers.* Texts that are written by the editorial board of a newspaper or magazine convey the opinion of the publisher. These editorials are intended to educate and persuade readers to agree with a specific idea and/or to take a specific action. The editorial boards of most newspapers reflect a conservative or liberal point of view through their editorials; for example, the editorial board of *The New York Times* has a reputation for being fairly liberal, while the editorial board of the *News-Gazette* of Champaign-Urbana, Illinois, has a reputation for being conservative.

**Audience**   Anyone with access to newspapers, magazines, television, radio, or the internet can read or watch editorials and opinion pieces. You might scan the opinion pages of newspapers regularly, or mainly during an election or controversy, in order to read the opinions, analysis, and interpretations of others on various issues. Writers of editorials keep their readers—primary and secondary audiences—in mind as they compose.

**Rhetorical appeals** Editorial and opinion piece writers rely most on ethos and logos to persuade readers of the validity of their positions. Writers are careful to avoid exaggeration and oversimplification to come across as credible (ethos), and they use evidence to appeal to readers' sense of logic (logos).

**Modes & media** Newspaper editorials and opinion pieces are usually presented as written texts; sometimes they're accompanied by a small photo of the writer to establish the writer's credibility. Some editorials include charts or other infographics. Some editorials are presented as audio texts, such as the commentaries offered by National Public Radio. Editorials and opinion pieces can be found both in print, such as in newspapers and magazines, and digitally, such as on the sites for *The New York Times* and NPR.

**Elements of the genre** Editorial and opinion piece writers do the following:

- *Clearly present their work as opinion writing.* The distinction between an editorial or opinion piece and a news article is important: Editorials or opinion pieces are opinions based on research and analysis, whereas news articles are objective reporting based on research. That is, editorials reflect a personal view, while news articles are supposed to be totally free of opinion. Editorials or opinion pieces are usually clearly labeled as *editorials* (or *opinion*, *viewpoint*, or *commentary*).

- *Write concisely.* An editorial or opinion piece is typically about five or so paragraphs long, which means the author needs to make their point quickly.

- *Identify and address counterarguments.* Editorial and opinion piece writers make their strongest cases when they anticipate objections and opposition to their views.

- *Offer potential solutions.* Often after explaining a problem, writers will examine potential solutions and suggest one over another.

- *Close with a simple but memorable statement.* For example, the editorial on page 241 by Grecia Sanchez closes with "It is an imperative for young people to acknowledge themselves for who and what they are, according to their own personal opinions."

- *Invite readers to respond.* Many online editorials become discussion starters in which hundreds or even thousands of readers post replies to the original editorial and to other posts.

**Style** Editorial and opinion piece writers do the following:

- *Include concise detail.* Writers use specific facts throughout their editorials to support their position. Because they are making a case, they need to use enough evidence to convince readers, but they still need to keep the entire piece fairly brief.

- *Use sound reasoning and avoid logical fallacies.* Opinion writers support their claims with quotations from experts. They also strive to avoid errors in reasoning known as logical fallacies. Here are some of the most common types:

  » *Red herring:* Distracting the reader from the real issue being argued: for example, "Global warming needs to be addressed, but people are struggling with gas prices."

» *Ad hominem*: Attacking the person making an argument instead of addressing the argument: for example, "She says women should have equal rights, but look at how ugly she is."

» *Hasty generalization*: Extrapolating unrealistically from one example: for example, "He lied; therefore all men are liars."

» *Slippery slope*: Assuming that if one step is taken, then all sorts of catastrophic results will inevitably follow: for example, "If we increase taxes by 1 percent today, tomorrow our children will be paying more in taxes than they take home."

» *Circular reasoning*: Defining a word by using the word, where the start is the same as the ending: for example, "The reason we should outlaw guns is that guns should be made illegal."

» *Post hoc*: Confusing chronology with causality: for example, "The cat peed on the bedspread because I just washed it."

- *Use analogies and refer to cultural and historical events.* Writers use comparisons to clarify the issue and refer to other events to help readers identify with it.

- *Use interesting language.* Opinion writers avoid jargon and instead use language that will appeal to readers who may not be familiar with the issue. They may also use rhetorical questions to spark readers' attention.

- *Convey a clear, personable voice and tone.* Writers use clear, persuasive language as they present their opinions and support them with facts. Editorial writers often write in the first person (I) and in a friendly, inviting tone to reach a wide readership.

**Design**   Editorial and opinion piece writers and the designers they work with do the following:

- *They write clear, interesting headlines.* Whether they're published in print or online, editorials, like news articles, are presented with a headline designed to get readers' attention and to make it clear what the editorialist is writing about. Editorials and opinion pieces are also clearly labeled as such, or with other terms, such as *opinions* or *commentaries*, that denote subjective writing.

- *They repeat design features on the page.* Whether you're reading an editorial or opinion piece in print or online, you'll see certain design elements on every page; these elements include the name of the newspaper, perhaps presented as a logo or otherwise branded, at the top and bottom of the page. This helps the writers and designers establish the news organization's identity. You might also find a heading indicating what part of the paper or site you've navigated to ("Editorial," "Opinion," etc.). The date also appears in these spots for easy reference.

**Sources**   Opinion writers refer to specific examples. They back up their generalizations by offering a variety of support from credible sources. They present evidence with attribution phrases that let readers know where the data came from.

# Guided Reading | Editorial

When she wrote this editorial, Grecia Sanchez was a student double-majoring in Philosophy and Multimedia Journalism at the University of Texas at El Paso. Her career goal was to work for a newspaper promoting ideas about social humanities. This opinion piece was published in *The Prospector*, the University of Texas at El Paso's student newspaper. Sanchez was a staff reporter for *The Prospector*. This editorial was published on September 13, 2016, and filed under the "Opinion" section of the site.

## Grecia Sanchez, *¿Es que acaso soy hispana?*

| RHETORICAL SITUATION & CHOICES | | GENRE CONVENTIONS | |
|---|---|---|---|

**PURPOSE**
Sanchez wants to convince readers that it should be up to individuals to decide how they want to identify their race or ethnicity.

**AUDIENCE**
Sanchez is writing for a college newspaper, so she knows her readers are college students. Her university is a Hispanic Serving Institution, which means that at least 25 percent of its students are Hispanic, so she knows that many of the paper's readers will be interested in her topic.

**RHETORICAL APPEALS**
Sanchez establishes her **ethos** by sharing that she was born in Mexico and that her first language was Spanish. She appeals to **logos** by presenting facts about the history of terms like *Latino, Hispanic,* and *Chicano.*

**MODES & MEDIA**
Mode = written:
Most editorials and opinion pieces are

◀ **What is the composer, Grecia Sanchez, doing?**

**How do I know this is** ▶ **an opinion piece?**

Grecia Sanchez, Staff Reporter
September 13, 2016
Filed under Opinion

Defining identity at an adolescent age can be a challenge, especially to those who are constantly interacting with a different culture than their own.

I was born and raised in Ciudad Juàrez, Mexico. My first language is Spanish and my only label in Juàrez was that of a Mexican girl. I only had to deal with one nationality and one term to define myself. I didn't realize that just across the border I was defined as something more than just Mexican.

My struggle began at the time I was applying to UTEP. Among the documents I had to deliver for my admission process was a requirement for a meningitis vaccine. I remember going to the pharmacy and having to fill out this form with the question "How do you identify yourself?" It even had optional answers showing Hispanic/Latino, Latinx, Chicano, Asian American, African American, among others.

The overall experience of it was overwhelming. I had to ask the pharmacist to define these terms for me because I had literally no idea what all of these meant. At the end, I just put "Mexican" with my own handwriting in the "Other" space.

Many Mexican students can relate to my experience since we are constantly labeled as Hispanic or Latino students, and though many of us think these terms are the same thing, in reality, they have differences regarding cultural, historical, political and social contexts.

According to the Pais Latino Web site, the term "Hispano" is used for all the people who come from countries that were once conquered by Hispania, or España (using modern

**ELEMENTS OF THE GENRE**
**Is clearly presented as opinion writing:**
Throughout her piece, Sanchez often asserts her opinions. For example, she says, "I shouldn't be pushed to decide," "one word invented by a large group of disrespectful people," and "it is important for other people to think about who they are."

**Is concisely written:**
Sanchez's sentences and language clearly convey her points. She uses only enough information to support her opinions. Although she has more paragraphs than one might typically see in an opinion piece, her paragraphs are short and follow journalistic conventions.

**Invites readers to respond:** In her closing statement, Sanchez asks her readers to "think about who they are and which term they identify with the most."

*(Continues on next page)*

Editorials & Opinion Pieces  **241**

written or audio pieces. Words are vital to editorialists or opinion columnists if they want to make their point because the specificity and clarity of the writer's position is so important.

**Medium = digital:** The column is available online, and at the bottom there's an option for a print-friendly version, which is formatted specifically to be printed on a standard 8.5" × 11" sheet of paper.

terminology). These countries include all the American countries from Mexico all the way down to South America, with the exception of Brazil, since it was conquered by Portugal.

The U.S. Census Bureau imposed the term in 1980 to define the people who would be later called Mexican Americans, unlike the term "Latino," which refers to the geography of Latin America and its inhabitants. This is used for people belonging to countries where the Romance languages are spoken (Spanish, Portuguese and French).

Both of these terms are politically and socially correct to use, as long as one has its definition and correct context in mind. However, Chicano is often used to depict Mexican Americans. It describes those who have Mexican heritage, and although it is a term that is recently accepted nowadays, there are still people who think of this term as a disrespectful one.

Alongside the LGBT movement in recent years, the term "Latinx" has been introduced into our society to refer to the gender-neutral alternative for Latino, Latina and Latin@. According to the *Huffington Post*'s Latino Voices article, "Why People are Using the Term Latinx," it is used as an inclusive term for intersecting identities of Latin American descendants.

Now that I know the differences between these words, I honestly do not consider them as part of my identity. I know I can be considered Hispana because I speak Spanish and I come from Mexico, which was conquered by España during colonial American times. I realize I can be a Latina because I belong to a Latin American country and I speak one of the Romance languages, and I also acknowledge I can be called Chicana because I have Mexican ascendency. But neither of these terms define me because of the simple fact that I was born and raised in Mexico.

Above all the differences, I am Mexican and I believe I shouldn't be pushed to decide whether I am Chicana, but not a Latina, or that I am Latinx, but not Hispanic; I am just a Mexican girl. I've heard that a lot of these terms were introduced by the U.S. government, which was driven by racism and disrespectful jokes toward Mexicans. This is another reason why I do not wish to recognize myself as one word invented by a large group of disrespectful people.

Although I do not identify myself with those terms, I do feel it is important for other people to think about who they are and which term they identify with the most, if they do at all. It is an imperative for young people to acknowledge themselves for who and what they are, according to their own personal opinions.

*Note from editors: ¿Es que acaso soy hispana? translates to "Is it that I am Hispanic?"*

**STYLE**
**Specific facts used as support:** Sanchez provides details from the U.S. Census Bureau and the Pais Latino website.

**Personal, informal tone:** Sanchez writes, "I just put 'Mexican' with my own handwriting in the 'Other' space."

**DESIGN**
**Clear, interesting headline:** The headline "¿Es que acaso soy hispana?" immediately signals that the subject of the opinion piece will relate to Hispanic identity.
**Byline, date of publication, and type of article at top.**

**SOURCES**
Sanchez refers to specific sources (Pais Latino website, U.S. Census Bureau, and *Huffington Post*). She also uses her own experiences throughout to help support her opinions.

**RHETORICAL SITUATION & CHOICES**

1. **Purpose.** Does Sanchez convince you that individuals should be able to make their own choices about their racial and ethnic identity? Why or why not?

2. **Audience.** How do you think a Caucasian person whose family has lived in the United States for many generations might respond to Sanchez's piece?

3. **Rhetorical appeals.** How effective do you think Sanchez's references to the origins of terms like *Hispanic*, *Latino*, and *Chicano* are?

4. **Rhetorical appeals.** How does Sanchez make her case? How does she appeal to her audience using ethos?

5. **Rhetorical appeals.** To what extent does Sanchez come across as authoritative and knowledgeable? What does she do to convince you that she is authoritative and knowledgeable, or alternatively, what does she do that makes you question her authority or knowledge?

**GENRE CONVENTIONS**

6. **Modes & media.** Imagine that Sanchez had included a map of Central and South America with each country labeled with the different terms the U.S. Census Bureau uses to identify people from that country. How would the addition of this image add to or detract from the effectiveness of this opinion piece?

7. **Elements of the genre.** Sanchez's piece doesn't have a clear, concise statement of her position until the very end. Where did you feel that you had a clear sense of her position? Why there? How would you characterize the tone of Sanchez's piece? How does it affect you as a reader?

8. **Style.** Would you consider Sanchez's language inflammatory? Why or why not?

9. **Style.** How does the fact that the title is in Spanish affect you? Do you think using Spanish for the title is appropriate for her subject and audience? Why or why not?

10. **Design.** If you go online to the piece, there is a button at the bottom to make the article print-friendly. How do the additional options benefit the audience?

11. **Sources.** While Sanchez does mention other sources, most of her piece relies on her own experiences as evidence. Are there areas where she might include more external sources to help convince the reader? What types of sources might help strengthen her position?

## CHECKLIST | Drafting an Editorial or Opinion Piece

Thinking of writing an editorial? Ask yourself the following questions:

### RHETORICAL SITUATION & CHOICES

☐ **Purpose.** What is my purpose? And what do I want to persuade others to think or do? Do I want readers to see things from a different perspective? To take action? Do I want them to completely change their minds on an issue? How feasible is it to try to change a person's mind?

☐ **Audience.** Who am I trying to persuade? What are my audience's concerns about the issue I'm writing about? What do they fear? What is their stake in the issue (what do they personally have to risk losing if they do what I want)?

☐ **Rhetorical appeals.** How will I establish myself as reasonable and authoritative on this issue? How can I use organization to appeal to my audience's sense of logos? Will my audience respond to emotional appeals, or will I seem manipulative if I appeal to pathos?

☐ **Modes & media.** Will I use written words or audio or video to convey my point? Based on the audience I have in mind, are they more likely to read or listen to an editorial in print, on the radio, or on the internet?

### GENRE CONVENTIONS

☐ **Elements of the genre.** How can I make it clear that I'm writing an opinion piece? How can I get my audience's attention immediately and show them how important and relevant this issue is to their lives? Which potential objections and counterarguments should I address? How can I make the closing of my editorial memorable?

☐ **Style.** Would it help to support my case by quoting experts? Are there analogies that I could use that would appeal to my readers? What types of rhetorical questions would be most compelling for my editorial? How will I keep my language persuasive yet friendly?

☐ **Design.** Do I want to design a heading or logo for my column to identify myself as the author? How can I use a heading, logo, or other design element to develop my ethos?

☐ **Sources.** What kinds of sources will be most useful and most interesting and persuasive to my audience? How might I bring in sources to address potential objections and opposing arguments?

---

### PRACTICE

## Writing to Persuade Fellow Citizens

Think about your position on an issue related to an aspect of identity, such as religion, sexual orientation, class, or ethnicity. Brainstorm a list of reasons you hold the position you do, and then consider the reasons someone might take a position different from yours. You might want to do additional research so you can bring in and respond to the perspectives of others. Then combine your research and ideas into an editorial or opinion piece that convinces your audience that your position is a valid one.

# Advertisements

An advertisement is any text created to persuade consumers to purchase a product or service. Print advertising is as old as the first newspapers, which appeared in England in the 1600s. Today, ads are everywhere and are presented in a variety of print and digital media. Advertisers spend large amounts of money to research potential customers and then tailor and distribute sales messages that will appeal to those consumers and translate into sales. The money they spend on digital advertising, in particular, is on the rise, especially for display ads (banners and video ads).

## Analyzing Advertisements

**Purpose**  To sell their products and services, companies need to publicize information about what they're offering. They also need to win business from competitors. Ultimately, an advertisement tries to persuade potential customers to use the company's product or service.

**Audience**  When advertising firms create ads, they have a clear picture of their target market, and they aim their branding, visuals, messages, and other persuasive tools squarely at that market. Maybelline created the ad for their mousse foundation shown on page 248.

**Rhetorical appeals**  Advertisers use appeals to ethos (authority), logos (logic), and pathos (emotion). Many ads that feature expert testimonials or celebrity endorsements, for example, do so to establish ethos. If you trust the expert giving the testimonial, you are more likely to trust the product. A product that has been long established may have its own built-in ethos, but advertisers may want to freshen that with a modern perspective or testimonial on a traditional brand. Advertisers also appeal to consumers' sense of pathos, tapping into their desire to buy the product, even though it may be a nonessential item.

**Modes & media**  As more reading and viewing happen online, more advertising will happen there too. A digital ad has the potential to spread through social media and YouTube, giving advertisers more "bang for the buck." In terms of the medium, some online ads are static (e.g., display ads that don't move), while others are videos or animations that incorporate sound. There are even reports of a new medium called "smell-vertising": a product's scent is broadcast in an area with potential consumers of the product.

**Elements of the genre**  The following are some features shared by advertisements. They present:

- *Headlines*. Advertisers use headlines to immediately attract the reader's attention. The headline often conveys the product's benefits through concise language. Additionally, advertisers pay special attention to the placement of the headline, ensuring that it is not obscured or overwhelmed by a visual element. In the case of some electronic ads, a headline may be read aloud by a narrator.

- *Visuals.* Graphics work together with the headline to attract the reader. They also illustrate the point or provide visual evidence that supports the product's claim. In television commercials, advertisers edit the visuals to hold viewers' attention, maintaining a quick pace and not lingering for too long on one image.

- *Ad copy.* Advertisers use the words of an advertisement, or ad copy, for specific purposes. They use a headline to get a consumer's attention and then draw the reader in further with an intriguing subheading. Copy that is not a headline or heading is called body text, and it tells about the benefits of the product or service and either implicitly or explicitly tells the consumer to make a purchase. Digital and TV ads also feature ad copy that can be spoken or animated on the screen.

- *Advertising slogans.* Advertisers often associate sayings or phrases with a product. For example, Nike's slogan is "Just Do It."

- *A signature.* Usually found toward the bottom of a print ad, the signature includes the advertiser name and contact information. In digital and TV ads, contact information is not normally provided, but the brand and product name is made clear.

**Style**   Advertisers make stylistic choices concerning the following:

- *Technique.* The writing tends to be brief and directive. For example, in the original Smokey the Bear advertisements, Smokey addresses the reader: "Only YOU can prevent forest fires!" Words are usually secondary to visuals. Visuals are carefully selected as persuasive tools (see "Design" below). Because digital and TV ads are very short (usually thirty seconds or less), words are limited.

- *Details.* Advertisers usually keep details (and words in general) to a minimum.

- *Voice and tone.* In a commercial, voice and tone can give the viewer an impression of the product's benefits. For example, if a company is promoting its product's ability to relieve stress, then the tone of the ad is usually soothing. If a financial company is advertising its services, then the tone is usually reassuring. Written ad copy conveys its tone through word choice and phrasing, while digital and TV ads convey tone through vocal intonation, pacing, and the qualities of the voice itself (male or female, deep or high, etc.).

**Design**   Creators of advertisements use design to reach audiences, including the following elements:

- *A visual of the product.* Advertisers need to provide an image of what they're selling so consumers can identify and purchase it. If the product is less tangible (or not an object), such as an auto insurance policy, then some kind of visual emphasizes the message. For example, in some Geico ads, a caveman is the main visual, emphasizing how easy it is to purchase auto insurance.

- *Additional pathos-building images.* Advertisers use visuals to convey ideas and tap into viewers' emotions. For example, in a commercial for Abilify (a drug used mainly to treat depression), the advertiser presents "before" and "after" images. The commercial begins with a series of people looking stressed, sad, and unable to do anything. The drug is introduced, followed by a series of visuals showing the same people engaged with life and smiling.

- *Color.* Advertisers can further appeal to pathos by using images and colors associated with particular emotions.

- *Product logos.* Advertisers carefully design product logos to convey particular ideas and values about a product. For example, the Nike swoosh indicates speed and movement. All Nike products and advertisements feature the swoosh, which is instantly identifiable and long established.

- *Layout.* In a print-based ad (or a static web ad), the layout orients the reader and establishes the most important pieces of information. The main visual and headline are the most prominent parts of the advertisement; contact info and fine print are usually somewhere toward the bottom of the piece. Advertisers use similar principles in digital and TV commercials to make the featured product and message clear and conspicuous.

**Sources** Advertising agencies conduct market research before creating ad campaigns so they can most efficiently identify and target their main audience and tailor their overall message accordingly. Once they've identified some possible directions for the content and design, they may ask a test audience to determine which ad will be most successful. Sources noted within an ad can include a company website where consumers can find more information about the product.

## Guided Reading | Advertisement

In the following advertisement, the Maybelline beauty product is promoted as "the newest dream sensation." The Maybelline Company, created in 1915, sells its cosmetics around the world. In 1996, the French cosmetic company L'Oréal purchased Maybelline. After this acquisition, the company moved its headquarters to New York City. This ad includes Maybelline's signature line, "Maybe she's born with it. Maybe it's Maybelline," which was changed in 2016 to "Make it happen." This ad was originally part of a 2010 U.S. and U.K. advertising campaign that ran in various magazines. Just like the product, the advertising campaign was aimed at women.

## Maybelline New York, *Baby-Smooth Perfection*

**RHETORICAL SITUATION & CHOICES**

What are the ▶
composers of the
ad, Maybelline,
doing?

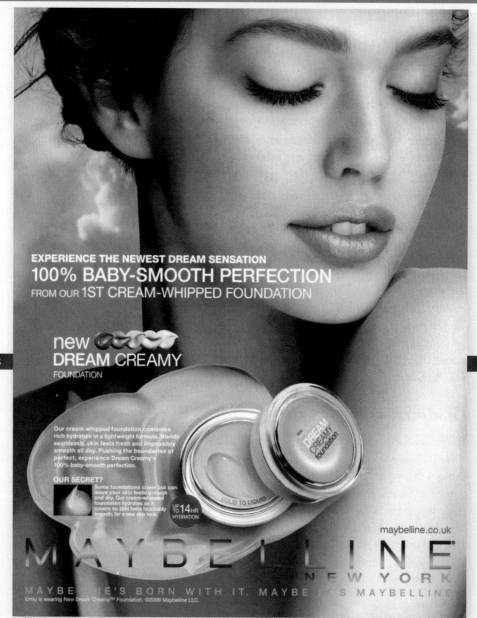

**GENRE CONVENTIONS**

How do I know ▶
this is an
advertisement?

Credit: The Advertising Archives.

## RHETORICAL SITUATION & CHOICES

### PURPOSE
Maybelline, the creators of this ad, hope to persuade consumers to buy their cosmetic product.

### AUDIENCE
The ad creators are aiming at women who want to keep their skin moist ("rich hydration") while appearing beautiful. The audience reads magazines (where the print ad appeared) and spends time online (notice the Maybelline URL in the ad copy).

### RHETORICAL APPEALS
The ad appeals mainly to readers' pathos (emotion) by displaying a woman's face that shows no age nor blemishes. The model's closed eyes imply a type of innocence, especially with the blue sky and ethereal lighting of the clouds in the background. Her nudity, along with a carefully made-up face (perfect mascara and lipstick), suggests sex. The ad copy that says "Our Secret?" appeals to a reader's sense that they are being let in on something not available to everyone.

The ad also conveys Maybelline's ethos through the presentation of the makeup and the emphasis on the company's branding.

### MODES & MEDIA
**Mode = written and visual:** The advertisers use visuals and a small amount of text to persuade viewers to purchase this Maybelline cosmetic. Maybelline's ad stresses the purity and benefits of this product, so both the visuals and text convey this point. The text emphasizes this through some of the headline copy ("100% baby-smooth perfection") and also the body copy ("Pushing the boundaries of perfect, experience baby- smooth perfection"). The visuals make the claim with a picture of a beautiful woman and blue skies.

**Medium = Print and Digital:** While this ad appeared in print magazines, it can also be found digitally on the internet. Maybelline's campaigns are designed not only for print but also for TV and the internet.

## GENRE CONVENTIONS

### ELEMENTS OF THE GENRE

**Argument:** This ad presents an argument (which is visual and textual) for purchasing a product.

The headline, "100% baby-smooth perfection," is brief and direct. The ad copy, "Our cream-whipped foundation," suggests the luxuriousness of the product and implies that Maybelline is the only company who produces this type of makeup.

Color is used to create a sense of tranquility, perfection, and allure. The writers and designers chose blue for the sky background to emphasize calmness and also to symbolize the trust that goes with a Maybelline product. Additionally a blue sky indicates a perfect day, much like the perfection that the Maybelline product delivers. The tan tones help make a connection between the sexual appeal of the model and the color of the foundation product.

**The layout focuses** on the woman's face and the upper part of her nude body; the composition suggests purity but also sexuality to entice consumers. The spatial arrangement emphasizes the woman's face since that is where the makeup will be applied. The placement of the woman below a beautiful blue sky with heavenly lighting through the clouds plays into the innocence suggested by the promise of "baby-smooth."

The use of a sans serif typeface suggests freshness and a contemporary quality.

The ad includes a visual of the product, the cream-whipped foundation, so it's easy for consumers to identify the product when they are shopping for makeup.

### SOURCES
Maybelline most likely conducted market research to figure out how to best appeal to a woman open to their product.

**RHETORICAL SITUATION & CHOICES**

1. **Purpose.** What information did the creators of the ad provide (textually and visually) about this Maybelline cosmetic? How interesting is the information? How persuasive is it? Explain.

2. **Audience.** How do the various images in the ad speak to its audience? Who is the primary target audience for this ad? Is there only one audience, or are several audiences being addressed? Why do you think so?

3. **Rhetorical appeals.** How many different ways is the concept of "purity" conveyed in the ad? How is this used to persuade the audience?

4. **Rhetorical appeals.** Why do the ad's creators focus on Maybelline's "baby-smooth perfection" properties? What does this suggest about Maybelline's target audience?

5. **Rhetorical appeals.** Look up the word *perfection* in a dictionary. Which of the definitions listed seems most appropriate in the case of the ad? Why?

**GENRE CONVENTIONS**

6. **Modes & media.** The ad is divided between the visual of the sky and woman for the top half and ad copy for the bottom. Why do you think the creators chose this particular balance of text and visuals?

7. **Elements of the genre.** The ad headline includes a reference to food—"cream-whipped." Why do you think composers included this in an advertisement for makeup?

8. **Style.** How would you characterize the tone of the ad copy? Does the tone fit the advertisement's purpose? Why or why not?

9. **Design.** Describe the visuals in the ad. What do the visuals suggest about what the advertisers want consumers to think, believe, or feel about Maybelline?

10. **Sources.** Is it effective to use an image of the sky and clouds for a cosmetics ad? Why or why not? What type of market research might have suggested this choice?

Thinking of creating an ad? Ask yourself the following questions:

## RHETORICAL SITUATION & CHOICES

☐ **Purpose.** What product do I use that I want to convince others to use? What are the reasons to use that product? Why would someone besides me want to use the product?

☐ **Audience.** Who are the people in my target audience? Who will use the product? When will they use the product? Where will they use the product? How will they use the product?

☐ **Rhetorical appeals.** How will I establish my credibility in my advertisement? How will I illustrate the product's reliability and ethos? How will I use emotions to persuade my reader to use the product? To what extent will I use logic to support my claim about the product?

☐ **Modes & media.** Will my ad be print-based, digital, or made for TV? How will I use visual images to persuade? Will I use one primary image or others that are secondary? How will my text work with my images? Will text explain visuals? Complement them? Will I use animation?

## GENRE CONVENTIONS

☐ **Elements of the genre.** Will my visuals be literal or symbolic? What type of catchy slogan can I create to make my product memorable? Will I use the slogan as my headline or within the ad copy?

☐ **Style.** What tone will work best for selling my product? How will my intended audience respond to my tone?

☐ **Design.** What typeface should I use? What size type will work best with my visuals? How can I use layout in order to feature the most important elements and leave the least important for final viewing? How can I use color and other design elements to guide my viewers' experience?

☐ **Sources.** What kind of market research will I conduct? Will I test out my headline or slogan on a potential audience? Will I show them a series of visuals to see which is most persuasive?

---

**PRACTICE**

## Selling a Product

Think of a product you consume or use, such as an energy drink, candy bar, computer, or article of clothing. Create a draft of a print advertisement that highlights a specific property or aspect of that product, such as the beautifying properties of Maybelline. Use symbolic visuals to sell your product, just as the Maybelline ad uses the model's nudity to convey purity and natural beauty. Use color to create the mood and focus viewers' attention. Alternatively, create a digital or TV ad in which you use images, sound, and text.

# *Wikipedia* Entries

Collecting facts has been a human pursuit for a long time. In the first century CE, a Roman author, naturalist, and military man named Pliny the Elder tried to record everything known about the natural world in his thirty-seven-volume *Naturalis Historia*, the world's first wiki-like document. (You can read it at the Perseus Digital Library in English or the original Latin.)

Pliny, like all wiki and encyclopedia authors, aimed to provide what was known about a specific or general topic in a way that worked best for his target audience. The *Encyclopaedia Britannica* is a source of general information on many topics; it's geared toward readers who want to gain a broad understanding of a given subject. More specialized encyclopedias, such as *The Encyclopedia of Women's History in America* by Kathryn Cullen-DuPont, may cover topics in more depth, assuming readers already have some understanding of the topic.

**WRITE**

How often do you refer to encyclopedias? What are the benefits and limitations of using an encyclopedia as a source? How often is the encyclopedia you refer to *Wikipedia*? What are the benefits and limitations of using *Wikipedia* as a source? How reliable do you consider *Wikipedia* to be? Make a list of the pros and cons of using *Wikipedia*.

*Wikipedia* is a kind of encyclopedia, thus the "pedia" part of the name. "Wiki" refers to the fact that entries are collaboratively produced online.

- *Wikipedia* entries exhibit many characteristics of typical encyclopedias: They are a general (or sometimes specialized) reference.
- They provide information that is considered true (meaning it is agreed upon by experts on the topic).
- They are compilations and syntheses of what others have said, rather than original research (that is, they are tertiary sources).
- They are organized into individual articles that are well researched and written by content experts, typically people with an academic degree related to the subject they're writing about.

However, *Wikipedia* differs from other encyclopedias in one key way: Instead of entries being written by scholars, entries can be written by anyone. *Wikipedia* is open access, meaning almost all of its entries can be edited by anyone who registers with the site.

## Analyzing *Wikipedia* Entries

**Purpose**  Encyclopedists, including those writing for *Wikipedia* (often referred to as *Wikipedians*), provide an overview of a subject so that readers can gain a general understanding of it. Some serve as a general reference source. Others are more specialized; they tend to be aimed at readers interested in a particular field.

**Audience**  Encyclopedists know that their primary audience is general readers looking for a reliable but quick snapshot of a topic. For example, writers for *Wikipedia* know their readers are mainly nonprofessionals. They know they must be accurate and fairly brief; they can link to additional resources with more in-depth information. Although they can write on specialized topics, they are not considered a final authority by the academic world on any of the topics.

**Rhetorical appeals**   Encyclopedists appeal to readers through ethos; they aim to present accurate information that will inform the reader. Readers can assume that a wiki entry is the result of someone's study and knowledge. Encyclopedists also appeal through logos, presenting content in a logical manner, often moving from general to more specific information. Writers begin by defining the topic and then often break it out into subtopics. The fact that keywords and subtopics are hyperlinked also contributes to the logos of the entry.

**Modes & media**   Wiki entries are written texts that appear in digital format. Before the digital age, a family would purchase an entire set of print encyclopedias; it's now more common to use free online resources such as *Encyclopedia.com* or *Wikipedia*.

**Elements of the genre**   Encyclopedia entries, including *Wikipedia* entries, are:

- *Well researched.* Encyclopedists gather, scrutinize, and synthesize information from many reliable sources to create an entry on a given topic. They convey information as objectively as possible, without the interference of opinion. In the case of *Wikipedia*, because anyone can edit what is in an entry, a kind of informal peer-review process takes place; when a reader encounters information in a *Wikipedia* entry that they think is inaccurate, they can correct it instantly.

- *Written by experts.* Most encyclopedists are knowledgeable of the topic of the entry to be written. In the case of *Wikipedia*, volunteer editors read new entries and new contributions to existing entries to check that sources are cited and when sources are not, they add a note to the entry that is visible to all readers, indicating that source citations are needed.

- *Clear.* Encyclopedists provide basic information in a direct and straightforward manner.

- *Brief.* Entries are not exhaustive; rather, they are intended as jumping-off points for further research. While some entries can be relatively long, they are still extremely short compared with the length of a book on the subject.

- *Accompanied by clear visuals.* Most wiki entries include visuals. An entry on the Grand Canal in China, for example, includes a photo and a map of the canal. Biographical entries include a photo of the person with the person's birth and death dates clearly indicated below.

**Style**   Encyclopedia entries use the following:

- *Just enough detail to inform general readers.* However, in a given entry, they mention related topics, concepts, and keywords that readers may want to pursue with further research.

- *Precise language and word choice.* Encyclopedists are specific and exact writers. They often use formal, academic language to bolster their authority and emphasize their seriousness. That means they avoid contractions, slang, and abbreviated forms such as "info" for "information."

- *The third person and a serious tone.* Encyclopedists write in the third person, which reinforces their ethos and reminds readers that the entries are based on shared knowledge, not just the perspective of one person. They use a serious tone to project credibility (ethos) to readers. Although the information in an entry might be informative *and also* funny, using humor as a rhetorical strategy in a wiki entry might undermine your authority and trustworthiness.

**Design**  Encyclopedia entries are:

- *Accessible and consistent.* Wiki entries are designed so that readers can quickly identify the parts of the entry. The introduction is followed by an outline of the different parts or headings, which are all hyperlinked so that readers can reach those parts quickly and choose which parts to read.

- *Clearly titled.* The name or title of the entry is in large letters at the top of the entry to clearly indicate the topic.

- *Hyperlinked to other entries.* The use of hyperlinks in an entry allows encyclopedists to provide more information without lengthening the entry itself. These links identify terminology (see "Just enough detail" on p. 253) and provide additional search terms to assist readers in narrowing their investigation of a broad subject.

**Sources**  *Wikipedia* entries contain documentation attributing the information to particular sources. At the end of the entry are sections entitled "Notes" and "References," which the reader can use to learn more about the subject.

## Guided Reading | Wiki Entry

The "Therapy Dog" entry on *Wikipedia* gives an overview of what a therapy dog is, presents information in a clear and accessible way to a general audience, and includes links to outside source material. You can see who has contributed to a *Wikipedia* entry by clicking on the "View history" tab at the top of the entry. Composers on *Wikipedia* are known by their usernames, which are generally not their real names, so you won't always be able to discover their credentials, but you can see other entries they've contributed to. *Wikipedia* has a page devoted to how to read the "View history" page (visit wikipedia.org).

# Wikipedia contributors, *Therapy Dog*

| RHETORICAL SITUATION & CHOICES | GENRE CONVENTIONS |
|---|---|

**PURPOSE**

The composers write to inform readers with documentable facts and uncontested ideas. Their writing is businesslike and factual.

**AUDIENCE**

The audience for *Wikipedia* and this entry is readers who want an overview on a topic, in this case therapy dogs. Readers are most likely from a general rather than an expert audience. They may use this entry as a jumping-off point for further research.

**RHETORICAL APPEALS**

The composers establish their ethos as experts through their clear writing, authoritative tone, and bibliography of sources.

The composers appeal to readers' sense of logos (logic) by presenting the information in an accessible way.

**NOTE:** Some *Wikipedia* entries, including this one, may have a notice posted at the top that asks readers who can contribute to add specific types of sources for credibility. In this case, the notice asks for medical references, which would be appropriate because "therapy" is a medical concept.

◄ **What are the composers doing?**

**How do I know this is a ► *Wikipedia* entry?**

**ELEMENTS OF THE GENRE**

**Gives an overview of the topic:** The entry provides established facts (e.g., facts about who originated the idea of therapy dogs and the contexts in which they are used).

**Serves as a starting point for further research:** The entry introduces related concepts (e.g., the distinction between therapy dogs and service dogs), but it does not get into detail.

**Is well researched:** The composers provide specific details and cite sources.

**STYLE**

The authors are precise, naming specific organizations and college campuses that have used therapy dogs. The authors use specific language, referring to "golden retrievers" rather than "certain breeds." The tone is neutral and the voice is professional; the entry is written in the third person.

**DESIGN**

The entry has a clear title and an organized layout. It includes images and is hyperlinked to other *Wikipedia* entries.

(Continues on next page)

## RHETORICAL SITUATION & CHOICES

## GENRE CONVENTIONS

### MODES & MEDIA

**Mode = written and visual:** The authors convey information in words, but also with images. For example, they use a photo of two golden retrievers to illustrate the type of dog typically trained as a therapy dog.

**Medium = digital:** There are pros and cons to providing information digitally. The pros are the many options for providing information. Digital encyclopedias also allow readers to connect through social media or other options. For example, *Wikipedia* readers can select the "talk" tab at the top of the entry to post comments about the entry. One con is the ads.

### SOURCES

There is a References list and a list of related links.

*Credit: WMF Marks are trademarks of WMF. WMF Marks are used under license from WMF. Text is licensed under Creative Commons.*

## QUESTIONS | Analyzing a *Wikipedia* Entry

### RHETORICAL SITUATION & CHOICES

1. **Purpose.** Although the value of therapy dogs is somewhat controversial, encyclopedists aim to inform—to take a neutral stance rather than try to persuade. What are some strategies the authors of the "therapy dog" entry use to avoid taking a position?

2. **Audience.** Who do you imagine is most likely to look up "therapy dog" in an online encyclopedia: a student, a businessperson, a therapist, or a scientist? What do you imagine his or her purpose might be?

3. **Rhetorical appeals.** Read an entry on a topic of your choice in *Wikipedia* and then read an

### GENRE CONVENTIONS

6. **Elements of the genre.** A wiki entry about therapy dogs is briefer than a book on the topic. As you read the *Wikipedia* entry, was there information you wished had been expanded upon? Why?

7. **Style.** Notice the neutral, third-person voice. How might your reading of this entry be different if the authors had written it in the first person?

entry on the same topic in another online encyclopedia. Compare the authors' techniques in the two entries. Do they use similar methods to develop their ethos? What differences do you notice? Which entry sounds more authoritative in your opinion? Why?

4. **Modes & media.** In what modes and media have you used encyclopedias? Do you have a preference for one mode or medium over another? Why?

5. **Elements of the genre.** As pointed out in the "Therapy Dog" annotations, encyclopedia entries serve as starting points for research. After reading the entry, what questions do you have about the topic? What might you want to research through more in-depth sources?

8. **Design.** The entry is consistently formatted and designed so that readers stay oriented. How important is it to you that information be easy to find in a reference work? Why? Can you think of examples of reference works that are not well designed?

9. **Sources.** In the *Wikipedia* entry, the authors rarely use attribution phrases such as "according to." How does this affect your reading of the entry? How might your experience as a reader be different if the entry were peppered with parenthetical notes and attribution phrases?

## CHECKLIST | Drafting a *Wikipedia* Entry

Are you thinking of drafting a *Wikipedia* entry? Ask yourself the following questions:

### RHETORICAL SITUATION & CHOICES

☐ **Purpose.** What specific topic do I want to write about? Which subtopics do I want to write about? How will I define my topic and subtopics? Writing an entry about "fashion" implies that I will cover fashion over the course of history. Writing about "street fashion," however, significantly narrows the time period I would need to cover.

☐ **Audience.** Who are my readers? How many of them are experts on my topic? Nonexperts who have a mild interest in my topic? What questions will they expect my entry to answer? Are there technical terms I may need to define or hyperlink to definitions? What kinds of examples will my readers relate to?

☐ **Rhetorical appeals.** How will I establish my authority as a writer? What kinds of vocabulary, diction, and examples will I use to convey authority?

☐ **Modes & media.** Do I want readers to experience my entry in print or digital format? Do I want to include images or videos? What should I provide hyperlinks to?

### GENRE CONVENTIONS

☐ **Elements of the genre.** To keep my entry relatively brief, I will need to summarize other, longer works on the topic. Which works will I summarize? (For more on summarizing effectively, see Chapter 13.) How will I make sure my writing is extremely precise? What terms might I need to carefully define?

☐ **Style.** How can I present everything in a neutral, third-person voice?

☐ **Design.** How can I use titles and subtitles to make my entry easy to access for readers? If I create a digital entry, how will I use hyperlinks to direct readers to other entries?

☐ **Sources.** In addition to a list of sources, will I want to include a list of "additional resources" for readers who want to do their own research?

## Contributing to a Public Reference

Are you an expert on a particular subject? Choose one you're well versed in, and draft a *Wikipedia* entry on that topic based on what you already know and what you can learn by doing some research (that does not involve *Wikipedia* or any encyclopedia). Remember to include only facts that are largely uncontested by others who are well versed in the subject. You may want to include visual features to illustrate key concepts. You'll find a helpful guide for *Wikipedia* authors on wikipedia.org. Note that the guide provides information about conventions that most *Wikipedia* entries follow—and yours should too.

# Photo Essays

A photo essay is a group of photos that tells a unified story or makes a unified argument. Some photo essayists provide supplementary text or brief captions for their images; others choose to present the images without words. Some photo essayists are journalists whose purpose is to convey a news or human-interest story or offer commentary on an event.

Photo essays can also be viewed as works of art that express ideas and evoke emotional responses in the viewer. You can find them online, in galleries and museums, and also in magazines such as *Life*, *Time*, and *National Geographic*. Photo essayists generally aim to make a particular point or argument; some make specific social commentaries.

## Analyzing Photo Essays

**Purpose**   Photo essayists aim to tell a story and/or to make a point. Usually their work is focused on a specific theme and intended to evoke an emotional response in the viewer.

**Audience**   Photo essayists know that their audiences are drawn to visual storytelling—and to the issues and themes of their works, which may be social and cultural, journalistic, and/or artistic. For example, photo essayist and documentarian Brenda Ann Kenneally, creator of an ongoing project called "Upstate Girls," aims her work at those interested in her intimate look at working-class women and their families. Norbert Wu targets his essay "Life Beneath Antarctic Ice" at an audience interested in nature.

**Rhetorical appeals**   Depending on their subject matter and composition, photo essayists may emphasize logos, pathos, or ethos to make their point. For instance, Andrew Testa's disturbing photo essays of Bangladeshi women who were scarred by acid for refusing to accept marriage proposals emphasize pathos by showing the women's scars close up; ethos is also important because viewers must trust that Testa has not used lighting or perspective to distort reality.

**Modes & media**   While photo essayists usually combine visuals with some written text, some also incorporate bits of audio, such as in *The New York Times* photo essay "One in 8 Million," which highlights the lives of ordinary New Yorkers. Photo essays can be print based, but they are also offered digitally, as is "Let Us Now Praise Famous Men"; or they can be created mainly for online publication, such as *Time* magazine's photo essays.

**Elements of the genre**   A photo essay can be used to tell a simple story, but the genre is often used to persuade viewers to sympathize with a point of view or to take a specific action. For example, through "Upstate Girls," Brenda Ann Kenneally hopes that viewers connect with the subjects' struggles and triumphs.

Some photo essayists include captions to provide context; others include more text, with a 50:50 text-to-image ratio. Photo essayists make rhetorical choices about their purpose and audience, and they choose images carefully, in the same way a writer chooses words, paragraphs, structure, and style. The photo essayist chooses each image with the viewer's intellectual, emotional, or other responses in mind. Similarly, a photo essay can be structured much like any persuasive essay. For example, the introductory images, which function like a written essay's introduction, need to establish the subject matter and further the purposes of the piece—to push the narrative or argument forward.

Photo essayists use some techniques that narrative essayists, storytellers, and persuasive writers do. They select and sequence their content in a way that will spark their readers' interest, keep them reading or viewing, and ultimately convince them of a particular point of view. Initial images may serve as an introduction, while those that follow may build in intensity to support the argument the photo essayist wants to make. (See "Design" below.)

**Style**   Photo essayists make the following stylistic choices. They consider:

- *Detail*. Most photo essayists do not provide much detail in the text of their essays. Usually captions give just enough information for readers to understand the story behind (and the location of) the related photo. The photos themselves can show varying degrees of detail—in some cases, capturing one element up close, such as a person's face, while in others, showing a panoramic view of a landscape.

- *Tone*. Photo essayists choose images that reflect the mood they want to convey. For example, a photo essayist who wants to stir readers to take action in response to an environmental disaster, such as an oil spill, might feature an image of someone rescuing and rehabilitating an oil-soaked bird.

**Design**   A successful photo essayist usually presents a variety of images from different perspectives and arranges the images in an order that builds emotion, furthers an argument, or advances a story. For example, a photo essayist who wants to tell a story might sequence the images from one event to the next, much like a narrative essayist would. In other cases, the photo essayist might not choose a linear progression, but might instead order images for maximum impact, especially when presenting an argument.

**Sources**   Photo essays always involve primary research, as the photographer is always witnessing the subject of the photos firsthand. Brenda Ann Kenneally's photo essay on working-class women, for example, is entirely informed by Kenneally's interviews with the women she photographed. Sometimes secondary research must be conducted as well, to fill in historical details or other information.

# Guided Reading | Photo Essay

*Time*, a weekly news and current events magazine, often features photo essays related to world events. In February 2006 the magazine commissioned and published an online photo essay titled "Life in the Googleplex." Presented as a slide show, the essay was created by photojournalist Eros Hoagland of Redux Pictures. Hoagland, who began his career reporting on the fallout of El Salvador's civil war, is also interested in showing the subtleties of place, something he clearly brought to the Googleplex project. Given the range of his subject matter, the quality of his work, and the publications he calls his clients (including *The New York Times* and *Newsweek*), Hoagland, like *Time* magazine, has some good ethos.

Hoagland's purpose in creating "Life in the Googleplex" was to give readers an inside look at what it's like to work at Google. By highlighting gadgets and leisure opportunities, Hoagland suggests that employees do serious work but also have plenty of time to play. Further, by showing the human side (and human faces) of Google, Hoagland establishes that the company is more than a search engine.

## Eros Hoagland, From *Life in the Googleplex*

| RHETORICAL SITUATION & CHOICES | | GENRE CONVENTIONS | |
|---|---|---|---|

**PURPOSE**
Hoagland (perhaps with the help of *Time* editors) set out to illustrate how a high-tech work environment, such as Google, can be filled with creativity and fun.

**AUDIENCE**
The audience for the photo essay is *Time* magazine readers, Google fans, and people interested in cultural trends related to technology and the workplace.

◀ What is the composer, Eros Hoagland, doing?

How do I know this is a ▶ photo essay?

**ELEMENTS OF THE GENRE**
**Is composed mainly of photos:** The photos are accompanied with some text.

**Is focused on a topic:** In this case, the topic is workers' play and leisure time at Google's offices.

**Tells a story:** This story is about a typical workday at Google.

**Makes an argument:** The photo essay wants to show that Google's workers are productive and inspired by creativity and recreation.

**TIME Photos**                                      200

Photo Essays | LightBox | Pictures of the Week | TIME Covers

## Photos: Life in the Googleplex
Inside Google Headquarters

Photographs by Eros Hoagland / Redux for TIME

Enter ▶

• In Search of The Real Google

**RHETORICAL APPEALS**
Hoagland uses logos to appeal to readers by building a logical case about how a creative work environment inspires workers' creativity. He establishes the essay's ethos by using photos of Google workers.

**MODES & MEDIA**
**Mode = written and visual:** Hoagland's primary goal was to visually portray a typical workday at Google. Adding written details tells a more complete story; it also provides a commentary about what is taking place, to persuade viewers that the workplace atmosphere is pleasant.

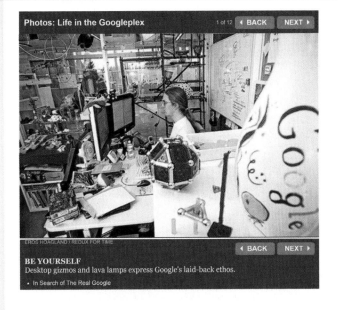

Photos: Life in the Googleplex          1 of 12  ◄ BACK   NEXT ►

EROS HOAGLAND / REDUX FOR TIME
◄ BACK   NEXT ►
**BE YOURSELF**
Desktop gizmos and lava lamps express Google's laid-back ethos.
• In Search of The Real Google

Photos: Life in the Googleplex          2 of 12  ◄ BACK   NEXT ►

EROS HOAGLAND / REDUX FOR TIME
◄ BACK   NEXT ►
**ASK THE HELP DESK**
Laptop on the fritz? Google keeps experts on site to fix computers and other digital gadgets.
• In Search of The Real Google

**Includes captions that explain the photos:** For example, the caption with the first image reads, "Be Yourself." Without it, viewers could assume the message is that the office is crowded and cluttered rather than supportive of individuality and expression.

**STYLE**
**Present tense:** The present tense reinforces the "this is happening now" feeling of the piece.

**Playful tone:** A light tone emphasizes that Google is a fun place to work. For example, the swimmer is referred to as a "Googler with Goggles."

*(Continues on next page)*

**Medium = digital:** Although *Time* publishes photo essays in their print edition, "Life in the Googleplex" was published digitally at *Time*'s website. Publishing this essay online is especially appropriate because Google is a digital company; further, the advantages of publishing online are obvious. As long as viewers have an internet connection, they can see and share the essay; if it were only in print form, they would need to locate a copy of that edition of the magazine.

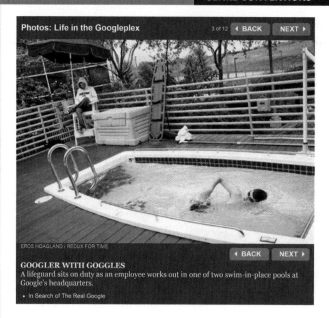

**DESIGN** The variety of the photos suggests the breadth of activities that can take place in the Googleplex. Elements of the text are highlighted by typeface choice and color. Captions consistently appear below the photos, and each caption has a pithy heading.

**SOURCES** Hoagland conducted primary research—spending time at Google, following around employees, trying to capture the elements of a typical day and different aspects of work and play.

Credit: All images on pp. 260–262: Eros Hoagland/Redux Pictures.

## QUESTIONS | Analyzing Hoagland's Photo Essay

### RHETORICAL SITUATION & CHOICES

1. **Purpose.** Explain in one sentence the unifying message of the three photos shown.

2. **Purpose.** Do the photos tend to focus more on people or objects? Why do you think Hoagland chose that emphasis?

3. **Audience.** What techniques did Hoagland use so that viewers would see the playful nature of working at Google?

### GENRE CONVENTIONS

6. **Elements of the genre.** In "Life in the Googleplex," do the photos illustrate the captions, or do the captions describe the photos? Explain your answer.

7. **Elements of the genre.** View the entire "Googleplex" slide show. Now that you've seen the whole thing, would you say that this essay is primarily telling a story or making an argument? Why?

4. **Rhetorical appeals.** Based on the three photos shown, what is your impression of the ethos of Hoagland and the *Time* editors he most likely worked with?

5. **Modes & media.** If there were no captions, what assumptions might you make about life at Google? Are there places where the image is able to fully convey its message without the text? Where and how? Is this essay best viewed digitally, rather than in print? Why or why not?

8. **Style.** How does the tone and voice of the writing emphasize the working environment at Google? How does the selection and presentation of photographs contribute to that tone? Use specific examples to illustrate your answer.

9. **Design.** View the entire "Googleplex" slide show again. Pay attention to how Hoagland and *Time* ordered the images. How might a different ordering of images impact the narrative? How do Hoagland and *Time* use organization of the images to build logic?

10. **Sources.** The photos were taken by Eros Hoagland, a professional photographer commissioned by *Time* magazine (Hoagland is the source of the images). Do you think someone working at Google would choose to highlight different aspects of working there? How?

## CHECKLIST | Sketching Out a Photo Essay

Are you thinking of composing a photo essay? Ask yourself the following questions:

### RHETORICAL SITUATION & CHOICES

☐ **Purpose.** What is my story, and why do I want to tell it? Or do I want to do more than tell a story? If so, what main point or argument do I want to make, and why?

☐ **Audience.** Who are my readers/viewers that I want to attract to my photo essay? Why will my photo essay matter to them? What do I want them to get out of it? How will I reach them?

☐ **Rhetorical appeals.** How will I use ethos, pathos, and logos to reach my audience? How will I establish my authority as a photographer and writer? Will I rely more on pathos or logos? How will my photos and text work together to appeal to my readers' sense of ethos, pathos, and/or logos?

### GENRE CONVENTIONS

☐ **Elements of the genre.** The best photo essays tell a story, but also put forth some type of argument. For example, in his "Googleplex" essay, Eros Hoagland asks viewers to see Google as a successful company in part because the workplace itself encourages creativity. How does this compare to what I want to do? What argument will I make in my photo essay, and how will I do it?

☐ **Style.** What tone do I want to strike? Playful, like in "Life in the Googleplex"? Or more serious, like in Kenneally's photo essay?

☐ **Design.** What order will I arrange the photos in, and how will the order affect how my viewers understand my story?

☐ **Modes & media.** Do I want to present my photo essay in hard-copy format, as in a photo album; or electronically, as on a website; or in some other way? How will these choices impact how my viewers experience my photo essay? For example, would it be better to present it online or as a collection of large photos matted and framed on the wall?

☐ **Sources.** Where will I need to go to take my photos? Will I want to photograph individuals and their possessions? Or perhaps historical sites? Will I need to request special permission to do so?

---

**PRACTICE**

## Making a Point with a Photo Essay

Just as Eros Hoagland conveys a sense of work life at Google in his photo essay, you might want to do something similar. What do you have to say about your own workplace, campus, or residence? Brainstorm about how people at one or more of those locations feel about that place; then take three to five photos of the place that convey that feeling. Your draft photo essay should offer some kind of commentary on the place you've chosen as your subject; it should not simply show it. Add brief captions similar to the ones in the "Googleplex" essay that help tell a story and offer perspective.

---

# Graphic Memoirs

The graphic memoir is an autobiographical or semiautobiographical story told through text and images, usually drawings. Sometimes there are more words than images, but usually it's the other way around. The graphic memoirist Alison Bechdel (p. 267) has described her process in interviews: First she writes her text; then she inks the images. Other graphic memoirists use different techniques, foregrounding the images in the panels and writing the text in later. You may already be familiar with graphic memoirs, a genre first made popular by Art Spiegelman's *Maus*, a graphic memoir about surviving the Holocaust. Graphic narratives now have a place as respected literary texts: They're the focus of college courses; they've won Pulitzer Prizes; and they've inspired successful movies, including *A History of Violence* and *Sin City*.

**WRITE**

What are your favorite graphic memoirs or novels? What aspects of the story are most memorable? Why?

# Analyzing Graphic Memoirs

**Purpose**  Like other memoirists, graphic memoirists tell the story of (or a story from) a writer's life. Using such literary devices as character (in this case, real people rather than fictional ones), dialogue, and setting, graphic memoirists connect their readers with their work. Graphic memoirs, which look something like extended comic strips, focus on transporting the reader to a world that is very different from everyday reality. Sometimes a graphic narrative, such as Marjane Satrapi's *Persepolis*, discloses elements of a culture—Satrapi's life growing up in Iran and later as an expatriate—showing readers a world that may be outside their own experience.

**Audience**  Graphic memoirists know that their audiences want a look into someone else's life, as told by that person. They know that their audiences are particularly drawn toward the visual, and perhaps grew up reading comic books, or really like illustrated texts or alternative narrative forms. As graphic memoirs are becoming more popular in academic settings, with instructors assigning them as part of their reading lists, or as an alternative to the print memoir in composition classes, more students are creating and reading them.

**Rhetorical appeals**  The play between visuals and text helps graphic memoirists emphasize certain aspects of the narrative to readers. Because memoirists want their readers to empathize with their experiences, they often use appeals to emotion to draw readers into their world. For example, when a story is meant to elicit shock, the shape of the letters and the use of bold graphics, along with the expressions on the character's face, can guide the reader's emotional response, emphasizing pathos. In a graphic memoir, ethos is a central concern because the audience must trust that the writer is accurately representing experience and events.

**Modes & media**  Graphic memoirs usually take print form but are sometimes digitized for the web. Graphic memoirs and novels are often adapted for film, reimagined as animated stories.

**Elements of the genre**  Like all memoirs, the graphic memoir has a real-life plot that revolves around a series of events, or a story line. The story line hinges on a central conflict driven by real people who function as characters do in fiction. The central conflict of Marjane Satrapi's *Persepolis*, for example, is her and her family's struggle to survive the Iranian Revolution of 1979, also known as the Islamic Revolution; at that time, the country's monarchy was overthrown and Iran became an Islamic republic with an increasingly repressive government.

To tell their stories, graphic memoirists use words—usually organized into short, simple sentences—that provide dialogue and move the plot along toward the conflict and its

WRITE

Consider Art Spiegelman's graphic memoir *Maus*, which is a Holocaust narrative and the story of Spiegelman's father. Freewrite about to what extent you think the graphic memoir is an appropriate genre for dealing with traumatic experiences.

resolution. The visuals, usually inked drawings, move the plot too, but also assist in creating the setting, atmosphere, and emotion of the memoir.

The written content of the graphic memoir often appears in boxes or in sentences interspersed among the visuals. Dialogue is usually placed in a bubble or box linked to the character's mouth. Most graphic composers do not present words and sentences in traditional paragraphs. The advantage is that by isolating a sentence in a box, the author creates a snapshot of a moment or of a series of moments, adding to the power of the story. Further, though the graphic narrative may not provide traditional transitions between ideas and scenes, there are some transitional expressions that help the visual memoirist move from one idea to the next.

Just as in comic strips, the visuals of a graphic memoir do a lot to relate the story and reinforce aspects of the written narrative. The visuals, which can focus in on a detail and pan out like a movie camera, for example, emphasize certain moments and allow readers to see what is happening. See the "Design" section below for more on how drawings function in a graphic memoir.

**Style**  The reader's experience depends on the written and visual style of the graphic memoirist—how much (and what kind of) detail and specific techniques he or she uses, and the quality of the visual story's voice and tone.

- *Tone and voice.* Graphic memoirists communicate the tone of their stories and their voices as storytellers through word choice, diction, visuals, the choice of typeface, and other graphics. For example, if a character is feeling exasperated, the writer might choose a font (such as Impact) to illustrate that mood.
- *Detail.* Depending on their target audience, graphic memoirists may use intricate, almost lifelike detail, as in Bechdel's *Fun Home* (p. 268). Other times, graphic memoirists might take a more cartoon/superhero approach, such as that of DC Comics' *Watchmen*. Typically, graphic memoirists limit their reliance on text, using it primarily to keep the plot moving. Sentences in a given panel tend to be short without much embellishment.

**Design**  Like comic strips, graphic memoirs are organized into visual panels, usually squares or rectangles that essentially freeze a moment in its own individual space. Like all graphic composers, graphic memoirists make choices about where to place panels, how large to make them, and what words from the written narrative to emphasize. They also decide how and where to place figures and objects within a panel in order to direct the reader. The size of one object next to another (scale), the direction an object is facing in relation to the page, and the cutting off of part of an object in a frame are all careful choices that create meaning for readers.

Other design choices include whether to use a font, real handwriting or lettering, or a font that mimics handwriting. Many graphic composers use block lettering, boldface, and italics when they want to show emphasis, and they use different graphical styles when needed (such as Courier or other distinctive fonts). Graphic memoirists also need to make decisions about the style, shape, and size of boxes, balloons, or other word-framing devices. Sometimes they assign specific shapes for specific speakers in the story. They also make choices about white space from panel to panel and within a frame of text. White space is used for aesthetic reasons but also to call attention to certain parts of the text, to provide a visual pause, or to represent the absence of something or someone.

**Sources** Most graphic memoirs are based on personal observation and experience. For this reason, graphic memoirists seldom cite outside sources. However, if someone were to write a graphic memoir of a group or an organization, that person would no doubt draw on historical documents, interviews, and other sources of information.

## Guided Reading | Graphic Memoir

Alison Bechdel gained notoriety in the comics scene in 1983 with her syndicated strip *Dykes to Watch Out For*. In her comic strip, Bechdel combined political commentary with the daily lives of mostly lesbian characters, narrating their love affairs, breakups, and adventures as attendees at such lesbian festivals as the Michigan Womyn's Music Festival. Bechdel wrote a graphic memoir, *Fun Home: A Family Tragicomic*, published in 2006. This was later adapted into a Broadway musical, which won the 2015 Tony Award for best musical.

▲ **BOOK COVER & AUTHOR PHOTO**
**Alison Bechdel,** *Fun Home: A Family Tragicomic.* Author photo: Liza Cowan.

Credit: From FUN HOME: A Family Tragicomic by Alison Bechdel. Copyright © 2006. Reprinted by permission of Houghton Mifflin Harcourt Publishing Company. All rights reserved.

In *Fun Home*, Bechdel tells the story of growing up with a closeted father who ran a funeral parlor and taught English. In this work, she conveys the importance of her father in her life. The section that we've excerpted here is from the book's first chapter. In it, Bechdel's own coming-out story is overshadowed by the death of her father.

As a graphic memoirist, Bechdel makes plenty of decisions about her purposes and how she will draw in her readers. She also works with many of the conventions of the graphic narrative, while using a style that is all her own.

# Alison Bechdel, From *Fun Home: A Family Tragicomic*

## PURPOSE

Bechdel's goal is to tell a story about her life, which includes childhood, coming out, and coming to terms with her father's identity and death.

## AUDIENCE

Bechdel knows her readers enjoy memoirs and are especially drawn to comics and graphic novels. They are also interested in the coming-of-age and sexual identity themes in *Fun Home*.

◀ What is the composer, Alison Bechdel, doing?

How do I know this ▶ is a graphic memoir?

## DESIGN

**Handwriting effect:** Bechdel's text font mimics handwriting, and she uses bold, italics, and other type effects to convey emotion.

**Varied layout:** For example, some panels are parallel to each other, while others are not aligned evenly.

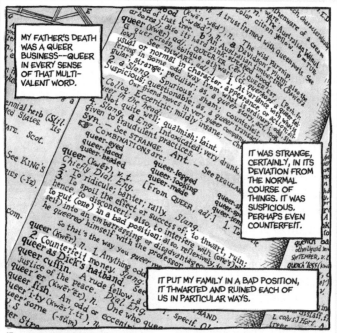

MY FATHER'S DEATH WAS A QUEER BUSINESS—QUEER IN EVERY SENSE OF THAT MULTI-VALENT WORD.

IT WAS STRANGE, CERTAINLY, IN ITS DEVIATION FROM THE NORMAL COURSE OF THINGS. IT WAS SUSPICIOUS, PERHAPS EVEN COUNTERFEIT.

IT PUT MY FAMILY IN A BAD POSITION, IT THWARTED AND RUINED EACH OF US IN PARTICULAR WAYS.

IT LEFT ME FEELING QUALMISH, FAINT, AND, ON OCCASION, DRUNK.

BUT MOST COMPELLINGLY AT THE TIME, HIS DEATH WAS BOUND UP FOR ME WITH THE ONE DEFINITION CONSPICUOUSLY MISSING FROM OUR MAMMOTH WEBSTER'S.

**RHETORICAL SITUATION & CHOICES**  **GENRE CONVENTIONS**

**RHETORICAL APPEALS**

Bechdel appeals to readers' emotions (pathos) by showing how her father's "queer death" caused her to feel "qualmish, faint, and, on occasion, drunk." The author uses events from her life to establish her ethos. Announcing "I am a lesbian" helps establish her ethos in what is partly a coming-out story.

ONLY FOUR MONTHS EARLIER, I HAD MADE AN ANNOUNCEMENT TO MY PARENTS.

MY HOMOSEXUALITY REMAINED AT THAT POINT PURELY THEORETICAL, AN UNTESTED HYPOTHESIS.

BUT IT WAS A HYPOTHESIS SO THOROUGH AND CONVINCING THAT I SAW NO REASON NOT TO SHARE IT IMMEDIATELY.

THE NEWS WAS NOT RECEIVED AS WELL AS I HAD HOPED. THERE WAS AN EXCHANGE OF DIFFICULT LETTERS WITH MY MOTHER.

THEN A PHONE CALL IN WHICH SHE DEALT A STAGGERING BLOW.

I'D BEEN UPSTAGED, DEMOTED FROM PROTAGONIST IN MY OWN DRAMA TO COMIC RELIEF IN MY PARENTS' TRAGEDY.

**Varied frame shapes:** These shapes around the text indicate what is thought, spoken, or narrated. Different shapes indicate who is speaking. In the last frame, the mother's dialogue appears in a jagged box that comes out of the phone.

**Different graphical styles:** Bechtel varies the graphical style to approximate reality. When the narrator types out, "I am a lesbian," Bechdel switches to Courier to approximate typing.

*(Continues on next page)*

Graphic Memoirs  **269**

## MODES & MEDIA

**Mode = written and visual:** Bechdel uses both the written and visual texts to communicate her story about coming out. Bechdel's use of visuals—such as when she mails a letter to her parents or talks on the phone with her mother—shows readers how Bechdel wants us to view her at that moment.

**Medium = print:** Just like traditional memoirs, graphic memoirs are available in both print and digital media. Bookstores, these days, have sections devoted to graphic novels, where you can also find graphic memoirs such as Bechdel's. There are, however, digital graphic novels and memoirs that are often created online. Websites such as Comic Master allow you to create your own short graphic novel or memoir online using their free software.

I HAD IMAGINED MY CONFESSION AS AN EMANCIPATION FROM MY PARENTS, BUT INSTEAD I WAS PULLED BACK INTO THEIR ORBIT.

AND WITH MY FATHER'S DEATH FOLLOWING SO HARD ON THE HEELS OF THIS DOLEFUL COMING-OUT PARTY, I COULD NOT HELP BUT ASSUME A CAUSE-AND-EFFECT RELATIONSHIP.

IF I HAD NOT FELT COMPELLED TO SHARE MY LITTLE SEXUAL DISCOVERY, PERHAPS THE SEMI WOULD HAVE PASSED WITHOUT INCIDENT FOUR MONTHS LATER.

(YES, IT REALLY WAS A SUNBEAM BREAD TRUCK.)

WHY HAD I TOLD THEM? I HADN'T EVEN HAD SEX WITH ANYONE YET. CONVERSELY, MY FATHER HAD BEEN HAVING SEX WITH MEN FOR YEARS AND NOT TELLING ANYONE.

WHY ARE YOU TELLING ME THIS AND NOT DAD?

YOUR FATHER TELL THE TRUTH? PLEASE.

THE LINE THAT DAD DREW BETWEEN REALITY AND FICTION WAS INDEED A BLURRY ONE. TO UNDERSTAND THIS, ONE HAD ONLY TO ENTER HIS LIBRARY.

## SOURCES

Bechdel's source is her own memory, so there are no citations to outside materials.

**RHETORICAL SITUATION & CHOICES**

1. **Purpose.** What parallels does Bechdel draw between her father's homosexuality and her own coming out?

2. **Audience.** Based on the short excerpt, who would you say is the audience for this graphic memoir? Why?

3. **Rhetorical appeals.** How do the visuals emphasize the main character's emotional state?

4. **Modes & media.** What different elements of the plot do the text and visuals emphasize?

5. **Elements of the genre.** Are there any places where the visuals and words seem to contradict each other or seem to be in tension with each other? If so, why do you think there is a contradiction or tension?

**GENRE CONVENTIONS**

6. **Elements of the genre.** How much time is covered in the pages shown? How does Bechdel show the passage of time?

7. **Elements of the genre.** Only three pages of the graphic memoir are represented here. Even though it is a small snapshot of the book, what sense do you get of Bechdel as the narrator of her own story? How do the different graphic elements, combined with words, give you that sense of her?

8. **Style.** How would you describe the level of detail Bechdel uses in her visuals? In her text? Does the level of detail serve different purposes? If so, how?

9. **Design.** Sometimes Bechdel chooses to sandwich the narrative text between the visual panels. Other times, she places the narrative text within its own box. What reasons might she have for this? Are the narrative pieces that are in a box more significant? Why?

10. **Sources.** The main source for the graphic memoir is Alison Bechdel's life and experience. How does this influence your reading of the work?

# CHECKLIST | Drafting a Graphic Memoir

Are you thinking of composing a graphic memoir? Ask yourself the following questions:

## RHETORICAL SITUATION & CHOICES

☐ **Purpose.** What specific moment in my life do I want to write about? Why? What questions do I have about that moment? How might I interpret that moment? What insights do I want to share with others? How would visuals illustrate the moment and make my experience more tangible for my reader?

☐ **Audience.** Who are my potential readers? Why will my memoir matter to them? What do I want them to get out of it? How old are they, and how will I reach them? How will I use visuals to do that?

☐ **Rhetorical appeals.** How will I establish my authority as a writer? How reliable will I be as a narrator? To what extent will I appeal to my readers' emotions? How might I use logic?

☐ **Modes & media.** Do I want to create my story first with graphics or text? What aspects will I represent visually, and what aspects will I represent in written form? Would my graphic memoir be appropriate to translate into a film? Do I want to create my story using ink on paper or using a digital program?

## GENRE CONVENTIONS

☐ **Elements of the genre.** How will I keep my writing true and accurate? How much will I disclose about myself and others in my graphic memoir? Will I write in the first person? What anecdotes will I use to tell my story, and why? How will I visually represent my characters? Will they be true-to-life or exaggerated? How will I balance the narrative with dialogue?

☐ **Style.** What tone will I take in my writing? Will my graphic memoir be funny? Serious? Tragic? What kind of language will I use? How much detail will I provide? How will I use the visuals to convey my tone?

☐ **Design.** What fonts will I use? How might I use shapes of boxes to indicate specific character voices? Will I vary the shapes of my panels?

☐ **Sources.** What specific memories will I draw on? Will I need to check my story with others from my life, or will I rely on my own recollections and interpretations? Will I need to research historical and cultural events related to the time period of my story?

---

**PRACTICE**

# Sharing Experience Through a Graphic Memoir

Identify a pivotal moment in your life. Sketch out a few panels of a graphic memoir that convey the moment and its importance. Think about how you want the key people who participated in the event to come across to readers and how you can convey those characteristics with visual details. Think about what you want to convey through dialogue and what you want to convey through internal reflection.

# Podcasts

A podcast is an audio file on the internet that users download and listen to. The word podcast, a portmanteau of "iPod" and "broadcast," refers to either an individual episode or an entire series. A variation of the podcast is the vlog, a video podcast. Podcasts focus on any topic imaginable, such as politics and current events, crime, self-improvement, movies, music, comedy, interviews, gaming, science, and observation and commentary about life. For example, you might decide to make your own podcast series about a passion of yours, such as pop culture, in which you offer your thoughts and commentary on new movies and music and do occasional interviews with people involved in the production of pop culture.

Podcasts take many different forms, from interview shows to conversations among cohosts to Q&A sessions in which listeners have tweeted or e-mailed questions on a particular topic to the podcaster, who then answers them. Podcasters can be anyone from a high school student to a journalist, like science reporter Shankar Vedantam, to a massive corporation like General Electric. Many podcasts have companion blogs, and many are financially supported by their fan base and sponsors through Patreon, a membership platform that allows listeners to make donations.

## Analyzing Podcasts

**Purpose**   Podcasters have many different purposes. A high schooler with a podcast about women's sports might have a purpose to highlight the achievements of female athletes. One of Shankar Vedantam's purposes in his podcast, *Hidden Brain*, is to persuade people to use social science research to "think about the news in unusual and interesting ways." A purpose of General Electric's podcast series, *Decoding Industry*, which offers TED-style talks by people who are considered geniuses in their fields, is to encourage innovation in industry.

**Audience**   A 2019 report indicated that 51 percent of Americans have listened to a podcast, with about a fifth of Americans listening to at least one podcast weekly. Listeners choose podcasts based on topics that interest them. Some listen to learn, others to escape. Many listeners use podcasts to stay informed about current events and politics.

**Rhetorical appeals**   Podcasters use ethos to establish themselves as credible on whatever topic they are speaking on. Shankar Vedantam, for example, often discusses his own curiosity in his podcast; this helps listeners understand him as someone driven by inquiry. It also helps him seem relatable to his audience, who is likely also curious about science. Podcasters often use pathos, expressing anger or disbelief about a current event, and encouraging listeners to express those same emotions. Other podcasters appeal to pathos through their use of humor. For podcasts that aim

WRITE

Do you listen to podcasts? If so, why? If not, what type of podcasts would interest you? Write one to two paragraphs that address these questions.

to persuade, logos is important. A podcast that aims to convince listeners that female athletes deserve higher salaries might present facts about female athletes' achievements and awards.

**Modes & media**   Podcasters rely on audio, but may also make text transcripts of their podcasts available. Podcasters usually use their own voices or those of people they interviewed. They may also use sound effects; for example, a podcast about coffee might feature the sounds of coffee beans being ground and then a cup of coffee being poured. Vlogs are similar to podcasts but also include video. Podcasts live on the internet and are digital.

**Elements of the genre**   Effective podcasters do the following:

- *A host or hosts who talks throughout the episode or conducts interviews with others.* Podcasters talk about their topics and with their guests.

- *Follow a similar format from episode to episode.* This means each episode will be roughly the same length and follow a pattern, such as opening with a summary of a current event, asking three different experts to weigh in on the event, and then closing with a bold prediction about a future consequence of the event.

- *Use sound bites and other sound elements beyond voices.* Podcasters often allow background noise to be heard to create a sense of place or ambience. A podcast about motorcycles may have the sounds of revving engines in the background, while a podcast about farm life might occasionally feature a pig snort.

- *Introduce guests with a specific and concise statement of their qualifications to speak on the topic.* A psychologist being interviewed about anxiety might be introduced with, "Dr. Muñoz has studied anxiety for over twenty years." This also helps contribute to the ethos of the podcast.

- *Invite listeners to contact the podcaster with feedback and ideas.* Many podcasters try to create rapport with listeners by being open to their comments and ideas for future podcasts.

**Style**   Effective podcasters do the following:

- *Open each episode with the same music.* Most podcasters use intro music to set the tone of their podcast. They choose music that fits the mood of their topic, their own personality, or their audience. A podcast about finances could use a song like Pink Floyd's "Money" to capture the topic, or it could use classical music to invoke a sense of respectability.

- *Share their personality.* While some podcasters are known for being goofy, even serious podcasters reveal bits of their personalities in their podcasts. Through voice inflection, laughter, and the judicious sharing of personal details, podcasters create rapport with their listeners.

- *Speak directly to listeners.* Many podcasters speak directly to their audience, either inviting their feedback or using the second person to make listeners feel like they are part of the conversation. A podcaster might say, "You guys know how much I love macaroni and cheese!" or "I can't wait to hear what you think about this!"

**Design** When listeners find podcasts on the internet or in Apple Podcasts, they see a podcast's cover art. The cover art should reflect the topic or mood of the podcast. Podcast cover art typically reflects these design features:

- *Adheres to the design specifications of the platform.* For example, Apple Podcasts require cover art to be in JPG or PNG format and have a minimum size.
- *Use colors and other visual elements to convey the topic and tone of the podcast.* A podcast about cold crime cases might use dark colors to conjure a sense of mystery.

**Sources** To come across as credible and persuasive, podcasters often do the following:

- *Draw on their own experience.* Podcasters usually talk about topics they are passionate about, and they mention their own experiences regularly. Shankar Vedantam regularly refers to experiences he's had that raised the questions he explores in his podcast.
- *Interview experts.* Podcasters interview people who have studied or had rich experiences with the subject matter, such as researchers, scientists, or professionals. Podcasters who host podcasts about music often interview musicians, for example. Dessert podcasters interview pastry chefs, bakery owners, and cookbook authors.
- *Refer to specific news articles, reports, books, or other reference material.* Podcasters often connect their topics to recent news or current events.

## Guided Reading | Podcast

The Planet Money podcast is produced by National Public Radio and features episodes on different aspects of the economy. It was created in 2008 by business journalists Alex Blumberg and Adam Davidson, who wanted to make economics accessible to people. Episodes are hosted by different people and have covered topics such as healthcare, insider trading, and oil production from an economic perspective. The following excerpt is from an episode entitled, "So, Should We Recycle?" and is hosted by journalists Sarah Gonzalez and Kenny Malone. The episode considers what happens to items we put into recycling bins (spoiler alert: They often end up in landfills).

# Planet Money, *So, Should We Recycle?*

| RHETORICAL SITUATION & CHOICES | GENRE CONVENTIONS |
|---|---|

**PURPOSE**
Gonzalez's and Malone's purpose is to explain why recycling may not necessarily be the best choice for the planet. To help listeners understand the counterintuitive idea that recycling a plastic bottle may hurt the environment more than throwing it in the trash, they give background about how recycling works.

◀ What are the composers, Sarah Gonzalez and Kenny Malone, doing?

How do I know this ▶ is a podcast?

**ELEMENTS OF THE GENRE**
Podcasters speak to their listeners and guests: Gonzalez and Malone talk to each other, their listeners, and their guests throughout, talking through the history of recycling and its effects.

**DESIGN**
The Planet Money cover art is a simple reference to the show's name: an astronaut against a green background. The astronaut refers to the "planet" and the green background refers to "money."

---

SARAH GONZALEZ, HOST:

This is part two of our series on recycling. Part one is the origin story of why we started recycling. You should go listen. It involves the mafia.

KENNY MALONE, HOST:

All right, let's just get this out of the way at the top here. The three R's—reduce, reuse, and then recycle. Recycling is the last option, although it sometimes feels like it is the main option. And it is broken in the United States. And to see just how bad it has gotten, you just need to go to any waste and recycling center.

GONZALEZ: Except those waste and recycling centers don't really like to talk about how broken recycling is. But we found one place that would—Nogales, Arizona.

MALONE: It's Thursday, recycling day, and a city truck has gone to everyone's house, picked up their recycling and brought them to a place called Tucson Recycling & Waste Services.

GONZALEZ: Beer bottles, water bottles—so water bottles, milk jugs, cardboard boxes. All this stuff tumbling out of the truck is carefully hand-sorted and hand-rinsed—soup cans and newspapers and peanut butter jars—from the upstanding citizens of Nogales, Arizona, who have made the effort to help save our planet and our oceans.

MALONE: And the guy overseeing all of this, Delbert Gallego, says that sorting and rinsing is, in fact, critical. Recycling is a delicate process. You need to do all that stuff.

DELBERT GALLEGO: You have to triple-rinse the plastic. And then, if it had the lids on it, that's considered contamination.

GONZALEZ: No lids?

GALLEGO: No lids.

GONZALEZ: Whoa. Oh, I've been doing that one wrong. So the city of Nogales went around to everyone's house this morning and picked up their recyclables.

**AUDIENCE**
Gonzalez's and
Malone's audience
is people who
are interested in
understanding
economics better or
understanding the
financial implications
of everyday decisions.

GALLEGO: Right.

GONZALEZ: And they brought them here. And where is all this going to go?

GALLEGO: It's dumped over here for right now.

GONZALEZ: And what's over here for?

GALLEGO: Trash.

GONZALEZ: The recycling is going into the trash. I am watching pristine beer bottles and juice cartons and cardboard boxes get smushed into a pile of wet, gooey, dripping food waste and soggy diapers.

KURT WAHL: Our wish would be to be able to recycle it, but we know we can't. We'll end up landfilling that waste.

MALONE: This is Kurt Wahl. He's Delbert's boss. And he says something has gone terribly wrong in the world of recycling.

GONZALEZ: And it's not just Nogales. Cities all over the United States are shoving their recyclables into the trash pile.

WAHL: Unfortunately, recycling is not—I'm not saying it's dead, but it's certainly—I wouldn't say life support, but it's critical (laughter). And I don't want to be the person to burst their bubble.

GONZALEZ: You will not be the one to burst people's bubble. I will burst their bubble.

(LAUGHTER)

GONZALEZ: Me and a bunch of cold-hearted economists.

(SOUNDBITE OF LEIGH MCALLISTER GRACIE'S "NUMBERS GAME")

GONZALEZ: Hello, and welcome to PLANET MONEY. I'm Sarah Gonzalez.

MALONE: And I'm Kenny Malone. Today on the show, recycling is on life support. Cities might be picking up your recyclables, but there is a very good chance they are not being recycled.

GONZALEZ: And that might be a good thing if you really care about the planet.

MALONE: (Imitating explosion).

(SOUNDBITE OF LEIGH MCALLISTER GRACIE'S "NUMBERS GAME")

*(Continues on next page)*

GONZALEZ: To understand what went wrong in the world of recycling, we called economist Bevin Ashenmiller at Occidental College.

BEVIN ASHENMILLER: So generally I teach environmental economics. I'm an environmental economist. And environmental economics is a pretty depressing class, so I—sometimes I teach a class called Marriage, Money and Motherhood.

GONZALEZ: I don't even want to know the findings of that.

ASHENMILLER: I have a really good friend who teaches it. And he's always like, I just love wage gaps. They just make me so excited. And I'm like . . .

GONZALEZ: You're like, yeah, it's not so cool on this end.

ASHENMILLER: Yeah.

(LAUGHTER)

GONZALEZ: OK, Bevin also knows a lot about the economics of recycling. And she says the first thing you need to know is that in economics, we have goods, and we have bads.

ASHENMILLER: A good is something that you pay money to get. That's why we call it a good. We're very simple people.

GONZALEZ: (Laughter).

ASHENMILLER: And a bad (laughter) is something that you pay money for somebody to take it away.

MALONE: Every time you make a good, like a jar of peanut butter, you also make a bad—an empty jar of peanut butter, something someone will need to dispose of.

GONZALEZ: But back in the 1990s, a few things happened that made all of our bads really attractive to China. China was making all this stuff and shipping it to the U.S. in these huge cargo ships.

ASHENMILLER: They were bringing a lot of tankers into the U.S. that were dropping off materials. And it doesn't make sense to bring a tanker back empty.

MALONE: So some smart person was like, well, then, why don't we just fill those cargo ships up with something useful then?

GONZALEZ: Like empty water bottles. China was like, we can turn those things into, like, polyester socks and sweaters, which are basically just woven out of really, really, really thin plastic bottles.

**Introduce guests:**
They introduce each guest succinctly, such as Bevin Ashenmiller, who they describe as an economist, and then Ashenmiller explains that she's an environmental economist.

**RHETORICAL APPEALS**
Gonzalez and Malone develop their ethos by mentioning how hard it was to find a recycling center that would talk to them about what's going wrong with recycling. They appeal to logos throughout by explaining how changes in China led to recycling in the United States becoming prohibitively expensive. They connect with listeners' sense of pathos by sharing how hard it is to see recyclables sitting in a trash pile.

MALONE: And thus, a market for our bads was born. And eventually, about half of the entire world's junk plastic was being sent to China, much of that coming from the U.S. And when this was working, it is what we imagine recycling to be—my peanut butter jar turning into freaking socks. I mean, that is a modern miracle. But then, just last year, something changed dramatically.

GONZALEZ: China said this isn't worth it for us anymore. Turning your peanut butter jar into socks is creating too much pollution. And frankly, it's just too much work for us now because you guys aren't as good at triple-rinsing your plastic as you think you are, and you're not even sorting it properly. There are milk jugs in with the peanut butter jars, lids still on, peanut butter still in the jar.

MALONE: A total mess. And it used to be worth it for China to just go ahead and clean this stuff up and sort it out on their end because, you know, labor was cheap, and so cleaning and then recycling our old plastic and aluminum was cheaper than creating new plastic and aluminum by drilling for oil and mining for bauxite in the ground, which is how we get plastic and aluminum.

GONZALEZ: But then, China's economy evolved. Labor got more expensive. And China said "we don't want to be the world's garbage dump"—an actual quote.

MALONE: And so China instituted a new plan called the National Sword—their name for it. And in this plan, China said we are only going to take recyclables if they are absolutely spotless and perfectly separated. Plus, we are going to stop taking 24 different kinds of junk, including some kinds of plastics, mixed paper and certain metals.

GONZALEZ: This sent shocks throughout the entire recycling world. Seemingly overnight, the biggest recycling market shriveled up.

MALONE: And you can see the impact that this had in Nogales, Ariz.

WAHL: You can see a lot of your really wet, nasty trash in there.

MALONE: Remember Kurt, that guy who didn't want to burst our recycling bubble? Here is the position he's in now. He collects all these recyclables, but he still needs to do something with them. And China used to buy recyclables. Kurt actually got paid for this stuff. But when China went away, there was no one to pay for it anymore. Now it is on Kurt to pay if he wants this stuff to get recycled.

*(Continues on next page)*

WAHL: Whenever you go from being paid for a product to having to pay, there's absolutely a sting and an awakening at that time.

GONZALEZ: So now, Kurt could either pay $200 to get one ton of plastic recycled, or he can pay $30 to get that same ton of plastic buried in a landfill.

WAHL: Obviously, I'm not going to bring it there for $200 a ton.

MALONE: It just simply didn't make financial sense to recycle anymore. And so he has started landfilling. And cities all over the U.S. are in the same position. Some are just canceling parts of their recycling programs altogether, like Douglas County, Ore., Franklin, N.H., Deltona, Fla.

GONZALEZ: Broadway, Va. There are entire cities that are saying we're not even going to bother to pick up your blue bin anymore. There are no more blue bins in entire towns.

MALONE: But in Nogales, Ariz., they're a little more optimistic. They're at least making sure people are going through the motions of recycling.

WAHL: We don't want to just discontinue. We don't want to just do away with it because I think, A, it'll be hard to retrain people to do what we think is the right thing. And we have the hopes that, at some point, it'll start up again.

GONZALEZ: It took Americans so long to pick up the habit of separating our paper and our plastic that if we stopped doing it, Kurt worries residents won't pick the habit back up once there is a market for plastic again. And sometimes when Kurt is all alone at night, and he sees a particularly clean batch of cardboard boxes, his heart goes out to them.

MALONE: It doesn't make financial sense, but, oh, these would make such great new boxes.

GONZALEZ: He opens up his wallet and pays for that stack of boxes to get recycled.

WAHL: Because again, I couldn't bear to see it just going into the landfill. To just throw it in the trash would not feel good at all.

MALONE: But then, eventually, Kurt says, he couldn't even pay anyone to take his cardboard.

WAHL: They wouldn't even take it. They wouldn't even take it because, again, they've got so much product, they had nowhere to go with it.

GONZALEZ: There have been piles of paper and cardboard stacking up all over the country, like actual warehouses full of water bottles and piles of paper just waiting for some buyer to come back on the scene. So we've got all these recyclables piling up.

MALONE: What we're going to do about it after the break.

MALONE [after break]: OK. So we've got piles of recycling piling up or getting landfilled because China doesn't want our dirty, poorly washed and sloppily sorted recycling anymore. So we wanted to talk to some experts about what our options are at this point.

GONZALEZ: It seems the main issue is that, like, if we had perfectly clean recyclables, then China would still buy it.

ASHENMILLER: Right.

GONZALEZ: And so we could just clean it ourselves.

ASHENMILLER: Yeah, but I'm not sure that would be—I mean, like, there's a water question here, right?

GONZALEZ: Again, Bevin Ashenmiller, who teaches all the depressing classes.

ASHENMILLER: This is the argument that people are constantly having. Like, do I spend all the water to clean my peanut butter container out?

GONZALEZ: It takes so long to clean out a peanut butter container.

ASHENMILLER: (Laughter) Right? And is that economically efficient for me to waste all that water cleaning out the stupid peanut butter thing so it can be recycled?

GONZALEZ: Bevin says in places like California where water is precious, no, you should not waste water on this. And hot water heated by burning fossil fuels—forget it. You will quickly undo the environmental benefits of recycling.

MALONE: So, OK, maybe we should not clean extra carefully and then ship our recycling to China. But all these recyclable things are piling up all over the U.S. So the U.S. is now looking for another country that maybe doesn't care as much if our stuff is dirty, you know, the way it used to be with China.

THOMAS KINNAMAN: So you expect the baton to be passed, and it has been passed.

MALONE: This is Thomas Kinnaman, an environmental economist at Bucknell University.

*(Continues on next page)*

KINNAMAN: Indonesia, India, Malaysia—these countries will accept some of this stuff, and they have been. And they'll go through the same process.

GONZALEZ: Of accepting it until they say, OK, never mind, we don't want it anymore.

KINNAMAN: Yeah. At some point, it looks like plastic, and at some other point, it starts looking like garbage. Yeah.

GONZALEZ: Is that, like, as the saying goes (laughter)?

KINNAMAN: I actually just made that up, so . . .

GONZALEZ: OK. Well, we'll trademark it to you.

MALONE: Thomas is kind of the economist when it comes to looking at all the financial and environmental costs and benefits of recycling. If you just landfill a peanut butter jar, obviously that has costs, and Thomas takes that into account. But he says there are also costs to recycling. Like, think about what it entails to recycle that peanut butter jar.

GONZALEZ: A giant truck has to come to your home to pick up your peanut butter jar and then drive it somewhere to get sorted and then drive it to a recycling center and then probably put it on a train, which takes it to a boat, which takes your jar halfway around the world.

MALONE: There are costs here. There are financial costs— paying the truck driver, the boat driver, the sorter—and there are, of course, environmental costs, like the pollution from trucks and trucks and trains and boats.

KINNAMAN: And that's where you start wondering, OK, wait a minute.

MALONE: Is recycling worth it? And when you crunch the numbers, Thomas says, more recycling isn't always better for the planet. Sometimes it is worse, including in ways that you may not have thought of.

KINNAMAN: Here's sort of the untold story is that China's ban may actually reduce the amount of plastic that ends up in the oceans. China was not very careful about what got into their ocean for a long period of time. And if some of the plastic piles were just too corrupted, they could do whatever they wanted with it.

GONZALEZ: They dumped them in the ocean.

KINNAMAN: So it's . . .

GONZALEZ: OK. We know that there is a big pile of plastic floating in the ocean, and Thomas is like, how do you think it got there? One bottle at a time, really?

KINNAMAN: You could imagine, oh, that big pile of plastic in the ocean came from the odd bottle being blown off the dock in San Francisco Bay and it went out there and joined all of its friends, and they're all hanging out out there off of the coast of Hawaii. That's probably a very tiny part of it. Countries historically dumped waste out in the ocean.

GONZALEZ: You guys, Thomas is saying that our valiant recycling efforts have been hurting the ocean.

MALONE: And those cute sea turtles.

KINNAMAN: If you're given two options if you're in the middle part of the country—there's a landfill about 50 miles away or put it on a boat to China—and ask yourself which plastic bottle is most likely to end up in the ocean, I'll let you answer that yourself.

GONZALEZ: Oh.

MALONE: And this gets us to the first of what is going to be several controversial Thomas Kinnaman ideas. And we're just going to save you the Googling. You can e-mail us your complaints to planetmoney@npr.org.

GONZALEZ: But hear Thomas out, OK? He is an environmental economist. He is interested in helping the planet. So I know it's hard to hear, but Thomas is saying that, at the moment, it is better for the planet if your plastic ends up in a landfill instead of on a boat shipped off to be recycled.

MALONE: And it's not just about falling in the ocean. This is about the overall environmental cost of that journey. And actually, his analysis finds that this is also true for glass. It's better if that ends up in the landfill. Paper, though, he finds it can go either way. Sometimes recycling is better; sometimes it's not.

GONZALEZ: But good news, everyone, you can still recycle some things. Certain materials, definitely, Thomas says, it is terrible if it ends up in a landfill, like metals, tin and aluminum. Think soup can and Coke can. Thomas says mining for new aluminum in the ground is worse for the environment than the environmental footprint that goes into recycling aluminum, even if we do ship them around the world.

KINNAMAN: Any time an aluminum can ends up in the landfill is a problem. So we should be targeting 100 percent for those materials.

(Continues on next page)

**MODES & MEDIA**
**Mode = audio:**
Gonzalez and Malone use their voices and those of the people they interview, as well as sound bites, such as the sound of a can being opened and someone slurping a beverage.

MALONE: As in, we should basically do everything we can to make sure aluminum and other metals do not ever end up in our landfills.

GONZALEZ: All this time, we've been demonizing water bottles, and LaCroix cans have been skating by.

(SOUNDBITE OF CAN OPENING)

MALONE: I'm going to watch you personally recycle that, Sarah Gonzalez.

GONZALEZ: (Laughter) I'm going to recycle it. Here's the twist. Tin and aluminum are still being recycled by the U.S. There is still a market for metal.

(SOUNDBITE OF SLURPING)

GONZALEZ: Do you want me to crack another bottle?

MALONE: Sarah.

GONZALEZ: (Laughter) I brought backups in case I didn't crack it properly.

MALONE: Moral of the story, Thomas says, Sarah is going to need to recycle all these cans, and she should bury her plastics.

KINNAMAN: Yeah. Put it all in the landfill or burn it, which is what's happening as well in parts of the world.

GONZALEZ: Hold on (laughter). It is better environmentally to burn plastic? That is not going to go down well with some of our listeners, I feel like.

KINNAMAN: Absolutely won't—not go down well in the United States. You have to travel to our other developed countries in the world.

GONZALEZ: So you are making the case for burning plastic.

KINNAMAN: It's going to be expensive.

MALONE: Actually, the most expensive way to dispose of waste, but Thomas says it is surprisingly the best for the environment at the moment—better than shipping to recycling places all over the world and better than landfilling.

KINNAMAN: In Germany and in the Netherlands and in Sweden, they've embraced a new form of incineration, which I refer to as incineration 2.0.

MALONE: Incineration 2.0 and Thomas says these newer, fancier incinerators actually give off fewer dangerous emissions than a backyard charcoal barbecue.

**Use sound effects:**
After discussing why aluminum is one material that should always be recycled, listeners hear a can being opened.

GONZALEZ: He calls incineration the Cadillac plan because he says it basically solves all of the problems. Incinerators generate electricity and hot water and the ashes are used for things like sidewalk tiles. It is very expensive, but he says incineration 2.0 is the future.

ERIC GOLDSTEIN: That's a ridiculous—that's a ridiculous . . .

GONZALEZ: (Laughter) Your face.

GOLDSTEIN: Yeah.

GONZALEZ: No? You're not buying it?

GOLDSTEIN: Ultimately . . .

GONZALEZ: This is Eric Goldstein, an attorney with the Natural Resources Defense Council. And Eric is so not down with incineration 2.0.

GOLDSTEIN: Well, some people have said that, I guess. They don't say it to me directly. They know that would be a mistake.

GONZALEZ: (Laughter).

GOLDSTEIN: Well . . .

MALONE: We wanted to talk to Eric and the NRDC because they represent another ideology on recycling. It's more absolutist.

GOLDSTEIN: Well, we like recycling.

MALONE: They say we owe it to the planet to find a way to make all kinds of recycling work.

GOLDSTEIN: Plastics are made from fossil fuels. If we continue to utilize every bit of coal and oil, petroleum that's buried under the ground, we're going to have a planet that is uninhabitable.

GONZALEZ: Eric says the minute you burn or landfill a plastic jar instead of recycling it, you just took a resource from the Earth—the oil to make the jar—and you didn't even try to use it as much as possible. You never gave that resource a second life—not good.

MALONE: And he says Thomas's calculations are based on how things are today where we have to ship things around the world to recycle them. If the U.S. were to invest in more recycling plants domestically, the calculations would change. It could make sense to recycle.

GOLDSTEIN: And we also need to recognize that maybe it shouldn't all be left up to municipalities to solve this problem and that manufacturers ought to bear more of the burden for figuring out how to deal with this ever-growing amount of waste that we're generating in the United States.

**SOURCES**
Gonzalez and Malone sources include guests who are experts on recycling and their own experiences with recycling.

*(Continues on next page)*

**Medium = digital:** The podcast is available on the NPR website and through the NPR app. Transcripts of episodes are also available on the NPR website.

GONZALEZ: Make less and use less—reduce. That is the best thing we can do. And our environmental economist Thomas Kinnaman totally agrees.

MALONE: It's just that right now a lot of things come in plastic—your shampoo, your peanut butter.

GONZALEZ: So what are we supposed to do?

KINNAMAN: It's OK to put it in the garbage pile, put it in the landfill and feel OK about it.

MALONE: And, look; we get it. Putting a plastic container into your trash can, it is going to feel bad.

GONZALEZ: You're going to want to pull it out and put it in the recycling bin. Thomas knows this urge very well.

KINNAMAN: I recycle, actually, all my plastic even though my own data suggests that it's not always good to.

GONZALEZ: You still recycle.

KINNAMAN: Yeah. I'll even clean it out a little bit before I put it into the container.

(SOUNDBITE OF ALESSANDRO RIZZO'S "FUNKY AND WESTERN")

GONZALEZ: If you have a story idea, send us an e-mail— planetmoney@npr.org.

MALONE: We also have a newsletter—just the right amount of economics for your inbox. You can subscribe by going to npr.org/planetmoneynewsletter. That is npr.org/planetmoneynewsletter. Today's show was produced by Alexi Horowitz Ghazi and Liza Yager. Bryant Urstadt edits our show.

GONZALEZ: And Alex Goldmark is our supervising producer. By the way, Kenny and I, we are still recycling. If you really want to be good to the environment, you're just going to have to do a little research, find out how your city is responding. I'm Sarah Gonzalez.

MALONE: I'm Kenny Malone.

GONZALEZ: And we have to give a special thanks to Lowell Harrelson of Mobile, Ala. He is basically the reason why the United States started residential recycling. And his story was part one of our series.

LOWELL HARRELSON: This is NPR, and we thank you for listening.

(SOUNDBITE OF ALESSANDRO RIZZO'S "FUNKY AND WESTERN")

**Style:** Gonzalez and Malone speak casually and conversationally throughout, joking with a guest and laughing frequently. They speak directly to listeners at the end, telling listeners with story ideas to e-mail them.

*Editor's Note: For the audio version of this podcast, visit www.npr.org/2019/07/12/741283641/ episode-926-so-should-we-recycle.*

**RHETORICAL SITUATION & CHOICES**

1. **Purpose.** How do Gonzalez and Malone use information about China's economy to explain why recycling in the United States isn't as profitable as it used to be?

2. **Audience.** What assumptions do you think Gonzalez and Malone make about their listeners' recycling habits? Do you think these assumptions are accurate?

3. **Rhetorical appeals.** How do Gonzalez and Malone appeal to listeners' sense of pathos throughout? Do you think their approach is effective?

4. **Rhetorical appeals.** How do Gonzalez and Malone's choice of guests affect your view of the podcast's credibility?

5. **Modes & media.** How is your experience of reading the podcast transcript different from your experience of listening to the podcast? Which do you prefer, and why?

**GENRE CONVENTIONS**

6. **Elements of the genre.** Listen through the entire podcast and notice the introductions Gonzalez and Malone offer for each guest. Do you find some introductions more useful than others? Why?

7. **Elements of the genre.** What are all the ways you notice Gonzalez and Malone building rapport with listeners? Do some ways seem more authentic than others? Do any seem forced?

8. **Style.** How do Gonzalez and Malone come across in terms of their personalities? How do they seem similar to each other and different from each other?

9. **Design.** The Planet Money cover art is very simplistic and simple. What does it convey to you about the podcast's approach to economics?

10. **Sources.** Gonzalez and Malone mention their own experiences and feelings about recycling throughout. Do you think their personal experiences with recycling are used appropriately as source material? Why or why not?

Thinking of drafting a podcast? Ask yourself the following questions:

## RHETORICAL SITUATION & CHOICES

☐ **Purpose.** What subjects am I passionate about? What am I an expert on? What am I curious about? Do I want to motivate my audience to do something? Do I want to teach them something? Do I want them to see things from a different perspective?

☐ **Audience.** Who am I talking to? What is the level of interest of my audience? What is the level of expertise of my audience? Why are they listening—for entertainment? Information? Something else?

☐ **Rhetorical appeals.** How will I establish my ethos? How can I choose guests who will help me establish ethos? How can I use pathos in a way that is appropriate for my audience and topic? How can I use logic to persuade my audience to see things my way?

☐ **Modes & media.** Will I make a transcript of my podcast available to listeners? Do I want to use Patreon to solicit listener support?

## GENRE CONVENTIONS

☐ **Elements of the genre.** What format do I want to use to best engage listeners and accommodate what I want my podcast to do? How do I want to introduce guests so that listeners know who they are, and why I am talking to them? What kinds of sound bites and sound effects can I incorporate to make my podcasts interesting? Are there sounds I can use that will help build my ethos or appeal to pathos?

☐ **Style.** What kind of music would best set the mood for my podcast? How do I want to let my personality shine through? How and when do I want to invite audience feedback?

☐ **Design.** Is my cover art simple and representative of my topic and approach to my topic? Am I using color and other design elements to convey the tone and theme of my podcast?

☐ **Sources.** Will my sources help me develop my ethos? How can I capitalize on my personal experience with the topic?

---

**PRACTICE**

# Describing the Elements of a Podcast

The range of podcasts is incredibly broad and you may find that some very closely adhere to the elements and conventions we outlined above, while others veer considerably away from them. Find a podcast on a topic you are interested in and listen to three episodes. After listening to all three, review the information above about podcasts. Based only on the three episodes you just listened to, how accurate is what we've said?

- If the information presented is entirely or mostly accurate, write an analysis of how the episodes you listened to do the things we've said podcasts do.

- If the information presented is entirely or mostly inaccurate, draft a list of elements of the genre and characteristics of the style, design, and sources you see in the episodes you analyzed. Just as we've done above, explain or provide examples for each item on your list.

# Fairy Tales

A fairy tale, in the simplest terms, is a story that conveys a moral or lesson, typically to children. Most have historical connections to folklore and oral tales; they are about magic and magical creatures and feature houses made of gingerbread, godmothers with magic wands, and animals that talk and wear human clothing. Many traditional fairy tales, such as "Cinderella," "Snow White," and "Sleeping Beauty," feature princesses in peril and princes saving the day. However, modern tales, such as Margaret Atwood's *The Handmaid's Tale*, offer a critique of society (in Atwood's novel, it's a feminist critique), and sometimes a grim view of the future.

As a child, you probably read or saw film versions of traditional fairy tales and learned social lessons from them. "Hansel and Gretel" and "Little Red Riding Hood" warn children of the dangers of going into the dark woods without a grown-up and reinforce the rule "don't talk to strangers." "The Three Little Pigs" enforces the idea that if something is worth doing, it's worth doing right.

As an adult—and as a reader and writer—you most likely encounter fairy tales from a different, more analytic angle. Use the guidelines that follow to read fairy tales and related genres critically. Understanding their conventions and rhetorical contexts are key to composing in them.

## Analyzing Fairy Tales

**Purpose**  Traditionally authors write fairy tales to entertain their readers and to teach morals or lessons to young audiences. Authors achieve these purposes in part through characters—often stock characters such as imperiled princesses and dangerous wolves that are easily identifiable and generic enough that a wide audience can relate to them. Authors of fairy tales entertain by keeping their stories brief and their pacing brisk and instruct by using every detail sentence and line of dialogue so it leads to the moral or lesson.

**Audience**  Authors of fairy tales create stories for children and, secondarily, for the adults who read to them at home or at school. Authors bring in fantasy elements, such as magic and talking animals, because these elements captivate children. The stories are written so that they're easy for young readers to understand and remember; authors tend to focus on universal human themes (such as curiosity, fear, and coming of age) to connect with as many readers as possible.

**Rhetorical appeals**  Authors of fairy tales most often rely on appeals based on pathos. Because their purpose is to teach a lesson to a young audience, writers rely on emotion to move the reader. In "Little Red Riding Hood," the reader needs to feel the danger of wolves in order to heed the warning of the tale. Authors also establish their credibility (ethos) by using the conventions of the genre, such as the stock opening of "Once upon a time" and a voice that sounds very assured.

**Modes & media**   Most often, we encounter fairy tales in anthologies such as *Grimms'* and *Mother Goose*. These print-based collections of tales are usually illustrated; sometimes individual tales are translated into film, such as Disney's *Snow White and the Seven Dwarfs* and *Sleeping Beauty*, or recorded as audiobooks.

**Elements of the genre**   Fairy tales are characterized by the following:

- *Typical elements of fiction.* Fairy tales are works of fiction, and like other works of fiction, they are typically structured around a few main elements. The plot is an arrangement of incidents that shape the action of a story. Authors also employ characters (the people involved in the story), a setting (the time, place, and atmosphere in which the story takes place), symbolism (the use of a person, object, image, word, or action that has a range of meaning beyond the literal), a point of view (who tells the story and how), and a theme (the story's central meaning or main idea).

- *Magical or fantasy elements.* Unlike most other types of fiction, fairy tales, as the genre's name implies, also feature fairies and magical creatures, such as the fairy godmother in "Cinderella"; magical elements, such as the decades-long naps in "Sleeping Beauty" and "Rip Van Winkle"; and/or magical objects, such as the talking mirror in "Snow White."

- *Stock characters.* Fairy-tale characters are usually one-dimensional, defined by only a few exaggerated details, such as greed, intelligence, or beauty. In "The Three Little Pigs," each pig is defined by one particular trait: The very lazy one builds a house of straw, the somewhat lazy one a house of sticks, and the hardworking one a house of bricks. Fairy-tale characters are usually completely good or completely evil (such as the "big bad" wolf in "Little Red Riding Hood"). They are often animals that the author has anthropomorphized—that is, the animals have human capabilities, such as being able to speak and wear clothing.

- *Conflict.* In most fairy tales, main characters have a task to fulfill or a journey to complete; often they are in danger.

- *Moral or lesson.* Conveying a moral or lesson—which is usually direct and obvious—is the main purpose of most fairy tales (don't go into the woods alone).

**Style**   Fairy tales are characterized by:

- *A conversational but often didactic tone.* Authors often use an informal tone (e.g., "Grandma, what big teeth you have"), but because they are writing to teach children a lesson, the tone can also be preachy. Traditional fairy tales do not feature irony or humor, though some modern versions do.

- *Simple prose.* Most authors of fairy tales use very straightforward language and sentence structure (e.g., "Once upon a time").

- *Repetition and rhythm.* Like poems or songs, fairy tales often include specific patterns of language and refrains (e.g., "I'll huff and I'll puff and I'll blow your house down.")

- *Sparse detail.* Authors tend to rely on just a few details, for example, describing a castle simply as "gloomy" or a forest as "dark." Details such as how large or old the castle is, or what kinds of trees grow in the forest, are usually not revealed.

**Design**   Although the details in the fairy tales themselves are usually spare, many are lavishly illustrated. Some are illustrated with realistic images, such as the Gustave Doré engravings that accompany some editions of Charles Perrault's version of "Little Red Riding Hood." In more modern books of fairy tales, illustrations are often colorful and fanciful looking; in *The Random House Book of Fairy Tales*, for example, each tale includes full-color images that illustrate key moments.

**Sources**   Fairy tales do not include footnotes or Works Cited pages, although most modern-day fairy tales are based on older stories that have been circulating in either oral or written form for generations. "Little Red Riding Hood," for instance, is connected to many European peasant tales that go back as far as the 1300s.

## Guided Reading | Fairy Tale

Charles Perrault (1628–1703) was a French writer during the reign of Louis XIV, and he told stories and tales, in part, to entertain the king and the royal court. Perrault's work did much to promote the fairy tale as a literary genre, and many of his versions of tales have been retold by other writers, including the Brothers Grimm. Presented here is Perrault's telling of "Little Red Riding Hood." Drawing on existing tales that had been passed on verbally through generations, he published the tale, originally titled "Le Petit Chaperon Rouge," in a collection of fairy tales in 1697. Our source for the Perrault text is a library of folklore and mythology at the University of Pittsburgh, hosted by Professor D. L. Ashliman, who has also gathered a collection of critical essays for each tale. The illustration on page 292 was created by Gustave Doré and is from a Perrault edition of "Le Petit Chaperon Rouge."

In the annotations that are shown, we've applied a possible analysis of the tale in terms of the author's rhetorical situation and the fairy tale's conventions as a genre. The analysis is meant not as an interpretation of the story, but as a tool for reading fairy tales and other narrative genres critically.

# Charles Perrault, *Little Red Riding Hood*

| RHETORICAL SITUATION & CHOICES | GENRE CONVENTIONS |
|---|---|

**◄ What is the composer, Charles Perrault, doing?**

**How do I know this is a fairy tale? ►**

## PURPOSE
Perrault's purpose is to convey a message or moral.

## AUDIENCE
Readers of fairy tales are usually children who are learning about how the world works.

## RHETORICAL APPEALS
Perrault establishes the tale's credibility by beginning with "Once upon a time," associating the tale with a venerable past (ethos). The author appeals to readers' pathos by implying that the child is in danger.

## MODES & MEDIA
**Mode = written:** Author Charles Perrault might have assumed two things about the audiences for his collected fairy tales: (1) that adults would read the stories silently to themselves, and (2) that adults would read the stories aloud for their children. Further, given the long oral tradition of telling tales and the limited options for entertainment (seventeenth century), it is also likely that

## ELEMENTS OF THE GENRE
This is a made-up story, geared toward children. It has a moral, which, in this case, is spelled out in the final paragraph. It includes magical elements, such as a talking animal. The main character has a task or journey to complete and is in potential danger. The tale features symbolism, in this case, a red cloak.

## STYLE
The story is set in the past; the author begins with the much-used opening "Once upon a time." Perrault tells the story simply but builds tension as he moves toward the conflict and the closing lesson that he wants to impart. The tale features a stock character (the big bad wolf). The setting has little detail.

## DESIGN
Perrault wrote text; editors of some editions of his text added illustrations, such as the one shown here.

Credit: Gustave Doré illustration from "Le Petit Chaperon Rouge."

Once upon a time there lived in a certain village a little country girl, the prettiest creature who was ever seen. Her mother was excessively fond of her; and her grandmother doted on her still more. This good woman had a little red riding hood made for her. It suited the girl so extremely well that everybody called her Little Red Riding Hood.

One day her mother, having made some cakes, said to her, "Go, my dear, and see how your grandmother is doing, for I hear she has been very ill. Take her a cake, and this little pot of butter."

Little Red Riding Hood set out immediately to go to her grandmother, who lived in another village.

As she was going through the wood, she met with a wolf, who had a very great mind to eat her up, but he dared not, because of some woodcutters working nearby in the forest. He asked her where she was going. The poor child, who did not know that it was dangerous to stay and talk to a wolf, said to him, "I am going to see my grandmother and carry her a cake and a little pot of butter from my mother."

"Does she live far off?" said the wolf.

"Oh I say," answered Little Red Riding Hood; "it is beyond that mill you see there, at the first house in the village."

"Well," said the wolf, "and I'll go and see her too. I'll go this way and you go that, and we shall see who will be there first."

the story would have been read aloud as a source of amusement for adults. So there are both written and verbal aspects to fairy tale modes.

**Medium = print:**
"Little Red Riding Hood" is presented here in print, and the assumption is that you will read it linearly, that is, from beginning to end. (In this case, you might be noticing the annotations in the margins as well.) Printed media are usually presented as pages that you turn; this gives an author the opportunity to create a mini-cliffhanger at the end of a page so that readers will turn the page and stay hooked. In contrast, a digital rendering of this tale might include hyperlinks that would allow you to skip around and read the story in whatever order you like.

The wolf ran as fast as he could, taking the shortest path, and the little girl took a roundabout way, entertaining herself by gathering nuts, running after butterflies, and gathering bouquets of little flowers. It was not long before the wolf arrived at the old woman's house. He knocked at the door: tap, tap.

"Who's there?"

"Your grandchild, Little Red Riding Hood," replied the wolf, counterfeiting her voice; "who has brought you a cake and a little pot of butter sent you by mother."

The good grandmother, who was in bed, because she was somewhat ill, cried out, "Pull the bobbin, and the latch will go up."

The wolf pulled the bobbin, and the door opened, and then he immediately fell upon the good woman and ate her up in a moment, for it had been more than three days since he had eaten. He then shut the door and got into the grandmother's bed, expecting Little Red Riding Hood, who came some time afterwards and knocked at the door: tap, tap.

"Who's there?"

Little Red Riding Hood, hearing the big voice of the wolf, was at first afraid; but believing her grandmother had a cold and was hoarse, answered, "It is your grandchild Little Red Riding Hood, who has brought you a cake and a little pot of butter mother sends you."

The wolf cried out to her, softening his voice as much as he could, "Pull the bobbin, and the latch will go up."

Little Red Riding Hood pulled the bobbin, and the door opened.

The wolf, seeing her come in, said to her, hiding himself under the bedclothes, "Put the cake and the little pot of butter upon the stool, and come get into bed with me."

Little Red Riding Hood took off her clothes and got into bed. She was greatly amazed to see how her grandmother looked in her nightclothes, and said to her, "Grandmother, what big arms you have!"

"All the better to hug you with, my dear."

"Grandmother, what big legs you have!"

"All the better to run with, my child."

"Grandmother, what big ears you have!"

"All the better to hear with, my child."

"Grandmother, what big eyes you have!"

"All the better to see with, my child."

"Grandmother, what big teeth you have got!"

"All the better to eat you up with."

And, saying these words, this wicked wolf fell upon Little Red Riding Hood, and ate her all up.

**SOURCES**
There are no footnotes or Works Cited list. There are many different sources and versions of this story. This one is the popular seventeenth-century Charles Perrault version, and its sources, in turn, probably date back to the fourteenth century. He is credited with being the first person to gather tales that had only been told orally in the past and to treat them as literature.

*(Continues on next page)*

> Moral: Children, especially attractive, well-bred young ladies, should never talk to strangers, for if they should do so, they may well provide dinner for a wolf. I say "wolf," but there are various kinds of wolves. There are also those who are charming, quiet, polite, unassuming, complacent, and sweet, who pursue young women at home and in the streets. And unfortunately, it is these gentle wolves who are the most dangerous ones of all.

## QUESTIONS | Analyzing Perrault's Fairy Tale

### RHETORICAL SITUATION & CHOICES

1. **Purpose.** Charles Perrault, in his telling of "Little Red Riding Hood," seeks to entertain and provide a lesson—in fact, he states the official moral at the end of the story. However, what other interpretations could be reached about the main character, the story, and the story's lessons? Which details support these alternative interpretations?

2. **Audience.** To what degree does Perrault gear his version of the tale toward children, and to what degree toward adults? What makes you think so? What are the ages of the children who are the primary targets of this tale, and how do you know? Which details or aspects of the story would appeal to different age groups?

3. **Rhetorical appeals.** Little Red Riding Hood seems to be an extremely naïve character, not quite recognizing that the creature in her grandmother's bed is not her grandmother. How does Little Red's naïveté function in terms of ethos, pathos, and logos?

4. **Rhetorical appeals.** How would the ethos of the tale be affected if, instead of beginning with "Once upon a time," it opened with a specific time and place, such as "Stockholm, Sweden; January 12, 1960"?

5. **Modes & media.** If you were to adapt "Little Red Riding Hood" for a digital format, what changes would you make? What might you hyperlink? Why?

### GENRE CONVENTIONS

6. **Elements of the genre.** Why is a wolf a fitting animal to play the role of the villain in this story? What other animals might adequately fulfill the role?

7. **Elements of the genre.** What is the significance of Little Red Riding Hood's red cape? What abstract or symbolic meaning might it have? Why do you think so?

8. **Style.** Sometimes the moral in a fairy tale is made explicit, as in this tale, and other times it's implied but not explicitly stated. What is the effect of the author stating the moral explicitly? And why does Perrault say that gentle wolves are the most dangerous?

9. **Style.** Identify the details of the story that convey the setting. To what extent do they contribute to your visualization of the story? To what extent do they add to the story's universality?

10. **Design.** How does Gustave Doré's woodblock illustration included with the text influence your reading of the story?

11. **Sources.** It's possible that oral stories served as inspiration for Perrault's tale and other similar tales. Can you think of more modern stories or films that may use this story as a source?

## CHECKLIST | Drafting a Fairy Tale

Thinking of drafting a fairy tale? Ask yourself the following questions:

### RHETORICAL SITUATION & CHOICES

☐ **Purpose.** What is my story, and why do I want to tell it? What message, main idea, or moral do I want to convey? What makes my message so important?

☐ **Audience.** Who are my readers? Why will my story matter to them? And how will I reach them?

☐ **Rhetorical appeals.** How will I use ethos, pathos, and logos to tell my tale and reach my audience? How will I establish my authority as a writer? To what extent will I appeal to my readers' emotions? What role, if any, will logic play in my tale?

☐ **Modes & media.** Will I compose my fairy tale in written, audio, or visual form? Will I present it in print, electronically, or face-to-face?

### GENRE CONVENTIONS

☐ **Elements of the genre.** How will I structure my plot? Who are my characters? What is going to happen to them? What is my story's setting? Who will narrate the story, and how? To what extent will I use symbols to convey meaning? How about magical objects? Talking animals? What is the central conflict of my tale? How will I get to my moral?

☐ **Style.** What tone will I take in my writing? Will my tale be funny? Preachy? Both? What kind of language will I use? How much detail?

☐ **Design.** How will I format my story? Will I include illustrations? If so, what kind? And for what key scenes? Why?

☐ **Sources.** Will my fairy tale connect to an existing tale? Will it connect with actual events in history? What sources, if any, will I draw on for my story? Why will I use those sources?

---

### PRACTICE

## Telling a Tale

Draft a brief fairy tale of your own in which a generic character defined by one trait (old, poor, silly, vain) experiences something that teaches a lesson. The lesson should connect in some way to a main trait of your character, just as Little Red's naïveté is connected to her ultimate demise. Alternatively, write your own version of "Little Red Riding Hood" or another popular traditional tale. What will be your main goal in rewriting the tale (perhaps you want to improve on it or make it more modern)? How will your rhetorical situation differ from that of the earlier authors of the tale? What conventions will you adhere to or adapt? How will your writing style compare to the original?

# PUBLIC GENRES

Now that you have reviewed a variety of different public genres, noticing their commonalities and differences, and practiced a few of the key moves made in these genres, you should feel ready to tackle some larger projects. Here we offer two extended project ideas for you to play with. The first invites you to create an Ignite presentation that persuades your viewer to embrace a behavior or activity. The second project invites you to create your own StoryCorps-style podcast.

## IN PRACTICE | Public Writing Projects

### Ignite Presentation

1. Think about Sunni Brown's presentation on doodling. What are some other behaviors or activities that people generally don't embrace as useful or that people look down on? For example, perhaps you believe that napping is a good use of time. Or maybe you believe that waking up and drinking coffee in bed for two hours puts you in the right frame of mind to go to work. Brainstorm a list of all these potential behaviors/activities.

2. Read through your list and choose a couple that you are passionate about. Freewrite for ten minutes about each of them. As you write, think about what makes you believe in these behaviors. What benefits do they provide?

3. Read over your freewrites and see which one has the most juice for you. Which one is most appealing to do some research on in order to discover what experts have to say?

4. Once you've chosen your topic for the presentation, do some research. Look up what others believe about it. For example, if you have chosen the art of napping, see whether there are statistics about what naps can do for someone. Are there famous people who indulged in napping? You might also check out the infographic on napping in this chapter. Gather all the evidence you might use to persuade your viewers that your behavior/activity is a worthy pursuit.

5. Rewatch the Sunni Brown presentation. How does she capture her viewer's attention? What strategies does she use to establish her ethos? Do a search for other Ignite presentations. Note the techniques used in ones you find most persuasive. Use these as models for yours.

6. Write out your speech. Figure out what it is you want to say to your audience. Make sure you aren't overwhelming your audience with lots of ideas. Focus on several key points.

7. Practice your speech for others. Have them time it (it shouldn't be longer than five minutes). Ask them for feedback. Revise based on that. Then ask them what types of visuals would help you make your case.

8. Begin to gather materials for your slide presentation. Remember that an Ignite presentation is a total of five minutes, with twenty slides that auto advance every fifteen seconds. Sketch out what you want on each slide. It's best to have one central idea for each slide. Make most of your slides visual. You are going to be speaking, so let your speaking be your text.

9. Create your slides. Then practice your speech as your slides are auto advancing. Do you need to pause more? Do you need to slow down? Are slides advancing while you're still speaking about their concept? Revise as needed.

10. Give your Ignite presentation in class. Thrill at the applause.

## StoryCorps-Style Podcast

1. Create a two to three minute podcast that meets the parameters of StoryCorps's mission statement: "StoryCorps's mission is to preserve and share humanity's stories in order to build connections between people and create a more just and compassionate world." Like the podcasts on the StoryCorps website and digital archive, your podcast should consist of an interview with someone in your life—ideally someone with a unique perspective on history, current events, American culture, or life in general.

2. Choose an interviewee you have a relationship with. This can be a parent, sibling, child, friend, maybe even that family "black sheep." In order to get stories out of a person, you need to build on familiarity and trust.

3. Plan your questions ahead of time. See the link to StoryCorps's "Great Questions" page (storycorps.org/participate/great-questions/) to help you get started. Come to your interview prepared with more questions than you think you'll get to.

4. Listen to some StoryCorps's podcasts to give you a sense of what makes a good story. Keep this in mind as you conduct your interview.

5. Practice recording ahead of time: Figure out what device/equipment you will be using, and test it out in the space you will be using for your interview (phones work fine for this if you get the right app. Hi-Q and Recorder Plus work well). Figure out how close you need to be to the microphone, how to limit background noise, and so on.

6. Record more than two to three minutes' worth of interview. You can get rid of the boring parts, and it's always better to have more to work with than less. Plus, it might take a while for your interviewee to get to the good stuff.

7. Apply everything you know about revising prose to audio editing your interview: Think about what feels like the real story, then ask yourself, "What distracts?" Edit your interview so that you keep the most compelling parts of the story.

8. If you want to include a music track, keep it subtle. You don't want it to take over your story. In fact, you might consider having music just in the beginning and the end, and using music that doesn't have lyrics. Keep in mind copyright/fair use rules.

9. Listen to your finished story/podcast. What do you like about it? What might you do differently next time? Consider sharing it with your interviewee.

# 10 ASSEMBLING A MULTIGENRE PROJECT

**W**hat is a multigenre project? It's a collection of three or more genre compositions, built around a single topic. A multigenre project is an opportunity to experiment. It also gives you the chance to practice in a variety of rhetorical situations, forms of composition, and types of media.

Let's look at an example. You've conducted research on the topic of, say, the significance of the bond between people and dogs. Through the course of your research, brainstorming, and drafting, you decide that you want to make the case that dogs were essential to the rise of civilization. You also want to present a history of the relationship between humans and canines, and perhaps even tell a story of a particular relationship. You are strong in a variety of genres and media (better at some than others). Your audience is one of general readers; that is, it's an unspecialized audience, but one with some interest in dogs and humanity. A multigenre project for your topic could include a few of these genres and media options:

- An **annotated timeline** tracing human-canine interactions from ancient times to the present
- A brief TED talk–style video **presentation** on how and why dogs were critical to human civilization
- A **story** of how dogs and humans relate now
- A **photo essay** or **slide show** that demonstrates how dogs benefit humans by reducing stress
- An **annotated map** locating where humans first settled and domesticated dogs
- An **interview** with a dog behaviorist, a therapy dog trainer, or a psychologist who uses dogs to treat humans
- An **Author's or Artist's Statement** that brings everything together

## The Possibilities of the Multigenre Project

Just like any research endeavor, a genre project allows you to join a conversation about a particular subject or issue. Whether you research and compose a single genre piece or multiple related pieces, you address a research question, make clear arguments, and draw on sources, all while keeping a strong sense of purpose and audience.

Unlike more traditional academic projects, genre projects let you break away from (or embrace, if you prefer) the usual forms such as the research paper. Multigenre projects go a step beyond: They open up unlimited channels and formats for you to convey your points. Nothing is out of bounds. Think handmade objects, videos, blogs, animations, photo essays, collages, and other visual arguments. Further, genre projects, and multigenre projects in particular, offer you the chance to connect with audiences beyond the classroom.

## Your Rhetorical Situation

When you begin thinking about creating a multigenre project, consider the following:

**Furthering your purpose**   You can do this by assembling a coherent collection. Think of each genre piece as a chapter that contributes to a whole. You will unify the pieces by building in relationships among them by choosing a sequence and package (more on this below—and by composing an Introduction that pulls everything together. For multigenre projects, we recommend that you compose a separate Author's or Artist's Statement for each of your individual genre pieces, and use the Introduction to discuss how the pieces work together. However, it also works to create one Author's or Artist's Statement for the entire project. Check with your instructor about specific preferences. (For more on Author's and Artist's Statements, see Chapter 6.

**Reaching your audience**   You might do this by providing different *perspectives*. As you decide on the genres to compose in, think about whether you want to convey multiple perspectives on your topic through each piece. For example, if you are presenting an argument, you could address a different point of view in each composition.

**Using rhetorical appeals to your advantage**   Imagine how you might use each genre piece to make your case through different rhetorical appeals. Maybe in one genre you emphasize ethos; in another, logos; and in another, pathos. Or maybe you want to organize your project around a single rhetorical appeal.

**Choosing modes and media**   Think about using a mix of modes and media throughout your pieces so your audience has different ways to connect with your message. Some of the best projects we've seen are a combination of textual, visual, and audio compositions.

## The Conventions of the Multigenre Project

Every multigenre project will be different—a culmination of one author's choices about which genres to mix together, which perspectives to represent, which voices or tones to incorporate. There are no conventions for a multigenre work beyond the use of multiple genres to convey ideas to an audience. Typically, we ask student composers of multigenre projects to provide an Introduction, a separate Author's or Artist's Statement for each individual piece, or a single statement in which they reflect on each of their genre pieces. The Statement(s) should include Works Cited or References lists.

# The Steps to Assembling a Multigenre Project

**1. Introduce your project and provide context**   Write a one- to two-page Introduction that gives your audience an overview of your topic, your scope, and what sparked your interest in your topic. Provide a brief explanation for your rationale for the sequence of your genre pieces (more on that below). You can provide more details—and cite and document your research—in your Author's or Artist's Statement(s), which is typically longer than the Introduction and includes a list of References or Works Cited. Alternatively, you can combine your Introduction and Statement into one document, as some of our students have done.

Your Introduction should also provide any context that your audience will need to fully understand your project and individual genre pieces. This means you may need to provide a brief history of your topic, the people who are key to its larger discussion, and the main controversies surrounding it.

**2. Sequence your genre pieces**   Do this in a way that will make sense to your audience. Each piece should prepare your audience for the one that follows it. Sequencing helps orient your audience, and it also helps you methodically achieve your purpose. Here are some scenarios:

- If your goal is to convince your audience to take action on a specific problem, begin with a composition that highlights that problem, and end with a piece that offers a possible solution and/or makes a direct call to action. An alternative approach could be to begin with a visual piece that shows what could happen if no one took action to solve the problem.

- If your purpose is to compare or contrast specific views on your topic, you might arrange your pieces to highlight differences and similarities.

- If one of your goals is to tell a story, sequence your pieces into a narrative structure (consider a beginning, middle, and end), and bring out narrative elements such as character and conflict.

- If you want to emphasize a particular rhetorical appeal, think about how the order of your genre pieces could do that. For example, to emphasize pathos, you could begin and end with the pieces that will evoke the most emotion in your audience.

---

ATTENTION, AUTHORS & ARTISTS

**Need some ideas for genres?**   Working on a multigenre project? Great. There are many genres to choose from. Here are just a few (they can be delivered in digital, print, and/or 3-D physical media): researched arguments, editorials, articles, user manuals, brochures, encyclopedia articles, obituaries, exposés, editorials, letters to the editor, interviews, book reviews, essays, surveys, business letters, poems, personal letters, short stories, scripts, journal entries, memoirs, advice columns, political speeches, eulogies, tabloid articles, restaurant menus, top 10 lists, résumés, directions, syllabi, web pages, photographs, collages, photo essays, charts, graphs, advertisements, comics, cartoons, posters, movie posters, skit performances, paintings, sketches, musical scores, musical performances, sculptures, audio essays, film clips, and scrapbook pages.

---

Alternatively, if establishing your ethos is more important, you might begin with a piece that establishes your expertise and credibility, such as a researched journal article.

**3. Title your project**   Your title should reflect your topic and your take on your topic. Create a title that will spark the interest of your target audience, a title that is memorable and provocative. The title should reflect your project's message but can go beyond simply stating it. Consider how the tone and word choice of the title will build expectations in readers' minds about what the project will or will not do.

Here are some titles our students have come up with:

- Dawson Swan's project on nature and mental health: "The Threat of Nature Deficit Disorder" (p. 310)
- Gwen Ganow's project on how the concept of superheroes intersects with "real life": "When Worlds Collide: Why Superheroes Matter" (p. 308)
- Scarlet Moody's project on Rwanda radio: "The Rwandan Genocide and Radio-Television's "Libre des Milles Collines"
- Emma Jones's project on Alzheimer's disease: "The Road of Life"

**4. Create an author's or artist's statement**   Use your Statement to discuss your research, explain your rhetorical choices, and evaluate your project overall. (See Chapter 6 for advice and examples.) We encourage our students to write a Statement for each genre piece, and provide an Introduction or project-wide Statement to unify their work.

**5. Package your project creatively**   While a standard research paper is generally packaged quite simply, with a cover page or perhaps in a folder, a multigenre project can be packaged more imaginatively. As with every other aspect of your project, your package and delivery will impact your audience and indicate your tone and angle on your subject. For example, a multigenre project packaged in a miniature black coffin indicates somberness, while a project presented in a miniature pink-polka-dotted coffin suggests a humorous and ironic approach.

Here are some ways students have packaged their projects in the past:

- A project on globalization: All the components were rolled up inside a mailing tube covered with stamps and postal marks from around the world.
- A project on the drinking age: All the genre pieces were presented in a wire wine bottle carrier.
- A project on education: The title page was designed to look like the cover of a teacher's grade book, and all the pieces inside had pale blue columns on the borders (like grade books have).

**Keep the following questions in mind.** Wherever you are in your composing process, it can be helpful to get feedback. Here are some more questions you might want to ask your respondents.

Note: There are no conventions for multigenre projects. However, there are conventions for individual genres. See Chapters 7–10 for advice and examples.

### RHETORICAL SITUATION & CHOICES

☐ **Purpose.** What is the overall purpose of my project? What are the purposes of my individual genre pieces? What is the effect of reading/viewing each piece in isolation versus reading/viewing each piece as a group? When all are experienced together, how is the effect different from reading/viewing each piece in isolation? How can I sequence or package my pieces to best achieve my overarching purpose? What title will signal my overall purpose to my readers?

☐ **Audience.** How do my Introduction and Author's/Artist's Statement work to draw my audience in? If I aim to persuade my audience, how does the sequencing encourage readers/viewers to accept my point of view? What kind of packaging will capture the attention of my audience?

☐ **Rhetorical appeals.** How do my individual genre compositions, Author's/Artist's Statements, and Introduction, taken together, establish my credibility (ethos)? Is there a clear logical aspect to the project (logos)? Is there something that will resonate emotionally (pathos) with readers? Given my audience, should I emphasize one appeal over another, perhaps highlighting it in my Introduction? Given my purpose, can I use sequencing to begin and end my project with a particular appeal?

☐ **Modes & media.** Have I used a mix of modes and media throughout my pieces so that my audience has different ways to connect with my message? Have I balanced one mode/medium with others so that the project overall isn't text-heavy or too visual?

# Examples of Multigenre Projects

Let's take a look at some student projects. We've annotated these to highlight the components of each project and how the student assembled them into a whole. We've also indicated how our students handled their rhetorical choices (regarding purpose, audience, rhetorical appeals, and modes and media) and the possibilities of the multigenre project (elements, style, design, and use of sources).

# Guided Reading | A Multigenre Project

One multigenre project will look very different from another. Here is student author Neil Carr's multigenre project on video games and violence.

## Neil Carr (STUDENT), *Video Games and Violence: Who Should We Blame When Kids Are Violent?*

**PURPOSE**
Neil wants to persuade his audience that video games and their makers should not be blamed for the violent real-life behavior of some players.

**AUDIENCE**
Neil identifies his primary audience as general readers who do not have specialized knowledge of video games. He's aiming at regular citizens/taxpayers. He sequences his compositions so that his audience will get a sense of the humanity of gamers themselves, as well as the escape aspects of gaming, before he moves on to more detailed research findings.

◄ **What is the author/artist, Neil Carr, doing?**

**What are the parts? How do ► they work together?**

▲ **STUDENT AUTHOR PHOTO**
Neil Carr.
*Credit: Neil Carr.*

**NEIL'S PROJECT CONSISTS OF**
A **researched essay** on studies of video games and violence.

An **audio diary** of a truancy officer (see recorder).

A narrative and persuasive **film script** of the story of two boys, one who plays video games and one who doesn't, comparing their tendencies toward violence.

The **film** (on DVD).

**To unify his project, Neil provides:**

An **Introduction** with contextual information.

## RHETORICAL APPEALS

Neil's choice to compose both a film script and an audio diary indicates that appealing to pathos and ethos is important to him.

## MODES & MEDIA

Neil chooses film and audio to engage his audience in a narrative, persuasive, and entertaining way. However, he opts to present his own views and research findings on the topic in a traditional research paper.

## MULTIGENRE CONVENTIONS

There are no conventions for multigenre projects. However, there are conventions for individual genres. See Chapters 7–10 for examples.

An **Author's Statement** in which he discusses his research, explains his rhetorical choices, and evaluates his project as a whole.

**Packaging** for his print pieces—a binder with an illustrated cover—and a recorder that contains his audio piece.

*Credit: Neil Carr.*

*(Continues on next page)*

Let's look at the audio diary from Neil's multigenre project.

**PURPOSE**

Neil channels the voice of a truancy officer to make a point about video gamers. This piece fits in with the broader purpose of his multigenre project: to persuade others that video games and their producers should not be blamed for the violent behavior of some gamers.

**AUDIENCE**

Neil's audience includes his classmates, his instructor, and a general audience.

If this had been a "real" audio diary by Officer Rendar, the audience could have been the court, if he'd been asked to submit his observations.

◄ What is the author/artist, Neil Carr, doing?

What makes this ► an audio diary?

**Neil Carr**

**Audio Diary of a Truancy Officer (transcript)**

March 31, 2013. This is truancy officer Mike Rendar, and this is the first entry of my audio diary. I've never done one of these before, but I decided to start because I've been put on a new duty—a pretty strange one. See, as a truancy officer, I usually patrol looking for kids trying to ditch their classes. When I find them, I ticket them—or rather, their parents—and get them to where they need to be. Well, I got called in by Sergeant Purser yesterday, on my day off, so he could tell me about my new assignment.

It seems that some kid named Thomas Miller was expelled from school yesterday for fighting. I guess with everything that's been going on lately . . . the school shootings and violence and all . . . Higher-ups must think the kid is gonna hurt someone.

I looked into the kid's profile, and I can see what they mean, but I just don't think it's gonna happen. Call it a hunch. [sigh] Oh, well. I'll begin my observation today . . . Here we go.

I spent all day yesterday watching this kid . . . nothing. He lives in a crappy little apartment with his dad. They live on the bottom floor, so I can go peek in the window sometime. At first, I waited in my car because the shades were all closed. Finally, the kid's dad opened the shades and left about 7:30 AM. Probably for work.

Once Dad left, I looked in to see what was going on. Nothing. Kid was probably sleeping. A couple hours later, I checked again. Kid was playing some video game. I checked again an hour later—same story. An hour later—no change.

That was when I realized this whole damn thing is political. The chief just doesn't want to get caught with his pants down . . . who can blame him. Anyway, the most exciting thing the kid did all day was switch from playing the video game to surfing the Net. I couldn't see what websites he was going to. Coulda been buying knitting needles . . . or looking up a recipe for a bomb.

April 1, 2013. It's morning again and I'm sitting in my car outside the kid's apartment . . . again. I've had way too much

**ELEMENTS OF THE GENRE**

A diary entry is a first-person narrative in which the writer records thoughts and observations.

**STYLE**

A diary entry is very casual; it often reads/sounds like a person's speaking voice. In this case, Neil has adapted some literary narrative elements, and has written this piece almost like dialogue or even a short scene from a play.

**DESIGN**

In this case, Neil has provided a transcript of the audio diary. He has formatted it as a Word document; it looks like an essay.

Neil clearly appeals to ethos by choosing a truancy officer to be the speaker in this creative audio diary. The officer has authority and knowledge of teen behavior. Neil also appeals to pathos by presenting the officer as a sympathetic character; he also uses humor.

**MODES & MEDIA**
Neil created an audio diary, which could just as easily have been a video diary. Either can be delivered in a digital environment. When he submitted his project, he included this paper transcript of the recording.

time to think just sitting here. I'm starting to wonder if what I'm doing is even legal. Course, even if it isn't, I wouldn't bring it up with Sergeant Purser. Up until now, I've enjoyed my job and I'd like to keep it. Besides, there's probably some new amendment to the Patriot Act.

But this kid never leaves the damn house. I wanna go invite him out to Denny's . . . McDonald's, 7-Eleven, anything! Who doesn't leave their house?

It's the end of the day. Another day this kid hasn't moved. Seems to be having fun with his games, though. At least one of us is having a good time. He went online again today. I hope the kid is getting a girlfriend or something. [chuckle]

I wonder if his dad even knows he's been expelled. Wouldn't surprise me if he didn't . . . They never talk to each other.

April 2, 2013. I think I got too many of my personal thoughts in this thing yesterday. I guess I forgot I may have to turn this over to a court someday. Hopefully not. Problem is, it might be the only thing keeping me sane on this job. Hmm, either way I gotta try and keep it more professional today.

I just checked on the Miller kid . . . like I do every hour. He's back at it, playing his game. His father left approximately forty-five minutes ago. I'm going to go approach the window and see what I can see.

Ah geez . . . I went up to the window, and I was being as sneaky as a person can be in daylight, but I think the kid might've seen me . . . [pause] Hmmm, you know, I didn't think about this before, but if he sees me . . . [chuckle] I won't have to do this crappy duty anymore. I'll lie low out here for a while, maybe he didn't notice me after all.

[laughing] Wow, now that was surprising. The kid walks out his door, looks me straight in the eye, and hocks a loogie from his patio to the hood of my car. Man, that kid has got range! Since he didn't pull a gun and blow me away, I doubt the kid's actually gonna hurt anyone. Still, he's got some nerve to go spitting on a cop car.

Anyway, my cover is blown so I'm heading back to Purser's office now . . . He'll probably rip me a new one, but that's better than working this job. What a waste. Rendar out.

*Credit: Neil Carr.*

Typically the source for a diary entry is the writer's own experience. In this case, however, Neil is channeling a truancy officer's voice and experience. He has also based this on his research on how gamers respond to video games, and what video games may or may not have to do with violence.

# Guided Reading | A Multigenre Project

In her multigenre project, "When Worlds Collide: Why Superheroes Matter," Gwen Ganow represents a variety of genres and media, as her table of contents shows (see below). To learn more about Gwen's project, see Chapters 4 and 5.

▲ STUDENT
AUTHOR PHOTO
**Gwen Ganow.**
*Credit: Gwen Dalynn Ganow.*

## Gwen Ganow (STUDENT), *When Worlds Collide: Why Superheroes Matter*

| GWEN'S RHETORICAL SITUATION & CHOICES | | MULTIGENRE PIECES |
| --- | --- | --- |

**PURPOSE**
Gwen's overall purpose is to persuade her audience that superheroes can help convey hope and strength to marginalized people who experience intolerance.

**AUDIENCE**
Gwen's primary audience is comic book readers; she sequenced the genre pieces to immerse readers in the world of the superhero right away.

**RHETORICAL APPEALS**
The film review, researched argument, and brochure rely on ethos and logos. The journal entry, memoir, and film review rely on pathos.

**MODES & MEDIA**
A mix of text and visuals help readers visualize, relate to, and interpret the world of the superhero.

◄ What is the author/artist, Gwen Ganow, doing?

What are the parts? ►
How do they work together?

---

**When Worlds Collide:
Why Superheroes Matter**

Gwen Ganow

**Project Contents**

1. Introduction 2
2. The Research: God, Superman, Batman, The Punisher, and Me 3
3. The Collage: Superheroes, Strength, Hope, and Justice 6
4. The Journal: The Worst Day of My Life 8
5. The Brochure: Gay/Straight Alliance: Be a Superhero 19
6. The Review: *X-Men*: Mutants R Us 22
7. The Presentation: We Are All Mutants: Why the Original *X-Men* Movie Still Matters 26
8. The Narrative: The Ties That Bind 29

*Credit: Gwen Dalynn Ganow.*

---

Gwen's project consists of:

A **researched argument**

A **journal entry**

A **brochure**

A **film review**

A **PowerPoint presentation**

A **memoir**

**To unify her project, Gwen provides:**

An **Introduction** that offers context. In it, she explains her research and rhetorical choices, and evaluates her project (item 1).

**Packaging.** Gwen puts her project together in a Word document that she can e-mail to her instructor. This format suits her project because some of her genre pieces—such as her film review and PowerPoint—include embedded links to film clips and other media.

Let's examine the brochure from Gwen's multigenre project.

## PURPOSE

In this brochure, Gwen makes a case for gay marriage, arguing for tolerance and presenting an invitation to a GSA (Gay/Straight Alliance) meeting. The brochure relates to her project on superheroes, "otherness," and acceptance.

## AUDIENCE

The audience for this piece is specifically gay teens, but Gwen also makes it relevant for her wider audience of comics/superhero fans as well as her classmates and instructor.

## RHETORICAL APPEALS

Gwen uses mainly pathos in this piece, both in her list (e.g., "Secrets hurt" and "You're not alone") and by choosing festive images of kissing couples.

## MODES & MEDIA

This piece can be used as a physical flyer or shared on digital media (in which case it can include links to the GSA, for example).

◀ What is the author/artist, Gwen Ganow, doing?

What makes this a persuasive ▶ brochure?

**Superhero GSA Brochure**
**Gay/Straight Alliance: Be a Superhero**

 Sometimes you are Superman, and sometimes you are just Clark Kent, but your gay identity should never be hidden within yourself.

 If your parents love you even though you're an alien/mutant/superhero, they'll still love you even if you're gay.

 All gay superheroes need a Fortress of Solitude. One can be found in your GLBT (Gay, Lesbian, Bisexual, and Transgender) resource center.

 Superheroes fight for what is right. This includes the coexistence of all religions, all skin colors, and all sexual orientations.

 Sticks and stones will not break your steel bones.

 Secrets hurt everyone, even superheroes.

 Bigotry and hatred can be just as deadly as kryptonite. Always stand up for yourself, and let strength and hope guide your path.

 You're not alone. Superheroes have to struggle and fight for what they believe in.

 Captain America fights for freedom, democracy, and the American way. He desires these things for ALL Americans.

Hear ye! Hear ye!
The GSA of Metropolis would like to invite all gay and straight superheroes to its first meeting of the year. Come as you are with an open heart and an open mind for a "brown bag" discussion on marriage in the twenty-first century. Through support for each other, we can lead the way for humanity.
The GSA meeting will be held at the time and place stated below:
GSA Headquarters
5655 W. Kent Ave.
Metropolis
Special Guest Speaker, Captain America
5-7 p.m.
Capes and refreshments will be provided.

*Credit: Gwen Dalynn Ganow.*

## ELEMENTS OF THE GENRE

Brochures are usually used to inform and/or persuade an audience, which is the case here. They are usually brief, to the point, and visual.

## STYLE

Gwen uses a casual but persuasive tone, and plays with the concept of the superhero to move readers/viewers to action.

## DESIGN

She works in two columns to present her content. In column 1 she chooses gay pride flags instead of bullets to telegraph the message behind the brochure. In column 2 she presents her eye-catching images and centers the invitation to the meeting.

## SOURCES

Gwen draws on the sources she has used in her research. See her Works Cited list in Chapter 5 (p. 83).

# Guided Reading | A Multigenre Project

In his multigenre project, Dawson Swan works with a variety of genres and media, as the image below shows.

▲ STUDENT
AUTHOR PHOTO

**Dawson Swan.**
*Credit: Dawson Swan.*

## Dawson Swan (STUDENT), *The Threat of Nature Deficit Disorder*

What is the ▶
author/artist,
Dawson Swan,
doing?

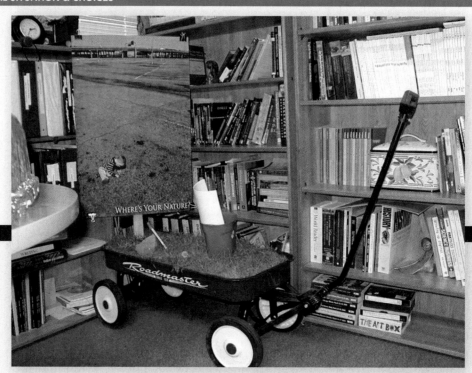

Credit: Dawson Swan.

**MULTIGENRE PIECES**

What are the ▶
parts? How do
they work
together?

### PURPOSE
Dawson's overall purpose is to persuade his audience that nature deficit disorder is real and that it should be taken seriously by parents, educators, and doctors.

### AUDIENCE
Dawson's primary audience is educated adults; his choice for packaging the components reflects his view that exposure to nature is important for all children.

### RHETORICAL APPEALS
Dawson's choice of the poster with a small child, the music CD, and the wagon used as packaging indicate that appeals to pathos are most important to him.

### MODES & MEDIA
Dawson's project includes print (the magazine article), audio (the CD), and visual pieces (the poster, the artwork with the CD, and the packaging).

### MULTIGENRE CONVENTIONS
There are no conventions for multigenre projects. However, there are conventions for individual genres. See Chapters 7–10 for examples.

### DAWSON'S PROJECT CONSISTS OF:
A **poster** (staked into a chunk of real dirt and grass, complete with a dandelion).

A **compilation CD,** leaning against a rock, of songs about nature, accompanied by liner notes that identify each song and the message it sends about nature.

A research-based **magazine article,** rolled up and "planted" in a green flowerpot.

### To unify his project, Dawson provides:

An **Introduction** that prepares his audience to experience his project and serves as his Author's/Artist's Statement. In it, he explains his research and rhetorical choices and evaluates his project (item 1).

**Packaging** consisting of a Roadmaster wagon, which represents childhood play and nature.

Let's take a closer look at Dawson's Introduction to his multigenre project.

**PURPOSE**
Dawson introduces his topic and argues for its importance.

**AUDIENCE**
The audience for this piece is people who don't understand the gravity of nature deficit disorder, so Dawson takes a serious tone.

**RHETORICAL APPEALS**
Dawson appeals to logos when he explains his genre choices and the order in which he wants them viewed/read and why.

**MODES & MEDIA**
The mode and medium were dictated by the assignment, which specified that the Introduction be a print-based essay. Dawson felt that visuals did not need to be part of the Introduction because the project itself was so eye-catching. So he used text exclusively to explain his decisions.

◀ What is the author/artist, Dawson Swan, doing?

What makes this an ▶ Introduction to a multigenre project?

**ELEMENTS OF THE GENRE**
Dawson begins by acknowledging that many people will initially view his topic as a joke; this helps him build rapport with his readers. He gives an overview of the different pieces in the project and prepares readers for what to expect.

**STYLE**
Dawson writes in a formal tone, which develops his ethos as someone who takes this issue seriously.

**DESIGN**
The design of Dawson's Introduction is minimal; he formats his Introduction into paragraphs for easy reading.

---

Dawson Swan

Introduction

**The Threat of Nature Deficit Disorder**

"Things are not like they used to be." I've heard this said many times in reference to technology, nature, parenting, music, and the world in general. That phrase will always be true because change is inevitable, but there is one change that is occurring unnoticed today that I believe requires our urgent attention. This change has resulted in a condition that has recently been identified as nature deficit disorder (NDD). Richard Louv introduced this condition in his book *Last Child in the Woods: Saving Our Children from Nature-Deficit Disorder*. Most people have never heard of this "disease," and when they do hear about it, their initial reaction is that it is a joke, just a clever play on words. Unfortunately NDD and the misery it causes are very real (pp. 22–24).

In today's society, it seems we no longer have time to relax, to take a walk outside and smell the roses. Instead, we are bombarded by tight schedules, economic pressures, and chronic stress. The former secretary of education Richard Riley was quoted as saying, "The top ten jobs that will be in demand in 2010 didn't exist in 2004. Students are being prepared for jobs that don't exist, using technologies that haven't been invented, to solve problems that we don't know about yet" (qtd. in Fisch). This shows how incredibly overwhelming it can be to simply live in our culture and to plan for the future, let alone find time to be outside.

Due to continually advancing technology, globalization is becoming a reality. The quantity of data created every day is increasing exponentially. Toddlers are learning to use technology scientists wouldn't have dreamed of thirty years ago. As a result, it is becoming vitally important to train our children about technology. Fortunately the young generations are easily able to learn to use technology, but there is always much more to be learned as technology continues to advance. The increasing need for technological "geeks" is drawing more and more of us into cyberspace and shoving nature off into a corner.

Ironically, going "green" is becoming increasingly popular. Our culture is reveling in new ways to better the environment and preserve nature, but it is seriously missing the point because the culture, particularly pop culture, has little firsthand knowledge of nature. We would rather stay inside and watch the hit TV show *Planet Earth* on our massive high-definition TVs than take a walk outside. Instead of climbing a mountain or sitting on our porch watching the sunset, we would rather sit in front of a computer monitor and look at beautiful photographs of exotic places. This misguided relationship with nature has created a synthetic environment and a secondhand relationship with the earth— an environment that is convenient and controlled. While those who have generated this environment are supposedly pursuing the natural, they have only created a vague reflection of the real thing. Our culture is sadly lacking in an understanding of the true meaning of "natural."

Now you may ask, "Why should I care? I get enough nature from the Discovery Channel and an occasional ski trip." Well, look at it this way. The generation that is currently approaching, or is already in, the child-rearing stage is the largest generation ever (Tapscott 20). The men and women of this generation are going to begin having children, and the decisions they make about how they raise their children will have a monumental impact on the future.

The logical next question you may ask is, "Is NDD a real threat?" Yes it is, and its effects can be devastating: obesity, ADD, emotional disorders, high blood pressure, and chronic pain that kids develop decades before they should. These conditions have always been there, but now they are disturbingly prevalent.

This project serves a couple of purposes: First, I want to inform people of NDD, and if they already know about it, I want to increase their knowledge and alert them to how urgent it is to take action. Second, I hope that this project gives inspiration to fight NDD. It can be as easy as walking outside, looking up at the stars, or smelling the fragrance of a wildflower in the night air.

I planned each part of the project to fit into a different category of media so I could communicate to more people. My first piece is a poster that can be displayed nearly anywhere, and it quickly draws people in—far more than an essay or a brochure can. A poster evokes emotion and thoughts of childhoods spent playing outside. This sets them up for my second piece.

*(Continues on next page)*

Dawson Swan, *The Threat of Nature Deficit Disorder*     **313**

The second and third pieces actually merge into a CD album, which can reach people on multiple levels. The artwork for the album is made up of photographs I have taken of nature during the last couple of years. These pictures grab the attention of the viewer and create a relaxing and thought-provoking environment for them to take part in as they experience the second half of the album—the music and lyrics (I searched through hundreds of songs to find specific songs about nature). I wrote an Introduction to the album that describes the purpose of each piece and its message. My fourth piece is a magazine article. It could appear in parenting magazines because my primary audience is people who are moving into, or are in, the childbearing years, and because children are most susceptible to NDD.

I have concluded that these pieces fit together best in a conference setting where the poster in a booth would initially draw people. Then they would see the CD. It could be considered a fund-raiser for my topic or maybe just a sampler. After leafing through the pages of artwork and listening to the music, people would want to know what it's all about, and they could read the magazine article. The article brings everything home and explains NDD in depth. Between these four pieces, a variety of media are used to grab people's attention, engaging both their minds and hearts. NDD is a compelling subject that affects everyone. Although a presentation of the simple facts of NDD would be enough to win people over, the potential of engaging them emotionally just as nature herself does, is fulfilled through photographs, poetry, and music.

————————

Works Cited

Fisch, Karl. "Did You Know 2.0?" YouTube, www.youtube.com/
    watch?v=pMcfrLYDm2U&feature=related. Accessed 13
    Oct. 2012.

Louv, Richard. *Last Child in the Woods: Saving Our Children
    from Nature-Deficit Disorder.* Algonquin, 2005, pp. 22–24.

Tapscott, Don. *Growing Up Digital: The Rise of the Net
    Generation. McGraw-Hill,* 1998, p. 20.

*Credit: Dawson Swan.*

**SOURCES**
Dawson incorporates three outside sources: two books and a video that went viral in 2007 about how the world is changing. He uses the MLA style of documentation, which requires parenthetical in-text citations that are, in turn, included in a Works Cited list. (See also MLA coverage in Chapter 13.)

# 11 EXPLORING TOPICS & CREATING A RESEARCH PROPOSAL

In this chapter, we will follow student Jasmine Huerta through her research process. Note that the process Jasmine uses is a typical research process, but it is not the only process. Many researchers do things in a different order, use different strategies, and so on. The more you research, the more you will tailor processes to fit you and what works for you.

# Considering Your Rhetorical Situation

As with everything you compose, you should start by thinking about your rhetorical situation—your purpose and audience. If you are responding to a research assignment, your instructor may have stipulated a particular purpose and audience, or you may be able to choose those on your own. Sometimes instructors also stipulate what types of sources you need to use. Be sure you understand what your instructor expects and how much latitude you have to make choices.

# Choosing a Topic Through Basic Research

The internet offers an unlimited source of topics, and beginning your reading can be exciting but overwhelming: You can easily locate millions of resources on any topic simply by doing a quick online search. That's why it's important to go about the process in an orderly fashion. This chapter will show you the steps you need to take.

Whenever you write—as a student in a composition classroom or a professional in a workplace—you focus on a specific topic. Sometimes you may be provided with a general theme or a specific topic or issue. For example, your instructor might ask you to respond to an essay you've read for class, or your manager at work might ask you to share your plans to improve business or increase sales in the next quarter. Other times, most often in the course of college work, you can start from scratch and choose a topic purely out of your own interest and curiosity.

So how do you choose a topic? Where should you start? One place might be this book. The Index of Themes (p. T-1) organizes every reading in this text by topic, and the Index of Genres (p. G-1) will help you see the relationship between topic choice and genre choice.

## 1. Brainstorm Topic Ideas | What Are You Curious About?

The best way to get started on identifying a topic that is meaningful to you is to get your ideas flowing. Whether you're composing from your own experience or composing based on research, you can use the same prewriting techniques that we discussed in Chapter 4: talk to people, make a brainstorm list, make a mind map, and freewrite.

In addition to those strategies, find out what others have already said about the topic, and discuss those ideas with others.

**Do some preliminary reading online, but be disciplined about it.**   Google a few things you are interested in to find some potential topics to research. You can find out what's in the news or what others are talking about by going to news sources, like *The New York Times* or the *Wall Street Journal*, and opinion sources, like *Salon* and *Slate*. If you want to skim scholarly sources, try Google Scholar (scholar.google.com). If you go to *Wikipedia*, be sure to look at the source links for the entries you read. That's where you'll find the best leads. And don't spend all day on it: Remember, you're generating ideas, not surfing mindlessly. To come up with a healthy list of topic ideas, try answering the following questions. Keep in mind any topic restrictions built into your assignment.

### ACTIVITY: GENERATING IDEAS FOR TOPICS

1. Ideas come out of conversations. What comes up in your talks with friends? What was the topic of your last discussion or disagreement? What are some of your unresolved questions about the topic?

2. Ideas come out of our passions. What are you passionate about?

3. Ideas come out of pet peeves. What bothers you on a regular basis? What would you change about your campus, town, state, country, or the world, if you were in charge?

4. Ideas come out of our curiosities. What are you curious about?

5. Ideas come out of our concerns. What do you worry about?

## 2. Explore Topic Ideas Through Preliminary Research | Ask Yourself, Who's Saying What?

Once you've identified a topic area, you're ready to dig a little deeper to better understand it. Keep a few possibilities in mind and conduct preliminary research on several related topics (or subtopics) so you can make an informed decision about which one to commit to; the viability of each topic will depend on what you find out at this point. As with the preliminary reading you did during brainstorming, you'll continue to draw on sources written for nonexperts. Later in your process, you'll move on to more specialized sources using scholarly databases. As you conduct preliminary research, focus on the following:

**Words and facts.**   Ask yourself some questions. Are there terms you need to define? And what are the facts?

**Opinions.**   Find out what others have to say on the subject, and notice what evidence they use to support their opinions. In addition to facts, what opinions surround your topic? Who writes about the topic, and why are they concerned? On what sources do they base their statements or arguments? What sources do they draw on? And what sources might you want to use too?

**Your perspective.**   Form your own arguments in response to others. As you research, you will begin to form your own ideas and opinions about your topic.

**Conflicting views.**   Notice those who disagree about your topic. When you begin reading sources related to your topic, you might begin to notice that there are viewpoints that stand opposed to each other. Furthermore, as you dig into these disagreements, you might realize that the differing viewpoints are well researched and should not be immediately dismissed. Discovering well-researched, well-reasoned opposing stances related to your topic forces you to accept that there is not necessarily one correct viewpoint; reasonable people can disagree.

**Irrational arguments.**   Avoid arguments that are just too out there. In the course of your research, you may stumble upon the ideas of people who are unreasonable, ill informed, or both. Keep a critical eye as you read sources.

**Key terms.**   As you conduct preliminary research, you'll notice that certain terms pop up. Follow up on these key terms by using them in your searches of the internet and library databases.

Following is an assignment we give our students during their preliminary research phase. It includes the responses of a student, Jasmine Huerta, whose research topic is diabetes. (Note: We will see more of her work on this project later in the chapter.)

▲ **STUDENT AUTHOR**

**Jasmine Huerta.** *In this chapter, we follow this student as she chooses and investigates a topic (diabetes). Jasmine appears next on page 325, Finding Facts About Diabetes.* Credit: Claudelle Girard/ iStock/Getty Images.

Through answering the assigned questions, Jasmine realizes that she has several interesting potential research questions to pursue. The list of key terms helped her continue and refine her research. She realized that the glycemic index is not 100 percent accepted, which surprised and intrigued her. By using the internet to find key terms, exploring some of these potential subtopics, previewing and reading sources, and then reflecting on her process and discoveries, Jasmine narrows her topic from diabetes to the role of nutrition in the diabetic patient.

ASSIGNMENT   **Jasmine Huerta** (STUDENT), *What Is Your Topic?*

**English 101**

Professor Braziller

September 26, 2019

Respond to the following questions to see how workable your topic may be.

1.  **What is the general topic area you are considering?**

    I am interested in researching and writing about diabetes.

◀ To the left, in blue type, are Jasmine's very early ideas about her diabetes project and some information on what she's discovered during preliminary research.

*(Continues on next page)*

2. **Why? Are you truly fascinated/curious/passionate about the topic? How did you become interested in this topic? (If your answer is no, explain why and then move on to the next topic without answering any more questions.)**

   Diabetes runs in my family, so it's something I want to understand more about in case I am faced with it at some point. My six-year-old cousin has type 1 diabetes. My mother had gestational diabetes when she was pregnant with me. Most recently, my grandfather, who is a bit overweight (as is my cousin), was diagnosed with diabetes. I'm wondering if I am just destined to develop it at some point because of my family history. I also wonder if perhaps there are things I can do to prevent the disease, since I presently don't have diabetes. I worry about both my cousin and grandfather, so I'd like to see if there are some things they could do to keep their diabetes under control, rather than just relying on traditional medicine.

3. **What surprising facts have you gathered so far about your topic? What further questions do you have that you need answered with data?**

   Surprising facts/data:
   - According to *Wikipedia*'s entry "Diabetes" (accessed on 9/20/19): "Diabetic patients with neuropathic symptoms such as numbness or tingling in feet or hands are twice as likely to be unemployed as those without the symptoms."
   - A link found on the American Diabetes Association to an article on SmartBrief.com stated that those who are exposed to secondhand smoke have a greater risk of contracting diabetes.
   - According to an article about lifestyle and home remedies, found on the Mayo Clinic's page, diabetes can contribute to gum infections.

4. **Do reasonable people disagree about the topic? If so, what aspects of the topic do they disagree about? Who disagrees with whom? Name names.**

   There seems to be a bit of a debate about what makes the best approach for a diabetic diet. While surfing around on the internet, one of the big debates I found discussed the glycemic index and how it relates to managing diabetes. It seems that people used to think you just had to avoid high-sugar foods, but after reading a few articles, I realized that many researchers want to look more closely at using the glycemic index (taking into account carbohydrates) in working with diabetic diets.

In an article titled "Low–Glycemic Index Diets in the Management of Diabetes," Miller et al. argue that this is a positive approach. I found an editorial written by Marion Franz in the publication *Diabetes Care* that argues with this approach: "The Glycemic Index: Not the most effective nutrition therapy intervention." in the Mayo Clinic's advice column, "Ask a Diabetes Specialist," someone wrote to Dr. Maria Collazo-Clavel, asking, "Is the glycemic-index diet useful for people with diabetes?" She responds that it's very complicated to use this as a measure, cautioning that it might not be the best approach for everybody.

5. **Is the topic researchable in the time you have?**

I don't see any issues with researching the topic this semester. In a short amount of time I was able to find many sources and potential ideas. I have a number of family members who deal with diabetes. I can easily interview them. I also would like to contact a doctor who treats people with diabetes and arrange an interview, perhaps by phone or e-mail.

6. **What are some subtopics that have emerged in your research?**

Nutrition to manage diabetes, medication to manage diabetes, alternative treatments for diabetes, prevention of diabetes, social issues connected to diabetes.

7. **What questions might you pursue in further research, based on what you've discovered during preliminary research?**

- What types of diets are best for people with diabetes?
- How can diet prevent someone from getting diabetes if he or she has a family history of diabetes?
- How can following certain nutritional guidelines make diabetes go away?
- How can alternative treatments or natural medications be used instead of insulin?
- What countries have the highest rate of diabetes? What contributes to the high rate?

8. **What are some key terms that keep coming up in relation to this topic?**

Glycemic index, metabolism, blood sugar, hypertension, obesity, glucose monitoring, insulin.

# 3. Commit to a Single Topic | What Are You Most Curious About?

Once you've identified a general topic area, it's time to commit to one specific topic within it. The "What Is Your Topic?" assignment (p. 319) can assist you with this choice, as can the following questions:

**Is your topic compatible with your assignment? And can you make a strong argument about it?**   If your instructor has given you an assignment, read it carefully and consider the degree to which your topic will work. If you've been asked to make an argument, you might find yourself gravitating toward controversial issues — such as gun control, abortion, and censorship. However, we urge you to consider other, less obvious topics. For example, if you are interested in the subject of gun control, rather than choosing the topic of concealed weapons and constitutional rights, you might take the topic of gun control and examine the power that gun control groups, such as the NRA, hold in the political arena.

**Do you like your topic enough to stick with it?**   If you are not truly curious about your topic, you probably won't remain interested in your research beyond the first week or so. Choose something you really want to learn about, that has some connection to you and your life.

**What is your deadline, and how will it affect your plans for research?**   If your completed project is due in two weeks, choose a topic for which there is plenty of information that you can access easily. If you have more time, say an entire fifteen-week semester, you have the luxury of using a range of sources, and conducting interviews or surveys, for example, so you can select your topic accordingly. On the other hand, if your topic is so obscure that your only sources need to be ordered through interlibrary loan (which can take several weeks), it is not a good topic for either a two-week or fifteen-week deadline.

---

ATTENTION, RESEARCHERS

**Looking for something to argue about? Almost any topic offers argumentative angles: The key is to find the angles.**

For example, while "reading" may not seem like the most provocative topic, a quick Google search reveals that it's the subject of much debate. Some questions around this debate include: Do college students read more or less than in the past? Is online reading cognitively different from reading books? What is the relationship between how much we read and our development of critical thinking skills?

The point is to keep an open mind to topics that seem vanilla. You may find some spice under the surface.

---

**Will you find appropriate sources for your topic?** Some topics are so current that there is little or no published research available. For example, a friend who works in the field of bioengineering might tell you that scientists are developing crops with deeper roots to reduce the amount of carbon dioxide in the atmosphere, but because the research has just begun, there are no published articles about it. In this case, you might want to shift your topic toward an aspect of bioengineering that is more researchable in the present.

# 4. Form a Working Research Question | Refine as You Go

**What's your general topic? What questions will move you from a basic, broad idea to more specific ideas?** Creating research questions focuses your attention from a general topic to a specific aspect of the topic, as follows:

| GENERAL TOPIC | Diabetes |
|---|---|
| WORKING RESEARCH QUESTIONS | What causes diabetes? |
| | What is the latest medical research on diabetes? |
| | How can people avoid getting diabetes? |

While you'll ask (and answer) lots of questions in your research, your research question is the big question, the one that you are ultimately interested in answering.

But as you discover more about your topic, you might revise your question to reflect what you're learning, as follows:

| REVISED RESEARCH QUESTION | What is the relationship between nutrition and diabetes? |
|---|---|

**What questions—focused on finding facts and defining terms—can move you toward a final research question?** As you begin your research, many of your questions will be focused on gathering facts and defining terms. If, as in the example above, you're researching the general topic of diabetes, you will ask questions at the outset such as the following:

| BASIC FACT-FINDING QUESTIONS | What causes diabetes? |
|---|---|
| | Who is affected by it, and why? |
| | What alternative treatments are there (as opposed to insulin)? |
| | What is the role of glucose and the glycemic index? |

WRITE

What is the general topic of your research? What are your questions about it so far? Which questions have to do with finding facts? Which ones are more about analysis? What, in your early research, has surprised you most?

Your research question, however, should focus on more complex *analysis*. Following are some examples of revised, more final research questions:

RESEARCH QUESTIONS

How can changes in diet help a person manage diabetes?

How can managing sugar and sodium intake help someone avoid taking insulin?

Why does the traditional medical establishment not promote alternatives to insulin injections?

Notice how these questions require extensive research and even speculation, especially the last question. These would make solid research questions, while the first set of questions would not, although they would be useful questions to ask in the course of researching one of the questions in the second list.

## CHECKLIST | Refining Your Research Question

What are the qualities of a really good research question? As you refine yours, ask yourself:

☐ **Is it appropriate for your rhetorical situation or assignment?**

☐ **Is it open-ended, meaning it cannot be answered with a simple yes, no, or maybe, or a single number?**

☐ **Are the terms of the question specific enough or too general?**

☐ **Can it be answered in the time you have— and with the resources you have access to?** You might have a fascinating and specific research question, but if you can't feasibly research it in the time you have, it just won't work.

☐ **Is it a question that you really want to find answers to?** The best research grows out of curiosity. No matter how good your research question is, if it isn't backed up by your genuine interest, it won't lead you to rich, interesting research.

# Moving from a Research Question to a Proposal

Now that you've got an understanding of how to explore a topic and form working research questions, let's look at some next steps.

While you may not follow every step that Jasmine takes as you work on your own research topic, tracing her process may give you ideas for how to proceed.

Ultimately, Jasmine moved from a research question to the argument she made in her final paper, which also became her title:

FINAL RESEARCH QUESTION

How can diet help someone with diabetes manage the disease and avoid taking insulin?

# Finding Facts About Diabetes

What was Jasmine's process? First, through her early reading, and as a person with a family history of the disease, Jasmine realizes that what interests her most are the dietary concerns of diabetics. With this in mind, she begins to explore a few more sources.

*Wikipedia* is her starting point. Even though her instructor has cautioned the class against using *Wikipedia* as a source (see our advice about *Wikipedia* in Step 1 earlier in this chapter), Jasmine sees it as a good starting point for general information, and perhaps some leads related to the dietary concerns of diabetics. She begins with the "Diabetes mellitus" page (when she typed in "Diabetes," she was redirected there).

After reading through the overview, Jasmine realizes that she needs information about the differences between type 1 diabetes and type 2 diabetes (which the entry explains is the more common form, and the one that can be treated through diet). She discovers she'll also need to explore diabetes in terms of blood glucose levels, metabolism, body weight, and insulin.

Of particular interest is the "References" section of the "Diabetes mellitus" page, which offers Jasmine a head start on exploring other sources.

▼ **WIKIPEDIA ENTRY**

**"Diabetes mellitus."** Jasmine reads through this entry with special attention to the "References" section for further resources for information on diet.

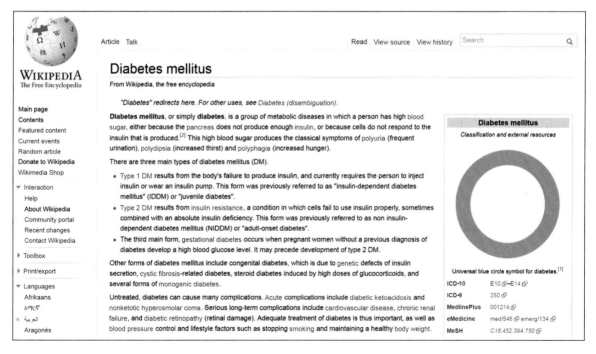

References

1. ^ "Diabetes Blue Circle Symbol" 🔗 International Diabetes Federation. 17 March 2006.

2. ^ "About diabetes" 🔗 World Health Organization. Archived from the original🔗 on 31 March 2014. Retrieved 4 April 2014.

3. ^ a b c d e f g h i j "Diabetes Fact sheet N°312" 🔗. WHO. October 2013. Archived from the original🔗 on 26 August 2013. Retrieved 25 March 2014.

4. ^ Kitabchi, AE; Umpierrez, GE; Miles, JM; Fisher, JN (Jul 2009). "Hyperglycemic crises in adult patients with diabetes." 🔗. Diabetes Care. 32 (7): 1335–43. doi:10.2337/dc09-9032🔗. PMC 2699725🔗. PMID 19564476🔗.

5. ^ a b c d e f Shoback, edited by David G. Gardner, Dolores (2011). "Chapter 17". Greenspan's basic & clinical endocrinology (9th ed.). New York: McGraw-Hill Medical. ISBN 0-07-162243-8.

6. ^ RSSDI textbook of diabetes mellitus. 🔗 (Rev. 2nd ed.). New Delhi: Jaypee Brothers Medical Publishers. 2012. p. 235. ISBN 9789350254899.

7. ^ a b c "The top 10 causes of death Fact sheet N°310" 🔗. World Health Organization. Oct 2013.

8. ^ Rippe, edited by Richard S. Irwin, James M. (2010). Manual of intensive care medicine🔗 (5th ed.). Philadelphia: Wolters Kluwer Health/Lippincott Williams & Wilkins. p. 549. ISBN 9780781799928.

9. ^ Picot, J; Jones, J; Colquitt, JL; Gospodarevskaya, E; Loveman, E; Baxter, L; Clegg, AJ (September 2009). "The clinical effectiveness and cost-effectiveness of bariatric (weight loss) surgery for obesity: a systematic review and economic evaluation". Health Technology Assessment (Winchester, England). 13 (41): 1–190, 215–357, iii–iv. doi:10.3310/hta13410🔗. PMID 19726018🔗.

10. ^ Cash, Jill (2014). Family Practice Guidelines🔗 (3rd ed.). Springer. p. 396. ISBN 9780826168757.

11. ^ a b "Update 2015" 🔗. IDF. International Diabetes Federation. p. 13. Retrieved 21 Mar 2016.

38. ^ Visser J, Rozing J, Sapone A, Lammers K, Fasano A (2009). "Tight junctions, intestinal permeability, and autoimmunity: celiac disease and type 1 diabetes paradigms." 🔗. Ann N Y Acad Sci. 1165: 195–205. doi:10.1111/j.1749-6632.2009.04037.x🔗. PMC 2886850🔗. PMID 19538307🔗.

39. ^ a b Risérus U, Willett WC, Hu FB (January 2009). "Dietary fats and prevention of type 2 diabetes" 🔗. Progress in Lipid Research. 48 (1): 44–51. doi:10.1016/j.plipres.2008.10.002🔗. PMC 2654180🔗. PMID 19032965🔗.

40. ^ Malik VS, Popkin BM, Bray GA, Després JP, Hu FB (2010-03-23). "Sugar Sweetened Beverages, Obesity, Type 2 Diabetes and Cardiovascular Disease risk" 🔗. Circulation. 121 (11): 1356–64. doi:10.1161/CIRCULATIONAHA.109.876185🔗. PMC 2862465🔗. PMID 20308626🔗.

41. ^ Malik VS, Popkin BM, Bray GA, Després JP, Willett WC, Hu FB (November 2010). "Sugar-Sweetened Beverages and Risk of Metabolic Syndrome and Type 2 Diabetes: A meta-analysis"🔗. Diabetes Care. 33 (11): 2477–83. doi:10.2337/dc10-1079🔗. PMC 2963518🔗. PMID 20693348🔗.

42. ^ Hu EA, Pan A, Malik V, Sun Q (2012-03-15). "White rice consumption and risk of type 2 diabetes: meta-analysis and systematic review" 🔗. BMJ (Clinical research ed.). 344: e1454. doi:10.1136/bmj.e1454🔗. PMC 3307808🔗. PMID 22422870🔗.

43. ^ Lee IM, Shiroma EJ, Lobelo F, Puska P, Blair SN, Katzmarzyk PT (1 July 2012). "Effect of physical inactivity on major non-communicable diseases worldwide: an analysis of burden of disease and life expectancy" 🔗. The Lancet. 380 (9838): 219–29. doi:10.1016/S0140-6736(12)61031-9🔗. PMC 3645500🔗. PMID 22818936🔗.

44. ^ a b "National Diabetes Clearinghouse (NDIC). National Diabetes Statistics 2011" 🔗. U.S. Department of Health and Human Services. Retrieved 22 April 2014.

Jasmine looks closely at the "External links" section of *Wikipedia* and decides to investigate the American Diabetes Association (ADA). She finds out that the ADA is a nonprofit group whose purpose is to control diabetes, especially through improving healthcare access, funding research, and prevention.

As Jasmine explores the ADA's page, she notices a "Food & Fitness section" that she's especially drawn to because of her interest in nutrition.

In the "Food & Fitness" section, Jasmine is surprised by the emphasis on recipes and meal planning as ways to control the disease. She finds the following information especially interesting:

- Beans, berries, and tomatoes are diabetes "superfoods."
- We shouldn't just look at the sugar content on food labels. It's more useful to examine the total carbohydrate number.
- Recipes for diabetics are not dull. The site includes recipes for Texas Tuna Burger, Asian Roast Pork Sliders, and Whole Wheat Pancakes.

As Jasmine continues to read through the ADA site, she gets more absorbed in the idea that eating specific kinds of foods can assist in managing diabetes. She decides her next step is to find more information on nutrition, maybe even some more recipes designed for diabetics. A hospital or research facility might be another good source, she thinks, and she decides to check out the Mayo Clinic site.

There she finds information on diabetes, along with meal plans and recipes. She gets even more interested in the relationship between diet and diabetes management.

Jasmine notices a recipe for Blackberry Iced Tea. The recipe itself, and the surrounding information, presents Jasmine with a few things to think about. First, the "Dietitian's tip" mentions that most herbal teas are caffeine-free, which makes her wonder about the connection between caffeine and the health of a diabetic. She also notices the use of cinnamon and ginger and wonders how these natural ingredients might benefit a diabetic. In the nutritional analysis of the recipe, Jasmine sees that the drink is low in calories and does not contain any sodium. She wonders if these are important concerns; before she started browsing recipes at the ADA and the Mayo Clinic, Jasmine knew that diabetics should avoid sugar, but she hadn't been taking sodium and calorie content into consideration.

Now that Jasmine has done some exploratory, informational reading, she's ready to see what scholars have to say about managing diabetes through diet. She moves on to look for sources that will offer viewpoints and arguments about diabetes and nutrition.

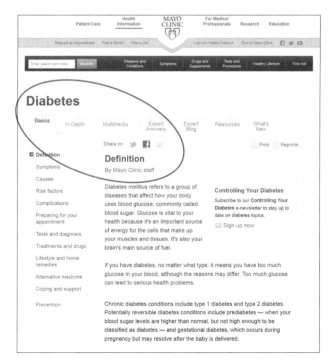

◀ **WEBSITE**

**Mayo Clinic.** On their "Diabetes" page, the Mayo Clinic provides a definition of the disease. Jasmine is interested to see how this information compares to that of the ADA.

*Credit: Mayo Foundation for Medical Education and Research.*

## Gathering Opinions About Diabetes

Jasmine looks for other sources—including a journal article, a website, and a YouTube video—to provide current viewpoints on nutrition as prevention/treatment for diabetes.

## 1. *Progress in Lipid Research* Article

When Jasmine looks at the references on the *Wikipedia* entry, she finds a peer-reviewed journal article entitled "Dietary Fats and Prevention of Type 2 Diabetes." When she goes to the article, she finds in the introduction this statement:

> Dietary composition could play a significant role in improving insulin sensitivity and reducing risk of diabetes and its composition. Risérus, Ulf, Walter C. Willett, and Frank B. Hu. "Dietary Fats and Prevention of Type 2 Diabetes."
>
> *Progress in Lipid Research*, vol. 48, issue 1, 2009, pp. 44–51.

## 2. The Joslin Diabetes Center

At this site, Jasmine reads the views of Amy Campbell, a Joslin nutritionist and the coauthor of a book titled *16 Myths of a Diabetic Diet*. Campbell states that there is no such thing as a "diabetic diet." Jasmine finds the following quote from Campbell on a Joslin page titled "The Truth About the So-Called 'Diabetes Diet'":

> A person with diabetes can eat anything a person without diabetes eats.
>
> **Amy Campbell,** from "The Truth About the So-Called 'Diabetes Diet'"

## 3. "Introduction to Clinical Nutrition and Diabetes" Video

On YouTube, Jasmine finds a video produced by USF Health (University of South Florida College of Public Health). In it, USF medical student Candace Haddox explains some of the connections between nutrition and diabetes management. In the video, "Introduction to Clinical Nutrition and Diabetes," Haddox suggests:

> You don't have to go straight to medication. There is something that you can do and it actually happens to be the most effective and that is a lifestyle modification: a little bit of weight loss, you know, fixing up the diet. . . .

## CHECKLIST | Narrowing a Topic

As you start your research, consider following these steps:

☐ **Brainstorm topic ideas.**
- ☐ Read what others have said.
- ☐ Google your topic (but stay focused).
- ☐ Discuss what you find with others.

☐ **Start writing informally.**
- ☐ Make a list of topics that interest you, double it, then double it again.
- ☐ Freewrite about your topic.
- ☐ Sketch out a mind map.

☐ **Do preliminary research.**
- ☐ Ask questions of fact and definition so that you will understand the more complex research you do later.
- ☐ What arguments have others made about your topic? How do they support their views?
- ☐ Note key terms to aid in later research.

☐ **Commit to a topic. Consider these factors:**
- ☐ Is the topic compatible with the assignment?
- ☐ Have you found an argumentative angle?
- ☐ Will you stay interested in this topic?
- ☐ Are there enough appropriate sources available for you to research in the time you have?

☐ **Form a research question. Consider these factors:**
- ☐ Does your question focus more on stating facts and defining terms? Or are you making an argument? Providing an analysis?
- ☐ Is your question open-ended?
- ☐ Is your question specific enough? If not, how will you move from a general question to a more specific one?
- ☐ Are you truly interested in finding answers to this question?
- ☐ What are some challenges you may come up against as you research this question, and how can you deal with these challenges?

Now that she's gathered some facts and arguments about diabetes, Jasmine decides to meet with her instructor to talk about a final research question and plan her research proposal.

## Creating a Research Proposal

A research proposal sets forth a writer's rationale for choosing a particular research question. For Jasmine, the proposal gives her an opportunity to fine-tune her research question and her focus. Your instructor may ask you to turn in a proposal or a working bibliography that outlines your sources (see Guided Process: How to Create a Bibliography on pp. 334–35). Or your instructor might simply ask you to think about your research before looking more carefully at sources.

Even if your instructor does not assign a formal research proposal, it can be a great tool for use in planning your project. Following is a research proposal assignment that we give our students.

► ASSIGNMENT

**Research Proposal.**
Creating a research proposal is a great way to help you focus and plan. See below for Jasmine's completed assignment.

**English 101**
**Professor Braziller**

**Research Proposal Assignment: What Is Your Focus?**
This proposal will help you solidify your ideas for your semester's research. Your proposal should be approximately two double-spaced pages in MLA manuscript format. Your proposal should include the following:

1. Your research question
2. A working title for your project
3. A summary of your project. Identify your topic and describe what you will be looking at in terms of the topic. Include some key terms and additional questions that will guide your research.
4. A description of your purpose for working on this project. Why did you choose this topic? What do you hope to learn from this project?
5. A discussion of the key challenges you will face or you imagine you will face. What concerns do you have regarding the research/project?

Following is Jasmine's research proposal, in response to the above assignment.

► ASSIGNMENT

**Research Proposal.**
Jasmine has explored her topic and gathered facts and opinions from some solid sources, and she is now ready to share her ideas for what she plans to do next.

**English 101**
**Professor Braziller**

**Research Proposal Assignment: What Is Your Focus?**
Jasmine Huerta
English 101
October 7, 2019

**Research Proposal**
1. Your research question

    How can diet—specifically, monitoring the intake of sugar, calories, and sodium—help someone with diabetes manage the disease and avoid taking insulin?

2. A working title for your project

    The working title for my project is "Living with Diabetes: Diet Is the answer."

3. A summary of your project. Identify your topic and describe what you will be looking at in terms of the topic. Include some key terms and additional questions that will guide your research.

I plan to research and write about different ways you can control diabetes through nutritional choices. While there are medications used to control the disease, such as insulin, I'm more curious about natural approaches, such as diet. I want my readers to understand that diabetes doesn't have to be a death sentence and that even if you are predisposed to it, there are some simple things you can do to keep it from taking over your life or causing other health issues.

I also think, based on my research, that diet and nutrition might be just as powerful as insulin for some people. I wonder if doctors are too quick to prescribe insulin.

Much of the debate around diabetes has to do with the connection between diabetes and obesity. I wonder to what extent diabetes can be prevented by a healthy diet, one that helps people avoid obesity. Also, are there specific foods that children need to avoid? Are these different from what older people should avoid?

Besides researching different diabetes-related diets, I want to find out how people learn about these diets. Are there specific programs, initiatives, or educational tools used to get this information out to the public? How might schools and doctors share this information?

Following are some **key terms** I've discovered during my preliminary research: *glycemic index*, *metabolism*, *blood sugar*, *hypertension*, *obesity*, *glucose monitoring*, and *insulin*.

Following are some of the **questions that will guide my research:**

- What diets are best for diabetics?
- What foods do diabetics need to avoid?
- Can diet cure diabetes? If so, how?
- Can diet prevent someone from getting diabetes, even if he or she has a family history of the disease? If so, how?
- Can diet prevent someone's diabetes from getting worse? If so, how?
- Can dietary changes prevent or reduce a diabetic's dependence on insulin?

4. **A description of your purpose for working on this project. Why did you choose this topic? What do you hope to learn from this project?**

Diabetes runs in my family, so it's something that is very close to me. My cousin, who is only six years old, has

*(Continues on next page)*

type 1 diabetes. Just last month, my grandfather, who is somewhat overweight, but definitely not obese, was diagnosed with diabetes. When my mother was pregnant with me, she had gestational diabetes.

I believe I may be predisposed toward the disease, and I want to find out what I can do to avoid it. I also want to help my family by sharing what I learn—especially in terms of natural alternatives rather than traditional medicine.

5. **A discussion of the key challenges you will face or you imagine you will face. What concerns do you have regarding the research/project?**

My biggest challenge so far has been making sense of some terms I've encountered in my research. Some articles go into a lot of detail about the relationship of the glycemic index to insulin levels. Authors of these pieces also use technical terms such as pancreatic *islet cells*, *resistant starches*, and *macronutrients*.

Another challenge I might face is that my topic may be too narrow. Based on my research so far, it seems that many sources say yes, diet does contribute to diabetes prevention and management. But how might I expand on that? Will I end up just listing foods to eat and not to eat?

I think that trying to figure out if nutritional changes can actually replace insulin as treatment gives my project a good argumentative angle, but I am a little worried that I may end up arguing more strongly against insulin than I really want to.

I am also afraid of getting sidetracked and focusing too much on the obesity problem, especially in regard to children, and losing my focus on diabetes. While obesity is related, I really want to focus on preventing and managing the disease—and not so much on the causes of diabetes. While it's important to understand some of the causes, especially as they relate to nutrition, I'm more interested in prevention and treatment.

Now that Jasmine has written her proposal and submitted it to her instructor, she is ready to begin the next stage of her research.

## CHECKLIST | Creating a Research Proposal

What does a good research proposal do?

- ☐ **It assists you in organizing your project, and includes five major components:**
  - ☐ Research question (the main thrust of your research)
  - ☐ Working title
  - ☐ Summary of the project (a sketch of the research you've done, the questions you've raised, and the possible direction you will take, including the potential argument you may make)
  - ☐ Overall purpose (why you want to pursue this topic and project)
  - ☐ Potential challenges

- ☐ **It shows that you have a clear focus for your research.** Your research question and working title are specific, showing your reader the angle you are researching. Throughout the proposal, you include details rather than vague generalities. For example, Jasmine doesn't just write, "I want to learn how people find out about these diets." She adds these details: "Are there specific programs, initiatives, or educational tools. . . ."

- ☐ **It illustrates that you have done some preliminary research.** Your summary includes key terms that you discovered while doing research. While Jasmine might have previously thought of the key terms *obesity* and *insulin*, she probably had not considered such terms as *glycemic index* and *glucose monitoring*.

- ☐ **It gives reasons why you have selected your area of research.** By communicating why you chose your topic, your reader understands your choice, and you see why this research matters to you. By articulating these reasons, you stay more engaged.

- ☐ **It shows that you have considered potential challenges.** Anticipating challenges prepares you for the bumps you might hit during research. Additionally, a good research proposal tells your reader about those challenges so that you might be given assistance. For example, when Jasmine writes that she has encountered technical terms such as *pancreatic islet cells*, her reader might point her to resources where she can get help deciphering these terms.

# Organizing Your Sources

## Guided Process | How to Create a Bibliography

**Jasmine Huerta** (STUDENT), *Diabetes Project: Bibliography*

We highly recommend that you create an annotated working bibliography. A working bibliography is simply a list of the sources you've gathered and plan to refer to. An annotated bibliography is a working bibliography (a list of your sources) that includes your own brief notes about each source. In your annotations, you summarize each source, capturing its essence in a few sentences. If the source is argumentative, you also note the main points of the writer's argument. In addition, note the potential reliability of the source: Is it from a reliable site, news organization, or publication? Was it created by a source you can trust? How well do the source and its author fit with your research? What might the source add? What might be its drawbacks? (For details on evaluating sources, see Chapter 12.)

Here is how Jasmine describes her process:

> I began each entry with a basic summary. In my summaries, I note specific examples, such as unfamiliar terms or important evidence. I've also indicated my evaluation of how dependable each source is. When I quoted exact language from a source, I used quotation marks. I also made connections among my sources.

**ATTENTION, BIBLIOGRAPHERS**

The latest MLA guidelines require writers to include source URLs without http:// as is shown in Jasmine's bibliographies. Including URLs (or embedding hyperlinks in your paper) leaves no room for confusion about where you obtained information, and makes it easier and faster for your readers to check your sources. For sources accessed through a database such as *JSTOR*, provide a DOI, if available, rather than a URL. (See also Chapter 13.)

For online sources that do not include a date, include in your Works Cited list an "Accessed" date, as Jasmine does.

**Huerta 1**

### Annotated Working Bibliography/Works Cited

Brand-Miller, Jennie, et al. "Low–Glycemic Index Diets in the Management of Diabetes." *Diabetes Care*, vol. 26, no. 8, 2003, pp. 2261–67, care.diabetesjournals.org/content/26/8/2261.long.

The authors explore the controversy about whether a low-glycemic diet actually helps someone manage his or her diabetes. The article presents the research methods used, along with the results. Ultimately, the results of their study show that a low-glycemic diet did help patients manage their diabetes—in contrast to patients whose diets consisted of high-glycemic foods. The article is filled with unfamiliar terms such as "acarbose therapy." At the end is a list of footnotes and references that will be useful as I continue my research. This is a very reliable source because *Diabetes Care* is a peer-reviewed journal; also, the use of documentation reinforces the authors' ethos.

"Glycemic Index and Diabetes." American Diabetes Association, www.diabetes.org/food-and-fitness/food/planning-meals/glycemic-index-and-diabetes.html. Accessed 26 Sept. 2019.

The ADA's page on the glycemic index and its relationship to diabetes is an informative summary on the topic. It has three subheads, so readers can immediately find information: "What is the glycemic index?" "What affects the GI of a food?" And, "Is the GI a better tool than carbohydrate counting?" The article discusses how the glycemic index is affected by many things and is not simply determined by a food's type. For example, factors such as length of ripening and cooking time affect a food's glycemic index. The article is written for a general reader, so I found that I could understand all its terms and get a beginning grasp of the glycemic index. This article, too, is very reliable since the American Diabetes Association is a respected and noted organization related to the field.

Risérus, Ulf, Walter C. Willett, and Frank B. Hu. "Dietary Fats and Prevention of Type 2 Diabetes." *Progress in Lipid Research*, vol. 48, issue 1, 2009, pp. 44–51.

This article summarizes the research on the connection between dietary fat and diabetes and then discusses the results of a study of how dietary fats affect insulin resistance. That study found that replacing foods high in saturated fats with foods that do not have hydrogenated or partially hydrogenated fats has a positive effect on diabetes. The article contains a lot of medical jargon and technical terms, but because I am already somewhat familiar with diabetes and the concept of glucose metabolism, I was able to understand most of it. I believe this is the most reliable source I have found so far because it appears in a peer-reviewed scientific journal and the authors have received prestigious grants for their research.

"Simple Steps to Preventing Diabetes." *The Nutrition Source*, Harvard School of Public Health, www.hsph.harvard.edu/nutritionsource/diabetes-prevention/preventing-diabetes-full-story/index.html. Accessed 26 Sept. 2019.

This article focuses on ways to prevent type 2 diabetes. It gives statistics on the number of people affected by the disease and lists illnesses that the disease may cause, such as blindness. Prevention strategies are offered, such as diet and exercise. The writers sum up these strategies by saying, "Stay lean and stay active." This article, like the Brand-Miller piece, also includes a list of references, so I will add that to my potential project sources. Since this piece was published by a Harvard University site, I trust the information presented.

# CHECKLIST | Beginning Your Research

As you begin drawing on sources, forming your research questions, drafting your research proposal, and creating a bibliography, ask yourself the following questions:

## RHETORICAL SITUATION & CHOICES

☐ **Purpose.** What am I learning as I research? And how can I develop what I'm learning into a solid research question? Does it simply focus on facts (if so, it's not refined enough)? Or is it geared toward analysis and argument (if so, I'm heading in the right direction)?

☐ **Audience.** What expectations will my readers (my instructor, classmates, and any audience beyond) have regarding the quality of my sources? (See Chapter 12 for more on evaluating source quality.) As I gather sources into an annotated bibliography, how can I make certain that my notes on each source show readers its potential usefulness?

☐ **Rhetorical appeals.** How will I know whether to trust an author and source? What about a given author and source gives me confidence, or doubts? What techniques and appeals do authors use that I can adopt for my own purposes? To what degree do they use logos (logic) and pathos (emotion) to reach readers?

☐ **Modes & media.** How do modes and media come into play as I'm reading and choosing sources? Do my sources represent a range of modes and media?

## GENRE CONVENTIONS

☐ **Elements of the genre.** Does the author of this source draw on other sources? Does the author document the work of others?

☐ **Style.** When I look at a potential source, how much attention should I pay to the author's style? Are informal first-person pieces the right fit for my topic? Do I need to gather sources written in a variety of styles? To what extent do tone and level of detail contribute to a source's reliability?

☐ **Design.** When I look at a potential source, how important are design considerations?

☐ **Sources.** What documentation style will I use (MLA, APA, *Chicago*, other)?

# Organizing Your Sources

Want to experiment? Draft a research proposal. Create an annotated working bibliography.

Find a topic that interests you and work through the points in the Refining Your Research Question checklist until you develop a workable research question. Then do the following:

1. Draft a research proposal for your professor that includes:
   - A working title for your project (you can always change the title later, when you have a better idea of what your finished project will actually cover).
   - A summary of the project, including which aspects of the topic you will research.
   - A list of the keywords you've identified in the research you've done so far.
   - A discussion of your purpose in working on the project. This is where you'll discuss why you are interested in answering the research question.
   - A discussion of the challenges you anticipate facing in your project and strategies you can use to deal with them.
2. Keep an annotated working bibliography of all the sources you use, even ones you think you won't refer to in your final written report. You never know.
3. Annotate three sources you find particularly interesting or thought-provoking. In your annotation, discuss:
   - What the summary is about
   - The argument the source makes
   - How reliable you judge this source to be and why
   - How this source might be used in your project

# 12

# EVALUATING & CHOOSING SOURCES

n Chapter 11, we discussed how to begin your research to explore topics—and ultimately to come up with a research question and proposal. We assume in this chapter that you've done your preliminary research, you have a topic, and you are ready to focus in on an important aspect of that topic. In the following pages, we will discuss research in greater depth, covering how to identify a source that is appropriate, reliable, and useful to you.

# Getting Started with Sources

## What Are Sources?

The word *source* comes from the Anglo-French word *surse*, which means "to rise or to begin." Think of a source as a starting point. To cook something you've never made before, you might first refer to a cookbook, an online recipe database, or the Food Network for inspiration. To plan a trip, you might begin with sources including maps, photos, and brochures. To begin a research paper, you might refer to Google and online databases such as *EBSCOhost* and *ProQuest*, and consult research librarians and professors to shape and define your ideas and narrow your topic. In the context of this book, we see everything you read (or view, or listen to, or experience in any way), every text you encounter, every conversation you have, as a potential source for your writing. When you compose—whether in college or on the job—you draw on sources for information and opinions. These sources do more than get you started; they are also the texts that you'll converse with throughout your composing process, from your earliest topic ideas to your final project. (For more on early topic ideas, see Chapter 11. For information on later stages of research and writing, see Chapter 13.)

ATTENTION, RESEARCHERS

What research have you done for other courses? Where did you seek advice? What sources worked especially well? What do you wish you'd done differently or better?

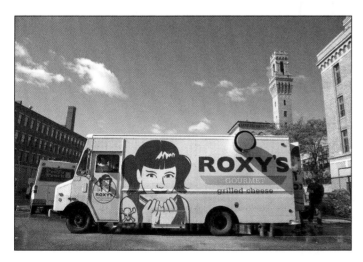

**◄ ARTIFACT**

**Roxy's Gourmet Grilled Cheese** is based in Boston. Researching food? A food truck or other eatery can be a valuable source of firsthand information.
*Credit: f 1.2/Alamy.*

Can a food truck be a source? Sure. Especially if you're researching the trend of food trucks, or the growing number of people who identify themselves as "foodies." Maybe you're interested in comparing the old-time ice-cream truck to the phenomenon of the food truck. Depending on your argument, you might use the truck as a starting point for your research, talking with its chef or operator to learn more about the business: its operation, clientele, and profitability. Or maybe about the food itself: the source of its ingredients and its nutritional value. (See roxysgrilledcheese.com.)

## Where Do I Find Sources?

Sources are everywhere. Imagine that a friend tells you about an upcoming debate about women's healthcare on campus; because she has provided you with information, your friend is a source. Let's say you become interested in the debate and decide to search your online campus newspaper for articles and editorials on the topic. Your campus paper and the materials it contains are sources. From there, you could learn

▶ STUDENT NEWSPAPER: EDITORIAL PAGE

**Accent: The Student Voice of Austin Community College.** Here a student offers a commentary on women's healthcare in the state of Texas, which has some of the most restrictive reproductive health policies in the country. Your own campus publication may provide an excellent source for ideas, facts, and opinions on your topic.

*Credit: The Accent.*

more by talking to a member of the campus health center staff, or a local activist organization supporting women's healthcare. The people you talk with and the discussions you have with them are sources.

## What Can Sources Do for Me?

For one thing, they help you make decisions. You use sources all the time—not only to inform your school and work projects, but to aid you in making informed choices. For example, you want to choose a movie to see this weekend. You'd probably consult a variety of sources: Maybe you'd read film reviews, watch current movie trailers, or talk with a film-buff friend. Or imagine you're shopping for a car. You would probably do some research; you would probably visit some manufacturers' sites, talk to your mechanic and other car owners, or visit dealerships for test drives. You might check out the advice at Cars.com.

Now that you have a sense of what sources are, the rest of this chapter will show you how to:

- Locate and preview sources
- Identify sources in terms of general versus specialized academic
- Read sources critically, with attention to author, purpose, audience, and other rhetorical concerns
- Evaluate what sources will be best for your own research and writing

## What's a General Source?
## What's a Specialized Academic Source?

ATTENTION, RESEARCHERS

When you look at a source, think about who created that text, and for what purpose and for what audience. That will guide you as to when and how to use that source.

**General Sources**  General sources are aimed at a general audience; that is, knowledgeable authors write them and nonexperts are meant to understand them. For example, a journalist who regularly covers local politics for your newspaper might write a piece to inform readers about a scandal at city hall. To get the gist of the story, you don't have to know anything about local politics or politicians. General sources help you:

- Begin to understand the overall topic
- Begin to see what the subtopics are
- Discover keywords
- Find the different conversations that are related to the topic
- Begin to explore your research questions

Did you ever start reading a source and realize that you were in over your head? What were the indicators? Have you ever had the opposite experience—you started reading a source and realized it was much too simple? What were the indicators?

An example of a general source is "The Truth About Beauty," an article written by Amy Alkon, a journalist and writer for the magazine *Psychology Today*. Alkon's purpose is to persuade her audience, primarily middle-aged women, about how men define beauty. Her ultimate goal in the article is to empower women so that they can understand their choices and the effects of their choices when it comes to beauty and landing a man.

**Specialized Academic Sources**   These sources are aimed at (you guessed it!) specialized academic readers. They are usually written by scholars and other experts—professors, scientists, doctors, and researchers—who have studied the subject extensively. An example of a specialized academic source is an article from *JAMA* (*The Journal of the American Medical Association*) on a new clinical trial and its success. Readers of such an article would include doctors interested in new treatments that they can incorporate in their own practice. Although academic articles are aimed at people with expertise on a given subject, that doesn't mean you should avoid these sources. They may include information that you can use—and may become easier to understand as you deepen your research and gain an understanding of your topic (and associated terms and vocabulary). You might turn to these sources once you've built a foundation of understanding with your general sources. Specialized academic sources help you:

- Delve into a topic in depth
- See how experts view the subject
- Access the latest research in the field
- Access critiques of research in the field
- Find other academic sources through Works Cited lists and bibliographies

An example of a specialized academic article is a piece on self-esteem development by Ruth Yasemin Erol and Ulrich Orth (see below), which appeared in the American Psychological Association's publication, the *Journal of Personality and Social Psychology*. In the article, the authors examine the ways that early self-esteem affects health and happiness in later life. The primary audience for this piece consists of psychology and sociology scholars interested in social behavior.

## How Do I Preview a Source Critically?

Previewing your sources before committing to them is worth the effort. Ask yourself the following questions to identify what you might expect from a particular source, and whether you will want to use it in your research.

▲ WEBSITE & ARTICLE: SPECIALIZED ACADEMIC SOURCE ▶

**American Psychological Association.** This article from the *Journal of Personality and Social Psychology* is aimed at an audience of experts.

## 1. What is the overall rhetorical situation?

What is the context of the source? Who wrote this piece, why, for whom, and how? And how does this impact the value of this text as a potential source?

Following is an example that we'll refer to throughout this section. It's an editorial published at Bloomberg.com.

▶ EDITORIAL, EXCERPTED

**Bloomberg.com.** An opinion piece by the editorial board of Bloomberg has a specific purpose and is written for a specific audience. These factors are important to consider when you are choosing sources.

Illustration by Bloomberg View

## Western U.S. Will Keep Burning Unless Fire Policy Changes

By the Editors | Jul 16, 2012 6:30 PM ET

22 COMMENTS ⊞ QUEUE

It is only mid-July, and Colorado has already had its most destructive wildfire in history -- some 350 houses in and near Colorado Springs burned, causing more than $110 million in damage.

This broke the previous state record, which was set earlier this summer in a fire farther up the Front Range of the Rockies. In May and June, New Mexico suffered its most devastating blaze ever -- worse than the one last year that threatened Los Alamos.

This is a scary trend.

In the 1960s, Colorado had about 460 fires a year that burned an average of 8,000 acres, according to a report compiled from state forest service records. In the past 10 years, the state averaged about 2,500 fires a year that consumed about 100,000 acres.

Climate change plays a role. Higher average temperatures mean the snowpack recedes earlier, and the fire season is extended in some places by almost two months. A study in Montana found that a rise of one degree in summer temperatures doubles costs of protecting a home against fire.

Yet hand-wringing about global climate patterns shouldn't distract us from dealing with the primary causes of the danger: human development and forest policy.

As more people moved to the so-called Wildland Urban Interface, where houses and forests intersect, the national policy of suppressing fires rather than letting them burn became more entrenched. That has meant fewer natural fires, which burn the underbrush but allow the mature trees to survive and propagate. In recent decades, fuel on the ground has built up, causing today's fires to burn more intensely, leaving a moonscape of ash.

Life and property have been lost in the fires, at unfathomable cost. But this can't be allowed to obscure the burden borne by U.S. taxpayers -- more than $3 billion annually. About half of the Forest Service's entire budget goes into fighting wildfires, up from 13 percent in 1995.

## What's the Rhetorical Situation?

**Bloomberg Editors, "Western U.S. Will Keep Burning Unless Fire Policy Changes"**

To get a sense of the rhetorical situation of this Bloomberg editorial—or any potential source—ask and answer some basic questions:

- **Who wrote this piece?** The editorial board at Bloomberg, an influential news organization focused on business and finance and with clout in both of these areas.
- **Why?** The Bloomberg editors wanted to address the disastrous Colorado fires of the summer of 2012. Their purpose was to persuade readers that the government could adopt a course of action that could prevent future fires—and also save taxpayers money.
- **For whom?** Bloomberg's audience includes general readers with internet access interested in business news and a business take on issues—both in Colorado and across the country—as well as business and government leaders who could do something about the problem.
- **How?** The editors collaborated to come up with their collective view on government policies regarding fires in the Rockies. They published their editorial in the opinion section of their website. The editorial includes hyperlinks to related materials, and there are options for commenting and linking to social networking.

As you look at sources, think about the rhetorical context of each by paying attention to the authors and their purposes, their target audiences and how they appeal to them, and the modes and media that they use for delivering their messages.

**Purpose**   First, ask yourself: Who is the author of this piece? What are his or her reasons for writing? What assumptions does the author make? How does all of this fit in with what I'm looking for? Keep in mind:

- *What is the author's background?* This information will give you a sense of the author's credibility (ethos) and his or her perspective on the topic at hand. Begin by reading any biographical information provided and see if there are links to any other writing the author has done on this topic. The authors of the editorial about fire policy (p. 344) are the members of Bloomberg's editorial board. Bloomberg is a well-respected news group focused on money and the marketplace, part of what makes this source a trustworthy one.

- *Is the author seeking to persuade?* Report information? Tell a story? All of the above? How does this fit with the type of information you're looking for? Begin by examining the title and then skim the piece with a critical eye.

- *What are the author's biases?* While you're skimming, keep an eye out for assumptions built into the text. The Bloomberg editorial represents the viewpoints of editors whose priorities are business growth and other financial concerns rather than the environment and other aspects of fire policy.

**Audience**   Ask yourself: Where did I find this text? Was it published in a popular magazine? A specialized academic journal? At a particular website? If so, who is the main audience for that magazine, journal, or website?

- *Am I part of the author's primary audience?* Based on the text's origin and a quick read of its contents, is the author aiming at a general readership or a narrower, more specialized audience? Evaluate the piece in terms of whether you find it readable, challenging, or perhaps oversimplified or condescending. Ask yourself: How much subject knowledge does the author assume readers have? As for the editors at Bloomberg, they write for businesspeople, not environmentalists, so their take on fire policy is likely going to mesh better with the concerns of the business community than those of tree huggers.

**Rhetorical appeals**   In general, what strategies does the author use to build his or her case and connect with readers?

- *Does the author use ethos, logos, and pathos to connect with readers?* How much authority does the author convey in the writing? Is the writing logical? To what extent does it appeal to your emotions? For example, you might realize as you analyze an author's appeal to pathos that his or her argument is not logical. At that point (unless you want a piece that is not logical, perhaps so you can critique it), you might decide not to use the source. In the case of the Bloomberg editorial, the numerical data particularly appeals to their business and government audience.

- *Does the author use humor?* Again, examine the title and skim the composition. If the author uses humor, does it work to strengthen the piece? How well does a humorous piece fit in with your topic and research?

**Modes & media**

- *Modes* In what mode was the source produced — written, audio, video, or something else? How does the composer's choice of mode contribute to the composition? What assumptions do you have about the mode? For example, it's fair to assume that hearing an audio essay, which features the composer's voice, is a more intimate experience than reading an article online. By considering mode, you're more aware of how the author appeals to his or her audience.

- *Media* In what medium is the source delivered — print, digital, or something else? What does the composer's choice of medium tell you about his or her assumptions about the audience? For example, digital sources are used primarily by audiences with access to computers or smartphones. Think, too, about the relationship between medium and the currency of information. A composer who publishes online can make revisions to the piece, adding links to newer articles on the topic at hand.

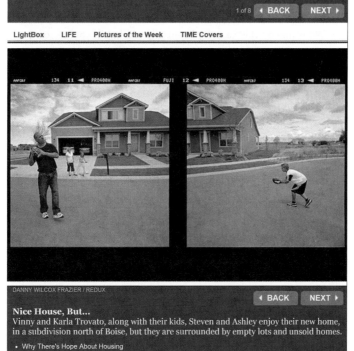

**Nice House, But...**
Vinny and Karla Trovato, along with their kids, Steven and Ashley enjoy their new home, in a subdivision north of Boise, but they are surrounded by empty lots and unsold homes.
- Why There's Hope About Housing

ATTENTION, RESEARCHERS
_____

Do you think that some modes are more reliable than others? For example, do you assume that printed sources are more authoritative than stories you hear on the radio? Why or why not?

◀ **PHOTO ESSAY**

*Time.* This photo essay, "In Boise, Housing Struggles to Emerge from Its Malaise," includes photos by Danny Wilcox Frazier of Redux, and captions by *Time* editors. As you consider sources, think about the genre of those sources (see the What's the Rhetorical Situation box on page 345).
*Credit: Danny Wilcox Frazier/Redux.*

## 2. What is the genre of the piece?

What are you looking at? What kind of composition is it? What qualities is this genre known for? What makes this text a potentially workable source, or not?

Following is an example that we'll refer to throughout this section. It's a photo essay published at *Time* magazine's website. The photos are by Danny Wilcox Frazier of Redux photography, and editors at *Time* wrote the text (see page 347).

---

### What's the Genre?

*Time* **and Danny Wilcox Frazier/Redux, "In Boise, Housing Struggles to Emerge from Its Malaise"**

When you look at a potential source, you want to understand its rhetorical situation (see the Bloomberg editorial on p. 344)—its authorship, purpose, audience, and so on.

You also want a sense of the genre that the composer chose—will it work for you?—as well as the style, design, and other sources drawn on. Ask and answer the following questions:

- **What am I looking at?** The image on page 347 is from a photo essay published online, created by *Time* editors and a photographer.

- **What qualities is this genre known for?** Photo essayists combine images and words to tell a story and/or to make an argument. Here, the editors at *Time* show the impact of an economic crisis—and hoped-for recovery—on a community. The title, "In Boise, Housing Struggles to Emerge from Its Malaise," suggests the argument being made.

- **What makes this text a potentially workable source, or not?** The authorship of this photo essay and its publication in a respected magazine make it a promising source. Also promising is that the journalists who composed the piece conducted interviews with residents. The genre makes it useful to a researcher looking for a persuasive visual/textual argument-based on experience.

---

**Elements of the genre**   Ask yourself: What do I know about the genre? What can I expect or assume about it? Keep in mind:

- *What is the scope of the information?* Different genres present different amounts and degrees of information: An encyclopedia entry provides an overview of information, while a peer-reviewed journal article provides in-depth treatment.

- *How reliable is the information?* Some genres are known for their reliability and objectivity, others less so. For example, in terms of factual accuracy, a peer-reviewed journal article is probably more reliable than a political ad. (See also Chapter 1, "Rhetorical Situations & Choices.")

- *What is the connection between genre and purpose?* Remember we talked in Chapter 2 about how genre is a social response to a rhetorical situation? For example, the authors of the *Time* photo essay (see p. 347) chose that genre for a reason. The *Time* editors and photographer Danny Wilcox Frazier, who collaborated on the photo essay, chose to focus on the human side of the housing crisis in Boise. Consider how differently the business-oriented Bloomberg editorial board might have dealt with the same issue, perhaps writing an opinion piece on the financial aspects of the crisis, rather than on how people deal with losing their homes.

**Style**   When evaluating a source, pay attention to the style of the author. Ask yourself:

- *How does the author use language?* As you skim, pay attention to the writer's word choice and vocabulary level. To what extent do they contribute to (or undermine) the author's ethos? How formal or informal is the language? Does the writer use slang? If so, keep in mind that slang is not an indicator of unreliability, just as formal language is not an indicator of reliability.

- *What is the author's tone? How does he or she use voice?* Describe the author's presence in the text. How does he or she use stylistic techniques to create a memorable voice and tone? For any source, pay attention to tone—some authors may be off-putting, while an author with an engaging voice and tone might get you to read a piece that you weren't initially sure about.

- *How well does the author's style work with the chosen genre?* Think of the author's style in the context of the genre the author composed in. For example, if the author has written an editorial, ask yourself: Is the style generally in keeping with other editorials? For example, is it direct and persuasive?

- *What special techniques does the author use? How much detail does he or she provide?* Does the author use literary techniques, such as dialogue, setting, and metaphor? How do these techniques get and keep your attention? How detailed does the author get? Paying attention to these factors will assist you in deciding whether to commit to the source; in the best cases, other authors provide examples of techniques that you can adapt in your own writing. Consider the *Time*/Frazier photo essay as a source (p. 347). The editors don't go into much detail in the textual part of the essay, but the photos they chose highlight the personal connections people have with their homes.

**Design**   All compositions—from the lowliest e-mail to the biggest-budget film—are designed. Ask yourself: Is the source I'm looking at presented in a way that draws me in?

- *How are text and images laid out?* How does the author use spatial arrangement to guide your reading? How does formatting, such as use of capital letters, bold, or special fonts, direct your attention or shape your understanding of the source's organization? Is color used to highlight information? As with style, you might notice how an author uses design elements to communicate with a reader and decide to try some of the same techniques yourself. Designs that you find annoying or gimmicky may turn you off to a source, and the opposite may happen too: Clever design that resonates with you can draw you in.

- *How are sound and other nontext/nonimage elements arranged?* How does the composer use sound to guide your listening? How does the composer use sound to evoke emotion? How do these elements direct your attention toward or away from aspects of the piece? Note, for example, how in the *Time*/Frazier photo essay (p. 347), the photos stand out against the black background.

ATTENTION, RESEARCHERS
——————
What is the price of drawing on unreliable sources? Have you ever lost faith in an author because of the sources he or she used? What were the sources? What made them seem unreliable?

**Sources**   When you preview a text, learn what you can about its author's research methods, and therefore the text's validity. Ask yourself:

- *How did the author gather and analyze data?* For example, if you're looking at an article that draws its data from surveys of large groups, you expect to encounter a lot of statistics and charts that compile the data. You'd also hope that the data is dependable. For example, the *Time* editors who created the photo essay on the housing situation in Idaho visited the location and conducted interviews, gathering information firsthand.

- *What types of sources did the author draw on?* Pay attention to where the author obtained the information on which the piece is based. Also, keep in mind the type of information you're looking for. For example, if you want facts on a specific topic and the source you're looking at is anecdotal or only relies on the author's experiences rather than on scientific research, you might decide the source won't be of use to you after all.

- *Did the author document sources?* Are sources listed in a bibliography or Works Cited list? Within the text, are specific details about sources given, such as page numbers and dates of publication for written sources? For example, in the *Time*/Frazier photo essay (p. 347), the writers refer to the names of the homeowners in the text of the piece.

- *Did the author not conduct research?* Not all authors conduct outside research, especially when they compose in particular genres such as the memoir. In the case of the memoir, the source that informs the piece is the author himself or herself—it's based on his or her own experiences.

# Previewing a Source

## Emily Kahn  |  Women in Comic Books Project

▲ STUDENT AUTHOR

**Emily Kahn.**
*Credit: megamix/Getty Images.*

Let's follow a student, Emily Kahn, as she previews a possible source. Emily is interested in comics and graphic novels, and she plans to write an academic argument about the portrayal of women in these works. She locates a promising looking article on the topic of women in graphic works in *Lightspeed: Science Fiction & Fantasy*, a weekly online magazine for fans of sci-fi and fantasy literature. The article, "The Objectification of Women in Comic Books," is by a writer named Jehanzeb.

Before Emily reads the article in depth or adds it to her working bibliography, she previews it. This means she'll dig around to better understand the context of the article.

Keeping in mind the factors outlined previously, Emily sets out to learn basic information about the publisher and author of the article—in addition to the author's purpose, audience, choice of genre, and more.

## 1. What is *Lightspeed* Magazine?

Emily first considers who publishes the magazine in which the article appears. She asks herself:

- What type of magazine is this?
- Who publishes it?
- What is the quality of the work presented there?
- Who is the main audience?
- Are the articles in the magazine peer-reviewed? Scholarly?

On the "About" page, she reads a note from the publisher (see below).

For Emily, the facts that *Lightspeed* has been nominated for a number of awards and that the editor seems to be knowledgeable are important selling points. While at first glance *Lightspeed* might look like a fanzine, she sees when she browses the contents that the nonfiction pieces published there seem sophisticated in terms of subject matter, cultural analysis, and the use of sources and Works Cited lists. *Lightspeed* may be more scholarly than she'd originally thought, though it's very readable for a general audience. She's not sure what to assume about it, so she reads on.

> ### ABOUT
>
> *Lightspeed* is an online science fiction and fantasy magazine. In its pages, you will find science fiction: from near-future, sociological soft SF, to far-future, star-spanning hard SF—and fantasy: from epic fantasy, sword-and-sorcery, and contemporary urban tales, to magical realism, science-fantasy, and folktales. No subject is off-limits, and we encourage our writers to take chances with their fiction and push the envelope.
>
> *Lightspeed* was a finalist for the 2011 & 2012 Hugo Awards, and stories from *Lightspeed* have been nominated for the Hugo Award, the Nebula Award, and the Theodore Sturgeon Award.
>
> Edited by bestselling anthologist John Joseph Adams, every month *Lightspeed* brings you a mix of originals and reprints, and featuring a variety of authors—from the bestsellers and award-winners you already know to the best new voices you haven't heard of yet. When you read *Lightspeed*, it is our hope that you'll see where science fiction and fantasy comes from, where it is now, and where it's going.

▲ MAGAZINE

*Lightspeed*.
"About" page. Emily begins her initial research by locating an article, "The Objectification of Women in Comic Books," in an online magazine for sci-fi fans, titled *Lightspeed*. She goes to the "About" page to learn more about the publication and the people behind it.

**A word about previewing.** When you find a source, do basic detective work before you commit to it. Start by getting to know its publisher and author. Ask yourself:

1. Where did the piece appear? Was it published by a scholarly journal? A well-known news outlet? An obscure but solid-looking blog? To what extent does the publisher have a specific point of view or agenda (e.g., *The Weekly Standard* states that it is a conservative publication)? How will this perspective fit in (or compare/contrast) with my project?
2. Who is the author? Someone I've heard of? Someone I don't know, but who seems to be a good writer?

## 2. Who are the editors & staff members at *Lightspeed* Magazine?

Emily scrolls down to the masthead to find out more about the magazine's editorial staff.

She asks herself:

- What can I learn about who runs the magazine?
- Who is the publisher or main editor? What are his or her credentials? Is this an independent company, or is a parent company in charge?
- Who are the other editors and regular contributors to the magazine? What else have they written, and for what publications?
- Are the editors and contributors scholars? Critics? Fans of the genres of science and fantasy fiction? Authors themselves?

Emily is curious about the publisher and editor-in-chief, John Joseph Adams, and sees that he has won several awards as an anthologist and also is affiliated with Wired.com. She notices that *Lightspeed*'s monthly sponsor is Orbit Books, an imprint of Hachette, which publishes books by authors she has read, so that adds to the magazine's credibility. Reading down the masthead, she sees that many editors are published authors themselves who also write critical articles for other magazines devoted to fantasy, science fiction, horror, culture, and comics. Emily is pleasantly surprised that the editors of *Lightspeed* are more than enthusiastic consumers of science fiction and fantasy: They are experts as well. From the information Emily reads on the "About," "Our Staff," and "Our Sponsor" pages, she finds that *Lightspeed* magazine may be an appropriate source for her paper.

## 3. Who Is Jehanzeb, the author of the article?

Emily sees that *Lightspeed* attributes the article to a writer named Jehanzeb, for whom no last name is given. She asks herself:

- How can I discover the last name of the author, so that I can learn more about this writer?
- Is there a biography somewhere? Maybe a link to a blog or personal website?
- What else has this author written—whether on this topic or others? And where has his or her work been published?
- How much credibility does the author convey?

Emily first needs to discover Jehanzeb's full name. She notices a brief biography at the end of the article, which links to Jehanzeb's blog, where the article was first published. She also sees that *Lightspeed* has published three other articles by Jehanzeb on the topic of women in comics. To learn more, Emily follows the link to Jehanzeb's *Broken Mystic* blog, where he posts poems, personal writing, and articles. There she links to a second blog, called *Muslim Reverie*, where Jehanzeb posts about "politics, current events, feminism, and media literacy." Here Emily discovers that his last name is Dar. She notices e-mail links at both blogs, so she can contact him directly. She thinks she might do that if she decides to use his article as a source in her research.

*Jehanzeb is a film student who writes about Islam, Feminism, Politics, and Media. This piece was originally published on his blog.*

**Tagged as:** comics

### Related Posts

- A Critique of Muslim Women in Comics -- AK Comics' Jalia and Aya
- A Critique of Muslim Women in Comics -- The 99
- Female, Muslim, and Mutant

◀ **AUTHOR PHOTO & BIO**

**Jehanzeb Dar.**
A photo from Jehanzeb's blog and a brief biographical note that appears with his article in *Lightspeed*. Emily begins to find out more about Dar, the author of the article she's interested in.
*Credit: Jehanzeb Dar.*

Now that Emily knows Jehanzeb's full name, she does a quick Google search to learn more about him. She wonders: Has Jehanzeb Dar published elsewhere—besides *Lightspeed* magazine and his blog? To what extent is he considered an expert on comics? A critic? She's interested to discover that the Associated Press interviewed Dar about the film *Prince of Persia*.

By tracking down information through the bio that appeared with the article, through Dar's blogs, and through a Google search, Emily has turned up some rich information. As her mental picture of Dar gets clearer—as a writer, and as a thinker and critic who takes part in larger, public conversations about the presentation of race in popular culture—she becomes more interested in his article on women in comics as a source for her paper.

### 4. What type of article is this? Will it work for my topic?

Now that Emily has a better sense of *Lightspeed* magazine and the writer Jehanzeb Dar, she's ready to do a closer reading of the article itself. Below is Dar's article, along with Emily's notes in the margins—you can see how she identifies her assumptions and also begins to read the piece closely and critically. At this point, she is still deciding on whether to use this source. Once she's done some annotating, she's ready to make her final call.

## Guided Process | How to Preview a Source

**Emily Kahn** (STUDENT), *Women in Comic Books Project: Previewing Jehanzeb Dar*

As she reads, Emily asks herself the following questions:

- What is Dar's main purpose? How does this fit in with my research questions?
- Who is his primary audience? Am I part of it? How does he connect with readers through rhetorical appeals?
- What genre is this piece? Based on what I know about the genre, what assumptions can I make?

- What is Dar's writing style? How do his techniques, voice, and tone affect me as a reader? How much detail does he use?

- Does the design of the article support what Dar seeks to achieve?

- What sources does he draw on? Does he document them? What types of sources are they—and how reliable are they?

**Emily's notes on Dar's essay**

**What genre is this?**
Definitely an article/essay. The title indicates the author is making an argument about sexism in comics. I know it's a researched argument because there is a references/Works Cited page at the end.

**What can I assume about this genre?**
I assume Dar will make claims (and maybe counterarguments) and support them with evidence from outside sources.

**What is the author's style?**
His style is serious and scholarly, but the tone is kind of entertaining—he uses terms such as "kick-butt." He also uses lots of detail.

**How does the author use design?**
I like the subheadings. They divide the article into sections on different portrayals of women in comics.

**How does the author work with sources?**
He cites sources in the text and in a References list. Looks like APA format.

Sources look to be from experts on comics and feminist and cultural critics. He also draws on comics themselves.

## Jehanzeb,
## The Objectification of Women in Comic Books

During World War II, a handsome American intelligence officer, Colonel Steve Trevor, crash-lands his plane on a mysterious island inhabited by the beautiful Amazons of Greek mythology. This new world is known as "Paradise Island" (what else would an island populated by Amazonian women be called, right?) and changes the course of human destiny. A princess by the name of Diana attends Trevor's wounds and subsequently falls in love with him. When she learns about the U.S. war against the Nazis, she dons a costume of America's red, white, and blue, and departs for the "Man's World." She becomes Wonder Woman—"beautiful as Aphrodite, wise as Athena, stronger than Hercules, and swifter than Mercury." She can fly like Superman and hurl heavy objects like the Hulk, and if you refuse to tell her the truth, she'll crack out her golden lasso and tie you up (especially if you're a heterosexual man).

At first glance, she may look like an empowered, kick-butt, feminist superheroine amidst a realm dominated by white heterosexual male superheroes. But is Wonder Woman really empowered? Is she really a symbol of feminism in comic books? Is her message really all about defending sisterhood, freedom, and democracy?

A historical overview is necessary to examine the role women have played in mainstream comic books as well as how intersecting dynamics of race and gender have impacted the way women are presented.

### 1. The Damsel in Distress
Originally, the only women that appeared in mainstream American comic books were white women, though they played very small roles. In the late 1930s, superpowered heroes like Superman and Captain Marvel dominated the stage while women scarcely had any presence. If women made

appearances, they were depicted as dependent and "damsels in distress"—victims (typically of male violence) needing to be rescued by the male protagonist (who typically exerts more violence over the male villain). The "damsel in distress" is not only a prize that needs to be won by either the male villain or hero, but also an object that measures the masculinity of the male characters. For example, Superman's "masculinity is defined by what it is not, namely 'feminine,' and by all its associated traits—hard *not* soft, strong *not* weak, reserved *not* emotional, active *not* passive" (Brown, 2001, p. 168). The manner in which women service masculinity is apparent in the first issue of *Superman*, where news reporter and future love interest Lois Lane is kidnapped by criminals and eventually saved by Superman. A romantic relationship is not developed between the two characters and nothing is learned about who Lois is—she is only a weak "feminine" body reinforcing Super-man's strong "masculinity" and "savior" role. Superman simply rescues her from villains, flies her to safety, and then flies away. Such one-dimensional portrayals were evident in other ways women were depicted: as the "girl-Friday . . . seductive vamp, or perhaps, the long-suffering girlfriend" (Lavin, 1998, p. 93). The stereotypical gender roles were quite obvious: men alone are capable of succeeding independently and being courageous, while women are dependent and weak beauties relegated to the background. These early attitudes toward women in comic books are quite suggestive of common sexist-defined role patterns where women are thought to be less intelligent than men and only have a place in the house as a caretaker and/or source of emotional support. As New York cartoonist Jules Feiffer states, "The ideal of masculine strength, whether Gary Cooper's, Lil Abner's, or Superman's, was for one to be so virile and handsome, to be in such a position of strength, that he need never go near girls. Except to help them" (1965).

## 2. Women as Sex Objects

The role of women changed dramatically during World War II when patriotic characters emerged and surprisingly attracted the interest of new readers, who were both men and women. Arguably, the most noteworthy female character was Wonder Woman. As mentioned above, she possesses enormous superhuman strength, has the ability to fly, and can overcome any obstacle

*(Continues on next page)*

**Emily's notes on Dar's essay**

**Who is the author?**
Dar is a writer concerned with comics and critical of the portrayal of women in them. He also writes about issues related to race and popular culture.

**What is the author's purpose?**
The title says to me that Dar wants to persuade readers that women are objectified in comic books. As I read further, I see that he argues that even strong female characters are created to be alluring.

**Who is the author writing for?**
For the editors and readers of *Lightspeed* magazine; the audience is mainly people who are experts on comics and interested in critical commentary about comics.

**How does the author use appeals?**
Dar appears to make his points using logic; he establishes his ethos/intelligence/expertise and uses sources. In this article he doesn't appeal to readers' emotions as a strategy.

that comes her way. Even more interesting is how her love interest, Colonel Trevor, is constantly being rescued by her, as if he is the male version of the aforementioned Lois Lane. Rather than the male rescuing the female in every episode, it is reversed in the Wonder Woman comics. In the following years, other strong superheroine characters surfaced like Miss America—the female version of Captain America—Mary Marvel, Supergirl, She-Hulk, and many others. They carried the symbolic message that "girls could do anything boys could do, and often better, especially if they stuck together" (Robbins, 2002).

However, despite these new portrayals of strong and powerful female characters like Wonder Woman, something else was occurring: they were being depicted as sex objects. As stated by Michael Lavin: "Powerful super-heroines like DC's Wonder Woman or Marvel's She-Hulk may easily overcome the most overwhelming threats and obstacles, but they are invariably depicted as alluring objects of desire, wearing the scantiest of costumes." The images of women with large bust sizes, hourglass figures, bare legs, and half-naked appearances became enormously popular after the success of Wonder Woman. Believe it or not, comic books were filled with so many sexual images of women that they were known as "headlight comic books" (crudely referring to the female anatomy). Comic book historian Ron Goulart writes: "In the days before the advent of *Playboy* and *Penthouse*, comic books offered one way to girl watch" (quoted in Lavin, p. 93). A prime example of "headlight comics" was in Bill Ward's *Torchy*, a series that ran from 1946 to 1950. The comic books contained dull and uninteresting storylines where the scriptwriters were merely making an excuse to draw Torchy as a tall, barelegged blonde, who walked around in her underwear.

The escalating amount of sex and violence in comic books eventually led to complaints, particularly by psychologist Fredric Wertham who held a symposium in 1948 on the "Psychopathology of Comic Books." He also wrote a book, *Seduction of the Innocent,* which correlated a connection between "juvenile delinquency and comic book reading" (Lavin, 1998, p. 95). As a result, the Comics Code Authority established a written code that set the guidelines for comic book publishing. During this time, the comic book industry took a remarkable new turn where the constant objectification of women was seized. The brief period where comic books were geared more toward teenage girls wouldn't last long, as superheroes reemerged in the late 1960s, along with their scantily clad superheroines and damsels in distress. Women were drawn in the same stereotypical fashion, but this time, the artists took it one step further on the skimpy scale. Consider the White Queen, a female villain who appeared in the *X-Men* comics during the 1980s. She was "the stuff of male sexual fantasy: a push-up bustier, panties, and high-heel boots, all in white" (Lavin, 1998, p. 94).

Today, women are becoming more and more sexualized. As described by Jones and Jacobs (1995, p. 341):

> Females, perpetually bending over, arching their backs, and heaving their anti-gravity breasts into readers' faces, defied all laws of physics . . . the Victoria's Secret catalogue became the Bible of every super-hero artist, an endless source of stilted poses ripe for swiping by boys who wanted their fantasies of women far removed from any human reality.

One study conducted by Jessica H. Zellers shows an examination of how women are depicted in eighteen comic books. She finds that "of the suggestively clad, partially clad, or naked individuals . . . about three times as many were women (296) than men (107)." From the comic book sample where there were 1,768 male characters and 786 female characters, only 6 percent of all males were suggestively clad, partially clad, or naked; while of all the females, 38 percent were suggestively clad, partially clad, or naked. Additionally, of all males, 2 percent were naked, while of all females, 24 percent were naked. Zellers writes: "It is incredible that almost one out of every four females was, at some point, depicted in the nude" (2005, p. 34). . . .

### References

Baughman, L. (1990). A psychoanalytic reading of a female comic book hero: Elektra: Assassin. Women and Language, 13.

Brown, J. A. (2001). Black superheroes, Milestone comics, and their fans. Jackson: University Press of Mississippi.

Brown, J. A. (2011). Dangerous curves: Action heroines, gender, fetishism, and popular culture. Jackson: University Press of Mississippi.

Donald, A., et al. (2003, September 9). The panel: "Why don't 'black books' sell?" Silver Bullet Comic Books. Retrieved from http://www.silverbulletcomicbooks.com/panel/1063121223602.htm. . . ."

**Emily's notes on Dar's essay**

**How do the mode & medium impact readers?**
The article appears online, so it probably has a wider potential audience than a print article would. This allows for hyperlinks to sources and other pages. Also, readers can add comments and interact with the author and each other.

**5. Should I add this source to my working bibliography?**

Emily is now satisfied that the author of the article is knowledgeable and that the article itself is interesting, readable, and potentially quite useful for her research project. She decides to add it to her working bibliography. She will return to the piece again later. Emily's next step is to create a research plan. (See Creating a Research Proposal on pp. 329–33 for information on research plans.)

# Evaluating a Source

Evaluating a source is much like previewing a source (see Previewing a Source on pp. 350–58), only with more depth and attention to specifics. Once you've decided that a source is a potential keeper, it's time to do a closer reading of it and decide whether it fits in with your research plan. Your main questions include:

- Is this a trustworthy source—do the author and publication convey an ethos of credibility?
- Will it work for my assignment—and further my purpose?

### Donovan Rodriguez | *Teenage Anxiety Project: Evaluating Three Sources*

▲ **STUDENT AUTHOR**
**Donovan Rodriguez.**
*Credit: Nithid/Shutterstock .com.*

In the following pages, we will follow student Donovan Rodriguez as he looks at three different sources related to his topic, teenage anxiety. These sources, which appear in the pages that follow, are:

- **Patti Neighmond's** "A Rise in Depression Among Teens and Young Adults Could Be Linked to Social Media Use," an article/transcript from NPR's "All Things Considered" news radio program.
- **Juliana Menasce Horowitz and Nikki Graf's** "Most U.S. Teens See Anxiety and Depression as a Major Problem Among Their Peers," a research report from the Pew Research Center.
- **SAMHA's,** "Support for Serious Mental Illness: Real Stories" a transcript from the "Real Stories" video series.

**Patti Neighmond, "A Rise in Depression Among Teens and Young Adults Could Be Linked to Social Media Use"**    Patti Neighmond, a journalist and a health policy reporter for NPR, regularly contributes to various NPR programs. Neighmond was educated at the University of Maryland and has received numerous journalism awards, including the George Foster Peabody Award. Neighmond's story aired on NPR on March 14, 2019. In the broadcast, Neighmond reports on a study of teen depression published in the *Journal of Abnormal Psychology*, examining the study's findings and discussing links between teenage anxiety and social media use. Neighmond's article appears on page 364.

**Juliana Menasce Horowitz and Nikki Graf, "Most U.S. Teens See Anxiety and Depression as a Major Problem Among Their Peers"** Juliana Menasce Horowitz works for the Pew Research Center, holding the position of Associate Director of Research. She manages major projects and analyzes data, interprets survey results, and presents her findings in researched reports. She studied at the University of Maryland, earning a PhD in political science. Nikki Graf also works for the Pew Research Center as a research associate. She holds a PhD in sociology from the University of Wisconsin. In their research report, based on a survey of U.S. teenagers aged thirteen to seventeen, they discuss different pressures experienced by teens, breaking down results by gender and socioeconomic background. The report was published on February 20, 2019. An excerpt from this report appears on page 368.

▲ AUTHOR PHOTO
**Nikki Graf.**
*Credit: Photo © David Hills.*

**SAMHSA, "Support for Serious Mental Illness: Real Stories"** SAMHSA is the Substance Abuse and Mental Health Services Administration, a section of the Department of Health and Human Services that is committed to reducing the impact of mental illness and substance abuse in the United States. They were established in 1992 by Congress and set strategic plans for reaching the public and supporting them in overcoming addiction and in coping with a wide variety of mental health concerns. One of their initiatives is a series of videos (shared through their YouTube channel) intended to put a face on mental illness and to point viewers to additional information and resources. A transcript of one of these videos appears on page 370.

▲ ORGANIZATION LOGO
**SAMHSA.**
*Credit: SAMHSA.*

Before we read these sources on teenage anxiety and depression in depth, we'll identify some guidelines for evaluating sources.

## How Do I Evaluate a Source? How Is This Different from Previewing?

While some of our advice overlaps with suggestions on previewing sources, we are asking you to do a more in-depth analysis of texts than you did earlier in the chapter. To evaluate whether a source is strong enough to draw upon for your own writing, ask yourself the questions posed in the following section:

**1. Is this source relevant to my project?** First, determine whether the source you're looking at is related to and useful for your project and research question(s). Ask yourself: Does the information in the source generate additional research questions related to my original question—does it get me deeper into my research? Does the source contribute to my knowledge on the topic—did I learn something new about the subject? In other words, does the author simply rehash what others have said, or does he or she say something new—or provide an alternative perspective? If the author simply duplicates knowledge, then the source is probably not a good choice for your project.

**2. What is the author's level of credibility?** When evaluating a source, you need to figure out how trustworthy the author is. Ask yourself:

- *What can I find out by Googling the author?* Learn about the author's education, degrees held, and any institutional, organizational, or professional affiliations. Find out whether the author is mentioned in other sources on the topic, and to what extent he or she is considered to be an expert on the subject by other experts in the field. Research other works by the author: One indicator of expertise is whether someone has published numerous times on the subject. However, don't discount the author's credibility just because this is the author's first piece on the subject—the author could be a rising expert in the field.

- *What if I can't figure out who the individual author is?* If there is no obvious author, look at the reliability of the organization sponsoring the website. For example, if the site is the American Diabetes Association, you can assume that the information presented is researched and reliable because it is an organization that publishes researched articles on diabetes. Additionally, this organization funds research on diabetes.

No matter how much you might agree with the viewpoint conveyed in a source or how much you might like the way the author has presented information, establishing the author's credibility is absolutely necessary if you are to use this source in your research. If you cannot trust the author, then you should not use the source.

**3. What is the author's purpose? To persuade? Inform? Tell a story? Some combination?** Identify the author's purpose by reading the source critically and carefully. As you read, ask yourself the following questions to determine the author's objectives:

- What is the author's purpose?
- Is the author trying to get me to agree with an opinion?
- Is the author presenting facts and information to teach me about the subject?
- Does the author use a narrative structure (include characters, conflict, setting)?

Once you have determined the purpose, ask yourself whether the author's purpose fits with your research question(s). For example, student Donovan Rodriguez's chosen sources are works in which authors seek to inform and persuade readers about teen anxiety and depression. One of these texts, Patti Neighmond's "A Rise in Depression Among Teens and Young Adults Could Be Linked to Social Media Use" (p. 364), presents research findings that suggest a possible link between teen depression and social media use, but the link isn't definitive. Donovan knows this because as he reads the transcript, he notes that one of the experts the reporter interviewed stipulated that the study "can only point out correlations, not causes." The expert goes on to say that the research does "help us narrow what the likely cause [of teen depression] might be."

**4. Who is the author's target audience? How does the author use rhetorical appeals to reach that audience?** When you preview a source, you determine the author's audience (see "Previewing a Source," p. 350). In order to determine the audience, ask yourself the following questions:

- Does the place of publication offer clues about audience? (For example, an editorial in *Bloomberg Businessweek* is clearly aimed at a business audience.)
- Does the author use a formal or informal tone?
- What level of detail is presented in the piece?
- Does the author include information that assumes previous knowledge?
- Does the author use jargon or vocabulary used by experts?

When Donovan reads the transcript of the SAMHSA video with individuals who have experienced anxiety and depression (p. 370), he notices that they use informal language and fillers, such as "you know" and "um." This tells Donovan that SAMHSA's primary audience is people concerned about how real individuals experience depression and mental illness and how they talk about it; this might include those struggling themselves, or family and friends.

Once you've determined the audience for the text, take a look at how the author appeals to that audience. Is the author establishing a sense of credibility that speaks to particular readers? Is the author using an emotional appeal to connect with the audience? Donovan notices that SAMHSA begins the video by establishing the value of sharing a personal story before showing individuals doing exactly that.

Besides identifying the audience and analyzing rhetorical appeals, you also need to examine the evidence the author provides and determine whether it is appropriate for his or her intended audience. Pay attention, too, to how the author keeps readers' perspectives in mind so that they will continue to read the piece. For example, when Donovan reads the research report by Horowitz and Graf, he sees that they begin with a claim about teens recognizing depression and anxiety as a major problem, a claim that they support with a reference to a Pew Research Study. This alerts audiences that the piece will draw on specific evidence.

**5. What is the source's genre? Does the author make the most of its conventions?** Let's say you're considering using a news and opinion blog as a source. As you evaluate it, look at a few other examples to see how other bloggers typically convey information—and the types of conventions they tend to adhere to. How does your potential source compare with other blogs? Does your blogger take advantage of the conventions of the genre? For example, does he clearly identify himself as the author? Does he embed hyperlinks to additional details or sources? Does he invite feedback? If not, you might want to consider using a different source. When an author chooses to ignore the traditional conventions of a genre, he may also ignore other things, such as using reliable evidence to support opinions.

**ATTENTION, READERS**

Do you read any blogs regularly? If so, think of two or three that you particularly enjoy. What do they have in common in terms of how the bloggers present information? Do they share design elements, such as headings and lists? Are there things that are done better on one blog than on the others?

**6. How does the author use evidence—and how reliable is that evidence?** As you evaluate a source, pay close attention to how the author supports his or her claims and arguments. Look at:

- *Sufficient support: Does the author use enough evidence?* If not, that's a problem. A skilled persuasive writer will back up each claim with an appropriate example. Read the source and (1) make a note every time the author makes a claim, and (2) also note whether the claim is supported. Notice also whether the evidence is vague and general, or specific and detailed. For example, Neighmond, the NPR reporter, quotes a clinical child psychiatrist who makes a claim about social media magnifying peer disapproval.

### CLAIM

"Fristad says kids are developmentally more worried about peer status and approval during pre-teen and teenage years. Social media exaggerates that process, she says, because it's so public, available, and highly visual."

The psychiatrist then gives an example—a generalized example about having a picture of yourself with bad hair posted on social media—that demonstrates how social media could magnify the results of peer disapproval. However, this doesn't sufficiently support the claim that social media does have this effect.

### INADEQUATE EVIDENCE

"For example, as opposed to 'going to school with "meh" hair, suddenly there's a picture of you with "meh" hair. Everybody's going to see it, can comment on it, make fun of you,' she says. These experiences resonate enormously during adolescence and can deeply affect teen's confidence and sense of self."

- *Timeliness: Is the source and evidence current?* In most cases, you'll want to draw on sources that are as recent as possible.

Timeliness mattered to Donovan Rodriguez when he conducted research on teen anxiety and depression. He knew he wanted very recent sources because he already knew from a psychology course he had taken that social media was being targeted as a potential cause of rising teen anxiety, so sources that predated social media wouldn't be particularly helpful.

If Donovan had been more interested in how teen anxiety and depression are diagnosed, sources that predate social media might have been relevant. Or if he had been curious about long-term effects of teenagers being prescribed antidepressant medications, he might have looked for sources written over a period of time. Depending on how you plan to use a source, its timeliness could make a difference.

**7. Does the author cite sources?** As you evaluate a source, ask yourself: Does the author give credit to others? Does he mention the work of others in the text

ATTENTION, RESEARCHERS

**A note about evidence.**
Wondering what we mean by "evidence"? Evidence is facts, examples, and source citations that authors use to illustrate and support each point they make in their compositions. Skilled authors use evidence to develop their arguments as well as their ethos. The type of evidence authors choose reflects upon them; for example, citing a celebrity gossip magazine as evidence suggests shallowness, while citing the *Wall Street Journal* suggests professionalism.

When you're evaluating a source, look at how the author uses evidence: Think of the evidence as the foundation upon which the argument is built. A shoddy foundation can cause even the most beautiful building to crumble.

itself—perhaps with hyperlinks or a list of credits? How easily can I tell where the author obtained his or her information? If you can't tell what sources the author drew on, it's possible that the information isn't well researched or can't be supported.

Citation conventions—and by this we mean the format in which an author identifies his sources—can vary across genres. Before you can judge whether an author has cited sources properly, you need to be aware of the documentation conventions for the genre you are looking at. For example:

- Authors of newspaper articles usually cite sources in the body of the article itself, by using quotations and naming people and publications they've drawn on.

- Authors of blogs usually cite sources by providing hyperlinks to them, assuming the sources are online sources.

- Authors of peer-reviewed journal articles usually use strict source-citing conventions; for example, *The American Journal of Family Therapy*, a peer-reviewed journal on family behavioral health, requires authors to cite sources in accordance with the *Publication Manual of the American Psychological Association*. (See Chapter 13 for information on APA documentation style.)

Once you know something about the citation conventions of a genre, ask yourself: Does the author of the source I'm evaluating cite sources the way she should? For example, a journalist who doesn't mention any sources in an article or editorial should raise eyebrows—but a blogger who uses hyperlinks (rather than an academic style such as APA) should not. In a reliable text, an author makes it clear where she drew from the material of others. The author provides this information in the format that is common to that genre. If the source you're looking at falls short on this score, you may want to look for a different one.

## Guided Process | How to Evaluate Sources

### Donovan Rodriguez (STUDENT), *Teenage Anxiety Project: Evaluating Three Sources*

Let's circle back to Donovan Rodriguez, who has identified a research question—and three sources that he's thinking of using.

#### RESEARCH QUESTION
What are reasons for the increase in depression/anxiety among teenagers?

Using the guidelines in the preceding pages, Donovan now evaluates his sources. His notes in the margins of each source show his thinking. He begins with Patti Neighmond's article for NPR. (For biographical information on Patti Neighmond, see p. 358.)

**Relevant to my topic?**

Yes. I want to look at teenage anxiety and its causes. Patti Neighmond's report on the study shows that there might be a link to teenage anxiety/depression and social media use.

**Credible author?**

Yes. Neighmond writes for NPR, so I trust she's a reliable journalist. She has won numerous journalism awards and regularly reports on health issues and policies. She is not just a reporter, but also a producer for NPR. When I do a search for Neighmond on Google, I find numerous links to other public radio stations that rebroadcast her NPR shows and links to many health-related articles she has authored.

**Author's purpose?**

Neighmond wants to inform readers about the rise in teenage depression/anxiety and its possible connection to social media use. She examines conclusions and interpretations of the study, such as Jean Twenge's belief that the "the rise in smartphone and social media use is a significant factor" in the rise of teenage depression/anxiety.

**Audience?**

Neighmond is writing for NPR listeners, especially people interested in issues related to teenage depression. Her listeners are also probably interested in psychology and health topics. Neighmond relies on ethos to appeal to listeners' concerns.

**Identifiable genre/mode/media?**

This article is a transcript from an NPR broadcast: Neighmond's column lists a heading of "Your Health" at the top. Its mode is written and audio, and it is published online. Essentially, Neighmond's article is primarily informative. She presents her information in short paragraphs and works in sources and quotes: This technique is common to radio news programs, editorials, and other journalistic writing.

## Patti Neighmond
### A Rise in Depression Among Teens and Young Adults Could Be Linked to Social Media Use

A study published Thursday in the *Journal of Abnormal Psychology* finds the percentage of U.S. teens and young adults reporting mental distress, depression and suicidal thoughts and actions has risen significantly over the past decade. While these problems also increased among adults 26 and older, the increase was not nearly as large as among younger people.

The study findings suggest a generational shift says psychologist Jean Twenge, with San Diego State University who headed the study and is author of the book *iGen*. To see a significant increase in negative psychological states "among our vulnerable population of teens and young adults is absolutely heartbreaking," she says.

Twenge and her colleagues analyzed data from the National Survey on Drug Use and Health, a government survey that tracks mental health and substance use in individuals age 12 and over in the U.S. They looked at survey responses from more than 200,000 adolescents ages 12 to 17 and almost 400,000 young adults ages 18 and over between 2005 and 2017.

They found the rate of individuals reporting symptoms consistent with major depression over the past year increased 52 percent in teens and 63 percent in young adults over a decade. Girls were more vulnerable than boys. By 2017 one out of every five teenage girls had experienced major depression in the last year.

Rates of psychological distress, which Twenge describes as "feeling nervous, hopeless or that everything in life is an effort" rose by 71 percent among people aged 18 to 25. Suicidal thoughts, plans and attempts also increased. Death from suicide increased by 56 percent among 18- to 19-year-olds between 2008 and 2017.

Understanding exactly why these trends are on the rise is always a challenge, says Twenge, since researchers can only point out correlations, not causes. But, she says, since the trends are "pretty large in a fairly short period of time, that helps us narrow what the likely cause might be."

She thinks the rise in smartphone and social media use is a significant factor. By 2012, smartphones had become widespread, she says, and it's around that same time that social media began to dominate young people's lives. For example, in 2009 about half of high school seniors visited social media sites every day. That's climbed to about 85 percent today, with Instagram and Snapchat replacing Facebook as the main "go to social media site," she says.

It's not just the phone or social media itself, says Twenge. It's the amount of time teens and young adults spend with it. As Twenge found in earlier research, the more time they spend, the greater the risk of depressive symptoms. Twenge says it's known from a body of research that in-person social contact is good for mental health. She questions whether spending that same amount of time on Instagram and Snapchat is just as beneficial, and says "it seems clear the answer is 'No.'"

"Spending time on social media tends not to be in real time," she says. "You're not having a real time conversation with someone—usually you're not seeing their face and you can't give them a hug; it's just not as emotionally fulfilling as seeing someone in person."

The findings of the new study ring "completely true" for clinical child psychologist Mary Fristad with the Department of Psychiatry and Behavioral Health at The Ohio State University, who was not involved in the study. Fristad, who treats children from age ten through to college age, says her patients are concerned "not about how much fun they look forward to having over the weekend, but about what event can they post on Snapchat so that other people will know they have friends."

Fristad says kids are developmentally more worried about peer status and approval during pre-teen and teenage years. Social media exaggerates that process, she says, because it's so public, available, and highly visual. It's like "taking what happens in typical adolescent development and putting it on steroids," she says.

For example, as opposed to "going to school with 'meh' hair suddenly there's a picture of you with 'meh' hair. Everybody's going to see it, can comment on it, make fun of you," she says.

(Continues on next page)

---

**Reliable evidence?**
Neighmond's sources are primarily the published journal study. She quotes statistics and key phrases from Jean Twenge, the head of the study. Additionally, she interviews other psychologists and researchers for their opinions on the study. That all seems solid.

Neighmond balances different ideas and includes various opinions on causes of the rise in teenage depression. She writes: "Another explanation could simply be that these teens and young adults are more willing to admit they are stressed, anxious, worried and even depressed. . . ." She supports this claim by reporting on other psychologists' beliefs on what has caused the increase. Are there others she could mention to back this statement more strongly?

**Sources cited?**
Neighmond attributes her information to sources when she quotes people and names them in the body of the transcript. She also provides hyperlinks so readers can get more information. For example, I clicked on the Jean Twenge link and it took me to her homepage that listed all the books Twenge has published and a link to her published research.

These experiences resonate enormously during adolescence and can deeply affect teen's confidence and sense of self.

Other researchers are less convinced of the connection between screen time and mood. It's important to keep in mind that while there has been an increase in negative psychological states, the majority of teens and young people are not depressed, notes Robert Croesner, a researcher in adolescent health and the chair of the Sociology Department at the University of Texas at Austin, who was not involved with the research.

And he adds, there could be many other things besides technology contributing to the rise.

"There really aren't data that show a strong connection between these two things," he says. "I think this increase in mental health issues is real and is something we need to be concerned about, but until we know exactly what's causing it, I don't think it's so easy for us to put the blame on any one thing."

Croesner says, to explain the phenomenon, you have to look at the entire context of the historic moment we're living in.

"I think we are living in a time of great uncertainty, where people are unsure about the future of the country but also their own futures," he says. "And that is anxiety provoking for anybody but it's especially true for young people whose whole future is ahead of them."

In the past economic pressures have been linked to increases in depression but Twenge notes that since 2012 the economy has been improving so a failing economy is not likely to blame.

Another explanation could simply be that these teens and young adults are more willing to admit they are stressed, anxious, worried and even depressed and that they need, and want help.

Psychologist Andrew Przybylski, an experimental psychologist at the University of Oxford in Oxford, England, is skeptical of the study findings. "The data is entirely descriptive," he wrote in an e-mail. "I find it very unfortunate that there is undue speculation about the effects of technology." He said the rise in mental health issues could be explained by other factors such as the opioid crisis.

Still Fristad thinks the impact of social media on mental health is a real issue for this age group. Fristad organized a focus group of college students at Ohio State. The students had all received smartphones when they were 13 or 14. What they told her was in line with current study's findings. The students described "another realm of things to worry about, pressure to build your brand, sharing too much and making unrealistic comparisons to other kids . . . being constantly on the phone and not engaging in face-to-face interactions."

"There's just a lot of heightened tension around this," says Fristad.

And the advice from her college students for younger kids? "Phones Off, Friends On."

Researcher and clinical psychologist Steve Ilardi, with the University of Kansas tries to help anxious and depressed kids feel better. The good news, he says, is that it's clear that they "intuitively grasp that how we live now is not ideal for us." Teens get that spending hours surfing, bringing their phones to bed, "this relentless cascade of stressful notifications and images is not good for them and they get it."

Ilardi developed a treatment approach, based in part on cognitive behavioral therapy, that helps young people make lifestyle changes, focusing on better diet and nutrition, exercise, exposure to sunlight and getting a good night's sleep, all of which have been shown to reduce depressive symptoms.

"Kids buy into it," says Ilardi, "when you lay it out for them and explain they can be empowered to make changes themselves that can make a big difference in how you feel, how your brain, mind and body functions."

He says behavior change can "help kids get unstuck from their perpetual sense of anxiety, stress and depression."

After reading through the informative piece on NPR, Donovan decided he wanted more research on the issues related to teenage anxiety and depression. He found a research report by Horowitz and Graf about how U.S. teens view depression and anxiety as a major problem. Additionally, he found that they provided some other potential causes behind the rise that might help his research. (For more biographical information on Juliana Menasce Horowitz and Nikki Graf, see p. 359.)

**Relevant to my topic?**
Yes. Horowitz and Graf focus on teenage anxiety
and depression, examining some of the reasons
behind the rise. Their findings will be a valuable
source for my research.

**Credible author?**
Yes. Both Horowitz and Graf hold doctorates in
fields that require research and interpretation
of statistics. They also both work for the Pew
Research Center whose mission is to "generate
a foundation of facts that enriches the public
dialogue and supports sound decision-making."

Because Pew regularly conducts unbiased
research, so I imagine that they are careful to
report their findings without inserting their own
opinions. This report allows me to see data on
how teens perceive issues related to anxiety and
depression without any bias from the authors.

**Authors' purpose?**
Horowitz and Graf write to inform readers that
"Anxiety and depression are on the rise among
America's youth and . . . seven-in-ten teens
today see them as major problems. . . ."

**Audience?**
Horowitz and Graf write for those interested in
teenage depression and anxiety. They appeal
to the audience with ethos (using evidence and
statistics from the report) and logos, organizing the
information in a way that supports their findings.

**Identifiable genre/mode/medium?**
Horowitz and Graf mix reported statistics and
charts. They use a combination of text and visuals.
They use report conventions such as listing their
methodology and acknowledgment of individuals
involved in the research and analysis.

**Sources cited?**
Horowitz and Graf attribute all the research to
the Pew Research Center survey conducted in
the fall of 2018. They provide a hyperlink to a
summary report of the survey.

**Juliana Menasce Horowitz and Nikki Graf**
**Most U.S. Teens See Anxiety and Depression as a**
**Major Problem Among Their Peers**

Anxiety and depression are on the rise among America's
youth, and whether they personally suffer from these conditions or not, seven-in-ten teens today see them as major problems among their peers. Concern about mental health cuts
across gender, racial and socio-economic lines, with roughly
equal shares of teens across demographic groups saying it is a
significant issue in their community.

Fewer teens, though still substantial shares, voice concern

**Teens see depression and anxiety as among the most common problems among their peers.**

*% of teens saying each of the following is a ___ among people their age in the community where they live*

■ Major problem  ■ Minor problem  ■ Not a problem

| | Major problem | Minor problem | Not a problem |
|---|---|---|---|
| Anxiety and depression | 70 | 26 | 4 |
| Bullying | 55 | 35 | 10 |
| Drug addiction | 51 | 35 | 13 |
| Drinking alcohol | 45 | 39 | 16 |
| Poverty | 40 | 47 | 13 |
| Teen pregnancy | 34 | 44 | 21 |
| Gangs | 33 | 38 | 29 |

Note: Share of respondents who didn't offer an answer not shown.
Source: Survey of U.S. teens ages 13 to 17 conducted Sept. 17–Nov.
25, 2018.
"Most U.S. Teens See Anxiety and Depression as a Major Problem
Among Their Peers"

over bullying, drug addiction, and alcohol consumption. More
than four-in-ten say these are major problems affecting people

their age in the area where they live, according to a Pew Research Center survey of U.S. teens ages thirteen to seventeen.

When it comes to the pressures teens face, academics tops the list: 61 percent of teens say they feel a lot of pressure to get good grades. By comparison, about three-in-ten say they feel a lot of pressure to look good (29 percent) and to fit in socially (28 percent), while roughly one-in-five feel similarly pressured to be involved in extracurricular activities and to be good at sports (21 percent each). And while about half of teens see drug addiction and alcohol consumption as major problems among people their age, fewer than one-in-ten say they personally feel a lot of pressure to use drugs (4 percent) or to drink alcohol (6 percent).

The pressure teens feel to do well in school is tied at least in part to their post-graduation goals. About six-in-ten teens (59 percent) say they plan to attend a four-year college after they finish high school, and these teens are more likely than those who have other plans to say they face a lot of pressure to get good grades.

**Reliable evidence?**
There is a good amount of evidence, and it's varied, including firsthand observations of teenagers. The survey results are timely, conducted within the past couple of years, so they are still relevant to today's teenage experience.

After realizing that Horowitz and Graf's research report contained a lot of evidence, Donovan decided that he wanted a more personal lens into the experiences of people coping with depression and anxiety. He found a YouTube video created by the Substance Abuse and Mental Health Services Administration, which goes by the acronym SAMHSA, that is intended to encourage those struggling with mental health issues and sharing some of their stories. Donovan believed this might help him understand how individuals viewed the reasons behind their anxiety and depression. (For information on the Substance Abuse and Mental Health Services Administration, see p. 359.)

## Donovan's notes on SAMHSA's video

**Relevant to my topic?**
Yes. I'm intrigued by hearing the voices of individuals struggling with mental health issues. In the transcript, I learn about how sharing personal struggles can be a good coping mechanism. This piece adds an angle that is different from the other two sources.

**Credible author?**
SAMHSA is a government-run organization, which helps with their credibility. In addition, they provide links and resources from other credible organizations.

**Authors' purpose?**
SAMHSA wants to inform listeners about how sharing your story can help you cope with depression and other mental illnesses. They want viewers to hear the voices of the individuals so that they understand the rise in depression from a personal, rather than a statistical perspective.

**Audience?**
The audience for SAMHSA's video series includes a general, popular audience interested in mental health. Since the program is focused on the voices of those coping with mental health concerns, the audience also more specifically includes individuals like those in the video and their family and friends.

**Identifiable genre/mode/medium?**
Yes. This is a transcript of a YouTube Video. The audio content features voices of individuals dealing with mental health concerns. The content is also available as a print transcript. It is broadcast through the internet and is available to anyone with access to a computer and an internet connection.

**Reliable evidence?**
Yes, the people in the video are providing their own experiences. Also, SAMHSA is an organization with a lot of experience in mental health, so they would know what information is important and how to present it effectively.

## SAMHSA
### Support for Serious Mental Illness: Real Stories

00:01

[Mike] There's something about sharing your story with other people that gives them a sense of hope that they're not alone. To be in a group with other people who are going through the same thing just makes it so much easier.

00:12

[Dan] For someone with depression, those connections are life-saving, they're, they're so important.

00:18

[Phil] Lots of people actually would contact me back, uh, after watching a few of my videos and say something like, uh, you gave me the words I didn't have.

00:27

[Victoria] And with the help of a good support team, doctor, psychiatrist, therapist, you could get through it and you can actually, um, be a stronger person because of it.

00:38

[Phil] My friends were, uh, were significantly important for my recovery.

00:42

[Dan] That's why oftentimes, uh, we need people around us. And with my wife and my daughter, you know, I mean I often say that they're my best antidepressants.

Full video available on SAMHSA's YouTube Channel: https://www.youtube.com/watch?v=jTquXGc_CO0

**Sources cited?**
The sources for this piece are the individuals themselves and the people they refer to in the video.

Following his evaluation of the works of Neighmond, Horowitz and Graf, and SAMHSA, Donovan maps his research out in a little more detail.

**Donovan Rodriguez** (STUDENT), *Teenage Anxiety Project*

**English 102**

**February 1, 2019**
**Research Plan**

1. Your research question.
   My research question is: What are reasons for the increase in depression/anxiety among teenagers?

2. Your goals.
   My starting point was to find out why it seems like all my friends in high school were experiencing depression and anxiety. I am thinking of majoring in psychology and in my intro course last semester, we learned that some researchers think social media is the reason for the increase in teen depression and anxiety. At the same time, my professor said it's possible that people are just more comfortable now talking about mental health issues, so it could be that there isn't actually more teen depression and anxiety but just more openness among teenagers in seeking help for it. One of my goals is to discover what research has been done on teen depression and anxiety and its causes.

   Another goal I have is more personal, and that is to be able to help my younger sister, who is sixteen and just got diagnosed with depression and anxiety. It's affecting her motivation to go to school and she's getting in trouble for absences and missing homework. She is on social media all the time. If I do find out that there's a meaningful connection between depression and anxiety and social media, maybe I could talk to her about her social media use.

   I believe my research would be considered inductive, because I truly haven't made up my mind about whether I think there is a social media connection, and the thoughts I have now are completely based on one lecture in my psychology course and the three sources I've read. The next source I read could make me see things differently.

3. Types of sources.
   I am interested in research on teen depression and anxiety, but I'm thinking that teen's opinions matter too. I'd like to find more sources like the interview with teenagers to get their perspectives. If teenagers themselves feel like social media is a way to reach out and get help, then I want to be able to weigh that against negatives of social media. I might look for blogs by teenagers or young adults experiencing anxiety and depression to learn more about what they think.

   For primary sources, I might interview my sister to find out from her perspective what might be contributing to her anxiety and depression. I could try to talk to some of my friends from high school about their experiences. Another idea I have is to survey everyone in this class and just find out who has anxiety and depression and maybe how much time they spend on average on social media. That might help me find a connection. I could also talk to my psychology professor from last semester.

4. Your timeline.
   - Find and read more sources and blogs: March 20–31
   - Schedule interview with Professor Hughes and sister: April 1
   - Write interview questions: April 5
   - Conduct interview with Professor Hughes: April 7–10
   - Conduct interview with sister: April 11–25
   - Draft: April 25–May 6
   - Revise: May 7–14
   - Edit: May 14
   - Submit: May 15

# 13

# INTEGRATING & DOCUMENTING SOURCES

In this chapter, we focus on two things: (1) how to integrate sources, and (2) how to cite and document sources using two popular documentation styles. First, we'll show you how to incorporate sources into your own compositions, through quotations, paraphrases, and summaries. As you'll discover, there are reasons for choosing one method over the others, or combining methods, depending on your purposes. We'll follow the processes of student writers as they work with their sources (see Guided Processes in this chapter). We will also take a look at the issue of plagiarism. Composers who plagiarize use a source unethically by, for example, using an idea or language from a source without giving credit to that source with an attribution, parenthetical citation, and bibliographical entry. Plagiarism is not always a deliberate act; it can simply be the result of sloppiness. Whether it's intentional or not, plagiarism is a serious offense in any academic setting. However, if you follow the advice in this chapter (especially the suggestions for avoiding plagiarism), you can be confident of your integrity and ethos as an author.

In the second part of the chapter, we will show you how to cite sources within the text of your own compositions, and how to document them in lists at the end of your paper. Because the documentation styles of the Modern Language Association (MLA) and American Psychological Association (APA) are the ones most typically used in the humanities and social sciences, we've provided detailed coverage of both (MLA, pp. 397–413; APA, pp. 414–32). There are other popular styles—such as *Chicago* style, used by some of the humanities disciplines, and the American Medical Association (AMA) style, used by health and medical fields. If you are using those styles, we refer you to chicagomanualofstyle.org and amamanualofstyle.com.

# Integrating Sources into Your Writing

When we talk about integrating sources, we mean a host of different and related activities. We mean using source material in our own compositions, perhaps to provide context for our ideas or evidence for our claims. We also mean showing how the source material we've used relates to other source material—does it agree with other sources? Does it contradict other sources? Does it provide a perspective missing in other sources? And finally, we mean citing our sources to credit outside sources throughout the text of our papers and documenting them in a Works Cited list (MLA) or References list (APA) so that interested readers can track the sources down for themselves.

## Using a Parenthetical Citation or Signal Phrase

Here are examples of how Emily Kahn (the student introduced in Chapter 12) integrated an article into a paper she wrote. She found the article, "The Objectification of Women in Comic Books" by Jehanzeb Dar, online in the fantasy magazine, *Lightspeed*.

In this first example, Emily presents Dar's name in what's called a parenthetical citation. Parenthetical citations must include the author's last name and the page number from the source that the material is taken from. Because Dar's article is from an online magazine, there are no page numbers to list.

EMILY'S IN-TEXT CITATION (MLA style—names author in parentheses)
The writer argues that the comic book industry may begin to attract female readers and readers of color if comics authors reject sexism and racism. He concludes: "As more female writers and artists make contributions to the industry, male writers and artists will need to be inspired to work against sexism, the objectification of women, and the sexualization of women of color" (Dar 000).

author's last name  ——— if there is a page number, it goes here

Alternatively, Emily could have cited Dar's article as follows, by naming him in a signal phrase.

EMILY'S IN-TEXT CITATION (MLA style—names author in a signal phrase)

author named
in signal phrase

Jehanzeb Dar argues that if the comic book industry wants to attract female readers, then comic book authors need to reject sexism and racism. He concludes: "As more female writers and artists make contributions to the industry, male writers and artists will need to be inspired to work against sexism, the objectification of women, and the sexualization of women of color" (00–00).

were this a print article, with page numbers, the page or pages referred to would go here

At the end of her paper, Emily provides a bibliographic entry for her references to Dar's article.

EMILY'S WORKS CITED ENTRY (MLA style)

author name:          title of          title of
last, first           article           magazine

Dar, Jehanzeb. "The Objectification of Women in Comic Books." *Lightspeed,*

              publication
publisher     date          article URL

John Joseph Adams, Aug. 2008, www.fantasy-magazine.com/non-fiction/articles/
the-objectification-of-women-in-graphic-novels/.

Using the MLA style of documentation, Emily:

- Cites Dar's article in the text of her paper, using an in-text citation that includes his name (no page number available)
- Documents Dar's article with a corresponding entry in her Works Cited list
- Avoids plagiarism by citing Dar's article in *both* the text of her paper *and* her Works Cited list

# Overview: Quoting, Paraphrasing, & Summarizing

**Quoting**    In the previous example, Emily quotes directly from Dar's article. To signify to her readers that she is using Dar's exact words, she surrounds his words with quotation marks:

**EMILY'S DIRECT QUOTATION FROM THE SOURCE (Dar)**
He concludes: "As more female writers and artists make contributions to the industry, male writers and artists will need to be inspired to work against sexism, the objectification of women, and the sexualization of women of color" (Dar).

Emily chooses to include a quotation in order to state the specifics of Dar's argument. The quotation also serves to back up her first sentence, in which she summarizes Dar's main argument.

**Paraphrasing**    Elsewhere in her paper, Emily paraphrases Dar's argument. To paraphrase, a writer takes the ideas of a source and puts them into his or her own words. A paraphrase rewords without significantly condensing a specific passage.

**ORIGINAL PASSAGE FROM SOURCE (Dar)**
The role of women changed dramatically during World War II when patriotic characters emerged and surprisingly attracted the interest of new readers, who were both men and women. Arguably, the most noteworthy female character was Wonder Woman.

**EMILY'S PARAPHRASE**
According to Dar, Wonder Woman was the most interesting character to come out of the comics of the World War II era.

Note that Emily rephrases Dar's sentences and condenses them into one. She also attributes the entire idea to Dar by naming him in a signal phrase: "According to Dar . . ." If the article were in print, she would also include a parenthetical note at the end with the page number on which the idea was mentioned.

**Summarizing**    In the example on page 374, Emily summarizes the main point of Dar's entire article in her first sentence:

**EMILY'S SUMMARY OF ENTIRE SOURCE**
Jehanzeb Dar argues that if the comic book industry wants to attract female readers, then comic book authors need to reject sexism and racism.

Emily manages to summarize in one sentence a point Dar makes in nine paragraphs. A summary condenses material significantly and focuses only on the point made, not the details that support or illustrate the point. Emily wants to reference Dar's central argument, so summary makes sense.

As you can see in the examples above, Emily always gives credit to Dar when she refers to his ideas, even if she changes his words, as in a summary or paraphrase.

**A little summary goes a long way.**   Although summarizing an entire work is occasionally the way to go, we recommend that you do this sparingly.

Choose summary to step back and give a "big picture" view to your readers, or to provide context.

In general, focus on specific points and passages of your sources; draw on these through quotations, paraphrases, or a combination of these. Support your arguments with specifics from your sources and your paper will be richer, more detailed, and ultimately more persuasive.

Integrating sources smoothly into your own writing allows you to maintain control over the authorial voice that your readers hear. For example, although the examples above show Emily referring to Dar's ideas, it is clear that she, not Dar, is the author of her paper. Dar's voice never overtakes Emily's. While she draws on the source through quotations, paraphrases, and summary, she does so smoothly. Like Emily, you'll need to decide how and when to use these methods of drawing on sources. You'll also need to decide whether you're going to cite them through signal phrases, such as "According to Dar," or through parenthetical citations, such as "(Dar 000)." And if your instructor has not requested that you use a particular documentation style, you'll need to decide which format to use: MLA, APA, or another method of documentation.

# Quoting

## What Does It Mean to Quote from a Source?

When you quote from a source, you provide a passage from that text—in the author's exact language. The best time to quote from a text is when the language from a passage contributes in a crucial way to the argument you are making.

When you quote from a passage, you should:

**Use the exact words from the original without alteration**   If you do need to alter the words for the sake of agreement of verb tense, use brackets to indicate what you've altered. To shorten a passage, use ellipses.

> **ORIGINAL PASSAGE FROM SOURCE**
> "Sexist undertones and stereotypical images are getting worse and increasingly sleazier."

> **EMILY'S ALTERED QUOTE (changes shown in brackets)**
> Dar points out that "[s]exist undertones . . . [have gotten] worse and increasingly sleaz[y]."

**Surround the quoted passage with quotation marks**   An exception is long quotes, which should be indented in a block. A long quote, per MLA, is more than four lines long; in APA style, it is more than forty words long.

**Give credit to the author of the source being quoted**   An attribution phrase, such as "Dar points out that," gives credit and cues readers to hear someone else's voice for a moment or two. Conventions for crediting sources differ. As with summaries and paraphrases, you may need to provide a parenthetical citation and/or a bibliographic entry if that is appropriate for the genre you are composing in.

Quote from other authors to present their specific language for good reasons; for example, if the original language is distinctive enough that paraphrasing would draw the meaning out.

Let's look at an example. Suppose a student named Omar Sadi is writing about the possible connection between extreme weather and climate change. One of his sources is *Yale Environment 360*, published by Yale University and its School of Forestry and Environmental Studies. In that journal, Omar finds an article that gathers the views of eight climate experts.

He decides that the experts' perspectives and voices will support his main argument, and he chooses to quote from the source a passage with memorable word choice.

### OMAR'S EFFECTIVE QUOTING

In a recent forum published by *Yale Environment 360*, a panel of experts addressed the question: Is extreme weather linked to climate change? Like many of the panelists, University of Colorado professor Roger A. Pielke Jr. said that because the Intergovernmental Panel on Climate Change defines climate change as a persistent change of weather that takes place over the course of thirty years or more, the question posed cannot be answered now. Instead, Pielke says, we need long-term studies and records to scientifically support a connection. He argues:

> "To suggest that particular extreme weather events are evidence of climate change is not just wrong, but wrongheaded. . . . Weather is not climate and short-term climate variability is not climate change."

quotation from a source

So how do scientists explain the extreme weather of recent years? And what are the best ways of evaluating the impact of global warming on the weather? . . .

---

### ATTENTION, WRITERS

**A caution against quoting too much.**   Remember that every time you quote an author, you are, in effect, turning over the microphone to someone else. So when should you let someone else take the microphone? Perhaps if the author makes a point in language so vivid it deserves a moment in the spotlight. Or if the author's language or phrasing is particularly precise, interesting, or humorous. Our point is this: Quote mindfully. Don't use quotations just because you think it will be too much work to paraphrase. Whether you choose to quote, paraphrase, or summarize from a source, be sure to credit it in the text of your paper and list it in your Works Cited (MLA) or References (APA) list.

---

# When Should I Quote from a Source?

A great time to quote from a source is when the ideas or language of the original is so striking that you can't truly capture them in a paraphrase or summary. For example, 9/11 hero Todd Beamer's words "let's roll" could be paraphrased as "we should act now," but such a paraphrase lacks the energy and emotion of the original. It would be best to quote Beamer. Here are some other instances when you might quote rather than paraphrase or summarize:

**Quote from a source when a paraphrase or summary would alter the author's meaning**   For example, this might be the case when your source is a legal document, as in the following:

STUDENT'S QUOTATION FROM A LEGAL DOCUMENT

In the Supreme Court's historical ruling on school segregation, Chief Justice Earl Warren offered the court's final opinion in *Brown v. Board of Education*, ruling for the plaintiffs:

quotation from a source

> We conclude that in the field of public education the doctrine of "separate but equal" has no place. Separate educational facilities are inherently unequal. Therefore, we hold that the plaintiffs and others similarly situated for whom the actions have been brought are, by reason of the segregation complained of, deprived of the equal protection of the laws guaranteed by the Fourteenth Amendment.

It was this ruling that changed . . .

Note: Because the quoted passage is long, it is "blocked" rather than run in with the text; there are no quotation marks in this case.

**Quote from a source when a paraphrase or summary would not capture the essence of the author's clear and memorable words and tone**   For example, supermodel Linda Evangelista once famously said, "I don't get out of bed for less than $10,000 a day." If you were to paraphrase this, you would lose the tone and spirit of her comment.

**Quote from a text if your purpose is to analyze that text**   For example, if you were writing an analysis of a work of literature, you would include in your paper specific passages to discuss. Let's say you want to comment on mystery writer Agatha Christie's use of an omniscient narrator and want to give an example from her writing to illustrate your point. You might write something like this:

STUDENT'S QUOTATION OF A PASSAGE FOR ANALYSIS

In *Secret Adversary*, Christie uses her narrator to convey a quick analysis of a character's true nature:

quotation from a source

> Although she was accustomed to take the lead, and to pride herself on her quick-wittedness, in reality she had relied upon Tommy more than she realized at the time. There was something so eminently sober and clear-headed about him, his common sense and soundness of vision were so unvarying, that without him Tuppence felt much like a rudderless ship (88).

The narrator's commentary on Tommy, conveyed through Tuppence's point of view, serves to . . .

# How Do I Quote from a Source?

To quote a source, do the following:

- Integrate the quote into your prose by providing a context for the quotation. In other words, don't simply plop the quote into the prose, expecting your reader to understand how it fits within the material that precedes and follows it.

- Signal the reader that a quote is coming. This is usually best done by using the author's name (Kleinfeld discusses "...").

- If the quote is shorter than four lines, integrate it into your sentences. If the quote is longer than four lines, use a blocked quote format.

## Guided Process | How to Quote from a Source

### Paul Pierre (STUDENT), *Nonviolent Protest Project: Quoting Gandhi*

Let's look at the process of student Paul Pierre. He's researching nonviolent protest and has come across some speeches by Mohandas K. Gandhi (known simply as Gandhi), the philosophical leader of the early twentieth-century independence movement in India. Gandhi became famous for using nonviolent protest strategies.

Paul decides to read some of Gandhi's writings and speeches, and to summarize and paraphrase them within his own writing. However, when he reads "The Doctrine of the Sword," in which Gandhi defines nonviolence, Paul decides that Gandhi's original words are powerful and that he should quote them directly.

Paul located the text of this 1920 article by Gandhi at the website of a research foundation dedicated to the author. Gandhi's article was originally published in his weekly journal, *Young India*.

▲ STUDENT AUTHOR
**Paul Pierre**
*Credit: Svetlana Prikhnenko/ Shutterstock.*

---

**M. K. Gandhi**
**The Doctrine of the Sword**

In this age of the rule of brute force, it is almost impossible for anyone to believe that anyone else could possibly reject the law of final supremacy of brute force. . . .

I do believe that where there is only a choice between cowardice and violence I would advise violence. Thus when my eldest son asked me what he should have done, had he been

---

**Paul's notes on Gandhi's article**

1. *I read the whole article* and chose the passage I thought was most significant to my argument about nonviolence.

2. *I thought about how this source works with my other sources.* In my research, I've looked into how well-known political figures define nonviolence. Gandhi, probably the best known of these figures, offers a perspective that I think is crucial to present.

present when I was almost fatally assaulted in 1908, whether he should have run away and seen me killed or whether he should have used his physical force which he could and wanted to use, and defended me, I told him that it was his duty to defend me even by using violence. . . .

I am not a visionary. I claim to be a practical idealist. The religion of nonviolence is not meant merely for the Rishis and saints. It is meant for the common people as well. Nonviolence is the law of our species as violence is the law of the brute. The spirit lies dormant in the brute and he knows no law but that of physical might. The dignity of man requires obedience to a higher law to the strength of the spirit.

I have therefore ventured to place before India the ancient law of self sacrifice. For Satyagrah and its off-shoots, non-cooperation and civil resistance are nothing but new names for the law of suffering. The Rishis, who discovered the law of non-violence in the midst of nonviolence, were greater geniuses than Newton. They were themselves greater warriors than Wellington. Having themselves known the use of arms, they realized their uselessness, and taught a weary world that its salvation lay not through violence, but through nonviolence.

Nonviolence in its dynamic condition means conscious suffering. It does not mean meek submission to the will of the evil-doer, but it means the putting of one's whole soul against the will of the tyrant. Working under this law of being, it is possible for a single individual to defy the whole might of an unjust empire to save his honor, his religion, his soul and lay the foundation for the empire's fall or its regeneration.

And so I am not pleading for India to practice nonviolence because it is weak. I want her to practice nonviolence being conscious of her strength and power. . . .

**Paul's notes on Gandhi's article**

3. *I tried paraphrasing Gandhi's words.* Here's what I came up with:

**MY PARAPHRASE**

Gandhi named in signal phrase, so no parenthetical citation needed

For Gandhi, nonviolence was a type of active defiance.

I don't think it works. My paraphrase is a lot less powerful than Gandhi's original words.

4. *I decided to quote Gandhi directly.* Here's what I wrote and included in my final audio essay:

**MY QUOTATION**

Gandhi named in signal phrase, so no parenthetical citation needed

Gandhi was adamant that nonviolence is different from being passive, explaining, "Nonviolence in its dynamic condition means conscious suffering. It does not mean meek submission to the will of the evil-doer, but it means the putting of one's whole soul against the will of the tyrant."

5. *I cited the Gandhi article as a source in my Works Cited list.* Even though I created an audio essay about nonviolent protest, my instructor asked me to formally cite all my sources. I submitted (with my audio essay) an Artist's Statement in which I documented all my research according to MLA style. Here's the entry that corresponds with my in-text citation of the Gandhi article.

**MY WORKS CITED ENTRY (MLA style)**

author name: last, first — title of short work from a website

Gandhi, M. K. "The Doctrine of the Sword."

date — title of site

1920. *Mahatma Gandhi Complete*

publisher

*Information Website*, Bombay Sarvodaya

URL

Mandal and Gandhi Research, www.mkgandhi

date of access

.org/nonviolence/D_sword.htm. Accessed 15

Sept. 2016.

Paul is satisfied that quoting is best in this case because Gandhi's distinct words indicate a tone and sensibility that would be lost in a summary or paraphrase.

# Paraphrasing

## What Does It Mean to Paraphrase a Source?

When you paraphrase a source, you basically restate what you've read from a text or a part of a text. Like when you summarize a source, you capture the author's main idea—usually the main idea behind an entire book or movie, for example—in your own words (for more on summary, see Summarizing on p. 386). However, when you *paraphrase* a source, you capture *all* of the author's ideas in your own words—including details and supporting evidence. Typically you won't paraphrase an entire source; instead you'll probably paraphrase a passage or a sentence or two.

Paraphrasing is handy when you want to share specifics but don't want to use the author's exact original wording. While quoting can be a good option (Quoting, pp. 376–80), there are times when you want the voice to be all your own. There are still other times when an author's tone is not a good fit for your purpose and audience; in these cases, use paraphrase to present that author's perspective smoothly.

A paraphrase should:

- Provide not only the big-picture message of a source, but also the details that the author uses to support his or her argument.
- Be in your own words and voice, with the same level of formality and vocabulary as the rest of your piece.
- Change both the words and the order of the ideas presented in the original.
- Usually end up being close to the same length as the original.
- Give credit to the author of the source you've paraphrased. If you are using MLA or APA conventions, be sure to credit your source with an in-text citation and correlating entry for the Works Cited or References list.

Let's look at an example. Shelby Prince, a student writing about therapeutic uses of music, found a blog called *The Contrapuntist*, where she read a post by Miguel Cano, titled "How Music Saved My Life, and Why Music Education Should Be Taken More Seriously." She wanted to integrate Cano's experience into her writing without shifting over to his voice. She decided to paraphrase.

### ORIGINAL PASSAGE FROM SOURCE
That sad instrument became my life; it became my outlet to express my frustration with teenage life. I took it everywhere, practiced everywhere and played for everyone. Like every other 15-year-old, my dream was to become a rock star. I wanted to be like my guitar heroes Alex Skolnick (from Testament), and Marty Friedman (formerly from Megadeth). Eventually, I became introduced to classical guitar music.

**SHELBY'S PARAPHRASE**

Before classical guitar music entered his life, the blogger fantasized about becoming a rock star like Alex Skolnick or Marty Friedman, and became almost physically attached to the guitar. That guitar enabled him to cope with his teenage angst (Cano).

parenthetical citation<br>names source

---

ATTENTION, WRITERS

**How to paraphrase fairly.**   When you paraphrase a passage from a source, make sure that the details you paraphrase are consistent with the "big picture" of your source; for example, if a source's author is positive overall about an experimental drug treatment, it would be unfair to paraphrase only the few negative details provided. However, it would be okay to mention the negative details, provided that you offer them in the context of the author's main (pro-treatment) argument.

---

# When Should I Paraphrase a Source?

Consider paraphrasing in the following situations:

**When you don't want to quote an author directly**   You may decide not to quote because you don't want too many competing voices in your piece. In this case, you could paraphrase the sentences from your source, keeping your voice dominant. (See "When Should I Quote from a Source?" on p. 379.)

**When *your* audience is very different from your source author's audience**   For example, the source you are using may have been written for a specialized or technical audience, and the language might not be suitable for your readers. That is the case in the first example below. A student is writing for an audience of nonexperts about various approaches to treating people convicted of crimes. However, one of her sources is very technical; it was written for criminologists who are familiar with legal terminology. This is an excellent opportunity to paraphrase. The following passage is from an article titled "A Comparative Recidivism Analysis of Releasees from Private and Public Prisons," by Lonn Lanza-Kaduce, Karen F. Parker, and Charles W. Thomas, from the journal *Crime & Delinquency*.

**ORIGINAL PASSAGE**

Recidivism was operationalized in alternative ways. FDOC records on arrest histories, sentencing, and the movement of inmates in and out of prison were the sources of the data, which were used to develop five different indicators of recidivism.

**STUDENT'S PARAPHRASE**

authors named in signal phrase; no parenthetical citation needed

Lanza-Kaduce, Parker, and Thomas examined the Florida Department of Correction's records, looking for signs that a prison releasee had returned to prison, such as a record of the releasee's being arrested again or sentenced to another prison term.

**You want your writing to flow with your own ideas and words; you want your tone to dominate**   Paraphrasing allows you to convey all of your source's information, but in your own consistent words and style. For example, imagine you are writing a blog entry in a very informal, snappy tone, and you want to paraphrase the very formal speech Queen Elizabeth II gave in Dublin in 2011.

> ### ORIGINAL PASSAGE
> Indeed, so much of this visit reminds us of the complexity of our history, its many layers and traditions, but also the importance of forbearance and conciliation. Of being able to bow to the past, but not be bound by it.
>
> ### STUDENT'S PARAPHRASE (with humorous intent)
> author named in signal phrase; no parenthetical citation needed
> The Queen remarked that you gotta remember the past, baby, but you can't let it hold you back. Our relationship's had problems, she told the Irish, but that don't mean it's gotta end.

Note: This paraphrase style can work for nonacademic genres; however, for formal research papers, we do not recommend this technique.

## How Do I Paraphrase a Source?

When you want to paraphrase a source, do the following:

**Read (or view or listen to) the passage**

**Put the source away and write down the passage from memory**   This ensures that you are articulating the ideas in your own words.

**Restate the sentence or passage in your own words — while maintaining the sense of the author's original words**   The following paraphrase retains the meaning of the original passage (from an article by Edison Elementary, "HG/HGT Education") while transforming it into a totally different voice and structure.

> ### ORIGINAL PASSAGE
> Giftedness is a collection of certain characteristics that have been displayed by remarkable adults and children past and present. Among the gifted there is great diversity; they are not a homogeneous group.
>
> ### STUDENT'S PARAPHRASE
> author named in signal phrase; no parenthetical citation needed
> According to educators at Edison Elementary, gifted adults or children are unique individuals who exhibit traits that make them stand out from their peers.

Think of paraphrasing as rephrasing. When you paraphrase, you do more than swap out key words with similar words. Following is an example of an unsuccessful paraphrase created through an inadvisable technique called "patch writing." When people patch write, they simply switch out key words and replace them with synonyms. The result is clunky at best.

The shaded words in the original (again, from the "HG/HGT Education" article by Edison Elementary) are the words the writer replaced with synonyms in the patch-written version.

**ORIGINAL PASSAGE**
Giftedness is a collection of certain characteristics that have been displayed by remarkable adults and children past and present.

**STUDENT'S UNSUCCESSFUL PARAPHRASE (what NOT to do)**
According to educators at Edison Elementary, specialness is a group of particular traits that have been shown by extraordinary people of all ages throughout time.

Notice how the patch-written version is not all that different from the original passage—only now it lacks style and voice. The writer chose to switch out words, for example, replacing *collection* with *group*. He also did not change the sentence structure or word order, and kept many of the smaller words (articles and prepositions) as they were in the original. The writer would have done better to use the original quote.

**Compare your sentence(s) to the original, making sure that you have altered the language and style enough so that the words are your own**

**Compare your sentence(s) to the original, making sure that you haven't altered the meaning or intent of the author**   Keep in mind that there are some words that you cannot change without changing the meaning of the author's content. Proper nouns and numbers, for example, should not be changed.

**Always, always, always attribute your paraphrase to its source**   Use the style that is appropriate to the genre you're composing in. For academic genres, see MLA and APA guidelines on pages 397–432.

## Guided Process | How to Paraphrase a Source

### Paul Pierre (STUDENT), *Nonviolent Protest Project: Paraphrasing Julia Bacha*

Paul, who is writing about nonviolent protest, finds a presentation by documentary filmmaker Julia Bacha. In it, Bacha argues that nonviolent protest is ignored by the media and tells a story about nonviolent protest in a Palestinian town, a story she portrays in her documentary *Budrus*. Following is a step-by-step look at how Paul paraphrased from this source. The image included is a still from Bacha's documentary film.

## BUDRUS
### Julie Bacha

**TRANSCRIPT:** I'm a filmmaker. For the last 8 years, I have dedicated my life to documenting the work of Israelis and Palestinians who are trying to end the conflict using peaceful means. When I travel with my work across Europe and the United States, one question always comes up: Where is the Palestinian Gandhi? Why aren't Palestinians using nonviolent resistance?

*Credit: Courtesy of Just Vision Media.*

The challenge I face when I hear this question is that often I have just returned from the Middle East where I spent my time filming dozens of Palestinians who are using nonviolence to defend their lands and water resources from Israeli soldiers and settlers. These leaders are trying to forge a massive national nonviolent movement to end the occupation and build peace in the region. Yet, most of you have probably never heard about them. This divide between what's happening on the ground and perceptions abroad is one of the key reasons why we don't have yet a Palestinian peaceful resistance movement that has been successful.

I'm [going to] talk about the power of attention, the power of your attention, and the emergence and development of nonviolent movements in the West Bank, Gaza and elsewhere—but . . . my case study is going to be Palestine. I believe that what's mostly missing for nonviolence to grow is not for Palestinians to start adopting nonviolence, but for us to start paying attention to those who already are. Allow me to illustrate this point by taking you to this village called Budrus.

About seven years ago, they faced extinction, because Israel announced it would build a separation barrier, and part of this barrier would be built on top of the village. They would lose 40 percent of their land and be surrounded, so they would lose free access to the rest of the West Bank. Through inspired local leadership, they launched a peaceful resistance campaign to stop that from happening.

## Paul's notes on Bacha's presentation

1. *I watched Bacha's entire presentation.* Then I watched it again. One section of what Bacha said really stood out for me—where she talks about a specific nonviolent protest in Budrus. I think I might want to use some of this in my audio essay. I watched that section of her talk a few times.

2. *Next, I read the transcript.* The entire text of Bacha's talk is available online. I focused especially on the passage that includes the Budrus story.

3. *I put the transcript aside, and paraphrased the passage from memory.* Here is what I came up with:

### MY DRAFT PARAPHRASE (of Bacha)

Violent and nonviolent protesters are similar in that to be effective, they need an audience to respond to them. When the media fails to cover nonviolent protest, they deprive nonviolent protestors of an audience (Bacha).

⌐‾‾‾‾‾‾‾‾‾⌐
parenthetical citation
names author of source

4. *I reread the passage in the transcript and evaluated my draft paraphrase.* I thought I could have done a better job in paraphrasing/restating what Bacha had to say.

5. *I revised and finalized my paraphrase.* I thought the wording of my draft paraphrase was not different enough from Bacha's original text, especially in voice and structure. Here's how I revised to correct those problems:

### MY IN-TEXT CITATION (paraphrase of Bacha)

Bacha named in signal phrase, so no parenthetical citation needed

Julia Bacha points out that all protesters—including nonviolent ones—need an audience in order to matter. It's a problem that violent protests are the ones we read about, the ones that get attention. When the media fails to cover nonviolent protest, she argues, they deprive peaceful protesters of an audience and of the potential to make a difference.

Let me show you some brief clips, so you have a sense for what that actually looked like on the ground.

FROM THE DOCUMENTARY *BUDRUS*:

*Palestinian Woman*: We were told the wall would separate Palestine from Israel. Here in Budrus, we realized the wall would steal our land.

Credit: Courtesy of Just Vision Media.

*Israeli Man:* The fence has, in fact, created a solution to terror.

*Man:* Today you're invited to a peaceful march. You are joined by dozens of your Israeli brothers and sisters.

**Paul's notes on Bacha's presentation**

6. *I cited Bacha as a source in my Works Cited list.* Although audio essays don't usually include a Works Cited list, my instructor asked me to submit one with my Artist's Statement. This caused me some strife because the MLA style for documenting digital sources is confusing to me. However, after consulting a handbook, I cited my source as follows:

**MY WORKS CITED ENTRY (MLA style)**

author name — publication date — title of short work from website — site title — URL — optional descriptive label

Bacha, Julia. "Budrus." *Just Vision,* Aug. 2011, www.justvision.org/budrus. Film clip.

In the paraphrase above (and in his summary on p. 389), Paul strips out references to Palestinians and Israelis. He believes Bacha's idea is relevant to conflicts outside of the Middle East, so he captures Bacha's comparison of violent and nonviolent protest but omits the details of the parties involved.

# Summarizing

## What Does It Mean to Summarize a Source?

When you summarize a source, you pare the whole thing down to its essence. You eliminate all specific details and give your reader the main point of what the source's author is saying. For example, you might summarize a source in the text of a paper you are writing when you want to investigate or compare the main ideas behind several different sources.

When you summarize, you should:

- Capture the ideas of the source's author.
- Be considerably shorter than the original work. For example, if you are summarizing a two-page article, your summary might be only a paragraph or less. (In the

## Susanne Mentzer
*Opera singer*

## The Catharsis of Song

Posted: 09/08/11 07:42 PM ET

The human singing voice has the power to release deep emotions. Many know of sounds that give us goosebumps. From the point of view of one who makes sounds, I refer to it as my primal scream therapy. The wonderfulness of singing can be the primal, super-human sound that pours out of one's body. It can also be humbling.

It is thought that hearing is the last sense to leave us when we die. Over the past year, I sang both my parents into the next world. In the ICU, for my mother, an amateur singer who was particularly proud of me, I think I sang my entire repertoire of hymns and arias, toned down to a low dynamic. At one point she awakened with a smile and said, in the slow, whispered voice of one who could barely breathe, "You were singing!" I am not sure if Dad heard me

in his last hours, but I would like to think so. It was a privilege that I would not trade for the world.

Even in my career I have had my own cathartic release of emotion. I once sang a matinee opera performance in Bonn, Germany, after having just put my 10-month old son and his father into a taxi to the airport to fly to the States. It was excruciatingly painful to let my child go but I was contractually obligated to stay. I went to the theater, sang my guts out, and became a blubbering idiot during curtain calls. (Fortunately, it was a dramatic role, the Composer in Strauss's Ariadne auf Naxos.) My colleagues mentioned that I was really "on" that show and that I gave so much emotion. Only then did I share what I was really crying about.

example below, a student writer summarizes twenty-one paragraphs in just one sentence.)

- Write in your own words—not the words of the source's author.

- Give credit to the author of the source summarized. Depending on the genre you compose in, the conventions for crediting sources differ. (In the example below, the student uses a signal phrase to name her source author.)

Let's return to Shelby, the student who is writing about therapeutic uses of music. She finds an article in the blog section of *The Huffington Post* by opera singer Susanne Mentzer, titled "The Catharsis of Song."

Shelby decides she wants to include the opera singer's perspective in her paper, but she wants to do so broadly and briefly, in her Introduction, to draw in her readers. Following are the first few paragraphs from Mentzer's post—as well as Shelby's summary of the post (which she read in its entirety at The *Huffington Post* blog).

### SHELBY'S SUMMARY OF AN ENTIRE ARTICLE

Opera singer Susanne Mentzer has used singing to alleviate both her own stress and tension and the stress and tension of others.

---

### ATTENTION, RESEARCHERS

**Summarizing versus paraphrasing.** When you summarize a passage from a source, you pick up on *the main points* the author is making and describe them in your own words. When you paraphrase, on the other hand, you do provide a type of summary—but one in which you restate/rephrase the author's words (not just the main points). Summarizing and paraphrasing are both subjective actions, and require you to retain the spirit of the author's meaning and ideas, even if you use them to contrast with your own.

---

# When Should I Summarize a Source?

As a researcher and writer, you might choose to summarize a source when you want to capture the main ideas of a source without going into details. As in the example of Shelby's summary on the previous page, the details of Mentzer's experiences, such as crying during rehearsal, are irrelevant to Shelby's point about the therapeutic nature of music; what matters to Shelby is that Mentzer, a professional singer, has experienced the therapeutic aspects of music in several different contexts.

# How Do I Summarize a Source?

To summarize a source, do the following:

- Read (or view or listen to) the source.
- Put the source away and write down the main ideas from memory. This ensures that you are articulating the ideas in your own words.
- Look over the main ideas you wrote down and organize them. For example, begin with a general statement and then move on to the supporting ideas.
- Also, make sure you're simply capturing the main ideas and arguments of the source's author, and not adding any of your own opinions.
- Go back and reread or re-listen to or review the original source. Compare it to what you've written to make sure you haven't distorted any of the points. Make sure you also haven't left out any of the central points.

Attribute your summary to its source. Do this not only in the text of your paper, but in your Works Cited or References list as well.

## Guided Process | How to Summarize a Source

**Paul Pierre** (STUDENT), *Nonviolent Protest Project: Summarizing Julia Bacha*

Paul, who earlier in this chapter paraphrased a passage from a talk by Julia Bacha, decides that he wants to summarize a different passage. Following are the steps he took:

## BUDRUS
### Julia Bacha

**TRANSCRIPT:** When I first heard about the story of Budrus, I was surprised that the international media had failed to cover the extraordinary set of events that happened seven years ago, in 2003. What was even more surprising was the fact that Budrus was successful. The residents, after 10 months

Credit: Courtesy of Just Vision Media.

of peaceful resistance, convinced the Israeli government to move the route of the barrier off their lands and to the green line, which is the internationally recognized boundary between Israel and the Palestinian Territories. The resistance in Budrus has since spread to villages across the West Bank and to Palestinian neighborhoods in Jerusalem. Yet the media remains mostly silent on these stories. This silence carries profound consequences for the likelihood that nonviolence can grow, or even survive, in Palestine.

Violent resistance and nonviolent resistance share one very important thing in common; they are both a form of theater seeking an audience to their cause. If violent actors are the only ones constantly getting front-page covers and attracting international attention to the Palestinian issue, it becomes very hard for nonviolent leaders to make the case to their communities that civil disobedience is a viable option in addressing their plight.

Credit: Just Vision Media.

**Paul's notes on Bacha's presentation**

1. *I revisited Bacha's talk*, and was struck by a passage in which she gives a viewpoint on Palestine and nonviolent resistance. I decided to include that material, in some way, in my audio essay.

2. *I reread the transcript*, focusing on the section on Palestine and nonviolent resistance. I decided that it might be best to summarize Bacha's argument.

3. *I drafted a summary of the passage.* To do this, I put the transcript away, and tried to provide an overview of what Bacha said in this part of her talk. Here is what I wrote:

**MY DRAFT SUMMARY (of Bacha's passage)**

*Bacha named in signal phrase, so no parenthetical citation needed*

Bacha says that residents of the Palestinian town of Budrus were able to successfully protest against the Israeli building of a fence using nonviolent strategies; however, the news reports of the conflict all focused on a few incidents that involved violence.

4. *Next, I re-viewed Bacha's talk.* I wanted to make sure I had accurately captured her point. Satisfied that I had, I put the summary away for the night.

5. *I revised my summary of Bacha's point.* The next day, when I reread my summary, I decided to cut back on some details of what Bacha had to say. Specifically, I opted not to mention that the Palestinians protested against Israel. For my audio essay, I wanted to stay focused on my main argument—that the media doesn't give enough attention to nonviolent protest—and didn't want to sidetrack my audience with the politics surrounding the protest itself. With this in mind, I revised as follows:

**MY REVISED SUMMARY (of Bacha's passage)**

Bacha describes and shows clips of protests in the Middle East that were completely nonviolent. This is in stark contrast to the media reports of the conflict, which failed to mention the nonviolent protests and focused on a handful of violent skirmishes.

6. *Next, I included my summary of Bacha's point in my audio essay.* I drew on Bacha's words to support my argument that nonviolent protest is more powerful than violent protest.

7. *I cited Bacha's talk as a source in my Works Cited list.*

**MY WORKS CITED ENTRY (MLA style)**

*author name* — *title of short work from website* — *site title*

Bacha, Julia. "Budrus." *Just Vision,*

*publication date* — *URL*

Aug. 2011, www.justvision.org/

*optional descriptive label*

budrus. Film transcript.

# Avoiding Plagiarism

Plagiarism is misrepresenting the ideas or words of others as your own. It includes submitting papers you didn't write, failing to adequately cite sources, and copying small bits and pieces from sources into your own work without properly documenting them. Plagiarism is unethical and committing an act of plagiarism can have serious consequences on your grade, your academic career, and your karma. Your school likely has a statement on academic integrity, defining penalties for acts of academic dishonesty. Be sure to familiarize yourself with the academic integrity policy at your school.

# Comparing Passages from a Source

Some plagiarism is unintentional. Writers may read several sources that express similar ideas and only cite one of these sources. Or writers may forget which source they got an idea from and not cite any source at all. Another all-too-common type of unintentional plagiarism occurs when a writer tries to paraphrase a source but doesn't significantly change the original source's language. Here are a couple of examples:

**Original passage**   From a podcast by Adam Hinterthuer, found online at *Scientific American*:

> Want to live a happier life? Try surrounding yourself with happy friends or at least find friends with happy friends. A study published online December 4th in the *British Medical Journal* says happiness can quickly go viral within your social network.

**Passage plagiarized**   The writer misrepresents the source; the source's author, Hinterthuer, is cited, but the writer has gotten the content wrong. Hinterthuer mentions only one study—not "a lot":

> There is a lot of research indicating that happiness is contagious. Simply surrounding yourself with happy friends can make you a happier person (Hinterthuer).

**Passage plagiarized**   In this case, the writer needs to provide an in-text citation. He or she has not shown that this information was obtained from the source, Hinterthuer:

> Recent research indicates that happiness is contagious. Simply surrounding yourself with happy friends can make you a happier person.

### Passage correctly presented with an in-text citation

**SUMMARY WITH MLA IN-TEXT CITATION**
Recent research indicates that happiness is contagious. Simply surrounding yourself with happy friends can make you a happier person (Hinterthuer).

### WORKS CITED ENTRY

Hinterthuer, Adam. "Happiness Is Contagious." *Scientific American*, 5 Dec. 2008, www.scientificamerican.com/podcast/episode.cfm?id=happiness-is-contagious-08-12-05 .MP3 file.

### SUMMARY WITH APA IN-TEXT CITATION

Recent research indicated that happiness is contagious. Simply surrounding yourself with happy friends can make you a happier person (Hinterthuer, 2008).

### REFERENCES LIST ENTRY

Hinterthuer, Adam. "Happiness is contagious." *Scientific American*. MP3 audio file.
  http://www.scientificamerican.com/podcast/episode.cfm?id=happiness-is-
  contagious-08-12-05.

It's important to realize that whether plagiarism is intentional or unintentional, it is a violation of academic ethics and most schools' codes of conduct. If in doubt about whether to cite a source, cite it. This will prevent you from unintentionally plagiarizing.

## CHECKLIST | Getting Help & Avoiding Plagiarism

☐ **Visit your writing center.** If you don't know how to properly summarize or paraphrase a source, consult your instructor or a writing-center tutor for help. It's never a good idea to plagiarize and then plan to apologize if caught. If you're not sure if you're using source material in a way that constitutes plagiarism, get help: Take your draft to your instructor or a tutor and explain what you're having trouble with. As long as you haven't yet turned in the paper, you haven't done anything wrong.

☐ **Use detection software.** If your school subscribes to a plagiarism-detection program like turnitin.com, you can submit a draft of your writing to the program and it will generate a report that indicates what percentage of the draft is from other sources. The report will alert you to places where you've used sources without properly citing them.

☐ **Manage your time.** Allow yourself enough time to complete your writing assignment. Sometimes students accidentally plagiarize because they don't give themselves time to properly double-check all their citations.

☐ **When in doubt, cite that source.** Remember, too, that using an image, audio clip, or video is just like quoting words from someone. These texts need to be cited just as any other source would be.

## How to Avoid Plagiarism During Your Research & Composing Process

There are certain crucial moments when researchers and writers can make mistakes that can lead to plagiarism. Please be especially careful at these points:

**When taking notes as you conduct research** Get in the habit of recording the source's bibliographic information and using quotation marks anytime you use the exact words of a source, even if you use just a few words from the source. For example, you might write in your notes:

> **Source:** *Our Stressful Lives* site, ourstressfullives.com/pets-and-stress-relief.html
> *About the source*: This site is authored by a "Certified Stress Management Coach," Jill Rheaume, who has also published a stress management workbook. She offers a variety of tips for stress management. I found the following article from the "Pets and Stress Relief: Other Benefits" section of the site, mainly from paragraph 9.

> **Notes:** Rheaume writes (in paragraph 3) that pets "make great listeners" and help reduce stress in many other ways. In paragraph 9 she writes: "Pets also increase the 'love chemical' oxytocin in our brains. In addition, they can also increase our serotonin, known as the 'happiness chemical.' Both of these things can help to reduce or even prevent stress and prove that our pets can increase our feelings of happiness and help to improve our moods."

Alternatively, you might want to create a screen capture of each source (or otherwise save the original content), so you can refer back to the original as you write.

**When quoting as you draft**   Always put quotation marks around the words you're using from the source. (In this case, there are quotation marks within quotation marks.)

> **MLA QUOTATION (no in-text cite needed because author is named)**
> Rheaume writes: "Pets also increase the 'love chemical' oxytocin in our brains."

> **WORKS CITED ENTRY**
> Rheaume, Jill. "Pets and Stress Relief: Other Benefits." *Our Stressful Lives,*
>    www.ourstressfullives.com/pets-and-stress-relief.html. Accessed 20 Aug. 2020.

> **APA IN-TEXT CITATION**
> Rheaume wrote: "Pets also increase the 'love chemical' oxytocin in our brains."

> **REFERENCES LIST ENTRY**
> Rheaume, Jill. "Pets and stress relief: Other benefits." OurStressfulLives.com. Retrieved
>    from http://www.ourstressfullives.com/pets-and-stress-relief.html.

**When paraphrasing as you draft**   Always credit the source you're paraphrasing. If you aren't sure if you've adequately rephrased the source's idea in your own words, ask a friend, classmate, or writing-center tutor to compare the original passage with your paraphrase. One trick to use when paraphrasing is to read the passage you want to paraphrase and then put the source out of sight and rewrite the idea in your own words. When you do this, you minimize the chance of accidentally using the words of the original. A paraphrase of the above content from Jill Rheaume's site follows. Note that even though we're not using Rheaume's exact words, we still provide the in-text citation.

> **PARAPHRASE WITH MLA IN-TEXT CITATION**
> Pets can make us healthier by raising the levels of oxytocin and serotonin in our brains (Rheaume).

**WORKS CITED ENTRY**

Rheaume, Jill. "Pets and Stress Relief: Other Benefits." *Our Stressful Lives*,
www.ourstressfullives.com/pets-and-stress-relief.html. Accessed 20 Aug. 2020.

**PARAPHRASE WITH APA IN-TEXT CITATION**

Pets can make us healthier by raising the levels of oxytocin and serotonin in our brains
(Rheaume).

**REFERENCES LIST ENTRY**

Rheaume, Jill. "Pets and stress relief: Other benefits." OurStressfulLives.com. Retrieved
from http://www.ourstressfullives.com/pets-and-stress-relief.html.

**When summarizing as you draft**   You can use the same strategies for summarizing
that you use for paraphrasing.

**SUMMARY IN MLA STYLE (no in-text citation needed because author is named)**

Stress management coach Jill Rheaume writes that interactions with our pets can make
us happier and more loving by altering levels of certain chemicals in the brain.

**WORKS CITED ENTRY**

Rheaume, Jill. "Pets and Stress Relief: Other Benefits." *Our Stressful Lives*,
www.ourstressfullives.com/pets-and-stress-relief.html. Accessed 20 Aug. 2020.

**SUMMARY WITH APA IN-TEXT CITATION**

Stress management coach Jill Rheaume wrote that interactions with our pets can
make us happier and more loving by altering levels of certain chemicals in the brain
(2008–2020, para. 9).

**REFERENCES LIST ENTRY**

Rheaume, Jill. "Pets and stress relief: Other benefits." OurStressfulLives.com. Retrieved
from http://www.ourstressfullives.com/pets-and-stress-relief.html.

**When drafting — without referring to notes**   Don't trust your memory! Writers
sometimes don't cite sources in their drafts, thinking they'll go back later and add citations. This is a dangerous practice because if you run out of time and end up not adding
those citations, you've plagiarized. *Always cite your sources*, even in a rough draft.

**When integrating sources**   When in doubt as to whether or not you should cite a
source, cite it. It's always better to give too much credit with source citations than to
give insufficient credit. You may wonder, for example, if a piece of information counts
as "general knowledge," and therefore doesn't need to be cited. If you're not sure if it
counts as "general knowledge," go ahead and cite a source.

## How to Avoid Plagiarism When Using Online Sources

As tempting as it is to copy and paste chunks of online sources into your notes or
drafts, minimize this practice because it greatly increases your chances of accidentally
plagiarizing. Get in the habit of putting quotation marks around every direct quote.

If you paraphrase or summarize, copy the original text into a document and indicate clearly—with color coding, highlighting, labeling, or some other device—that it is the original content from your source, and then work on your composition in a separate document. Another strategy is to create screen captures of each online source, always accompanied by the URL that will lead you back to that content.

## How to Avoid Plagiarism When Composing a Multigenre/Multimodal Project

All the above guidelines apply to multigenre/multimodal projects: Cite your sources in drafts, give credit generously, and be meticulous about using quotation marks around quoted material in your notes. Even if you are composing in a genre or mode that doesn't use the MLA or APA format for citations, you still need to credit your sources in ways that are appropriate to the genre or mode of your composition. Additionally, your instructor may want you to submit a Works Cited list or an Author's or Artist's Statement that includes MLA or APA citations. (See Chapter 5, p. 91, for example.)

## DOCUMENTING SOURCES
# A Guide to MLA & APA Styles

Documenting (or citing) a source means giving credit to the authors of any texts—including images, video, sound, or any other composition—that inform your writing, whether you're writing a research paper or creating other types of research-based compositions.

When you document sources, you show your audience where you got your information. You also develop your ethos as an author by showing that you've used reliable source material. Failing to give credit to your sources is a form of dishonesty and is considered plagiarism; it leads readers to conclude that all of the ideas and facts that you state come from your own independent thinking or research.

Whether you quote, paraphrase, or summarize from a source, you need to cite it. (For more on quoting, see pp. 376–80; for paraphrasing, see pp. 381–86; for summarizing, see pp. 386–94.)

As composers, when we cite sources, we do so using specific documentation styles. The documentation style you will use depends on the audience you're writing for: Are you writing for an academic audience, your peers, or a general/popular audience? Another factor is the subject matter you're writing about—and the discipline associated with that subject. For example, are your target readers associated with the humanities, social sciences, or sciences? The style you choose also depends on the genre you're composing in (e.g., whether you're writing a straight-up research paper or something else). Following are some guidelines for choosing a documentation style.

**Why don't musicians document their sources when they sample music?**   Many hip-hop musicians use sampling (taking a part of a song) when they create their songs. For example, Nas's song "Can't Forget About You" includes a sample from Nat King Cole's classic "Unforgettable." Not only does the sample figure in the song, but clearly Nas's title was inspired by Nat King Cole. He doesn't provide formal documentation because it is a convention within the music industry that some sampling is deemed appropriate. This, however, is subject to legal interpretation if the original composer wants to challenge the originality of the composition. To avoid potential legal issues, most musicians will obtain permission prior to including samples in their own compositions—and include some kind of credit in the liner notes if there *are* liner notes.

Composers of other genres often draw upon other sources; however, because of the conventions of the genres they're working in, they might not use formal academic documentation. Such genres include obituaries, memoirs, sets of instructions, and poems.

# How to Choose a Documentation Style

**Are you writing a research paper for a specific academic discipline?**

- For papers for an English course or other humanities course, you will almost always use the documentation style of the Modern Language Association (MLA; mla.org). However, in some English courses that focus on writing in or across disciplines, you might use the documentation style that is associated with your major area of study.

- For papers for a social science course, you will probably use the format of the American Psychological Association (APA; apastyle.org).

- For papers for a history course, you will likely use *Chicago* style, based on *The Chicago Manual of Style* (chicagomanualofstyle.org).

- For papers for a science course, you will probably use the style specified by the Council of Science Editors in *Scientific Style and Format: The CSE Manual for Authors, Editors, and Publishers* (councilscienceeditors.org).

**Are you composing a photo essay, ad, or documentary, or in some other alternative genre? And are your subject and audience based in the humanities, social sciences, or sciences?**   While MLA tends to be the default documentation style of the English composition course, and is likely the format your instructor may require, you might have the option of deciding for yourself which documentation style would be best for your composition and chosen subject. For example, if your topic involves criminal justice or gender studies, you could make a case for using APA style. If you are creating a lab report or doctor's notes, you might use the CSE documentation style.

Most of our students submit MLA-style Works Cited lists with their compositions, though some, depending on their chosen genres, subjects, and major areas of study, use APA, *Chicago*, or CSE. If you plan to use one of these styles, you might want to discuss it with your instructor first, and make a case for why that style would be best.

**Are you composing an Author's Statement to accompany your genre composition?** If you are creating an Author's Statement to accompany your composition (whether it's a research paper or alternative genre project), we recommend the MLA style of documentation, unless you've made a case for using APA, *Chicago*, or CSE. (For more on the Author's Statement—the reflective piece that can be submitted with any genre composition—see Chapter 6.)

While there are several documentation styles for you to choose from, the following sections of this chapter provide basic guidance for using MLA and APA styles, as these are the styles you are most likely to use in conjunction with this textbook.

# MLA Style

The MLA style of documentation is presented in the *MLA Handbook*, 8th ed. (MLA, 2016). It is commonly used in English courses and other courses in the humanities. This style has been around a long time, but it has evolved to take into account the many types of sources we work with today.

The MLA style of documentation has two main components:

1. In-text citations
2. List of Works Cited (a.k.a. Works Cited list)

**The in-text citation**    Each time you cite a source in your paper—whether through a signal phrase or a parenthetical reference—you cue readers to a corresponding entry in your Works Cited list. When you include an in-text citation, you:

- Name the author of your source (or title if author is not provided)
- Provide a page number for that source (if there is one)
- Make sure you have a corresponding entry in your Works Cited list

**The list of Works Cited**    In your Works Cited list, at the end of your paper, you:

- Provide publication information about each source (for web sources that don't provide publication dates, provide an "Accessed" date)
- Alphabetize your sources by authors' last names (or by title if an author is not provided)
- Include a URL for each online source (for more on this, see the box on p. 400)

Following is an example of an in-text citation along with its corresponding entry in the Works Cited list.

IN-TEXT CITATION

"Parents with this philosophy know there may be things their daughter hides from them, but they don't take it as a personal insult or an indication that their relationship with their daughter is weak" (Wiseman 54).
       author        exact page that quotation is from

WORKS CITED ENTRY

           author:
last name, first name          title of book                    publisher
 Wiseman, Rosalind. *Queen Bees and Wannabes*. 3rd ed., Penguin Random House,
publicaton
   year        page number
 2016, p. 54.

**In-text citations: General guidelines**   There are two main ways to handle an in-text citation: by using a signal phrase or a parenthetical reference (or some combination).

SIGNAL PHRASE (author named in phrase)

author

Wiseman suggests that "parents with this philosophy know there may be things their daughter hides from them, but they don't take it as a personal insult or an indication that their relationship with their daughter is weak" (54).

exact page that quotation is from

PARENTHETICAL REFERENCE (author cited in parentheses)

"Parents with this philosophy know there may be things their daughter hides from them, but they don't take it as a personal insult or an indication that their relationship with their daughter is weak" (Wiseman 54).

author        exact page that quotation is from

**Works Cited entries: General guidelines**   For each in-text citation in your paper, you need to provide a corresponding entry in your Works Cited list. The following guidelines provide the basic format for the MLA Works Cited entry.

- Name the author by last name, followed by first name.

author        book title        publisher        publication year        page range        descriptive label (optional, for clarity)

Mezrich, Ben. *Bitcoin Billionaires.* Flatiron Books, 2019, pp. 1–12. Kindle.*

- For works by three or more authors or editors, list the name that appears first on the cover or title page, followed by "et al." (See also page 402 example 5.) Note that for university presses, you should use the abbreviation "UP."

lead author or editor: last name, first name, then et al.        spell out "editors"        book title

Valentine, Scott Victor, et al., editors. *After Tobacco: What Would Happen If Americans*

publication year        page range        publisher

*Stopped Smoking?* Columbia UP, 2011, pp. 30–36.

- Present the titles of long works—books or entire websites—in italics.

author        book title        publisher        publication year        page range

Orlean, Susan. *The Library Book.* Simon and Schuster, 2018, pp. 113–17.

author        website title        publisher

Sullivan, Andrew. *The Dish: Biased & Balanced.*  The Daily Beast,

URL        in the absence of a publication date, provide an access date

andrewsullivan.thedailybeast.com/. Accessed 8 Sept. 2020.

*Provide a page range if your source is an e-book with numbered pages.

- Present the titles of short works—articles or other short pieces from books or periodicals—in quotation marks.

  author      article title

  Tiffany, Kaitlyn. "Managing Your Friendships, with Software."
  periodical    publication    page
  title      date      range

  *The Atlantic*, Nov. 2019, pp. 38–41.

  author          article title

  Vagianos, Alanna. "The First Person on Mars Could Be a Woman, NASA Says?"
  periodical and     publication
  site title         date            URL

  *The Huffington Post*, 28 Oct. 2019, www.huffpost.com/entry/the-first-person-on-

  mars-could-be-a-woman-nasa-says_n_5daf0bdae4b0422422cc1f8a.

- Present titles with initial capital letters—except in the case of articles (*a, the*, etc.), prepositions (*to, from, with*, etc.), or coordinating conjunctions (*and, but, or, for*, etc.), unless these words come first or last.

                           publication    page
  author        book title     publisher   year    range

  Hemingway, Ernest. *To Have and Have Not.* Scribner's, 1937, pp. 1–4.
                                          publication
  author        book title          publisher     year

  Bryson, Bill. *The Body: A Guide for Occupants.* Knopf Doubleday Publishing, 2019,
  page    descriptive label
  range    (optional, for clarity)

  pp. 12–13. Nook.

- For print works, include the publisher's name as it appears on the title page. If no publisher is given on the title page, then see the copyright page.

                                  publication    page
  author        book title      publisher      year    range

  Lahiri, Jhumpa. *Unaccustomed Earth.* Bloomsbury Publishing, 2008, pp. 52–56.

- For both print and online works, provide the date that the piece was published. For online sources, if no publication date is provided, include the date you accessed the source. For online sources, provide the URL at the end of the entry (omitting https://).

  author          article title

  Wu, Katherine J. "From Ashes to AI: How Technology Puts a New Lens on Ancient Texts."
  publication           publication
  title     publisher    date            URL

  *NOVA*, PBS, 5 Nov. 2019, www.pbs.org/wgbh/nova/article/scan-image-process-

  translate-ancient-text/.

- When needed to clarify a source, you can include a descriptive label. MLA makes this practice optional. Whatever you decide, be consistent.

author               book title

Gates, Henry Louis, Jr. *Life upon These Shores: Looking at African American History:*

publication page      descriptive label
publisher    year    range    (optional, for clarity)

*1513–2008.* Alfred A. Knopf, 2011, pp. 112–14. Kindle.

publication    descriptive label
developer    title    publisher    year    (optional for clarity)

Auroch Digital Ltd. *Megaquarium.* Microsoft Studios, 18 Oct. 2019. Video game.

Organize your Works Cited list alphabetically. For entries of more than one line, indent additional lines five spaces (this is called hanging indentation).

---

Works Cited

Auroch Digital Ltd. *Megaquarium.* Microsoft Studios, 18 Oct. 2019. Video game.

Bryson, Bill. *The Body: A Guide for Occupants.* Knopf Doubleday Publishing, 2019, pp. 12–13. Nook.

Gates, Henry Louis, Jr. *Life upon These Shores: Looking at African American History: 1513–2008.* Alfred A. Knopf, 2011, pp. 112–14. Kindle.

Hemingway, Ernest. *To Have and Have Not.* Scribner's, 1937, pp. 1–4.

Lahiri, Jhumpa. *Unaccustomed Earth.* Bloomsbury Publishing, 2008, pp. 52–56

Mezrich, Ben. *Bitcoin Billionaires.* Flatiron Books, 2019, pp. 1–12. Kindle.

Orlean, Susan. *The Library Book.* Simon and Schuster, 2018, pp. 113–17.

Sullivan, Andrew. *The Dish: Biased & Balanced. The Daily Beast,* andrewsullivan.thedailybeast.com/. Accessed 8 Sept. 2020.

Tiffany, Kaitlyn. "Managing Your Friendships, with Software." *The Atlantic,* Nov. 2019, pp. 38–41.

Vagianos, Alanna. "The First Person on Mars Could Be a Woman, NASA Says?" *The Huffington Post,* 28 Oct. 2019, www.huffpost.com/entry/the-first-person-on-mars-could-be-a-woman-nasa-says_n_5daf0bdae4b0422422cc1f8a.

Valentine, Scott Victor, et al., editors. *After Tobacco: What Would Happen If Americans Stopped Smoking?* Columbia UP, 2011, pp. 30–36.

Wiseman, Rosalind. *Queen Bees and Wannabes.* 3rd ed., Penguin Random House, 2016, p. 54.

Wu, Katherine J. "From Ashes to AI: How Technology Puts a New Lens on Ancient Texts." *NOVA,* PBS, 5 Nov. 2019, www.pbs.org/wgbh/nova/article/scan-image-process-translate-ancient-text/.

---

# MLA Models

## Models for Basic Situations

**1. Author is named in a signal phrase**   When citing a source in the text of your paper, you need to name your author. You can do this in a signal phrase or in a parenthetical reference (along with the source's page number) following your citation. It's simplest to name the author in a signal phrase and keep the parenthetical reference brief. The following citation refers to material from Ben Goldfarb's book *Eager: The Surprising, Secret Life of Beavers and Why They Matter* (Chelsea Green Publishing, 2019).

> IN-TEXT CITATION
> Ben Goldfarb doesn't mince words when discussing European settlers in North America. "You're probably familiar with most of the colonists' original environmental sins," he writes: "They wielded an axe against every tree, lowered a net to catch every fish, turned livestock onto every pasture, churned the prairie to dust" (9).

> WORKS CITED ENTRY
> Goldfarb, Ben. *Eager: The Surprising, Secret Life of Beavers and Why They Matter.*
>     Chelsea Green Publishing, 2019, pp. 9–22.

**2. Author is named in parentheses**   If you decide not to name your author in a signal phrase, then name the author in your parenthetical reference along with the page number; don't use any punctuation between the name and page number.

> IN-TEXT CITATION
> Goldfarb goes on to argue that Europeans "began despoiling" any part of the North American landscape they touched "the moment they set boots on the stony shore of the New World" (Goldfarb 9).

> WORKS CITED ENTRY
> Goldfarb, Ben. *Eager: The Surprising, Secret Life of Beavers and Why They Matter.*
>     Chelsea Green Publishing, 2019, pp. 9–22.

**3. Individual author name is not provided**   If you cannot locate an author's name for your source, use the title. Provide the complete title of the text (or video, etc.) in a signal phrase—or give a shortened version of the title in the parenthetical reference. (Note: If the author is an organization, see example 6 on p. 403.) Following are sample citations for an article titled "Beavers have an impact on the climate" that appears on Phys.org.

> IN-TEXT CITATION (title in signal phrase; no page number available)
> According to a recent *Phys.org* article, "Beavers Have an Impact on the Climate," beavers can be sources of carbon emissions, but can also cause rising water levels that cause carbon to be dissolved into the soil, keeping the greenhouse gas from rising to the ozone.

OR (shortened title in parentheses; no page number available)

Beaver habitats are capable of releasing *or* sinking hundreds of thousands of tons of carbon annually ("Beavers Have").

WORKS CITED ENTRY

"Beavers Have an Impact on the Climate." Phys.org, Aug. 2018, phys.org/news/2018-08-beavers-impact-climate.html.

**4. Author identified by screen name only**   Some online sources identify an author, but not by a traditional first and last name. For example, the author of this VICE article is simply identified as "VICE Sports."

IN-TEXT CITATION (no page number available)

In 2016, Arsene Wenger celebrated 20 years as the manager of Arsenal Football Club (VICE Sports).

WORKS CITED ENTRY

VICE Sports. "An Arbitrary Milestone for Arsene Wenger: Reflections on His 20 Years at Arsenal." *VICE*, 30 Sept. 2016, www.vice.com/en_us/article/aebkxa/an-arbitrary-milestone-for-arsene-wenger-reflections-on-his-20-years-at-arsenal.

**5. More than one author**   Some sources have multiple authors. If your source has *two authors*, include both of their names. Following is a reference to *Three Days at the Brink: FDR's Daring Gamble to Win World War II*, a book by Bret Baier and Catherine Whitney (William Morrow, 2019).

IN-TEXT CITATION (two authors)

FDR surprised some with his decision to move his family to Albany upon winning his district's State Senate seat (Baier and Whitney 38).

WORKS CITED ENTRY

Baier, Bret, and Catherine Whitney. *Three Days at the Brink: FDR's Daring Gamble to Win World War II*. William Morrow, 2019, p. 38.

For *three or more authors*, use the phrase "et al." (short for the Latin phrase *et alia*, which means "and others"). Following is a reference to an article published in *European Journal of Sport Science* titled "Immune Nutrition and Exercise: Narrative Review and Practical Recommendations." It was written by Neil C. Williams, Sophie C. Killer, Ida Siobhan Svendsen, and Arwel Wyn Jones.

IN-TEXT CITATION (four or more authors; no page number available)

According to a 2018 review, athletes pushing themselves to maintain long periods of overly-intense training may be impairing their immune cell function (Williams et al.).

WORKS CITED ENTRY

Williams, Neil C., et al. "Immune Nutrition and Exercise: Narrative Review and Practical Recommendations." *European Journal of Sport Science*, vol. 19, no. 1, 2019, doi.org/10.1080/17461391.2018.1490458.

ATTENTION, RESEARCHERS USING MLA

**Does your source have no page numbers?**   Many digital sources do not have page numbers. When using these sources, do your best to meet MLA's requirements:

Provide the author, title, publisher/publication title, date of publication, and if no publication date is given, provide your access date. Also, please note: While MLA does not require you to provide descriptive labels such as "photograph," "chart," "map," "cartoon," "episode," and so on, you can choose to do so if you think this would be helpful to your readers. The Works Cited entry for an episode of *The Colbert Report* that you found online could look like this:

**WORKS CITED ENTRY (for online clip)**

Host — episode title — name of show/series

Colbert, Stephen, host. "Nancy Pelosi." *The Late Show with Stephen Colbert,*

publisher — episode date — URL

CBS, 31 Oct. 2019, www.cbs.com/shows/the-late-show-with-stephen-colbert/

video/28ajlHgnaNk1_eijHCeU6PcVcJV5VsNM/the-late-show-10-31-19-

descriptive label (optional for clarity)

nancy-pelosi-/. Episode.

The Works Cited entry for a film you saw in a theater could look like this:

**WORKS CITED ENTRY (for movie)**

director — movie title — major performers

Eggers, Robert, director. *The Lighthouse.* Performances by Robert Pattinson and

publisher — release date — descriptive label (optional, for clarity)

Willem Dafoe, A24, 2019. Film.

**6. Author is an organization**   Follow the same basic format as for sources with any other type of author.

IN-TEXT CITATION (no page number available)

Mental health is a human and civil rights issue (Mental Health America).

WORKS CITED ENTRY

Mental Health America. "Position Statement 21: Rights of Persons with Mental Health and Substance Use Conditions." *Mental Health America,* nmha.org/go/position-statements/21. Accessed 30 Sept. 2013.

**7. No page numbers**   Many online sources (unless the source is a PDF) have no page numbers. The example above and examples 3 and 4 (pp. 401–402) show how to handle entries for sources without page numbers.

Another example: A TED Talk on video games.

IN-TEXT CITATION

Narula discusses how the current experience of video games and how they interact with reality has been heretofore "woefully limited" (Narula).

WORKS CITED ENTRY

Narula, Herman. "The Transformative Power of Video Games." *TED*, 31 Oct. 2019, ted
.com/talks/herman_narula_the_transformative_power_of_video_games.

**8. Source used more than once in a paragraph**   If you refer to a source multiple
times in one paragraph, you can provide the author's name(s) just once, as long as it's
clear it's still the same source. For example, see the citation for the article titled "Panic
Disorder" from *The Journal of the American Medical Association*. The authors are Janet
M. Torpy, Alison E. Burke, and Robert M. Golub.

IN-TEXT CITATION

According to research published in *The Journal of the American Medical Association*,
not everyone who has a panic attack gets diagnosed with panic disorder (Torpy et al.).
Still, as the article makes clear, many Americans suffer from mental health issues.

WORKS CITED ENTRY

Torpy, Janet M., et al. "Panic Disorder." *Journal of the American Medical
Association*, vol. 305, no. 12, 2011, pp. 20–30, jama.jamanetwork.com/article
.aspx?articleid=646264.

## Models for Specific Types of Sources

**9. Book**   For more in-text citation models for books, see examples 1, 2, and 5 (pp. 401
and 402). The following is from *Blowout: Corrupted Democracy, Rogue State Russia, and the
Richest, Most Destructive Industry on Earth* by Rachel Maddow.

IN-TEXT CITATION

Rockefeller's new company, Standard Oil, grew rapidly: "By 1875, thanks to the fire
sale that followed the first frightening financial panic and depression in industrialized
America, Rockefeller had taken control of every major refining center in the country"
(Maddow 23).

WORKS CITED ENTRY

Maddow, Rachel. *Blowout: Corrupted Democracy, Rogue State Russia, and the Richest,
Most Destructive Industry on Earth*. Crown, 2019, p. 23.

**10. Article or essay**   The following model shows how to cite an article from an online
periodical. In November 2019, *National Geographic* published an article by Erin Blakemore
titled "Idealistic and Tough, Catherine the Great Sought to Modernize Russia."

IN-TEXT CITATION (article from online magazine)

Catherine the Great expanded Russia's borders significantly during her 34-year rule,
managing to almost double the Russian population (Blakemore).

Blakemore, Erin. "Idealistic and Tough, Catherine the Great Sought to Modernize Russia." *National Geographic*, Nov. 2019, www.nationalgeographic.com/history/reference/people/who-was-catherine-great/.

The following model shows how to cite an article from a database.

IN-TEXT CITATION (article from a database)

Some images have the power to "spur a revolution" (Childs).

WORKS CITED ENTRY

Childs, Arcynta Ali. "The Power of Imagery in Advancing Civil Rights." *Smithsonian*, Oct. 2011, pp. 40–41. *OmniFile Full Text Select*, web.b.ebscohost.com.ezproxy.bpl.org/.

**11. Source quoted in another source**   The following models show how to cite a source that is quoted in another source. "Living with the Kincade Fire" by Clinton Cargill was published in *The New York Times* (on November 4, 2019). Cargill's article features quotations from residents of Sonoma County, California. To cite one of those quotations, use the phrase "qtd. in" to indicate that you did not read the quoted source itself, but rather found the quoted material in another source.

IN-TEXT CITATION

The worsening wildfires in California have taken on an almost biblical quality for California residents affected by the recurring natural disaster. One truck driver described it as "a dragon breathing fire. That's the only way I can describe it. I didn't think that the firemen were going to be able to stop it." (qtd. in Cargill).

WORKS CITED ENTRY

Cargill, Clinton. "Is Anybody Out There?" *The New York Times*, The New York Times Company, Nov. 2019, www.nytimes.com/2019/11/04/opinion/california-wildfires.html?action=click&module=Opinion&pgtype=Homepage.

**12. Encyclopedia or dictionary entry — or wiki entry**   In your signal phrase or parenthetical reference, provide the word or phrase that you looked up in the dictionary or encyclopedia. If the work or entry has an author, provide that also. For the following example, there is no author provided by *Encyclopaedia Britannica*. Also, because the source (*Encyclopaedia Britannica*) and publisher (Encyclopaedia Britannica, Inc.) are essentially the same, MLA does not require that the publisher name be included in the Works Cited list.

IN-TEXT CITATION (for online encyclopedia)

Though a beautiful building in its own right, the Taj Mahal is also a mausoleum, housing the remains of the wife of Mughal emperor Shah Jahān ("Taj Mahal").

WORKS CITED ENTRY

"Taj Mahal." *Encyclopaedia Britannica*, www.britannica.com/topic/Taj-Mahal. Accessed 17 Aug. 2019.

**IN-TEXT CITATION (for online source)**

During the Battle of Wabash of the Northwest Indian War, the Western Confederacy of Native Americans dealt the American military a devastating defeat ("St. Clair's Defeat").

**WORKS CITED ENTRY**

"St. Clair's Defeat." *Wikipedia*, en.wikipedia.org/wiki/St._Clair%27s_defeat. Accessed 4 Nov. 2019.

---

**ATTENTION, *WIKIPEDIA* LOVERS**

Check with your instructor about using *Wikipedia* as a source. It is a public wiki that can be edited by anyone. Tip: *Wikipedia* can be a great place to start your research, especially because the "Reference," "Further Reading," and "External Links" sections can often lead you to excellent and reliable sources to use in your research project. For example, the "St. Clair's defeat" entry provides links to the U.S. Army Heritage and Education Center, books authored by historians, and websites hosting versions of a folk song composed about the defeat. See also *Wikipedia*'s entry (or go to wikipedia.org and type in "Researching with Wikipedia").

---

**13. Entire website**   In the rare instance that you will want to cite an entire website — rather than a specific portion of it, such as an article — use the following model. (For information on citing a short work from a website, see example 14 on page 407.) MLA requires that you provide a website's author. Note that an author can be an organization such as a library or museum. If no author is provided, begin your Works Cited entry with the title of the site.

### Website with no author

**IN-TEXT CITATION**

It is possible for an internet radio station, drawing from a database and using your preferences for artists, songs, and genres, to personalize your experience, playing only the music you want to hear (Pandora).
                                                          └─────┘
                                                        website title

**WORKS CITED ENTRY**

*Pandora*. Music Genome Project and Pandora Media Inc., pandora.com/. Accessed 2 Sept. 2019.

### Website with author or editor

**IN-TEXT CITATION**

As the national conversation becomes more hostile and divisive with each passing day, many Americans find themselves turning to sites like FactCheck.org to provide a clearer, less partisan take on the news (Robertson et al.).
                                                    └──────────────┘
                                                     website editors

**WORKS CITED ENTRY**

Robertson, Lori, et al., editors. *FactCheck.org*, factcheck.org/. Accessed 4 Aug. 2019.

**14. Short work from a website**   Most of what you cite from the internet can be categorized as a "short work from a website." A short work is any text (of any type and medium) that is not book length or that appears as an internal page or section of a website. A short work can be an article, report, poem, song, video, and so on.

### Short work with no author

IN-TEXT CITATION

Before you invest in travel insurance, make sure what you're getting isn't something already covered by your employer or certain credit cards ("The 10 Best Travel Tips for 2019").

title of short work from a website

WORKS CITED ENTRY

"The 10 Best Travel Tips for 2019." *The Cultureur,* thecultureur.com/best-travel-tips-
for-2019/. Accessed 30 Sept. 2019.

### Short work with an author

IN-TEXT CITATION

Though it may be tempting to argue or lash out when an editor rejects a piece you've submitted, it's in one's best interest to accept such rejection with grace or even silence (Monks).

author

WORKS CITED ENTRY

Monks, Christopher. "Don't Be a Jerk to Your Online Humor Editor." *Vulture,* 4 Nov.
2019, www.vulture.com/2019/11/mcsweeneys-editor-chris-monks-advice-jerks.html.

**15. Video, movie, or TV show**   In general, cite these sources as you would a short work from a website (see example 14). When citing a movie or any work that includes a director, begin with the title and then identify the director, as shown below. Note: Although MLA style does not require it, keep in mind that you can add a descriptive label to your Works Cited entry if you think that would be helpful to your readers. For example, you can add words to indicate a source's type, such as "episode," "advertise-ment," "cartoon," "pamphlet," "photograph," "painting," and so on.

IN-TEXT CITATION

The first episode of the second season of *The Handmaid's Tale* starts the season with its signature nail-biting intensity (Barker).

director

WORKS CITED ENTRY (for online episode)

Barker, Mike, director. "June." *The Handmaid's Tale,* Hulu, 25 April 2018, www.hulu
.com/series/the-handmaids-tale-565d8976-9d26-4e63-866c-40f8a137ce5f. Episode.

**16. Video game, online game, or software**   To cite an entire video game, follow the format for an entire website (see example 13). For a clip from a video game, follow the format for a short work from a website. As noted in example 15, you can include descriptive labels such as *game*, *software*, and so on.

### Entire video game

IN-TEXT CITATION

It's quite common in video games for the premise to be based on an alternate historical timeline—*Outer Worlds'* universe predicates its existence on the failure of presidential assassin Leon Czolgosz to murder President William McKinley, thereby creating a future where Theodore Roosevelt was never president (Outer Worlds).

video game title

WORKS CITED ENTRY

*Outer Worlds*. Obsidian Entertainment, 2019, Windows. Game.

### Clip from video game

IN-TEXT CITATION

In *Outer Worlds'* opening cutscene, players are quickly introduced to a setting both advanced and dystopian ("Opening Cinematic Cutscene").

video game clip title

WORKS CITED ENTRY

clip title

"Opening Cinematic Cutscene." *Outer Worlds*. Obsidian Entertainment, 2019,
Windows. Game clip.

**17. Visuals (photos, maps, charts, posters)**    Cite these as you would a short work from a website (see example 14) or other, longer work. Include the following, if available: author's or artist's name, title of the work, name of publication, and date of publication. You also have the option to note the type of the composition that your source is, for example, "photograph," "map," "chart," or "poster."

IN-TEXT CITATION

The photo shows neurologist Francisco Lopera gazing searchingly at a slide as though it alone may hold the answer to preventing dementia (Ríos).

photographer

WORKS CITED ENTRY

Ríos Escobar, Frederico. "Francisco Lopera, a Neurologist at the University of Antioquia in
Medellin, Colombia, Has Been Painstakingly Collecting Brains, Birth and Death Records
from One Sprawling Colombian Family to Study Alzheimer's." *The New York Times*,
4 Nov. 2019, www.nytimes.com/2019/11/04/health/alzheimers-treatment-genetics
.html?action=click&module=Top%20Stories&pgtype=Homepage. Photograph.

**18. Comic strip/graphic work**    Think of comic strips as short works—from longer works such as websites, magazines, and so on—and cite them as you would a short work or article from a website (see example 14), online journal, book, or other source.

As an option, you can include the label "cartoon" or "comic strip" at the end of your Works Cited entry if you think that would benefit your readers. For graphic novels (fiction) or memoirs (nonfiction), follow the format that you would for a book. In some cases, the author is also the illustrator; when that is not the case, be sure to include the name of the illustrator, preceded by the phrase "Illustrated by" (see example below).

### Comic strip

IN-TEXT CITATION

Parrish's irreverent take on revered literature lends the works she references a jocular relatability that contrasts with their often deadly serious tones (Parrish).

author/artist

WORKS CITED ENTRY

Parrish, R.E. "The Sick Rhymes of the Ancient Mariner" *ReParrish Comics*, 1 Jul. 2019, reparrishcomics.com/image/185986699343. Comic strip.

### Excerpt from a graphic memoir (author is also illustrator)

IN-TEXT CITATION

Bechdel weaves references to mythology and literature into the loose narrative throughout her graphic memoir, comparing her father to figures such as Icarus and Daedalus (Bechdel 7).

author/artist

WORKS CITED ENTRY

Bechdel, Alison. *Fun Home*. Mariner Books, 2007, p. 7. Graphic memoir.

### Excerpt from a graphic novel (with an author and an illustrator)

IN-TEXT CITATION

The story opens with a journal entry that makes clear the character's obsessions with gore, filth, and death, not to mention Communists and intellectuals (Moore 1).

author

WORKS CITED ENTRY

artist

Moore, Alan. *Watchmen*. Illustrated by Dave Gibbons, DC Comics, 2008, pp. 1–32. Graphic novel.

**19. Advertisement**   To cite an ad, give the name of the product being advertised. Following are the in-text citation and Works Cited entry for an ad for oVertone Coloring Conditioner, found at the company website. For the in-text citation, provide a shortened version of the product name.

IN-TEXT CITATION

A recent ad campaign for color-depositing conditioner claims to color and soften hair, promising vibrant color "sans damage and cold showers" (oVertone Coloring Conditioner).

ad title (shortened)

oVertone Coloring Conditioner. *oVertone*. https://overtone.co/. Accessed 30 Oct. 2019. Advertisement.

**20. Personal e-mail, text message, letter, or interview**   To cite an e-mail message (that you've written or received), provide the writer's name and the subject line. Next, provide the words "Received by" followed by the name of the recipient and the date the message was received. It is optional to include the descriptive label "E-mail" at the end. For a text message you've received, provide the writer's name followed by "Received by the author," followed by the date the text was received. For a letter you've received, provide the author's name and the phrase "Received by the author," followed by the date it was received. To cite an interview that you've conducted, provide the interviewee's name and "Interview by the author" followed by the date. Please note that MLA style calls for the word *e-mail* to be hyphenated.

### E-mail *(received)*

IN-TEXT CITATION

Once customers search for a flight, hotel, or car, the organization e-mails periodic pricing updates, which can lead to a better deal for the consumer (Hotwire).

author of e-mail

WORKS CITED ENTRY

Hotwire. "Another Way to Save on Portsmouth Hotels." Received by the author, 15 Sept. 2019. E-mail.

### Text Message *(received)*

IN-TEXT CITATION

At the rally, a student was pepper-sprayed (Tamura).

author of text message

WORKS CITED ENTRY

Tamura, Annika. Received by the author, 1 Oct. 2020. Text message.

### Letter *(received)*

IN-TEXT CITATION

I received an unsettling report of suspicious activity involving my personal credit information (Experian).

author of letter

WORKS CITED ENTRY

Experian National Consumer Assistance Center. Received by the author, 15 Jan. 2020. Letter.

### Interview (conducted)

IN-TEXT CITATION

The world-traveling journalist admitted that while she might have wanted to stay home on her couch eating Ben and Jerry's Chunky Monkey, she did not have the time: Moscow, Afghanistan, and Cairo awaited (Amanpour).

person interviewed

WORKS CITED ENTRY

Amanpour, Christiane. Interview with the author, 21 Feb. 2020.

**21. Blog post or social media posting**   Cite as you would a short work from a website (see example 14); if the entry has no title, create a brief title based on the first line of the entry. For Twitter posts, however, MLA requires the full text of the tweet, presented without changes, in place of the title.

IN-TEXT CITATION

The National Interagency Fire Center declared on Monday that the National Preparedness Level for wildfires would be moving from PL-1 to PL-2 later in the day (National Interagency Fire Center).

author

WORKS CITED ENTRY

National Interagency Fire Center. "Due to adequate resource availability and the decreasing potential for emerging significant wildland fires in multiple geographical areas, the National Preparedness Level will move to PL-1 at 2pm MST today." *Twitter*, 4 Nov. 2019, twitter.com/NIFCfire.

**22. Audio recording or podcast from the web**   Cite audio recordings or podcasts that you've accessed online in the same way you would a short work from a website (see example 14).

### Podcast

IN-TEXT CITATION

Aaron Mahnke expounds on the price humans are willing to pay for answers in a divination-themed episode of *Lore* (Episode 128).

episode title

WORKS CITED ENTRY

"Episode 128: A Hole in the Head." *Lore*. Narrated by Aaron Mahnke, 28 Oct. 2019, www.lorepodcast.com/episodes/128. Podcast.

### Song

IN-TEXT CITATION

The artist utilizes the whispery moans and frenetic beat that fans have come to expect from his solo work (Yorke).

**WORKS CITED ENTRY**

Yorke, Thom. "*I Am a Very Rude Person.*" *Anima*, Unsustainabubble Ltd, 2019, play.google
.com/store/music/album/ANIMA?id=Biptxw23d5oufctd2fe2uvqnczi&hl=en_US. Song.

**23. Phone app**    Cite a phone app as you would a website, or if you're referring to
part of the app, cite it as you would a short work from a website (see example 14). It is
optional to include the descriptive label "Phone app."

**IN-TEXT CITATION**

The Associated Press allows users of its app to choose the types of stories—such as
sports, finance, or U.S. politics—about which to receive notifications (AP News).

app title

**WORKS CITED ENTRY**

*AP News*. Version 3.2 for iPhone. The Associated Press, iTunes, 5 Nov. 2019, apps
.apple.com/us/app/ap-news/id364677107. Phone app.

**24. Government or business document**    For a government document, provide the
author, title, and date. If there is no author, provide the name of the government agency
(and department, if any). Follow the rules for a short work from a longer work (e.g., a
book, journal, or website). For a historical document, such as the one included below,
provide the title in italics.

*Government document*

**IN-TEXT CITATION**

He wrote: "[A]ll persons held as slaves within any State or designated part of a State,
the people whereof shall then be in rebellion against the United States, shall be then,
thenceforward, and forever free" (Lincoln).

author

**WORKS CITED ENTRY**

title of document

Lincoln, Abraham. *Emancipation Proclamation*. 1 Jan. 1863. The Library of Congress,
loc.gov/pictures/item/97507511/resource/cph.3b53030/?sid=40c1ec586dad
774d8a08ebfbf8cdff07. Accessed 12 Sept. 2020.

*Business document (annual report)*

**IN-TEXT CITATION**

Microsoft has thrived under these economic conditions, making 2019 a "record-
breaking year" for the company (Nadella).

author

**WORKS CITED ENTRY**

title of document

Nadella, Satya. "Microsoft Corporation: Annual Report 2019." Microsoft, 16 Oct. 2019,
www.microsoft.com/investor/reports/ar19/index.html#.

**25. Literary work (novel, poem, fairy tale, etc.)** Provide the author, title, publisher, and date. For web sources, provide a URL. For e-books, it is optional to include a descriptive label, for example "Kindle" or "Nook," to identify for readers the brand platform.

### Novel (print)

WORKS CITED ENTRY

Coates, Ta-Nehisi. *The Water Dancer*. One World, 2019.

### Novel (e-book)

WORKS CITED ENTRY

Coates, Ta-Nehisi. *The Water Dancer*. One World, 24 Sept. 2019. Nook.

### Poem

WORKS CITED ENTRY

Su, Adrienne. "Lychee Express." *Poetry Foundation*, www.poetryfoundation.org/
poetrymagazine/poems/148684/lychee-express. Accessed 11 Apr. 2020.

**26. Selection from an anthology or textbook** Begin with the selection author and title, followed by the anthology or textbook title, editors, publisher, year, and page range.

IN-TEXT CITATION

The internet uses a variety of sensory inputs to re-condition our brains to interface with

content (Carr).

author of selection (shortened)

WORKS CITED ENTRY

author of selection

Nicholas Carr. "The Juggler's Brain." *The Bedford Book of Genres*, edited by Amy
Braziller and Elizabeth Kleinfeld, 3rd ed., Bedford/St. Martin's, 2021, p. 502.

information on textbook where selection appears

**27. Object/artifact (cereal box, etc.)** If you find an object or artifact online, cite it as a short work from a website (see example 14). As an option, you can include a descriptive label for the item in your Works Cited entry.

IN-TEXT CITATION

Children might be drawn to the sunny yellow box, but parents likely focus on the red
heart and the soft claim about lowering cholesterol (Cheerios).

Name of object

### Object (found online)

WORKS CITED ENTRY

"Cheerios." General Mills, www.cheerios.com/Products/Cheerios. Accessed 10 Sept.
2019. Cereal box.

### Object (found in physical world)

WORKS CITED ENTRY

"Cheerios." General Mills. Cereal box.

▲ OBJECT
Cheerios box.

# APA Style

The APA style of documentation is the style presented in the *Publication Manual of the American Psychological Association*, 7th ed. (Washington: APA, 2019). It is commonly used in the behavioral and social science disciplines, which include courses in psychology and in sociology, and some English and cultural studies courses.

The APA style of documentation has two main components:

1. In-text citations
2. List of References

**The in-text citation**   Your in-text citations refer your readers to your list. Each time you cite a source in your paper—whether through a signal phrase or a parenthetical reference—you cue readers to a corresponding entry in your References list. When you include an in-text citation, you:

- Name the author of your source
- Provide the source's year of publication—and a corresponding page number
- Make sure you have a corresponding entry (for each in-text citation) in your References list

**The References list**   In your References list, at the end of your paper, you:

- Provide publication information about each source
- Alphabetize your sources by authors' last names (or by title if an author is not provided)

The following example shows an in-text citation along with its corresponding entry in the References list.

IN-TEXT CITATION

As students who visit our writing centers are working with multimodal

author        publication year

compositions (Sheridan, 2010), it makes sense to open up our

idea of what it means to help with the entire composing processes (p. 3).

exact page where information is from

---

**ATTENTION, RESEARCHERS**

**A note about APA & tense.**   When you use a signal phrase to discuss a source, you must introduce the source by using the past or present perfect tenses. For example: "Lady Gaga (2020) said," or "Lady Gaga (2020) has argued." For more examples, see the APA in-text citation models provided in this chapter (pp. 418–32).

Note that MLA dictates a different approach, and requires you to use the present tense. For example: "Lady Gaga (2020) says," or "Lady Gaga (2020) argues." See pages 401–13 for MLA models.

---

## REFERENCES LIST ENTRY

publication
author      year              title of chapter             editors

Sheridan, D. M. (2010). Writing centers and the multimodal turn. In D. M. Sheridan &

title of book

J. A. Inman (Eds.), *Multiliteracy centers: Writing center work, new media, and multimodal rhetoric* (pp. 1–22). Hampton Press.

page range    publisher
of chapter

**In-text citations: General guidelines**    There are two main ways to handle an in-text citation: by using a signal phrase or a parenthetical reference (or some combination).

**SIGNAL PHRASE (author named in phrase)**

publication
authors      year

Kingsolver et al. (2007) explained to readers that they "had come to the farmland to eat deliberately" (p. 23).

exact page that quotation is from

**PARENTHETICAL REFERENCE (author named in parentheses)**

"When academics are strongly motivated to teach and are satisfied with and take pride in their teaching," those positive feelings carry over into their feelings about the schools at which they teach (Zhang, 2019, para. 3).

author  publication    for this online source, no page number is available,
year         but source has paragraph numbers

**References entries: General guidelines**    Provide a corresponding entry in your References list for each in-text citation in your paper. The following guidelines provide the basic format for the APA References list entry.

- Give the author's last name, followed by initials for all first and middle names. Provide additional authors' names with each last name followed by initials for first and middle names.

author: last      publication
name + initial(s)   year         title of book

Ben-Shahar, T. (2007). *Happier: Learn the secrets to daily joy and lasting fulfillment.*

publisher

McGraw-Hill.

authors: last    publication
name + initial(s)   year       title of article

Ganegoda, D. B., & Bordia, P. (2019). I can be happy for you, but not all the time:

title of journal

A contingency model of envy and positive empathy in the workplace. *Journal of*

page
volume  range           DOI

*Applied Psychology, 104*(6), 776–795. https://doi.org/10.1037/apl0000377

issue

- Present the titles of long works—books or entire websites—in italics. Capitalize the first word of the title; other words in the title (except proper nouns) are lowercased. If there is a subtitle, capitalize the first word of the subtitle.

author: last name + initial(s)     publication year     title of book

Deutsch, D. (2011). *The beginning of infinity: Explanations that transform the world.*

publisher

Viking Penguin.

- Present the titles of short works from books or websites without quotation marks or italics. Capitalize the first word of the title; other words are lowercased (though be sure to retain the capitalization of proper nouns). If there is a subtitle, capitalize the first word of the subtitle. IMPORTANT: For all online sources, include the URL. APA suggests you provide the exact URL for the specific article or other work you're referring to. For example, the article cited below is from Wired.com. The URL takes readers to the page for the article itself, not Wired's homepage.

author: last name + initial(s)   publication year, month, day   title of article   title of magazine   paragraph range

Vlahos, J. (2019, March). Alexa, I want answers. *Wired,* 58–65.

article URL

https://www.wired.com/story/amazon-alexa-search-for-the-one-perfect-answer/

- For print works, omit the city and state of publication, and spell out the entire name of the publisher.

author: last name + initial(s)   Publication year   title of book

Dugatkin, L. A. & Trut, L. (2017). *How to tame a fox (and build a dog).*

publisher

Chicago University Press.

- For both print and online works, provide the date that the piece was published. For online sources, provide the URL, but not the access date—unless there is a chance the content of the source may change.

author: last name + initial(s)   publication year   title of book

Gazzaniga, M. S. (2019). *The consciousness instinct: Unraveling the mystery of how the*

publisher

*brain makes the mind.* Farrar, Straus and Giroux.

author: last name + initial(s)   publication year, month, day   title of article   descriptive label

Gladwell, M. (2019, January 14). Is marijuana as safe as we think? [Editorial].

title of magazine     article URL

*The New Yorker.* https://www.newyorker.com/magazine/2019/01/14/

is-marijuana-as-safe-as-we-think

- If your source is a work that would benefit from clarification, provide that term in brackets. (See models for these on pp. 426–32.)

publication year,<br>
author      month, day      title of newspaper editorial

Los Angeles Times Editorial Board. (2019, September 4). Gavin Newsom wants to stop

descriptive label

rent gouging. Will lawmakers finally stand up for tenants? [Editorial].

title of newspaper      editorial URL

Los Angeles Times. https://lat.ms/2lBlRm1

Organize your References list alphabetically. For entries of more than one line, indent additional lines five spaces (this is called hanging indentation).

References

Ben-Shahar, T. (2007). *Happier: Learn the secrets to daily joy and lasting fulfillment.* McGraw-Hill.

Deutsch, D. (2011). *The beginning of infinity: Explanations that transform the world.* Viking Penguin.

Dugatkin, L. A. & Trut, L. (2017). *How to tame a fox (and build a dog).* Chicago University Press.

Ganegoda, D. B., & Bordia, P. (2019). I can be happy for you, but not all the time: A contingency model of envy and positive empathy in the workplace. *Journal of Applied Psychology, 104*(6), 776–795. https://doi.org/10.1037/apl0000377

Gazzaniga, M. S. (2019). *The consciousness instinct: Unraveling the mystery of how the brain makes the mind.* Farrar, Straus and Giroux.

Gladwell, M. (2019, January 14). Is marijuana as safe as we think? [Editorial]. *The New Yorker.* https://www.newyorker.com/magazine/2019/01/14/is-marijuana-as-safe-as-we-think

Los Angeles Times Editorial Board. (2019, September 4). Gavin Newsom wants to stop rent gouging. Will lawmakers finally stand up for tenants? [Editorial]. *Los Angeles Times.* https://lat.ms/2lBlRm1

Sheridan, D. M. (2010). Writing centers and the multimodal turn. In D. M. Sheridan & J. A. Inman (Eds.), *Multiliteracy centers: Writing center work, new media, and multimodal rhetoric* (pp. 1–22). Hampton Press.

Vlahos, J. (2019, March). Alexa, I want answers. *Wired,* 58–65. https://www.wired.com/story/amazon-alexa-search-for-the-one-perfect-answer/

# APA Models

## Models for Basic Situations

**1. Author is named in a signal phrase**   When citing a source, name your author in a signal phrase—that is, name the author in the body of your text, and provide the source publication year and page number in parentheses. Or use a parenthetical reference—as shown in the example below—and provide everything in parentheses: the author's last name, the source publication year, and page number.

The simplest, cleanest method is to name the author in a signal phrase and keep the parenthetical reference brief:

**IN-TEXT CITATION**

Bruns (2017) showed that "the consequences of incarceration spill over into family life, impacting the employment of not only currently and formerly incarcerated men but also their female partners" (p. 211).

**REFERENCES LIST ENTRY**

Bruns, A. (2017). Consequences of partner incarceration for women's employment. *Journal of Marriage and Family, 79*(5), 1331–1352. https://doi.org/10.1111/jomf.12412

**2. Author is named in parentheses**   If you don't name your author in a signal phrase, then do so in your parenthetical reference along with the publication year and page number; use commas between the name, year, and page number.

**IN-TEXT CITATION**

Part of what has made the study relevant is the focus on the impact of incarceration on romantic partners rather than the impact on those who have been incarcerated, which has already been studied extensively and is well understood (Bruns, 2017, p. 1340).

**REFERENCES LIST ENTRY**

Bruns, A. (2017). Consequences of partner incarceration for women's employment. *Journal of Marriage and Family, 79*(5), 1331–1352. https://doi.org/10.1111/jomf.12412

**3. Individual author name is not provided**   In the rare case that you cannot locate an author name for your source, use the title (or the first word or two of the title) in parentheses. (Note: If the author is an organization, see example 6.) Following are sample citations for a brief article titled "Pushed Out" that appears in *The Economist*.

**IN-TEXT CITATION (title in signal phrase; no page number available)**

According to a current *Economist* article, "Pushed Out" (2019, August 24), "there were an estimated 2.4 m[illion] eviction cases" in the United States in 2016 (para. 2).

OR (shortened title in parentheses; no page number available)

Evictions are part of the cause of poverty ("Pushed," 2019, August 24, para. 2).

REFERENCES LIST ENTRY

Pushed out. (2019, August 24). *The Economist*. https://www.economist.com/
united-states/2019/08/24/new-research-probes-evictions-causes-and-consequences

ALTERNATIVE APPROACH: If you consider the publisher, *The Economist*, as the author, here is how the in-text citation and References list entry would work:

IN-TEXT CITATION (organization treated as author)

Typically, the only lawyers present in eviction cases are representing the landlords (*The Economist*, 2019, August 24, para. 2).

REFERENCES LIST ENTRY

The Economist. Pushed out. (2019, August 24). *The Economist*. https://www.economist.com/
united-states/2019/08/24/new-research-probes-evictions-causes-and-consequences

**4. Author identified by screen name only**   Some online sources identify an author, but not by a traditional first and last name. For example, the author of an eHow article is simply identified as an "eHow Contributor."

IN-TEXT CITATION (no page number available)

Among the suggestions for improving memory were doing crossword puzzles, reading, and playing word games (eHow Contributor, 2020).

REFERENCES LIST ENTRY

eHow Contributor. (2020, September 6). 7 creative hobbies that keep your memory
sharp. *eHow*. https://www.ehow.com/how_12343803_7-creative-hobbies-boost-
memory.html

**5. More than one author**   Some sources have multiple authors. In general, you will list only up to two names in your in-text citations; for your References list, you can list up to twenty authors, using an "&" just before the final name. Below is a reference to an article from the *Journal of Applied Psychology*.

IN-TEXT CITATION (two authors)

To better understand the back and forth of author relationships, the authors explore the interplay between positive empathy and envy in employees across a variety of different workplaces (Ganegoda & Bordia, 2019, p. 777).

REFERENCES LIST ENTRY

Ganegoda, D. B. & Bordia, P. (2019). I can be happy for you, but not all the time: A contingency model of envy and positive empathy in the workplace. *Journal of Applied
Psychology, 104*(6), 776–795. https://doi.org/10.1037/apl0000377

*For three or more authors*, use only the first author's name and the phrase "et al." (short for the Latin phrase *et alia*, which means "and others"). Note: The article cited in the examples below is from a database; many databases provide a DOI number for use in your References list entry. If there is no DOI, then include the URL.

**IN-TEXT CITATION (three or more authors)**

A recent study found a boost in girl power in India, thanks to affirmative action laws that gave women leadership roles in their village councils. In terms of career goals, the gender gap for teen girls in the villages with women leaders closed by 32 percent (Beaman et al., 2012, pp. 582–586).

**REFERENCES LIST ENTRY (article retrieved from database with DOI)**

Beaman, L., Duflo, E., Pande, R., & Topalova, P. (2012, February 3). Female leadership raises aspirations and educational attainment for girls: A policy experiment in India. *Science, 335*, 582–586. https://doi.org/10.1126/science.1212382

**REFERENCES LIST ENTRY (article from publisher site, abstract or summary only)**

Beaman, L., Duflo, E., Pande, R., & Topalova, P. (2012, February 3). Female leadership raises aspirations and educational attainment for girls: A policy experiment in India [Abstract]. *Science, 335*, 582–586. http://www.sciencemag.org/content/335/6068/582.abstract

In your References list entry, list up to twenty authors. If there are more than twenty authors, list the first nineteen followed by three ellipsis dots and the last author's name. Following is a reference to an article published in a developmental biology journal *Development* titled "Mapping a Multiplexed Zoo of mRNA Expression."

**IN-TEXT CITATION (twenty-one or more authors)**

The authors explore how HCR can help researchers in their attempts to map mRNA across a variety of imaging settings (Choi et al., 2016, October 1, p. 3633).

**REFERENCES LIST ENTRY (twenty-one or more authors)**

Choi, H. M, Calvert, C. R., Husain, N., Barsi, J. C., Deverman, B. E., Hunter, R. C., Kato, M., Lee, S. M, Abelin, A. C, Rosenthal, A. Z, Akbari, O. S., Li, Y., Hay, B. A., Sternberg, P. W., Patterson, P. H., Davidson, E. H., Mazmanian, S. K., Prober, D. A., van de Rijn, M., . . . Pierce, N. A. (2016, October 1). Mapping a multiplexed zoo of mRNA expression. *Development, 143*(19), 3632–3637. https://doi.org/10.1242/dev.140137

**6. Author is an organization**   Follow the same basic format as for sources with any other type of author.

**IN-TEXT CITATION**

The American Civil Liberties Union argued that since 9/11, our civil liberties have "undergone constant erosion" thanks to expanded powers of government security agencies (ACLU, 2012, para. 1).

**OR**

Since 9/11, Americans' civil liberties, especially in the digital realm, have been under attack by security agencies such as the NSA and FBI (American Civil Liberties Union [ACLU], 2012, para. 1).

LATER CITATIONS
(ACLU, 2012)

REFERENCES LIST ENTRY

American Civil Liberties Union. (2012). Protecting civil liberties in the digital age,

paras. 1–3. http://www.aclu.org/protecting-civil-liberties-digital-age

**7. No page numbers**   Most print sources have numbered pages, but unless your online source is provided as a PDF file, it probably will not include page numbers. APA calls for paragraph numbers or heading titles in any sources that do not include page numbers.

IN-TEXT CITATION

Citing federal data, *The New York Times* reported a 30 percent drop in "people entering teacher preparation programs" between 2010 and 2014 (Rich, 2015, para. 10).

REFERENCES LIST ENTRY

Rich, M. (2015, August 9). Teacher shortages spur a nationwide hiring scramble

(credentials optional). *The New York Times.* https://nyti.ms/1WaaV7a

**8. Source used more than once in a paragraph**   Let's say that you give the author's name in a signal phrase in the text of your paper (and the publication date and page number in parentheses). To refer to that same source later in the same paragraph, simply provide the page number (or paragraph number).

## For a print source

The example below refers to a book by Malcolm Gladwell about human interactions. It was published in 2019 by Little, Brown and Company.

IN-TEXT CITATION

The trope of the introvert has gained a lot of traction in recent years, but Gladwell (2019) makes a case for engaging with people—not only family and friends, but complete strangers (22). While online shopping and the ease of having food delivered to your house makes it easier than ever to avoid casual interactions, Gladwell reminds us that these small interactions shouldn't be high-pressure situations, designed to form lasting new relationships. Instead, he makes the case that "[s]ometimes the best conversations between strangers allow the stranger to remain a stranger" (xii).

REFERENCES LIST ENTRY

Gladwell, M. (2019). *Talking to strangers: What we should know about the people we*

*don't know.* Little, Brown and Company.

## For an online source

The next example refers to an article by Michael Johnson of NASA. Note that while there are no page numbers for this source, we have provided paragraph numbers. APA

---

**ATTENTION, RESEARCHERS**

**A note about APA style.**   Like language, documentation styles are always evolving. APA style changes from edition to edition, of APA's manual, and even daily on the organization's blog. Our best advice:

1. Provide readers with the information they'll need to identify and find your sources.
2. If you aren't sure how to cite a particular source, and you don't see a model for it here, find a similar source and adapt the model provided.

also suggests that particularly long URLs be replaced in citations with biy.ly or other shortened URLs, as you see in the example below.

### IN-TEXT CITATION

Michael Johnson (2019) underscores the importance for astronauts in knowing "how fire spreads and behaves in space" (para. 1). As with many of the innovations prompted by NASA's need to keep their astronauts safe and to discover how best to explore our universe, research into the way that fire operates in space are useful here on earth as well. The big takeaway, of course, is in generating energy, which is often done through combustion (para. 4).

### REFERENCES LIST ENTRY

Conover, E. (2019, June 22). Space flames may hold secrets to soot-free fire. *Science News, 195*(11), 5. https://bit.ly/2p0Xj89

---

### ATTENTION, RESEARCHERS USING APA

**Does your source have no page numbers?** For most online sources (anything that's not a PDF), you will not be able to provide page numbers. However, for online articles and other text-based digital sources, you can provide paragraph numbers. Paragraph numbers help your readers see exactly where you drew from a source.

For sources you cannot provide paragraph numbers for—videos, audio recordings, and many other types of digital media—we (and APA) recommend that you do your best to provide whatever information will guide your audience to a particular moment in that video or audio recording. You can provide a time range, for example.

Let's look at a model from a video. Here is how you might cite a particular moment from that source.

### IN-TEXT CITATION

According to Erik Qualman's (2011) video on the role of social media, "If Facebook were a country it'd be the world's 3rd largest" (0:42–0:44).

Let's say that elsewhere in your paper you refer to other moments of the video, which is two minutes and thirty-five seconds long. This is what a very precise References list entry would look like.

### REFERENCES LIST ENTRY

Qualman, E. (2011, June 8). Social media revolution 2011 [Video file]. http://www.youtube.com/watch?v=3SuNx0UrnEo (0:01–2:35)

---

# Models for Specific Types of Sources

**9. Book**  The following is from *The Heartbeat of Wounded Knee* by David Treuer.

---

ATTENTION, RESEARCHERS

**Citing entire works is a rarity.**  When working with sources, 99.9 percent of the time you refer to specific passages and pages from a source—and include them in both your in-text citation and the corresponding References list entry. In the *extremely* rare instance that you need to summarize an entire work (as shown in the example below), you do not need to provide specific page numbers. Unless you are creating an annotated bibliography, we do not recommend that you make a practice of summarizing entire sources.

---

IN-TEXT CITATION (that summarizes entire work)

In his exploration of the Battle at Wounded Knee and its aftermath on Native America into the present day, David Treuer (2019) traces an important timeline in American history that sheds important light on the social and political structure of Native American life today.

REFERENCES LIST ENTRY

Treuer, D. (2019). *The heartbeat of Wounded Knee: Native America from 1890 to the present*. Riverhead Books.

IN-TEXT CITATION (that quotes from a specific passage)

Treuer (2019) writes that instead of direct confrontations, the U.S. government "switched tactics . . . [and] encouraged widespread encroachment by settlers . . . reneged on treaty promises of food and clothing, and funded the wholesale destruction of the once vast buffalo herds of the Plains" (p. 3).

REFERENCES LIST ENTRY

Treuer, D. (2019). *The heartbeat of Wounded Knee: Native America from 1890 to the present*. Riverhead Books. 1–12.

IN-TEXT CITATION (that paraphrases a specific passage)

Parts of the bison killed were shipped to the East Coast to be used in manufacturing (Treuer, 2019, p. 3).

REFERENCES LIST ENTRY

Treuer, D. (2019). *The heartbeat of Wounded Knee: Native America from 1890 to the present*. Riverhead Books. 1–12.

**10. Article or essay**  The following models show how to cite online and print articles. In October 2019, a magazine called *Scientific American* published an article by Kristof Koch—"Is Death Reversible?"—in two forms: online and in print.

IN-TEXT CITATION (article from an online magazine)

According to Koch (2019, October), "[a]n experiment that partially revived slaughterhouse pig brains raises questions about the precise end point of life" (para. 1).

REFERENCES LIST ENTRY
Koch, C. (2019, October). Is death reversible? *Scientific American*. https://www
    .scientificamerican.com/article/is-death-reversible/

IN-TEXT CITATION (article from a print magazine)
According to Koch (2019, October), "[a]n experiment that partially revived slaughter-house pig brains raises questions about the precise end point of life (p. 34).

REFERENCES LIST ENTRY
Koch, C. (2019, October). Is death reversible? *Scientific American, 321*(4), 34–37.

**11. Source quoted in another source**   The following models show how to cite a source that is quoted in another source, whether online or print. "What It Takes to Be a Space Pilot" by Mara Johnson-Groh was published by *Discover* magazine in two different forms—in a print edition (in its November 2019 issue) and online at discovermagazine. com (on November 8, 2019). Johnson-Groh's article features several quotations from working pilots. To cite one of those quotations, you need to use the phrase "as cited in" to indicate that you did not read the quoted source itself, but rather found the quoted material in another source.

IN-TEXT CITATION (article from an online magazine)
According to David Mackay, Virgin Galactic's chief pilot, the more experience a person has flying, the greater their chances of encountering "situations that are more challenging" (as cited in Johnson-Groh).

REFERENCES LIST ENTRY
Johnson-Groh, M. (2019, November 8). "What it takes to be a space pilot." *Discover*
    (para. 4). http://blogs.discovermagazine.com/crux/2019/11/08/what-it-takes-to-be-
    a-space-pilot/#.Xcm-xVdKiUk

IN-TEXT CITATION (article from a print magazine)
According to David Mackay, Virgin Galactic's chief pilot, the more experience a person has flying, the greater their chances of encountering "situations that are more challenging" (as cited in Johnson-Groh, 2019).

REFERENCES LIST ENTRY
Johnson-Groh, M. (2019, November). What it takes to be a space pilot. *Discover, 49*–51.

---

ATTENTION, *WIKIPEDIA* LOVERS

Check with your instructor about using *Wikipedia* as a source. It is a public wiki that can be edited by anyone. Tip: *Wikipedia* can be a great place to start your research, especially because the "Reference," "Further Reading," and "External Links" sections can often lead you to excellent and reliable sources to use in your research project. For example, the "Racial segregation" entry provides links to *The Washington Post*, *The American Historical Review*, and books authored by experts on apartheid. You can also go to wikipedia.org and type in "Researching with Wikipedia."

---

**12. Encyclopedia or dictionary entry — or wiki entry**   When the author or authors of an entry are named, follow the format that you would for an article (see example 10). When no author is named, use the name of the publisher or publication — or begin the citation with the title of the entry. If there is a publication date, provide it. If not, then indicate that there is no date by using "n.d." in parentheses following the author's name.

> IN-TEXT CITATION (for online dictionary)
>
> publisher name
>
> According to *Merriam-Webster* (2019), psychoanalysis is used to "treat emotional disorders."
>
> REFERENCES LIST ENTRY
>
> *Merriam-Webster.* (2019). Psychoanalysis. http://www.merriam-webster.com/
> dictionary/psychoanalysis

Unlike *Merriam-Webster*, *Wikipedia* is a multiple-authored wiki: This means that the authors and the content itself change all the time. Following is a model for citing a *Wikipedia* entry. We've included a "Retrieved from" date because any *Wikipedia* entry cited today may be quite different by tomorrow.

> IN-TEXT CITATION (for a wiki)
>
> Racial segregation (2019), according to *Wikipedia*, is defined as "the separation of humans into racial groups in daily life" (para. 1).
>
> REFERENCES LIST ENTRY
>
> *Wikipedia.* (2019, February 6). Racial Segregation. Retrieved February 8, 2019, from
> http://en.wikipedia.org/wiki/Racial_segregation (para. 1)

**13. Entire website**   In the extremely rare instance that you will want to cite an entire website — rather than a specific portion of it, such as an article — use the following model. (For information on citing a short work from a website, see example 14 on page 426.) APA requires that for web sources, you provide the name of the organization that authored the page, the publication date, if there is one, the name of the site, and the URL. If content is likely to change regularly, include a "Retrieved" date for the information.

*Website with an organization as author*

> IN-TEXT CITATION
>
> website sponsor/publisher
>
> Fastweb (2020) divided its scholarship links into categories including "Art Scholarships," "Hispanic Scholarships," and "Scholarships for College Freshmen."
>
> REFERENCES LIST ENTRY
>
> Fastweb. Retrieved October 21, 2020, from http://www.fastweb.com

**14. Short work from a website**   Most of what you cite from the internet can be categorized as a "short work from a website." A short work is any text (of any type and medium) that is not book length or that appears as an internal page or section of a website. A short work can be an article, report, poem, song, video, and so on. In some cases, you will include a descriptive label (see example 15).

### Short work with an organization as author

IN-TEXT CITATION

website sponsor/publisher

The WebMD entry "Anxiety Disorders" (2020) defined various types of disorders, such as panic disorder and social anxiety disorder.

REFERENCES LIST ENTRY

WebMD (2020). Anxiety disorders. http://www.webmd.com/anxiety-panic/guide
    /mental-health-anxiety-disorders

### Short work with an individual author

IN-TEXT CITATION

In an evaluation of the new Netflix series "Devil Next Door," Stevens (2019) explores the ability of the show "to raise big-picture questions tied to seemingly universal fears" (para. 1).

REFERENCES LIST ENTRY

Stevens, A. D. (2019, November 8). Devil next door: Was a Nazi among us? *Salon*.
    https://www.salon.com/2019/11/08/netflix-the-devil-next-door-review-nazi-
    john-demjanjuk/

**15. Video, movie, or TV show**   In general, if you find these sources online, cite them as you would a short work from a website (see also example 14). Include an identifying label in brackets: "Television series episode," "Film," and so on.

IN-TEXT CITATION

During the *Fleabag* episode "The Provocative Request," the title character learns about her friend Claire's crush (Waller-Bridge & Bradbeer, 2019).

REFERENCES LIST ENTRY (for a TV episode)

Waller-Bridge, P. (Writer), & Bradbeer, H. (Director). (2019, March 18). The provocative
    request (Season 2, Episode 3) [TV series episode]. In P. Waller-Bridge, H. Williams,
    & J. Williams (Executive Producers), *Fleabag*. Two Brothers Pictures; BBC.

REFERENCES LIST ENTRY (for a different episode, online)

Waller-Bridge, P. (Writer), & Bradbeer, H. (Director). (2019, March 18). The provocative
    request (Season 2, Episode 3) [TV series episode]. In P. Waller-Bridge, H. Williams, &
    J. Williams (Executive Producers), *Fleabag*. https://www.amazon.com/gp/video/detail
    /B07QBD39W7/ref=atv_dp

**16. Video game, online game, or software**   To cite an entire video game, follow the format for an entire website and include a description—"Video game," "Online game," or "Computer software"—in brackets. For a clip from a video game, follow the format for a short work from a website (see example 14 on page 427).

### Entire video game

IN-TEXT CITATION

The goal of one popular game was to plow, plant, and harvest on "your own" virtual land (ConcernedApe, 2016).
        video game publisher

REFERENCES LIST ENTRY

ConcernedApe. (2016). *Stardew Valley* [Video game]. Chucklefish.

### Clip from video game

IN-TEXT CITATION

In *Outer Worlds'* opening cutscene, players are quickly introduced to a setting both advanced and dystopian ("Opening Cinematic Cutscene, 2019").
        video game clip title

WORKS CITED ENTRY

        format

"Opening Cinematic Cutscene." (2019). *Outer Worlds.* [Game Clip]. Obsidian
    Entertainment.

**17. Visuals (photos, maps, charts, posters)**   Cite these works as you would a short work from a website (see example 14 on page 427), or other longer work. Include the following, if available: author's or artist's name, date of composition, title of the work, and publication's name. Also note the medium of the composition—"Photograph," "Map," "Chart," "Poster," and so on—in brackets.

IN-TEXT CITATION

Most visitors spend time in the capital city of Kuala Lumpur, located in the southwestern part of the country (Lonely Planet, 2019).
        author of map

REFERENCES LIST ENTRY

Lonely Planet. (2019). Malaysia [Map]. http://www.lonelyplanet.com/maps/asia
    /malaysia/

**18. Comic strip/graphic work**   Think of comic strips as short works—from longer works such as websites, magazines, and so on—and cite them as you would a short work or article from a website, online journal, book, or other source. Include the description—"Cartoon" or "Comic strip"—in brackets. For graphic novels (fiction) or memoirs (nonfiction), follow the format that you would for a book. In some cases, the author is also the illustrator; when that is not the case, in parentheses after the title, indicate the illustrator's name followed by the word "illustrator."

### Comic strip

**IN-TEXT CITATION**

author/artist

Thomas's (2012) comic strip offered a commentary on the mentality of social media users.

**REFERENCES LIST ENTRY**

Thomas, C. (2012, February 5). Watch your head [Comic strip]. *The Washington Post Writer's Group.* http://www.cartoonistgroup.com/properties/wpwg .php?id=106&today=2012-02-05

### Excerpt from a graphic memoir *(author is also illustrator)*

**IN-TEXT CITATION**

author/artist

In his graphic memoir, Hart (2016) explores the untimely death of his daughter, Rosalie.

**REFERENCES LIST ENTRY**

Hart, T. (2016). *Rosalie Lightning: A graphic memoir.* St. Martin's Press.

### Excerpt from a graphic novel *(with an author and an illustrator)*

**IN-TEXT CITATION**

author

Scott (2019) offers a playful glimpse into the castle of Darth Vader through the eyes of young heroes.

**REFERENCES LIST ENTRY**

artist

Scott, C. (2019). *Star Wars Adventures: Tales from Vader's Castle.* (Derek Charm, Chris Fenoglio, Kelley Jones, & Corin Howell, illustrators.) IDW Publishing.

**19. Advertisement**   To cite an ad, name the product being advertised, along with the word "Advertisement" in brackets. Following are the in-text citation and References list entry for an ad that appeared in a print magazine, *The Atlantic.*

**IN-TEXT CITATION**

*The Atlantic* supports itself in part through advertising on a variety of topics, including prescription drugs. (America's Biopharmaceutical Companies, 2018).

author of ad

**REFERENCES LIST ENTRY**

America's Biopharmaceutical Companies [Advertisement]. (2018, September). *The Atlantic, 322*(2), 2.

**20. Personal e-mail, letter, or interview**  Even though APA does not require you to list e-mails, personal interviews, letters, memos, or other personal communications in your References list, we recommend you do so for the sake of clarity. To cite an item in the text of your paper, include the author's first and middle initials (if known) and last name and the term "personal communication" (regardless of whether it was an interview, letter, or e-mail), and then the full date of the communication. In your References list, you can indicate in brackets the medium of the item, such as "E-mail."

### E-mail (received)

IN-TEXT CITATION

Metro State's next Undergraduate Research Conference was scheduled to take place in April (P. Ansburg, personal communication, February 9, 2020).
author of e-mail

REFERENCES LIST ENTRY

Ansburg, P. (2020, February 9). Next annual metro state undergraduate research conference [E-mail].

### Interview (conducted)

IN-TEXT CITATION

person interviewed

I spoke to one tutor who described a method known as "glossing" (P. Calzia, personal communication, May 2, 2020).

REFERENCES LIST ENTRY

Calzia, P. (2020, May 2). Writing center discussion [Interview by E. Kleinfeld].

**21. Blog post or social media posting**  Cite postings as you would any short work from a website (see example 14). In your References list entry, add in brackets a brief description of the item: "Web log," "Facebook post," "Twitter post," and so on. Note: APA requires that you use the term "Web log" instead of "blog." As with example 4, use the author's screen name if that is all that is provided.

IN-TEXT CITATION

author

Marino (2019) used social media to convey some of the items on his bucket list.

REFERENCES LIST ENTRY

Marino, B. (2019). Bucket list [Facebook post]. Retrieved from http://www.facebook .com/billy.marino1

**22. Audio recording or podcast from the web**  Cite podcasts that you've accessed online in the same way you would cite a short work from a website (see example 14). Audio recordings should be cited similarly to works of art, regardless of whether they are downloaded from the web or not.

### Podcast from web

**IN-TEXT CITATION**

West (2018) introduced listeners to the philosophical concept of logical positivism.

**REFERENCES LIST ENTRY**

West, S. (Host). (2018, July 27). Logical positivism (No. 120) [Audio podcast episode]. In *Philosophize this!* https://philosophizethis.org/logical-positivists/

### Song from the web (via iTunes)

**IN-TEXT CITATION**

Gomez's (2019) song "Lose You to Love Me" explored one of her recurring themes about moving on from a difficult relationship.

**REFERENCES LIST ENTRY**

Gomez, S. (2019). Lose you to love me [Song]. Interscope Records. https://music.apple .com/us/album/lose-you-to-love-me/1484383006?i=1484383177

**23. Phone app** Cite a phone app as you would an advertisement, but include "Phone app" or "Mobile App" in brackets. Use the date of the most recent iteration of the phone app as the publication date. Put the developer's or publisher's name where you would put an author for a print source.

**IN-TEXT CITATION**

A cartographic app with a global scale, Google Earth allows you to zoom in and out almost anywhere on the planet (Google LLC, 2019).

app publisher

**REFERENCES LIST ENTRY**

Google LLC. (2019). *Google earth* (Version 9.3.3) [Mobile app]. App Store. https://apps. apple.com/us/app/google-earth/id293622097

**24. Government or business document** For a government document, provide the author, the most specific government organization or department, the title, and the date, as well as publication information. If there is no author, provide the name of the government agency (and department, if any).

### Government document

**IN-TEXT CITATION**

One of the top concerns of organizers of farmers' markets was the availability of parking for customers (Ragland & Tropp, 2014, pp. 6–10).

authors

**REFERENCES LIST ENTRY**

Ragland, E., & Tropp, D. U.S. Department of Agriculture, Agricultural Marketing Service. (2014). *USDA national farmers market managers survey*. U.S. Department of Agriculture, 6–10.        └ title of document

### Business document *(annual report)*

IN-TEXT CITATION (for document found online; no page numbers)

The company that makes Clif Bars is investing in solar energy (Pham & Hammond, 2010).

editors

REFERENCES LIST ENTRY

title of document

Pham, T., & Hammond, E. (Eds.). Clif Bar & Company (2018). All aspirations: Clif Bar & Company annual report [PDF file]. https://issuu.com/clifbar/docs/clif_bar_all_ aspirations_report_201_41d449fdd34e27

## 25. Literary work (novel, poem, fairy tale, etc.)   Provide the author, date, title, and publisher. For a selection (such as an essay) within a longer work (such as a collection of essays), provide the selection title before the full title.

IN-TEXT CITATION

Drawing on traditional fairy tale elements, Novik (2018) uses evocative language and begins with a winter where "[t]he cold kept stealing out of the woods earlier and earlier, eating at our crops" (2).

### Novel *(print)*

REFERENCES LIST ENTRY

Novik, N. (2018). *Spinning silver.* Random House.

### Novel *(e-book)*

REFERENCES LIST ENTRY

Novik, N. (2018). *Spinning silver* [Kindle version]. https://www.amazon.com/ Spinning-Silver-Novel-Naomi-Novik-ebook/dp/B077WXP3KG

## 26. Selection from an anthology or textbook   Include the selection author, publication date, and selection title, followed by the anthology editors, anthology title, page range of selection, and publisher.

IN-TEXT CITATION

The internet uses a variety of sensory inputs to re-condition our brains to interface with content (Carr, 2011).

author of selection

REFERENCES LIST ENTRY

author of selection

Carr, N. (2011). The juggler's brain. In A. Braziller & E. Kleinfeld (Eds.), *The Bedford book of genres,* Third Edition (p. 502). Bedford/St. Martin's.

information on textbook where selection appears

## 27. Object/artifact (cereal box, etc.)   If you find an object or artifact online, cite it as a short work from a website, but include a description of the item in brackets. If you

find such a source in the physical world, cite it as a work with an author and include a descriptor in brackets.

**IN-TEXT CITATION**

The box is a cheerful sunny yellow meant to attract children, but parents likely focus on the red heart and the soft claim about lowering cholesterol (General Mills, 2019).

author is an organization

## Object *(found online)*

**REFERENCES LIST ENTRY**

General Mills. (n.d.). Cheerios [Cereal box]. http://www.cheerios.com/Products/
   Cheerios

## Object *(found in physical world)*

**REFERENCES LIST ENTRY**

General Mills. (n.d.). Cheerios [Cereal box].

# 14

## COMPOSING:
## DRAWING ON IN-DEPTH RESEARCH:
## A Student Case Study

In this chapter, Michael Kipp, a writer and artist who studied at Red Rocks Community College and who currently works at the school's Communication Lab, shows how he researched and composed a multimodal project. Michael will walk us through his process of gathering sources; evaluating, annotating, and choosing sources; composing and integrating sources; and documenting those sources in his composition.

# Project Overview

▲ STUDENT
AUTHOR

**Michael Kipp.**

*Credit: Michael Kipp.*

## My Assignment & Topic

"Gratitude for Happiness" is a multimodal, multigenre project that uses positive psychology research to show how gratitude can make us happier and more fulfilled. It looks at the benefits of gratitude, shares a few methods for practicing gratitude, and encourages us to take responsibility for our happiness through conscious gratitude practice.

## My Rhetorical Situation

Thinking about hypothetical, real-world applications of audience analysis in the classroom can be hard. We think of our instructors as the only audience because our feedback comes in the form of a grade. But whether it's art, blogs, or business, the audience is a co-creator. They inform our entire process. Because of this, I spent a lot of time considering who I'm speaking to in my work.

Although I am a male author, I recognized that the emotional nature of my topic leans my audience toward a female majority. I also imagined most would be in the college-age and early adult years between eighteen and twenty-eight, when people are struggling with life transitions, moving out, getting jobs, and going to school. They're also developing their sense of identity, and considering difficult, fundamental questions about their desires, direction in life, and survival. Many will have struggles with mental health, as depression, anxiety, and other mental health challenges are common. My audience would also be diverse in ethnic and racial backgrounds, diverse socioeconomically, have had varying educational advantages, and be mostly from city and suburban neighborhoods. This makes my audience similar to myself and many people I know. If my topic were different, this may not be the case.

My purpose varied from genre to genre, but when considered collectively, the project was meant to be persuasive: I wanted my audience to use gratitude to become happier. Individually, the memoir told a story, the online magazine article was informative, and the advertisements were persuasive.

The collage's primary purpose is harder to put in a box. It is intended to inform the audience by showing the concept of gratitude through a visual description of this woman's mindset. But it also persuades them to think about how gratitude requires changing your frame of mind, and shares her mental and emotional story through symbolism.

Like the collage, the other genres also used all three. The informative, online magazine article, for instance, also tries to persuade the audience to practice gratitude themselves.

# My Research Plan & First Steps

After I chose my topic, I began to gather sources. Getting organized at this stage is important. For most of us, the creative process is not linear and can seem chaotic. This is especially true if we are unfamiliar with our personal creative process, which we can adapt to and optimize with practice.

Getting organized seems like extra work, but taking the time in the beginning and maintaining your organization systems throughout the process will save you enormous amounts of time and stress in the long run. That said, you will not always do this, and this is okay. It's important to be realistic and not expect perfection. Procrastination and resistance are mighty foes, and your best weapon next to self-discipline is self-compassion.

# Potential Sources

## What Information Do I Need?

With any project, I start by looking for potential sources, and I ask, "If I used this source later, what information would I need?" I would want to know:

- The type of source
- How to access that source again
- What that source is about
- How to cite the source

So I create a digital document called "Potential Sources" to store this information. I organize the document by source type (scholarly, book, interview, etc.). Then I list them alphabetically, as it will be in the Works Cited, under each type and include:

- The title and author
- A link to the source (if it is digital)
- Obvious citation information
- A summary of the source

In the case of a peer-reviewed, scholarly journal source, this process is simple. Most databases have a "citation" feature that allows you to select a citation style (like MLA) and copy the information for an at-a-glance look at the info you will include in your final citation.

However, it's not unusual for these to be out of date or contain errors, so you must double-check these later.

Studies also come with their own summary: the abstract. This can be copied over to the document as well.

## Types of Sources

But how do I decide what sources to look for? I create a list of source types to step through:

- Scholarly journals (studies)
- Books (digital and physical)
- News articles
- Interviews (text, audio, or video)
- Videos (documentaries, lectures, talks, etc.)
- Podcasts
- Blogs and opinion pieces
- Infographics and charts
- Other

I begin with the types of sources most likely to be credible, like studies, books, and interviews with experts. If I see an expert or author that shows up more than once, I'll search for other works or research by that person.

## Where Do I Look?

**Databases**   The first place I look is the database resources I can access through my campus. Because my topic used positive psychology research, studies were the first thing I wanted to gather.

After I've used the database(s), I move to both Google Scholar and Google's general search to look for other studies. Sometimes it is a struggle to find free access to the full-text of a study, and after trying to locate it on the school's database(s), you may need to ask a librarian for help.

If I'm struggling to find credible sources, or if I know of someone whose opinion about the topic I value, I may ask for source recommendations from that person or for help from a librarian. This is not something I needed to do for the "Gratitude for Happiness" project.

**Books**   After I have exhausted peer-reviewed sources, I look at books. I will often start with Google Books, which has previews of many books, so you can quickly check for relevancy.

I also do a general search online to locate books on the topic, as well as through the school and local library. I prefer digital texts I can access anywhere, so I focus on locating those first. Print books have their advantages as well.

**Other sources**   Then I move to other types of sources. A search engine, or even library search, can get access to videos, websites, news articles, and opinion pieces.

Throughout this process of finding potential sources, I keep anything that seems even remotely relevant. I spend the minimum amount of time determining source relevancy and credibility because I know I'll go back to look at them more closely.

Although I do most of this gathering at the beginning of the project, I usually go back and do this several times. While composing and evaluating, I often find holes in my research, find out sources weren't as relevant as they seemed, or change the way I'm framing my topic. I also look for sources that are cited within other sources. This means I move through this process multiple times during the project.

## My Working Bibliography

Below is one scholarly source I chose for my project. In the annotations, you'll see how I kept track of the source and laid the groundwork for integrating it into my project.

The type of source

**SCHOLARLY**

1. Algoe, Sara B., et al.
   "Putting the 'You' in 'Thank You': Examining Other-Praising Behavior as the Active Relational Ingredient in Expressed Gratitude"
   Link: http://spp.sagepub.com/content/7/7/658

Abstract quoted to use for summary. I often go back and edit this to make it easier to understand once I've read the article.

**Summary:**
"Although positive emotions as a class can build interpersonal resources, recent evidence suggests a unique and direct role for gratitude. In the current research, we shine the spotlight on what happens between a grateful person and the benefactor to illuminate what can build a bridge between them. Specifically, we draw on work calling gratitude an 'other-praising' emotion. In an original study and a conceptual replication that included two independent samples, couples had video-recorded conversations in which one member expressed gratitude to the other ($n = 370$).

Expressers' other-praising behavior was robustly positively associated with the benefactor's postinteraction perception of expresser responsiveness, personal good feelings in general, and felt loving in particular. Several practical and theoretical alternative explanations are ruled out. By clarifying the specific behavioral and subjective psychological mechanisms through which expressed gratitude promotes relationships, this work advances affective and relationship science, two domains that cut across disciplines within psychology."

Basic information taken from the website for reference. This is neither all the information nor the correct format for the Works Cited page, and it should always be double-checked.

**Citation Details:**

Sara B. Algoe, Laura E. Kurtz, and Nicole M. Hilaire
"Putting the 'You' in 'Thank You': Examining Other-Praising Behavior as the Active Relational Ingredient in Expressed Gratitude"
*Social Psychological and Personality Science*, vol. 7 no. 7, https://doi.org/10.1177/1948550616651681

Sometimes logging into a database is inconvenient. I downloaded the full text PDF and stored it on Google Drive.

2. Diebel, Tara, et al.
"Establishing the Effectiveness of a Gratitude Diary Intervention on Children's Sense of School Belonging"
Link: https://drive.google.com/open?id=0B-KDbYpALgJPRngxbFZFaTUxYjg

Original Link: https://drive.google.com/open?id=0B-KDbYpALgJPbm1wNDEwOF83Tmc

I kept the original database link for access and for my citation.

# Evaluating, Annotating, & Choosing Sources

## Evaluating My Sources

After I've gathered my list of potential sources, I begin to evaluate them. I begin at the top of the "Potential Sources" document and work my way down, starting with digital sources. This means I begin with scholarly articles.

To evaluate scholarly sources, I reread the abstract, focusing on the conclusion, and ask myself whether the results support my claim, or whether it's evidence against my claim that I should acknowledge in my work. I also look at what journal it was published in to see who the journal's audience is (a coaching journal is going to be different from a positive psychology journal), and whether the journal seems credible. There are a surprising number of journals with poor reputations.

*Techniques and Approaches section*
# Positive psychology techniques – gratitude

Jonathan Passmore & Lindsay G. Oades

*This article builds on a descriptive paper on positive psychology coaching and several previous techniques papers. This paper explores the application of gratitude, with its associated benefits, as a part of positive psychology coaching practice.*
**Keywords:** *gratitude; positive psychology coaching.*

*Gratitude*

This technique can form a regular routine that the coachee can develop and help build positivity and manage workplace stress, challenging times or difficult situations. This can be done through using a 'gratitude diary' or letters. Which of these tools to use will depend on the individual and their situation, with Emmons (2008) suggesting that we need to be cautious in offering only one 'gratitude' technique.

Research by Seligman et al. (2005) found individuals who did this task daily become bored, whilst those asked to write down their

## Conclusion

This short technique of gratitude can help which can be used to both coaches and coachees in the development of positivity, potentially leading to enhanced well-being,

## Correspondence
### Dr Jonathan Passmore
E-mail: jonathancpassmore@yahoo.co.uk

## References
Emmons, R. (2008). *Thanks. How practicing gratitude can make you happier.* Houghton Mifflin.

McCullough, M. E., Emmons, R. & Tsang. J. (2002).

Once I've considered those, I look at the full text. At this point, I'm not reading the entire thing, but skimming for indications that it's credible and relevant. Sometimes all it takes is a quick glance to realize a text isn't relevant.

If I need to go deeper, I will usually read the conclusion and the section describing limitations. I may also examine the methods, if they aren't clear in the abstract and parts I've already read. If a study was published about a population in a particular culture, I'll evaluate whether it's still relevant to my topic, and if a study is a translation, whether the translation seems clear. I alternate between skimming and reading more carefully. It's likely I'll still eliminate more sources later, but I want to get rid of the obvious ones.

During this, I maintain the organization of my sources document and update the summaries to make things clearer, as needed. If I eliminate a source, I remove it and put it in a separate document called "Eliminated Sources." In the event I change my mind, I can still access it.

Here is an example of a source I decided was useful:

# Establishing the effectiveness of a gratitude diary intervention on children's sense of school belonging

Tara Diebel, Colin Woodcock, Claire Cooper & Catherine Brignell

*Aim:* The promotion of well-being in schools using evidence-based interventions from the field of positive psychology is a growing area of interest. These interventions are based on the principle that sustainable changes in well-being can be achieved through regularly engaging in simple and intentional activities. This study examines the effectiveness of a school-based gratitude diary intervention to promote school belonging for primary school aged pupils (age range 7 to 11 years).
*Method:* The intervention took place in a one-form entry primary school for four weeks and involved participants writing a diary about things that they were either grateful for in school that day or about neutral school events.
*Findings:* Participants who completed the gratitude intervention demonstrated enhanced school belonging and gratitude relative to the control group, although this was moderated by gender with the gratitude diary showing clearer benefits for males. Increases in gratitude were positively correlated with increases in school belonging.
*Limitations:* The lack of a follow-up measure meant that it was not determined whether positive outcomes were maintained. Participants' diary entries were not analysed for content.
*Conclusions:* The findings extend the evidence base concerning the use of gratitude diaries with children and indicate that this intervention can be beneficial for children younger than research has previously demonstrated. This study also illustrates how a gratitude diary intervention can be used to build social resources and makes a novel connection between gratitude and sense of belonging. Implications for how this simple intervention has the potential to have a systemic impact on the well-being of pupils and staff are discussed.
*Keywords:* gratitude; gratitude intervention; sense of school belonging.

design. In addition, while the gratitude manipulation appeared to protect female pupils from the fall in gratitude observed in the control group, only males showed a significant increase in gratitude scores following the gratitude diary intervention. This was an unexpected finding insofar as the literature on gender differences in the expression of gratitude suggests that males are less inclined to this activity than females (e.g., Kashdan et al., 2009; Thompson et al., 2015). It is possible gratitude was already at ceiling level in the girls in our study, however there was no evidence that baseline levels of gratitude were effected by gender. Most such effect on both gratitude and SoSB. This would make the control group in the current study comparable to the hassle diary in both Emmons and McCullough (2003) and Froh et al. (2008). However, in these studies significant declines were not observed. A coded analysis of diary entries would be needed to establish the content of the diary entries and explore these hypotheses. Finally, the fact that the gratitude diary intervention and the control intervention were occurring in the same classes could have been an issue, if participants became aware that they were in different groups.

## Annotating My Sources

There are several ways I've annotated my sources. I actually used two ways during this project, as I experimented to see what worked best. I haven't settled on a method, and I think each person will be drawn to a different one.

The first method was on paper. I printed off the articles to have physical copies and took a highlighter and pen to them. The benefit of this was readability and retention. The downside was that if I did not have them with me, I couldn't reference my annotations. But I did find it easier to keep track of information and engage with the texts than with digital copies. If you find yourself easily distracted, having trouble keeping track of things, or if your eyes hurt reading digitally, this method may work for you.

The second method was digital. Many of the studies were PDFs, and many PDF-viewing programs have a highlighter feature. So I digitally highlighted them, if the feature was available. Other programs allow you to do this with other kinds of sources, and some allow you to take notes or make comments.

As I highlighted, I also did something a little unusual: I took screenshots. I already have a "Potential Sources" document and an "Eliminated Sources" document at this stage. Now, I added one more: a "Screenshots of Sources" document. In this document, I put the title and author of the source, and below it I included the screenshots of all my highlights. Here, I could take notes if I wanted to or leave comments.

What this allowed me to do was keep everything I found relevant in *one place*. I could look at it at a glance and find the information I wanted. If I needed more context, I had a summary in the "Potential Sources" document or could access the full text. This saved me from having to go back and forth between documents as often, which I find makes it difficult to track information. I also felt like I could make connections between different sources more easily. The one improvement I'd make on this method is using a program that can search text in images, which would make keyword searches possible. But this wasn't necessary.

## Digital Highlighting

Here is an example of how I highlighted text I was particularly interested in.

*Credit: From "Establishing the effectiveness of a gratitude diary intervention on children's sense of school belonging" by Diebel, T., Woodcock, C., Cooper, C. & Brignell, C. in Educational & Child Psychology, 33(2), 2016. Copyright © 2016 by The British Psychological Society. Reproduced with permission of the Licensor through PLSclear.*

that aims to gain greater understanding of how positive emotions and character traits can contribute to positive well-being (Seligman et al., 2005). Advocates of positive psychology assert that interventions that prompt people to engage in simple intentional activities can be more effective in increase levels of the sense of school belongingness (SoSB).

Gratitude arises following help from others, but is also a process that involves awareness of and appreciation on positive aspects of life (Wood, Froh & Geraghty, 2010). The empirical literature concerning

## Digital Highlighting with Notes

And here is an example of how I added notes to the margins once I highlighted the text.

*Credit: From "Establishing the effectiveness of a gratitude diary intervention on children's sense of school belonging" by Diebel, T., Woodcock, C., Cooper, C. & Brignell, C. in Educational & Child Psychology, 33(2), 2016. Copyright © 2016 by The British Psychological Society. Reproduced with permission of the Licensor through PLSclear.*

**Studies:**

1. "Establishing the Effectiveness of a Gratitude Diary Intervention on Children's Sense of School Belonging"

Diebel, Tara, et al.

Notes and Quotes:

**Discussion**

The present study represents the first to use a gratitude diary intervention that requires children to write specifically about school. There have also only been two published studies to date that have used gratitude diaries with primary school aged children. As predicted, the study found the gratitude diary intervention had a beneficial effect on both gratitude towards school and SoSB. Improvements in gratitude due to die grati-

Gratitude diary with children.

Beneficial for:
* Sense of belonging
* Gratitude toward school

Annotating and highlighting sources is something I do throughout the process. During my initial evaluation of sources, I may do it as I skim or read portions. Then when I read the full text, this is where the most annotation happens. But as I'm composing and integrating sources, I may reread a source or portions of it, and may add more annotations. The process of engaging with the source is continuous. As I have said, the creative process is not linear.

## Choosing My Sources

Once I've gathered sources and done an initial evaluation, I begin to examine them in full. This is where I read the entire text of a study. As mentioned, it's also where the bulk of annotation happens. Often, I end up eliminating sources again. When examined more deeply, I may realize a source isn't as relevant as it seemed, or I may think it's poorer quality than my first examination indicated.

After I've gone through all my sources, I update the "Potential Sources" document with correct MLA citation format. I do this early, so that I can add correct in-text citations as I go to save time. Like the other stages of interacting with sources, I come back to this one often. I don't ever truly know what sources I'm going to choose until I begin the process of composing, when the ideas and knowledge from my research combine with my own ideas.

# Composing & Integrating Sources

## Drafting

By the time I'm ready to do an initial draft, I've read many or all of my potential sources and eliminated poor quality or irrelevant ones. I've also spent some time annotating, highlighting, and drawing connections between different sources. Because of this, sometimes I have a very clear idea of what I want to talk about and can create an outline to follow. Other times I'm better off doing a brain dump and organizing later.

For "Gratitude for Happiness," I went with the brain dump method. I had a purpose, knew my audience, had chosen a genre, and I knew what the research said about my topic. All the pieces were inside my head and only needed to come out. So I would do a first draft where I didn't filter myself. Usually, the organization would come intuitively, and I'd just need to clean it up. This involved several drafts and revisions.

## Integrating Sources

As I'm doing my initial draft, because I've read my sources and I'm familiar with them, I find myself drawing on the research naturally. If I want to make a point, I'll back it up with the source or sources I remember that support it. Because I'm doing this during my draft and I want to keep track of what sources I use, I put the in-text citation in immediately. I try to format it correctly, but always check during the revision.

After I've done that first draft, I add more sources as I revise. I'll ask myself if there are other sources to support a point, and if there are other points that I need to make and sources to include with them. Sometimes I feel like there isn't enough support, and I'll start at the beginning of the process, looking for more sources.

Integrating sources in the genre pieces was different than integrating sources in my author's and artist's statements. Not all the genre pieces had references in the genre piece itself. The online magazine article had links, but the memoir, collage, and advertisements don't reference the research in the piece itself. This meant I kept my

that aims to gain greater understanding of how positive emotions and character traits can contribute to positive well-being (Seligman et al., 2005). Advocates of positive psychology assert that interventions that prompt people to engage in simple intentional activities can be more effective in increase levels of the sense of school belongingness (SoSB).

Gratitude arises following help from others, but is also a process that involves awareness of and appreciation on positive aspects of life (Wood, Froh & Geraghty, 2010). The empirical literature concerning

One's life" (277).

For Nelson and Lyubomirsky, this difference between gratitude and appreciation lies in interpersonal context (277). They believe that gratitude involves an interpersonal exchange, contrasting it with appreciation as a generalized gratitude for one's life blessings (277). Similarly, Jane Taylor Wilson says that gratitude "refers to an ability to recognize and appreciate the benefits received from others" (2); and Nancy S. Fagley describes a model for appreciation as an umbrella term broken into eight aspects, one of which is gratitude (71). Here it is defined as, "being grateful to others for benefits they provided or tried to provide" (71). However, not all people in the field adhere to the definition of gratitude as a subset of appreciation or as a description limited to an interpersonal context. For example, Tara Diebel et al. remark that, "Gratitude arises following help from others, but is also a process that involves awareness of and appreciation on positive aspects of life" (117).

Because the definition of gratitude is still being clarified amongst psychological researchers, and because the lay definition includes both interpersonal contexts and an appreciation for the positive aspects of a person's life (Nelson and Lyubomirsky 277), this project will recognize gratitude in both interpersonal exchanges and in general life circumstances, and will not distinguish between appreciation and gratitude.

In this project I decided to use a series of advertisements by a fictional organization called "Gratitude4Happiness" to guide the flow of concepts. The organization's purpose is to persuade the readers to believe that gratitude is one tool for happiness, and that they should take action to improve their well-being by practicing it themselves. These advertisements connect with the genre piece following them, serve to highlight points made in the other genre, and create a thread throughout the project that brings all of the genres together.

Each of the genre pieces, including the last advertisement, has an accompanying research in mind as I composed it, and then I integrated the research into the author or artist's statement that accompanied it, which explained my thought process. The integration of the research in the genre pieces was indirect—it informed my composition, but wasn't demonstrated in the piece. In contrast, the author's and artist's statements directly integrated the research and it was cited within.

To give an example, the study "Establishing the Effectiveness of a Gratitude Diary Intervention on Children's Sense of School Belonging" by Tara Diebel et al. was used as a source in three sections of my project: the Introduction, Chapter 1 ("The Benefits of Gratitude"), and Chapter 2 ("Ways to Practice Gratitude"). Here's how I did it:

iour but did not find any significant outcomes. Finally, Lambert et al. (2010) investigated the impact of a gratitude intervention on communal strength, the sense of responsibility the participant feels for their partner's welfare. The study used a novel intervention and asked participants to increase the frequency that they expressed gratitude to their partner. The results indicated that this intervention yielded significantly higher increases in communal strength compared to paying attention to grateful events or sharing positive events with a partner. No information was reported

### Chapter 1: The Benefits of Gratitude

My highlighted sources, as discussed on p. 441.

*Credit: From "Establishing the effectiveness of a gratitude diary intervention on children's sense of school belonging" by Diebel, T., Woodcock, C., Cooper, C. & Brignell, C. in Educational & Child Psychology, 33(2), 2016. Copyright © 2016 by The British Psychological Society. Reproduced with permission of the Licensor through PLSclear.*

Fredrickson). Research has also linked gratitude to well-being through the building of social resources such as increasing feelings of connectedness (Froh, Bono & Emmons, 2010), prosocial emotions such as forgiveness, compassion, trust and empathy (Dunn & Schweitzer, 2005; Hill & Allemand, 2011; McCullough et al., 2001) and increasing perception of social support (Algoe, Haidt & Gable, 2008; Wood et al., 2008).

*Findings: Participants who completed the gratitude intervention demonstrated enhanced school belonging and gratitude relative to the control group although this was moderated by gender with the gratitude diary showing clearer benefits for males. Increases in gratitude were positively correlated with increases in school belonging.*

At the beginning of the study, Tara Diebel et al. discuss what gratitude is. I also wanted to talk about how positive psychology defines gratitude in my own project to give my readers a foundation for understanding the rest of it. This study used a definition of gratitude that contrasted with some other studies, and I wanted to highlight that. Tara Diebel et al.'s definition itself drew off past research, which is common in studies that build upon existing literature.

**Chapter 2: Ways to Practice Gratitude**

My highlighted source, as discussed on p. 441.

ical feelings of belonging. Research on school belonging has shown it is inversely related to school dropout and linked with engagement and interest in school positive relationships (Bond et al., 2007) intrinsic motivation and academic achievement (Goodenow, 1993; Osterman, 2000).

significant others rated the participants in the gratitude group as more helpful than the participants in the other groups (31–32). Emmons and McCullough also say, "In a sample of adults with neuromuscular disease, a 21-day gratitude intervention resulted in . . . a greater sense of feeling connected to others . . ." ("Highlights"). Furthermore, Tara Diebel et al. discuss that research has linked gratitude to increased feelings of connection, prosocial emotions, and sense of social support (118), and that another study showed expressing gratitude to one's partner more often increased communal strength (the level of responsibility a partner feels for the other's welfare) more than noticing grateful events or sharing positive events (119). These findings support the idea that grateful people are more connected, helpful, and involved with others, and I tried to show this in my memoir.

In the second section, I describe the day I dropped out of high school. Tara Diebel et al.'s study showed students experienced increased feelings of school belonging (117), which has been connected to decreased dropout rates and increased intrinsic motivation and academic achievement (121). Gratitude was something I rarely experienced during this time, and I wanted to show I also had a lack of motivation, energy, and goals; experienced negative physical symptoms; and was disconnected from others. Emmons and McCullough say that study participants who kept gratitude lists made more progress toward personal goals, including academic, interpersonal, and health-based goals, and young adults reported higher levels of positive states, including alertness, enthusiasm, determination, attentiveness, and energy. They also write that participants who kept a weekly gratitude journal "exercised more regularly, reported fewer physical symptoms, felt better about their lives as a whole, and were more optimistic about the upcoming week compared to those who recorded hassles or neutral life events. . . ."

Tying social connection and experiences of poor physical health, one recent study

**Integrated Source**

An example of how I integrated my source into my project.

*Findings: Participants who completed the gratitude intervention demonstrated enhanced school belonging and gratitude relative to the control group although this was moderated by gender with the gratitude diary showing clearer benefits for males. Increases in gratitude were positively correlated with increases in school belonging.*

well as, *Thanks! How the New Science of Gratitude Can Make You Happier,* which details his study more in depth (27–35). I wanted to highlight the gratitude journal both because it's well known, and because of its benefits. Emmons's and McCullough's studies found that people had increased life satisfaction, felt more energetic and alert, and felt more opti- mistic when doing the exercise ("Highlights"). In support of these findings, a more recent study on children in school showed the gratitude diary resulted in an increase in gratitude and sense of belonging, although the findings suggested gender may be a moderating factor and more research needs to be done exploring this possibility (Diebel et al. 117). The quote by Chris Peterson (from Aaronson's *Psychology Today* article), which says the gratitude exercise "can be done with skepticism, but not with cynicism," reinforces the ideas discussed above, because it says that it must be done authentically, with genuine intent. Meditating briefly on the feeling helps achieve this.

In the next section, I referenced *Authentic Happiness* by Martin Seligman. In his book he describes how to carry out a "gratitude visit," and I paraphrased his instructions for the visit (74). I also reference a study by Sara B. Algoe et al., where increased oth- er-praising behavior is shown to be a key component in the expression of gratitude, caus- ing the target to feel more positive emotions, perceive the expresser as more responsive, and feel more "loving." In contrast, the self-benefit behavior did not have any association with the target's perception of responsiveness, general positive emotions, or experience of love (661). This is important, because increasing the positivity of the experience for the person for whom someone is grateful for encourages social bonds and relational growth (658, 664), and high-quality relationships are a part of living a happy life.

**Integrated Source**

An example of how I integrated my source into my project.

Here, I paraphrased Tara Diebel et al.'s summaries of previous research. I wanted to illustrate in my project the connection between gratitude and my involvement in school. Diebel et al.'s study supported my personal experience in the memoir, and their summaries provide more evidence of the connection. The research they reference is also part of the support for their own hypothesis and its results.

et al., 2010). Gratitude is also thought to promote resilience as it provides an adaptive coping mechanism for dealing with negative life events (Lambert et al., 2012; Watkins et al., 2008). These hypotheses

Gratitude has been found to be negatively correlated with stress (Wood et al., 2008) burnout (Chan, 2010) and buffer the effect of two suicide risk factors: hopelessness and depressive symptoms (Kleiman et al., 2013).

In the second paragraph, I use Diebel et al.'s research to discuss school belonging and dropouts in the context of my own choice to drop out of school. I want to show that the connection between low gratitude and low sense of school belonging may have been a factor in my choice to drop out.

The first citation (117) is the results of their study. The second citation (121) is a paraphrase of summarized results from a former study that they used to support their own research.

The online article recommends the gratitude journal, so in my author's statement, I expanded on the research supporting it as an effective gratitude intervention. The results of Tara Diebel et al.'s study are in direct support of the exercise.

However, I also wanted to note that the study showed gender may be a moderating factor. It's important to represent the results of a study with as much accuracy as possible, rather than twisting the results to support a claim. Rather than weakening my point, including this adds credibility.

eye forward and to a higher point. A Spanish study confirmed that positive affect rises in persons who practice gratitude, which validated what was found in a previous study (Martinez-Marti 893). Gratitude has also been tied to resilience, providing a coping mechanism in challenging times, and it buffers the effect of hopelessness and depressive symptoms, which are risk factors for suicide (Diebel et al. 118). Also, the landscape refers to the fact that grateful people experience a positive memory bias—they are more likely to recall positive memories, similar to the negative memory bias experienced in depression (Watkins et al. 63). The idea of creation is also shown in the plant, whose roots surround her head. Her efforts to be thankful and practice gratitude are nourishing the plant, who grows upward, changing her reality, subjective and objective, for the better.

**Integrated Source**
An example of how I integrated my source into my project.

In the collage, I'm showing the impact a grateful mindset and practice has on one's perception of reality, and that this positive shift in perception has objective benefits. In this part, I'm specifically describing the rise of the landscape and rainbow as symbolism for that positivity. Tara Diebel et al. summarize in their study some research linking gratitude and resilience, and its positive effect on depressive symptoms. This supports what I wanted to symbolize in the collage.

## Documenting Sources in MLA Style

When I'm wrapping up any project, and it's time to formally document my sources, I'm never sorry that I kept thorough records and notes along the way. As Amy and Elizabeth write in "A Guide to MLA & APA Sources" on p. 394, "When you document sources, you show your audience where you got your information. You also develop your ethos as an author by showing that you've used reliable source material." Properly and accurately documenting sources—and showing that you've used quality sources in the first place—is worth the work.

For a detailed guide, including models, on documenting in MLA and APA style, see Chapter 13.

# Reader

# 15

## IDENTITIES:
## THE CULTURE OF IDENTITY

## CONTENTS

**W**hat do our online profiles, tattoos, or bumper stickers say about who we are? How about the magazines and blogs we read? The things we carry and the things we wear? And how do we define and represent ourselves in other genres and media—such as music, poems, movies, advertisements, or national slogans?

As individuals and as members of a larger community, we may define ourselves based on where we live, our religion, heritage, race, class, gender, and sexual orientation. We may also identify ourselves through favorite activities or sports teams, educational major, or profession, for example.

When we express something about identity, we create. What we create depends on what we want to say and the people we want to say it to—and also on how we say it. In other words, our creative expression depends not only on our choices about our purpose, message, and audience but also on the genres and media that we choose as vehicles for that expression.

For example, if you wanted to share something about your own identity with your friends, you might create a musical mixtape or playlist. As you compile that music, would you choose songs that reflect where you're from? Would the lyrics say something about your likes and dislikes, or some other aspect of you?

Now, imagine that instead you've decided to say something about who you are in the form of a narrative essay, or through a poem, blog, or YouTube video. What might change? What different choices would you need to make in order to represent your ideas about identity through these genres?

In this chapter, you will encounter a range of voices commenting on personal and cultural identity. You'll read a variety of genres: infographic, ad, editorial, article, blog, and book excerpt. As you read, pay attention to how these authors use different types of compositions and media to present ideas and arguments about identity.

The readings explore such ideas as how we represent ourselves online, with an infographic about our digital identities. Consider how you would define your digital identity. For example, do you tend to be someone who holds back information when you're online? Does what you share depend upon the platform you use? Other readings examine social aspects of identity. How does your access to social media determine your social life? How does where we live now affect who we are? Laura Robinson suggests that digital inequality can influence our social life and Marisa Kabas details the reasons behind a Muslim woman hiding her identity upon moving to the United States.

Closing the chapter is David Sedaris's humorous examination of how language influences our identity. As you read through all the pieces in this chapter, consider different ways these pieces resonate with your own experiences.

# ▼ Infographic

## ACMA, *The Secret (Online) Life of Us*

The Secret (Online) Life of Us infographic is based on a short research report titled "Managing Your Digital Identity: Digital Footprints and Identities Research." The Australian Communications and Media Authority (ACMA), conducted this research, examining challenges and actions that Australians experienced when going online.

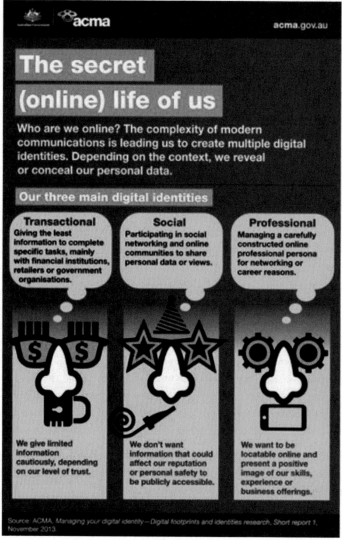

Credit: ACMA.

1. How does the infographic use visuals to support the text?
2. What features in the infographic's design make it effective for understanding digital identities?

## COMPOSING PROJECT | Create an Infographic

Think about your own digital identity. What categories would you use to define it? How would you represent it with visuals and text? Create your own infographic to illustrate who you are online.

## ▼ Ads

### Spotify, *Various Advertisements*

The Spotify advertisements are from their 2018 ("Love What You Love") campaign. These ads hope to show how Spotify is for a wide variety of users/music lovers. This campaign focused on Spotify's belief that all music lovers should have some free access to their favorite songs.

*Credit: Michael Nagle/Bloomberg/Getty Images.*

Credit: Michael Nagle/Bloomberg/Getty Images.

## QUESTIONS

1. What are some of the ways the Spotify ads convey the sensibilities of people who use the app?

2. How do the ads use lighting, contrast, and framing to convey their message?

## COMPOSING PROJECT | Design an Ad

Redesign the Spotify ad for a different audience than the ones intended in the ads shown here. You might consider redesigning the ad for an older audience that uses the Spotify app.

## ▼ Editorial

### The Occidental Editorial Board, *Identity Ought to Be Self-Decided*

*The Occidental* is the student newspaper of Occidental College, a liberal arts college in Los Angeles. The paper is completely student run and provides news, information, and opinions on issues of interest to the students, faculty, and staff of Occidental College as well as the local community.

Credit: Occidental News *Editorial Board*, "Identity Ought to Be Self-Decided" Occidental News, March 28, 2017. Reprinted by permission.

*The Weekly* believes in stepping away from standard journalistic tradition and allowing students and sources in our community to define their own gender pronouns.

Last week, the Associated Press (AP) Stylebook expanded their use of the pronoun "they" to include those who do not fit into the "he" or "she" categories. The actual entry makes clear that the pronoun should only be used in clauses that are impossible to reword or rephrase, because most readers might not understand that "they" can be used to describe a singular person, according to Paula Froke, lead editor for the AP Stylebook.

We applaud the more nuanced, albeit still conservative, reflection of changing times and the increased open-mindedness of the Associated Press. Yet, we believe that the twin tenets of the Code of Journalistic Ethics, "identifying sources clearly" and "giving voice to the voiceless" are not in contradiction as much as the AP Style suggests. We call on the AP Stylebook to go further.

Although we see the necessity of clear labeling and the potential confusion of using "they" as a singular pronoun, we think that the journalistic commitment to truth necessitates that this change be more dramatic than the current style changes reflect. To acknowledge and perpetuate the notion that there is a gender binary that must be upheld, particularly in reporting news, is to simplify a complex set of stereotypes and sociological tools that have been used to promote sexism and homophobia.

As we have investigated news stories and found that the truth is never a simple "yes" or "no," we understand that we cannot hold the truth of gender identity to a simple "he" or "she" either. Larger news outlets generally feel as if they do not have the freedom to make substantial changes reflective of changing ideas and the changing world. Their audiences are not at the forefront of progressive ideas the way most college campuses are. The worry that held the AP back from making these changes previously was that to allow sources to go by "they" would confuse the reader, even to the extent of misleading the story.

Our response to this argument is that the reader must take on the responsibility of learning how to use "they." Words have the power to resist oppression. In supporting our students, faculty, and staff who identify as "they," we hope that others who disagree with this motion explore the oppression that occurs when we attempt to define others using our own terms. We hope that discarding the gender binary in our writing shows our readers that we have deemed it no longer accurate, useful or truthful to depict the stories and information of this community in such rigid terms. We hope that the changes in the AP Stylebook give readers the opportunity to learn and grow kinder to those whose identity has been devalued for so long.

> **Words have the power to resist oppression.**

## QUESTIONS

1. What is the central purpose of the editorial, "Identity Ought to Be Self-Decided"? What evidence does the editorial board use to support its point?

2. How does the editorial board establish their ethos? What are some of the strategies they use in the editorial to build their credibility?

## COMPOSING PROJECT | Create an Editorial

Do a quick perusal of your school's website to determine how gender identity is articulated on the website. Using the Occidental Editorial Board's editorial as a model, create your own editorial that makes an argument about how your school should indicate gender on its website. You might argue that your school should keep doing what they are doing or that they should make changes.

## ▼ Article

### Marisa Kabas, *She Hid Her Muslim Identity for 15 Years*

Marisa Kabas is a freelance writer and blogger. She often writes for Fusion, an online media outlet that describes itself as "the media brand for a young, diverse, and inclusive world." Fusion is where the story below appeared. In it, Kabas tells the story of a Somali immigrant to the United States who kept her Muslim identity a secret from even her closest friends for fifteen years.

Credit: Marisa Kabas, "This Woman Hid her Muslim Identity for 15 Years. Here's Why She Came Out," Gawker, May 20, 2016. Copyright © 2016 G/O Media Inc. Reprinted by permission.

When Elhan moved to Washington, D.C. from Somalia, the United States was not at war with Iraq and Afghanistan and the Twin Towers still dominated the New York skyline. But just a few weeks later, on September 11, 2001, everything changed. Overnight, "Muslim" became a dirty word—and Elhan became "Amy."

With this one day of terror, the nation's attitudes toward followers of Islam went from fairly neutral to vitriolic, after the perpetrators of the most deadly terrorist attack on U.S. soil were revealed to be Muslim. Elhan, a high school freshman at the time, could see the change happening before her eyes.

That's when she decided that in public she'd be "Amy," a normal American teenager.

For the next 15 years, Amy would go to school, hang out with her friends, and go to parties, never letting on that she was deeply attached to her religion. When she wasn't at school, though, she was at her mosque, where she prayed regularly and engaged with a close-knit community as Elhan. Never did these two lives meet, she said—not even any close calls.

That all changed earlier this year, however, when Elhan finally worked up the courage to come clean to her friends about her double life—and the entire world.

"It felt like a very heavy rock was on my chest. I just didn't know how to get out of it," Elhan, now 32, told me in a phone conversation last week. "I was stuck. I got so used to it being my daily routine and it became a normal thing to be 'Amy' once I was outside the door."

Not only did Elhan decide she was going to finally share her secret, but she elected to do it on the season two premiere of the Pivot network docu-series *Secret Life of Americans*.

Each week on the show, a different subject reveals something personal they've been hiding from loved ones. On Friday's episode, viewers follow Elhan on her self-filmed journey toward revealing her religious, Muslim self to her friends—and her secular identity as "Amy" to her family.

"My whole adult life, I've been living in fear," she tells the camera, set in selfie mode. "Fear of rejection from society. Fear of being labeled as a terrorist. Fear that someone might hurt me because I'm Muslim. That fear is still there."

While not all Muslims go to the lengths Elhan did to hide their religious identity, her story provides a vivid example of the conflict many Muslims feel in simply navigating daily life in this country. In the years since 9/11, racial tensions have arguably gotten worse, not better. This climate of intolerance has forced many, like Elhan, to hide in shame. But perhaps leading by example will encourage others to come out from the shadow of hate.

> " Never did these two lives meet, she said—not even any close calls. "

In the days following 9/11, Elhan made a few practical decisions that would affect her life and identity for the decade-and-a-half to come: She asked school administrators to officially address her as Amy and she began changing out of her traditional garments and into jeans and T-shirts before school. Once she began hearing mean-spirited jokes in the wake of 9/11, including insults about how Muslims look and dress, she became convinced this superficial assimilation was the only way to live a peaceful existence in this country.

"It's not like I had two different personalities," she tells me. "I was still the same girl." But one of those girls—the real her—was only seen within the safety of her home and at her mosque. It was never a question of her commitment or love of her faith, but rather a paralyzing fear that left her, and so many like her, she says, feeling like she would be put in harm's way by simply being herself.

This fear was not unfounded. According to 2015 numbers from the FBI's Uniform Crime Reports program, the county has seen five times more annual hate crimes against Muslims since 9/11. The group estimates that 100 to 150 have occurred per year, in contrast with 20 to 30 per year before the attacks.

Merely "looking" Muslim isn't the only thing Elhan and fellow followers of Islam need to worry about—so-called "Muslim-sounding" names can also impact how others perceive you. In a 2014 study that analyzed the way employers respond to prospective employees whose résumés indicate a religious affiliation, the researchers found that résumés with one of the seven religions tested "received [on average] 29 percent fewer e-mails and 33 percent fewer phone calls than the control group." But Muslims fared even worse, receiving 38 percent fewer e-mails and a staggering 54 percent fewer phone calls.

Despite these discouraging odds, earlier this year Elhan took the bold step of embracing her religion and lifestyle in public after the big reveal to her family and friends. She'd been contemplating it for the past few years since being diagnosed with relapsing Multiple Sclerosis and realized the stress of concealing her true identity was not only bad for her emotionally, but also bad for her health. These days, she can once again be seen everywhere she goes donning the headscarf and traditional garment she had worn in Somalia, from her regular Starbucks to the gas station and over to her friend's places. As far as she's concerned, the hardest part about "coming out" as Muslim is over, which was telling her friends. Before she told them, she feared that not only would they not accept her because of her religion but, above all, they'd be angry she lied to them for all of these years.

When she finally told them, tears streaming down her face, they understandably had some questions. "Why didn't you tell us before?" "How have you been able to party with us when Muslims don't drink?"—a common misconception. But she says that since the initial shock wore off, they've all been accepting and supportive. It's other Americans that still need some help. . . .

"So many communities are being swooped to the side because they want to be free, want to be themselves," she said, pointing to the embattled transgender community as an example. "We're Americans no matter what we are. And all we need is to be loved."

## QUESTIONS

1. Sometimes Kabas quotes Elhan, and other times she summarizes what Elhan said. Do you think the quotations Kabas chose to include are effective? Why or why not?

2. How do you think Kabas's article would have to be changed for a media outlet that doesn't gear itself toward a "young, diverse, and inclusive world"?

## COMPOSING PROJECT | Write a Researched Essay or Blog Entry

Kabas mentions that Elhan's decision to "come out" was motivated in part by the toll that hiding her identity was taking on her health. Research coming out and the different reasons people give for coming out or not coming out. Present your findings to your classmates in a researched essay or blog entry.

## ▼ Blog

### Erin B. Taylor, *The Curation of the Self in the Age of the Internet*

Erin B. Taylor is an economic anthropologist and consumer finance research consultant, as well as the author of the 2013 book *Materializing Poverty: How the Poor Transform Their Lives*. She has consulted for the British Museum and done field work in Haiti and the Dominican Republic, among other places. She blogs about consumer finance at erinbtaylor.com.

Erin B. Taylor, "The Curation of the Self in the Age of the Internet" https://erinbtaylor.com/entry/the-curation-of-the-self-in-the-age-of-the-internet. Reprinted by permission of the author.

In his famous 1936 essay, "The Work of Art in the Age of Mechanical Reproduction," Walter Benjamin describes how art was historically used for ritual purposes. Because the ritual value of art was tied up with its uniqueness, it was unthinkable to reproduce a work of art.

In some respects, this phenomenon continues to exist today, particularly in religious contexts. Every year, up to a million pilgrims walk to the town of Fátima in Portugal to witness a parade in which the statue of Our Lady of Fátima is displayed.

The development of technologies of mechanical reproduction means that it would technically be possible to produce a close copy of this statue, and of course, with photography, millions of images of the Lady circulate around the world freely.

However, as Benjamin explains, the use of original art works in ritual contexts gives them a uniqueness that is not replicable; none of these reproductions can ever capture the "aura" of the original. People travel from far and wide to see the Lady in her original, miraculous form.

Of course, the vast majority of works of art that we produce and consume today are not originals and arguably never were. This is particularly true of digital technologies, which unlike film stock can be copied without losing quality. Does this mean that the images we use are not authentic? By using reproductions, are we losing sight of tradition?

Walter Benjamin argues that when we consume reproductions we are indeed moving away from tradition. For him, this shift has both positive and negative implications. It is potentially revolutionary because when works of art are disembedded from their ritual context they also become independent from authority.

This means that they can be appropriated to make political statements and spread a diversity of messages. But the easy replicability of images also makes them more vulnerable to appropriation by totalitarian forces. For example, nationalist discourses depend heavily on images to convey a sense of collectivity.

## Popular Culture in the Age of Mechanical Reproduction

Today, artworks and photographs are heavily appropriated by commercial interests. At times it seems that there is truly nothing sacred any more. *The Mona Lisa*, Van Gogh's *Starry Night*, Che Guevara and Bob Marley can all be found printed on mugs, toilets, and T-shirts. They are made into dolls and featured in advertisements for completely unrelated products.

Does this endless reproduction signify the dilution of the original art, its tradition and politics? Or is it a sign of democratization? After all, commercialization plays a key role in bringing art out of the galleries and into popular culture.

In this paper I draw upon a material culture perspective to explore the implications of digital reproduction. I'd like to suggest that the internet has brought something new to our engagement with art and popular culture, something that does grant us a significant ability to appropriate images and bestow them with our own meanings, despite the existence of widespread commoditization and the continued existence of an artistic elite. The internet allows us to display our own collections of aesthetic forms publicly in a way that was never possible before.

I have come to think of this process as the "curation of the self." By this I don't mean to claim that everything that everyone posts online is a kind of curation. The word "curation" implies that different aesthetic objects are put together deliberately to create a cohesive story.

Simply posting the odd picture on Facebook, or even a collection on Flickr, may not count as curation in the sense that we normally associate with galleries and museums, because many pictures are posted without a great deal of thought about how they fit into an existing collection. However, there is a certain sense in which we are always engaging in curation, because when we appropriate aesthetic forms we are generally constructing a story about ourselves.

## Popular Culture as Material Culture

This appropriation of forms is a topic that anthropologists who study material culture have covered in detail. In his work on material culture, Daniel Miller has discussed at length how we use material forms, such as clothes, bags, tattoos, and hairstyles to create our social identities. Our use of material forms for social purposes is one of the most prominent characteristics that separates humans from other animals.

Unlike Benjamin, who views reproduction as a negation of authenticity, Miller argues that the mass production of consumer goods expands our possibilities for self-creation because it gives us access to an almost endless array of goods that we can combine in the expression of our own, unique identities.

The fact that we might choose to wear a pair of jeans or a headband that are worn by thousands of people worldwide does not detract from our original identity, because when we appropriate goods we invest them with our own meanings. The result is creativity, not homogenization.

This doesn't just apply to the things we wear. We use a wide variety of aesthetic forms, drawn from a wide variety of sources, to engage in self-creation and to express ourselves socially. These include images, sounds, textures, and tastes. Some of these we make ourselves, some we buy, others we borrow.

We incorporate some of these forms more consciously than others, and what we choose to represent ourselves can change on a daily basis. But, together, this aesthetic collection helps us to feel human, and to express ourselves as social beings.

## Images and the Internet

Before the internet, curatorship was dominated by a tiny subsection of the global populace, made up of professional curators, television executives, big studios, and perhaps the occasional renegade street artist. Most people had very little choice of how to display their aesthetic preferences, or to whom.

The development of mass techniques of reproduction meant that people could display art works and family portraits on the walls of their own homes, but they had very little impact outside of the domestic sphere.

The internet breaks down those boundaries. No longer confined to the prints sold in the local shop, or the photographs that one can produce oneself, today we have access to millions of artworks and billions of images. By displaying our curated collections on sites such as Facebook, Flickr, and Pinterest, we expand our potential audience to the entirety of the internet's user base. And for the first time ever, we are not dependent upon a creative elite in order to do this.

> [I]t gives us an unprecedented ability to curate our own collections and present them to a global public.

But the internet doesn't just open up a smorgasbord of images that we can use for self-creation. It is a game-changer, because it gives us an unprecedented ability to curate our own collections and present them to a global public. This is a truly new phenomenon. I've chosen to use the term "curation" in order to emphasize the importance of this capacity to display a particular kind of self.

This is not to say that the elite have ceased to be important in the art world. In fact, one of the primary effects of mechanical reproduction has been to increase the price value of original works of art. It's hard to imagine that the *Mona Lisa* would become invaluable if it hadn't become famous through its reproduction. And elite curators, collectors, and dealers are still dominant players in setting the symbolic and quantitative value of original works of art.

But the curation of the self using the internet doesn't depend upon our ability to pay, once we have access. This gives us an independence from the art world elites. We don't need cash to appropriate images and show them to others. So, how are we using this newfound ability?

## Selfies

If recent media attention is anything to go by, we seem to be using social media a lot to post pictures of ourselves. In fact, I'd argue that selfies today are the quintessential popular culture. What could be more popular than the mass production, dissemination, and consumption of images of the self?

Some people take selfies so seriously that they have built careers out of it, mimicking the much older phenomenon of the socialite. In a recent article on *PopAnth*, Crystal Abidin discusses how Singaporean lifestyle bloggers use photographs and hashtags to document their daily lives. Of all the selfies that circulate on the internet, these carefully-crafted images probably come closest to being a truly curated collection.

Celebrity bloggers such as Naomi Neo are followed by thousands of fans, and receive lucrative sponsorships that can amount to close to a million dollars a year. Neo admits to having "no idea what am I known for in majority's eyes."

But what people like Neo are doing is essentially creating their own aura and sharing it through social media. Neo's aura is expressed through numerous photos and texts, and her audience demands new material to learn more about her story. Just like a painting whose value is increased by the fact that millions of reproduction have made it famous, Neo's value rises as she shares her self with the world.

The selfie has been accused of being the product of an individualistic, self-obsessed culture. It's sometimes seen to represent the worst of the internet, as a space characterized by shallow social interactions and not much more than a vehicle for self-promotion. But others argue that there's far more to the selfie than the self.

In an article in "The Conversation," Marianne Hardey (2013) claims, "The selfie is not just a narcissistic exercise, it has become part of our social interactions and a way to place ourselves in our surroundings."

Hardey explains that as we interact online, we often lose control of how we're portrayed, and the selfie is a way of taking back that control. Through the selfie we can display ourselves as we see ourselves and as we wish to be seen.

In fact, selfies are nothing new. Artists have been making self-portraits throughout the history of art. That today the vast majority of the world's population can make and share their own selfies doesn't negate this continuity with artistic tradition.

## Curating the Self

But there's far more to the curation of the self than just selfies. People are creating collections using different kinds of images to express their social selves. They post them over multiple media: different platforms engender different kinds of collections. We can read the images together, in a similar way that you might analyze the material contents of a handbag or a house.

Of all the social media platforms, Facebook is probably the one that most fulfills the function of the family photo album. It's where many of us post photos of our holidays, major life events such as weddings and new babies, and i"s where we record your participation in collective ritual events such as Christmas.

Facebook timelines, irrespective of their privacy settings, tend to have an intimate, domestic feel to them. Depending on an individual's friending strategies and privacy settings, these collections are generally at least semipublic.

But Facebook timelines are also a major site for engagement with popular culture. Memes, popular music, street art, DJ-ing cats, films, and the latest twerks of Miley Cyrus all end mixed together with the intimate sphere of the self.

It's also important to note that collections cross social media platforms. For example, Facebook timelines link with Twitter feeds, feature reposts of people's favorite songs from SoundCloud, and integrate with personal blogs.

Software such as Buffer helps people to coordinate their posts, so that they can manage multiple social media platforms simultaneously. People can create posts ahead of time and Buffer will post them for automatically at pre-set times of day.

These posts are often carefully crafted to look spontaneous, even though they're pre-planned. The result is that a collection of posts that does not look curated to its audience may have been very carefully thought through.

This is an apt point to return again to Walter Benjamin. Benjamin talked about how film can seem to represent reality more than paintings. Although films are made up of all kinds of different elements, the way they're brought together as a final product gives the audience a sense that the events taking place are real.

Benjamin argues that this is because films obscure the nature of their production. In contrast, with paintings, you can see that it is just a representation of reality. This is evident in things like its static nature and the visibility of brush strokes.

Social media are a bit more like an unedited film: they often appear to be random collections of things that people posted spontaneously. Hence, like paintings, they reveal the elements that create the whole. But like film, there is a whole production mechanism behind these posts that is often unseen. In a sense, then, one purpose of curation is to mask itself.

## Curating the Future Self

Pinterest is designed to be largely visual, using little text. Users create collections of images around themes by pinning images to boards. These can be anything, but a common use is to make "boards" featuring products and experiences that one would like to consume in the future. Wedding paraphernalia, exotic travel destinations, handbags, art, and domestic items are some of the more common themes, especially by female users.

Although Pinterest is a highly commercial social media platform, the collections that people create tend to be more aesthetically-driven, and more highly curated, than collections on other social media.

Whereas Facebook helps us to tell a story about our current lives, Pinterest tends to be used to imagine and communicate out aspirations. Material culture studies have generally focused on how people use the things they possess to represent themselves in the present. With Pinterest, we have a window into how people would like to construct themselves as future consumers if they could afford to do so.

This doesn't mean that users are not constructing an image of themselves in the present. Even though users in many cases don't own the things they post, and may never buy them, users curate collections very carefully to create a certain aesthetic and promote themselves as people who possess taste and style. As a result, many of the more vulgar, banal, or tongue-in-cheek aspects of popular culture get left out.

This is a rather different way of gaining "distinction" than that discussed by Pierre Bourdieu. Pinterest users may not own the items they post, and may never be able to afford them, but appropriating the images is a way of consuming without having to pay the price of the goods in question.

This is a good example of how the lowering of monetary barriers allows for the broad dissemination of cultural products. These become the materials of popular culture.

## Art and the Self in Community

Sharing images via social media is also a way to engage with forms of popular culture and expand their reach. Street art is a great example of this. By definition, street art is a public, popular art that does not depend upon elite-controlled spaces and fashions. Long before the internet existed, street art has provided a way to extend the material presence of the self beyond the body and the domestic sphere.

The internet has tended to expand street art's public audience, blurring the online/offline spaces as people curate collections of street art images and encourage each other's work. For example, "De mi barrio a tu barrio" is a project involving around 300 artists from Mexico, Central America, and the Caribbean. They are running an online competition to create murals in a number of countries around the world. Local artists, designers, and cartoonists can send in proposals for the murals.

This project takes communities as its point of reference, making the assumption that art painted on walls in communities is not the property or product of any single individual, but of all of a community's residents. Here, the self is situated as part of a collective, with the curated artworks acting as a metaphor for social relations.

The kind of community reflected in the group's Facebook posts is one that is connected, politically engaged, and democratic. It encourages a creativity that is dependent neither upon elites nor upon commercial interests. As such it represents quite a different kind of curation to personal Facebook timelines, which are focused on a kind of expanded domesticity, and Pinterest boards, which posit a future consumer.

## The Implications of Online Curation

So, these examples show three very different forms of the appropriation and popularization of images. Each medium provides different tools for self-expression, and different ways of connecting to audiences. Through them, people engage in self-curation and build traditions. In the age of the internet, *we* are the authentic original.

But this does not mean that our online representations are somehow inauthentic. Material culture theory states that our personal identities are created out of a fusion of ourselves (the subject) and the things we use (the objects). Similarly, it makes little sense to claim that our physical selves are the authentic original and our online selves are simply partial mirrors. Rather, subject and object create the whole.

What does this mean for art and popular culture? Online curation doesn't really pose a challenge to the world of elite art, in which the aura of the original still influences its price. But nor does the capacity for auto-curation depend upon this market.

This is why self-curation in the age of the internet matters: Irrespective of the elite forces of production of art and popular culture, it is a space in which people can engage with art and popular culture at will, and put these forms to their own social uses.

### Acknowledgments

This paper was presented at the IUAES/JASCA conference in Tokyo on May 16, 2014. Thanks to the AAA for inviting me onto the panel. Thanks to John McCreery for early comments on my paper plan, Gawain Lynch for listening to me think aloud, and to Catherine Eagleton for helping me think through what curation actually is!

### Further Reading

Benjamin, Walter. 1936. *The Work of Art in the Age of Mechanical Reproduction.*

Hardey, Mariann. 2013. "Note to Selfie: You're More than Just a Narcissist's Plaything." *The Conversation*, November 21.

Miller, Daniel. 2014. "The No-Makeup Selfie." UCL Social Networking Blog, April 29.

Miller, Daniel. 1987. *Material Culture and Mass Consumption.* Oxford UK and Cambridge USA: Blackwell.

Sinanan, Jolynna, Connor Graham and Kua Zhong Jie. 2014. Crafted Assemblage: Young Women's 'Lifestyle' Blogs, Consumerism and Citizenship in Singapore. *Visual Studies* 29(2): 201–213.

## QUESTIONS

1. Taylor claims that "we are always engaging in curation, because when we appropriate aesthetic forms we are generally constructing a story about ourselves." Think about your own recent social media activity, including the posting of selfies, the sharing of images, and the like. Do you see yourself constructing a story about yourself? In what ways?

2. Taylor refers specifically to Pinterest, Facebook, Flickr, SoundCloud, and Twitter to bolster her points. Can you think of other social media platforms that could be used to either support or contradict her argument?

## COMPOSING PROJECT | Construct a Curated Collection

Do some research to find out whether your city or town has any street art. If it does, make a pilgrimage to go see it. If street art is not to be found in your town, try wandering around campus looking for posters, flyers, and other artistic forms. Take pictures of anything that captures your interest and post them to the social media platform of your choice. What story about you might this collection of images tell?

# ▼ Humorous Essay

## David Sedaris, *Me Talk Pretty One Day*

David Sedaris is a humor writer and author of numerous books and essay collections. He also frequently contributes to radio programs such as National Public Radio's *This American Life*. In his book, *Me Talk Pretty One Day*, Sedaris chronicles his experiences prior to moving to France and his escapades living in France. In the excerpt below, Sedaris recollects the struggles he and others faced in a French class.

*Credit: From Me Talk Pretty One Day by David Sedaris, copyright © 2000. Reprinted by permission of Little, Brown, and Company, an imprint of Hachette Book Group, Inc., and Don Congdon Associates, Inc. Copyright © 2000 by David Sedaris*

At the age of forty-one, I am returning to school and having to think of myself as what my French textbook calls "a true debutant." After paying my tuition, I was issued a student ID, which allows me a discounted entry fee at movie theaters, puppet shows, and Festyland, a far-flung amusement park that advertises with billboards picturing a cartoon stegosaurus sitting in a canoe and eating what appears to be a ham sandwich.

I've moved to Paris in order to learn the language. My school is the Alliance Française, and on the first day of class, I arrived early, watching as the returning students greeted one another in the school lobby. Vacations were recounted, and questions were raised concerning mutual friends with names like Kang and Vlatnya. Regardless of their nationalities, everyone spoke what sounded to me like excellent French. Some accents were better than others, but the students exhibited an ease and confidence I found intimidating. As an added discomfort, they were all young, attractive, and well dressed, causing me to feel not unlike Pa Kettle trapped backstage after a fashion show.

I remind myself that I am now a full-grown man. No one will ever again card me for a drink or demand that I weave a floor mat out of newspapers. At my age, a reasonable person should have completed his sentence in the prison of the nervous and the insecure—isn't that the great promise of adulthood? I can't help but think that, somewhere along the way, I made a wrong turn. My fears have not vanished. Rather, they have seasoned and multiplied with age. I am now twice as frightened as I was when, at the age of twenty, I allowed a failed nursing student to inject me with a horse tranquilizer, and eight times more anxious than I was the day my kindergarten teacher pried my fingers off my mother's ankle and led me screaming toward my desk. "You'll get used to it," the woman had said.

I'm still waiting.

The first day of class was nerve-racking, because I knew I'd be expected to perform. That's the way they do it here—everyone into the language pool, sink or swim. The teacher marched in, deeply tanned from a recent vacation, and rattled off a series of administrative announcements. I've spent some time in Normandy, and I took a monthlong French class last summer in New York. I'm not completely in the dark, yet I understood only half of what this teacher was saying.

"If you have not meismslsxp by this time, you should not be in this room. Has everybody apzkiubjxow? Everyone? Good, we shall proceed." She spread out her lesson plan and sighed, saying, "All right, then, who knows the alphabet?"

It was startling, because a) I hadn't been asked that question in a while, and b) I realized, while laughing, that I myself did not know the alphabet. They're the same letters, but they're pronounced differently.

"Ahh." The teacher went to the board and sketched the letter a. "Do we have anyone in the room whose first name commences with an ahh?"

Two Polish Annas raised their hands, and the teacher instructed them to present themselves, giving their names, nationalities, occupations, and a list of things they liked and disliked in this world. The first Anna hailed from an industrial town outside of Warsaw and had front teeth the size of tombstones. She worked as a seamstress, enjoyed quiet times with friends, and hated the mosquito.

"Oh, really," the teacher said. "How very interesting. I thought that everyone loved the mosquito, but here, in front of all the world, you claim to detest him. How is it that we've been blessed with someone as unique and original as you? Tell us, please."

The seamstress did not understand what was being said, but she knew that this was an occasion for shame. Her rabbity mouth huffed for breath, and she stared down at her lap as though the appropriate comeback were stitched somewhere alongside the zipper of her slacks.

The second Anna learned from the first and claimed to love sunshine and detest lies. It sounded like a translation of one of those Playmate of the Month data sheets, the answers always written in the same loopy handwriting: "Turn-ons: Mom's famous five-alarm chili! Turnoffs: Insincerity and guys who come on too strong!!!"

The two Polish women surely had clear notions of what they liked and disliked, but, like the rest of us, they were limited in terms of vocabulary, and this made them appear less than sophisticated. The teacher forged on, and we learned that Carlos, the Argentine bandonion player, loved wine, music, and, in his words, "Making sex with the women of the world." Next came a beautiful young Yugoslavian who identified herself as an optimist, saying that she loved everything life had to offer.

The teacher licked her lips, revealing a hint of the sadist we would later come to know. She crouched low for her attack, placed her hands on the young woman's desk, and said, "Oh, yeah? And do you love your little war?"

While the optimist struggled to defend herself, I scrambled to think of an answer to what had obviously become a trick question. How often are you asked what you love in this world? More important, how often are you asked and then publicly ridiculed for your answer? I recalled my mother, flushed with wine, pounding the table late one night, saying, "Love? I love a good steak cooked rare. I love my cat, and I love . . ." My sisters and I leaned forward, waiting to hear our names. "Tums," our mother said. "I love Tums."

The teacher killed some time accusing the Yugoslavian girl of masterminding a program of genocide, and I jotted frantic notes in the margins of my pad. While I can honestly say that I love leafing through medical textbooks devoted to severe dermatological conditions, it is beyond the reach of my French vocabulary, and acting it out would only have invited unwanted attention.

When called upon, I delivered an effortless list of things I detest: blood sausage, intestinal pâté, brain pudding. I'd learned these words the hard way. Having given it some thought, I then declared my love for IBM typewriters, the French word for "bruise," and my electric floor waxer. It was a short list, but still I managed to mispronounce IBM and afford the wrong gender to both the floor waxer and the typewriter. Her reaction led me to believe that these mistakes were capital crimes in the country of France.

"Were you always this palicmkrexjs?" she asked. "Even a fiuscrzsws tociwegixp knows that a typewriter is feminine."

I absorbed as much of her abuse as I could understand, thinking, but not saying, that I find it ridiculous to assign a gender to an inanimate object incapable of disrobing and making an occasional fool of itself. Why refer to Lady Flesh Wound or Good Sir Dishrag when these things could never deliver in the sack?

The teacher proceeded to belittle everyone from German Eva, who hated laziness, to Japanese Yukari, who loved paintbrushes and soap. Italian, Thai, Dutch, Korean, Chinese—we all left class foolishly believing that the worst was over. We didn't know it then, but the coming months would teach us what it is like to spend time in the presence of a wild animal. We soon learned to dodge chalk and to cover our heads and stomachs whenever she approached us with a question. She hadn't yet punched anyone, but it seemed wise to prepare ourselves against the inevitable.

Though we were forbidden to speak anything but French, the teacher would occasionally use us to practice any of her five fluent languages.

"I hate you," she said to me one afternoon. Her English was flawless. "I really, really hate you." Call me sensitive, but I couldn't help taking it personally.

Learning French is a lot like joining a gang in that it involves a long and intensive period of hazing. And it wasn't just my teacher; the entire population seemed to be in on it. Following brutal encounters with my local butcher and the concierge of my building, I'd head off to class, where the teacher would hold my corrected paperwork high above her head, shouting, "Here's proof that David is an ignorant and uninspired ensigiejsokhjx."

Refusing to stand convicted on the teacher's charges of laziness, I'd spend four hours a night on my homework, working even longer whenever we were assigned an essay. I suppose I could have gotten by with less, but I was determined to create some sort of an identity for myself. We'd have one of those "complete the sentence" exercises, and I'd fool with the thing for hours, invariably settling on something like, "A quick run around the lake? I'd love to. Just give me a minute to strap on my wooden leg." The teacher, through word and action, conveyed the message that, if this was my idea of an identity, she wanted nothing to do with it.

My fear and discomfort crept beyond the borders of my classroom and accompanied me out onto the wide boulevards, where, no matter how hard I tried, there was no escaping the feeling of terror I felt whenever anyone asked me a question. I was safe in any kind of a store, as, at least in my neighborhood, one can stand beside the cash register for hours on end without being asked something so trivial as, "May I help you?" or "How would you like to pay for that?"

My only comfort was the knowledge that I was not alone. Huddled in the smoky hallways and making the most of our pathetic French, my fellow students and I engaged in the sort of conversation commonly overheard in refugee camps.

"Sometimes me cry alone at night."

"That is common for me also, but be more strong, you. Much work, and someday you talk pretty. People stop hate you soon. Maybe tomorrow, okay?"

Unlike other classes I have taken, here there was no sense of competition. When the teacher poked a shy Korean woman in the eyelid with a freshly sharpened pencil, we took no comfort in the fact that, unlike Hyeyoon Cho, we all knew the irregular past tense of the verb "to defeat." In all fairness, the teacher hadn't meant to hurt the woman, but neither did she spend much time apologizing, saying only, "Well, you should have been paying more attention."

Over time, it became impossible to believe that any of us would ever improve. Fall arrived, and it rained every day. It was mid-October when the teacher singled me out, saying, "Every day spent with you is like having a cesarean section." And it struck me that, for the first time since arriving in France, I could understand every word that someone was saying.

Understanding doesn't mean that you can suddenly speak the language. Far from it. It's a small step, nothing more, yet its rewards are intoxicating and deceptive. The teacher continued her diatribe, and I settled back, bathing in the subtle beauty of each new curse and insult.

"You exhaust me with your foolishness and reward my efforts with nothing but pain, do you understand me?"

> "If you have not meismslsxp by this time, you should not be in this room. Has everybody apzkiubjxow? Everyone? Good, we shall proceed."

The world opened up, and it was with great joy that I responded, "I know the thing what you speak exact now. Talk me more, plus, please, plus."

## QUESTIONS

1. Throughout the essay, Sedaris tries to place us directly in his experience. How does he do this? What are some of the techniques he uses to make us feel as if we are there, learning the language with him and other students?

2. Why do you think we chose to include this essay in a chapter on identity? Give specific examples from the essay to support your answer.

## COMPOSING PROJECT | Create a Humorous Comic

Think of a time you felt like you were in over your head—you had no idea what was going on. Create a comic strip poking fun at yourself or someone you perceived to be an antagonist in that situation.

## LONG-TERM PROJECTS | Identity

1. **Investigate & analyze how a subculture you identify with uses social media.**

   a. **Identify a subculture group that you are a member of**, perhaps computer nerds, hunters, skateboarders, parents, chess players, organic food eaters, or bluegrass music fans.

   b. **Track your social media usage for seven consecutive days & take notes on your purposes for using it.** Pay particular attention to how you use social media in relation to the subculture you identified yourself being a member of above. Consider:
   - Which platforms are you using and why?
   - Who are you communicating with on those platforms?
   - Are there purposes you have that the platforms easily support? For example, if you post something on Twitter about wanting advice, do you get the advice you are hoping for?
   - Are their purposes you have that the platforms don't seem to support? Does a request on Reddit for information on a new organic brand of yogurt yield useful results?

   c. **Interview three to four people you know who are members of the same subculture about their social media usage**, asking them questions similar to the ones you asked yourself above.

   d. **Review all your notes & tracked social media usage.** What generalizations can you make about how members of your subculture use social media? What inferences can you make or what conclusions can you draw based on the information you've collected? Answer the following questions:
   - Why do people use these social media platforms? What needs or desires draw them there?
   - What sort of people use these social media platforms? How do they behave within this space?
   - What types of behaviors seem to be encouraged or discouraged on these social media platforms, based on what you've observed?

- What roles do socializing and consumption seem to play on the platforms?

e. **Write an essay** that proposes a new social media platform that would better meet the needs of the members of the subculture you focused on, providing screen shots from social media and quotations and references to details from your observations throughout to support your point. Your finished essay should **include a variety of media, such as a mixture of text, photographs, drawings, sketches**, and so on.

2. **Brand your family: create a motto, logo, & illustrated history.** Your family reunion is coming up and you've been nominated to put together a family history. The history will ultimately take the form of a paper scrapbook, web page, or blog. You've also been asked to design a T-shirt that family members will wear for a group portrait. The T-shirt needs to feature a slogan that makes a statement about your family.

- **Brainstorm a motto that** signifies your family's identity. For example, Amy might design a T-shirt that says "The Brazillers: Even the Adults Are Children," to reflect the playful nature of her extended family.
- **Interview at least three family members** and ask them to consider your motto. Does it ring true for them? Would they identify your family with some other phrase or slogan? Ask interviewees to recall at least three memorable family episodes that support or refute your motto, and have them share photos with you (and video, if you have multimedia access).

- **Write up the best anecdotes** and/or include transcripts of your family interviews. Illustrate the stories (and/or transcripts) with family photos. If you have multimedia access, include audio and video recordings of your interviews, as well as any multimedia materials you gather from family members.
- **Revise your motto as needed**, based on feedback from interviewees.
- **Design a logo** that complements your family motto. Perhaps you'll use one of the photos you've collected or another image that works for your slogan and family history. For example, Amy could create a logo that portrays stick-figure people playing on a seesaw to illustrate the playful nature of her family, or work with a photo of family members at play.
- **Assemble your motto, logo, & illustrated family history** in a paper scrapbook or on a web page or blog.
- **Write a reflective essay** that explains the choices you made along the way in your project. How did your audience (family) and purpose (to tell family stories and reflect family identity) affect your decisions and revisions? To what extent does what you've created offer a true picture of your family?
- **Alternative project:** Adapt the above assignment so that it's about you and a group of your friends.

# 16 MIND & BODY: CONNECTIONS

How do we define ourselves in relation to our minds and bodies? Are we what we eat—the healthy green salad and the late-night extra-cheesy mac and cheese? Are we our muscles? Our belly fat? Our illnesses and addictions? Our physical disabilities? Evidence of our attitudes toward our minds and bodies can be found in various genres of everyday life. Consider these questions: What do our food labels say about how we fortify our bodies? How do we represent our bodies in advertising, and in art and literature? How do our (dis)abilities define us, and how do others use them to define us?

Opening this chapter is a poem celebrating the body by the famous American poet Walt Whitman. Focusing on the brain, a piece by Nicholas Carr looks at how technology might be changing our most important organ. This is followed by Elizabeth Segran's blog about Halloween costumes for children living with disabilities.

The chapter ends with Dwayne Godwin and Jorge Cham's comic about addiction and Emily Sohn's article about the health benefits of having friends.

As you work through this chapter, consider the different perspectives on what a "normal" body or mind is, and how the genre choices of these authors can be seen as responses to social situations.

## ▼ Poem

### Walt Whitman, From "I Sing the Body Electric"

Walt Whitman's poem "I Sing the Body Electric" was originally published in 1855 as part of his collection *Leaves of Grass*, which was labeled obscene by some because of its explicit sexuality. In "I Sing the Body Electric," Whitman celebrates both the male and female body through physical and spiritual imagery.

O my body! I dare not desert the likes of you in other men and women, nor the likes of the parts of you,

I believe the likes of you are to stand or fall with the likes of the soul, (and that they are the soul,)

I believe the likes of you shall stand or fall with my poems—and that they are poems.

Man's, woman's, child's, youth's, wife's, husband's, mother's, father's, young man's, young woman's poems.

Head, neck, hair, ears, drop and tympan of the ears.

Eyes, eye-fringes, iris of the eye, eye-brows, and the waking or sleeping of the lids,

Mouth, tongue, lips, teeth, roof of the mouth, jaws, and the jaw-hinges,

Nose, nostrils of the nose, and the partition,

Cheeks, temples, forehead, chin, throat, back of the neck, neck-slue,

Strong shoulders, manly beard, scapula, hind-shoulders, and the ample side-round
of the chest.

Upper-arm, arm-pit, elbow-socket, lower-arm, arm-sinews, arm-bones,

Wrist and wrist-joints, hand, palm, knuckles, thumb, fore-finger, finger-balls, finger-joints,
finger-nails,

Broad breast-front, curling hair of the breast, breast-bone, breast-side,

Ribs, belly, back-bone, joints of the back-bone,

Hips, hip-sockets, hip-strength, inward and outward round, man-balls, man-root,

Strong set of thighs, well carrying the trunk above,

Leg-fibers, knee, knee-pan, upper-leg, under-leg,

Ankles, instep, foot-ball, toes, toe-joints, the heel;

All attitudes, all the shapeliness, all the belongings of my or your body or of any one's
body, male or female,

The lung-sponges, the stomach-sac, the bowels sweet and clean,

The brain in its folds inside the skull-frame,

Sympathies, heart-valves, palate-valves, sexuality, maternity,

Womanhood, and all that is a woman, and the man that comes from woman,

The womb, the teats, nipples, breast-milk, tears, laughter, weeping, love-looks, love-pertur-
bations and risings,

The voice, articulation, language, whispering, shouting aloud,

Food, drink, pulse, digestion, sweat, sleep, walking, swimming,

Poise on the hips, leaping, reclining, embracing, arm-curving and tightening,

The continual changes of the flex of the mouth, and around the eyes,

The skin, the sun-burnt shade, freckles, hair,

The curious sympathy one feels, when feeling with the hand the naked meat of the body,

The circling rivers, the breath, and breathing it in and out,

The beauty of the waist, and thence of the hips, and thence downward toward the knees,

The thin red jellies within you, or within me, the bones, and the marrow in the bones,

The exquisite realization of health;

O I say these are not the parts and poems of the body only, but of the soul,

O I say now these are the soul!

## QUESTIONS

1. In his poem, Walt Whitman compares the body and the soul. In what ways does he find the body similar to the soul? What does he mean by the line "I believe the likes of you are to stand or fall with the likes of the soul, (and that they are the soul)"?

2. In his poem, Whitman lists various parts of the body. Sometimes he is just naming the part of the body ("Ribs, belly, back-bone") and sometimes he is more descriptive ("brain in its folds inside the skull-frame"). What effect does this have for the reader?

## COMPOSING PROJECT | Revise the Poem

Take several of the lines in Whitman's poem where he just lists the body parts and revise them to read more like the lines "brain in its folds inside the skull-frame" and "the bowels sweet and clean."

## ▼ Book Excerpt

### Nicholas Carr, *The Juggler's Brain*

Nicholas Carr is an author and journalist who writes about technology. The excerpt below is from his book *The Shallows: What the Internet Is Doing to Our Brains*, which was a finalist for the 2011 Pulitzer Prize in nonfiction.

Credit: From The Shallows: What the Internet Is Doing to Our Brains by Nicholas Carr. Copyright © 2010 by Nicholas Carr. Used by permission of W. W. Norton & Company, Inc.

What can science tell us about the actual effects that internet use is having on the way our minds work? No doubt, this question will be the subject of a great deal of research in the years ahead. Already, though, there is much we know or can surmise. The news is even more disturbing than I had suspected. Dozens of studies by psychologists, neurobiologists, educators, and web designers point to the same conclusion: when we go online, we enter an environment that promotes cursory reading, hurried and distracted thinking, and superficial learning. It's possible to think deeply while surfing the Net, just as it's possible to think shallowly while reading a book, but that's not the type of thinking the technology encourages and rewards.

One thing is very clear: if, knowing what we know today about the brain's plasticity, you were to set out to invent a medium that would rewire our mental circuits as quickly and thoroughly as possible, you would probably end up designing something that looks and works a lot like the internet. It's not just that we tend to use the Net regularly, even obsessively. It's that the Net delivers precisely the kind of sensory and cognitive stimuli — repetitive, intensive, interactive, addictive — that have been shown to result in strong and rapid alterations in brain circuits and functions. With the exception of alphabets and number systems, the Net may well be the single most powerful mind-altering technology that has ever come into general use. At the very least, it's the most powerful that has come along since the book.

During the course of a day, most of us with access to the web spend at least a couple of hours online — sometimes much more — and during that time, we tend to repeat the same or similar actions over and over again, usually at a high rate of speed and often in response to cues delivered through a screen or a speaker. Some of the actions are physical ones. We tap the keys on our PC keyboard. We drag a mouse and click its left and right buttons and spin its scroll wheel. We draw the tips of our fingers across a trackpad. We use our thumbs to punch out text on the real or simulated keypads of our BlackBerrys or mobile phones. We rotate our iPhones, iPods, and iPads to shift between "landscape" and "portrait" modes while manipulating the icons on their touch-sensitive screens.

> **With the exception of alphabets and number systems, the Net may well be the single most powerful mind-altering technology that has ever come into general use.**

As we go through these motions, the Net delivers a steady stream of inputs to our visual, somatosensory, and auditory cortices. There are the sensations that come through our hands and fingers as we click and scroll, type and touch. There are the many audio signals delivered through our ears, such as the chime that announces the arrival of a new e-mail or instant message and the various ringtones that our mobile phones use to alert us to different events. And, of course, there are the myriad visual cues that flash across our retinas as we navigate the online world: not just the ever-changing arrays of text and pictures and videos but also the hyperlinks distinguished by underlining or colored text, the cursors that change shape depending on their function, the new e-mail subject lines highlighted in bold type, the virtual buttons that call out to be clicked, the icons and other screen elements that beg to be dragged and dropped, the forms that require filling out, the pop-up ads and windows that need to be read or dismissed. The Net engages all of our senses — except, so far, those of smell and taste — and it engages them simultaneously.

The Net also provides a high-speed system for delivering responses and rewards — "positive reinforcements," in psychological terms — which encourage the repetition of both physical and mental actions. When we click a link, we get something new to look at and evaluate. When we Google a keyword, we receive, in the blink of an eye, a list of interesting information to appraise. When we send a text or an instant message or an e-mail, we often get a reply in a matter of seconds or minutes. When we use Facebook, we attract new friends or form closer bonds with old ones. When we send a tweet through Twitter, we gain new followers. When we write a blog post, we get comments from readers or links from other bloggers. The Net's interactivity gives us powerful new tools for finding information, expressing ourselves, and conversing with others. It also turns us into lab rats constantly pressing levers to get tiny pellets of social or intellectual nourishment.

## QUESTIONS

1. In the last sentence of the excerpt, Carr says that the internet "turns us into lab rats." What connotations does the term "lab rat" have? What is your reaction to being compared with a lab rat?

2. Carr gives a detailed list of the activities we engage in when we are on the internet: tapping on keyboards, clicking on links, hearing sounds, and more. Why do you suppose he gives such elaborate descriptions of these activities instead of simply saying that the internet engages multiple senses?

## COMPOSING PROJECT | Create a Tip Guide for Reading on the Internet

Carr writes that "dozens of studies by psychologists, neurobiologists, educators, and web designers point to the same conclusion: when we go online, we enter an environment that promotes cursory reading, hurried and distracted thinking, and superficial learning." Do some research to find several of these studies (you might start by going to Google Scholar and searching "internet effects on reading comprehension") and read them. Then create a list of tips for college students to help them read text on the internet with the same level of concentration and thought that reading offline encourages. You might find that the research articles you read include tips; feel free to use those with citations, but also come up with your own.

## ▼ Blog

### Elizabeth Segran, *Target Just Launched Halloween Costumes for Kids with Disabilities*

Elizabeth Segran is a senior staff writer for *Fast Company*, a business magazine. Her work has been published in other magazines, including *The Atlantic* and *Foreign Affairs*, and she is the author of the 2012 book, *The River Speaks*.

Credit: Elizabeth Segran, "Target Just Launched Halloween Costumes for Kids with Disabilities," Courtesy of Fast Company. Fast Company is registered trademark of Mansueto Ventures LLC.

For kids with disabilities—whether that involves sensory or mobility issues—finding a Halloween costume can be hard work. Since it's close to impossible to find a costume off the rack at a store, parents need to make something themselves or find an organization that will help them.

Parenting blogs offer creative ideas for kids in wheelchairs, but many require real carpentry skills. An adorable Mr. Rogers trolley, for instance, requires attaching cardboard to the wheelchair with dowels and adding a caving headlamp to the device, too. There is also a nonprofit called Magic Wheelchair that builds epic costumes for kids in wheelchairs at no cost to families. The organization relies on donations and fundraising to create incredible costumes, including a Captain America rocket ship and a Cinderella carriage. You can also buy an adaptive costume from Etsy, but that can be pricey and you will have to order it months in advance.

All of this takes a lot of time, effort, and planning, which is hard for parents who already feel stretched thin. But Target is here to save the day. The brand has launched an affordable line of adaptive Halloween costumes that allow kids with a range of disabilities to trick or treat in style.

For kids in wheelchairs, there's a princess dress and carriage, or a pirate outfit and ship. Target's designers put a lot of thought into making these costumes easy to assemble and put on. The outfits, which cost between $20 and $25, have openings in the back that make them easier to put on. The ship and carriage wheelchair covers, which cost $45 each, are designed to fit easily onto wheelchairs of various sizes using a hook-and-loop closure.

Meanwhile, for children with autism or other sensory issues, Halloween can be a difficult holiday to navigate. They might find costumes with rough textures, buttons, and zippers uncomfortable and overstimulating. And trick or treating can also be overwhelming, since it involves visiting new places or interacting with new people. To make the holiday easier for kids with sensory issues, Target created a unicorn and shark costume, at $30 each, that are designed to be extra soft and contain flat seams with no tags. There is also a hidden opening in the front for convenient abdominal access for children who might have special needs that require access for medical equipment.

## QUESTIONS

1. Segran's article is designed to shine light on the challenges of finding a Halloween costume for a child living with a disability. What are some of the challenges, and how does Segran present them?

2. What tone does Segran use for her article? Why do you believe she chose this tone to get across her point?

## COMPOSING PROJECT | Write a Letter

Go to your campus disability services office and find out what materials it has related to a disability you or a loved one lives with. Read over the materials, and if you need more information, interview the head of disability services. Then compose a letter to the chair of the department you're majoring in that offers information and advice about supporting students with that disability.

## ▼ Comic

### Dwayne Godwin and Jorge Cham, *Understanding Addiction*

Dwayne Godwin is a neuroscientist and professor at Wake Forest University School of Medicine. Jorge Cham earned his PhD in mechanical engineering from Stanford University and is the creator of the comic strip *Piled High and Deeper*. Together, Godwin and Cham create comic strips related to the brain for *Scientific American*.

# ADDICTION

BY DWAYNE GODWIN & JORGE CHAM

ADDICTION COSTS AMERICANS OVER $700 BILLION EACH YEAR IN LOST WORK, TREATMENT AND DRUG-RELATED CRIME.

BUT WHAT IS ADDICTION... AND HOW DO WE BREAK IT?

ADDICTION HAS ITS ROOTS IN THE BRAIN'S REWARD SYSTEM.

FEEL GOOD

FOOD, SEX

IT'S THE SYSTEM MEANT TO REINFORCE BEHAVIORS NEEDED FOR SURVIVAL SUCH AS EATING AND HAVING SEX.

ONE IMPORTANT COMPONENT IN THIS SYSTEM IS THE MESOLIMBIC PATHWAY ...

... A COLLECTION OF NEURONS THAT PRODUCES AND RELEASES DOPAMINE WHENEVER YOU ENGAGE IN A POSITIVE ACTIVITY.

DOPAMINE IS A NEUROTRANSMITTER THAT, AMONG MANY OTHER THINGS, GIVES YOU THE SENSATION OF PLEASURE WHEN RELEASED IN CERTAIN BRAIN AREAS.

ADDICTION CAN OCCUR WHEN THIS PATHWAY IS HIJACKED REPEATEDLY BY DRUGS OR OTHER STIMULI, CREATING CHANGES IN THE SYNAPTIC CONNECTION THAT ARE HARD TO REVERSE.

DRUGS OR OTHER STIMULI EXAGGERATE DOPAMINE INCREASES ...

RECEIVING NEURON

DOPAMINE RECEPTORS

DOPAMINE

TRANSMITTING NEURON

SYNAPSE

... WHICH ALTERS THE NUMBER OF DOPAMINE RECEPTORS.

THIS CHANGED PATHWAY, ALONG WITH INCREASED STRESS DURING WITHDRAWAL, CAUSES ADDICTS TO COMPULSIVELY SEEK OUT THE STIMULUS ...

... DESPITE LONG-TERM NEGATIVE CONSEQUENCES.

NOT ALL DRUGS OR ADDICTS ARE THE SAME. SOME PEOPLE ARE GENETICALLY MORE SUSCEPTIBLE TO ADDICTION ...

... AND A DRUG'S ADDICTIVENESS SEEMS TO DEPEND ON HOW RAPIDLY IT ACTS ON YOUR SYSTEM.

HEALING ADDICTION IS A DIFFICULT PROCESS, AIDED BY GROUP EFFORT.

THE BEST WAY TO BEAT A HARMFUL DEPENDENCY IS BY DEPENDING ON OTHERS.

Credit: Dwayne Godwin and Jorge Cham.

## QUESTIONS

1. The comic illustrates the complicated disease of addiction in several concise panels. How do the creators take a scientific process and make it understandable to someone who doesn't have a scientific background?

2. "Understanding Addiction" is text heavy for a comic. Why do you think the creators chose to include so much text? Could this have less text and convey the same information to the same audience? Why or why not?

## COMPOSING PROJECT | Create a Comic

Think about a complicated process you know something about. Perhaps it is in a field you are studying. Maybe it's a skill you have. Then create a comic that illustrates this process to a general audience. Consider how you will use text along with your visuals.

## ▼ Researched Essay

**Emily Sohn,** *More and More Research Shows Friends Are Good for Your Health*

Emily Sohn is a freelance journalist whose work has appeared in many newspapers and magazines, including the *Washington Post*, where this article was published. In this piece, Sohn summarizes recent research on the health benefits of having a circle of friends.

Credit: Emily Sohn, "More and More Research Shows Friends Are Good for Your Health," Washington Post, May 26, 2016. Used with permission of Emily Sohn, Tide Pools LLC.

Overwhelmed recently by the stress of an impending move—along with the usual demands of a busy life—I turned to the people I love.

In small chunks of time between tasks on my to-do list, I called and texted with my sister, my parents, local friends and old friends scattered around the country. Some conversations turned my stress into laughter. Others made me cry. One friend came over to clean out my closet. Then she took our kids for four hours so we could pack without interruption.

With each hug, conversation and gesture of support, I started to feel better. As it turns out, those feelings may be paying long-term dividends, too: According to accumulating evidence, strong relationships breed better health, with benefits that include resilience against heart disease and a longer life.

It's encouraging research that's worth paying attention to. When life gets hectic, making time for friends can be a challenge. And some studies suggest that many of us have fewer friends today than our parents did a generation ago.

Those obstacles make prioritizing relationships all the more important, experts say.

"A good friendship is a wonderful antidepressant," says psychologist Janice Kiecolt-Glaser, director of the Institute for Behavioral Medicine Research at the Ohio State University College of Medicine in Columbus. "Relationships are so powerful, we don't always appreciate the many levels at which they affect us."

Ever since researchers began to make links between loneliness and poor health about twenty-five years ago, the scientific literature on the value of friendship has exploded. Today, the data make a convincing case: Having people who care about us is good for us.

In a 2010 meta-analysis that combined data on more than 308,000 people across 148 studies, for example, researchers found a strong connection between social relationships and life span. The size of the effect rivaled that of better-known health-related behaviors such as smoking and exercise.

Because the studies used different methods, the analysis couldn't say exactly how many more years of life we might gain by having true pals, says lead author Julianne Holt-Lunstad, a psychologist at Brigham Young University in Provo, Utah.

But in a 2015 analysis that compiled data on more than 3.4 million people across seventy studies, she and colleagues found that the absence of social connections carried the same health risk as smoking up to fifteen cigarettes a day. Loneliness led to worse outcomes than obesity. And the findings held true for people of all ages.

Early on, it seemed possible that healthier people might simply make more friends. But a growing body of research suggests instead that good relationships actually lead to better health. One clue comes from studies that begin with a large group of healthy people and follow them for decades. Experimental work on animals has also linked isolation with earlier death.

And plenty of studies have revealed biological theories that may explain what makes us healthier when we feel supported: lower blood pressure, better hormone function, stronger immune systems and possibly lower levels of inflammation.

Meanwhile, friends can influence health-related behaviors through peer pressure that values healthy eating, exercise, taking prescriptions and going to doctor's appointments, Holt-Lundstad adds. True friendships can also give us a sense of purpose, making us more motivated to take care of ourselves.

But even as evidence piles up to support the value of bonding, the nature of friendship seems to be changing, says Glenn Sparks, a communications professor at Purdue University in West Lafayette, Ind., who studies how media affect people. One reason is that people move more frequently than they used to. And for many people, a focus on display screens has replaced a focus on faces.

Sparks remembers arriving at Purdue in 1986 and marveling at a stretch of sidewalk on campus dubbed the "Hello Walk." The point was to smile and say hello to the people you passed there, and that's what students did.

"Today, you walk down that sidewalk and people are staring at their iPhones and iPads and in some cases even their laptops," says Sparks, co-author of "Refrigerator Rights: Creating Connections and Restoring Relationships." "Their ear buds are in and they're gone into some virtual space. We think that really takes a toll on the relational health of any community."

Technology isn't necessarily all bad, he adds. Facebook and Skype can help keep people connected from afar, and science hasn't yet caught up with the nuanced ways that digital devices might alter relationships. But a confluence of factors seems to be threatening the potential for connection.

According to a long-term study published in 2006, people had an average of about three friends they felt they could discuss important things with in 1984. By 2005, the average number of confidants had dropped to about two. At the end of the study, close to 25 percent of respondents said they didn't have anyone they could truly trust, triple the proportion from two decades earlier.

More recently, a 2010 study by AARP surveyed more than 3,000 people age forty-five and older and found that 35 percent scored in the lonely category. Another survey, published this year by researchers at the University of Oxford, included more than 3,300 British people and found that, even though respondents averaged 155 Facebook connections, the number they felt they could approach in times of extreme distress was just four.

It's not necessarily important to have a lot of friends, though some studies suggest that more might be better than fewer. The AARP survey found that loneliness rates were highest in people who had fewer than three close friends, and having five or more was better than having three or four.

What is clear is that quality trumps quantity. Just as strong relationships can improve health measures, toxic or stressful relationships can lead to depression, high blood pressure and other negative outcomes.

In one recent study, Kiecolt-Glaser and colleagues asked married couples to discuss something they disagreed about. Over the next day, pairs that both included someone with a history of depression and had argued with hostility burned fewer calories than did those who talked to each other with more kindness. That suggests that relationship quality can affect metabolism. So how can we cultivate more and stronger relationships? Science can't yet say. Studies that have randomly assigned patients in hospitals to be part of a support group or have sent visitors to sit with lonely people have produced mixed results, probably because of chemistry: There's no guarantee that two people will click.

> **Today, the data make a convincing case: Having people who care about us is good for us.**

A better strategy, Holt-Lundstad suspects, is to try volunteering or joining activities that allow for interaction with a wide variety of people. It's also worth making a conscious effort to be the kind of friend you'd like people to be for you, Kiecolt-Glaser says. That includes being supportive, being there when friends need you, having fun together and making an effort to listen, even when you're busy or stressed-out.

In my case, I'm going to try to remember how much it meant to me when friends helped us with our move. And if I can organize a closet or even show up to give a hug, I'll do my best to be there. After all, there's something in it for me, too.

## QUESTIONS

1. What do you think Sohn's central argument is? What are the main pieces of support she offers for it? What objections to her central argument can you think of that she doesn't deal with?

2. Sohn is not a researcher or expert on friendship. What does she do to build her ethos? Are there things she doesn't do that you think she should have done to develop her ethos?

## COMPOSING PROJECT | Create a Collage

Go through your photos of yourself with friends. Notice which ones document important moments, which ones seem to capture the spirit of a particular friendship, and which ones reflect the personality or values or something else of you or your friend(s). Select your favorites and create a collage that illustrates the role friendship has played in your life.

## LONG-TERM PROJECTS    Mind & Body

1. **Create a marketing campaign for self-care.** Imagine you work for a marketing firm or ad agency hired by your city or state to promote the benefits of self-care. Perhaps your city has asked you to promote and celebrate being well hydrated, getting enough sleep, lowering your stress. Or maybe your state has hired you to "sell" citizens on the benefits of meditation and forest bathing.

   a. To begin your project, **choose a particular self-care practice**. Then research the techniques and benefits. Do some primary research by trying some of the things you discovered in your research.

   b. **Conduct a survey or several interviews** with residents of your city or state to find answers to these questions:
      - Who are they, in terms of age, race, education level, income level, etc.?

      - Do they typically integrate self-care regularly into their lives? Do they follow any particular practices? Why?
      - Are there financial barriers that keep them from adopting any of these practices?
      - Are there time barriers that keep them from performing self-care?
      - Are there stigmas or logistical barriers that prevent them from integrating self-care into their lives?

   c. Next, review the survey results or interview notes you collected. **Decide what group of citizens you want to target** with your marketing. **Consider these questions:** How will you entice them to appreciate the self-care practice? How can you appeal to their needs and values?

d. Then take this information and create the pieces of your marketing campaign. Your ultimate goal is to sell your campaign in a presentation to your class (who will pose as your peers at the marketing firm or ad agency and/or as the city or state officials who have hired your firm). **Create at least three different pieces for your campaign**, perhaps a series of print ads, storyboards for television ads, scripts for radio ads, slogans for bumper stickers or billboards, or YouTube videos. Your final presentation to your class should include the following:

- A description of your target group
- Your specific goal and message
- A rationale for the marketing campaign (including the needs and wants of the target group)
- A presentation of the pieces of the marketing campaign that you created

2. **Create an illustrated timeline.** Begin by researching advertisements past and present for a particular addictive substance, such as tobacco (cigarettes, vape pens), alcohol, or prescription drugs (oxycontin, codeine). How has the substance/product been advertised over time?

a. Research and create the timeline:
- **Identify and print out** as many images of ads as you can find online, keeping careful track of the original dates of each. Make sure your ads represent a wide time span, from the nineteenth century to the present if possible. As you search, you might want to use the search terms "Vintage Medicine Ads" or "Vintage Codeine Advertisements" (if you're researching codeine).
- **Choose four or five** of the most interesting ads, again keeping in mind the desired time range. Remember that you want to illustrate the ways this substance/product has been advertised over time.
- **Research the historical, political, and cultural events** that were taking place as your substance/product was advertised.
- **Create a timeline** that incorporates the ads with the corresponding historical, political, and cultural events you have identified.

b. Analyze:
- **Look for ways that history, politics, and culture affected your product's ad campaign.** For example, do ads from the Great Depression reflect the nation's economic desperation in any way? Are certain social or ethnic groups represented in new or different ways? Are products geared toward certain afflictions that reflect the time period? Try to make connections between the ads and what was happening at that time.
- **Write an essay** to accompany your timeline. Be sure to write about each ad and each point in your timeline. **Analyze** how history, politics, and culture impacted the way your product was advertised over time. Alternatively, you can write analytical annotations to accompany your timeline.

# 17

## ACTIVISM:
## MAKING YOUR VOICE HEARD

What does it mean to be an activist? Are you writing a letter to the editor urging drivers to be mindful of cyclists on the road? Perhaps you are joining thousands of marchers in your city and around the world protesting for an environmental change. You might even be sitting at a table on your campus on World AIDS Day (December 1), passing out pamphlets and answering questions.

Activism takes on all forms. You might participate in a shopping boycott, choosing only to support small businesses on a particular day, rather than support major corporations. You could write a play and perform it to raise awareness about an issue, as Eve Ensler did with *The Vagina Monologues*. Or you could attend a local open mic and perform a piece of spoken-word poetry that challenges the audience's notion of privilege.

Margaret Mead, a U.S. anthropologist, once said, "Never doubt that a small group of committed people can change the world. Indeed, it is the only thing that ever has." This chapter explores different ways activists have expressed their ideas and made their mark on the world. You'll examine photographs and protest signs, analyze fact sheets and speeches, and explore organizational sites and their messages.

The chapter begins with photographs of the activists Martin Luther King Jr., Marsh P. Johnson, and Greta Thunberg. This is followed by two websites: the "What We Do" page from the City Year organization, which shows the various activities of the organization; and the United Nations' "Sustainable Development Goals" page, which includes a list entitled "The Lazy Person's Guide to Saving the World."

The chapter then moves on to congressional testimony from Hasan Minhaj, a comedian, about the student debt crisis, a poster and fact sheet from the Mine Safety and Health Administration, and soccer player/activist Abby Wambach's commencement speech at Barnard College. This is followed by a series of three protest signs from three different movements: the Women's March, Build the Wall, and the Climate Strike.

Ending the chapter are a speech by the actress Ellen Page given at the Human Rights Campaign Foundation Conference and an article celebrating the birthday and accomplishments of the activist Malala Yousafzai.

As you read through the chapter, consider what different forms activism takes and how you might define activism.

## ▼ Photo

**Getty Images,** *Martin Luther King Jr.*

This photo captures Dr. Martin Luther King Jr. after he delivered his "I Have a Dream" speech in Washington, D.C., on August 28, 1963. The occasion was the March on Washington for Jobs and Freedom, a civil rights event that called for an end to racial discrimination. In his speech, King expressed his hope: "I have a dream that one day this nation will rise up and live out the true meaning of its creed: 'We hold these truths to be self-evident, that all men are created equal.'" While there were many photographs taken that day, this one was taken by an unidentified photographer and provided to us by Getty Images from its database.

*Credit: CNP/Hulton Archive/Getty Images.*

## ▼ Photo

**Netflix,** *Marsha P. Johnson*

Marsha P. Johnson (1945–1992) is usually credited for throwing the first brick that started the Stonewall Riots in 1969. Johnson, along with other members of the gay community, rioted to protest against a police raid at the Stonewall Inn. Johnson was a transgender woman and a leading advocate for LGBTQ rights, especially trans people of color. Her activism also included issues related to sex workers, homeless youth, and HIV/AIDS. She co-founded Street Transvestite Action Revolutionaries, performed drag, and held the informal title of mayor of Christopher Street. The photo is taken from a 2017 documentary, *The Death and Life of Marsha P. Johnson.*

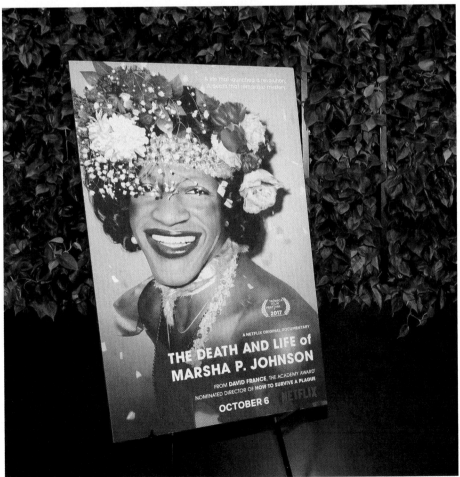

Credit: Tibrina Hobson/Getty Images Entertainment/Getty Images.

## ▼ Photo

### Kyodo News, *Greta Thunberg's Arrival in New York*

Greta Thunberg (b. 2003) is an environmental climate change activist from Sweden. She began to be noticed as an activist in 2018, when she inspired other students with her protest sign that urged students to strike to bring attention to the issues of climate change. Over the course of a year, this movement became known as Fridays for Future, with student walkouts taking place worldwide. In 2019, Thunberg earned a place on the cover of *Time* magazine as a "next generation leader," and also received a Nobel Peace Prize nomination. In September of 2019, Thunberg addressed leaders from around the world at the UN Climate Action Summit.

She said:

> "This is all wrong. I shouldn't be up here. I should be back in school on the other side of the ocean. Yet you all come to us young people for hope? *How dare you!* You have stolen my dreams and my childhood with your empty words. And yet I'm one of the lucky ones. People are suffering. People are dying. Entire ecosystems are collapsing. We are in the beginning of a mass extinction. And all you can talk about is money and fairytales of eternal economic growth. How dare you!"

This photo was taken by Kyodo News, a leading news organization in Japan who circulates news to various news organizations around the world. In this image, Greta Thunberg waves from a boat as she arrives in New York City on August 28, 2019.

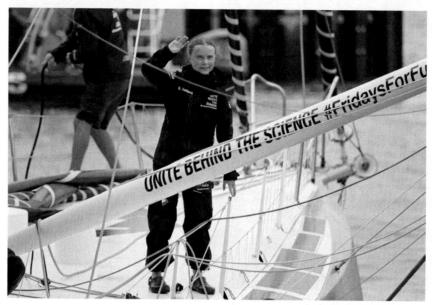

*Credit: Kyodo News/Getty Images.*

## QUESTIONS

1. These three photos portray noted activists. How do the photos emphasize their activism or historic stature?

2. Do you find one photo more compelling than another? Why?

## COMPOSING PROJECT | Create a Photo Essay

Research the civil rights movement of the 1950s and 1960s, the history of the gay rights movement from the Stonewall Rebellion (1969) to the Supreme Court ruling on same-sex marriage (2015), or climate change activism. Find pictures of people and events that display the activism involved in the movement you've chosen to research. Create a photo essay that tells the story and conveys the spirit of one of these movements.

## ▼ Website

### Volunteer.gov, *America's Natural and Cultural Resources Volunteer Portal*

Volunteer.gov is a site dedicated to connecting people with government-sponsored volunteer opportunities. Created in 2002, this site helps potential volunteers to learn about opportunities based on their interests and location.

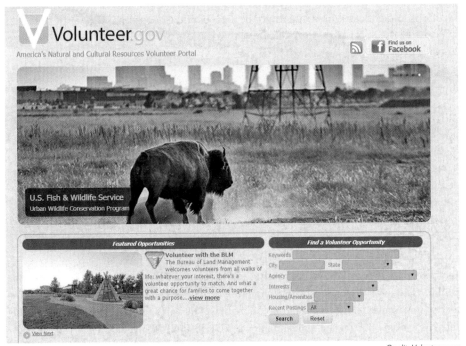

**Featured Opportunities**
Highlights a particular government organization with opportunities open, giving visitors to the site an idea of what sort of work might be available.

**Find a Volunteer Opportunity**
A search feature built directly into the main page so that site visitors do not need to navigate to multiple pages to begin searching.

Credit: Volunteer.gov.

**Events Calendar and Find Opportunities by State**

Allows site visitors to sort opportunities based on their availability or location.

**Links**

Allows site visitors to log their volunteer hours

Credit: Volunteer.gov.

## QUESTIONS

1. How do the images on the page set the tone and help convey the section's purpose? Are they effective? Would you have chosen different ones? Why or why not?

2. Do you think the main page provides sufficient information and resources? Why or why not?

## COMPOSING PROJECT | Create a Web Page

Review some websites of nonprofit volunteer organizations devoted to volunteering, such as Volunteer.org, CityYear.org, or PeaceCorps.gov. Then create a web page that helps recent college graduates find volunteer opportunities. Think of the web page as a general resource where someone can go to learn information about these various organizations and choose which one might be the best fit. Choose an image or images that will convey the spirit of that organization.

## ▼ List

### United Nations, *The Lazy Person's Guide to Saving the World*

On the United Nations' "Sustainable Development Goals" page, there is a list of activities people can do that will positively impact the earth. The list is geared toward lazy people, since, according to the site, "Every human on earth—even the most indifferent, laziest person among us—is part of the solution." The list is divided into three categories: Sofa Superstar, Household Hero, and Neighborhood Nice Guy.

Credit: From THE LAZY PERSON'S GUIDE TO SAVING THE WORLD by The United Nations. Copyright © The United Nations. Reprinted with the permission of the United Nations.

End extreme poverty. Fight inequality and injustice. Fix climate change. Whoa. The Global Goals are important, world-changing objectives that will require cooperation among governments, international organizations and world leaders. It seems impossible that the average person can make an impact. Should you just give up?

No! Change starts with you. Seriously. Every human on earth—even the most indifferent, laziest person among us—is part of the solution. Fortunately, there are some super easy things we can adopt into our routines that, if we all do it, will make a big difference.

We've made it easy for you and compiled just a few of the many things you can do to make an impact.

## Level 1: Sofa Superstar
### Things you can do from your couch

- Save electricity by plugging appliances into a power strip and turning them off completely when not in use, including your computer.

- Stop paper bank statements and pay your bills online or via mobile. No paper, no need for forest destruction.

- Share, don't just like. If you see an interesting social media post about women's rights or climate change, share it so folks in your network see it too.

- Speak up! Ask your local and national authorities to engage in initiatives that don't harm people or the planet. You can also voice your support for the Paris Agreement and ask your country to ratify it or sign it if it hasn't yet.

- Don't print. See something online you need to remember? Jot it down in a notebook or better yet a digital post-it note and spare the paper.

- Turn off the lights. Your TV or computer screen provides a cozy glow, so turn off other lights if you don't need them.

- Do a bit of online research and buy only from companies that you know have sustainable practices and don't harm the environment.

- Report online bullies. If you notice harassment on a message board or in a chat room, flag that person.

- Stay informed. Follow your local news and stay in touch with the Global Goals online or on social media at @GlobalGoalsUN.

> **Every human on earth—even the most indifferent, laziest person among us—is part of the solution.**

- Tell us about your actions to achieve the global goals by using the hashtag #globalgoals on social networks.

- Offset your carbon emissions! You can calculate your carbon footprint and purchase climate credit from Climate Neutral Now. In this way, you help reduce global emissions faster!

## Level 2: Household Hero
### Things you can do at home

- Air dry. Let your hair and clothes dry naturally instead of running a machine. If you do wash your clothes, make sure the load is full.

- Take short showers. Bathtubs require gallons more water than a 5–10 minute shower.

- Eat less meat, poultry, and fish. More resources are used to provide meat than plants.

- Freeze fresh produce and leftovers if you don't have the chance to eat them before they go bad. You can also do this with takeaway or delivered food, if you know you will not feel like eating it the next day. You will save food and money.
- Compost—composting food scraps can reduce climate impact while also recycling nutrients.
- Recycling paper, plastic, glass, & aluminum keeps landfills from growing.
- Buy minimally packaged goods.
- Avoid preheating the oven. Unless you need a precise baking temperature, start heating your food right when you turn on the oven.
- Plug air leaks in windows and doors to increase energy efficiency.
- Adjust your thermostat, lower in winter, higher in summer.
- Replace old appliances with energy efficient models and light bulbs.
- If you have the option, install solar panels in your house. This will also reduce your electricity bill!
- Get a rug. Carpets and rugs keep your house warm and your thermostat low.
- Don't rinse. If you use a dishwasher, stop rinsing your plates before you run the machine.
- Choose a better diaper option. Swaddle your baby in cloth diapers or a new, environmentally responsible disposable brand.
- Shovel snow manually. Avoid the noisy, exhaust-churning snowblower and get some exercise.
- Use cardboard matches. They don't require any petroleum, unlike plastic gas-filled lighters.

### Level 3: Neighborhood Nice Guy
**Things you can do outside your house**

- Shop local. Supporting neighborhood businesses keeps people employed and helps prevent trucks from driving far distances.
- Shop Smart—plan meals, use shopping lists and avoid impulse buys. Don't succumb to marketing tricks that lead you to buy more food than you need, particularly for perishable items. Though these may be less expensive per ounce, they can be more expensive overall if much of that food is discarded.
- Buy Funny Fruit—many fruits and vegetables are thrown out because their size, shape, or color are not "right." Buying these perfectly good funny fruit, at the farmer's market or elsewhere, utilizes food that might otherwise go to waste.
- When you go to a restaurant and are ordering seafood always ask: "Do you serve sustainable seafood?" Let your favorite businesses know that ocean-friendly sea-food's on your shopping list.
- Shop only for sustainable seafood. There are now many apps like this one that will tell you what is safe to consume.
- Bike, walk or take public transport. Save the car trips for when you've got a big group.

- Use a refillable water bottle and coffee cup. Cut down on waste and maybe even save money at the coffee shop.
- Bring your own bag when you shop. Pass on the plastic bag and start carrying your own reusable totes.
- Take fewer napkins. You don't need a handful of napkins to eat your takeout. Take just what you need.
- Shop vintage. Brand-new isn't necessarily best. See what you can repurpose from second-hand shops.
- Maintain your car. A well-tuned car will emit fewer toxic fumes.
- Donate what you don't use. Local charities will give your gently used clothes, books and furniture a new life.
- Vaccinate yourself and your kids. Protecting your family from disease also aids public health.
- Take advantage of your right to elect the leaders in your country and local community.

These are only a few of the things you can do. Explore this site to find out more about the goals you care most about and other ways to engage more actively.

## QUESTIONS

1. Are the actions organized in a particular way under each category? If so, how would you describe the pattern of organization? If you don't feel they are arranged in a particular order, how might you rearrange them?

2. Are there actions you would add to any of the categories? What are they?

## COMPOSING PROJECT | Create an Activism Diary

Take "The Lazy Person's Guide to Saving the World" list and note which actions you already do. Then choose five more that you will do in the course of a week (you can always do more than that). Keep a diary of what you did and when. Note in your entry the date, time, and what you did. Then write a paragraph noting how it felt to take that particular action. Is this something you will continue to do? Why or why not?

## ▼ Congressional Testimony

### Hasan Minhaj, *A $1.5 Trillion Crisis: Protecting Student Borrowers and Holding Student Loan Servers Accountable*

Hasan Minhaj is a comedian and host of *Patriot Act*, a Netflix talk show devoted to current political and cultural issues. In Season 2, Episode 3, Minhaj focused on student loans, showing the widespread enormity of student loan debt and deceitful practices of providers. He testified before the House Financial Services Committee in September of 2019 about the student debt crisis and the practices of loan providers.

### Testimony of Hasan Minhaj, 09/10/19

Thank you so much. I want to thank Chairwoman Maxine Waters for the opportunity to testify. And I'd like to thank ranking member Patrick McHenry for quietly tolerating it. Ladies and gentlemen, my name is Hasan Minhaj. Chairwoman Waters invited me to speak today because I host a show on Netflix called "Patriot Act." We recently did an episode covering the student loan crisis, and it really hit home with our audience. And it's probably because 44 million Americans owe more than 1.6 trillion dollars of student loan debt. In fact, the day we shot our episode, we surveyed our studio audience—which is only about 200 people—that room alone had over 6 million dollars of student debt. Granted my audience is mainly Asian dental students. But still. That's a lot.

Now I have a confession to make. I was extremely lucky to leave school without debt because I have immigrant parents, and they forced me to live at home during college. So I don't have crippling financial debt. I have crippling emotional debt. And Congress has yet to do anything about that. But you don't need to be drowning in debt to understand that this issue is sidelining millions of Americans. Marriage. Kids. Homeownership. And retirement are all being put on hold because of this crisis. Especially for my generation. Growing up, it was drilled into our heads, "You need to get a college education to get a middle-class job." We even tell kids today, "If you don't go to college, you might as well get a face tattoo. And we all can't be Post Malone."

> ❝ **We've put up a paywall to the middle class.** ❞

And it's true! Two thirds of all jobs in America require some college or a bachelor's degree. This is the standard now. But that wasn't the case when you went to college. And by you, I mean the members of Congress on this committee. Most of you grew up in a time when middle class jobs didn't require a Bachelor's. And you all paid far less for your degrees. College has become two to three times more expensive. In that same period, wages have only gone up about 16 percent.

People aren't making more money and college is way more expensive. We've put up a paywall to the middle class. And if there's one thing Americans hate—it's paywalls. That's why we put our entire show for free on YouTube. Because we care about the viewers. Also, because you can't find anything on Netflix. I'm sorry, I'm not just gonna talk into my Roku remote, "Roku: play 'Santa Clarita Diet'." But despite these numbers, we keep hearing the same talking point: "if student borrowers just took more 'personal responsibility,' they wouldn't be in this predicament." But they're trying to get ahead by doing the most responsible thing they can—invest in education.

And yet many of them are treated like deadbeats because the government is putting their financial futures in the hands of predatory, for-profit, loan servicers. Companies like Navient give borrowers terrible customer service and push them into repayment plans that add billions in interest to their loans. And the worst part is—you don't even get to choose your loan servicer. The department of education chooses one for you. So there's no competition to force these companies to provide better service.

Look—the deck is stacked against borrowers in ways it wasn't even ten or fifteen years ago. Why are we punishing student borrowers? Why aren't we giving them basic protections? At the very least, why can't we treat our borrowers the same way we treat our banks? Because 44 million Americans—that's too big to fail. In a country this wealthy, any American seeking higher education should never have to go bankrupt, they should never be preyed upon, and they should never have to live with my parents.

## QUESTIONS

1. Make a reverse outline of the main ideas in Minhaj's testimony. Do you see other ways Minhaj could have organized his ideas? Do you think he chose the most effective order to present his ideas? Why or why not?

2. Minhaj's primary audience is members of the U.S. Congress. Since Minhaj is a comedian, he brings some of his comedy into his testimony. Does this work for his audience? Why or why not? How does he temper his comedy to account for the needs and concerns of his audience?

## COMPOSING PROJECT | Craft Your Testimony

Imagine you have been invited to testify before Congress on an issue that is important to you. Draft the comments you would make, beginning by introducing yourself and explaining your connection to the issue. Then, as Minhaj does, explain how the issue has affected people and what you would like to see done about it. The Association for Career and Technical Education website (acteonline.org) has helpful information about testifying before policymakers.

## ▼ Poster & Fact Sheet

### Mine Safety and Health Administration, *End Black Lung & MSHA's Final Rule to Lower Miners' Exposure to Respirable Coal Mine Dust*

The Mine Safety and Health Administration (MSHA) is a branch of the U.S. Department of Labor charged with ensuring that mines comply with safety and health standards. Mining is a very dangerous activity for workers; in addition to facing death and dismemberment on the job, miners often suffer from maladies such as black lung or coal workers' pneumoconiosis, an ailment caused by exposure to coal dust. As the poster on page 502 indicates, black lung is both fatal and preventable. The fact sheet that follows describes a new rule designed to help prevent new cases of black lung.

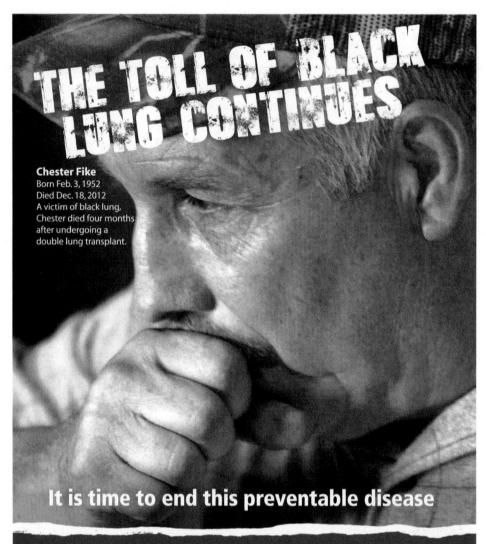

Credit: Mine Safety and Health Administration

Fact Sheet

## MSHA's Final Rule to Lower Miners' Exposure to

## Respirable Coal Mine Dust

According to data from the National Institute for Occupational Safety and Health (NIOSH), coal workers' pneumoconiosis (also known as black lung) was a cause or contributing factor in the death of more than 76,000 miners since 1968. Caused by breathing unhealthy coal mine dust, this disease has cost more than $45 billion dollars in federal compensation benefits. Evidence shows that miners continue to get the disease, even younger miners.

The Mine Safety and Health Administration has taken a historic step forward in the effort to end black lung disease by issuing a final rule to reduce miners' exposure to respirable coal dust. The new rule takes effect August 1, 2014 and accomplishes the following:

- Lowers the concentration of dust in the air that miners breathe and improves sampling practices to better reflect actual working conditions and protect all miners from overexposures;

- Increases sampling and makes use of cutting-edge technology developed for the mining environment to provide real-time information about dust levels, allowing miners and operators to identify problems and make necessary adjustments instead of letting overexposures languish. Requires immediate corrective action for excessive levels of dust; and

- Has a common sense phase-in over a two-year period to give the industry the time it needs to adjust to the new requirements, acquire monitoring equipment, and obtain compliance assistance from MSHA.

## Highlights of the final rule

**Lowers dust concentration levels:** Reduces the overall dust standards in coal mines from 2 to 1.5 milligrams per cubic meter of air; cuts in half the existing standard for air in entries used to ventilate places where miners work, and for Part 90 miners (those who have evidence of pneumoconiosis).

**Further lowers dust levels by eliminating loopholes that masked overexposures and improves sampling for more accurate measurements:**

- Changes the current practice of averaging dust samples, which allows miners on some shifts to be exposed to levels above the standard;

- Mandates immediate action by mine operators when dust levels are high instead of allowing miners to be exposed to unhealthy dust levels for days or weeks;

- Requires more frequent sampling of areas known to have high dust levels, such as those closest to the production area;

- Requires sampling for the full shift a miner works to ensure protection for all working hours rather than stopping measurement after 8 hours, as is the existing requirement;

- Requires sampling on all shifts;

- Requires dust samples to be taken when mines are operating at 80 percent of production or more, as opposed to the existing 50 percent requirement, so that samples are more representative of actual working conditions; and

- Requires more thorough examinations of the dust controls on mining sections each shift with records of the exams signed by mine officials.

**Utilizes cutting-edge technology to measure dust levels:** Requires use of the continuous personal dust monitor (CPDM), a device developed with mining industry involvement to provide real-time sampling results. The CPDM is to be worn by miners in high-risk occupations. It continuously evaluates dust levels and provides operators with readings they can use to take immediate action to correct dust conditions, instead of waiting days for lab results, as is necessary with current sampling methods.

**Improves the early warning system for the disease:** Expands the medical surveillance program to include surface as well as underground coal miners, and adds lung function testing as well as x-rays.

### Background

> **The persistence of black lung disease has long troubled health researchers, labor advocates and responsible industry leaders.**

The persistence of black lung disease has long troubled health researchers, labor advocates and responsible industry leaders. In separate reports in the mid-1990s, the Centers for Disease Control's National Institute for Occupational Safety and Health, and a Secretary of Labor's Advisory Committee of industry, labor and government representatives recommended changes to exposure limits and enforcement protocols, many of which are included in the new rule.

The rule builds on years of research and was developed with the input of industry, labor, and health professionals. It is the centerpiece of the agency's campaign to End Black Lung, launched in 2009, which seeks to fulfill a promise originally made by Congress in passing the Federal Coal Mine Health and Safety Act of 1969.

MSHA proposed the rule in October 2010 and followed its announcement with an extensive period of public outreach that included seven hearings in coal-producing regions and at its headquarters in Arlington, VA. About 2,000 pages of comments were received over an 8-month period. The final rule is responsive to the comments.

### Extensive training and outreach will prepare miners and operators

MSHA will provide extensive guidance and support to mine operators and miners, including:

- Outreach to all coal mine operators during the implementation period;
- Stakeholders meeting at MSHA headquarters in Arlington, VA;

- Field seminars in coal mining regions, including in Beckley, WV; Washington, PA; Hazard, KY; Birmingham, AL; Evansville, IN; and Grand Junction, CO; and

- Comprehensive compliance assistance material, including distribution of guidance documents.

More outreach sessions will be scheduled. During these sessions, MSHA representatives will highlight the major provisions and effective dates, and describe best practices for controlling dust and reducing exposures. Training will be provided to MSHA enforcement personnel before implementation, and training materials will be available on the MSHA website for operators and miners.

**For more information, visit www.msha.gov/endblacklung**

## QUESTIONS

1. These two documents convey the idea that Black Lung can be prevented, but they do it in quite different ways. Who do you think the audience is for each piece and why?

2. The fact sheet uses bulleted lists to convey much of the information. How do the bullets help you read the information? Would you prefer that the bulleted information be conveyed in full paragraphs? Why or why not?

## COMPOSING PROJECT | Create an Infographic

Notice that the poster is almost purely visual and the fact sheet is purely text-based. Create a third piece that combines visuals (find or create your own or use the image from the poster) and some of the text from the fact sheet into an infographic designed for college students or an audience other than the ones you identified in question 1 above.

## ▼ Speech

### Abby Wambach, *We Are the Wolves*

Abby Wambach played on the U.S. Women's soccer team and scored more goals than any other player on the team. She is the world record holder for international goals scored, and was the 2012 FIFA Player of the Year. She played in both the World Cup and the Olympics. She retired from soccer in 2015. Her autobiography, *Forward*, was a *New York Times* bestseller. She also helped lead the fight for U.S. women soccer players to be paid the same as men. She delivered the following speech at Barnard College's 2018 graduation.

Credit line: Commencement 2018. Remarks as Delivered by Abby Wambach. Used with Permission from Barnard College. Accessed at https://barnard.edu/commencement/archives/2018/abby-wambach-remarks

Greetings to President Beilock, Barnard faculty, trustees, and honorees: Katherine Johnson, Anna Quindlen, and Rhea Suh.

And to each of the 619 bad-ass women of the Barnard graduating class of 2018: Congratulations! Doesn't it feel like the second you figure anything out in life, it ends and you're forced to start all over again?

Experts call these times of life "transitions." I call them terrifying. I went through a terrifying transition recently when I retired from soccer. The world tries to distract us from our fear during these transitions by creating fancy ceremonies for us. This graduation is your fancy ceremony. Mine was the ESPYs, a nationally televised sports award show. I had to get dressed up for that just like you got dressed up for this, but they sent me a really expensive fancy stylist. It doesn't look like you all got one. Sorry about that.

So it went like this: ESPN called and told me they were going to honor me with their inaugural icon award. I was humbled, of course, to be regarded as an icon. Did I mention that I'm an icon? I received my award along with two other incredible athletes: basketball's Kobe Bryant and football's Peyton Manning. We all stood on stage together and watched highlights of our careers with the cameras rolling and the fans cheering—and I looked around and had a moment of awe. I felt so grateful to be there—included in the company of Kobe and Peyton. I had a momentary feeling of having arrived: like we women had finally made it.

Then the applause ended and it was time for the three of us to exit stage left. And as I watched those men walk off the stage, it dawned on me that the three of us were stepping away into very different futures.

Each of us, Kobe, Peyton and I—we made the same sacrifices, we shed the same amount of blood sweat and tears, we'd left it all on the field for decades with the same ferocity, talent and commitment—but our retirements wouldn't be the same at all. Because Kobe and Peyton walked away from their careers with something I didn't have: enormous bank accounts. Because of that they had something else I didn't have: freedom. Their hustling days were over; mine were just beginning.

Later that night, back in my hotel room, I laid in bed and thought: this isn't just about me, and this isn't just about soccer. We talk a lot about the pay gap. We talk about how we U.S. women overall still earn only 80 cents on the dollar compared to men, and black women make only 63 cents, while Latinas make 54 cents. What we need to talk about more is the aggregate and compounding effects of the pay gap on women's lives. Over time, the pay gap means women are able to invest less and save less so they have to work longer. When we talk about what the pay gap costs us, let's be clear. It costs us our very lives.

And it hit me that I'd spent most of my time during my career the same way I'd spent my time on that ESPYs stage. Just feeling grateful. Grateful to be one of the only women to have a seat at the table. I was so grateful to receive any respect at all for myself that I often missed opportunities to demand equality for all of us.

But as you know, women of Barnard—CHANGE. IS. HERE.

Women have learned that we can be grateful for what we have while also demanding what we deserve. Like all little girls, I was taught to be grateful. I was taught to keep my head down, stay on the path, and get my job done. I was freaking Little Red Riding Hood.

You know the fairy tale: It's just one iteration of the warning stories girls are told the world over. Little Red Riding Hood heads off through the woods and is given strict instructions: Stay on the path. Don't talk to anybody. Keep your head down hidden underneath your Handmaid's Tale cape.

And she does . . . at first. But then she dares to get a little curious and she ventures off the path. That's of course when she encounters the Big Bad Wolf and all hell breaks loose. The message is clear: Don't be curious, don't make trouble, don't say too much or BAD THINGS WILL HAPPEN.

I stayed on the path out of fear, not of being eaten by a wolf, but of being cut, being benched, losing my paycheck. If I could go back and tell my younger self one thing it would be this: "Abby, you were never Little Red Riding Hood; you were always the wolf."

So when I was entrusted with the honor of speaking here today, I decided that the most important thing for me to say to you is this:

**BARNARD WOMEN—CLASS OF 2018—WE. ARE. THE. WOLVES.**

In 1995, around the year of your birth, wolves were re-introduced into Yellowstone National Park after being absent for seventy years. In those years, the number of deer had skyrocketed because they were unchallenged, alone at the top of the food chain. They grazed away and reduced the vegetation, so much that the river banks were eroding. Once the wolves arrived, they thinned out the deer through hunting. But more significantly, their presence changed the behavior of the deer.

Wisely, the deer started avoiding the valleys, and the vegetation in those places regenerated. Trees quintupled in just six years. Birds and beavers started moving in. The river dams the beavers built provided habitats for otters and ducks and fish. The animal ecosystem regenerated. But that wasn't all. The rivers actually changed as well. The plant regeneration stabilized the river banks so they stopped collapsing. The rivers steadied—all because of the wolves' presence.

See what happened here?

The wolves, who were feared as a threat to the system, turned out to be its salvation. Barnard women, are you picking up what I'm laying down here?

Women are feared as a threat to our system—and we will also be our society's salvation. Our landscape is overrun with archaic ways of thinking about women, about people of color, about the "other," about the rich and the poor, about the powerful and the powerless—and these ways of thinking are destroying us.

We are the ones we've been waiting for.

We will not Little Red Riding Hood our way through life. We will unite our pack, storm the valley together and change the whole bloody system.

Throughout my life, my pack has been my team. Teams need a unifying structure, and the best way to create one collective heartbeat is to establish rules for your team to live by. It doesn't matter what specific page you're all on, just as long as you're all on the same one.

Here are four rules I've used to unite my pack and lead them to gold.

**Rule One: MAKE FAILURE YOUR FUEL**

Here's something the best athletes understand, but seems like a hard concept for non-athletes to grasp. Non-athletes don't know what to do with the gift of failure. So they hide it, pretend it never happened, reject it outright—and they end up wasting it.

Listen: Failure is not something to be ashamed of, it's something to be POWERED by. Failure is the highest octane fuel your life can run on. You gotta learn to make failure your fuel.

When I was on the Youth National Team, only dreaming of playing alongside Mia Hamm. You know her? Good. I had the opportunity to visit the National Team's locker room. The thing that struck me most wasn't my heroes' grass-stained cleats or their names and numbers hanging above their lockers—it was a picture. It was a picture that someone had taped next to the door so that it would be the last thing every player saw before she headed out to the training pitch.

You might guess it was a picture of their last big win, of them standing on a podium accepting gold medals—but it wasn't. It was a picture of their longtime rival—the Norwegian national team—celebrating after having just beaten the USA in the 1995 World Cup.

In that locker room, I learned that in order to become my very best—on the pitch and off—I'd need to spend my life letting the feelings and lessons of failure transform into my power. Failure is fuel. Fuel is power. Women, listen to me. We must embrace failure as our fuel instead of accepting it as our destruction.

As Michelle Obama recently said: "I wish that girls could fail as well as men do and be okay. Because let me tell you watching men fail up—it's frustrating. It's frustrating to see men blow it and win. And we hold ourselves to these crazy, crazy standards."

**Wolf Pack: Fail up. Blow it, and win.**

**Rule Two: LEAD FROM THE BENCH**

Imagine this: You've scored more goals than any human being on the planet—female or male. You've co-captained and led Team USA in almost every category for the past decade. And you and your coach sit down and decide together that you won't be a starter in your last World Cup for Team USA.

So . . . that sucked.

You'll feel benched sometimes, too. You'll be passed over for the promotion, taken off the project—you might even find yourself holding a baby instead of a briefcase—watching your colleagues "get ahead." Here's what's important. You are allowed to be disappointed when it feels like life's benched you. What you aren't allowed to do is miss your opportunity to lead from the bench.

During that last World Cup, my teammates told me that my presence, my support, my vocal and relentless belief in them from the bench is what gave them the confidence they needed to win us that championship. If you're not a leader on the bench, don't call yourself a leader on the field. You're either a leader everywhere or nowhere.

And by the way: the fiercest leading I've ever seen has been done between mother and child. Parenting is no bench. It just might be the big game.

**Wolf Pack: Wherever you're put, lead from there.**

**Rule Three: CHAMPION EACH OTHER**

During every 90-minute soccer match there are a few magical moments when the ball actually hits the back of the net and a goal is scored. When this happens, it means that everything has come together perfectly—the perfect pass, the perfectly timed run, every player in the right place at exactly the right time: all of this culminating in a moment in which one player scores that goal.

What happens next on the field is what transforms a bunch of individual women into a team. Teammates from all over the field rush toward the goal scorer. It appears that we're celebrating her: but what we're REALLY celebrating is every player, every coach, every practice, every sprint, every doubt, and every failure that this one single goal represents.

> **Let's claim infinite joy, success, and power—together.**

You will not always be the goal scorer. And when you are not—you better be rushing toward her.

Women must champion each other. This can be difficult for us. Women have been pitted against each other since the beginning of time for that one seat at the table. Scarcity has been planted inside of us and among us. This scarcity is not our fault. But it is our problem. And it is within our power to create abundance for women where scarcity used to live.

As you go out into the world: Amplify each others' voices. Demand seats for women, people of color and all marginalized people at every table where decisions are made. Call out each other's wins and just like we do on the field: claim the success of one woman, as a collective success for all women.

Joy. Success. Power. These are not pies where a bigger slice for her means a smaller slice for you. These are infinite. In any revolution, the way to make something true starts with believing it is. Let's claim infinite joy, success, and power—together.

**Wolf Pack: Her Victory is your Victory. Celebrate it.**

**Rule Four: DEMAND THE BALL**

When I was a teenager, I was lucky enough to play with one of my heroes, Michelle Akers. She needed a place to train since there was not yet a women's professional league. Michelle was tall like I am, built like I'd be built, and the most courageous soccer player I'd ever seen play. She personified every one of my dreams.

We were playing a small sided scrimmage—five against five. We were eighteen-year-olds and she was—Michelle Akers—a chiseled, thirty-year-old powerhouse. For the first three quarters of the game, she was taking it easy on us, coaching us, teaching us about spacing, timing and the tactics of the game.

By the fourth quarter, she realized that because of all of this coaching, her team was losing by three goals. In that moment, a light switched on inside of her. She ran back to her own goalkeeper, stood one yard away from her, and screamed:

GIVE. ME. THE. EFFING. BALL.

And the goalkeeper gave her the effing ball. And she took that ball and she dribbled through our entire effing team and she scored. Now this game was winner's keepers, so if you scored you got the ball back. So, as soon as Michelle scored, she ran back to her goalie, stood a yard away from her and screamed:

GIVE ME THE BALL.

The keeper did. And again she dribbled though us and scored. And then she did it again. And she took her team to victory.

Michelle Akers knew what her team needed from her at every moment of that game. Don't forget that until the fourth quarter, leadership had required Michelle to help, support, and teach, but eventually leadership called her to demand the ball.

Women. At this moment in history leadership is calling us to say:

GIVE ME THE EFFING BALL.

GIVE ME THE EFFING JOB.

GIVE ME THE SAME PAY THAT THE GUY NEXT TO ME GETS.

GIVE ME THE PROMOTION.

GIVE ME THE MICROPHONE.

GIVE ME THE OVAL OFFICE.

GIVE ME THE RESPECT I'VE EARNED AND GIVE IT TO MY WOLF PACK TOO.

In closing, I want to leave you with the most important thing I've learned since leaving soccer. When I retired, my sponsor Gatorade surprised me at a meeting with the plan for my send-off commercial. The message was this: Forget Me.

They'd nailed it. They knew I wanted my legacy to be ensuring the future success of the sport I'd dedicated my life to. If my name were forgotten, that would mean that the women who came behind me were breaking records, winning championships and pushing the game to new heights. When I shot that commercial I cried.

A year later, I found myself coaching my ten-year-old daughter's soccer team. I'd coached them all the way to the championship. (#Humblebrag.) One day I was warming the team up, doing a little shooting drill. I was telling them a story about when I retired. And one of those little girls looked up at me and said: "So what did you retire from?" And I looked down at her and I said, "SOCCER." And she said, "Oh. Who did you play for?" And I said, "THE. UNITED. STATES. OF. AMERICA." And she said, "Oh. Does that mean you know Alex Morgan?"

Be careful what you wish for, Barnard. They forgot me. But that's okay. Being forgotten in my retirement didn't scare me. What scared me was losing the identity the game gave me. I defined myself as Abby Wambach, soccer player—the one who showed up and gave 100 percent to my team and fought alongside my wolf pack to make a better future for the next generation. Without soccer who would I be?

A few months after retirement, I began creating my new life. I met Glennon and our three children and I became a wife, a mother, a business owner and an activist. And you know who I am now? I'm still the same Abby. I still show up and give 100 percent—now to my new pack—and I still fight every day to make a better future for the next generation.

You see, soccer didn't make me who I was. I brought who I was to soccer, and I get to bring who I am wherever I go. And guess what? So do you.

As you leave here today and everyday going forward: Don't just ask yourself, "What do I want to do?" Ask yourself: "WHO do I want to be?" Because the most important thing I've learned is that what you do will never define you. Who you are always will.

And who you are—Barnard women—are the wolves.

Surrounding you today is your wolf pack. Look around.

Don't lose each other.

Leave these sacred grounds united, storm the valleys together, and be our salvation.

## QUESTIONS

1. In her speech, Wambach says that instead of asking what you want to do, you should ask who you want to be. Why does she believe you should ask that question? What evidence does she offer to support this?

2. How would you describe the tone of her speech? Why? Does it stay consistent throughout or does it change? If so, what are the changes?

## COMPOSING PROJECT | Compose an Activism Speech

Think about something you're passionate about, something you would protest for. This could be an issue on campus or in your community. It might be environmental, political, or sports related. Compose a speech that brings the issue into focus for your audience. Try to use some of the techniques Wambach used to evoke the urgency of the situation. After you have written out the speech, read it aloud to a few classmates. You might also consider recording it.

## ▼ Protest Sign

### Carsten Koall, *Women's March Berlin*

On January 19, 2019, people gathered near the Brandenburg Gate in Berlin for the second anniversary of the Women's March. The Berlin march was just one of many held around the world. The photo below was taken at the rally.

*Credit: Carsten Koall/Getty Images New/Getty Images.*

## ▼ Protest Sign

### Tom Williams, *"Build the Wall" Sign*

On September 7, 2019, a man supporting Donald Trump's proposed wall between Mexico and the United States stands in front of the White House with his protest sign. Below is the photo.

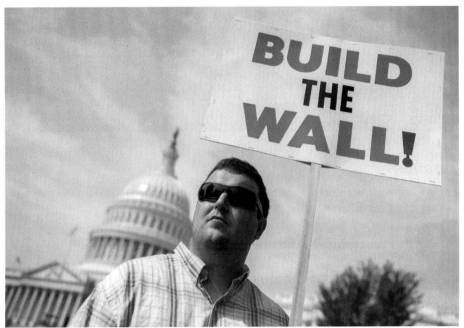

Credit: Tom Williams/CQ-Roll Call, Inc./Getty Images.

## ▼ Protest Sign

### SOPA Images, *Climate Strike in Los Angeles*

On May 24, 2019, hundreds of thousands of students participated in a worldwide climate strike, inspired by Greta Thunberg. This was the second Global Climate Strike, with participants from more than 100 countries. In Los Angeles, students gathered at Pershing Square and marched to City Hall. Some of the demands listed on the event's Facebook page were "Pass 2500 ft setback between oil extraction sites and homes, and zero emissions economy by 2025." The photo on the following page is from the Los Angeles Climate Strike.

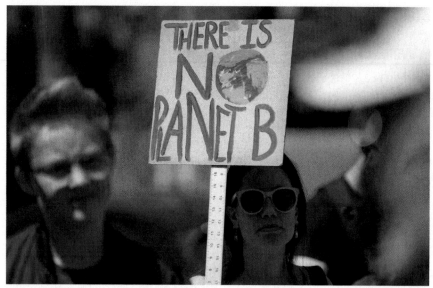

Credit: SOPA Images/LightRocket/Getty Images.

## QUESTIONS

1. What are some similarities you notice in the protest signs? Besides the message, are there key differences?

2. Do some brief research on each march or movement. Then look at each protest sign. Is it representative of the march/movement's intent? Why or why not?

## COMPOSING PROJECT | Create a Collage

Choose a social justice movement (e.g., women's rights, LGBTQ rights, immigration rights, climate change). Find photos from different protests related to that movement (you might want to focus on just one march or several marches). Choose photos that represent different faces of the movement/march. Then assemble them into a collage that conveys the story of the march(es).

## ▼ Speech

### Ellen Page, *Speech at Time to THRIVE Conference*

Ellen Page is a TV and film actor who has starred in films including *X-Men: The Last Stand*, *Inception*, and *Juno*, for which she was nominated for several awards, including an Oscar. She delivered the following speech at the 2014 Time to THRIVE conference, an event organized by the Human Rights Campaign Foundation. The conference aims to support LGBTQ youth.

Credit: Actress Ellen Page Speech at Human Rights Campaign Foundation Conference. Reprinted with permission.

Thank you, Chad, for those kind words, and for the even kinder work that you and the Human Rights Campaign Foundation do every day on behalf of the lesbian, gay, bisexual, and transgendered young people here and across America.

It is such an honor to be here at the inaugural Time to THRIVE Conference. But it's a little weird, too. Here I am in this room because of an organization whose work I deeply, deeply admire, and I'm surrounded by people who make it their life's work to make other people's lives better—profoundly better. Some of you teach young people. Some of you help young people to heal and find their voice. Some of you listen. Some of you take action. Some of you are young people yourselves, in which case it's even weirder for a young person like me to be speaking to you.

It's weird because here I am, an actress, representing at least in some sense an industry that places crushing standards on all of us—and not just young people, everyone. Standards of beauty, of a good life, of success; standards that I hate to admit have affected me. You have ideas planted in your head—thoughts you never had before—that tell you how you have to act, how you have to dress, and who you have to be. And I've been trying to push back to be authentic and follow my heart, but it can be hard. But that's why I'm here, in this room. All of you, all of us, can do so much more together than any one person can do alone. And I hope that that thought bolsters you as much as it does me. I hope that the workshops you go to over the next few days give you strength, because I can only imagine that there are days when you've worked longer hours than your boss realizes or cares about just to help a kid who you know can make it. Days where you feel completely alone, undermined, or hopeless.

> **If we took just five minutes to recognize each other's beauty instead of attacking each other for our differences—that's not hard, it's really an easier and better way to live.**

And I know that there are people in this room who go to school every day and get treated like shit for no reason. Or you go home and you feel like you can't tell your parents the whole truth about yourself. And beyond putting yourself in one box or another, you worry about the future, about college, or work, or even your physical safety. And trying to create that mental picture of your life, of what on earth is going to happen to you, can crush you a little bit every day. And it is toxic, and painful, and deeply unfair. And sometimes it's the little, insignificant stuff that can tear you down.

Now, I try not to read gossip as a rule. But the other day, a website ran an article with a picture of me wearing sweatpants on the way to the gym. And the writer asked, "Why does this petite beauty insist on dressing like a massive man?" Because I like to be comfortable. There are pervasive stereotypes about masculinity and femininity that define how we're all supposed to act, dress, and speak, and they serve no one. Anyone who defies these so-called "norms" becomes worthy of comment and scrutiny, and the LGBT community knows this all too well. Yet there is courage all around us. The football hero Michael Sam; the actress Laverne Cox; the musicians Tegan and Sara Quinn; the family that supports their daughter or son who has come out. And there is courage in this room. All of you.

And I'm inspired to be in this room because every single one of you is here for the same reason: you're here because you've adopted, as a core motivation, the simple fact that this world would be a whole lot better if we just made an effort to be less horrible to one another.

If we took just five minutes to recognize each other's beauty instead of attacking each other for our differences—that's not hard, it's really an easier and better way to live. And ultimately, it saves lives. Then again, it can be the hardest thing—because loving other people starts with loving ourselves and accepting ourselves. And I know many of you have struggled with this, and I draw upon your strength and your support in ways that you will never know.

And I am here today because I am gay. And because maybe I can make a difference to help others have an easier and more hopeful time. Regardless, for me, I feel a personal obligation and a social responsibility. I also do it selfishly, because I'm tired of hiding. And I'm tired of lying by omission. I suffered for years because I was scared to be out. My spirit suffered, my mental health suffered, and my relationships suffered. And I'm standing here today, with all of you, on the other side of that pain. And I am young, yes. But what I have learned is that love—the beauty of it, the joy of it, and yes, even the pain of it—is the most incredible gift to give and to receive as a human being. And we deserve to experience love fully, equally, without shame, and without compromise. There are too many kids out there suffering from bullying, rejection, or simply being mistreated because of who they are. Too many dropouts. Too much abuse. Too many homeless. Too many suicides. You can change that, and you are changing it. But you never needed me to tell you that, and that's why this was a little bit weird.

The only thing that I can really say is what I have been building up to for the past five minutes: thank you. Thank you for inspiring me. Thank you for giving me hope. And please keep changing the world for people like me. Happy Valentine's Day, I love you all.

## QUESTIONS

1. What do you think Page's purpose is? To inspire? To motivate? To share her story? What are some details and examples from her speech that support your idea?

2. Were you surprised to see the phrase "treated like shit" in Page's speech? Why or why not? Why do you think Page decided to use that colloquialism rather than a more formal statement to express her idea?

## COMPOSING PROJECT | Write a Speech

Imagine you have been invited to give a speech at a conference on an issue of interest to you. Consider your audience and the point you want to make. Write a speech, carefully considering how much of yourself and your personal story you want to share with a room full of strangers, what kind of language you want to use, and what message you want to send.

## Amy Davidson, *Happy Birthday, Malala*

Amy Davidson is a senior editor and writer for *The New Yorker*. She worked as a fact-checker for *The New Yorker* before becoming an editor. Davidson has written about topics such as immigration and politics. In the piece below, she uses the occasion of Malala Yousafzai's sixteenth birthday to remind readers of the difference that educating one child can make.

Credit: Amy Davidson, "Happy Birthday, Malala" From The New Yorker, July 12, 2013. © Conde Nast. Reprinted by permission.

A sixteen-year-old girl wearing three shades of pink stood in front of the United Nations on Friday. She was introduced by Gordon Brown, Britain's former Prime Minister—a broad, lumbering man who nonetheless seemed as slight as a pencil sketch next to her. "Let me repeat the words," Brown said. "The words the Taliban never wanted her to hear: happy sixteenth birthday, Malala."

It was Malala Day at the U.N.'s Youth Assembly, in honor of Malala Yousafzai, the girl who wanted to go to school. Less than a year ago, she was on a school bus in Pakistan when a man with a gun got on and said, "Where is Malala?" He shot her in the face; the bullet entered near an eye and ended up near her left shoulder. "They shot my friends, too," Yousafzai told the audience at the United Nations.

> They thought that the bullet would silence us. But they failed. And out of that silence came thousands of voices. The terrorists thought they would change my aims and stop my ambitions, but nothing changed in my life except this: weakness, fear, and hopelessness died. Strength, power, and courage was born.

Those qualities were born in this young woman, one has the sense, the moment she came into the world. They might have been wasted. She had the luck of having parents who believed in her education, and the great barrier of an armed group that thought it would be better if she were dead. Among Yousafzai's many gifts is the ability to convey both how extraordinary she herself is and how many other children might be, too, if someone taught them how to read and write. "So here I stand. So here I stand, one girl among many," she said. "I am here to speak up for the rights of education for every child."

Yousafzai's delivery was as compelling as her words—watch the video. She has an air of control about her, and self-possession, that goes beyond fearlessness. Speaking of the Taliban gunman who tried to kill her, she said that she was not seeking revenge. "Even if there is a gun in my hand, and he stands in front of me, I would not shoot him," she said—and one believed her, not because as a child she would be too meek or gentle but because she knew, intuitively, that

> **And out of that silence came thousands of voices.**

it was not the way to impose her will. "The power of education frightens them. They are afraid of women. The power of the voice of women frightens them." She knew that she, in the end, was the stronger one.

And yet Yousafzai can't go home; nor, as the *Times* has reported, has there been a pause in attacks on schools that educate girls in Pakistan. Many have been bombed. British doctors saved Yousafzai's life, and she is now in school in Birmingham.

"I am the same Malala. My ambitions are the same. My hopes are the same. My dreams are the same," Yousafzai said. One hopes that those ambitions will remain limitless. She was wearing a shawl, she said, that Benazir Bhutto, the former Prime Minister of Pakistan, had worn before she was murdered. Yousafzai could run a country someday; she might do almost anything. "One child, one teacher, one book, and one pen can change the world," she said. "Education is the only solution. Education first." With time, perhaps, for a birthday party.

## QUESTIONS

1. About midway through the piece, Davidson says, "Yousafzai's delivery was as compelling as the words—watch the video." You can watch the video on YouTube. After watching the video, do you agree with Davidson's assessment of Yousafzai's delivery? What is the effect of having a piece in one mode—print, in this case—refer you to a piece in another mode?

2. Davidson uses several quotations from Yousafzai throughout the short piece and also quotes Britain's former prime minister, Gordon Brown. Despite the liberal use of quotations, does Davidson maintain her own voice as the controlling voice in this piece, or did you forget that the piece was written by someone other than Yousafzai?

## COMPOSING PROJECT | Write a Tribute

Think of someone you admire in your life: perhaps a friend, relative, or coworker. Compose a one- to two-page tribute to that person and a particular quality of that person you wish the world had more of. Then try to connect the person and the quality to a bigger issue, just as Davidson connects Yousafzai's fearlessness and self-possession to the importance of education for children.

## LONG-TERM PROJECTS | Activism

1. **Create an activist campaign.** For this project, you will choose an issue you care about. This might be something related to your community, such as fighting against a new highway that is going to be built through a poor neighborhood. Perhaps it's something related to the environment, such as a company's use of nonsustainable palm oil and its connection to deforestation. Or maybe you want to focus more broadly on a topic such as racism,

such as fighting mass incarceration of young black males.

Part I: Preliminary Steps.

a. To begin your project, **brainstorm a list of causes** you're passionate about. Share this list with classmates, discussing why you chose to put some items on the list.

b. Choose the cause you want to focus on for the activist campaign. **Research** your cause to find out the various issues related to it. Are there leaders on a global, national, state, or community level? Who are they? What are they doing? Why do some people support the cause? Why are some people opposed to the cause?

c. **Create a five-minute oral presentation** for your class. In the presentation, you want to describe your issue to students and your teacher, demonstrating why they should care and be involved. Ultimately, you want to persuade them to join you in the movement.

Part II: The Campaign.

a. **Design a protest sign.** Do a Google image search for protest signs and see the varying ways people represent causes. You will need cardboard, poster board, glue, markers, and possibly photos/images. Remember that your phrase/text should only be a few words—people will want to be able to read it quickly and remember it.

b. Choose a place where you would hold a march and/or rally. Research how you would go about getting a permit for your event. If you are holding a rally, decide what speakers you might have. Do you want any musicians/poets? Do you want any religious leaders? Would it be appropriate to have politicians speak?

c. Decide how you are going to advertise your event. Will you have a hashtag for Twitter? Will there be a Facebook page, and if so, what will you call the page? Are there other ways you might get the word out?

d. **Create a leaflet** to hand out at your march/rally that describes the issues related to your cause.

e. Put together a **ten-minute oral presentation** for your class. In the presentation, show your protest sign and pass around your leaflet. Describe to the class where you are going to hold your march/rally and why you've chosen that location. Who is going to be present at the march/rally? How are you going to get the word out about the event?

f. **Write up a one- to two-page paper** that describes your cause and campaign for your teacher. Include the information that you are presenting and make sure to articulate why you made certain decisions (such as why you chose the phrase for your protest sign, why you chose particular speakers).

2. **Create a poster and fact sheet for an environmental issue.** Research an environmental issue that interests you, such as overfishing, climate change, deforestation, or ocean pollution.

a. Choose one environmental issue to investigate. Your goal is to formulate an innovative response that helps mitigate the environmental issue's impact. For example, the Coca-Cola company has formed partnerships with the communities their plants are in to protect the water supplies.

b. As you research the issue, consider the following:
   - How has the environmental issue affected local economies?
   - How has the environmental issue shaped legislation?
   - How has tourism been affected by the environmental issue?
   - What business practices have been developed in response to the environmental issue?
   - What have been some innovative responses to the environmental issue?

c. Next, consider what innovative response you might suggest. For example, you might have an idea for a program to prevent overfishing from getting worse, a plan to rebuild the rain forests or a campaign to make the public aware of how they contribute to the problem. Once you decide on your response, produce:

- A fact sheet that conveys facts about the issue, its impacts, and the innovative response you have come up with.
- A poster that gets people's attention and highlights a few compelling facts about the issue and its impacts.

# 18

## CREATIVITY:
## IT'S COMPLICATED

What does it mean to be "creative"? While we often associate creativity with artsy types, anyone who creates anything new can be said to be creative. When you think about it that way, doesn't "creative" apply to all of us? Whether you create poems, flower arrangements, baby blankets, grilled specialties, tattoos, hairstyles, or something else, you are making something that did not previously exist—creating.

When we are inspired to create, to combine ingredients in a bold new way or to carve a hunk of wood into some never-before-seen shape, it can feel magical. Perhaps you recall a time when you awoke from a dream, knew your dream had a fantastic story line, and sat down at your computer and furiously typed out a rough plot for a short story. Or maybe you went to the farmers' market, purchased a wide assortment of vegetables, and then went home and invented a new dish with many of them, delighted in the new taste combinations you had created.

Sometimes our creative juices flow. Is it magic? Everyone at some point, though, experiences the frustration of not being able to create. Writers call it writer's block, which is defined as the inability to write. We may not have a fancy term to describe the lack of inspiration a flower arranger may feel when he struggles to figure out his next bouquet—flower arranger's block just doesn't have a great ring to it—but we know that every person involved in creative endeavors has that awful feeling occasionally (or more often) of just being completely stumped by what to do next. Sometimes creators even wonder if they will ever be able to create again. Staring at a bare canvas or empty page or collection of ingredients with a blank mind can be intimidating enough to paralyze even the most seasoned creator.

While we typically celebrate success and try to hide our failures, the burgeoning failure movement asks us to not only acknowledge our failures but to recognize them as learning experiences and honor them. By publicizing our failures, we can normalize the idea that defeat is often a precursor to success. Appreciating failure also helps us understand the value of a less-than-smooth process.

The beginning of the chapter focuses on creative impulses and processes. Anne Lamott suggests that the secret to creativity is to not aim for brilliance. A meme expresses what a fine line there is between being blocked and simply lacking motivation. Emily Temple presents the advice of thirteen well-known writers on beating writer's block. New York Book Editors suggest that writer's block may boil down to procrastination. Jordan Sargent evaluates how Janelle Monáe's latest album shows a more personal side of the artist.

The chapter ends with a look at forces that crush creativity and ways to free ourselves of those forces. Philosopher Alan Watts suggests that the education system's emphasis on grade completion causes us to not pay attention to the journey, which to his mind, is the inspiration. Johannes Haushofer and the Aalto Entrepreneurship Society urge us to embrace failure as part of the process of getting to success.

# ▼ Style Book Excerpt

## Anne Lamott, *Shitty First Drafts*

Anne Lamott is a nonfiction writer and novelist. In her book *Bird by Bird: Some Instructions on Writing and Life*, she guides writers to move beyond their writing blocks, helping them to get words onto the page. She shares some of her own experiences with the writing process, allowing readers to see that a prolific writer also battles with writing demons. In the excerpt below, Lamott concentrates on ways to get that initial draft out of your head and onto the page.

Now, practically even better news than that of short assignments is the idea of shitty first drafts. All good writers write them. This is how they end up with good second drafts and terrific third drafts. People tend to look at successful writers, writers who are getting their books published and maybe even doing well financially, and think that they sit down at their desks every morning feeling like a million dollars, feeling great about who they are and how much talent they have and what a great story they have to tell; that they take in a few deep breaths, push back their sleeves, roll their necks a few times to get all the cricks out, and dive in, typing fully formed passages as fast as a court reporter. But this is just the fantasy of the uninitiated. I know some very great writers, writers you love who write beautifully and have made a great deal of money, and not *one* of them sits down routinely feeling wildly enthusiastic and confident. Not one of them writes elegant first drafts. All right, one of them does, but we do not like her very much. We do not think that she has a rich inner life or that God likes her or can even stand her. (Although when I mentioned this to my priest friend Tom, he said you can safely assume you've created God in your own image when it turns out that God hates all the same people you do.)

Very few writers really know what they are doing until they've done it. Nor do they go about their business feeling dewy and thrilled. They do not type a few stiff warm-up sentences and then find themselves bounding along like huskies across the snow. One writer I know tells me that he sits down every morning and says to himself nicely, "It's not like you don't have a choice, because you do—you can either type or kill yourself." We all often feel like we are pulling teeth, even those writers whose prose ends up being the most natural and fluid. The right words and sentences just do not come pouring out like ticker tape most of the time. Now, Muriel Spark is said to have felt that she was taking dictation from God every morning—sitting there, one supposes, plugged into a Dicta-phone, typing away, humming. But this is a very hostile and aggressive position. One might hope for bad things to rain down on a person like this.

For me and most of the other writers I know, writing is not rapturous. In fact, the only way I can get anything written at all is to write really, really shitty first drafts.

The first draft is the child's draft, where you let it all pour out and then let it romp all over the place, knowing that no one is going to see it and that you can shape it later. You just let this childlike part of you channel whatever voices and visions come through and onto the page. If one of the characters wants to say, "Well, so what, Mr. Poopy Pants?," you let her. No one is going to see it. If the kid wants to get into really sentimental, weepy, emotional territory, you let him. Just get it all down on paper, because there may be something great in those six crazy pages that you would never have gotten to by more rational, grown-up means. There may be something in the very last line of the very last paragraph on page six that you just love, that is so beautiful or wild that you now know what you're supposed to be writing about, more or less, or in what direction you might go—but there was no way to get to this without first getting through the first five and a half pages.

I used to write food reviews for *California* magazine before it folded. (My writing food reviews had nothing to do with the magazine folding, although every single review did cause a couple of canceled subscriptions. Some readers took umbrage at my comparing mounds of vegetable puree with various ex-presidents' brains.) These reviews always took two days to write. First I'd go to a restaurant several times with a few opinionated, articulate friends in tow. I'd sit there writing down everything anyone said that was at all interesting or funny.

> A friend of mine says that the first draft is the down draft—you just get it down. The second draft is the up draft—you fix it up.

Then on the following Monday I'd sit down at my desk with my notes, and try to write the review. Even after I'd been doing this for years, panic would set in. I'd try to write a lead, but instead I'd write a couple of dreadful sentences, xx them out, try again, xx everything out, and then feel despair and worry settle on my chest like an x-ray apron. It's over, I'd think, calmly, I'm not going to be able to get the magic to work this time. I'm ruined. I'm through. I'm toast. Maybe, I'd think, I can get my old job back as a clerk-typist. But probably not. I'd get up and study my teeth in the mirror for a while. Then I'd stop, remember to breathe, make a few phone calls, hit the kitchen and chow down. Eventually I'd go back and sit down at my desk, and sigh for the next ten minutes. Finally I would pick up my one-inch picture frame, stare into it as if for the answer, and every time the answer would come: all I had to do was to write a really shitty first draft of, say, the opening paragraph. And no one was going to see it.

So I'd start writing without reining myself in. It was almost just typing, just making my fingers move. And the writing would be *terrible*. I'd write a lead paragraph that was a whole page, even though the entire review could only be three pages long, and then I'd start writing up descriptions of the food, one dish at a time, bird by bird, and the critics would be sitting on my shoulders, commenting like cartoon characters. They'd be pretending to snore, or rolling their eyes at my overwrought descriptions, no matter how hard I tried to tone those descriptions down, no matter how conscious I was of what a friend said to me gently in my early days of restaurant reviewing. "Annie," she said, "it is just a piece of *chicken*. It is just a bit of *cake*."

But because by then I had been writing for so long, I would eventually let myself trust the process—sort of, more or less. I'd write a first draft that was maybe twice as long as it should be, with a self-indulgent and boring beginning, stupefying descriptions of the meal, lots of quotes from my black-humored friends that made them sound more like the Manson girls than food lovers, and no ending to speak of. The whole thing would be so long and incoherent and hideous that for the rest of the day I'd obsess about getting creamed by a car before I could write a decent second draft. I'd worry that people would read what I'd written and believe that the accident had really been a suicide, that I had panicked because my talent was waning and my mind was shot.

The next day, though, I'd sit down, go through it all with a colored pen, take out everything I possibly could, find a new lead somewhere on the second page, figure out a kicky place to end it, and then write a second draft. It always turned out fine, sometimes even funny and weird and helpful. I'd go over it one more time and mail it in.

Then, a month later, when it was time for another review, the whole process would start again, complete with the fears that people would find my first draft before I could rewrite it.

Almost all good writing begins with terrible first efforts. You need to start somewhere. Start by getting something—anything—down on paper. A friend of mine says that the first draft is the down draft—you just get it down. The second draft is the up draft—you fix it up. You try to say what you have to say more accurately. And the third draft is the dental draft, where you check every tooth, to see if it's loose or cramped or decayed, or even, God help us, healthy.

What I've learned to do when I sit down to work on a shitty first draft is to quiet the voices in my head. First there's the vinegar-lipped Reader Lady, who says primly, "Well, *that's* not very interesting, is it?" And there's the emaciated German male who writes these Orwellian memos detailing your thought crimes. And there are your parents, agonizing over your lack of loyalty and discretion; and there's William Burroughs, dozing off or shooting up because he finds you as bold and articulate as a houseplant; and so on. And there are also the dogs: let's not forget the dogs, the dogs in their pen who will surely hurtle and snarl their way out if you ever *stop* writing, because writing is, for some of us, the latch that keeps the door of the pen closed, keeps those crazy ravenous dogs contained.

Quieting these voices is at least half the battle I fight daily. But this is better than it used to be. It used to be 87 percent. Left to its own devices, my mind spends much of its time having conversations with people who aren't there. I walk along defending myself to people, or exchanging repartee with them, or rationalizing my behavior, or seducing them with gossip, or pretending I'm on their TV talk show or whatever. I speed or run an aging yellow light or don't come to a full stop, and one nanosecond later am explaining to imaginary cops exactly why I had to do what I did, or insisting that I did not in fact do it.

I happened to mention this to a hypnotist I saw many years ago, and he looked at me very nicely. At first I thought he was feeling around on the floor for the silent alarm button, but then he gave me the following exercise, which I still use to this day.

Close your eyes and get quiet for a minute, until the chatter starts up. Then isolate one of the voices and imagine the person speaking as a mouse. Pick it up by the tail and drop it into a mason jar. Then isolate another voice, pick it up by the tail, drop it in the jar. And so on. Drop in any high-maintenance parental units, drop in any contractors, lawyers, colleagues, children, anyone who is whining in your head. Then put the lid on, and watch all these mouse people clawing at the glass, jabbering away, trying to make you feel like shit because you won't do what they want—won't give them more money, won't be more successful, won't see them more often. Then imagine that there is a volume-control button on the bottle. Turn it all the way up for a minute, and listen to the stream of angry, neglected, guilt-mongering voices. Then turn it all the way down and watch the frantic mice lunge at the glass, trying to get to you. Leave it down, and get back to your shitty first draft.

A writer friend of mine suggests opening the jar and shooting them all in the head. But I think he's a little angry, and I'm sure nothing like this would ever occur to you.

## QUESTIONS

1. Throughout this excerpt, Anne Lamott attempts to alleviate the frustration a writer encounters when beginning to write. What strategies does she use? Are they effective? Why or why not?

2. How would you characterize Lamott's tone? Why do you believe she chose this particular tone? Use specific examples to support your answer.

## COMPOSING PROJECT | Write an Advice Column

You have been given the role of writing an advice column for writers struggling to get words on the page. Write a series of three to four entries for the advice column. Use your own experiences and some of the ideas from Lamott's piece.

## ▼ Meme

### Unknown Author, *Writer's Block*

The meme on the facing page depicts Fry, the lead character in the animated TV series *Futurama*, pondering his inability to write. Since memes are easily created, replicated, and modified, many users do not consider themselves the owner of the composition. In this example, the author is anonymous.

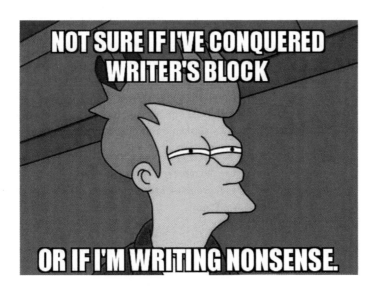

**QUESTIONS**

1. The creator of this meme is anonymous. How does this anonymity affect the piece's credibility? In what ways does the meme establish its ethos?

2. What makes this meme humorous? Do you have to be familiar with the TV show the character is from to find this funny?

**COMPOSING PROJECT** | Create a Meme

Using the meme in this chapter, create two new versions. For one of the versions, change the visual. You could use another figure from pop culture, a celebrity, an animal, or any other idea you feel could fit the existing text. For the other version, change the text.

## ▼ Article

**Emily Temple,** *13 Famous Writers on Overcoming Writer's Block*

Emily Temple writes fiction and nonfiction. Many of her nonfiction pieces have appeared on *Flavorwire*, an online magazine that focuses on film, art, music, and other culturally relevant topics. In her article "13 Famous Writers on Overcoming Writer's Block," she includes a variety of tips to help inspire writers. Many of the quotes give specific strategies for overcoming writer's block, such as Hilary Mantel's recommendation to "Take a walk, take a bath, go to sleep, make a pie, draw, listen to music, meditate, exercise. . . ."

*Credit: Emily Temple, 13 Famous Writers on Overcoming Writer's Block. Used with permission of Falvorpill Media.*

It's the first weekend of November, and for all you aspiring writers out there, that might just mean that you're flexing your fingers for your first crack at this year's NaNoWriMo (that's National Novel Writing Month). The philosophy behind NaNoWriMo is pretty simple: get the words—50,000 of them, to be exact—on the page. But what if you experience that dreaded writer's block while you're chipping away at your "Great Frantic Novel"? Never fear, you're not alone. After the jump, take comfort in the words of thirteen famous writers who've been there, done that—and add your own words of encouragement in the comments!

"What I try to do is write. I may write for two weeks 'the cat sat on the mat, that is that, not a rat.' And it might be just the most boring and awful stuff. But I try. When I'm writing, I write. And then it's as if the muse is convinced that I'm serious and says, 'Okay. Okay. I'll come.' "—**Maya Angelou**

"Suggestions? Put it aside for a few days, or longer, do other things, try not to think about it. Then sit down and read it (printouts are best I find, but that's just me) as if you've never seen it before. Start at the beginning. Scribble on the manuscript as you go if you see anything you want to change. And often, when you get to the end you'll be both enthusiastic about it and know what the next few words are. And you do it all one word at a time."—**Neil Gaiman**

"I encourage my students at times like these to get one page of anything written, three hundred words of memories or dreams or stream of consciousness on how much they hate writing—just for the hell of it, just to keep their fingers from becoming too arthritic, just because they have made a commitment to try to write three hundred words every day. Then, on bad days and weeks, let things go at that. . . . Your unconscious can't work when you are breathing down its neck. You'll sit there going, 'Are you done in there yet, are you done in there yet?' But it is trying to tell you nicely, 'Shut up and go away.' "—**Anne Lamott, *Bird by Bird***

"Now, what I'm thinking of is, people always saying 'Well, what do we do about a sudden blockage in your writing? What if you have a blockage and you don't know what to do about it?' Well, it's obvious you're doing the wrong thing, don't you? In the middle of writing something you go blank and your mind says: 'No, that's it.' Ok. You're being warned, aren't you? Your subconscious is saying 'I don't like you anymore. You're writing about things I don't give a damn for.' You're being political, or you're being socially aware. You're writing things that will benefit the world. To hell with that! I don't write things to benefit the world. If it happens that they do, swell. I didn't set out to do that. I set out to have a hell of a lot of fun.

> **What you do then is MAKE IT UP.**

"I've never worked a day in my life. I've never worked a day in my life. The joy of writing has propelled me from day to day and year to year. I want you to envy me, my joy. Get out of here tonight and say: 'Am I being joyful?' And if you've got a writer's block, you can cure it this evening by stopping whatever you're writing and doing something else. You picked the wrong subject."—**Ray Bradbury at The Sixth Annual Writer's Symposium by the Sea, 2001**

"The secret of getting ahead is getting started. The secret of getting started is breaking your complex overwhelming tasks into small manageable tasks, and then starting on the first one."—**Mark Twain**

"The best way is always to stop when you are going good and when you know what will happen next. If you do that every day . . . you will never be stuck. Always stop while you are going good and don't think about it or worry about it until you start to write the next day. That way your subconscious will work on it all the time. But if you think about it consciously or worry about it you will kill it and your brain will be tired before you start."—**Ernest Hemingway**

"Writer's block is my unconscious mind telling me that something I've just written is either unbelievable or unimportant to me, and I solve it by going back and reinventing some part of what I've already written so that when I write it again, it is believable and interesting to me. Then I can go on. Writer's block is never solved by forcing oneself to 'write through it,' because you haven't solved the problem that caused your unconscious mind to rebel against the story, so it still won't work—for you or for the reader."—**Orson Scott Card at Fiction**

"Many years ago, I met John Steinbeck at a party in Sag Harbor, and told him that I had writer's block. And he said something which I've always remembered, and which works. He said, 'Pretend that you're writing not to your editor or to an audience or to a readership, but to someone close, like your sister, or your mother, or someone that you like.' And at the time I was enamored of Jean Seberg, the actress, and I had to write an article about taking Marianne Moore to a baseball game, and I started it off, 'Dear Jean . . . ,' and wrote this piece with some ease, I must say. And to my astonishment that's the way it appeared in *Harper's Magazine*. 'Dear Jean . . . ,' Which surprised her, I think, and me, and very likely Marianne Moore."—**John Steinbeck by way of George Plimpton**

"Over the years, I've found one rule. It is the only one I give on those occasions when I talk about writing. A simple rule. If you tell yourself you are going to be at your desk tomorrow, you are by that declaration asking your unconscious to prepare the material. You are, in effect, contracting to pick up such valuables at a given time. Count on me, you are saying to a few forces below: I will be there to write."—**Norman Mailer in** *The Spooky Art: Some Thoughts on Writing*

"If you get stuck, get away from your desk. Take a walk, take a bath, go to sleep, make a pie, draw, listen to music, meditate, exercise; whatever you do, don't just stick there scowling at the problem. But don't make telephone calls or go to a party; if you do, other people's words will pour in where your lost words should be. Open a gap for them, create a space. Be patient."—**Hilary Mantel**

"[When] the thoughts rise heavily and pass gummous through my pen . . . I never stand conferring with pen and ink one moment; for if a pinch of snuff or a stride or two across the room will not do the business for me— . . . I take a razor at once; and have tried the edge of it upon the palm of my hand, without further ceremony, except that of first lathering my beard, I shave it off, taking care that if I do leave hair, that it not be a grey one: this done, I change my shirt—put on a better coat—send for my last wig—put my topaz ring upon my finger; and in a word, dress myself from one end to the other of me, after my best fashion."—**Laurence Sterne**

"I learned to produce whether I wanted to or not. It would be easy to say oh, I have writer's block, oh, I have to wait for my muse. I don't. Chain that muse to your desk and get the job done."—**Barbara Kingsolver**

"Writer's block . . . a lot of howling nonsense would be avoided if, in every sentence containing the word WRITER, that word was taken out and the word PLUMBER substituted; and the result examined for the sense it makes. Do plumbers get plumber's block? What would you think of a plumber who used that as an excuse not to do any work that day? The fact is that writing is hard work, and sometimes you don't want to do it, and you can't think of what to write next, and you're fed up with the whole damn business. Do you think plumbers don't feel like that about their work from time to time? Of course there will be days when the stuff is not flowing freely. What you do then is MAKE IT UP. I like the reply of the composer Shostakovich to a student who complained that he couldn't find a theme for his second movement. 'Never mind the theme! Just write the movement!' he said. Writer's block is a condition that affects amateurs and people who aren't serious about writing. So is the opposite, namely inspiration, which amateurs are also very fond of. Putting it another way: a professional writer is someone who writes just as well when they're not inspired as when they are."—**Philip Pullman**

## QUESTIONS

1. Emily Temple selected several quotes from famous authors to help convey her point. What is the overall message? How can you tell?

2. Why do you think she chose these particular authors and quotes? Are there other authors/quotes that you would add to her list?

## COMPOSING PROJECT | Make a List

Brainstorm what unleashes your creativity. When and where do you feel most creative? Least creative? Are there activities or people that seem to bring out your creativity? Make a list that reflects your creative world.

## ▼ Poster

### New York Book Editors, *Got Writer's Block?*

New York Book Editors, a group of experienced editors who have worked for some of New York City's major publishing houses, created an informative visual map to help creative writers extricate themselves from writer's block. The map provides a series of yes/no pathways in response to questions about plot and character. All the paths in the visual lead to one final bit of advice: "Stop procrastinating. Keep writing."

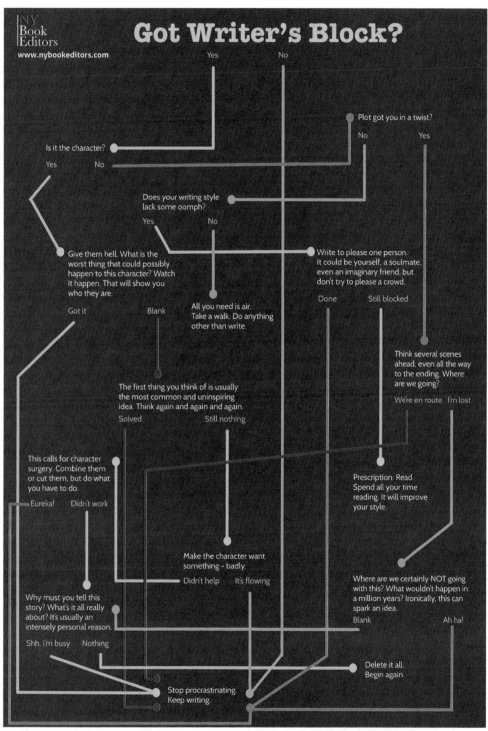

# Got Writer's Block?

N Y
Book
Editors
www.nybookeditors.com

Yes    No

Plot got you in a twist?

No    Yes

Is it the character?

Yes    No

Does your writing style
lack some oomph?

Yes    No

Give them hell. What is the
worst thing that could possibly
happen to this character? Watch
it happen. That will show you
who they are.

Write to please one person.
It could be yourself, a soulmate,
even an imaginary friend, but
don't try to please a crowd.

Done    Still blocked

Got it    Blank

All you need is air.
Take a walk. Do anything
other than write.

Think several scenes
ahead, even all the way
to the ending. Where
are we going?

We're en route   I'm lost

The first thing you think of is usually
the most common and uninspiring
idea. Think again and again and again.

Solved    Still nothing

This calls for character
surgery. Combine them
or cut them, but do what
you have to do.

Prescription: Read.
Spend all your time
reading. It will improve
your style.

Eureka!    Didn't work

Make the character want
something - badly.

Didn't help    It's flowing

Where are we certainly NOT going
with this? What wouldn't happen in
a million years? Ironically, this can
spark an idea.

Why must you tell this
story? What's it all really
about? It's usually an
intensely personal reason.

Blank    Ah ha!

Shh, I'm busy    Nothing

Delete it all.
Begin again.

Stop procrastinating.
Keep writing.

*Credit: New York Book Editors.*

1. The creators of this piece used a flowchart approach for their visual. Is this an effective strategy for communicating their ideas? Why or why not? What other approaches might have worked in this poster?

2. How would you characterize the language used in the chart? Do you think it is effective? How might the chart strike you differently if the tone were more formal?

## COMPOSING PROJECT | Create a Poster

Using the New York Book Editors' poster as your model, create your own flowchart titled "Need Musical Inspiration?" In the poster, use a series of prompts/questions to help your reader make choices about the types of music to listen to that might inspire the creative process.

## ▼ Review

### Jordan Sargent, Dirty Computer *Is a Typical Janelle Monáe Album, Except When It's Not*

Jordan Sargent is a freelance writer and a former senior editor for *Spin*, a webzine devoted to covering contemporary music. His writing focus has included music, pop culture, and sports. In his review of Janelle Monáe's album, *Dirty Computer*, he shows how this album is a departure from her previous work.

Credit: Jordan Sargent, "Dirty Computer *Is a Typical Janelle Monáe Album, Except When It's Not,*" Spin, May 3, 2018. https://www.spin.com/2018/05/review-janelle-m

Janelle Monáe occupies rarified air. She is an instantly recognizable face—magazine covers, Super Bowl commercials—but has no hit singles; a canonized artist without a classic album. She exists in a space shared by artists like Lady Gaga and Bruno Mars as old school capital-p Performers who restore your parents' faith in modern music, but without any of the ubiquity. Frankly, it sounds great.

Existing in the outer orbit of superstardom has allowed Monáe ample room to chase her muse. The result has been records that could have been made by nobody else: Afrofuturistic epics about an android who falls in love with a human, presented nonlinearly and with the help of collaborators ranging from Of Montreal and Saul Williams to Prince and Erykah Badu. But that doesn't mean Monáe ever quite found herself. As unique as those projects were, the narrative could be inscrutable to the uninvested; and for as ambitious as she was as a storyteller, her music is generally the opposite: studious homages to the greats of soul and funk.

She is now aiming to change that. "I knew I needed to make this album, and I have put it off because the subject is Janelle Monáe," she told the *New York Times* magazine. It's not that her previous albums had none of her in them—they were centered around a character, Cindi Mayweather, whose love was denied by the government, encouraging the listener to draw a connection to Monáe, who recently came out as pansexual. But the pomp of her career—the multi-suite albums, the tuxedos, the Performing—presented her as someone incubated in a lab to entertain. Whether she lived a life away from the character was if not unclear, then at least irrelevant.

This is remedied overtly on *Dirty Computer*, her newest album. "A-Town, we made it out there / Straight out of Kansas City, yeah we made it out there," she says, cleverly summarizing her personal come-up. "Mama was a G, she was cleaning hotels / Papa was a driver, I was working retail." These lines are rapped on the song "Django Jane," which helped introduce the album along with fellow lead single "Make Me Feel." As a single, "Django Jane" was odd and awkward, offering up something—a Janelle Monáe rap song—that nobody really asked for. But within the context of the album it works as a moment of true triumph. It bleeds out of "Screwed," a song about how sex can be both an escape and a protest during the apocalypse, and presented this way "Django Jane" feels less like a frivolity and more like a lynchpin of the album, with the blending of the personal and political heightening the impact of both.

If there's any success unique to *Dirty Computer*, it's Monáe merging her world and ours in a way that feels natural, even if it's not always exactly coherent. "Everything is sex / Except sex, which is power / You know power / Is just sex / Now ask yourself who is screwing you," she raps on "Screwed," a fun little tongue twister that actually reveals truths when you begin to unravel it. Less provoking is that song's outro, another rap verse that hinges on lines like, "Fake news, fake boobs, fake food, what's real? / Still in the Matrix eating on the blue pills"—spaced-out mumbo jumbo that is more the province of people whose lives are disconnected from any tangible problems. Elsewhere, her sloganeering is blunt. The song "I Got the Juice" contains a refrain that goes "If you try and grab my pussy cat, this pussy grab you back," and though it lacks a certain nuance, it nonetheless feels like an era-appropriate moment of catharsis.

> "[T]hough it lacks a certain nuance, it nonetheless feels like an era-appropriate moment of catharsis."

The album is best in its meatiest section, a run of songs in the middle of the tracklist that remind us that Monáe and her team—including the writers and producers Nate Wonder and Chuck Lightning—have the songwriting chops to justify their reverence. This extends even to "Make Me Feel," the single produced by pop machine cogs Mattman & Robin and co-written by radio maestros Julia Michaels and Justin Tranter. As a standalone it's far too reminiscent of Prince (Monáe seemed to mount a defense against this criticism by inferring that Prince was actually involved in its creation), but sounds much better when entered into a continuum of her own work, sandwiched by the pleasingly elastic "Pynk" and "I Got the Juice."

Things do get ponderous at the end. "Don't Judge Me"—which shares a soft shuffle and airiness with "Pink Cashmere"—is a naked admission of self-doubt, but drags at six minutes. "Americans," in which Monáe sings from both the perspective of a chauvinist and a revolutionary, is a muddled and ineffective attempt at a subversive anthem. That it just makes you want to listen to "Let's Go Crazy" doesn't really help either.

*Dirty Computer* is a different Monáe album — explicitly personal and political — but it's also not. Her ability to transcend her influences has always been song-to-song, and that's true here, too. But it also feels like she is inching closer to a breakthrough: an album that fully lives up to her reputation and ambition.

### QUESTIONS

1. In his review of Janelle Monáe's *Dirty Computer*, Sargent states, "*Dirty Computer* is a different Monáe album — explicitly personal and political — but it's also not." What evidence does he provide in his review to support this point?

2. Do you have to be familiar with Monáe's album to get meaning from this review? Why or why not?

### COMPOSING PROJECT | Write an Album Review

Find an album that you believe exemplifies amazing artistry. In your review, highlight what makes this particular musical endeavor worthy of listening and attention. Try to bring the album and its contents to life for a reader that perhaps has not encountered that artist before.

## ▼ Podcast Transcript

### Alan Watts, *Music Is Life*

Alan Watts was a British-born philosopher who wrote many books and articles on Eastern and Western religion. He was most associated with Buddhism. The excerpt below is from *Learning the Human Game*, a recording that captures four of his lectures on the human condition. The excerpt plays with the idea that our schooling system cheats us out of the real experience of education by making us focus on the destination rather than the journey itself.

*Credit: Used by permission from Alan Watts.*

In music, though, one doesn't make the end of the composition the **point** of the composition. If that were so, the best conductors would be those who played fastest; and there would be composers who only wrote finales. People go to concerts only to hear one crashing chord — because that's the end. Same way in dancing — you don't aim at a particular spot in the room; that's where you should arrive. The whole point of the dancing is the dance.

Now, but we don't see that as something brought by our education into our everyday conduct. We've got a system of schooling which gives a completely different impression. It's all graded—and what we do is we put the child into the corridor of this grade system, with a kind of "c'mon kitty kitty kitty . . ." And yeah, you go to kindergarten, and that's a great thing, because when you finish that, you'll get into first grade. And then c'mon, first grade leads to second grade, and so on . . . And then you get out of grade school you go to high school—and it's revving up, the thing is coming . . . Then you're going to go to college, and by jove then you get into graduate school, and when you're through with graduate school, you'll go out to join the world. And then you get into some racket where you're selling insurance. And they've got that quota to make. And you're going to make that.

> " **The whole point of the dancing is the dance.** "

And all the time, this thing is coming, it's coming, it's coming—that great thing, the success you're working for. Then when you wake up one day about forty years old, you say "My God! I've arrived! I'm there!" And you don't feel very different from what you always felt. And there's a slight letdown, because you feel there's a hoax. And there was a hoax. A dreadful hoax.

They made you miss everything. By expectation. Look at the people who live to retire, and put those savings away. And then when they're sixty-five, and they don't have any energy left, they're more or less impotent, they go and rot in an old people's "senior citizens" community. Because we've simply cheated ourselves, the whole way down the line. We thought of life by analogy was a journey, was a pilgrimage, which had a serious purpose at the end.

And the thing was to get to that end. Success, or whatever it is, or maybe heaven after you're dead. But we missed the point the whole way along. It was a musical thing, and you were supposed to sing, or to dance, while the music was being played.

## QUESTIONS

1. How effective do you think Watts's use of music and dance as metaphors is? Can you think of other metaphors he could have used that would have been more effective?

2. How would you describe Watts's voice in this piece? Does he sound like someone you would like to hang out with? Trust? Why or why not?

## COMPOSING PROJECT | Write a Letter to the Principal of Your Former High School

What are some changes that could be made at the high school you went to that would help students there focus on the journey as much as the destination? Write a letter to your high school's principal in which you suggest a few changes that could be implemented.

## ▼ Curriculum Vitae

### Johannes Haushofer, *CV of Failures*

Johannes Haushofer is an assistant professor of psychology and public affairs at Princeton University. His research and publications focus on poverty. Although Haushofer's résumé is brimming with impressive successes, his "CV of Failures," below, focuses on his unsuccessful attempts to get grants, jobs, and publications. (Note: CV stands for "curriculum vitae," a form of résumé used in academia.)

*Credit: Used by permission of Johannes Haushofer.*

Most of what I try fails, but these failures are often invisible, while the successes are visible. I have noticed that this sometimes gives others the impression that most things work out for me. As a result, they are more likely to attribute their own failures to themselves, rather than the fact that the world is stochastic, applications are crapshoots, and selection committees and referees have bad days. This CV of Failures is an attempt to balance the record and provide some perspective.

**This idea is not mine**, but due to a wonderful article in *Nature* by **Melanie I. Stefan**, who is a Lecturer in the School of Biomedical Sciences at the University of Edinburgh. You can find her original article here, her website here, her publications here, and follow her on Twitter under *@MelanieIStefan.*

**I am also not the first academic to post their CV of Failures.** Earlier examples are here, here, here, and here.

This CV is unlikely to be complete—it was written from memory and probably omits a lot of stuff. So if it's shorter than yours, it's likely because you have better memory, or because you're better at trying things than me.

### Degree Programs I Did Not Get Into

| | |
|---|---|
| 2008 | PhD Program in Economics, Stockholm School of Economics |
| 2003 | Graduate Course in Medicine, Cambridge University |
| | Graduate Course in Medicine, UCL |
| | PhD Program in Psychology, Harvard University |
| | PhD Program in Neuroscience and Psychology, Stanford University |
| 1999 | BA in International Relations, London School of Economics |

### Academic Positions and Fellowships I Did Not Get

| | |
|---|---|
| 2014 | Harvard Kennedy School Assistant Professorship |
| | UC Berkeley Agricultural and Resource Economics Assistant Professorship |

MIT Brain & Cognitive Sciences Assistant Professorship

This list is restricted to institutions where I had campus visits; the list of places where I had first-round interviews but wasn't invited for a campus visit, and where I wasn't invited to interview in the first place, is much longer and I will write it up when I get a chance. The list also shrouds the fact that I didn't apply to most of the top economics departments (Harvard, MIT, Yale, Stanford, Princeton, Chicago, Berkeley, LSE) because one of my advisors felt they could not write a strong letter for them.

## Awards and Scholarships I Did Not Get

2011    Swiss Network for International Studies PhD Award

2010    Society of Fellows, Harvard University
        Society in Science Scholarship
        University of Zurich Research Scholarship

2009    Human Frontiers Fellowship

2007    Mind-Brain-Behavior Award (Harvard University)

2006    Mind-Brain-Behavior Award (Harvard University)

2003    Fulbright Scholarship
        Haniel Scholarship (German National Merit Foundation)

## Paper Rejections from Academic Journals

2016    QJE, Experimental Economics

2015    AER × 2

2013    PNAS, Experimental Economics, Science, Neuron

2009    AER

2008    Science, Neuron, Nature Neuroscience, Journal of Neuroscience, Journal of Vision

## Research Funding I Did Not Get

2016    MQ Mental Health Research Grant

2015    Russell Sage Research Grant (two separate ones)

2013    National Science Foundation Research Grant

2010    University of Zurich Research Grant
        Swiss National Science Foundation Research Grant

2009    Financial Innovation Grant
        International Labor Organization Research Grant
        3ie Research Grant

## Meta-Failures

2016    This darn CV of Failures has received way more attention than my entire body of
        academic work

### QUESTIONS

1.  Who do you think Haushofer sees as the audience for his "CV of Failures"—students,
    faculty, or someone else? Why do you think so?

2.  What purpose do you think the introductory note on the "CV of Failures" serves?
    How would you read and understand the piece differently if it didn't have the
    introductory note?

### COMPOSING PROJECT | Create a CV of Failures

List jobs you've applied for but not gotten, colleges that rejected you, perhaps courses
or assignments you've failed, relationships that have ended, scholarships you didn't
get, fraternities or sororities that rejected you, and other disappointments. What can
you learn about yourself by looking at this list?

## ▼ Blog

### Aalto Entrepreneurship Society, *International Day for Failure*

The first official Day for Failure was celebrated in Finland on October 13, 2010. The
day calls attention to all the ways we learn and grow from being unsuccessful at
something. The "Day for Failure" web page invites people to share their failure stories via social media. The day is sponsored by the Aalto Entrepreneurship Society, a
Finnish student organization that encourages start-up culture.

Credit: Used by permission of Aalto Entrepreneurship Society.

### Quotes

"Only those who dare to fail greatly can ever achieve greatly."— **Robert F. Kennedy**

"A person who never made a mistake never tried anything new." —**Albert Einstein**

"There is only one thing that makes a dream impossible to achieve: fear of failure."
—**Paulo Coelho**

## The Steps

1. Fail. How? You'll find your own personal way to do it.

2. Tweet your failure with hashtag #dayforfailure or read a bunch of fails from other human beings. We human beings are used to failing.

3. Buy great ingredients, read recipe, prepare everything, and burn your food. Serve when you (and the food) are cooled down.

4. Share your failphoto on Instagram. On the 13th, #skateboardingbruises, #blush, and #faces will be paired with #dayforfailure.

5. Do a bankruptcy. Money isn't everything, they say. Right?

6. Ask that boy/girl/anyone out.

7. Go to YouTube and search "fail." Remember, no one on the videos planned failing. It's just something that usually occurs after trying. Still, why so many videos?

8. Use Facebook as you use it every day. Share a story about your day. The more embarrassing, the more likes it usually gains. People are weird.

9. Don't share this awesome ACTIONBOOK.

10. Learn from your failure.

## QUESTIONS

1. Go to dayforfailure.com, which is where the steps are from. How does the layout of the "Day for Failure" web page direct your attention? What did you notice first? Why do you think the creators might have wanted your attention to go there first?

2. Are there steps for failing listed here that you think are not really in the spirit of celebrating failure? Which one(s)? What sets those steps apart from others?

## COMPOSING PROJECT | Conduct an Interview

Interview a very successful person you know to find out what role failure has played in that person's life. How has he or she built upon failures or learned from them? Does the person consider some failures as turning points?

## LONG-TERM PROJECTS | Creativity

1. **Conduct a poster session in your class.** Conferences held by many disciplines and organizations feature discussion panels and presentations; they also include poster sessions. In a poster session, researchers present their research methods and findings on a poster that combines text and images to quickly convey information to people walking around the poster session venue. You can find examples of posters used in poster sessions at projects.ncsu .edu/project/posters/ExamplePosters.html.

   a. For this project, pair up with a classmate to create a poster for a poster session on strategies for alleviating creative blocks. Your task will be to test a theory or piece of advice about overcoming writer's block or finding inspiration, such as Hilary Mantel's suggestion that you should get away from your desk and bake a pie. To gather a reasonable amount of data for analysis, you will need to implement the advice on at least three occasions, so if you are baking a pie to spur your creativity, you will need to bake a pie on at least three separate occasions and track how that affected your ability to write. Ultimately, you will present a poster detailing the results of your experiments to the class.

b. Begin by choosing a particular strategy to try. You might select one from the readings in this chapter, or you can do further research to find out about other strategies. For example, Elizabeth Gilbert, author of the best-selling memoir *Eat, Pray, Love*, has a popular TED talk, "Your Elusive Creative Genius," in which she suggests that creative types could relieve a lot of the pressure on themselves by reframing where inspiration comes from.

c. Next, decide what your measure of success will be for the strategy. For example, if you test the idea that baking a pie can help with writer's block, the measure of success needs to relate to your ability after baking the pie to write productively, rather than to show how delicious the pie is.

d. Then, conduct your test. Take detailed notes. For example, in the case of baking, note whether your attitude toward your creative endeavor changed as you baked and to what extent and when. Remember that you'll need to conduct your test at least three times to make sure that the results are consistent.

e. After you've conducted your test, analyze the results and create a three-panel poster for the class. In your analysis, you might consider:
   • How effective the strategy was
   • Pros and cons of the strategy
   • Changes you might make to your experimental protocol to get more accurate results

2. **Conduct a study of your creative processes.** For this project, you and your creativity are the subject. To better understand patterns in your own creative processes, carefully and systematically study yourself. What makes you productive? Are there specific activities that help spur your creativity? Are there times during the day that you are most creative?

a. To begin your project, devote a section of a notebook or purchase a journal to detail your creativity. Alternatively, you can create a spreadsheet on your computer or phone.

b. Observe and take detailed notes daily over the course of three weeks about the following:
   • What creative acts did you do that day? Write down as many details as you can about what you did, where you were, and how you felt at the moment. Include even unrelated details, such as what you ate or drank and how well rested you were.
   • Note the times that you engaged in creative endeavors. If you are a writer, when did you produce writing? If you act, when did an idea for a performance capture your imagination? If you cook, what time of day did you feel most inspired to try something new?
   • Detail any things that happened during the day that seemed to impede your creative juices. For example, were you sick? Stressed out about bills? Distracted by an upcoming event?

c. After three weeks, review your notes. What patterns do you notice about your creativity? Are there particular days and times when you were more creative? Do you see any variables that tend to make you more or less productive? Are there things that occurred right before you were inspired? Are there things that occurred that gave you a creative block? What conclusions might you draw about your creative process?

d. Take all the information and compose a written draft of your study. Use these categories: Introduction, Materials and Methods, Results.

# INDEX OF GENRES

## Student Newspapers/Journals

## Student Work

## Videos

## Websites

## Wiki Entries

# INDEX OF THEMES

## Education

## Environment & Nature

## Fairy Tales, Fantasy, & Science Fiction

## Family

# INDEX

Modes (*continued*)
    for poster presentations, 142, 145
    for presentations, 217, 223
    for press release, 41
    for proposals, 204, 206
    reading to understand, 13
    for researched argument, 115, 118–119
    for rhetorical analyses, 148, 152
    of sources, 347
    understanding, 11
    for *Wikipedia* entries, 253, 256
Mooney, Sherry, 195–196
Moral lessons, in fairy tales, 290
"More and More Research Shows Friends Are Good
    for Your Health" (Sohn), 485–488
"Most U.S. Teens See Anxiety and Depression as a
    Major Problem Among Their Peers" (Horowitz
    and Graf), 358, 359, 368–369
Movies
    APA models for, 426
    MLA models for, 407
MSNBC, 231
Multigenre projects, 298–314
    avoiding plagiarism and, 394
    conventions of, 300
    examples of, 303–314
    possibilities of, 299–300
    steps to assembling, 300–303
Multimodal, 11
Multimodal/multigenre project, student case study,
    434–449
"Music Is Life" (Watts), 534–535
Music sampling, 395

**N**

Nakata, Ashleigh, 144–145
Narrative genres, 36–38
*Narrative of the Life of Frederick Douglass, an American
    Slave, Written by Himself* (Douglass), 37
Nas, 395
National Public Radio, 231, 275
*Naturalis Historia* (Pliny the Elder), 252
*Nature*, 123
Neighmond, Patti, 358, 364–367
Netflix, 493
News articles, 229–237

*See also* Articles
    analyzing, 230–233, 236
    drafting, 237
    guided reading of, 233–236
    understanding, 229–230
New York Book Editors, 530–532
*New York Times*, 230, 233, 258–259
Nollen, Julia, 183–189
"Nonviolent Protest Project" (Pierre), 379–380,
    384–386, 388–389
Note taking, during research process, 391–392
Notre-Dame Cathedral, 29
Novels
    APA models for, 431
    MLA models for, 413
Numbered lists
    in business memos, 194
    in proposals, 205

**O**

Obama, Barack, 37
Obama, Michelle, 29
Obituaries, 37
"Objectification of Women in Comic Books, The"
    (Dar), 350–358, 373–374
Objects/artifacts
    APA models for, 431–432
    MLA models for, 413
Occidental Editorial Board, 458–459
"On Composing Happiness: How and Why I Created
    My Collage *Thank You*" (Kipp), 106–107
"$1.5 Trillion Crisis: Protecting Student Borrowers
    and Holding Student Loan Servers
    Accountable" (Minhaj), 499–501
"One in 8 Million," 258–259
Online games
    APA models for, 427
    MLA models for, 407–408
Online news publications, 231
Online sources, 334
    APA models for, 421–422
    avoiding plagiarism and, 393–394
    MLA models for, 403–404
Opinion pieces, 238–244
    analyzing, 238–240
    drafting, 244